# Reprise

## A French Grammar Review Worktext

SECOND EDITION

David M. Stillman, Ph.D.
*The College of New Jersey*

Ronni L. Gordon, Ph.D.

Boston   Burr Ridge, IL   Dubuque, IA   Madison, WI   New York
San Francisco   St. Louis   Bangkok   Bogotá   Caracas   Kuala Lumpur
Lisbon   London   Madrid   Mexico City   Milan   Montreal   New Delhi
Santiago   Seoul   Singapore   Sydney   Taipei   Toronto

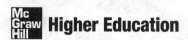

## Higher Education

Published by McGraw-Hill, an imprint of The McGraw-Hill Companies, Inc., 1221 Avenue of the Americas. Copyright © 2007 by The McGraw-Hill Companies, Inc. All rights reserved. Printed in the United States of America. Except as permitted under the United States Copyright Act of 1976, no part of this publication may be reproduced or distributed in any form or by any means, or stored in a database or retrieval system, without the prior written permission of the publisher.

Editor-in-chief: *Emily Barrosse*
Publisher: *William R. Glass*
Director of development: *Susan Blatty*
Sponsoring editor: *Katherine Crouch*
Development editor: *Connie Anderson*
Executive marketing manager: *Nick Agnew*

Production editor: *Mel Valentin*
Production supervisor: *Tandra Jorgensen*
Design manager: *Violeta Díaz*
Interior designer: *Susan Breitbard*
Compositor: *ICC Macmillan Inc.*
Printer: *RR Donnelley*

Printed in the United States of America.

ISBN-10: 0-07-353541-9
ISBN-13: 978-0-07-353541-8

12 13 14 CUS/CUS 20 19 18 17 16

# About the Authors

**David M. Stillman,** Ph.D., teaches at The College of New Jersey where he has given courses in Spanish, French, Italian, and Hebrew, and where he supervises conversation hours in French, German, Italian, Chinese, Japanese, and Arabic. He is a well-known writer of foreign language textbooks, multimedia courses, and reference books and is co-author of the acclaimed *The Ultimate Spanish Review and Practice: Mastering Spanish Grammar for Confident Communication* and *The Big Red Book of Spanish Verbs.* He is President of Mediatheque Publisher Services, a leader in the development of foreign language instructional materials. He received a Ph.D. in Spanish linguistics from the University of Illinois and taught at Harvard University, Boston University, and Cornell University. He has been appointed to national committees devoted to the improvement of teacher training.

**Ronni L. Gordon,** Ph.D., is a prominent author of foreign language textbooks, reference books, and materials for multimedia. She is co-author of the acclaimed *The Ultimate Spanish Review and Practice: Mastering Spanish Grammar for Confident Communication* and *The Big Red Book of Spanish Verbs.* She is Vice President of Mediatheque Publisher Services, a leader in the development of foreign language instructional materials. She received a Ph.D. in Spanish language and Spanish and Latin American literature and history from Rutgers University, and taught at Harvard University and Boston University. She has read in foreign languages for the National Endowment for the Humanities, spoken at the U.S. Department of Education, and founded the Committee for Quality Education, an organization devoted to the improvement of academic standards in the public schools. She is an education consultant specializing in curriculum development and is an associate scholar with a Philadelphia-based think tank.

By the same authors

The Ultimate French Verb Review and Practice: Mastering Verbs and Sentence Building for Confident Communication
The Ultimate French Review and Practice: Mastering French Grammar for Confident Communication
The Ultimate French Review and Practice: Mastering French Grammar for Confident Communication, CD Edition
The Big Blue Book of French Verbs + CD-ROM
The Blue Pocket Book of French Verbs

The Ultimate Spanish Verb Review and Practice: Mastering Verbs and Sentence Building for Confident Communication
The Ultimate Spanish Review and Practice: Mastering Spanish Grammar for Confident Communication
The Ultimate Spanish Review and Practice: Mastering Spanish Grammar for Confident Communication, CD Edition
The Big Red Book of Spanish Verbs + CD-ROM
The Red Pocket Book of Spanish Verbs

# TABLE OF CONTENTS

# PRÉFACE

**Reprise—A French Grammar Review Worktext**

Like everything metaphysical the harmony between thought and reality is to be found in the grammar of the language.

—Ludwig Wittgenstein

*Reprise—A French Grammar Review Worktext,* is a powerful tool for review and progress in French. This new college edition incorporates the suggestions of teachers who use *Reprise* with their classes. *Reprise* is organized into 25 chapters offering intermediate through advanced learners of French clear, concise, and well-organized grammar explanations. Examples come from everyday usage, most often in the format of conversational exchanges. These presentations of structure are easy to read and understand and encourage students to see grammar as a stepping-stone to communication. The activities in *Reprise* provide practice in all the grammar topics that learners of French at these levels should know. *Reprise* bridges grammar practice and communication by emphasizing authentic language use in contextualized structural activities. Instructions for the activities are written in French, which helps to set the scene and prepare students for the task at hand.

Thematic vocabulary boxes linked to some of the activities provide a review of the vocabulary common to most elementary and intermediate French textbooks and present additional current vocabulary that empowers learners to express themselves on a broad range of topics. The activities encourage learners to use the target grammar and vocabulary to express their own ideas. For convenient student reference, the Appendix of *Reprise* supplies easy-to-read verb charts. Also included in the Appendix are a review of numbers, telling time, and dates, conjugations of the French literary tenses (the imperfect and pluperfect subjunctives and the past anterior), lists of verb + infinitive and verb + preposition + infinitive constructions, and a section on written conventions, which explains French rules of spelling and punctuation. There is an end vocabulary that contains most of the words used in the activities.

*Reprise* is ideal for use in a classroom setting or for assigned self-study outside the classroom. The clearly written grammatical explanations enable students to review on their own, thus saving class time for other activities. Chapters may be covered in any order, allowing teachers to individualize grammar practice. The Answer Key provided at the end of the book allows students to check their work. Practical, inviting, and easy to use, *Reprise* will help learners acquire knowledge that will increase their confidence in using and comprehending French in a wide variety of contexts and situations.

David M. Stillman, Ph.D.

Ronni L. Gordon, Ph.D.

# PREMIÈRE PARTIE  VERBS: FORMS AND USES

## CHAPITRES

# PRESENT TENSE OF REGULAR VERBS

Verbs are presented in conjugation paradigms that summarize the forms that the verbs have in each tense. French verbs change their form for person and number. Verbs are said to have three persons: the speaker, the person spoken to, and a third person, referring neither to the speaker nor the person spoken to. French has two numbers: singular and plural.

I.   The following chart lists the English persons of the verb and their corresponding pronouns.

|  | SINGULAR | PLURAL |
|---|---|---|
| **FIRST PERSON** | *I* | *we* |
| **SECOND PERSON** | *you* | *you* |
| **THIRD PERSON** | *he/she/it* | *they* |

The following chart lists the French persons of the verb and their corresponding pronouns.

|  | SINGULAR | PLURAL |
|---|---|---|
| **FIRST PERSON** | je | nous |
| **SECOND PERSON** | tu | vous |
| **THIRD PERSON** | il/elle/on | ils/elles |

II.  Differences between the two languages:

1.  English has only one form for *you;* French has two. **Tu** is a singular form and is informal. It is used to address one person with whom you have an informal relationship: a family member, a close friend, a fellow student, small children, and pets. **Vous** is both the plural of **tu** and a formal singular form. It is used to address one person with whom you have a formal relationship: a stranger, a customer, a colleague at work, and so on.

2.  French does not have a separate pronoun for *it.* **Il** and **elle** can refer both to people and to things; all that matters is the grammatical gender of the noun. Thus, the masculine nouns **le garçon** and **le sac** may both be replaced by **il.** Similarly, the feminine nouns **la femme** and **la ville** may be replaced by the pronoun **elle.**

3. The pronoun **on** has two main uses in French.

   a. It is used as a general subject similar to the English *one, people, you, they*, or the passive voice.

   | | |
   |---|---|
   | **On s'amuse** bien à Paris. | *People have a good time in Paris.* |
   | Ici **on parle** français. | *French is spoken here.* |

   b. In contemporary French, **on** replaces **nous** in everyday speech and writing. Note that even when **on** is used to mean *we* it takes a third-person singular verb form.

   | | |
   |---|---|
   | Toi et ta famille, vous restez en ville? | *Are you and your family staying in town?* |
   | Non, **on part** en vacances. | *No, we're leaving on vacation.* |

4. French makes a gender distinction in the third-person plural. **Ils** refers to masculine plural nouns; **elles** refers to feminine plural nouns. **Ils** also refers to groups of males and females; **elles** refers to groups consisting of females or feminine nouns only.

   | | |
   |---|---|
   | —Où sont Luc et Marie? | *Where are Luc and Marie?* |
   | —**Ils** sont là. | *They're here.* |
   | —Où sont Christine et Marie? | *Where are Christine and Marie?* |
   | —**Elles** sont là. | *They're here.* |

5. In French, most verbs are divided into three classes, or conjugations, according to the ending of the infinitive.

   FIRST CONJUGATION: **-er** verbs like **parler**

   SECOND CONJUGATION: **-ir** verbs like **finir**

   THIRD CONJUGATION: **-re** verbs like **rendre**

6. The present tense is formed by dropping the infinitive ending (**-er, -ir,** or **-re**) and adding the appropriate present-tense ending. Verbs that follow these patterns are called *regular verbs*.

## First conjugation: -er verbs

Verbs of the first conjugation (**-er** verbs) are conjugated like **parler** (*to speak*).

| | SINGULAR | PLURAL |
|---|---|---|
| **FIRST PERSON** | je parl**e** | nous parl**ons** |
| **SECOND PERSON** | tu parl**es** | vous parl**ez** |
| **THIRD PERSON** | il/elle/on parl**e** | ils/elles parl**ent** |

### Some common **-er** verbs

**accepter** *to accept*
**accompagner** *to accompany*
**adorer** *to adore, love*
**aider** *to help*

**aimer** *to like, love*
**allumer** *to light, turn on (appliance)*
**apporter** *to bring*

**apprécier** *to appreciate, value, rate highly*
**arriver** *to arrive; to succeed*
**bavarder** *to chat*

*(continued)*

**casser** *to break*
**cesser** *to stop*
**chanter** *to sing*
**chercher** *to look for*
**cliquer** *to click (computers)*
**continuer** *to continue*
**copier** *to copy*
**créer** *to create*
**danser** *to dance*
**décider** *to decide*
**déjeuner** *to have lunch*
**demander** *to ask, ask for*
**dépenser** *to spend (money)*
**désirer** *to desire, want*
**dessiner** *to draw*
**détester** *to hate*
**dîner** *to have dinner*
**discuter** *to discuss*
**donner** *to give*
**écouter** *to listen to*
**éditer** *to edit*
**emporter** *to carry/take away, carry off*
**emprunter** *to borrow*
**enseigner** *to teach*
**entrer** *to go/come in, enter*
**étudier** *to study*
**fermer** *to close*
**fonder** *to found*
**formater** *to format*

**frapper** *to strike, hit*
**gagner** *to earn, win*
**garder** *to keep*
**habiter** *to live (reside)*
**hésiter** *to hesitate*
**imprimer** *to print*
**installer** *to install*
**inviter** *to invite*
**jouer** *to play*
**laisser** *to leave, let*
**laver** *to wash*
**marcher** *to walk*
**monter** *to go up (stairs)*
**montrer** *to show*
**naviguer (sur Internet)** *to surf (the Web)*
**organiser** *to organize*
**oublier** *to forget*
**parler** *to speak*
**passer** *to pass; to spend (time)*
**penser** *to think*
**photocopier** *to photocopy, xerox*
**porter** *to carry, wear*
**pousser** *to push*
**pratiquer** *to practice*
**préparer** *to prepare*
**présenter** *to present*
**prêter** *to lend*
**quitter** *to leave (a person or place)*

**raconter** *to tell, tell about, relate*
**refuser** *to refuse*
**regarder** *to look at*
**remercier** *to thank*
**rencontrer** *to meet (by chance)*
**rentrer** *to return, go back*
**retourner** *to return, come/go back*
**retrouver** *to meet (by appointment)*
**rouler** *to move, travel (of a vehicle)*
**saluer** *to greet*
**sauvegarder** *to save (computer file)*
**supporter** *to bear, stand*
**supprimer** *to eliminate (a job); to erase (a computer file); to cancel (train, flight)*
**surfer (sur) le Web** *to surf the Web*
**téléphoner (à)** *to phone*
**terminer** *to end, finish*
**tourner** *to turn*
**travailler** *to work*
**traverser** *to cross*
**trouver** *to find*
**voler** *to fly*

## Second conjugation: -ir verbs

Verbs of the second conjugation (**-ir** verbs) are conjugated like **finir** (*to finish*).

|  | SINGULAR | | PLURAL | |
| --- | --- | --- | --- | --- |
| **FIRST PERSON** | je | fin**is** | nous | fin**issons** |
| **SECOND PERSON** | tu | fin**is** | vous | fin**issez** |
| **THIRD PERSON** | il/elle/on | fin**it** | ils/elles | fin**issent** |

### Some common -ir verbs

**agir** *to act*
**applaudir** *to applaud*
**atterrir** *to land*
**avertir** *to warn*
**bâtir** *to build*
**choisir** *to choose*
**désobéir** *to disobey*

**établir** *to establish*
**finir** *to finish*
**gémir** *to moan*
**grossir** *to get fat*
**guérir** *to cure, make better*
**maigrir** *to get thin*
**mincir** *to get thin*

**obéir** *to obey*
**périr** *to perish*
**réfléchir** *to think, reflect*
**remplir** *to fill*
**réussir** *to succeed*
**rougir** *to blush*
**salir** *to make dirty*

# Third conjugation: -re verbs

Verbs of the third conjugation (-re verbs) are conjugated like **rendre** (*to give back*).

|  | SINGULAR |  | PLURAL |  |
|---|---|---|---|---|
| FIRST PERSON | je | rend**s** | nous | rend**ons** |
| SECOND PERSON | tu | rend**s** | vous | rend**ez** |
| THIRD PERSON | il/elle/on | rend | ils/elles | rend**ent** |

## Some common -re verbs

**attendre** *to wait for*
**confondre** *to confuse*
**défendre** *to forbid*
**descendre** *to go down (stairs); to get off (bus, train)*
**entendre** *to hear*

**interrompre** *to interrupt*
**mordre** *to bite*
**perdre** *to lose*
**prétendre** *to claim*
**rendre** *to give back*
**répondre** *to answer*

**rompre** *to break, break off (relationship)*
**tendre** *to stretch out; to offer; to tend to*
**tordre** *to twist*
**vendre** *to sell*

**NOTES**

- If the verb begins with a vowel or a mute **h**, then **je** becomes **j'**.

  j'arrive       j'entends       j'habite

- The subject pronoun **on** refers to people in general or to a nonspecific subject. It is often equivalent to the passive voice in English.

  Ici **on parle** français.          *French is spoken here.*
  **On cherche** un secrétaire.        *Secretary wanted.*

  In colloquial language, **on** + a third-person singular verb means *we*.

  Aujourd'hui **on dîne** au restaurant.   *Today we're having dinner at a restaurant.*

  **On habite** à Paris maintenant.       *We live in Paris now.*

- Most verbs of the third conjugation (-re verbs) have a stem ending in **d** like **vendre**. Those few whose stems don't end in **d**, such as **rompre** (*to break*) and **interrompre** (*to interrupt*), add a **-t** in the third-person singular.

  **il/elle** romp**t**                  **il/elle** interromp**t**

**Activité 1**   **Une soirée en famille.** Hélène Poiret décrit une soirée passée en famille. Formez des phrases pour savoir ce qu'elle dit.

MODÈLE   nous / passer la soirée / à la maison
Nous passons la soirée à la maison.

1. moi, je / préparer / un bon dîner

2.  papa / finir / son livre

   _____

3.  ma fille Lise / attendre / un coup de téléphone

   _____

4.  mon fils / écouter / un nouveau CD

   _____

5.  on / inviter nos cousins / à prendre le dessert avec nous

   _____

6.  mon cousin Philippe / jouer de la guitare

   _____

7.  nous / chanter / ensemble

   _____

8.  nous / applaudir

   _____

**Activité 2**  **Des invités.** Les Trichard ont invité l'oncle Charles à dîner. Complétez les phrases de Robert Trichard avec la forme correcte des verbes entre parenthèses pour savoir ce qui se passe.

1.  Nous _____ l'arrivée de l'oncle Charles et sa famille. (attendre)

2.  Ils _____ chez nous. (dîner)

3.  Ils _____ à sept heures. (arriver)

4.  Je _____ nos invités. (saluer)

5.  L'oncle Charles _____ des fleurs et des bonbons. (apporter)

6.  Ma mère _____ son frère. (remercier)

7.  Tout le monde _____ à la salle à manger. (passer)

8.  Mon père _____ les verres. (remplir)

**Activité 3**  **À la fac.** Comment est la classe de littérature de Raoul? Pour savoir, complétez les phrases avec la forme correcte des verbes entre parenthèses.

1.  Le professeur _____ dans la salle de classe. (entrer)

2.  Nous _____ un poème à analyser. (choisir)

3.  Les étudiants _____ leurs livres. (regarder)

4.  Moi, je _____ mon cahier. (chercher)

5.  Tout le monde _____ l'explication du professeur. (écouter)

6. Je demande à mon amie Anne-Laure, «Tu _____ à comprendre ce poème?» (arriver)

7. Elle _____ que oui. (répondre)

8. Le cours _____ à dix heures et quart. (finir)

9. Nous _____ nos livres. (fermer)

10. Nous _____ la fin de l'heure avec impatience. (attendre)

## Spelling changes in the present tense of regular -er verbs

1. First conjugation verbs whose stems end in **c, g,** or **y** have spelling changes in the present tense. These changes are required by the rules of French spelling.

2. The letter **c** in French represents the sound /s/ before **e** and **i,** but before **a, o,** and **u** it represents the sound /k/. Compare the pronunciation of the initial **c** in **casser** and **cesser.** For the letter **c** to represent the sound /s/ before **a, o,** and **u,** a cedilla is added under the **c.** Therefore, verbs whose stems end in **c,** such as **commencer** (*to begin*), add a cedilla under the **c** (**ç**) before the **o** of the ending of the **nous** form: commençons. The cedilla indicates that the **nous** form of the verb has the same soft /s/ sound as the rest of the conjugation (e.g., je **commence, tu commences,** etc.).

|  | SINGULAR | PLURAL |
|---|---|---|
| **FIRST PERSON** | je commence | nous commençons |
| **SECOND PERSON** | tu commences | vous commencez |
| **THIRD PERSON** | il/elle/on commence | ils/elles commencent |

### Verbs like **commencer**

**annoncer** *to announce*  
**avancer** *to advance*  
**divorcer** *to divorce*  
**effacer** *to erase*  

**lancer** *to launch*  
**menacer** *to threaten*  
**placer** *to place, invest*  
**prononcer** *to pronounce*  

**remplacer** *to replace*  
**renoncer** *to resign, quit*

3. The letter **g** in French represents the sound /zh/ (like the English **s** in *pleasure*) before **e** and **i,** but before **a, o,** and **u** it represents the sound /g/. Compare the pronunciation of the initial **g** in **garder** and **geler.** For the letter **g** to represent the sound /zh/ before **a, o,** and **u,** an **e** is added after the **g.** Therefore, verbs whose stems end in **-g,** such as **manger** (*to eat*), add an **e** after the **g** before the **o** of the ending of the **nous** form: mangeons. This change allows the pronunciation of the **nous** form of the verb to have the soft /zh/ sound that characterizes the rest of the conjugation (e.g., **je mange, tu manges,** etc.).

|  | SINGULAR | PLURAL |
|---|---|---|
| **FIRST PERSON** | je mange | nous mang**e**ons |
| **SECOND PERSON** | tu manges | vous mangez |
| **THIRD PERSON** | il/elle/on mange | ils/elles mangent |

## Verbs like **manger**

**aménager** *to fix up, convert (a room, etc.)*
**arranger** *to arrange*
**changer** *to change*
**corriger** *to correct*
**décourager** *to discourage*
**déménager** *to move (change residence)*

**déranger** *to bother*
**diriger** *to direct*
**encourager** *to encourage*
**engager** *to hire*
**loger** *to house, put someone up*
**nager** *to swim*
**partager** *to share*

**plonger** *to dive*
**ranger** *to put away*
**rédiger** *to draft, write*
**télécharger** *to download*
**voyager** *to travel*

4. Verbs whose stems end in **y,** such as **nettoyer** (*to clean*), change the **y** to **i** before a mute **e** ending (all singular forms and the third-person plural).

|  | SINGULAR | PLURAL |
|---|---|---|
| **FIRST PERSON** | je netto**i**e | nous nettoyons |
| **SECOND PERSON** | tu netto**i**es | vous nettoyez |
| **THIRD PERSON** | il/elle/on netto**i**e | ils/elles netto**i**ent |

**NOTE** Verbs ending in **-ayer** may either make the preceding change or keep the **y** in all forms: **je paie** or **je paye,** although the change of **y → i** is more common. Verbs in **-oyer** and **-uyer** must change **y → i** before a mute **e** ending.

## Some common verbs whose stems end in **y**

**appuyer** *to lean, press, support*
**balayer** *to sweep*
**effrayer** *to frighten*
**employer** *to use*
**ennuyer** *to bore*

**envoyer** *to send*
**essayer** *to try, try on*
**essuyer** *to wipe*
**nettoyer** *to clean*
**noyer** *to drown*
**payer** *to pay*

**rayer** *to cross out*
**renvoyer** *to send back, dismiss*
**tutoyer** *to use the **tu** form to address someone*
**vouvoyer** *to use the **vous** form to address someone*

**Activité 4** **On fait le ménage.** Complétez les phrases suivantes avec la forme correcte des verbes entre parenthèses pour savoir ce que font Claudette Legrand et sa famille pour mettre la maison en ordre avant l'arrivée de leurs cousins.

1. Ma sœur et moi, nous _____ nos affaires. (ranger)

2. Ma mère _____ le salon. (balayer)

3. Mon père _____ la cuisine. (nettoyer)

4. Mon frère et moi, nous _____ à travailler dans le jardin. (commencer)

5. Mes grands-parents _____ les tables. (essuyer)

6. J'_____ d'aider tout le monde. (essayer)

**Activité 5** **Est-ce que c'est comme ça dans votre classe de français?** Répondez à ces questions à propos de votre classe de français. Utilisez **nous** comme sujet dans chaque réponse.

1. Est-ce que vous commencez à lire des livres en français?

   _____

2. Est-ce que vous corrigez vos copies en classe?

   _____

3. Est-ce que vous effacez les mots mal écrits?

   _____

4. Est-ce que vous employez le français dans vos conversations?

   _____

5. Est-ce que vous dérangez les autres étudiants?

   _____

6. Est-ce que vous tutoyez le professeur?

   _____

7. Est-ce que vous prononcez correctement?

   _____

8. Est-ce que vous rédigez des courriels en français?

   _____

## First conjugation (-er) verbs with mute e or é as the stem vowel

1. a. First conjugation verbs that have mute **e** as their stem vowel, such as **acheter** (*to buy*), change the mute **e** to **è** in those forms in which the ending has a mute **e.** This spelling change reflects an important pronunciation change. The **e** in **nous achetons, vous achetez,** and in the infinitive **acheter** is a mute **e** and is usually not pronounced in these forms:/ashtõ/,/ashté/. The vowel **è** represents the sound/ɛ/, as in **tête** and **lettre,** and is a full-fledged vowel that is always pronounced.

|  | SINGULAR | PLURAL |
|---|---|---|
| **FIRST PERSON** | j' ach**è**te | nous achetons |
| **SECOND PERSON** | tu ach**è**tes | vous achetez |
| **THIRD PERSON** | il/elle/on ach**è**te | ils/elles ach**è**tent |

### Verbs like **acheter**

| | | |
|---|---|---|
| **amener** *to bring* (*someone*) | **geler** *to freeze* | **peser** *to weigh* |
| **emmener** *to take* (*someone*) | **lever** *to pick up, raise* | **promener** *to take for a walk* |
| **enlever** *to remove, take off* | **mener** *to lead* | *or drive* (*person, dog*) |

b. Verbs like **appeler** (*to call*) double the consonant after the mute **e** instead of changing **e** to **è**. The **e** before the single consonant represents a mute **e** that is often dropped in spoken French: **nous appelons**/nu za plõ/, **vous jetez**/ vu shté/.

|  | SINGULAR | PLURAL |
|---|---|---|
| **FIRST PERSON** | j' appe**ll**e | nous appelons |
| **SECOND PERSON** | tu appe**ll**es | vous appelez |
| **THIRD PERSON** | il/elle/on appe**ll**e | ils/elles appe**ll**ent |

### Verbs like **appeler**

| | | |
|---|---|---|
| **épeler** *to spell* | **projeter** *to project, throw,* | **rejeter** *to reject* |
| **feuilleter** *to leaf through* | *plan* | **renouveler** *to renew* |
| **jeter** *to throw* | **rappeler** *to call back* | |

2. a. Verbs that have **é** as the stem vowel, such as **espérer** (*to hope*), change **é** to **è** when the ending has a mute **e**.

|  | SINGULAR | PLURAL |
|---|---|---|
| **FIRST PERSON** | j' esp**è**re | nous espérons |
| **SECOND PERSON** | tu esp**è**res | vous espérez |
| **THIRD PERSON** | il/elle/on esp**è**re | ils/elles esp**è**rent |

b. In verbs that have **é** twice in their stem, such as **préférer** (*to prefer*), only the second **é** changes to **è**.

|  | SINGULAR | PLURAL |
|---|---|---|
| **FIRST PERSON** | je préf**è**re | nous préférons |
| **SECOND PERSON** | tu préf**è**res | vous préférez |
| **THIRD PERSON** | il/elle/on préf**è**re | ils/elles préf**è**rent |

## Verbs like **espérer** and **préférer**

**céder** *to yield*  
**célébrer** *to celebrate*  
**compléter** *to complete*

**protéger** *to protect*  
**refléter** *to reflect*

**répéter** *to repeat*  
**révéler** *to reveal*

**Activité 6**  **Entre amis.** Reformulez les questions suivantes en remplaçant le pronom **vous** par le pronom **tu**.

1. Est-que vous préférez travailler en été ou en hiver?

   _____

2. Qu'est-ce que vous espérez faire après l'université?

   _____

3. Combien est-ce que vous pesez?

   _____

4. Comment est-ce que vous épelez votre nom?

   _____

5. Est-ce que vous rejetez les idées extrémistes?

   _____

6. Où est-ce que vous achetez les livres pour les cours?

   _____

**Activité 7**  **Portrait de Jean-Claude.** Jean-Claude est un jeune homme dynamique. Formez les phrases indiquées pour savoir quels sont ses projets.

1. Jean-Claude / espérer devenir interprète

   _____

2. il / préférer les langues

   _____

3. il / projeter un voyage aux États-Unis

_____

4. il / feuilleter des brochures de l'agence de voyages

_____

5. il / renouveler son passeport

_____

6. ses idées / refléter l'influence de sa mère

_____

7. elle / lui répéter toujours l'importance d'une orientation internationale

_____

## Uses of the present tense

1. The present tense in French has several meanings. It generally expresses what is happening now.

   En général **nous nageons** dans une piscine, mais aujourd'hui **nous nageons** dans la mer.

   *We generally **swim** in a pool, but today **we are swimming** in the ocean.*

2. The French present tense can also express the future, especially if an expression in the sentence refers to future time.

   **Je t'emmène** en ville demain. Merci, tu es gentil. Mais demain **je travaille.**

   *I'll **take you** downtown tomorrow. Thanks, that's nice of you. But tomorrow **I'm working.***

3. Note that French has no equivalent for the English auxiliary *do, does* in questions or negative sentences.

   Quelle langue étudiez-vous? L'allemand?

   *What language do you study? German?*

   Non, je n'étudie pas l'allemand. J'apprends le français.

   *No, I don't study German. I'm learning French.*

4. French uses the present tense to refer to actions that began in the past but continue into the present, whereas English uses the present perfect (*have done something*) or present perfect progressive (*have been doing something*) for this function. The French construction consists of the following elements.

   a. To ask a question about how long something has been going on:
   **Depuis combien de temps** + verb in present tense

   **Depuis combien de temps** est-ce que vous habitez ce quartier?

   *How long have you been living in this neighborhood?*

There are also informal versions of this question.

**Il y a combien de temps que** vous habitez ce quartier?

**Ça fait combien (de temps) que** vous habitez ce quartier?

b. To tell how long something has been going on:
Verb in present tense + **depuis** + expression of time

**J'habite** ce quartier **depuis** un an.

There are also informal versions of this response pattern.

**Il y a un an que j'habite** ce
quartier.

**Voilà un an que j'habite** ce
quartier.

**Ça fait un an que j'habite** ce
quartier.

*I've been living* in this
neighborhood *for a year.*

c. To specify the starting point of an action that began in the past and
continues into the present, use **depuis quand** in the question and
**depuis** in the answer.

**Depuis quand** est-ce que vous
attendez le train?

J'attends **depuis** midi.

*Since when* have you been waiting
*for the train?*
*I've been waiting **since** noon.*

**Activité 8**  **Problèmes de bureau.** Françoise n'aime pas son travail. Pour savoir
ce qui se passe dans son bureau, complétez les phrases avec la forme
correcte des verbes entre parenthèses.

1. Demain je _____ de travail. (changer)

2. Il y a deux ans que je _____ dans le même bureau. (travailler)

3. Je _____ le même salaire depuis dix-huit mois. (gagner)

4. Ça fait dix mois que je _____ une augmentation.
   (demander)

5. Et ça fait dix mois que mon patron _____ la même
   réponse: Non. (répéter)

6. Tous mes collègues _____ de nouveaux emplois. (chercher)

7. Il y a longtemps qu'ils _____ renoncer à leur travail ici.
   (désirer)

8. La semaine prochaine ils _____ leur décision au patron.
   (annoncer)

**Activité 9**  **Un professeur dynamique.** Formez des phrases pour connaître les efforts
que Mme Ferron, professeur de langues, fait pour envoyer ses étudiants
faire des études à l'étranger. Employez **ça fait, depuis, il y a** ou **voilà** et
variez les constructions.

| MODÈLE | Mme Ferron / huit ans / envoyer des étudiants à l'étranger |
|---|---|
| | Il y a (Voilà) huit ans que Mme Ferron envoie des étudiants à l'étranger. |
| | *ou* |
| | Mme Ferron envoie des étudiants à l'étranger depuis huit ans. |

1. Mme Ferron / dix ans / enseigner dans notre université

   _____

2. elle / huit ans / encourager les étudiants à étudier à l'étranger

   _____

3. elle / huit ans / organiser des voyages pour les étudiants

   _____

4. les étudiants / quatre ans / passer un semestre au Québec chaque année

   _____

5. mon ami Charles / trois ans / étudier l'allemand

   _____

6. il / deux mois / projeter un voyage d'études en Allemagne

   _____

7. Charles / six semaines / feuilleter des brochures

   _____

8. Mme Ferron / un mois / chercher le programme idéal pour Charles

   _____

**Activité 10**    **Activité orale.** Demandez à un(e) ami(e) trois choses qu'il/elle aime faire et depuis combien de temps il/elle les fait. Racontez ce que cet(te) ami(e) vous dit à un(e) autre camarade de classe.

# PRESENT TENSE of irregular verbs

## Common irregular verbs

1. Irregular verbs are those that do not follow the patterns of regular **-er, -ir,** and **-re** verbs. Two of the most important irregular verbs are **avoir** (*to have*) and **être** (*to be*).

| AVOIR | | | |
|---|---|---|---|
| j' | **ai** | nous | **avons** |
| tu | **as** | vous | **avez** |
| il/elle/on | **a** | ils/elles | **ont** |

| ÊTRE | | | |
|---|---|---|---|
| je | **suis** | nous | **sommes** |
| tu | **es** | vous | **êtes** |
| il/elle/on | **est** | ils/elles | **sont** |

2. The verbs **aller** (*to go*) and **faire** (*to make, do*) are also irregular.

| ALLER | | | |
|---|---|---|---|
| je | **vais** | nous | **allons** |
| tu | **vas** | vous | **allez** |
| il/elle/on | **va** | ils/elles | **vont** |

| FAIRE | | | |
|---|---|---|---|
| je | **fais** | nous | **faisons*** |
| tu | **fais** | vous | **faites** |
| il/elle/on | **fait** | ils/elles | **font** |

Compounds of irregular verbs, such as **défaire** (*to undo*) and **refaire** (*to redo*), are conjugated like the simple verb.

*Note that the **ai** in **nous faisons** is pronounced / ə /, like the **e** of **le.**

3. The irregular verb **prendre** (*to take*) and its compounds are frequently used. **Prendre** resembles a regular **-re** verb only in the singular verb forms.

| PRENDRE | | | |
|---|---|---|---|
| je | **prends** | nous | **prenons** |
| tu | **prends** | vous | **prenez** |
| il/elle/on | **prend** | ils/elles | **prennent** |

Conjugated like **prendre: apprendre** (*to learn*), **comprendre** (*to understand*), **entreprendre** (*to undertake*), **reprendre** (*to resume*), **surprendre** (*to surprise*).

4. Verbs like **venir** (*to come*) have the following forms.

| VENIR | | | |
|---|---|---|---|
| je | **viens** | nous | **venons** |
| tu | **viens** | vous | **venez** |
| il/elle/on | **vient** | ils/elles | **viennent** |

Conjugated like **venir: appartenir** (*to belong*), **devenir** (*to become*), **maintenir** (*to maintain, support* [financially]), **obtenir** (*to obtain*), **retenir** (*to retain, hold back*), **revenir** (*to return*), **soutenir** (*to support, hold up*), **tenir** (*to hold*).

**NOTE**  The singular forms of **prendre** and **venir** end in a nasal vowel. The third-person plural has the vowel /ɛ/ + the nasal consonant /n/, and the **nous** and **vous** forms have the sound /ə/ as in **le**.

5. The verbs **devoir** (*to owe; should, ought, must*), **pouvoir** (*to be able to; can*), and **vouloir** (*to want*) are also irregular and may be followed by an infinitive.

| DEVOIR | | | |
|---|---|---|---|
| je | **dois** | nous | **devons** |
| tu | **dois** | vous | **devez** |
| il/elle/on | **doit** | ils/elles | **doivent** |

| POUVOIR | | | |
|---|---|---|---|
| je | **peux** | nous | **pouvons** |
| tu | **peux** | vous | **pouvez** |
| il/elle/on | **peut** | ils/elles | **peuvent** |

| VOULOIR | | | |
|---|---|---|---|
| je | **veux** | nous | **voulons** |
| tu | **veux** | vous | **voulez** |
| il/elle/on | **veut** | ils/elles | **veulent** |

**Activité 1** *Devoir* **n'est pas toujours** *vouloir.* Ces gens doivent faire certaines choses, même s'ils ne veulent pas. Répondez aux questions avec **devoir** et **vouloir** selon le modèle.

> MODÈLE    Martine travaille?
> Elle doit travailler, mais elle ne veut pas.

1. Tu passes la journée à la bibliothèque?

   _____

2. Catherine reste à la maison aujourd'hui?

   _____

3. Jean-Claude et Philippe vont chez le médecin?

   _____

4. Tes amis et toi, vous rentrez tôt?

   _____

5. Moi, je prépare le dîner?

   _____

6. Solange et moi, nous prenons un taxi?

   _____

**Activité 2** **Qui fait quoi chez Hélène?** Hélène et Sylvie se parlent de leur famille, qui est assez grande. Chacun fait une partie des travaux du ménage. Utilisez les éléments proposés pour savoir ce qu'elles disent.

**Vocabulaire**

## Des travaux ménagers

**faire les carreaux** *to do the windows*
**faire les courses** *to do the shopping/marketing*
**faire la cuisine** *to do the cooking*
**faire le jardin** *to do the gardening*

**faire le linge, faire la lessive** *to do the laundry*
**faire le(s) lit(s)** *to make the bed(s)*
**faire le ménage** *to do the housework*
**faire la vaisselle** *to do the dishes*

1. papa et moi / la vaisselle

   _____

2. les parents / le jardin

   _____

3. David et moi / les courses

   _____

4. grand-mère / la lessive

   _____

*(continued)*

5. moi / les carreaux

_____

6. maman et toi / les lits

_____

**Activité 3** *Vouloir* n'est pas toujours *pouvoir*. Ces gens veulent faire certaines choses, même s'ils ne peuvent pas. Répondez aux questions avec **vouloir** et **pouvoir** selon le modèle.

> MODÈLE   Philippe et toi, vous sortez ce soir?
> Nous voulons sortir ce soir, mais nous ne pouvons pas.

1. Tu vas au concert ce soir?

_____

2. Claire et Jean-Paul nous accompagnent au café?

_____

3. Sylvaine passe ses vacances à Tahiti?

_____

4. Moi, je cherche Laurent à la gare?

_____

5. Pauline et toi, vous regardez un film à la télé?

_____

6. Diane et Christine font du shopping?

_____

# Expressions with avoir, être, faire, and prendre

## Expressions with avoir

**avoir... ans** *to be . . . years old*
**avoir besoin de quelque chose** *to need something*
**avoir de la chance** *to be lucky*
**avoir envie de faire quelque chose** *to feel like doing something*
**avoir envie de quelque chose** *to feel like (having) something*

**avoir faim/soif/sommeil/ chaud/froid** *to be hungry/ thirsty/sleepy/warm/cold*
**avoir honte** *to be ashamed*
**avoir l'air + *adjective*** *to look . . .*
**avoir l'air d'un(e) + *noun*** *to look like a . . .*
**avoir l'intention de faire quelque chose** *to intend to do something*

**avoir mal à la tête / aux yeux / à l'estomac** *to have a headache / sore eyes / a stomachache*
**avoir mal au cœur** *to feel nauseous*
**avoir peur** *to be afraid*
**avoir raison** *to be right*
**avoir tort** *to be wrong*

| Quel âge avez-vous? | How old are you? |
|---|---|
| **J'ai dix-huit ans.** | *I'm eighteen years old.* |
| **Il a l'air triste, intelligent, distrait.** | *He looks sad, intelligent, absent-minded.* |
| **Elle a l'air d'une artiste, d'un professeur.** | *She looks like an artist, a teacher.* |

**Activité 4**  **Après l'accident.** Un groupe d'amis a eu un accident de voiture. L'un d'eux raconte où chacun a mal.

> MODÈLE    Marthe / tête
> Marthe a mal à la tête.

1. Pierre et Michèle / jambes

   _____

2. Frédéric / bras

   _____

3. Rachelle / dos

   _____

4. toi / épaule droite

   _____

5. moi / genoux

   _____

6. Alfred et moi / pieds

   _____

**Activité 5**  **Synonymes.** Écrivez sous chaque phrase une autre phrase formée avec une des expressions avec le verbe **avoir** qui a le même sens ou qui explique pourquoi le sujet a réalisé l'action.

1. Il veut dormir.

   _____

2. Je veux manger.

   _____

3. Nous voulons boire.

   _____

4. Elles mettent la climatisation.

   _____

5. Tu mets un pull-over.

   _____

(continued)

6. Il entend des pas dans son appartement.

_____

7. Vous donnez la réponse correcte.

_____

8. On rougit.

_____

9. Tu dis quelque chose qui n'est pas correct.

_____

10. Elle a gagné un voyage en Tunisie.

_____

## Expressions with être

**être à l'heure** _to be on time_
**être à quelqu'un** _to belong to someone; to give one's attention to someone_
**être à quelqu'un de faire quelque chose** _to be someone's turn (or responsibility) to do something_
**être au régime** _to be on a diet_

**être bien** _to be nice looking; to be comfortable_
**être d'accord avec quelqu'un** _to agree with someone_
**être de bonne/mauvaise humeur** _to be in a good/bad mood_
**être de retour** _to be back_
**être en avance** _to be early_
**être en colère** _to be angry_

**être en retard** _to be late_
**être en train de faire quelque chose** _to be busy doing something_
**être en vacances** _to be on vacation_
**être pressé(e)** _to be in a hurry_
**être sur le point de faire quelque chose** _to be about to do something_

À qui est ce stylo? — _Who(m) does this pen belong to?_
C'est (Il est) à Yvette. — _It's Yvette's. (It belongs to Yvette.)_

C'est à qui de jouer? — _Whose turn is it to play?_
C'est à vous d'en parler au directeur. — _It's up to you to talk to the manager about it._

Je suis à vous dans un instant. — _I'll be with you in just a moment._

## Expressions with faire

**Il fait beau/mauvais.**
_The weather's good/bad._
**Il fait chaud/froid.**
_It's hot/cold (outside)._
**Il fait du soleil/vent.**
_It's sunny/windy._
**Il fait jour/nuit.**
_It's daytime/nighttime._
**Il fait un sale temps.**
_The weather is lousy._
**Il fait 30 degrés.** _It's 30 degrees._

**Quelle température fait-il?**
_What's the temperature?_
**Quel temps fait-il?** _What's the weather like?_
**faire attention** _to pay attention_
**faire des projets** _to make plans_
**faire du sport, du jogging, du vélo** _to play sports, jog, bike ride_

**faire sa toilette** _to wash and get dressed (especially in the morning)_
**faire un voyage** _to take a trip_
**faire une promenade à pied / en voiture** _to go for a walk/ride_
**faire 10 kilomètres** _to travel/cover 10 kilometers_

## Expressions with prendre

**prendre de l'essence** *to get (buy) gasoline*
**prendre du poids** *to put on weight*
**prendre froid, prendre un rhume** *to catch cold*
**prendre le petit déjeuner** *to have breakfast*

**passer prendre quelqu'un** *to go pick someone up*
**prendre quelque chose à manger / à boire** *to have (meals, food, drink)*
**prendre quelqu'un pour un autre** *to mistake someone for somebody else*

**prendre un café / un thé / un coca / une glace** *to have coffee / tea / a soft drink / an ice cream*

**Activité 6**    **Un voyage dans le Midi.** Complétez les phrases suivantes avec la forme correcte du verbe **avoir, être, faire** ou **prendre,** pour savoir comment les Duverger et leurs enfants passent leurs vacances.

1. Les Duverger et leurs deux enfants _____ en vacances.

2. Ils _____ envie de connaître Marseille.

3. «On _____ un voyage dans le Midi!» décide la famille.

4. Ils voyagent en TGV. Le train _____ 800 kilomètres en moins de 4 heures.

5. Les Duverger _____ soif quand ils arrivent à Marseille.

6. Ils _____ une limonade dans le café de la gare.

7. Ils cherchent un guide. Les Duverger _____ attention quand le guide parle.

8. Le guide propose, «Aujourd'hui vous _____ une promenade en voiture pour connaître la ville.»

9. Les Duverger trouvent que c'est une excellente idée. Ils _____ de l'essence et ils partent à la découverte de Marseille.

**Activité 7**    **Comparons!** Parlez avec un(e) camarade de sujets divers.

> MODÈLE    Moi, j'ai envie de sortir. Et Jean?
> Lui aussi, il a envie de sortir.

1. Moi, je prends un café. Et Philippe et Yves?

   _____

2. Moi, j'ai faim. Et Camille et toi?

   _____

3. Céline et moi, nous faisons les courses maintenant. Et Paul et Christophe?

   _____

*(continued)*

4. David et toi, vous avez vingt ans. Et Marie et Quentin?

   _____

5. Claire et Chrystelle, elles sont en vacances la semaine prochaine. Et Émilie et moi?

   _____

6. Je suis en retard. Et Daniel?

   _____

7. Kevin et Stéphanie prennent du poids en hiver. Et toi?

   _____

8. Aurore et Gabriel ont raison. Et moi?

   _____

**Activité 8**  **Où ça?** Utilisez la forme correcte du verbe **être** pour décrire où se trouvent les personnes ou les choses par rapport aux endroits indiqués dans chaque cas.

> MODÈLE  le chien / à côté de / cinéma
> Le chien est à côté du cinéma.

**Vocabulaire**

## Les prépositions

| | | | |
|---|---|---|---|
| **à** _to, at_ | | **près de** _near_ | |
| **dans** _in_ | | **loin de** _far from_ | |
| **sur** _on_ | | **à côté de** _next to_ | |
| **sous** _under_ | | **en face de** _across from_ | |
| **devant** _in front of_ | | **entre** _between_ | |
| **derrière** _in back of_ | | **parmi** _among_ | |

_Note the following contractions._

**à + le → au**           **de + le → du**
**à + les → aux**          **de + les → des**

1. le journal / sous / le banc

   _____

2. moi / à côté de / le banc

   _____

3. mes amis / assis sur / le banc

   _____

4. les arbres / derrière / le banc

   _____

5. toi et moi / près de / le lac

_____

6. nous / en face de / le café

_____

7. le lac / entre / la forêt et le pré (*meadow*)

_____

8. vous / à / le café

_____

**Activité 9** **C'est une belle journée qui commence!** Chantal ne travaille pas aujourd'hui. Elle est très contente. Complétez ces phrases avec la forme correcte du verbe **avoir, être, faire** ou **prendre,** pour savoir comment elle se prépare pour sortir.

1. Il est sept heures. Il _____ très beau aujourd'hui.

2. Il _____ chaud.

3. Je ne travaille pas aujourd'hui et je _____ de très bonne humeur.

4. J' _____ envie de sortir.

5. Je _____ ma toilette.

6. Je _____ le petit déjeuner.

7. Je _____ des projets pour la journée.

8. Mon ami François va passer la journée avec moi. Le matin, nous

   _____ du jogging.

9. L'après-midi nous _____ une promenade en voiture.

10. Le soir nous _____ une bière ensemble dans un café.

# Irregular verbs resembling regular verbs

1. A small group of **-ir** verbs has the same endings as those of **-er** verbs in the present tense. Study the conjugation of **ouvrir** (*to open*).

| OUVRIR | | | |
|---|---|---|---|
| j' | ouvr**e** | nous | ouvr**ons** |
| tu | ouvr**es** | vous | ouvr**ez** |
| il/elle/on | ouvr**e** | ils/elles | ouvr**ent** |

However, **-ir** verbs in this group don't necessarily share the same verb stems. Conjugated like **ouvrir: couvrir** (*to cover*), **découvrir** (*to discover*), **rouvrir** (*to reopen*), but also the verbs **cueillir** (*to gather, pick* [flowers]), **accueillir** (*to welcome*), and **souffrir** (*to suffer*).

2. Another group of **-ir** verbs is conjugated like **-re** verbs, but omits the final consonant from the stem (in writing as well as speech) in the first- and second-person singular and replaces it with a **t** in the third-person singular. Study the conjugation of **dormir** (*to sleep*).

| DORMIR | | | |
|---|---|---|---|
| je | **dor**s | nous | **dorm**ons |
| tu | **dor**s | vous | **dorm**ez |
| il/elle/on | **dor**t | ils/elles | **dorm**ent |

Conjugated like **dormir: mentir** (*to lie*), **partir** (*to leave, set out*), **repartir** (*to leave again*), **sentir** (*to feel*), **servir** (*to serve*), **sortir** (*to go out*).

3. The verbs **mettre** (*to put*) and **battre** (*to beat*) and their compounds are conjugated like **-re** verbs, but lose one **t** in the singular.

| METTRE | | | |
|---|---|---|---|
| je | **met**s | nous | **mett**ons |
| tu | **met**s | vous | **mett**ez |
| il/elle/on | **met** | ils/elles | **mett**ent |

Conjugated like **mettre** and **battre: combattre** (*to fight, combat*), **débattre** (*to debate*), **omettre** (*to omit*), **permettre** (*to permit*), **promettre** (*to promise*). The singular forms of these verbs all end in a vowel sound in speech.

4. The verbs **convaincre** (*to convince*) and **vaincre** (*to conquer*) have two stems. The singular stem ends in **c,** and the plural stem ends in **qu.**

| CONVAINCRE | | | |
|---|---|---|---|
| je | **convainc**s | nous | **convainqu**ons |
| tu | **convainc**s | vous | **convainqu**ez |
| il/elle/on | **convainc** | ils/elles | **convainqu**ent |

5. Verbs with infinitives ending in **-aindre, -eindre,** and **-oindre** have two stems. The singular stem ends in **n,** and the plural stem ends in **gn.** These verbs follow the pattern of the verb **craindre** (*to fear*).

| CRAINDRE | | | |
|---|---|---|---|
| je | **crain**s | nous | **craign**ons |
| tu | **crain**s | vous | **craign**ez |
| il/elle/on | **crain**t | ils/elles | **craign**ent |

Conjugated like **craindre: atteindre** (*to reach, attain*), **éteindre** (*to put out, turn off, extinguish*), **étreindre** (*to embrace*), **joindre** (*to join, to reach someone by phone*), **peindre** (*to paint*), **plaindre** (*to pity*), **rejoindre** (*to rejoin, to meet up with someone, a group*).

6. Verbs like **connaître** (*to know* [*person, place*]) have a singular stem ending in **ai**. In the third-person singular form, the **i** changes to **î**. The plural stem ends in **ss**.

| CONNAÎTRE | | | |
|---|---|---|---|
| je | **connai**s | nous | **connaiss**ons |
| tu | **connai**s | vous | **connaiss**ez |
| il/elle/on | ***connaî**t* | ils/elles | **connaiss**ent |

Conjugated like **connaître: apparaître** (*to appear*), **disparaître** (*to disappear*), **paraître** (*to seem, appear*), **reconnaître** (*to recognize*).

7. Verbs with infinitives ending in **-uire** like **construire** (*to build*) have two stems. The singular stem ends in **i,** and the plural stem ends in **s**.

| CONSTRUIRE | | | |
|---|---|---|---|
| je | **construi**s | nous | **construis**ons |
| tu | **construi**s | vous | **construis**ez |
| il/elle/on | **construi**t | ils/elles | **construis**ent |

Conjugated like **construire: conduire** (*to drive*), **détruire** (*to destroy*), **introduire** (*to introduce*), **produire** (*to produce*), **traduire** (*to translate*).

8. The verb **recevoir** (*to receive*) is conjugated similarly to **devoir**. Note the change of **c** to **ç** before **o**.

| RECEVOIR | | | |
|---|---|---|---|
| je | **reçoi**s | nous | **recev**ons |
| tu | **reçoi**s | vous | **recev**ez |
| il/elle/on | **reçoi**t | ils/elles | **reçoiv**ent |

Conjugated like **recevoir: apercevoir** (*to notice*), **décevoir** (*to disappoint*).

**Activité 10** **Rien!** Jean-Baptiste a une attitude très négative aujourd'hui, comme vous pouvez le voir par ses réponses. Suivez le modèle.

> MODÈLE   Vous servez quelque chose?
> Non, je ne sers rien.

1. Vous craignez quelque chose?

_____

2. Vous recevez quelque chose?

_____

3. Vous devez quelque chose?

_____

(*continued*)

4. Vous construisez quelque chose?

_____

5. Vous reconnaissez quelque chose?

_____

6. Vous peignez quelque chose?

_____

7. Vous traduisez quelque chose?

_____

8. Vous découvrez quelque chose?

_____

**Activité 11**  **Un peintre qui réussit.** L'art de Nicole évolue avec beaucoup de succès. Formez les phrases indiquées pour savoir comment.

1. Nicole / peindre / tous les jours

_____

2. la nature / apparaître / dans ses tableaux

_____

3. nous / apercevoir / son talent

_____

4. nous / découvrir / de nouveaux thèmes

_____

5. maintenant / Nicole / introduire / la vie de la ville dans son art

_____

6. ses nouveaux tableaux / ne pas décevoir

_____

7. le public / accueillir / son art avec enthousiasme

_____

**Activité 12**  **Moi aussi.** Dans une conversation avec M. et Mme Sauvignon, Mme Dulac découvre qu'elle a beaucoup en commun avec eux. Suivez le modèle.

> MODÈLE   M. et Mme Sauvignon: Nous sortons le week-end.
> Mme Dulac: Moi aussi, je sors le week-end.

1. En été nous ouvrons toutes les fenêtres.

_____

2. Nous accueillons souvent des étudiants étrangers à la maison.

_____

3. Nous mettons toutes les plantes à l'extérieur au mois de mars.

_____

4. Nous découvrons de nouveaux paysages.

_____

5. Nous souffrons du dos quand il fait froid et humide.

_____

6. Nous partons en vacances au mois de juillet.

_____

7. Nous dormons dans le jardin quand il fait beau.

_____

8. Nous permettons aux enfants de jouer sur la pelouse.

_____

**Activité 13**    **Des vacances dans le désert.** Refaites cette petite histoire pour qu'elle raconte les aventures (et mésaventures!) de Josette.

> MODÈLE    Alain et Marc ne travaillent pas cette semaine.
> Josette ne travaille pas cette semaine.

1. Alain et Marc partent en vacances.

   Josette _____.

2. Ils rejoignent des amis.

   Elle _____.

3. Ils conduisent une vieille voiture.

   Elle _____.

4. Ils dorment dans des hôtels très modestes.

   Elle _____.

5. Ils arrivent dans le désert.

   Elle _____.

6. Ils sentent la chaleur.

   Elle _____.

7. Ils souffrent d'allergies.

   Elle _____.

8. Ils repartent à la maison.

   Elle _____.

# Other irregular verbs with two stems

1. In the conjugations of the verbs **écrire** (*to write*) and **boire** (*to drink*), the consonant **v** appears in the plural stem.

| ÉCRIRE | | | |
|---|---|---|---|
| j' | **écris** | nous | **écrivons** |
| tu | **écris** | vous | **écrivez** |
| il/elle/on | **écrit** | ils/elles | **écrivent** |

| BOIRE | | | |
|---|---|---|---|
| je | **bois** | nous | **buvons** |
| tu | **bois** | vous | **buvez** |
| il/elle/on | **boit** | ils/elles | **boivent** |

2. With the verbs **vivre** (*to live*), **savoir** (*to know*), and **suivre** (*to follow*), the **v** is absent from the singular stem.

| VIVRE | | | |
|---|---|---|---|
| je | **vis** | nous | **vivons** |
| tu | **vis** | vous | **vivez** |
| il/elle/on | **vit** | ils/elles | **vivent** |

| SAVOIR | | | |
|---|---|---|---|
| je | **sais** | nous | **savons** |
| tu | **sais** | vous | **savez** |
| il/elle/on | **sait** | ils/elles | **savent** |

| SUIVRE | | | |
|---|---|---|---|
| je | **suis** | nous | **suivons** |
| tu | **suis** | vous | **suivez** |
| il/elle/on | **suit** | ils/elles | **suivent** |

**NOTE**

Expressions with **suivre: suivre bien à l'école** (*to be a good student*), **suivre l'actualité** (*to keep up with the news*), **suivre un cours** (*to take a course*), **suivre un régime** (*to be on a diet*).

3. **Dire** (*to say, tell*), **lire** (*to read*), **mourir** (*to die*)

| DIRE | | | |
|---|---|---|---|
| je | **dis** | nous | **disons** |
| tu | **dis** | vous | *dites* |
| il/elle/on | **dit** | ils/elles | **disent** |

| LIRE | | | |
|---|---|---|---|
| je | **lis** | nous | **lisons** |
| tu | **lis** | vous | **lisez** |
| il/elle/on | **lit** | ils/elles | **lisent** |

| MOURIR | | | |
|---|---|---|---|
| je | **meurs** | nous | **mourons** |
| tu | **meurs** | vous | **mourez** |
| il/elle/on | **meurt** | ils/elles | **meurent** |

**NOTES**

- Note the irregular second-person plural form of the verb **dire: vous** *dites*.

- In its infinitive form, **courir** resembles **mourir**. However, unlike **mourir**, **courir** has only one stem in its conjugation, **cour-** (**je cours, il court, nous courons** etc.).

4. **Voir** (*to see*), **croire** (*to believe*)

| VOIR | | | |
|---|---|---|---|
| je | **vois** | nous | **voyons** |
| tu | **vois** | vous | **voyez** |
| il/elle/on | **voit** | ils/elles | **voient** |

| CROIRE | | | |
|---|---|---|---|
| je | **crois** | nous | **croyons** |
| tu | **crois** | vous | **croyez** |
| il/elle/on | **croit** | ils/elles | **croient** |

**Activité 14**   **Maintenant il s'agit de vacances à la plage.** Racontez l'expérience de Josette.

> MODÈLE   Les cousins de Josette veulent aller au bord de la mer.
> Josette veut aller au bord de la mer.

1. Ils croient que ça va être amusant.

   Elle _____.

2. Ils écrivent des courriels aux copains pour les inviter.

   Elle _____.

3. Ils savent arriver à la plage.

   Elle _____.

4. Ils boivent de l'eau parce qu'il fait chaud.

   Elle _____.

5. Ils meurent de soif.

   Elle _____.

6. Ils courent sur la plage pour faire de l'exercice.

   Elle _____.

7. Ils voient le coucher du soleil (*sunset*) sur la mer.

   Elle _____.

8. Ils disent que c'est très joli.

   Elle _____.

9. Le soir, ils lisent des blagues en ligne.

   Le soir, elle _____.

10. Ils suivent l'actualité à la télé.

    Elle _____.

11. Ils vivent des jours heureux au bord de la mer.

    Elle _____.

# Verbal constructions: verb + infinitive; verb + preposition + infinitive

1. When **aller** is followed by an infinitive, it expresses future time, like the English *to be going to.*

| | |
|---|---|
| À quelle heure est-ce que vous **allez prendre** un café avec nos amis? | *What time **are you going to have** a cup of coffee with our friends?* |
| Je **vais arriver** au café à midi. | *I'm **going to get** to the café at noon.* |

2. The present tense of **venir** + **de** + *infinitive* expresses an action that has just taken place.

| | |
|---|---|
| Je **viens de voir** Élise. | *I **just saw** Élise.* |
| Elle **vient de recevoir** un courriel de son frère. | *She **just received** an email from her brother.* |

3. The verbs **devoir, pouvoir,** and **vouloir** may be followed directly by an infinitive.

| | |
|---|---|
| Je **dois partir.** | *I **have to leave.*** |
| Je **ne peux pas sortir** aujourd'hui. | *I **can't go out** today.* |
| Tu **veux jouer** au football avec nous? | *Do you **want to play** soccer with us?* |

4. When **savoir** is followed by an infinitive, it means *to know how to do something.*

| | |
|---|---|
| Tu **sais nager?** | *Do you **know how to swim?*** |
| Oui, mais je **ne sais pas plonger.** | *Yes, but I **don't know how to dive.*** |
| Elle **ne sait pas monter** à bicyclette. | *She **doesn't know how to ride** a bike.* |
| Mais elle **sait conduire.** | *But she **knows how to drive.*** |

5. Verbs of motion, such as **descendre, sortir, venir,** and **monter,** can also be followed directly by an infinitive.

| | |
|---|---|
| Je **descends faire** les courses. | *I'm **going down to do** the shopping.* |
| Et moi, je **sors prendre** les billets pour le concert de demain soir. | *And I'm **going out to buy** the tickets for tomorrow night's concert.* |
| Marc **vient chercher** son livre. | *Marc **is coming to get** his book.* |
| Il est dans ma chambre. Il **peut monter le chercher,** s'il veut. | *It's in my room. He **can go upstairs to get it,** if he wants.* |

6. **Apprendre** is followed by **à** before an infinitive.

| | |
|---|---|
| Tu **apprends à jouer** de la flûte? | *Are you **learning to play** the flute?* |
| Non, je joue déjà de la flûte. J'**apprends à jouer** du piano. | *No, I already play the flute. I'm **learning to play** the piano.* |

**Activité 15** **Moi aussi.** Dites ce que votre camarade apprend à faire. Puis, dites-lui que vous voulez faire la même chose.

> MODÈLE  parler russe
> J'apprends à parler russe. Tu sais parler russe, toi?
> Non, pas encore, mais je veux parler russe.

1. danser le tango

_____

_____

2. jouer au golf

_____

_____

3. chanter du jazz

_____

_____

4. conduire une Ferrari

_____

_____

5. faire la cuisine

_____

_____

6. programmer l'ordinateur

_____

_____

**Activité 16** **C'est déjà fait.** Formez des échanges avec **aller** et **venir de** selon le modèle.

> MODÈLE   Baudouin / prendre un verre
> Est-ce que Baudouin va prendre un verre?
> Mais il vient de prendre un verre!

1. toi / faire du jogging

_____

_____

2. les gestionnaires / placer cet argent

_____

_____

3. vous deux / télécharger un document

_____

_____

(continued)

4. Christine / téléphoner à ses parents

_____

_____

5. nous / visiter les monuments

_____

_____

6. moi / voir un film

_____

_____

**Activité 17**   **Même pas pour la santé.**  Ces gens savent ce qu'ils doivent faire pour être en forme, mais ils ne le font pas. Exprimez leur refus en suivant le modèle.

> MODÈLE   Jean-Pierre doit courir tous les jours.
> Il sait qu'il doit courir, mais il dit qu'il ne peut pas et qu'il ne veut pas.

1. Mes parents doivent marcher tous les jours.

_____

_____

2. Mes amis, vous devez faire de l'exercice.

_____

_____

3. Je dois nager une heure tous les jours.

_____

_____

4. Tu dois faire du sport.

_____

_____

5. Catherine doit suivre un régime pour maigrir.

_____

_____

6. Ma sœur et moi, nous devons faire du vélo.

_____

_____

**Activité 18**   **Activité orale.**  Avec un(e) camarade, parlez de votre journée—quand vous avez faim et soif, ce que vous prenez quand vous sortez et quand vous êtes de retour, combien d'heures vous dormez, et ainsi de suite (*et cetera*).

# PASSÉ COMPOSÉ

## Passé composé with avoir

The **passé composé** (*literally,* compound past) is one of the two past tenses in modern French. It is used to express an action completed in the past; it may sometimes be translated into English using the present perfect: *have/has done something.* Both the **passé composé** and the English present perfect consist of an auxiliary verb conjugated in the present tense followed by a past participle.

Here is the conjugation of **parler** (*to speak*), which is conjugated in the **passé composé** with the auxiliary **avoir.**

| PARLER | | | |
|---|---|---|---|
| j' | **ai parlé** | nous | **avons parlé** |
| tu | **as parlé** | vous | **avez parlé** |
| il/elle/on | **a parlé** | ils/elles | **ont parlé** |

The past participle endings differ according to verb group.

**-ER** verbs: The **-er** infinitive ending is replaced with **-é.**

march**er** → march**é** (*walked*)

parl**er** → parl**é** (*spoken*)

**-IR** verbs: The **-ir** infinitive ending is replaced with **-i.**

chois**ir** → chois**i** (*chosen*)

fin**ir** → fin**i** (*finished*)

**-RE** verbs: The **-re** infinitive ending is replaced with **-u.**

interromp**re** → interromp**u** (*interrupted*)

vend**re** → vend**u** (*sold*)

### Verbs with irregular past participles

apprendre → **appris**
atteindre → **atteint**
avoir → **eu**
boire → **bu**
comprendre → **compris**
conduire → **conduit**

connaître → **connu**
construire → **construit**
courir → **couru**
couvrir → **couvert**
craindre → **craint**
croire → **cru**

cuire → **cuit**
découvrir → **découvert**
devoir → **dû**
dire → **dit**
écrire → **écrit**
être → **été**

*(continued)*

| | | |
|---|---|---|
| faire → **fait** | peindre → **peint** | suivre → **suivi** |
| instruire → **instruit** | pouvoir → **pu** | tenir → **tenu** |
| joindre → **joint** | prendre → **pris** | venir → **venu** |
| lire → **lu** | produire → **produit** | vivre → **vécu** |
| mettre → **mis** | recevoir → **reçu** | voir → **vu** |
| ouvrir → **ouvert** | savoir → **su** | vouloir → **voulu** |
| paraître → **paru** | souffrir → **souffert** | |

1. Negation in the **passé composé** is formed by placing **ne** before the conjugated form of **avoir** followed by **pas** (or most negative words).

Tu **n'**as **pas** encore fait tes devoirs?    *Haven't you done your homework yet?*
Non, je **n'**ai **rien** écrit. Je **n'**ai **jamais**    *No, I haven't written **anything.** I've*
eu tant de difficulté.    ***never** had so much trouble.*

2. However, **personne** and **nulle part** follow the past participle.

Tu **n'**as vu **personne** hier soir?    *Didn't you see **anyone** last night?*
Non. J'ai cherché mes amis partout,    *No. I looked for my friends everywhere,*
mais je **n'**ai rencontré **personne**    *but I didn't run into **anyone***
**nulle part.**    ***anywhere.***

3. When inversion is used to ask a question in the **passé composé,** the subject pronoun and the auxiliary verb are inverted. In negative questions, the **ne** and **pas** (or other negative words, except for **personne** and **nulle part**) are placed around the inverted auxiliary verb and pronoun, before the past participle. Negative questions with inversion in the **passé composé** are limited to formal language.

**Les Durand ont-ils décidé** de    ***Have the Durands decided** to*
vendre leur appartement?    *sell their apartment?*
Oui. **N'avez-vous pas vu** l'annonce    *Yes. **Didn't you see** the advertisement*
dans le journal?    *in the newspaper?*

**Activité 1**    **C'était hier.** Vous faites la même réponse à toutes les questions de votre ami(e). Employez le passé composé pour lui dire que tout le monde a tout fait hier. Suivez le modèle.

> MODÈLE    Vous travaillez aujourd'hui?
> Non. Mais j'ai travaillé hier.

1. Jean nage aujourd'hui?

_____

2. Christine et toi, vous déjeunez en ville aujourd'hui?

_____

3. Marc prend de l'essence aujourd'hui?

_____

4. Toi et moi, nous nettoyons notre chambre aujourd'hui?

_____

5. Les étudiants rédigent un thème aujourd'hui?

_____

6. Tu apprends le vocabulaire aujourd'hui?

_____

7. Jacquot fait le linge aujourd'hui?

_____

8. Vous finissez le travail aujourd'hui, vous deux?

_____

9. Tu attends tes amis aujourd'hui?

_____

10. Alice répond en classe aujourd'hui?

_____

11. Les étudiants obtiennent les résultats de l'examen aujourd'hui?

_____

12. Le film reprend aujourd'hui?

_____

13. Tu as mal à l'estomac aujourd'hui?

_____

14. Je suis en avance aujourd'hui?

_____

15. Il fait un gâteau aujourd'hui?

_____

**Activité 2** **Une aventure routière.** Jean-Pierre a pris la voiture hier, mais il a eu des difficultés. Réécrivez son histoire au passé composé pour savoir ce qui lui est arrivé.

**Vocabulaire**

## L'automobile

**au bord de la rue** _at the side of the street_
**avoir un pneu crevé** _to have a flat tire_
**l'essence** (_f._) _gasoline_
**faire le plein** _to fill the gas tank_

**faire une promenade en voiture** _to go for a ride in the car_
**garer la voiture** _to park the car_
**pousser la voiture** _to push the car_
**la station-service** _gas station_

1. J'invite mon copain Serge à faire une promenade en voiture avec moi.

   _____

2. Serge veut faire le plein avant de partir.

   _____

3. Tout d'un coup, nous entendons un bruit.

   _____

4. Nous avons un pneu crevé.

   _____

5. Nous poussons la voiture au bord de la rue.

   _____

6. Nous achetons un nouveau pneu à la station-service.

   _____

7. Nous devons dépenser tout notre argent.

   _____

8. Nous ne pouvons pas aller à la campagne.

   _____

9. Nous remontons la rue.

   _____

10. Tu nous vois de la fenêtre.

    _____

11. Je gare la voiture devant mon immeuble.

    _____

12. Sylvie et toi, vous riez de notre histoire.

    _____

**Activité 3**  **Un nouvel ordinateur.**  Colette raconte comment elle a acheté un nouvel ordinateur. Réécrivez son histoire au passé composé.

1. Je convaincs mon père d'acheter un nouvel ordinateur.

   _____

2. Mon père et moi, nous lisons une brochure ensemble.

   _____

3. Nous demandons d'autres brochures.

   _____

4. Mon père trouve un revendeur (clerk) bien informé.

   _____

5. Nous posons beaucoup de questions au revendeur.

   _____

6. Il répond patiemment à nos questions.

   _____

7. Nous choisissons une imprimante aussi.

   _____

8. J'achète des logiciels (*software packages*).

   _____

9. Mon père trouve des CD-ROM intéressants.

   _____

10. Je mets le nouvel ordinateur dans ma chambre.

    _____

**Activité 4** **Un courriel de son cousin.** Marie reçoit un courriel de son cousin François. Pour savoir de quoi il s'agit, formez des phrases au passé composé avec les éléments proposés.

1. Marie / recevoir un courriel

   _____

2. elle / ouvrir le message

   _____

3. elle / lire le texte

   _____

4. son cousin François / écrire le courriel

   _____

5. il / joindre une photo au courriel

   _____

6. il / être malade pendant un mois

   _____

7. il / passer deux semaines à l'hôpital

   _____

8. Marie / imprimer le courriel pour ses parents

   _____

9. ils / dire à Marie de téléphoner à François

   _____

(*continued*)

10. elle / inviter François à passer les vacances chez elle

_____

11. il / être très content d'accepter son invitation

_____

12. il / promettre d'arriver au début du mois de juillet

_____

## Passé composé with être

1. A group of French verbs forms the **passé composé** with **être** rather than with **avoir**. Most of these verbs express motion or describe a change of state. When the **passé composé** is formed with **être**, the past participle agrees in gender and number with the subject. Study the **passé composé** of **aller**.

| ALLER | | | |
|---|---|---|---|
| je | **suis** allé(e) | nous | **sommes** allé(e)s |
| tu | **es** allé(e) | vous | **êtes** allé(e)(s) |
| il | **est** allé | ils | **sont** allés |
| elle | **est** allée | elles | **sont** allées |

The following verbs are conjugated with **être** as the auxiliary in the **passé composé**.

arriver → je **suis arrivé(e)**            partir → je **suis parti(e)**
descendre → je **suis descendu(e)**        rentrer → je **suis rentré(e)**
devenir → je **suis devenu(e)**            rester → je **suis resté(e)**
entrer → je **suis entré(e)**              retourner → je **suis retourné(e)**
monter → je **suis monté(e)**              sortir → je **suis sorti(e)**
mourir → il (elle) **est mort(e)**         tomber → je **suis tombé(e)**
naître → je **suis né(e)**                 venir → je **suis venu(e)**

These verbs are also conjugated with **être** when a prefix is added.

redescendre → je **suis redescendu(e)** _I went_       repartir → je **suis reparti(e)** _I left again_
   _back down_                                          revenir → je **suis revenu(e)** _I came back_
remonter → je **suis remonté(e)** _I went_
   _back up_

2. **Être** verbs form the negative and interrogative in the **passé composé** the same way that **avoir** verbs do.

Negatives:

Elle **n'**est **pas** montée.          _She didn't go upstairs._
Je **n'**y suis **jamais** retourné.    _I **never** went back there._
Ils **ne** sont allés **nulle part.**   _They didn't go **anywhere.**_

Interrogatives and negative interrogatives:

> Quand **vos invités sont-ils partis**?  *When **did your guests leave**?*
> **N'est-elle pas encore venue**?  *Hasn't she come yet?*

Questions with inversion, especially negative questions, are limited to formal styles.

**Activité 5**  **Ma soirée.** Marie-Noëlle raconte ce qu'elle a fait hier soir. Pour savoir ce qu'elle a fait, formez des phrases au passé composé avec l'auxiliaire **être** selon les éléments proposés.

1. je / arriver chez moi vers cinq heures et demie

   _____

2. je / repartir à six heures

   _____

3. je / aller au supermarché pour acheter quelque chose à manger

   _____

4. je / rentrer tout de suite

   _____

5. Lise et Solange / venir chez moi vers sept heures

   _____

6. elles / rester une heure

   _____

7. elles / partir à huit heures

   _____

8. je / monter dans ma chambre faire mes devoirs

   _____

9. je / redescendre regarder les informations à la télé

   _____

10. je / remonter dans ma chambre pour me coucher

    _____

11. je / tomber dans mon lit, épuisée (*exhausted*)

    _____

**Activité 6**  **Pas cette fois.** Hélène est sortie avec Robert et Richard, les jumeaux. Elle explique à son amie Elvire que cette fois tout a été différent de ce qui se passe d'habitude. Utilisez le passé composé en employant l'auxiliaire correcte pour savoir ce qu'Hélène dit. Suivez le modèle.

> MODÈLE  Robert et Richard mangent toujours au restaurant. (au bistrot du coin)
>  Cette fois ils ont mangé au bistrot du coin.

1. Robert et Richard arrivent toujours en retard. (en avance)

   _____

2. Ils prennent toujours le bus. (le métro)

   _____

3. Robert et Richard parlent toujours du football. (de leurs cours)

   _____

4. Ils lisent toujours le journal sportif. (*Le Monde*)

   _____

5. Ils commandent toujours un sandwich. (un steak-frites)

   _____

6. Ils boivent toujours beaucoup de coca avec le repas. (beaucoup d'eau minérale)

   _____

7. Robert et Richard mangent toujours vite. (lentement)

   _____

8. Ils restent toujours cinq minutes après le repas. (une demi-heure)

   _____

9. Ils laissent toujours un pourboire d'un euro. (de deux euros)

   _____

10. Ils vont toujours à la fac après le déjeuner. (en ville)

    _____

**Activité 7**   **Dormir à la belle étoile.**   Nicolas et ses amis sont allés faire du camping. Ils ont eu une mauvaise surprise dans la forêt de Fontainebleau. Pour savoir ce qui s'est passé, formez des phrases au passé composé avec les éléments proposés.

**Vocabulaire**

## À la campagne

**à la belle étoile** *under the stars*
**affreux** *horrible*
**coucher, dormir à la belle étoile**
   *to sleep outdoors*
**dresser la tente** *to set up the tent*
**en courant** *running*
**épuisé** *exhausted*
**être pris de panique** *to be overcome by panic*
**faire un feu de camp** *to make a campfire*

**ne pas fermer l'œil de la nuit**
   *not to sleep a wink all night*
**hurler** *to scream*
**installer son camp** *to set up camp*
**plier la tente** *to fold up the tent*
**ramper** *to creep*
**rentrer sous la tente** *to go back in the tent*
**le ruisseau** *stream*
**le sac de couchage** *sleeping bag*

Trois de mes amis et moi, nous _____ (vouloir) coucher
1

à la belle étoile. Nous _____ (aller) à la campagne.
2

Nous _____ (installer) notre camp à côté du ruisseau.
3

Claude et moi, nous _____ (faire) un feu de camp.
4

Marc et Philippe _____ (dresser) les tentes.
5

Nous _____ (manger) autour du feu de camp. Vers
6

neuf heures, nous _____ (entrer) sous nos tentes.
7

Chacun _____ (entrer) dans son sac de couchage.
8

Soudain, je/j' _____ (entendre) un cri affreux.
9

Marc _____ (remarquer) un serpent sous la tente.
10

Philippe et lui _____ (sortir) de la tente en
11

courant. Nous _____ (être) pris de panique. Le
12

serpent _____ (partir) en rampant. Je crois que le pauvre
13

serpent _____ (avoir) peur. Nous _____
14                                                              15

(arrêter) de hurler. Chacun _____ (rentrer) sous sa tente.
16

Personne ne/n' _____ (fermer) l'œil de la nuit. Le matin
17

nous _____ (plier) les tentes. Nous _____
18                                                            19

(retourner) chez nous. Tout le monde _____ (être) épuisé.
20

## Verbs conjugated with avoir and être in the passé composé

Several verbs usually conjugated with **être** in the **passé composé** are conjugated
with **avoir** when they have direct objects. Note the changes in meaning.

1. **monter, descendre**

   | | |
   |---|---|
   | Le chasseur **a monté nos bagages.** | *The bellhop **took up our luggage.*** |
   | Mais nous **avons descendu nos valises** tout seuls. | *But we **brought our suitcases down** by ourselves.* |

2. **entrer, rentrer, sortir**

   | | |
   |---|---|
   | Je **n'ai pas encore entré les données.** | *I haven't yet entered the data.* |
   | Qui **a rentré le journal**? | *Who **brought in the newspaper**?* |
   | Elle **a sorti son porte-clés.** | *She **took out her key ring.*** |

3. The verb **passer** is conjugated with **être** in the **passé composé** when it
   means *to come by, stop by to see, visit, be over.*

   | | |
   |---|---|
   | Le facteur **est** déjà **passé.** | *The mail carrier **has already come by.*** |
   | Hier ma cousine **est passée** me voir. | *My cousin **came by** to see me yesterday.* |
   | Le pire **est passé.** | *The worst **is over**.* |

In most other cases, **passer** is conjugated with **avoir**.

Ils **ont passé** une année en Suisse.    *They **spent** a year in Switzerland.*
Elle **a passé** son permis de conduire.    *She **took** her driving test.*

**NOTE**    The expression **passer un examen** (*to take an exam*) is not to be confused with **réussir un examen** (*to pass an exam*).

**Activité 8**    **Quelle journée!** Les Vaillancourt ont eu une journée très fatigante hier. Pour savoir ce qui s'est passé, complétez les phrases suivantes avec le passé composé des verbes entre parenthèses, en faisant attention au choix d'auxiliaire et à l'accord du participe passé si l'auxiliaire **être** est nécessaire.

**Vocabulaire**

## Des mots utiles

**à toute vitesse** *in a hurry*
**l'aîné(e)** *the older child*
**le/la cadet(te)** *the younger child*

**étendre le linge sur le fil**
  *to hang the clothes on the line*
**les travaux** *road work*

M. Vaillancourt _____ (sortir) la voiture du garage à cinq heures du matin. Il _____ (partir) au travail. Il _____ (monter) la rue de la République, comme toujours. Mais aujourd'hui il _____ (voir) qu'il y avait des travaux. Il _____ (devoir) changer de route. Il _____ (arriver) en retard.

Mme Vaillancourt _____ (demander) à ses filles de l'aider à la maison. Elle _____ (sortir) du bureau. L'aînée _____ (faire) le linge. La cadette _____ (étendre) le linge sur le fil. Ensuite, les deux sœurs _____ (descendre) faire les courses. Elles _____ (descendre) l'escalier de l'immeuble. Elles _____ (rentrer) en une demi-heure. Elles _____ (monter) les paquets. Quand elles _____ (entrer) dans l'appartement, il _____ (commencer) à pleuvoir. «Le linge!» _____ (dire) l'aînée. Les deux _____ (rentrer) le linge à toute vitesse.

# Agreement of the past participle

1. The past participle of a verb conjugated with **avoir** agrees in gender and number with the direct object when the direct object precedes the verb. The direct object may be a noun, an object pronoun, or a relative pronoun.

| | |
|---|---|
| Quelle **pièce** avez-vous vu**e**? | *Which **play** did you see?* |
| Combien de **sandwichs** a-t-il mang**és**? | *How many **sandwiches** did he eat?* |
| Elle a acheté une nouvelle robe. Elle **l'**a mis**e** aujourd'hui. | *She bought a new dress. She wore **it** today.* |
| Les fenêtres sont fermées. Personne ne **les** a ouver**tes** aujourd'hui. | *The windows are closed. No one opened **them** today.* |
| Voilà **les articles qu'**il a lu**s**. | *Here are **the articles that** he read.* |
| On va publier **les histoires qu'**elle a écri**tes**. | *They're going to publish **the stories that** she wrote.* |

2. Note that the past participle does not agree with a preceding indirect object.

| | |
|---|---|
| Marthe? Je **lui** ai téléphoné. | *Marthe? I called **her.*** |
| Et tes parents? Tu **leur** as écrit? | *What about your parents? Did you write **to them**?* |

**Activité 9**  **Élisabeth s'installe à Paris.**  Complétez l'histoire suivante avec le participe passé des verbes entre parenthèses. Faites les accords nécessaires.

Élisabeth a _____ (quitter) le Québec pour la France.

On lui a _____ (offrir) un bon emploi et elle

l'a _____ (accepter). Elle a _____

(faire) ses valises et elle a _____ (prendre) l'avion. Elle est

_____ (arriver) à Paris il y a un mois. Elle a tout de suite

_____ (commencer) à chercher un appartement. Les annonces

qu'elle a _____ (lire) dans le journal promettaient beaucoup,

mais les appartements qu'elle a _____ (voir) n'étaient pas très

jolis et étaient très chers. Quelqu'un lui a _____ (donner)

l'adresse d'une agence immobilière. Quand elle l'a _____

(trouver), elle est _____ (entrer) et a _____

(demander) de l'aide. Les appartements qu'on lui a _____

(montrer) n'étaient pas mal. L'appartement qu'elle a _____

(choisir) n'était pas loin de son travail. Il se trouvait dans une petite rue

qu'elle a _____ (trouver) très agréable. Après,

*(continued)*

elle a _____ (commencer) à travailler. Au bureau, on
                  17

l'a _____ (présenter) à tout le monde, et on l'a
                 18

_____ (accueillir) très amicalement. Elle est très contente
              19

à Paris maintenant.

**Activité 10**  **Lequel?**  Votre ami(e) s'intéresse à vos affaires. Dans chaque cas
demandez-lui s'il s'agit de la chose que vous avez faite hier. Employez le
verbe entre parenthèses dans votre réponse et faites attention à l'accord du
participe passé.

> MODÈLE  Fais voir ta calculatrice. (acheter)
> La calculatrice que j'ai achetée hier?

1. Montre-moi tes devoirs. (faire)

   _____

2. Je peux lire la lettre de Michèle? (recevoir)

   _____

3. Où est ta composition? (rédiger)

   _____

4. Tu as un nouveau sac à dos? (acheter)

   _____

5. Fais voir ton appareil-photo. (utiliser)

   _____

6. Montre-moi ton nouveau DVD. (regarder)

   _____

7. Je peux écouter tes nouveaux CD? (écouter)

   _____

8. Fais voir tes nouvelles chaussures. (mettre)

   _____

9. Je veux voir tes lunettes de soleil. (porter)

   _____

10. Tu me prêtes les revues? (lire)

    _____

**Activité 11**  **Activité orale.**  Avec un(e) camarade parlez des choses que vous avez faites
hier. Après, racontez à un(e) autre camarade les choses que vous avez
faites tous les deux. Employez le passé composé dans votre conversation.

# 4 IMPERFECT

## Forms of the imperfect

1. The imperfect tense is used to describe background actions or situations, (but not events) in the past. Its formation is simple because the imperfect endings are the same for all verbs: **-ais, -ais, -ait, -ions, -iez,** and **-aient.** The stem to which the imperfect endings are added is the **nous** form of the present tense minus the **-ons** ending.

   Study the imperfect of these three regular verbs.

| PARLER | | | |
|---|---|---|---|
| je | parl**ais** | nous | parl**ions** |
| tu | parl**ais** | vous | parl**iez** |
| il/elle/on | parl**ait** | ils/elles | parl**aient** |

| FINIR | | | |
|---|---|---|---|
| je | finiss**ais** | nous | finiss**ions** |
| tu | finiss**ais** | vous | finiss**iez** |
| il/elle/on | finiss**ait** | ils/elles | finiss**aient** |

| RENDRE | | | |
|---|---|---|---|
| je | rend**ais** | nous | rend**ions** |
| tu | rend**ais** | vous | rend**iez** |
| il/elle/on | rend**ait** | ils/elles | rend**aient** |

2. Irregular verbs also form their imperfect stems from the **nous** form.

| INFINITIVE | PRESENT TENSE, *nous* FORM | IMPERFECT STEM | CONJUGATION EXAMPLE |
|---|---|---|---|
| avoir | nous avons | **av-** | **j'avais** |
| boire | nous buvons | **buv-** | **tu buvais** |
| craindre | nous craignons | **craign-** | **on craignait** |
| étudier | nous étudions | **étudi-** | **nous étud*i*ions** |

*(continued)*

| INFINITIVE | PRESENT TENSE, *nous* FORM | IMPERFECT STEM | CONJUGATION EXAMPLE |
|---|---|---|---|
| lire | nous lisons | **lis-** | vous lisiez |
| prendre | nous prenons | **pren-** | ils prenaient |
| recevoir | nous recevons | **recev-** | elles recevaient |

**NOTE**

Like the verb **étudier,** all verbs whose stems end in **i** have a double **i** (**ii**) in the **nous** and **vous** forms of the imperfect.

> **crier** → nous criions        **rire** → vous riiez

3. Verbs with a spelling change in the **nous** form of the present tense, such as **manger** and **commencer,** have the same spelling change before imperfect endings that begin with **a.**

| MANGER | | | |
|---|---|---|---|
| je | mang**e**ais | nous | mangions |
| tu | mang**e**ais | vous | mangiez |
| il/elle/on | mang**e**ait | ils/elles | mang**e**aient |

| COMMENCER | | | |
|---|---|---|---|
| je | commen**ç**ais | nous | commencions |
| tu | commen**ç**ais | vous | commenciez |
| il/elle/on | commen**ç**ait | ils/elles | commen**ç**aient |

4. Only the verb **être** has an irregular stem in the imperfect.

| ÊTRE | | | |
|---|---|---|---|
| j' | **ét**ais | nous | **ét**ions |
| tu | **ét**ais | vous | **ét**iez |
| il/elle/on | **ét**ait | ils/elles | **ét**aient |

**Activité 1**   **Avant, c'était différent.** Formez des phrases au présent et à l'imparfait pour expliquer que tout a changé. Suivez le modèle.

> MODÈLE   je / travailler tous les jours
> Je ne travaille plus tous les jours. Avant, je travaillais tous les jours.

1. vous / croire à cette histoire

_____

2. il / lire en allemand

_____

3. elles / faire les carreaux

   _____

4. tu / habiter en ville

   _____

5. ils / vivre bien

   _____

6. mon chien / obéir

   _____

7. elle / rougir

   _____

8. je / répondre en classe

   _____

9. tu / voyager

   _____

10. elle / prononcer correctement

    _____

11. vous / apprécier la musique classique

    _____

12. ils / ranger leurs affaires

    _____

**Activité 2**  **Ma jeunesse.** Caroline parle de son enfance. Formez des phrases à l'imparfait pour savoir comment elle vivait à l'époque.

1. nous / avoir une maison dans un quartier tranquille

   _____

2. elle / être grande

   _____

3. la maison / avoir dix pièces

   _____

4. mes parents / travailler en ville

   _____

5. ils / aller au bureau en bus

   _____

(continued)

6. l'arrêt / être au coin de la rue

_____

7. beaucoup d'autres jeunes filles / habiter dans notre rue

_____

8. je / jouer avec elles

_____

9. nous / aller à l'école ensemble

_____

10. je / garder souvent ma petite sœur Marguerite

_____

11. maman / nous conduire au parc

_____

12. nous / être tous très contents

_____

**Activité 3** **Grand-mère évoque son enfance.** La grand-mère de Nicolas raconte ses souvenirs. Formez des phrases à l'imparfait pour savoir ce qu'elle dit.

1. nous / vivre à la campagne

_____

2. je / partager une chambre avec ma sœur

_____

3. nous / ne pas avoir beaucoup d'argent

_____

4. mais on / être heureux

_____

5. je / nager dans le lac

_____

6. mes parents / élever des vaches

_____

7. les enfants / boire le lait frais

_____

8. nous / vendre le lait

_____

9. ton grand-père / commencer à passer me voir

_____

10. je / avoir dix-huit ans

_____

**Activité 4**    **Nos vacances à l'époque.** Un groupe d'amis évoque les souvenirs de leurs vacances quand ils étaient jeunes. Formez des phrases à l'imparfait pour savoir comment ils passaient leurs vacances. Faites attention au placement des adverbes de temps dans les phrases.

> MODÈLE    Alfred: tous les ans / nous / aller / à la campagne
> Nous allions tous les ans à la campagne.

1. Lise: souvent / je / passer les vacances / chez ma tante

_____

2. Michel: toujours / je / vouloir / aller au bord de la mer

_____

3. Christine: chaque été / ma famille et moi, nous / visiter / une région de France

_____

4. Paul: tous les ans / mes cousins / m'inviter / chez eux

_____

5. Marianne: le plus souvent / nous, on / prendre les vacances en hiver

_____

6. Robert: en général / ma cousine Élisabeth / venir / chez nous à Paris

_____

7. Françoise: d'habitude / nous / partir / en Suisse

_____

8. Guy: tous les étés / mon père / louer / un appartement à Nice

_____

9. Sabine: chaque année pour Noël / ma famille / aller / chez nos grands-parents

_____

10. Olivier: toutes les semaines / nous / passer le week-end / à la ferme

_____

# Uses of the imperfect tense; imperfect vs. passé composé

1. The imperfect tense focuses on past actions or conditions as ongoing processes rather than as completed events. It emphasizes the action or condition itself rather than its beginning or end. One use of the imperfect is to express repeated or ongoing actions in the past.

| | |
|---|---|
| Qu'est-ce que tu **faisais** quand tu **habitais** à Cannes? | What **did you use to do** when you **lived** in Cannes? |
| J'**allais** tous les jours à la plage. | I **went** to the beach every day. |
| Est-ce que tu **avais** des cours l'après-midi? | **Did** you **use to have** classes in the afternoon? |
| Non, j'**étais** à la faculté le matin. L'après-midi j'**allais** au travail. | No, I **used to be** at the university in the morning. In the afternoon I **would go** to work. |

2. The imperfect is also used to describe a past state or condition.

| | |
|---|---|
| Mes amis **étaient** tous diligents. Ils **étudiaient** sérieusement et **s'intéressaient** à leur travail. Mais ils **savaient** s'amuser aussi. Ils **étaient** tous très gentils et les professeurs les **trouvaient** sympathiques et intelligents. | My friends **were** all diligent. They **studied** seriously and **took an interest** in their work. But they **knew how** to have a good time too. They **were** all very nice, and the teachers **found** them pleasant and intelligent. |

3. The **passé composé,** in contrast to the imperfect, expresses specific actions and events that were started and completed at a specific time in the past.

| | |
|---|---|
| J'**ai pris** le petit déjeuner, j'**ai mis** mon manteau et je **suis sorti.** | I **had** breakfast, **put on** my coat, and **left** the house. |

4. The imperfect and the **passé composé** can appear in the same sentence. The imperfect provides the background for the event stated in the **passé composé.** In such instances, the imperfect may describe time, weather, or an action that was going on when an event happened.

| | |
|---|---|
| Il **était** sept heures et demie quand elle **est rentrée.** | It **was** seven-thirty when she **returned** home. |
| Quand on **est sortis** du restaurant, il **pleuvait.** | When we **left** the restaurant, it **was raining.** |
| Je **lisais** quand Jacques **a frappé** à la porte. | I **was reading** when Jacques **knocked** at the door. |

**Activité 5** **Un temps trop variable.** Jeannine a vu plusieurs changements atmosphériques pendant sa journée. Formez des phrases avec les éléments proposés en employant un imparfait et un passé composé pour savoir ce qui lui est arrivé. Suivez le modèle.

> MODÈLE  faire du soleil / je / descendre prendre le bus
> Il faisait du soleil quand je suis descendue prendre le bus.

### Vocabulaire

## Le temps

**faire du vent** *to be windy*  **neiger** *to snow*
**geler** *to freeze*  **pleuviner** *to drizzle*
**grêler** *to hail*  **tonner** *to thunder*

1. faire du vent / je / arriver à l'arrêt

   _____

2. pleuviner / le bus / arriver

   _____

3. pleuvoir / je / monter dans le bus

   _____

4. geler / je / arriver à la faculté

   _____

5. grêler / je / retrouver mon amie Hélène

   _____

6. neiger / nous / entrer dans l'amphithéâtre

   _____

7. tonner / le professeur / commencer sa conférence

   _____

8. grêler / nous / sortir de l'amphithéâtre

   _____

**Activité 6**  **Quand ça?** Jean-Marc donne un aperçu de sa journée par ordre chronologique. Formez des phrases avec les éléments proposés en employant l'imparfait et le passé composé pour savoir ce qu'il a fait et quand il le faisait. Suivez le modèle.

> MODÈLE  tôt / je / sortir
> Il était tôt quand je suis sorti.

1. huit heures et demie / mon train / venir

   _____

2. neuf heures pile / je / arriver en ville

   _____

3. un peu tard / je / arriver au bureau

   _____

4. midi / mon collègue / m'inviter à déjeuner

   _____

*(continued)*

*Imperfect*  **51**

5. une heure et demie / nous / finir de manger

_____

6. tard dans l'après-midi / je / quitter le bureau

_____

7. déjà sept heures / je / retrouver ma fiancée pour dîner

_____

8. presque minuit / je / rentrer chez moi

_____

**Activité 7**  **Comment faire le ménage?** M. Fournier a profité de quelques moments de solitude pour faire le ménage. Suivez le modèle pour savoir ce que faisaient les autres membres de la famille pendant qu'il faisait le ménage. Chaque phrase aura un imparfait et un passé composé.

> MODÈLE  laver le plancher / sa femme / dormir
> Il a lavé le plancher pendant que sa femme dormait.

1. nettoyer la cuisine / les enfants / jouer dans le jardin

_____

2. faire le linge / sa mère / promener le chien

_____

3. préparer le dîner / sa sœur / faire les courses

_____

4. mettre la table / son fils aîné / réparer la voiture

_____

5. étudier ses dossiers / sa fille / bricoler (*to fix things, tinker*) au sous-sol (*basement*)

_____

6. cirer (*to polish*) les meubles / son frère / lire le journal

_____

**Activité 8**  **Des explications.** Pourquoi est-ce que ces amis n'ont pas fait les choses qu'ils devaient faire? Formez des phrases pour expliquer leur manque d'action en écrivant ce qu'ils n'ont pas fait au passé composé et la raison pour laquelle ils ne l'ont pas fait à l'imparfait. Suivez le modèle.

| MODÈLE | QUI? | QUOI? | POURQUOI? |
|---|---|---|---|
| | vous | prendre l'avion | avoir peur |

> Vous n'avez pas pris l'avion parce que vous aviez peur.

|  | QUI? | QUOI? | POURQUOI? |
|---|---|---|---|
| 1. | je | aller au restaurant | ne pas avoir envie de sortir |
| 2. | nous | faire une promenade | ne pas avoir le temps |
| 3. | je | lire le chapitre | avoir mal à la tête |
| 4. | Albert | prendre le petit déjeuner | être trop pressé |
| 5. | Chantal | venir à la réunion | travailler |
| 6. | nos copains | aller au concert | ne pas avoir d'argent |
| 7. | les voisins | sortir | leur voiture être en panne |
| 8. | tu | répondre au professeur | ne pas faire attention à sa question |

1. _____

2. _____

3. _____

4. _____

5. _____

6. _____

7. _____

8. _____

**Activité 9**   **Dormir (mal) à la campagne.**  Alain et Guy ont passé une mauvaise nuit sous leur tente à cause du mauvais temps qu'il faisait. Formez des phrases pour raconter leur mésaventure. Les deux propositions (*clauses*) seront à l'imparfait.

> MODÈLE   faire du soleil / Guy et Alain / voyager en voiture
> Il faisait du soleil pendant qu'ils voyageaient en voiture.

1. le ciel / être couvert / ils / chercher un endroit pour camper

   _____

2. pleuviner / les deux garçons / dresser leur tente

   _____

3. pleuvoir / Guy / faire un feu de camp

   _____

4. faire du vent / Alain / cuisiner

   _____

5. la température / baisser / ils / manger

   _____

(*continued*)

6. des éclairs / illuminer le ciel / ils / ouvrir les sacs de couchage

_____

7. tonner / les deux garçons / essayer de dormir

_____

8. mais le matin / faire beau / ils / plier leur tente

_____

## Other uses of the imperfect tense

1. The imperfect is used with time expressions to describe an action that began in the past and was still going on when another action occurred. The English translations of these sentences usually have the structure _had been doing something for a certain amount of time, when something else happened._

Combien de temps y avait-il que **vous habitiez** à Paris quand on vous a offert le poste à Perpignan?

_ou_

Depuis combien de temps **habitiez-vous** à Paris quand on vous a offert le poste à Perpignan?

*How long **had you been living** in Paris when you were offered the job in Perpignan?*

Il y avait dix ans que **j'étais** à Paris quand je suis parti pour Perpignan.

_ou_

**J'étais** à Paris depuis dix ans quand je suis parti pour Perpignan.

***I had been** in Paris for ten years when I left for Perpignan.*

Note that the phrases used before the time expressions are also in the imperfect: **combien de temps y avait-il que, il y avait dix ans que.**

2. **Si** plus the imperfect tense makes a suggestion, similar to _How about . . . ?_ or _What if . . . ?_ in English. It is especially common with either **nous** or **on** as the subject. With **tu** or **vous** this construction can express extreme impatience or irritation.

| | |
|---|---|
| **Si** nous **sortions**? | *How about if we go out?* |
| **Si** on **partait** déjà? | *What if we leave now?* |
| **Si** nous nous **dépêchions** un peu? | *How about if we hurry up?* (Could we hurry up, please?) |
| Et **si** tu te **taisais**? | *And **supposing** you **kept quiet**?* |

**Activité 10**  **L'imprévu.** Dites combien de temps ces gens faisaient ce qu'ils étaient en train de faire quand quelque chose d'imprévu est arrivé. Traduisez les phrases en anglais.

> MODÈLE  je / regarder la télé / une heure // Mon ami a frappé à la porte.
> Je regardais la télé depuis une heure quand mon ami a frappé à la porte.
>
> *ou*
>
> Il y avait (Ça faisait) une heure que je regardais la télé quand mon ami a frappé à la porte.
> *I had been watching TV for an hour when my friend knocked at the door.*

1. vous / attendre le bus / vingt minutes // Jean-Claude est venu vous prendre avec sa voiture.

   _____

   _____

2. nous / étudier à la bibliothèque / six heures // Christine nous a invités à dîner chez elle.

   _____

   _____

3. Odile / dormir / dix minutes // Le téléphone a sonné.

   _____

   _____

4. Sylvain / entrer des données / deux heures // Il y a eu une panne d'électricité (*power failure*).

   _____

   _____

5. Brigitte / faire du jogging / une heure // Il a commencé à pleuvoir.

   _____

   _____

6. Alain / ranger ses affaires / dix minutes // Ses amis l'ont appelé pour jouer au football.

   _____

   _____

**Activité 11**  **J'ai une idée!** Laëtitia s'ennuie. Son amie Claire lui propose des activités. Écrivez deux fois ses idées—une fois avec **nous**, la seconde avec **on**. Suivez le modèle.

> MODÈLE  aller au cinéma
> **a.** Si nous allions au cinéma?
> **b.** Si on allait au cinéma?

1. naviguer sur Internet

   **a.** _____

   **b.** _____

2. acheter le journal

   a. _____

   b. _____

3. passer chez Françoise

   a. _____

   b. _____

4. regarder une vidéo

   a. _____

   b. _____

5. manger au restaurant

   a. _____

   b. _____

6. commencer nos devoirs

   a. _____

   b. _____

## Special meanings of certain verbs

Some verbs have different meanings in the imperfect and the **passé composé.** In general, the imperfect describes a continuing condition, whereas the **passé composé** refers to a particular moment when a change of state occurred.

1. **avoir**

| | |
|---|---|
| Elle **avait** faim. | *She **was** hungry.* |
| Elle **a eu** faim. | *She **got** hungry.* |

2. **connaître, savoir**

| | |
|---|---|
| Tu **connaissais** mon voisin? | ***Did** you **know** my neighbor?* |
| Tu **as connu** mon voisin? | ***Did** you **meet** my neighbor?* |
| Il **savait** qu'elle était là. | *He **knew** that she was here.* |
| Il **a su** qu'elle était là. | *He **found out** that she was here.* |

3. **pouvoir, vouloir**

| | |
|---|---|
| Il **ne pouvait pas** la joindre hier. | *He **couldn't** reach her yesterday. (He had other things to do.)* |
| Il **n'a pas pu** la joindre hier. | *He **didn't succeed** in reaching her yesterday. (He tried, but she wasn't in.)* |
| Je **voulais** partir. | *I **wanted** to leave.* |
| J'**ai voulu** partir. | *I **tried** to leave.* |
| Je **ne voulais pas** partir. | *I **didn't want** to leave.* |
| Je **n'ai pas voulu** partir. | *I **refused** to leave.* |

**NOTE** The imperfect forms of **pouvoir** and **vouloir** imply that the action of the infinitive may not have taken place.

**Activité 12** **Une visite au musée.** Racontez cette histoire au passé en choisissant pour chaque verbe soit l'imparfait, soit le passé composé selon le cas.

Je _____**suis allé(e)**_____ (aller) au musée. Je/J' _____
(vouloir) voir les peintures de la Renaissance. Je/J' _____
(entrer) d'abord dans les salles italiennes qui _____ (être)
à côté des salles françaises. Il y _____ (avoir) beaucoup de
tableaux très intéressants. Je/J' _____ (voir) des peintures
fabuleuses. Après, je/j' _____ (passer) aux salles françaises.
Ensuite, je/j' _____ (monter) voir l'art du vingtième siècle.
J'y _____ (trouver) des œuvres fantastiques. Après une
heure, je/j' _____ (descendre) à la librairie parce que je/j'
_____ (vouloir) acheter des cartes postales. J'y _____
(remarquer) deux livres sur l'art qui me/m' _____ (intéresser)
beaucoup, mais je ne/n' _____ (avoir) pas assez d'argent
pour les acheter. Je ne/n' _____ (acheter) que deux cartes
postales. Je/J' _____ (décider) de rentrer demain pour acheter
les deux livres.

**Activité 13** **Fernand cherche du travail.** Racontez cette histoire au passé en choisissant pour chaque verbe soit l'imparfait, soit le passé composé selon le cas.

Fernand Bercot _____**voulait**_____ (vouloir) travailler à Paris. Donc,
il _____ (quitter) son petit village dans la Gironde et il
_____ (prendre) le train pour Paris. Il _____
(arriver) dans la capitale il y a trois ans. Il n' _____ (avoir)
même pas une chambre et il n'y _____ (connaître) personne.
Mais dans une semaine il _____ (trouver) un poste de
serveur. Il _____ (falloir) travailler beaucoup, mais il
_____ (recevoir) pas mal de pourboires. Il _____
(vivre) dans une chambre d'hôtel très modeste pour faire des économies.

*(continued)*

Après un an et demi il _____ (renoncer) à son travail. Il
_____ (inviter) son frère Joseph à le rejoindre à Paris. Fernand
_____ (mettre) assez d'argent de côté pour monter un café.
Son frère et lui _____ (ouvrir) un petit bistrot dans le
quinzième arrondissement. Ils _____ (être) ouvriers, mais
maintenant ils _____ (devenir) propriétaires d'un café!

---

**Activité 14**  **Activité orale.** Causez avec un(e) camarade au sujet de la journée que
vous (et vos copains) avez passée hier. Pour chaque (ou pour presque
chaque) action que vous mentionnez, décrivez aussi les circonstances:
l'heure, le temps qu'il faisait, les actions des autres, et ainsi de suite.
Comparez votre journée avec celle de votre camarade.

# FUTURE AND CONDITIONAL

## Forms of the future tense

1. The future tense of regular verbs is formed by adding the following endings to the infinitive: **-ai, -as, -a, -ons, -ez, -ont.**

| PARLER | | | |
|---|---|---|---|
| je | parler**ai** | nous | parler**ons** |
| tu | parler**as** | vous | parler**ez** |
| il/elle/on | parler**a** | ils/elles | parler**ont** |

| FINIR | | | |
|---|---|---|---|
| je | finir**ai** | nous | finir**ons** |
| tu | finir**as** | vous | finir**ez** |
| il/elle/on | finir**a** | ils/elles | finir**ont** |

2. Verbs whose infinitive ends in **-re** drop their final **e** before the endings of the future.

| RENDRE | | | |
|---|---|---|---|
| je | rendr**ai** | nous | rendr**ons** |
| tu | rendr**as** | vous | rendr**ez** |
| il/elle/on | rendr**a** | ils/elles | rendr**ont** |

3. Some verbs have an irregular stem or modified infinitive in the future tense. Nevertheless, the endings are regular for all verbs.

| | | | | | |
|---|---|---|---|---|---|
| avoir | j'**aur**ai | acquérir | nous **acquérr**ons | décevoir | je **décevr**ai |
| aller | tu **ir**as | courir | nous **cour**rons | devoir | tu **devr**as |
| être | il **ser**a | envoyer | vous **enverr**ez | falloir | il **faudr**a |
| faire | elle **fer**a | mourir | vous **mourr**ez | pleuvoir | il **pleuvr**a |
| savoir | on **saur**a | pouvoir | ils **pour**ront | recevoir | nous **recevr**ons |
| | | voir | elles **verr**ont | tenir | vous **tiendr**ez |
| | | | | venir | ils **viendr**ont |
| | | | | vouloir | elles **voudr**ont |

Compounds of the preceding verbs have the same irregularities in their stems.

| | | | |
|---|---|---|---|
| devenir | je **deviendr**ai | revenir | je **reviendr**ai |

4. The future of **il faut** is **il faudra.** The future of **il y a** is **il y aura.**

5. Verbs that change a mute **e** to **è** before a mute **e** in the present tense (such as **acheter**) also change **e** to **è** in all forms of the future tense. Verbs that double their final consonant before a mute **e** in the present tense (such as **appeler**) have the same change in all persons of the future tense.

| | | | |
|---|---|---|---|
| acheter | j'**achèter**ai | appeler | j'**appeller**ai |
| amener | j'**amèner**ai | jeter | je **jetter**ai |

6. However, verbs such as **espérer** and **préférer** that have an **é** in the infinitive retain the **é** in the future tense.

| | | | |
|---|---|---|---|
| espérer | j'**espérer**ai | préférer | je **préférer**ai |

**NOTE**  The future of **s'asseoir** is either **je m'assiérai** or **je m'assoirai** (without the **e** of the infinitive).

7. The simple future tense in French contrasts with the **futur proche,** a compound tense consisting of **aller** + infinitive. The **futur proche** resembles the English construction *to be going to do something*. It stresses that the action of the verb will be completed in the near future, whereas the simple future does not focus on the completion of the action. This difference in meaning is not easily conveyed in English.

Je **vais** lui **dire que** vous l'attendez.  *I'll tell him you're waiting for him.*
Je lui **dirai** que vous l'attendez.  *I'll tell him (at some later time) you're waiting for him.*

A receptionist speaking with someone who has just arrived in the office would be more likely to say the first sentence.

When an expression of time appears in the sentence, either the simple future or the **futur proche** may be used interchangeably.

Ils arriveront dans une heure.
Ils vont arriver dans une heure. } *They will arrive in an hour.*

**Activité 1**  **C'est pour demain.**  Tout ce qu'on allait faire aujourd'hui, on a remis (*postponed*) pour demain. Répondez à ces questions en suivant le modèle.

> MODÈLE  Jean ne fait pas les courses aujourd'hui?
> Non, il fera les courses demain.

1. Mademoiselle, vous ne faites pas le ménage aujourd'hui?

_____

2. Tes parents ne reviennent pas aujourd'hui?

_____

3. Ton ami ne va pas à la fac aujourd'hui?

_____

4. Je ne travaille pas aujourd'hui, monsieur?

_____

5. Je ne réponds pas aujourd'hui?

_____

6. Tu ne sais pas la réponse aujourd'hui?

_____

7. Papa, je n'envoie pas le colis aujourd'hui?

_____

8. Nous n'emmenons pas les enfants au zoo aujourd'hui?

_____

9. Les autres professeurs et vous, vous ne projetez pas le film aujourd'hui?

_____

10. Les étudiants ne complètent pas leur travail aujourd'hui?

_____

**Activité 2** **Je crois.** Serge, optimiste, parle avec un copain impatient. Serge croit que tout se réalisera. Écrivez ses réponses en suivant le modèle.

| MODÈLE | Un copain: | Le prof vient ou ne vient pas? |
|---|---|---|
| | Serge: | Je crois qu'il viendra. |

1. Je réussis ou je ne réussis pas?

_____

2. Nos copains descendent ou ne descendent pas?

_____

3. Théo va ou ne va pas en cours?

_____

4. Il neige ou il ne neige pas?

_____

5. Tu sors ou tu ne sors pas?

_____

6. Marie et moi, nous arrivons à l'heure ou nous n'arrivons pas à l'heure?

_____

(continued)

7. Tes parents nous prêtent la voiture ou ne nous prêtent pas la voiture?

_____

8. Tu complètes tes devoirs ou tu ne complètes pas tes devoirs?

_____

**Activité 3** **Je ne sais pas.** Dans chaque cas, dites que vous ne savez pas si l'action arrivera. Suivez le modèle.

> MODÈLE Est-ce qu'il vient demain?
> Je ne sais pas s'il viendra.

1. Est-ce qu'ils partent demain?

_____

2. Est-ce que vous travaillez demain?

_____

3. Est-ce que je passe l'examen demain?

_____

4. Est-ce que le professeur revient demain?

_____

5. Est-ce que les hommes d'affaires vont à la réunion demain?

_____

6. Est-ce que tu conduis demain?

_____

7. Est-ce que les étudiants lisent demain?

_____

8. Est-ce qu'on projette un film demain?

_____

9. Est-ce que tu veux venir demain?

_____

10. Est-ce que ton copain peut rentrer demain?

_____

**Activité 4** **Des projets pour l'été.** La famille Ramonet est très nombreuse. Le départ en Normandie pour passer l'été n'est donc pas facile. Formez des phrases au futur à partir des éléments donnés pour dire ce que chaque membre de la famille fera pour faciliter ce départ.

1. le fils aîné / faire les valises

_____

2. papa / s'occuper des petits

_____

3. maman / se charger de la voiture

_____

4. tout le monde / se réveiller à sept heures du matin

_____

5. tous les membres de la famille / se dépêcher

_____

6. personne / regarder la télé

_____

7. les enfants / s'aider mutuellement

_____

8. les grands-parents / préparer le petit déjeuner

_____

9. personne / voir le temps passer

_____

10. les Ramonet / se mettre en route vers dix heures du matin

_____

## Use of the future after **quand** and other conjunctions of time

The future tense is used after **quand, lorsque** (*when*), **dès que** (*as soon as*), **aussitôt que** (*as soon as*), and **après que** (*after*) when a future event is implied, in other words, when the main clause (**la proposition principale**) of the sentence is in the future or the imperative.

Téléphone-moi **quand tu seras** prêt.
*Call me **when you're** ready.*

Je passerai te prendre **dès que tu m'appelleras.**
*I'll come by and pick you up **as soon as you call me.***

**Quand tu verras** ma voiture, descends.
*When you see my car, come downstairs.*

Je te ramènerai **aussitôt que la réunion finira.**
*I'll bring you back **as soon as the meeting is over.***

**NOTE**  English uses the present tense, not the future, after these conjunctions.

**Activité 5**  **On se met en route.** Odile Dulac explique quand sa famille fera le nécessaire pour partir à Strasbourg. Formez des phrases à partir des éléments donnés pour voir ce qu'elle dit. Mettez les propositions principales au futur.

1. je / faire ma valise / dès que / le linge / être sec

   _____

2. les enfants / s'habiller / quand / ils / rentrer de l'école

   _____

3. nous / manger / quand / maman / revenir du marché

   _____

4. mon frère / mettre les valises dans la voiture / aussitôt que / papa / revenir de la station-service

   _____

5. nous / choisir la route / quand / je / trouver la carte

   _____

6. nous / partir / quand / il / faire beau

   _____

7. nous / chercher un hôtel / lorsque / nous / arriver à Strasbourg

   _____

8. je / se coucher / aussitôt que / nous / être à l'hôtel

   _____

**Activité 6** **Conseils et ordres.** Employez l'impératif et le futur simple pour donner des conseils et des ordres. Suivez le modèle.*

| MODÈLE | CONSEIL/ORDRE | QUAND |
|---|---|---|
| | (à ton ami Pierre) s'asseoir | quand / le professeur / entrer |
| | Assieds-toi quand le professeur entrera. | |

| CONSEIL/ORDRE | QUAND |
|---|---|
| 1. (à tes amis) sortir | dès que / la cloche / sonner |
| 2. (à ton amie Lise) téléphoner | aussitôt que / Albert / arriver |
| 3. (à tes camarades) se mettre à prendre des notes | quand / le professeur / commencer sa conférence |
| 4. (à ton petit frère) descendre à la cuisine | quand / je / t'appeler |
| 5. (à Jean-Luc et Ghislaine) venir me voir | quand / vous / pouvoir |
| 6. (à ta sœur) fermer la porte à clé | quand / tu / s'en aller |
| 7. (à Mme Chiclet) dire bonjour de ma part à votre fils | quand / vous / le voir |
| 8. (à tes parents) lire ma lettre | dès que / vous / la recevoir |
| 9. (à ton frère) ne pas faire de bruit | après que / le bébé / s'endormir |

*For a review of the imperative, see Chapter 6.

1. _____

2. _____

3. _____

4. _____

5. _____

6. _____

7. _____

8. _____

9. _____

## Forms of the conditional

1. The conditional expresses what might happen or what would happen if certain conditions existed. It is formed by adding the endings of the imperfect tense to the future tense stem.

| PARLER | | | |
|---|---|---|---|
| je | parler**ais** | nous | parler**ions** |
| tu | parler**ais** | vous | parler**iez** |
| il/elle/on | parler**ait** | ils/elles | parler**aient** |

| FINIR | | | |
|---|---|---|---|
| je | finir**ais** | nous | finir**ions** |
| tu | finir**ais** | vous | finir**iez** |
| il/elle/on | finir**ait** | ils/elles | finir**aient** |

| RENDRE | | | |
|---|---|---|---|
| je | rendr**ais** | nous | rendr**ions** |
| tu | rendr**ais** | vous | rendr**iez** |
| il/elle/on | rendr**ait** | ils/elles | rendr**aient** |

| ÊTRE | | | |
|---|---|---|---|
| je | ser**ais** | nous | ser**ions** |
| tu | ser**ais** | vous | ser**iez** |
| il/elle/on | ser**ait** | ils/elles | ser**aient** |

2. The same spelling changes that appear in the future stems appear in the conditional stems.

   acheter  j'**achèter**ais     appeler  j'**appeller**ais     préférer  je **préférer**ais

3. Those verbs that have an irregular stem or modified infinitive in the future, have the same stem in the conditional. (See the list on p. 59.)

4. The conditional of **il faut** is **il faudrait.** The conditional of **il y a** is **il y aurait.**

5. The conditional tense is the equivalent of English *would + verb.* It should not be confused with the use of *would* to describe a repeated action in the past (imperfect tense in French). Compare the use of the imperfect and the conditional in the following sentences.

J'**allais** à la plage chaque week-end
   quand j'étais jeune.
J'**irais** à la plage chaque week-end
   si je pouvais.

*I **would go** to the beach every
   weekend when I was young.*
*I **would go** to the beach every
   weekend if I could.*

6. The conditional is often used to make polite requests, suggestions, and refusals, or to ask for favors.

**Pourriez**-vous m'accompagner?
**Voudriez**-vous prendre un verre
   avec nous?

***Could** you go with me?*
***Would** you like to have a drink
   with us?*

---

**Activité 7**   **Si on pouvait.**   On ferait les choses dont on a envie, si on pouvait. Employez le conditionnel du verbe principal et l'imparfait du verbe **pouvoir** pour exprimer cette idée, en suivant le modèle.

> MODÈLE   Jean a envie de partir.
> Oui, il partirait s'il pouvait.

1. J'ai envie de rentrer.

   _____

2. Monique et Danielle ont envie de faire du ski.

   _____

3. Tu as envie de devenir programmeur.

   _____

4. Aimée et moi, nous avons envie de nous voir tous les jours.

   _____

5. J'ai envie de me mettre en route.

   _____

6. Richard a envie de se promener.

   _____

7. Sylvie et toi, vous avez envie d'acheter du pain.

   _____

8. Mon copain et moi, nous avons envie d'être chez nous.

   _____

**Activité 8** **Moi non plus.** Quand on vous dit ce que vos amis n'ont pas fait, dites dans chaque cas que vous ne feriez pas ces choses non plus. Employez le conditionnel dans vos réponses, en suivant le modèle.

> MODÈLE  Je ne me suis pas baigné dans ce lac.
> Moi non plus, je ne me baignerais pas dans ce lac.

1. Charles n'a pas pris la voiture.

   _____

2. Martin n'a pas fait la vaisselle.

   _____

3. Olivier et Chantal ne se sont pas assis dans le jardin.

   _____

4. Je n'ai pas regardé la télé aujourd'hui.

   _____

5. Les enfants n'ont pas enlevé leur pull.

   _____

6. Le cinéma n'a pas projeté ce film.

   _____

7. Les étudiants n'ont pas répété ces slogans.

   _____

8. Solange n'a pas couru.

   _____

**Activité 9** **Impossible!** Employez le conditionnel pour dire dans chaque cas que la nouvelle qu'on vient de vous annoncer est sûrement fausse.

> MODÈLE  On dit que Pierre est parti.
> Impossible! Il ne partirait pas.

1. On dit que vous avez renoncé à votre travail.

   _____

2. On dit que Catherine a rejeté notre offre.

   _____

3. On dit que Philippe s'est levé pendant la classe.

   _____

4. On dit que les professeurs ont fait grève.

   _____

(continued)

5. On dit que tu exagères.

   _____

6. On dit que j'ai perdu les billets.

   _____

7. On dit que Laurent est tombé en faisant du ski.

   _____

8. On dit que le petit Baudouin a jeté son dîner à la poubelle (*garbage can*).

   _____

## Conditional with si clauses

1. A conditional sentence consists of two clauses: an "if" (or **si**) clause and a result clause. If an event is likely to happen, the present tense is used in the **si** clause and the present, future, or imperative is used in the result clause.

   | | |
   |---|---|
   | S'il **pleut,** nous **restons** chez nous. | *If it **rains**, we **stay** home.* |
   | Si tu **t'en vas,** le prof **se fâchera.** | *If you **leave**, the professor will get angry.* |
   | **Viens** me voir si tu **as** le temps. | *Come see me if you **have** time.* |

2. If an event is unlikely to happen or is contrary to fact, the imperfect is used in the **si** clause and the conditional is used in the result clause.

   | | |
   |---|---|
   | Je t'**aiderais** si je **pouvais.** | *I'd **help** you if I **could.** (Fact: I can't help you. But if I could, I would.)* |
   | S'il **était** plus ouvert, il **s'habituerait** à la vie mexicaine. | *If he **were** more open, he **would get accustomed** to Mexican life. (Fact: He isn't open to the culture. But if he were, he would get used to Mexican life.)* |

| SUMMARY OF TENSES IN CONDITIONAL SENTENCES | |
|---|---|
| SUPPOSITION (**si** CLAUSE) | MAIN CLAUSE (PROPOSITION PRINCIPALE) |
| Present | Present, future, or imperative |
| Imperfect | Conditional |

**Activité 10** **Du progrès personnel pour Jean-Pierre.** Jean-Pierre doit se transformer pour être un jeune homme branché (*"with it"*). Employez des phrases composées d'une supposition (**si**) à l'imparfait et d'une proposition principale au conditionnel pour exprimer ce que Jean-Pierre doit faire.

> MODÈLE  Jean-Pierre ne lit jamais le journal. Il ne sait pas ce qui se passe dans le monde.
> Si Jean-Pierre lisait le journal, il saurait ce qui se passe dans le monde.

1. Jean-Pierre ne s'habille pas bien. Les autres étudiants se moquent de lui.

   _____

2. Jean-Pierre ne fait pas de sport. Il ne connaît pas beaucoup de monde.

   _____

3. Jean-Pierre ne s'intéresse pas à ses études. Il n'est pas préparé en classe.

   _____

4. Jean-Pierre s'absente souvent. Les professeurs se fâchent contre lui.

   _____

5. Jean-Pierre lit des bandes dessinées (*comics*) en classe. Les profs sont furieux.

   _____

6. Jean-Pierre mange toujours seul. Il ne parle pas avec les autres étudiants.

   _____

**Activité 11** **Déménagement.** Les Fantin essaient de décider où placer leurs meubles dans leur nouvelle maison. Exprimez leurs idées avec une phrase composée d'une supposition au présent et d'une proposition principale au futur. Suivez le modèle.

> MODÈLE on / mettre la télé dans le séjour / on / pouvoir regarder
>   des émissions ensemble
> Si on met la télé dans le séjour, on pourra regarder des
>   émissions ensemble.

1. vous / installer la machine à laver au sous-sol / nous / avoir plus de place dans la cuisine

   _____

2. je / mettre la lampe à côté du fauteuil / je / pouvoir lire

   _____

3. nous / nettoyer le tapis / nous / le mettre dans le salon

   _____

4. tu / trouver la table en plastique / tu / pouvoir la mettre sur la terrasse

   _____

5. on / laisser l'ordinateur dans ma chambre / je / faire mes devoirs sans déranger (*bother*) les autres

   _____

6. les déménageurs / monter une étagère dans ma chambre / je / ranger tous mes livres

   _____

**Activité 12**  **Il y a toujours des problèmes quand on déménage.** Employez des phrases composées d'une supposition avec **si** à l'imparfait et d'une proposition principale au conditionnel pour exprimer tout ce qui manque dans la nouvelle maison des Didier. Suivez le modèle.

> MODÈLE   On n'a pas de lave-vaisselle. On fait la vaisselle à la main.
> Si on avait un lave-vaisselle, on ne ferait pas la vaisselle à la main.

1. On n'a pas deux télés. On ne peut pas regarder la télé dans le séjour.

   _____

2. Cette maison n'a pas de grenier (*attic*). Il n'y a pas de place pour les boîtes.

   _____

3. La cheminée ne fonctionne pas. Nous ne pouvons pas faire un feu.

   _____

4. On n'a pas de tableaux dans le salon. Le salon n'est pas douillet (*cozy*).

   _____

5. Je n'ai pas de lecteur CD dans ma chambre. J'écoute mes CD dans le séjour.

   _____

6. Le frigo est tellement petit. Papa fait les courses plusieurs fois par semaine.

   _____

7. Tu ne décroches (*take down*) pas les rideaux. Je ne peux pas les laver.

   _____

8. Cette fenêtre ne se ferme pas bien. Il fait froid dans ma chambre.

   _____

**Activité 13**  **Problèmes de santé.** Quelles seraient les réactions de ces amis à des problèmes de santé hypothétiques? Composez des phrases avec une supposition à l'imparfait et une proposition principale au conditionnel à partir des éléments donnés. Suivez le modèle.

| MODÈLE | SUPPOSITION (si) | PROPOSITION PRINCIPALE |
|---|---|---|
| | Marie / se couper le doigt | elle / mettre un pansement |

> Si Marie se coupait le doigt, elle mettrait un pansement.

**Vocabulaire**

## Comment est-ce qu'on se soignerait?

**aller pieds nus** *to go barefoot*
**attraper un rhume** *to catch a cold*
**avoir mal à la tête** *to have a headache*
**le comprimé d'aspirine** *aspirin tablet*
**se couper le doigt** *to cut one's finger*

**être en forme** *to be in shape*
**se faire mal (au pied)** *to hurt oneself (one's foot)*
**maigrir** *to lose weight*
**mettre un pansement** *to put on a bandage*
**ordonner** *to prescribe*
**tomber malade** *to get sick*

| SUPPOSITION (SI) | PROPOSITION PRINCIPALE |
|---|---|
| 1. je / se sentir mal | je / aller chez le médecin |
| 2. je / ne manger que des légumes et des fruits | je / maigrir |
| 3. il / sortir sous la pluie | il / attraper un rhume |
| 4. elle / tomber malade | elle / se reposer |
| 5. nous / aller pieds nus | nous / se faire mal aux pieds |
| 6. tu / avoir mal à la tête | tu / prendre des comprimés d'aspirine |
| 7. le médecin / m'ordonner des antibiotiques | je / les prendre |
| 8. je / être en forme | je / ne pas se fatiguer tellement |

1. _____
2. _____
3. _____
4. _____
5. _____
6. _____
7. _____
8. _____

**Activité 14** **Activité orale.** Discutez avec un(e) camarade vos projets pour l'avenir. Employez le futur pour les choses que vous comptez faire et des suppositions avec **si** pour exprimer les circonstances nécessaires pour réaliser vos projets. Faites attention à l'emploi du futur après **quand, lorsque, après que,** et à l'emploi du conditionnel et de l'imparfait.

MODÈLE  Quand j'aurai dix-huit ans, j'irai à l'université.
Si j'ai de la chance, on me donnera une bourse d'études.
Si j'étais riche, je n'aurais pas besoin d'une bourse d'études.

## Imperative

1. The imperative is used to give a command or to make a request. For most verbs, the imperative is formed by using the **tu, vous,** or **nous** form of the present tense without the subject pronoun. This is true of both affirmative and negative commands.

| | |
|---|---|
| **Finis** tes devoirs. **Ne perds pas** ton temps. | *Finish your homework. **Don't waste** your time.* |
| **Attendez** un moment. **Ne partez pas.** | ***Wait** a moment. **Don't leave.*** |
| **Rentrons** maintenant. **Ne passons plus** de temps ici. | ***Let's go back home** now. **Let's not spend any more** time here.* |

2. In the informal imperative (**tu** form) of regular **-er** verbs, the final **-s** of the present tense form is dropped. The **-s** is also dropped in the imperative **tu** forms of **aller** and of **-ir** verbs conjugated like **-er** verbs, such as **ouvrir** and **souffrir.**

| | |
|---|---|
| **Téléphone** à tes parents. **N'oublie pas.** | *Call your parents. **Don't forget.*** |
| On sonne. **Va. Ouvre** la porte. | *The doorbell is ringing. **Go open** the door.* |

3. Four common verbs have irregular imperative forms.

| | |
|---|---|
| être: | **sois, soyons, soyez** |
| avoir: | **aie, ayons, ayez** |
| savoir: | **sache, sachons, sachez** |
| vouloir: | **veuille, veuillez*** |

**Activité 1** **Projets de vacances.** Jean-Claude et Arlette parlent de leurs vacances. À chaque idée de Jean-Claude, Arlette propose une autre possibilité. Employez l'impératif pour reproduire leur conversation. Suivez le modèle.

> MODÈLE   On reste à Paris? (aller en Italie)
> Non, ne restons pas à Paris. Allons en Italie.

*The command forms of **vouloir** are very formal and generally limited to written formulaic expressions (often for closing business letters). In spoken language, **Tu veux… ?** or **Vous voulez… ?** followed by an infinitive, is more common: **Voulez-vous patienter?** (*Please hold* [on the phone]).

1. On part la semaine prochaine? (attendre la fin du mois)

   _____

2. On prend l'avion? (prendre le train)

   _____

3. On descend dans un hôtel de luxe? (choisir une auberge)

   _____

4. On visite les monuments en taxi? (louer une voiture)

   _____

5. On assiste à un concert? (aller voir une pièce de théâtre)

   _____

6. On mange dans le restaurant de l'hôtel? (dîner dans un restaurant en ville)

   _____

**Activité 2**  **Des conseils à une amie qui part.** Michèle dit à son amie Ghislaine ce qu'il faut faire avant de partir aux Antilles. Refaites les phrases suivantes à l'impératif familier. Suivez le modèle.

> MODÈLE   Il faut faire des projets précis.
>          Fais des projets précis.

1. D'abord, il faut descendre dans la rue.

   _____

2. Ensuite, il faut chercher une librairie.

   _____

3. Là-bas, il faut demander un livre sur les Antilles.

   _____

4. Il faut rentrer tout de suite à ton appartement.

   _____

5. Après, il faut lire le livre.

   _____

6. Il faut choisir ton itinéraire.

   _____

7. Après, il faut réserver une place dans l'avion et une chambre d'hôtel sur Internet.

   _____

8. Finalement, il faut faire les valises.

   _____

**Activité 3**  **De mère en fille.** Mme Élouard explique à sa fille ce qu'il faut faire pour acheter une nouvelle robe. Écrivez ses conseils en employant l'impératif familier des verbes indiqués.

> MODÈLE  prendre le journal
> Prends le journal.

1. lire les annonces

2. savoir ce que tu veux

3. regarder les soldes (*sales*)

4. aller aux grands magasins

5. essayer les vêtements qui te plaisent

6. être patiente

7. choisir une robe

8. payer avec la carte de crédit

9. revenir à la maison

10. mettre ta nouvelle robe

**Activité 4**  **On fait des projets.** Richard et Zoë vont passer la journée ensemble. Ils expriment leurs idées en employant l'impératif. Suivez le modèle.

> MODÈLE  passer la journée ensemble
> Passons la journée ensemble.

1. aller en ville

2. prendre le train de neuf heures

3. descendre à la gare centrale

    _____

4. faire une promenade

    _____

5. déjeuner dans un bon restaurant

    _____

6. chercher un bon film

    _____

7. acheter des livres dans une librairie

    _____

8. rentrer par le train de cinq heures

    _____

**Activité 5** **Ce qu'on doit faire.** Véronique donne des conseils à son ami Marc. À chaque question de son ami il répond par un impératif négatif suivi de l'impératif affirmatif du verbe entre parenthèses. Écrivez les réponses en suivant le modèle.

> MODÈLE  Je dois attendre? (partir tout de suite)
> Non, n'attends pas. Pars tout de suite.

1. Je dois mentir? (dire la vérité)

    _____

2. Je dois descendre? (rester en haut)

    _____

3. Je dois lire le texte? (écrire la composition)

    _____

4. Je dois suivre ce régime? (faire du sport)

    _____

5. Je dois mincir? (prendre du poids)

    _____

6. Je dois préparer le déjeuner? (faire la vaisselle)

    _____

7. Je dois nettoyer la cuisine? (balayer [*to sweep*] l'escalier)

    _____

8. Je dois jeter cette cravate? (offrir les vieux vêtements aux voisins)

    _____

**Activité 6** **On a des invités ce soir.** Les Lary ont invité leurs amis à dîner ce soir. Employez le pronom **vous** de l'impératif pour écrire ce que Mme Lary demande à ses fils de faire. Suivez le modèle.

> MODÈLE    acheter du pain et du vin
> Achetez du pain et du vin.

1. descendre à six heures et demie

   _____

2. aller à la boulangerie

   _____

3. faire les courses

   _____

4. choisir des légumes frais chez le marchand

   _____

5. prendre un kilo d'asperges et de la salade

   _____

6. être de retour à la maison avant sept heures et demie

   _____

7. sortir les verres et mettre le couvert (*set the table*)

   _____

8. commencer à préparer le dîner

   _____

9. savoir que les invités arriveront sûrement en retard

   _____

**Activité 7** **Comment est-ce que ça se dit?** Quels conseils donneriez-vous à un(e) camarade ou à deux camarades pour réussir dans la classe de français? Employez l'impératif.

1. *Arrive on time.*

   À un(e) camarade: _____

   À deux camarades: _____

2. *Listen to the teacher.*

   À un(e) camarade: _____

   À deux camarades: _____

3. *Don't sleep in class.*

   À un(e) camarade: _____

   À deux camarades: _____

4. *Never forget the book.*

   À un(e) camarade: _____

   À deux camarades: _____

5. *Answer the questions.*

   À un(e) camarade: _____

   À deux camarades: _____

6. *Repeat after the teacher.*

   À un(e) camarade: _____

   À deux camarades: _____

7. *Try to understand the teacher.*

   À un(e) camarade: _____

   À deux camarades: _____

8. *Don't bother the other students.*

   À un(e) camarade: _____

   À deux camarades: _____

**Activité 8**  **Activité orale.**  Avec un(e) camarade, jouez une des scènes suivantes.

1. Une mère donne des conseils à son fils quand il commence ses études à la fac.

2. Un professeur en colère dit à ses élèves ce qu'ils doivent faire pour avoir une bonne note.

3. Un épicier dit à son employé(e) ce qu'il/elle doit faire avant l'ouverture du magasin.

4. Deux amis se proposent des activités pour la semaine de vacances en décembre.

# 7 Reflexive verbs

## Present tense of reflexive verbs

Reflexive verbs are called **les verbes pronominaux** in French, because they always appear with an object pronoun that refers to the same person or thing as the subject. For example, note the verb **se réveiller** (*to wake up*).

| SE RÉVEILLER | | | |
|---|---|---|---|
| je | **me** réveille | nous | **nous** réveillons |
| tu | **te** réveilles | vous | **vous** réveillez |
| il/elle/on | **se** réveille | ils/elles | **se** réveillent |

The reflexive pronoun precedes the conjugated verb.

Je **me lève** toujours de bonne heure.    *I always **get up** early.*
Et est-ce que tu **te couches** aussi de bonne heure?    *And do you also **go to bed** early?*
Oui, mais je ne **m'endors** pas avant minuit.    *Yes, but I don't **fall asleep** before midnight.*

 **NOTE** In a negative sentence, **ne** precedes the reflexive pronoun and **pas** follows the conjugated verb.

### Reflexive verbs used to express one's daily routine

**se brosser les cheveux** *to brush one's hair*
**se brosser les dents** *to brush one's teeth*
**se coucher** *to go to bed*
**se couper les cheveux** *to cut one's hair*
**se couper / se limer les ongles** *to cut/file one's nails*

**se déshabiller** *to get undressed*
**s'endormir** *to fall asleep*
**se fatiguer** *to get tired*
**s'habiller** *to get dressed*
**se laver** *to wash*
**se laver les cheveux / la tête** *to wash one's hair*
**se laver les mains, la figure** *to wash one's hands, face*

**se lever** *to get up*
**se maquiller** *to put on makeup*
**se peigner** *to comb one's hair*
**se raser** *to shave*
**se reposer** *to rest*
**se sécher les cheveux** *to dry one's hair*
**se soigner** *to take care of oneself*

**NOTE** When a body part receives the action of a reflexive verb, the definite article is used to express possession.

**Il se brosse** *les dents.*   **Elles se lavent** *les cheveux.*

**Activité 1** **Jumeaux (*Twins*).** Paul et Jérôme sont des jumeaux. Paul décrit leur journée. Suivez le modèle.

> MODÈLE   se réveiller à sept heures
> Je me réveille à sept heures.
> Jérôme se réveille à sept heures aussi.

**Le matin**

1. se lever tout de suite

   _____

   _____

2. se brosser les dents

   _____

   _____

3. se peigner

   _____

   _____

4. se raser

   _____

   _____

5. s'habiller

   _____

   _____

**Le soir**

6. se laver les mains

   _____

   _____

7. se laver la figure

   _____

   _____

8. se reposer

   _____

   _____

(*continued*)

9. se coucher à onze heures

_____

_____

10. s'endormir tout de suite

_____

_____

**Activité 2**   **C'est la mère des jumeaux qui parle.** Maintenant c'est la mère de Paul et de Jérôme qui décrit une journée typique. Suivez le modèle.

> MODÈLE   se réveiller à sept heures
> Ils se réveillent à sept heures.

### Le matin

1. se lever tout de suite

_____

2. se brosser les dents

_____

3. se peigner

_____

4. se raser

_____

5. s'habiller

_____

### Le soir

6. se laver les mains

_____

7. se laver la figure

_____

8. se reposer

_____

9. se coucher à onze heures

_____

10. s'endormir tout de suite

_____

**Activité 3** **Notre journée.** Marthe et Vivienne décrivent une matinée typique. Employez dans chaque cas le pronom **nous** pour savoir ce qu'elles font. Suivez le modèle.

> MODÈLE    se réveiller de bonne heure
> Nous nous réveillons de bonne heure.

1. se lever immédiatement

   _____

2. se laver les mains et la figure

   _____

3. se brosser les dents

   _____

4. se laver les cheveux

   _____

5. se sécher les cheveux

   _____

6. se maquiller

   _____

7. se peigner

   _____

8. se brosser les cheveux

   _____

9. se limer les ongles

   _____

10. s'habiller avec soin

    _____

**Activité 4** **Au cinéma.** Jacques raconte sa sortie au cinéma avec ses copains. Formez des phrases avec les éléments donnés pour voir ce qui se passe.

**Vocabulaire**

## Les actions

**s'approcher de** *to approach*
**s'arrêter** *to stop*
**s'asseoir** *to sit down*
**se dépêcher** *to hurry up*
**se diriger vers** *to head toward*
**s'éloigner de** *to move away from*

**s'installer** *to move in, settle in*
**se joindre à** *to join up with*
**se promener** *to take a walk*
**se réunir** *to get together*
**se trouver** *to be located*

1. je / se joindre / à mes copains

   _____

2. ils / se trouver / dans un café du centre

   _____

3. je / s'approcher / du café

   _____

4. mes copains / se lever

   _____

5. nous / s'éloigner du café

   _____

6. nous / se diriger / vers le cinéma

   _____

7. nous / se dépêcher

   _____

8. nous / s'arrêter au guichet (*ticket window*) pour prendre les billets

   _____

9. nous entrons dans le cinéma et nous / s'asseoir

   _____

## Infinitive of reflexive verbs

1. When the infinitive of a reflexive verb is used with another verb, such as **aller, devoir, pouvoir,** or **vouloir,** the reflexive pronoun immediately precedes the infinitive and agrees with the subject.

   | | |
   |---|---|
   | **Tu** vas **te** promener? | *Are **you** going to take a walk?* |
   | **Je** veux **me** promener, mais je ne peux pas. | *I want to take a walk, but I can't.* |
   | **Vous** devez **vous** dépêcher. | *You must hurry up.* |
   | **Nous** allons **nous** énerver si vous ne vous calmez pas. | *We're going to get upset if you don't calm down.* |

2. Such constructions are negated by putting **ne... pas** around the conjugated verb. Note that the reflexive pronoun and verb function as a single unit that comes after the second half of the negation (**pas**).

   | | |
   |---|---|
   | Je **ne** vais **pas** me promener. | *I'm **not** going to take a walk.* |
   | Nous **ne** voulons **pas** nous dépêcher. | *We don't want to hurry.* |

**Activité 5** **Sentiments.** Exprimez les sentiments et les réactions indiqués en mettant le deuxième verbe à l'infinitif. Suivez le modèle.

> MODÈLE   Jean / aller / s'amuser
> Jean va s'amuser.

**Vocabulaire**

## Les émotions

**s'amuser**  *to have a good time*
**s'animer**  *to feel/act more lively*
**se calmer**  *to calm down*
**s'embêter**  *to be/get bored*
**s'énerver**  *to get nervous, upset*
**s'ennuyer**  *to be/get bored*
**s'enthousiasmer**  *to get enthusiastic*
**s'exprimer**  *to express oneself*
**se fâcher**  *to get angry*

**s'impatienter**  *to get impatient*
**s'inquiéter**  *to worry*
**se mettre en colère**  *to get angry*
**s'offenser**  *to be/get offended*
**se réjouir (de)**  *to be thrilled (about)*
**se passionner (pour)**  *to get excited (about)*
**se préoccuper**  *to worry*
**se sentir**  *to feel*

1. je / ne pas vouloir / s'inquiéter

_____

2. vous / devoir / se calmer

_____

3. il / ne pas pouvoir / se sentir triste

_____

4. elles / ne pas vouloir / s'ennuyer

_____

5. tu / ne pas devoir / se mettre en colère

_____

6. nous / ne pas aller / s'offenser

_____

7. le professeur / aller / s'impatienter

_____

8. tu / devoir / s'animer

_____

**Activité 6** **Cette fois-ci, ça va être différent.** Employez **aller** suivi d'un infinitif pour exprimer que cette fois-ci les sentiments vont changer. Suivez le modèle.

> MODÈLE  il / s'amuser
> En général, il ne s'amuse pas, mais cette fois-ci il va s'amuser.

1. je / se fâcher

_____

2. elles / s'énerver

_____

3. tu / s'impatienter

_____

4. il / s'offenser

_____

5. nous / s'inquiéter

_____

6. vous / s'embêter

_____

7. je / se sentir de trop (*in the way*)

_____

8. tu / se passionner

_____

**Activité 7**  **Conseils psychologiques.** Employez le verbe **devoir** suivi d'un infinitif pour suggérer comment maîtriser les émotions. Suivez le modèle.

> MODÈLE    tu / ne pas devoir / s'énerver
> Tu ne dois pas t'énerver.

1. vous / devoir / se calmer

_____

2. elle / devoir / s'amuser un peu

_____

3. je / devoir / se sentir heureux(-se)

_____

4. nous / ne pas devoir / se mettre en colère

_____

5. ils / devoir / s'enthousiasmer

_____

6. tu / ne pas devoir / s'impatienter

_____

7. je / devoir / s'animer un peu

_____

8. vous / ne pas devoir / s'offenser

_____

# Passé composé of reflexive verbs

1. All reflexive verbs are conjugated with **être** in the **passé composé.** The reflexive pronoun is placed immediately before the conjugated form of **être,** and the past participle agrees in gender and number with the subject if the reflexive pronoun is a direct object, as it is here with the verb **se laver** (*to wash*).

| SE LAVER | | | |
|---|---|---|---|
| je | me suis lav**é(e)** | nous | nous sommes lav**é(e)s** |
| tu | t'es lav**é(e)** | vous | vous êtes lav**é(e)(s)** |
| il | s'est lav**é** | ils | se sont lav**és** |
| elle | s'est lav**ée** | elles | se sont lav**ées** |

Note that in the **passé composé,** the **on** form of the verb is often used in speech to mean **nous,** hence past participle agreement is often made:

| | |
|---|---|
| Nous, on s'est lav**és.** | *We washed up.* |
| On s'est baign**és** dans le lac hier avec les enfants. | *We went swimming in the lake with the children yesterday.* |
| J'ai vu Jean hier. On est all**és** au cinéma ensemble. | *I saw Jean yesterday. We went to see a movie together.* |

2. When a direct object follows a reflexive verb (as in **se laver les mains**), the reflexive pronoun is an indirect object. In such cases the past participle does not agree with the subject.

| je | me suis lav**é** les mains | nous | nous sommes lav**é** les mains |
|---|---|---|---|
| tu | t'es lav**é** les mains | vous | vous êtes lav**é** les mains |
| il | s'est lav**é** les mains | ils | se sont lav**é** les mains |
| elle | s'est lav**é** les mains | elles | se sont lav**é** les mains |

3. In the negative, **ne** precedes the reflexive pronoun and **pas** follows the conjugated form of **être.**

| | |
|---|---|
| Nicole **ne** s'est **pas** couchée de bonne heure et elle **ne** s'est **pas** réveillée de bonne heure non plus. | *Nicole didn't go to bed early, and she didn't wake up early either.* |

**Activité 8** **Ne t'impatiente pas!** Formez de petites conversations entre ces deux copines. La première veut savoir quand les choses vont se faire. La seconde lui répond qu'on les a déjà faites. Faites attention à l'accord du participe passé au féminin. Suivez le modèle.

> MODÈLE les enfants / se laver
> Solange: Quand est-ce que les enfants vont se laver?
> Annick: Ils se sont déjà lavés.

**Vocabulaire**

### Des verbes

**se charger de quelque chose** *to take charge of something, be responsible for something*
**se détendre** *to relax*
**se fatiguer** *to get tired*
**s'intéresser à quelqu'un / à quelque chose** *to be interested in someone/something*

**se mettre à faire quelque chose** *to begin to do something*
**se mettre en route** *to get going*
**s'occuper de quelque chose / quelqu'un** *to take care of something/someone*

1. tu / se mettre à préparer le dîner

   _____

   _____

2. les enfants / se coucher

   _____

   _____

3. Josette et toi / s'occuper du linge

   _____

   _____

4. tu / se reposer

   _____

   _____

5. Elvire / se laver les cheveux

   _____

   _____

6. tu / se limer les ongles

   _____

   _____

7. Carole et Paulette / se calmer

   _____

   _____

8. je / se brosser les cheveux

   _____

   _____

**Activité 9** **Pas encore.** Mme Goulet est pressée parce que sa famille doit partir en vacances, mais personne n'est prêt. Utilisez le passé composé avec **pas encore** pour exprimer les réponses à ses questions. Suivez le modèle.

> MODÈLE Marc, tu viens de te laver, n'est-ce pas?
> Non, je ne me suis pas encore lavé.

1. Christine, tu viens de te lever, n'est-ce pas?

   _____

2. Chéri, tu viens de te raser, n'est-ce pas?

   _____

3. Marc et Christine, vous venez de vous brosser les dents, n'est-ce pas?

   _____

4. Marc, tu viens de te laver les cheveux, n'est-ce pas?

   _____

5. Chéri, tu viens de t'habiller, n'est-ce pas?

   _____

6. Marc et Christine, vous venez de vous peigner, n'est-ce pas?

   _____

**Activité 10** **Une excursion de l'université.** L'université a organisé une excursion pour les étudiants. Décrivez leur départ en formant des phrases au passé composé à partir des éléments donnés.

1. Olivier et Jean / se réveiller de bonne heure

   _____

2. Christine / se laver les cheveux

   _____

3. Monique et Véronique / se préparer pour le départ

   _____

4. Mireille / se dépêcher comme une folle

   _____

5. Christian et Pierre / se charger de la nourriture

   _____

6. tous les étudiants / se réunir devant la Faculté des Lettres

   _____

*(continued)*

7. ils / s'asseoir dans les autocars

_____

8. les autocars / s'éloigner de l'université

_____

**Activité 11**  **Zéro de conduite.** Grand-mère se plaint de la conduite de ses petits-enfants hier, quand toute la famille est venue lui rendre visite. Formulez des phrases au passé composé pour voir ce qui est arrivé.

**Vocabulaire**

## La mauvaise conduite

**se cacher**  _to hide_
**s'échapper de**  _to run away from,_
  _escape from_
**se mettre en panique**  _to fly into_
  _a panic_
**se moquer de quelqu'un /_
  **quelque chose**  _to make fun of_
  _someone/something_

**se mouiller**  _to get wet_
**se plaindre de quelqu'un /_
  **quelque chose**  _to complain_
  _about someone/something_
**se salir**  _to get dirty_

1. le petit Claude / se mouiller la chemise en buvant un coca

_____

2. Marlise / se salir dans le garage

_____

3. les jumeaux / se moquer du voisin

_____

4. les parents de Philippe / se mettre en panique

_____

5. leur fils / s'échapper de la maison

_____

6. Caroline / se plaindre de tout

_____

7. le petit Baudouin / se cacher au sous-sol

_____

8. Odile / se couper le doigt avec un couteau

_____

9. moi / se fatiguer

_____

10. je / se coucher de bonne heure

_____

# Reciprocal reflexive verbs

1. A plural reflexive verb form may express reciprocity (English *each other*).

Vous **vous parlez** souvent?  
Oui, nous **nous téléphonons** tous les jours.

*Do you **speak to each other** often?*  
*Yes, we **call each other** every day.*

Marc et Constance **se voient** souvent?  
Oui, ils **se donnent rendez-vous** après leur cours.

*Do Marc and Constance **see each other** often?*  
*Yes, they **agree to see each other** after their class.*

2. The **passé composé** of a reciprocal verb is formed like the **passé composé** of any other reflexive verb. To determine whether agreement of the past participle is necessary, consider whether the corresponding nonreflexive verb takes a direct object. If you need **à** between the verb and the object, then the verb takes an indirect object. Only reflexive pronouns that are direct objects may agree with the past participle.

(Pierre a vu Christophe.) Ils **se sont vus.**

*They saw each other.*

(Pierre a parlé **à** Christophe.) Ils **se sont parlé.**

*They spoke **to** each other.*

## Des verbes réciproques

*s'acheter des cadeaux* to buy gifts for each other  
**s'aider, s'entraider** to help each other  
**s'aimer** to love each other  
**se comprendre** to understand each other  
**se connaître** to know each other  
**se détester** to hate each other  

*se donner rendez-vous* to agree to meet (friends)  
*s'écrire* to write to each other  
*s'envoyer (des courriels)* to send each other (emails)  
*se mentir* to lie to each other  
*se parler* to speak to each other  
*se plaire* to like each other  

*se poser des questions* to ask each other questions  
**se regarder** to look at each other  
**se rencontrer** to meet; to run into each other  
*se ressembler* to look alike  
*se téléphoner* to call each other  
**se voir** to see each other  

**Activité 12** **Pas hier.** Répondez à l'affirmatif aux questions qu'on vous pose, mais dites que hier c'était différent. Utilisez le passé composé et faites attention à l'accord du participe. Suivez le modèle.

MODÈLE Vous vous rencontrez souvent?  
Oui, mais hier nous ne nous sommes pas rencontrés.

*The reflexive pronoun of this verb is an *indirect* object: no agreement of the participle in the **passé composé.**

1. Vous vous voyez souvent?

   _____

2. Vous vous écrivez souvent?

   _____

3. Vous vous parlez souvent?

   _____

4. Vous vous téléphonez souvent?

   _____

5. Vous vous donnez souvent rendez-vous?

   _____

6. Vous vous aidez souvent?

   _____

7. Vous vous envoyez souvent des courriels?

   _____

8. Vous vous posez souvent des questions?

   _____

**Activité 13**  **Histoire d'amour.** Racontez le triste amour de Félix et Geneviève. Utilisez le pronom **ils** et le passé composé dans chaque phrase. Remarquez qu'il y a des verbes qui ne sont pas pronominaux.

## Les rapports humains

**Vocabulaire**

**se disputer**  *to argue*
**s'entendre bien/mal avec quelqu'un**  *to get along well / not get along with someone*
**se fiancer (avec quelqu'un)** *to get engaged (to someone)*
**se marier (avec quelqu'un)**  *to get married (to someone)*

**plaire à (quelqu'un)** *to be pleasing to (someone), to like or be drawn to (someone)*
**rompre (avec quelqu'un)** *to break off (with someone)*
**tomber amoureux (amoureuse) de quelqu'un** *to fall in love with someone*

1. se voir

   _____

2. se connaître

   _____

3. se parler

   _____

4.  se comprendre

_____

5.  se plaire

_____

6.  tomber amoureux

_____

7.  s'acheter de petits cadeaux

_____

8.  se fiancer

_____

9.  après un temps / se disputer

_____

10. se mentir

_____

11. rompre

_____

12. ne pas se marier

_____


## Imperative of reflexive verbs

1.  In negative commands, the reflexive pronoun precedes the verb.

    Ne **t'énerve** pas!                  *Don't get upset!*
    Ne **vous levez** pas.                *Don't get up.*
    Ne **nous approchons** pas.           *Let's not get closer.*

2.  In affirmative commands, the reflexive pronoun is placed after the verb and is connected to it by a hyphen. **Te** changes to **toi** when placed after the verb.

    **Asseyez-vous.**                     *Sit down.*
    **Dépêchons-nous.**                   *Let's hurry up.*
    **Habille-toi** et **mets-toi** à étudier.   *Get dressed and start studying.*

**Activité 14** **Quelle lenteur!** Employez l'impératif des verbes pronominaux pour dire à un(e) ami(e) (et à deux amis) ce qu'ils doivent faire pour ne pas être en retard. Suivez le modèle.

| MODÈLE | se réveiller | |
|---|---|---|
| À UN(E) AMI(E): | Réveille-toi. | |
| À DEUX AMIS: | Réveillez-vous. | |

|  | À UN(E) AMI(E) | À DEUX AMIS |
|---|---|---|
| 1. se lever | _____ | _____ |
| 2. s'habiller | _____ | _____ |
| 3. se dépêcher | _____ | _____ |
| 4. se laver les mains | _____ | _____ |
| 5. ne pas s'énerver | _____ | _____ |
| 6. ne plus se reposer | _____ | _____ |
| 7. ne pas se disputer | _____ | _____ |
| 8. ne pas se recoucher | _____ | _____ |
| 9. se diriger vers la porte | _____ | _____ |
| 10. se préparer pour partir | _____ | _____ |

**Activité 15**   **On s'encourage.** Employez l'impératif avec le pronom **nous** pour dire à un(e) ami(e) ce qu'il faut faire pour ne pas être en retard. Suivez le modèle.

> MODÈLE   se lever
> Levons-nous.

1. s'habiller _____

2. se dépêcher _____

3. se laver les mains _____

4. ne pas s'énerver _____

5. ne plus se reposer _____

6. ne pas se disputer _____

7. s'aider _____

8. se diriger vers la porte _____

9. se préparer pour partir _____

## Other reflexive constructions and reflexive verbs

1. When inversion is used to form questions with reflexive verbs, the subject pronoun is placed after the verb; the reflexive pronoun remains before the verb. The use of inversion to form questions with reflexive verbs is limited to formal written style and very formal speech.

| | |
|---|---|
| **Vous intéressez-vous** à l'art moderne? | *Are you interested in modern art?* |
| Les prisonniers **se sont-ils échappés?** | *Did the prisoners escape?* |
| **Ne vous efforcez-vous pas** de progresser? | *Aren't you striving to make progress?* |
| **Ne se sont-elles pas vues** dans le Midi? | *Didn't they see each other in the south of France?* |

2. A reflexive verb in the third-person singular can be the equivalent of the English passive voice.

| | |
|---|---|
| Ça ne **se fait** pas. | *That's not **done.*** |
| C'est un livre qui **se lit** beaucoup. | *It's a book that **is read** a lot.* |
| Cette ville **s'appelle** Valence. | *This city **is called** Valence.* |

## Useful reflexive verbs

**s'adresser à quelqu'un** *to address, speak to, be aimed at*

**s'apercevoir de quelque chose** *to notice something*

**s'attendre à quelque chose** *to expect something*

**se débarrasser de quelqu'un / de quelque chose** *to get rid of someone/something*

**se demander** *to wonder*

**se donner la peine de faire quelque chose** *to bother to, take the trouble to do something*

**s'en aller** *to go away*

**se fier à quelqu'un / quelque chose** *to trust someone/something*

**s'habituer à quelque chose** *to get used to / accustomed to something*

**se méfier de quelqu'un / quelque chose** *to distrust / be wary of someone/something*

**se passer de quelque chose** *to do without something*

**se perdre** *to get lost*

**se priver de quelque chose** *to deprive oneself of something*

**se rappeler quelque chose** *to recall, remember something*

**se servir de quelque chose** *to use something*

**se soucier de quelqu'un / quelque chose** *to worry, be concerned about someone/something*

**se souvenir de quelqu'un / quelque chose** *to remember someone/ something*

**se tromper de quelque chose** *to make a mistake, be wrong about something*

**Activité 16** **Posez vos questions!** Refaites ces questions dans un langage soutenu (*formal*) en employant l'inversion.

1. Est-ce que ce produit se vend bien?

   _____

2. Est-ce que les étudiants s'amusent au bal?

   _____

3. Est-ce que vous ne vous dirigez pas vers la sortie (*the exit*)?

   _____

4. Est-ce qu'ils se sont approchés du guichet?

   _____

5. Est-ce que nous ne nous éloignons pas du centre de la ville?

   _____

6. Pourquoi est-ce que vos amis ne se voient plus?

   _____

7. Pourquoi est-ce que tu ne t'intéresses plus au cinéma?

   _____

*(continued)*

8. À quelle heure est-ce qu'elles se sont mises en route?

   _____

9. Est-ce qu'ils ne se sont pas offensés?

   _____

10. Est-ce qu'elle s'est souvenue de moi?

    _____

11. Pourquoi est-ce qu'elle ne s'est pas habituée à la vie française?

    _____

12. Est-ce que vous vous attendez à le voir?

    _____

**Activité 17**   **Activité orale.** Avec un(e) camarade décrivez votre journée—ce que vous faites le matin, comment vous arrivez à la fac, les gens que vous y voyez, vos sentiments, ce que vous faites en rentrant chez vous, et ainsi de suite. Votre camarade décrira la sienne. Comparez les deux journées et présentez les différences et les similarités à une troisième personne.

The pluperfect, the future perfect, and the past conditional are compound tenses, like the **passé composé.** They consist of an auxiliary verb (**avoir** or **être**) followed by the past participle. The auxiliary verb indicates tense: it may be in the imperfect, future, or conditional. Verbs will use the same auxiliary, either **avoir** or **être,** as they do in the **passé composé.**

## The pluperfect (le plus-que-parfait)

1. The pluperfect tense (English: *had done something*) consists of the imperfect of the auxiliary verb (either **avoir** or **être**), followed by the past participle.

| CHERCHER | | | |
|---|---|---|---|
| j' | **avais cherché** | nous | **avions cherché** |
| tu | **avais cherché** | vous | **aviez cherché** |
| il/elle/on | **avait cherché** | ils/elles | **avaient cherché** |

| ARRIVER | | | |
|---|---|---|---|
| j' | **étais arrivé(e)** | nous | **étions arrivé(e)s** |
| tu | **étais arrivé(e)** | vous | **étiez arrivé(e)(s)** |
| il | **était arrivé** | ils | **étaient arrivés** |
| elle | **était arrivée** | elles | **étaient arrivées** |

Reflexive verbs are conjugated with **être** in the pluperfect, just as they are in the **passé composé.**

| SE RÉVEILLER | | | |
|---|---|---|---|
| je | **m'étais réveillé(e)** | nous | **nous étions réveillé(e)s** |
| tu | **t'étais réveillé(e)** | vous | **vous étiez réveillé(e)(s)** |
| il | **s'était réveillé** | ils | **s'étaient réveillés** |
| elle | **s'était réveillée** | elles | **s'étaient réveillées** |

The rules for agreement of the past participle in all the compound tenses are the same as in the **passé composé.** See Chapter 3.

2. The pluperfect expresses a past action that occurred prior to another past action that is either mentioned in the same sentence or understood from the context.

Jean n'a pas mangé avec vous?
Non. Quand Jean est arrivé, nous **avions** déjà **mangé.**

*Jean didn't eat with you?*
*No. When Jean arrived, we **had** already **eaten.***

Pourquoi est-ce que tu n'as pas répondu au téléphone? Tu **ne t'étais pas** encore **réveillé**?
Si, je **m'étais** déjà **levé.**

*Why didn't you answer the telephone?* ***Hadn't** you **awakened** yet?*

*Yes, I **had** already **gotten up.***

Je lui ai demandé s'il **avait lu** le livre.
Il m'a répondu qu'il ne l'**avait** pas encore **acheté.**

*I asked him if he **had read** the book.*

*He answered me that he **hadn't** yet **bought** it.*

---

**Activité 1**  **Jacques était absent.**  Lisez l'histoire de la classe du professeur Jourdain ce matin. Refaites chaque phrase au passé. Les verbes au présent passeront au passé composé; les verbes au passé composé passeront au plus-que-parfait, suivant le modèle.

> MODÈLE  Nous voyons que le professeur Jourdain a déjà commencé la leçon.
> Nous avons vu que le professeur Jourdain avait déjà commencé la leçon.

1. Le professeur demande pourquoi Jacques n'est pas venu.

   _____

2. Les étudiants répondent que Jacques est resté chez lui.

   _____

3. Le professeur veut savoir si Jacques est tombé malade.

   _____

4. On nous dit que Jacques est arrivé à la cantine.

   _____

5. Jacques nous demande si nous avons assisté à la classe du professeur Jourdain.

   _____

6. Hélène lui répond que nous avons tous été présents.

   _____

7. Je lui prête les notes que j'ai prises.

   _____

**Activité 2** **Explications.** On n'a pas fait ces choses hier parce qu'on les avait déjà faites avant-hier. Employez le plus-que-parfait dans vos explications. Suivez le modèle.

> MODÈLE Pourquoi est-ce que Claude n'a pas apporté les fleurs hier?
> C'est qu'il avait déjà apporté les fleurs avant-hier.

1. Pourquoi est-ce que Joëlle ne t'a pas téléphoné hier?

   _____

2. Pourquoi est-ce que Renée n'est pas venue te voir hier?

   _____

3. Pourquoi est-ce que les garçons n'ont pas demandé le nom du médecin hier?

   _____

4. Pourquoi est-ce que tu n'as pas passé ton permis de conduire hier?

   _____

5. Pourquoi est-ce que Jeanne et Martine n'ont pas fait leur travail hier?

   _____

6. Pourquoi est-ce que tu n'as pas posté la lettre hier?

   _____

7. Pourquoi est-ce que Charles n'a pas fait le plein hier?

   _____

8. Pourquoi est-ce que ton colocataire (*roommate*) et toi n'avez pas balayé la chambre hier?

   _____

**Activité 3** **Déjà fait à huit heures et demie du matin.** Employez le plus-que-parfait pour exprimer tout ce qu'on avait déjà fait à huit heures et demie quand les amis ont sonné à la porte. Suivez le modèle.

> MODÈLE je / se réveiller
> À huit heures et demie, je m'étais déjà réveillé(e).

1. ma sœur / prendre une douche

   _____

2. ma mère / préparer le petit déjeuner

   _____

3. je / se lever

   _____

*(continued)*

4. mon amie Ghislaine / téléphoner deux fois

_____

5. mon père / ne pas encore partir pour le bureau

_____

6. je / relire mes notes de biologie

_____

7. mes frères / mettre leurs papiers dans leurs serviettes (*briefcases*)

_____

8. je / ne pas encore s'habiller

_____

## The future perfect (le futur antérieur)

1. The future perfect tense (English: *will have done something*) consists of the future of the auxiliary verb (**avoir** or **être**), followed by the past participle.

| CHERCHER | | | |
|---|---|---|---|
| j' | **aurai cherché** | nous | **aurons cherché** |
| tu | **auras cherché** | vous | **aurez cherché** |
| il/elle/on | **aura cherché** | ils/elles | **auront cherché** |

| ARRIVER | | | |
|---|---|---|---|
| je | **serai arrivé(e)** | nous | **serons arrivé(e)s** |
| tu | **seras arrivé(e)** | vous | **serez arrivé(e)(s)** |
| il | **sera arrivé** | ils | **seront arrivés** |
| elle | **sera arrivée** | elles | **seront arrivées** |

| SE RÉVEILLER | | | |
|---|---|---|---|
| je | **me serai réveillé(e)** | nous | **nous serons réveillé(e)s** |
| tu | **te seras réveillé(e)** | vous | **vous serez réveillé(e)(s)** |
| il | **se sera réveillé** | ils | **se seront réveillés** |
| elle | **se sera réveillée** | elles | **se seront réveillées** |

2. The future perfect expresses a future action that will have been completed before another future event takes place at or before an implied or specified point in time in the future.

J'**aurai fini** vers cinq heures du soir.　　　*I **will have finished** around five o'clock in the evening.*

Elle **sera arrivée** avant nous.　　　*She **will have arrived** before us.*

Ils **se seront installés** avant le mois de septembre.　　　*They **will have moved in** by the month of September.*

3. The future perfect is used after the conjunctions **quand, lorsque, dès que, aussitôt que,** and **après que** when the verb in the main clause is in the future tense.

Je te téléphonerai **quand** les courriels **seront arrivés.**

*I'll call you **when** the emails **arrive.***

Nous partirons **aussitôt que** Chantal **aura fini** son travail.

*We'll leave **as soon as** Chantal **has finished** her work.*

**Activité 4**  **Qui aura fait quoi?** Vous et votre ami, vous vous approchez de la grande fête de fin d'année. Vous expliquez à votre ami que tout devrait marcher comme sur des roulettes (*come off beautifully*) parce que tout a été très bien organisé. Employez le futur antérieur pour lui dire qui se sera chargé de chaque tâche importante. Suivez le modèle.

> MODÈLE  Marie-France / préparer les hors-d'œuvre
> Marie-France aura préparé les hors-d'œuvre.

1. Claude et Alain / chercher les boissons

   _____

2. Sylvie / mettre le couvert

   _____

3. Jean-Paul / choisir les DVD

   _____

4. Sophie et Odile / inviter tout le monde

   _____

5. Hervé et Nathalie / décorer la salle

   _____

6. Marguerite / acheter les gobelets (*paper cups*)

   _____

7. Robert / organiser les attractions (*entertainment*)

   _____

**Activité 5**  **Trop tard.** Utilisez le futur antérieur après **après que** pour dire que dans chaque cas il sera trop tard. Employez le futur dans la proposition principale. Suivez le modèle.

> MODÈLE  tu / arriver / je / sortir
> Tu arriveras après que je serai sorti.

1. il / m'offrir un coup de main (*a helping hand*) / je / finir

   _____

2. elle / sonner à la porte / nous / se coucher

   _____

3. tu / venir / tout le monde / partir

_____

4. ils / trouver la carte routière / nous / se perdre

_____

5. nous / arriver / ils / fermer le restaurant

_____

6. il / nous renseigner / nous / trouver la solution

_____

7. elle / apporter le pain / nous / finir de manger

_____

8. vous / venir nous prendre en voiture / nous / partir en autocar

_____

**Activité 6**   **Récompensé ou puni?** Expliquez pourquoi ces gens seront récompensés ou punis, à partir des éléments proposés. Employez le futur dans la proposition principale et le futur antérieur dans la proposition annoncée par **parce que.** Suivez le modèle.

> MODÈLE   tu / être grondé parce que tu / ne rien faire
> Tu seras grondé parce que tu n'auras rien fait.

**Vocabulaire**

## Actions, récompenses et punitions

| | |
|---|---|
| **agir** *to act* | **se faire gronder** *to get scolded* |
| **comme il faut** *properly* | **louer** *to praise* |
| **se conduire** *to behave* | **récompenser** *to reward* |
| **donner un prix** *to give a prize* | **sécher un cours** *to cut class* |

1. tu / recevoir une bonne note parce que tu / étudier sérieusement

_____

2. on / donner un prix à Marc parce qu'il / rédiger la meilleure composition

_____

3. on / récompenser les étudiants parce qu'ils / se conduire comme il faut

_____

4. les journaux / louer cet agent de police parce qu'il / agir héroïquement

_____

5. le petit Pierrot / être grondé parce qu'il / ne pas ranger ses affaires

_____

6. Michèle / se faire gronder par ses parents parce qu'elle / sécher ses cours

_____

7. je / répondre à toutes les questions à l'examen parce que je / comprendre la matière

_____

8. tout le monde / être déçu parce que nos cousins / ne pas arriver avant le match

_____

**Activité 7**  **En famille.** Laurent Duval raconte une soirée que sa famille passera ensemble. Formez des phrases à partir des éléments proposés pour savoir ce qu'il dit. Employez le futur dans la proposition principale et le futur antérieur dans la proposition subordonnée. Faites attention à l'accord du participe passé. Suivez le modèle.

> MODÈLE  nous / prendre les hors-d'œuvre que ma sœur et moi / préparer
> Nous prendrons les hors-d'œuvre que ma sœur et moi
> aurons prépar**és.**

1. nous / manger un dîner magnifique que nous / cuisiner

_____

2. je / écouter le CD que je / acheter

_____

3. papa / servir un dessert formidable avec la pâtisserie qu'il / acheter

_____

4. ma sœur / nous raconter l'histoire du roman qu'elle / lire

_____

5. ma mère / lire des articles dans la revue qu'elle / acheter

_____

6. nous / regarder le film que nous / louer

_____

7. ma mère et moi, nous / parler des articles qu'elle / lire

_____

8. mon frère / chanter les nouvelles chansons qu'il / apprendre à l'école

_____

# The conditional perfect (le conditionnel passé)

1. The conditional perfect (English: *would have done something*) consists of the conditional of the auxiliary verb (**avoir** or **être**), followed by the past participle.

| CHERCHER | | | |
|---|---|---|---|
| j' | **aurais cherché** | nous | **aurions cherché** |
| tu | **aurais cherché** | vous | **auriez cherché** |
| il/elle/on | **aurait cherché** | ils/elles | **auraient cherché** |

| ARRIVER | | | |
|---|---|---|---|
| je | **serais arrivé(e)** | nous | **serions arrivé(e)s** |
| tu | **serais arrivé(e)** | vous | **seriez arrivé(e)(s)** |
| il | **serait arrivé** | ils | **seraient arrivés** |
| elle | **serait arrivée** | elles | **seraient arrivées** |

| SE RÉVEILLER | | | |
|---|---|---|---|
| je | **me serais réveillé(e)** | nous | **nous serions réveillé(e)s** |
| tu | **te serais réveillé(e)** | vous | **vous seriez réveillé(e)(s)** |
| il | **se serait réveillé** | ils | **se seraient réveillés** |
| elle | **se serait réveillée** | elles | **se seraient réveillées** |

2. The conditional perfect usually refers to an event that *did not take place* in the past.

Tu **m'aurais aidé**?
J'**aurais** tout **fait** pour t'aider.

*Would you have helped me?*
*I would have done everything to help you.*

Vous **vous seriez souvenu** de lui?
Non, je **ne l'aurais pas reconnu.**

*Would you have remembered him?*
*No, I wouldn't have recognized him.*

**Activité 8** **Je n'aurais pas fait une chose pareille.** Vous n'auriez pas fait tout ce que vos copains ont fait. Dites-le en employant le conditionnel passé, selon le modèle.

MODÈLE   Christophe s'est baigné dans le fleuve.
Moi, je ne me serais pas baigné(e) dans le fleuve.

1. Philippe s'est couché à cinq heures du matin.

_____

2. Claudette a pris rendez-vous avec le professeur Bouvard.

_____

3. Mireille et Louis se sont mis en route sous la pluie.

_____

4. Alain a fait dix kilomètres à pied.

_____

5. Christine a cueilli des fleurs dans le jardin public.

_____

6. Serge et Frédéric ont cru à l'histoire que Marc a racontée.

_____

7. Lise et Blanche ont dépensé tout leur argent.

_____

8. Chantal a oublié la date de la réception.

_____

**Activité 9**  **Eux, ils l'auraient fait.** Marcel avait peur de faire beaucoup de choses. Les autres copains n'auraient pas eu peur. Exprimez cette idée en employant le conditionnel passé, selon le modèle.

> MODÈLE   J'avais peur de parler avec le professeur. (Cécile)
> Vraiment? Cécile aurait parlé avec le professeur.

1. J'avais peur de conduire la voiture d'André. (Guillaume)

_____

2. J'avais peur de descendre. (Jacqueline et Martin)

_____

3. J'avais peur d'interrompre. (Vincent et moi)

_____

4. J'avais peur de m'exprimer. (moi)

_____

5. J'avais peur d'employer ce mot. (Albert)

_____

6. J'avais peur de plonger. (Simone et moi)

_____

7. J'avais peur de répondre à Georges. (Ségolène)

_____

8. J'avais peur de me disputer avec lui. (Solange et Marie)

_____

# Si clauses with perfect tenses

To express a hypothetical situation situated in the past, which is contrary to fact, French uses the pluperfect in the **si** clause and the conditional perfect in the result clause.

| SUMMARY OF TENSES IN PERFECT CONDITIONAL SENTENCES | |
|---|---|
| SUPPOSITION (si CLAUSE) | MAIN CLAUSE (OR "RESULT" CLAUSE) |
| Pluperfect | Conditional Perfect |

—Jean-Claude n'est pas arrivé.
—S'il **était arrivé,** nous **aurions dîné** ensemble.

*Jean-Claude hasn't arrived.*
*If he **had arrived,** we **would have had dinner** together.*

—Je n'ai pas étudié.
—Si tu **avais étudié,** tu **aurais réussi** les examens.

*I didn't study.*
*If you **had studied,** you **would have passed** the exams.*

—Alice ne nous a pas vus.
—C'est vrai. Si elle nous **avait vus,** elle **se serait approchée** de notre table.

*Alice didn't see us.*
*That's true. If she **had seen** us, she **would have come over** to our table.*

**Activité 10**    **Moi, je l'aurais fait aussi.** Dites que vous auriez fait toutes ces choses si Berthe les avait faites. Suivez le modèle.

> MODÈLE   Berthe n'est pas sortie hier.
> Mais si elle était sortie hier, moi aussi je serais sorti(e).

1. Berthe n'est pas allée en ville hier.

   _____

2. Berthe n'a pas acheté le logiciel hier.

   _____

3. Berthe ne s'est pas promenée hier.

   _____

4. Berthe n'a pas envoyé ses paquets hier.

   _____

5. Berthe n'a pas pris son billet hier.

   _____

6. Berthe ne s'est pas préparée pour partir hier.

   _____

7. Berthe n'a pas écouté le CD hier.

   _____

8. Berthe n'a pas travaillé hier.

   _____

**Activité 11**  **Si on avait fini notre travail!** Qu'est-ce que les copains auraient fait s'ils avaient fini leurs devoirs? Employez une phrase avec une supposition au plus-que-parfait et une proposition principale au conditionnel passé exprimant le résultat. Suivez le modèle.

> MODÈLE  Marc n'a pas appris le nouveau vocabulaire. (aller au cinéma)
> Si Marc avait appris le nouveau vocabulaire, il serait allé au cinéma.

1. Rachelle n'a pas rédigé sa composition. (se réunir avec ses amis)

   _____

2. Philippe n'a pas relu ses leçons de chimie. (jouer au football)

   _____

3. Louise et Danielle n'ont pas préparé le compte rendu. (aller aux grands magasins)

   _____

4. Olivier et Jean-Luc ne sont pas allés au laboratoire de langues. (assister au concert)

   _____

5. Françoise et Guy n'ont pas étudié l'histoire du dix-septième siècle. (aller danser)

   _____

6. Mireille n'a pas fait les problèmes de maths. (sortir avec Charles)

   _____

7. Monique et Édouard n'ont pas révisé (*to review*) leurs notes de littérature française. (dîner en ville)

   _____

8. Jean-François n'a pas appris le poème par cœur. (jouer aux jeux vidéo)

   _____

**Activité 12**  **Résumés.** Résumez chaque échange par une phrase composée d'une supposition au plus-que-parfait et une proposition principale au conditionnel passé. Suivez le modèle.

> MODÈLE  THIERRY: Pourquoi est-ce que tu n'as pas répondu à ma lettre?
> GEORGES: Je ne l'ai pas reçue.
> Georges aurait répondu à la lettre de Thierry s'il l'avait reçue.

1.   YVES: Pourquoi est-ce que tu ne m'as pas salué à la cantine?
   MICHÈLE: Je ne t'ai pas vu.

   _____

2.    ROGER:   Pourquoi est-ce que tu ne m'as pas téléphoné?

        SYLVIE:   J'ai passé toute la journée à la bibliothèque.

---

3.    JUDITH:   Pourquoi est-ce que tu ne m'a pas dit qu'il y avait un examen aujourd'hui?

   DAMIEN:   Je ne m'en suis pas souvenu.

---

4.    JULIE:   Pourquoi est-ce que tu n'as pas suivi ton régime?

   ARIANE:   J'ai eu envie de manger du chocolat.

---

5.    SONIA:   Pourquoi est-ce que tu n'as pas fait le ménage?

   NICOLAS:   Je n'ai pas eu le temps.

---

6.    ROLAND:   Pourquoi est-ce que tu n'as pas pris ta bicyclette?

   PATRICK:   Je me suis foulé la cheville (*sprained my ankle*).

---

7.   GRÉGOIRE:   Pourquoi est-ce que toi et Virginie, vous n'êtes pas sortis?

    PAUL:   Nous avons dû étudier.

---

8.   HÉLÈNE:   Pourquoi est-ce que tu n'es pas venu à la faculté?

    LOUIS:   Je suis allé chez le médecin.

---

**Activité 13**   **Création.** Les personnes indiquées ont fait des choses surprenantes. Créez des réponses en employant une phrase composée d'une supposition au plus-que-parfait et une proposition principale au conditionnel passé exprimant le résultat.

> MODÈLE   Le professeur ne s'est pas fâché contre Pierrot.
> Il se serait fâché contre Pierrot s'il avait entendu ses paroles.

1. Christine ne s'est pas amusée à la fête.

---

2. Les touristes ne se sont pas mis en route hier.

---

3. M. Marsaud ne s'est pas chargé de la collecte.

---

4. Tu n'as pas assisté au concert.

---

5. Le médecin ne m'a pas ordonné des antibiotiques.

_____

6. Émile n'a pas ses devoirs.

_____

7. Charlotte n'est pas venue nous voir.

_____

8. Bernard et Stéphane n'ont pas joué au basket aujourd'hui.

_____

**Activité 14** **Activité orale.** Avec un groupe de deux ou trois camarades, parlez de comment votre vie aurait été différente si votre famille et vous aviez fait les choses différemment. Employez des phrases avec **si** pour exprimer les possibilités.

## The **passé simple** of regular verbs

1.  The **passé simple** is a literary tense used only in formal speeches and literary and journalistic writing. Like the **passé composé,** it expresses an action that was completed in the past. The **passé simple** of regular **-er** verbs is formed by dropping the **-er** from the infinitive and adding the endings **-ai, -as, -a, -âmes, -âtes, -èrent.**

| PARLER | | | |
|---|---|---|---|
| je | parl**ai** | nous | parl**âmes** |
| tu | parl**as** | vous | parl**âtes** |
| il/elle/on | parl**a** | ils/elles | parl**èrent** |

2.  In the **passé simple, aller** is conjugated like a regular **-er** verb.

3.  Infinitives that end in **-cer** change **c** to **ç**, and infinitives that end in **-ger** insert an **e** before the ending in all forms of the **passé simple** except the **ils/elles** form.

| LANCER | | | |
|---|---|---|---|
| je | lan**ç**ai | nous | lan**ç**âmes |
| tu | lan**ç**as | vous | lan**ç**âtes |
| il/elle/on | lan**ç**a | ils/elles | lancèrent |

| MANGER | | | |
|---|---|---|---|
| je | mang**e**ai | nous | mang**e**âmes |
| tu | mang**e**as | vous | mang**e**âtes |
| il/elle/on | mang**e**a | ils/elles | mangèrent |

4.  The **passé simple** of regular **-ir** and **-re** verbs is formed by dropping the infinitive ending and adding **-is, -is, -it, -îmes, -îtes, -irent.**

| FINIR | | | |
|---|---|---|---|
| je | fin**is** | nous | fin**îmes** |
| tu | fin**is** | vous | fin**îtes** |
| il/elle/on | fin**it** | ils/elles | fin**irent** |

| RENDRE | | | |
|---|---|---|---|
| je | rend**is** | nous | rend**îmes** |
| tu | rend**is** | vous | rend**îtes** |
| il/elle/on | rend**it** | ils/elles | rend**irent** |

Irregular **-ir** verbs such as **dormir** and **partir** form the **passé simple** in the same way as **finir: je dormis, je partis.** Irregular **-re** verbs such as **battre** and **suivre** form the **passé simple** in the same way as **rendre: je battis, je suivis.**

**Activité 1**  **Au passé simple.** Transformez ces verbes du passé composé au passé simple.

1. j'ai gagné

   _____

2. tu as commencé

   _____

3. elle a choisi

   _____

4. elles ont attendu

   _____

5. vous avez espéré

   _____

6. tu as nagé

   _____

7. il a encouragé

   _____

8. nous avons déménagé

   _____

9. je suis descendu(e)

   _____

10. tu as annoncé

    _____

11. ils ont rangé

    _____

12. elles ont défendu

    _____

13. vous avez obéi

    _____

14. nous avons entendu

    _____

15. j'ai remplacé

    _____

16. on a rédigé

    _____

17. nous avons réfléchi

    _____

18. vous avez essayé

    _____

19. tu es allé(e)

    _____

20. nous avons partagé

    _____

# The **passé simple** of irregular verbs

1. Some irregular verbs form the **passé simple** using the same endings as regular **-ir** and **-re** verbs.

| INFINITIVE | STEM | PASSÉ SIMPLE |
|---|---|---|
| s'asseoir | **ass-** | je **m'assis** |
| conduire | **conduis-** | je **conduisis** |
| dire | **d-** | je **dis** |
| écrire | **écriv-** | j'**écrivis** |
| faire | **f-** | je **fis** |
| joindre | **joign-** | je **joignis** |
| mettre | **m-** | je **mis** |
| naître | **naqu-** | je **naquis** |
| peindre | **peign-** | je **peignis** |
| prendre | **pr-** | je **pris** |
| rire | **r-** | je **ris** |
| voir | **v-** | je **vis** |

2. Most irregular verbs that have a past participle ending in **-u** have a stem that resembles their past participle. The endings for such verbs are **-s, -s, -t, -^mes, -^tes, -rent.** They follow the pattern of **avoir.**

| AVOIR | | | |
|---|---|---|---|
| j' | **eus** | nous | **eûmes** |
| tu | **eus** | vous | **eûtes** |
| il/elle/on | **eut** | ils/elles | **eurent** |

| INFINITIVE | STEM | PASSÉ SIMPLE |
|---|---|---|
| boire | **bu-** | je **bus** |
| connaître | **connu-** | je **connus** |
| courir | **couru-** | je **courus** |
| croire | **cru-** | je **crus** |
| devoir | **du-** | je **dus** |
| falloir | **fallu-** | il **fallut** |
| lire | **lu-** | je **lus** |
| pleuvoir | **plu-** | il **plut** |
| pouvoir | **pu-** | je **pus** |
| recevoir | **reçu-** | je **reçus** |
| savoir | **su-** | je **sus** |
| valoir | **valu-** | il **valut** |
| vivre | **vécu-** | je **vécus** |
| vouloir | **voulu-** | je **voulus** |

Some verbs have special forms in the passé simple.

être:          **je fus, tu fus, il/elle/on fut, nous fûmes, vous fûtes, ils/elles furent***

mourir:        **je mourus, tu mourus, il/elle/on mourut, nous mourûmes, vous mourûtes, ils/elles moururent**

*verbs like* venir:  **je vins, tu vins, il/elle/on vint, nous vînmes, vous vîntes, ils/elles vinrent**

**Activité 2**   **Transformation.**  Refaites cette petite histoire au passé simple.

La nuit est tombée sur Versailles et son château. La ville est devenue silencieuse. Les habitants sont rentrés chez eux. On a fermé les magasins. Je suis entré dans un bistrot. Je me suis assis à une petite table. J'ai attendu Michèle. Elle a voulu me voir. Elle m'a rejoint à sept heures. Nous avons pris un café ensemble. Nous sommes sortis. Nous nous sommes promenés près du château. Après, nous sommes rentrés chez nous.

_____

_____

_____

_____

_____

_____

_____

**Activité 3**   **Transformation.**  Refaites l'histoire ci-dessous au passé composé.

Le soleil se leva. Le ciel bleu devint écarlate et les nuages pâles se couchèrent derrière la montagne. Sylvaine fut sublime dans cette lumière pourpre et Baptiste ne put pas s'empêcher de (*help himself from*) lui en toucher un mot (*letting her know*). «Vous naquîtes sous un soleil céleste, Sylvaine», lui dit-il. Elle sourit en entendant ces mots, mais elle n'y répondit point (pas). Il fallut des remarques plus étincelantes (*scintillating*) pour retenir l'attention de la jeune rêveuse. Elle descendit la route qui la mena vers la ville. Sa tête se remplit d'images d'une vie sophistiquée et suave. Baptiste voulut la suivre, mais il n'eut pas le courage.

_____

_____

_____

_____

_____

_____

_____

_____

*The verbs **faire** and **être** are quite similar in the **passé simple.** Be sure not to confuse **je fis** (*I did*) and **je fus** (*I was*), as well as all the other forms of **faire** and **être** in this tense (**nous fîmes, nous fûmes,** etc.).

# 10 Participles and infinitives

## The present participle

1. The French present participle (**le participe présent**) corresponds to the English *-ing* form of a verb (*going, seeing, doing*). The present participle of most verbs is formed by dropping **-ons** from the present-tense **nous** form and adding **-ant.**

| INFINITIVE | PRESENT TENSE, *nous* FORM | PRESENT PARTICIPLE STEM | PRESENT PARTICIPLE |
|---|---|---|---|
| parler | nous parlons | **parl-** | **parlant** |
| étudier | nous étudions | **étudi-** | **étudiant** |
| écrire | nous écrivons | **écriv-** | **écrivant** |
| finir | nous finissons | **finiss-** | **finissant** |
| lire | nous lisons | **lis-** | **lisant** |
| prendre | nous prenons | **pren-** | **prenant** |
| recevoir | nous recevons | **recev-** | **recevant** |
| rendre | nous rendons | **rend-** | **rendant** |

Only three verbs have irregular present participles.

avoir → **ayant**　　　　être → **étant**　　　　savoir → **sachant**

2. A present participle may be used as an adjective or a verb. When used as an adjective, a present participle usually follows the noun or pronoun it modifies and agrees with it in gender and number.

| | |
|---|---|
| de l'eau **courante** (courir) | *running* water |
| les numéros **gagnants** (gagner) | the *winning* numbers |
| des histoires **touchantes** (toucher) | *touching* stories |

3. When used as a verb, the present participle often follows the preposition **en.** This construction consisting of **en** + present participle is called **le gérondif.**

a. **En** + *present participle* may express an action that is happening at the same time as the action of the main verb.

Ici on ne parle pas **en travaillant.**    *Here people don't talk **while working.***

**En entrant** dans le café, nous avons vu notre amie Diane.    *Upon entering the café, we saw our friend Diane.*

b.  **En** + *present participle* may also express the causal relationship between an action and its result.

On ne maigrit pas **en mangeant** des glaces.    *You don't get thinner **by eating** ice cream.*

J'ai fait des progrès en français **en lisant** beaucoup.    *I made progress in French **by reading** a lot.*

c.  The present participle may also be used without **en.**

**Ayant peur** d'arriver en retard, nous sommes partis de très bonne heure.    ***Being afraid** to arrive late, we left very early.*

**NOTE**  The implied subject of the **gérondif** *must* be the same as the subject of the main clause.

4.  The present participle may be used instead of a relative clause. In this case it is invariable. This construction is typical of formal speech and writing.

les trains **venant** de l'étranger (**venant** = qui viennent)    *trains **coming** from abroad*

des employés **parlant** français (**parlant** = qui parlent)    *employees **speaking** French*

un autobus **montant** le boulevard (**montant** = qui monte)    *a bus **going up** the boulevard*

**Activité 1**  **Des conseils.** Marie-Josette donne des conseils à son frère cadet qui entre au collège. Refaites chacune de ses phrases en changeant la supposition commençant par **si** au gérondif. Suivez le modèle.

> MODÈLE  Tu apprendras beaucoup si tu fais attention.
> Tu apprendras beaucoup en faisant attention.

1.  Tu auras une bonne note si tu fais tes devoirs de maths tous les jours.

   _____

2.  Tu arriveras à l'heure si tu quittes la maison à sept heures et demie.

   _____

3.  Si on apprend toutes les dates par cœur, on évite beaucoup de problèmes dans le cours d'histoire.

   _____

(continued)

4. Si tu écoutes des programmes en anglais sur Internet, tu te prépareras pour l'examen oral.

_____

5. On évite la fatigue si on organise son travail.

_____

6. Si on regarde très peu la télé, on peut toujours finir son travail.

_____

**Activité 2**  **La langue administrative.** Pour écrire des phrases typiques des annonces officielles, remplacez la proposition subordonnée par le participe présent correspondant. Puisque ce participe est une forme verbale, il ne s'accorde pas avec le substantif (*noun*).

> MODÈLE   Les visiteurs qui désirent visiter le musée sont priés d'attendre à gauche.
> Les visiteurs désirant visiter le musée sont priés d'attendre à gauche.

1. Les voyageurs qui partent pour le Nord sont priés de passer au quai (*platform*) numéro 3.

_____

2. Nous annonçons un retard pour tous les avions qui proviennent d'Afrique.

_____

3. Le docteur Gobert verra les malades qui souffrent d'un problème gastrique.

_____

4. Les étudiants qui passent leurs examens demain doivent arriver à l'université à huit heures.

_____

5. C'est un manuel d'anglais qui contient tout le vocabulaire essentiel.

_____

6. Voici une carte qui montre le site des centrales nucléaires.

_____

## Infinitives

1. In French, the infinitive can serve as the subject of a sentence. English usually uses a gerund (the *-ing* form of the verb) in this case.

| | |
|---|---|
| **Voir,** c'est **croire.** | *Seeing* is *believing.* |
| **Apprendre** le français en six mois n'est pas facile! | *Learning* French in six months is *not easy!* |
| **Vivre** à Paris, c'est mon rêve. | *Living* in Paris is my dream. |

2. The infinitive can also serve as the complement of a verb, much the way direct or indirect object nouns do. Some verbs can be followed directly by an infinitive; others require a preposition before an infinitive used as a complement.

Il **doit** finir.    Il **essaie de** finir.    Il **réussit à** finir.

The following verbs do not take a preposition before an infinitive.

| | | |
|---|---|---|
| **aimer** *to like* | **désirer** *to want* | **penser** *to intend* |
| **aimer mieux** *to prefer* | **détester** *to hate* | **pouvoir** *to be able* |
| **aller** *to be going* | **devoir** *should, must,* | **préférer** *to prefer* |
| **avoir beau** *to do* (*something*) | *ought* | **savoir** *to know how* |
| *in vain* | **espérer** *to hope* | **vouloir** *to want* |
| **compter** *to intend* | **oser** *to dare* | |

**Tu comptes partir** en vacances en février? *Do you intend to leave for vacation in February?*

Non, **je déteste voyager** en hiver. *No, I hate traveling in the winter.*

**Tu préfères y aller** en été? *Do you prefer to go in the summer?*

**J'aime mieux prendre** mes vacances au printemps. *I prefer to take my vacation in the springtime.*

3. Verbs of movement and direction are followed directly by an infinitive.

**Je descends faire les courses.** Tu as besoin de quelque chose? *I'm going down to do the shopping. Do you need anything?*

**Tu peux aller** me **chercher** un journal français? *Can you go get me a French newspaper?*

4. The expressions **il faut** (*one must, you have to*) and **il vaut mieux** (*it's better to*) are also followed directly by the infinitive. These expressions are not conjugated for person: the impersonal **il** is the only possible subject. However, these expressions are conjugated for tense.

imperfect: **il fallait, il valait mieux**

passé composé: **il a fallu, il a mieux valu**

future: **il faudra, il vaudra mieux**

conditional: **il faudrait, il vaudrait mieux**

**Activité 3**  **Les fêtes et les célébrations.** Employez la construction **verbe** + **infinitif** en ajoutant les verbes entre parenthèses aux phrases. Vous verrez comment les Maurois et leurs amis passent les fêtes durant l'année. Suivez le modèle.

MODÈLE   Les Maurois restent chez eux le jour de Noël. (préférer)
Les Maurois préfèrent rester chez eux le jour de Noël.

1. Les Maurois font un grand réveillon pour la Saint-Sylvestre (*New Year's Eve*). (aimer)

_____

2. Ils s'offrent des étrennes (*New Year gifts*) le jour de l'An. (aller)

_____

3. Le 6 janvier ils invitent des amis pour la fête des Rois. (espérer)

   _____

4. La grand-mère passe le dimanche de Pâques (*Easter*) avec eux. (vouloir)

   _____

5. Le 8 mai, ils vont en Normandie pour commémorer la victoire des Alliés en 1945. (compter)

   _____

6. Pour Noël, ils sont dans leur maison à la campagne. (désirer)

   _____

7. Ils vont fleurir les tombes (*graves*) de leurs parents décédés (*deceased*) le 2 novembre. (devoir)

   _____

8. Ils vont à la messe de minuit (*midnight mass*) le 24 décembre. (aller)

   _____

**Activité 4**   **Au bord de la mer.** Ajoutez les verbes entre parenthèses à ces phrases pour voir comment un groupe d'amis a passé leurs vacances au bord de la mer. Employez le même temps verbal que celui de la phrase donnée. Suivez le modèle.

> MODÈLE   Philippe nageait tous les jours. (vouloir)
> Philippe voulait nager tous les jours.

1. Alice et Géraldine ont fait du tourisme. (pouvoir)

   _____

2. Georges ne nageait pas très bien. (savoir)

   _____

3. Il s'éloignait de la plage. (ne pas oser)

   _____

4. Claudette et Brigitte jouaient au tennis. (préférer)

   _____

5. Louis visitait les petits villages en dehors de la ville. (aimer)

   _____

6. Solange a acheté des souvenirs. (ne pas pouvoir)

   _____

7. Richard a envoyé beaucoup de courriels. (devoir)

   _____

# Verb + à + infinitive

1. When followed by an infinitive, some verbs require the preposition **à**.

| | | |
|---|---|---|
| **s'amuser à** *to enjoy oneself (by doing)* | **s'ennuyer à** *to get/be bored (doing something)* | **penser à** *to be thinking of (doing something)* |
| **apprendre à** *to learn how to* | **s'exercer à** *to practice* | **se préparer à** *to get ready to* |
| **arriver à** *to manage to* | **s'habituer à** *to get used to* | |
| **s'attendre à** *to expect to* | **hésiter à** *to hesitate to* | **se résigner à** *to resign oneself to* |
| **avoir à** *to have to* | **s'intéresser à** *to be interested in* | **réussir à** *to succeed in* |
| **chercher à** *to try to* | | **songer à** *to be thinking of (doing something)* |
| **commencer à** *to begin to* | **se mettre à** *to begin to* | |
| **se consacrer à** *to devote oneself* | **s'obstiner à** *to persist stubbornly in* | **tendre à** *to tend to* |
| **consentir à** *to consent to* | **parvenir à** *to manage to, succeed in* | **tenir à** *to insist on* |
| **continuer à** *to continue* | | |
| **se décider à** *to make up one's mind to* | **passer son temps à** *to spend one's time (doing something)* | |

Henri **s'obstine à causer** avec tous les touristes allemands.
Il **s'exerce à parler** allemand.
Il **parviendra à chasser** tous les touristes de Paris.
Tu exagères. Les touristes **s'amusent à converser** avec lui.

*Henri **insists on chatting** with all the German tourists.*
*He's **practicing speaking** German.*
*He'll **succeed in chasing** all the tourists away from Paris.*
*You're exaggerating. The tourists **enjoy talking** with him.*

2. Some verbs that require the preposition **à** before an infinitive used as a complement usually have a direct object as well.

| | |
|---|---|
| **aider quelqu'un à faire quelque chose** *to help someone do something* | **forcer quelqu'un à faire quelque chose** *to force someone to do something* |
| **autoriser quelqu'un à faire quelque chose** *to authorize someone to do something* | **inviter quelqu'un à faire quelque chose** *to invite someone to do something* |
| **encourager quelqu'un à faire quelque chose** *to encourage someone to do something* | |
| **engager quelqu'un à faire quelque chose** *to urge someone to do something* | **obliger quelqu'un à faire quelque chose** *to oblige someone to do something* |

**J'ai invité les Deschênes à passer** la soirée avec nous.
**Ils vous aideront à préparer** le repas. Ils adorent faire la cuisine.

*I **invited** the Deschênes **to spend** the evening with us.*
*They'll **help you prepare** the meal. They love to cook.*

3. **Enseigner** and **apprendre** (when it means *to teach*) take an indirect object, when they are followed by **à** + infinitive.

| |
|---|
| **enseigner/apprendre à quelqu'un à faire quelque chose**   *to teach someone to do something* |

**Qui lui a appris à parler français?**   *Who taught him/her to speak French?*

**Activité 5**  **La fête de Marthe.**  Marthe veut organiser une fête chez elle. Complétez le récit de ses préparatifs en ajoutant la préposition **à** si elle est nécessaire. Si on n'a pas besoin d'ajouter la préposition **à**, écrivez **X**.

1. Nous pensons _____ organiser une fête.

2. Je tiens _____ donner une fête formidable.

3. Michèle va _____ préparer des sandwichs.

4. Alfred et Robert doivent _____ s'occuper des boissons.

5. Ils tendent _____ oublier tout ce qu'ils ont à acheter.

6. Olivier invitera ses amis _____ venir.

7. Moi, je me consacrerai _____ mettre de l'ordre dans notre appartement.

8. Lise sait _____ faire une délicieuse tarte au citron.

**Activité 6**  **On modifie un peu le message.**  Refaites chacune des phrases avec les éléments proposés entre parenthèses pour connaître les occupations et les préoccupations d'un groupe d'étudiants.

> MODÈLES   Vous sortez. (pouvoir)
> Vous pouvez sortir.
>
> Vous sortez. (on / obliger)
> On vous oblige à sortir.

1. Nous lisons un livre par semaine. (le professeur / encourager)

   _____

2. Je fais mes recherches sur Internet. (aimer mieux)

   _____

3. Jacques finira son compte rendu demain. (réussir)

   _____

4. Philomène fait de l'allemand. (son patron / engager)

   _____

5. Vous cherchez du travail. (l'administration de l'école / autoriser)

   _____

6. Henri et Jules reçoivent une mauvaise note en maths. (se résigner)

   _____

7. Chantal révise ses notes d'informatique (*computer science*). (continuer)

   _____

8. Odile recopie ses notes. (passer son temps)

   _____

# Verb + **de** + infinitive

1. Some verbs are joined to a following infinitive by the preposition **de.**

| | | |
|---|---|---|
| **s'abstenir de** *to refrain from* | **décider de** *to decide* | **oublier de** *to forget* |
| **accepter de** *to agree* | **se dépêcher de** *to hurry* | **parler de** *to talk about* |
| **s'arrêter de** *to stop* | **s'empêcher de** *to refrain* | **promettre de** *to promise* |
| **avoir l'intention de** *to* | *from* | **se proposer de** *to set out,* |
| *intend* | **s'empresser de** *to hurry, rush* | *mean, intend, propose* |
| **avoir peur de** *to be afraid* | **entreprendre de** *to undertake* | *(an idea)* |
| **avoir raison de** *to be right* | **essayer de** *to try* | **refuser de** *to refuse* |
| **avoir tort de** *to be wrong* | **s'étonner de** *to marvel at* | **regretter de** *to regret* |
| **brûler de** *to be dying to* | **éviter de** *to avoid* | **se réjouir de** *to be* |
| **se charger de** *to make sure* | **s'excuser de** *to apologize for* | *delighted to* |
| *to, see to it (that some-* | **finir de** *to finish* | **résoudre de** *to resolve* |
| *thing is done)* | **se flatter de** *to claim to* | **risquer de** *to risk, run the* |
| **choisir de** *to choose* | *(be able)* | *risk of* |
| **craindre de** *to fear* | **mériter de** *to deserve* | **se souvenir de** *to remember* |

**Venir de** means *to have just done something.*

**Je viens de voir** Jacquot. *I **have just seen** Jacquot.*

2. When **finir** and **commencer** are followed by the preposition **par**, their meaning changes.

| | |
|---|---|
| **finir par** *to wind up doing something* | **commencer par** *to begin by doing something* |

Study the following pairs of contrasting examples.

Il **commence à chercher** du travail.    *He's **beginning to look for** work.*
Il **commence par chercher** du    *He **starts by looking for** work.*
   travail.

Il **a fini de** nous **aider.**    *He **finished helping** us.*
Il **a fini par** nous **aider.**    *He **wound up helping** us.*

**Activité 7**   **Élections à l'université.** Nous essayons d'organiser les élections au conseil d'administration de l'université (*university governance council*), mais ce n'est pas facile. Complétez les phrases suivantes avec les prépositions qui manquent pour savoir ce qui se passe. Si la phrase est complète telle qu'elle est, écrivez **X.**

1. Les étudiants se proposent _____ organiser les élections au conseil d'administration.

2. Ils se mettent _____ chercher des candidats.

3. Ils comptent _____ procéder aux élections au mois de novembre.

*(continued)*

4. Antoinette Dubois veut _____ se porter candidate.

5. Elle ne mérite pas _____ être élue.

6. Nous encourageons d'autres étudiants _____ se présenter.

7. Mais ils ne s'empressent pas _____ se porter candidats.

8. Je viens _____ parler avec Lise Léotard.

9. Elle s'intéresse un peu _____ participer au conseil.

10–11. Si elle se décide _____ se présenter, il faudra _____ organiser sa campagne.

12. Mais en ce moment, nous craignons _____ ne pas avoir assez de candidats.

**Activité 8** | **Dix jours à Paris.** La classe de français de Mme Richard passe dix jours à Paris. Les étudiants sont pressés de tout voir et de tout faire, et chacun s'intéresse à quelque chose de différent. Formez des phrases avec les éléments donnés pour voir comment ils profitent de leur séjour.

1. Loïc et Charles / tenir / voir un match de football

   _____

2. Marie-Noëlle / s'empresser / s'acheter des livres

   _____

3. Albert / se flatter / connaître parfaitement toutes les lignes de métro

   _____

4. Berthe et Christine / entreprendre / organiser une sortie aux cabarets

   _____

5. Philippe / compter / visiter la Cité des Sciences et de l'Industrie (*Museum of Science and Industry*)

   _____

6. Chantal / passer son temps / regarder les robes aux grands magasins

   _____

7. tous les étudiants / brûler / visiter le Louvre

   _____

8. Paulette et Mireille / espérer / avoir le temps de voir Montmartre

   _____

## Verb + direct object + de + infinitive

Several verbs that take **de** and that are followed by an infinitive take a direct object as well.

| | |
|---|---|
| **accuser quelqu'un de faire quelque chose** *to accuse someone of doing something* **convaincre quelqu'un de faire quelque chose** *to convince someone to do something* **décourager quelqu'un de faire quelque chose** *to discourage someone from doing something* **empêcher quelqu'un de faire quelque chose** *to prevent someone from doing something* **féliciter quelqu'un d'avoir fait quelque chose** *to congratulate someone for having done something* | **persuader quelqu'un de faire quelque chose** *to persuade someone to do something* **prier quelqu'un de faire quelque chose** *to beg someone to do something* **remercier quelqu'un de faire quelque chose** *to thank someone for doing something* **soupçonner quelqu'un de faire quelque chose** *to suspect someone of doing something* |

Several verbs that take **de** and that are followed by an infinitive take an indirect object.

| | |
|---|---|
| **commander/ordonner à quelqu'un de faire quelque chose** *to order someone to do something* **conseiller à quelqu'un de faire quelque chose** *to advise someone to do something* **déconseiller à quelqu'un de faire quelque chose** *to advise someone not to do something* **défendre/interdire à quelqu'un de faire quelque chose** *to forbid someone to do something* **demander à quelqu'un de faire quelque chose** *to ask someone to do something* **dire à quelqu'un de faire quelque chose** *to tell someone to do something* | **pardonner à quelqu'un d'avoir fait quelque chose** *to forgive someone for having done something* **permettre à quelqu'un de faire quelque chose** *to allow someone to do something* **promettre à quelqu'un de faire quelque chose** *to promise someone to do something* **proposer/suggérer à quelqu'un de faire quelque chose** *to suggest to someone to do something* **reprocher à quelqu'un de faire quelque chose** *to reproach someone for doing something* |

**Activité 9** **Comment aider nos amis?** Il y a beaucoup de copains qui ont des difficultés à l'université. Sophie et Daniel essaient de trouver des idées pour les aider. Écrivez leurs solutions en utilisant **il faut** et les mots proposés entre parenthèses, selon le modèle. Faites attention aux objets directs et indirects et aux prépositions employées devant l'infinitif.

> MODÈLE    Marc n'ouvre jamais le manuel d'histoire. (convaincre / le lire)
> Il faut le convaincre de le lire.

1. Régine ne révise jamais son vocabulaire anglais. (encourager / apprendre les mots)

   _____

2. Christophe s'endort en classe. (convaincre / faire attention)

   _____

3. Brigitte n'est jamais chez elle et elle n'étudie pas. (déconseiller / sortir tous les jours)

   _____

*(continued)*

4. Olivier ne participe pas aux discussions. (persuader / participer en classe)

   _____

5. Chantal et Robert parlent tout le temps pendant la classe. (dire / se taire)

   _____

6. Gérard et Louis ne pensent qu'au football. (conseiller / se concentrer sur leurs études)

   _____

7. Philippe dit qu'il ne comprend rien à l'informatique. (aider / résoudre les problèmes)

   _____

8. Olivier et Micheline pensent s'absenter le jour de l'examen. (dissuader / le faire)

   _____

**Activité 10**  **En famille.** Les membres de la famille Chéron s'aiment bien et essaient de s'aider mutuellement et de se conseiller. Utilisez les éléments proposés pour décrire leurs rapports familiaux. Employez le passé composé.

> MODÈLE  la tante Rosette / conseiller / son neveu Pierrot / se coucher tôt
> La tante Rosette a conseillé à son neveu Pierrot de se coucher tôt.

1. le grand-père / convaincre / son gendre (*son-in law*) Guillaume / ne pas quitter son travail

   _____

2. les enfants de Guillaume et Sylvie / s'empresser / apporter des fleurs à la tante Émilie

   _____

3. le petit Bertrand / demander / sa mère / lui acheter une bicyclette

   _____

4. la grand-mère / pardonner / sa petite-fille Giselle / avoir oublié son anniversaire

   _____

5. Guillaume et Sylvie / féliciter leur fille Christine / avoir eu la meilleure note de la classe en biologie

   _____

6. l'oncle François / enseigner / sa nièce / se servir de l'ordinateur

   _____

7. Anne-Marie / interdire / sa fille Mireille / sortir avec Frédéric

   _____

8. Nadine / prier / ses parents / l'emmener au bord de la mer

_____

9. Sylvie / inviter ses beaux-parents (*in-laws*) / dîner

_____

10. Guillaume / proposer / ses parents / passer leurs vacances avec sa famille

_____

## Adjective or noun + preposition + infinitive

1. Most adjectives and nouns take **de** when followed by an infinitive.

| | |
|---|---|
| Tu étais **surprise d'apprendre** que notre équipe a perdu le match? | *Were you **surprised to learn** that our team lost the game?* |
| Oui. Mais ils sont **sûrs de gagner** le match de dimanche. | *Yes. But they're **sure to win** the game on Sunday.* |
| Sans doute. Ils ont **un** grand **désir de gagner.** | *No doubt. They have **a** great **desire to win.*** |

2. However, some adjectives and nouns take **à.**

---

**être déterminé(e) à** *to be determined to*
**être le(la) premier(-ère) / le(la) troisième / le(la) seul(e) / le(la) dernier(-ère) à** *to be the first/third/only/last to*

**être prêt(e) à** *to be ready to*

---

| | |
|---|---|
| Je suis **déterminée à recevoir** la meilleure note de la classe. | *I'm **determined to get** the best grade in the class.* |

3. Adjectives modified by **trop** or **assez** take **pour** before a following infinitive.

| | |
|---|---|
| Pierrot est **trop petit pour comprendre.** | *Pierrot is **too young to understand.*** |
| Mais il est **assez intelligent pour se conduire** comme il faut. | *But he is **intelligent enough to behave** the way he ought to.* |

**Activité 11**  **À compléter.** Complétez les phrases suivantes avec la préposition qui convient.

1. Marie n'est pas prête _____ passer son examen de chimie.

2. Elle dit qu'elle est sûre _____ ne pas y réussir.

3. Mais elle est déterminée _____ passer l'été à réviser ses cours de chimie.

4. Je serais enchanté _____ vous aider à réparer la voiture.

5. Je serais le premier _____ vous aider si je pouvais.

6. Mais je suis trop maladroit (*clumsy*) _____ vous être utile.

*(continued)*

7. Je ne suis pas heureux _____ voir le petit Albert jouer aux jeux vidéo.

8. C'est une mauvaise idée _____ laisser un enfant perdre son temps.

9. Il est le seul élève de sa classe _____ passer tant de temps devant la télé.

10. Il est assez intelligent _____ comprendre l'importance de ce que je lui dis.

## Faire + infinitive (le causatif)

1. To express the idea that one person has, gets, or causes another person to do something, French uses the verb **faire** followed by an infinitive.

| | |
|---|---|
| Tu **as fait redécorer** ton appartement? | **Did** you **have** your apartment **redecorated?** |
| J'**ai fait repeindre** le salon, c'est tout. | **I had** the living room **repainted,** that's all. |
| La voiture est en panne. Je ne peux pas la **faire démarrer.** | The car is not working. I can't **get** it **to start.** |
| Alors, il faut la **faire réparer.** | Then it **has to be repaired.** |

2. The person you have do the work or perform the action may appear at the end of the sentence as the direct object, if there is no other object present.

| | |
|---|---|
| Mme Ducros fait étudier **ses enfants.** | Mrs. Ducros makes **her children** study. |
| L'institutrice fait chanter **ses élèves.** | The schoolteacher has **her pupils** sing. |

3. When the sentence contains two objects, the object of the infinitive is direct and the object of **faire** is indirect. The indirect object may be preceded by **par** or **à.**

J'ai fait repeindre la maison **par M. Jollivet.**
J'ai fait repeindre la maison **à M. Jollivet.**

*I had **Mr. Jollivet** repaint the house.*

4. One or both of the objects in the preceding example may be replaced by an object pronoun. The object pronouns always precede **faire.**

Je la **lui** ai fait repeindre.   *I had **him** repaint it.*

The past participle of **faire** does not agree with a preceding direct object in this construction.

**Activité 12**   **Problèmes du logement.** Les Giraud viennent d'acheter une maison. La maison est charmante, mais les Giraud découvrent qu'il y a beaucoup de travail à faire. Lisez la liste des problèmes et employez **il faut** et le causatif pour dire ce qu'il faut faire dans chaque cas pour rendre la maison habitable.

MODÈLE   La peinture de la cuisine est vieille. (repeindre)
Il faut la faire repeindre.

**Vocabulaire**

## Pour aménager une maison

**crevassé** *cracked (ground)*
**débarrasser** *to clear*
**se décoller** *to peel off, become detached*
**installer** *to install*
**insuffisant** *insufficient*
**se lézarder** *to crack (wall)*
**la lumière** *light*

**marcher** *to work (appliance)*
**le papier (peint)** *wallpaper*
**paver** *to pave*
**le plancher** *floor*
**plâtrer** *to plaster*
**remplacer** *to replace*
**retapisser** *to repaper; to reupholster*

1. Le papier du salon se décolle. (retapisser)

   _____

2. La lumière dans la salle à manger ne marche pas. (réparer)

   _____

3. Le plancher des chambres est très sale. (nettoyer)

   _____

4. La fenêtre du balcon est cassée. (remplacer)

   _____

5. Le trottoir est crevassé. (paver)

   _____

6. Les murs se lézardent. (plâtrer)

   _____

7. Le garage est plein de vieux meubles. (débarrasser)

   _____

**Activité 13** **Une institutrice de première classe (*first-rate*).** Mlle Arnaud est une institutrice excellente qui sait faire progresser ses élèves. Employez le causatif pour exprimer sa façon de résoudre les problèmes de ses élèves et d'organiser sa classe. Suivez le modèle.

> MODÈLE   Jérôme jette des papiers par terre. (balayer la salle de classe)
> Mlle Arnaud lui fait balayer la salle de classe.

1. Catherine n'aime pas parler en classe. (réciter des poèmes)

   _____

2. André a peur de parler devant tout le monde. (présenter son travail devant un petit groupe)

   _____

3. Luc et Claude bavardent en classe. (écrire une composition)

_____

4. Samuel ne comprend pas les problèmes de maths. (relire l'explication dans son livre)

_____

5. Les élèves sont fatigués après un examen. (regarder un film)

_____

6. Quelques élèves apprennent plus vite que les autres. (aider leurs camarades)

_____

7. Le directeur de l'école arrive à la porte de sa salle de classe. (observer une leçon de français)

_____

8. Nous nous intéressons à la musique. (écouter la chanson que les élèves ont apprise)

_____

**Activité 14**  **Les causes.** Votre ami fait des observations. Vous lui signalez la personne ou la chose qui est la cause des actions qu'il remarque. Suivez le modèle.

> MODÈLE  Les étudiants travaillaient. (leur professeur)
> Leur professeur les a fait travailler.

**Vocabulaire**

## Quelques actions

**démarrer** _to start (car)_
**grelotter** _to shiver_
**pleurer** _to cry_
**pousser** _to grow_
**rager** _to fume (with anger)_

**rire** _to laugh_
**soupirer** _to sigh_
**sourire** _to smile_
**trembler** _to shake, tremble_

1. Élise pleurait. (son petit ami)

_____

2. Les fenêtres tremblaient. (le vent)

_____

3. De belles roses poussaient chez ton voisin. (mon voisin)

_____

4. Les élèves lisaient. (leur institutrice)

_____

5. Les enfants riaient. (le clown)

_____

6. La voiture démarrait. (le mécanicien)

_____

7. La mère souriait. (ses enfants)

_____

8. La vieille dame soupirait. (la chaleur)

_____

9. Le chien grelottait. (le froid)

_____

10. Le client rageait. (la vendeuse)

_____

**Activité 15** **Activité orale.** Posez des questions à un(e) camarade sur ce qu'on l'encourage à faire, sur ce qu'on lui permet de faire, sur ce qu'on lui demande de faire, sur ce qu'on lui fait faire, et ainsi de suite. Employez des tournures (*expressions*) avec l'infinitif. Votre camarade vous répondra en employant ces structures et vous posera des questions pareilles à son tour.

# 11 PASSIVE VOICE

## The passive voice (la voix passive)

The passive voice is similar in formation and function in both French and English. It serves to move the focus from the performer of the action (usually the subject of the active sentence) to the action itself. To understand this, it is helpful to see passive sentences as deriving from active ones.

1. The direct object of the sentence in the active voice becomes the subject of the passive sentence. The subject of the original sentence in the active voice can be added to the corresponding passive sentence in a phrase beginning with **par.** This is called *the agent phrase.*

---

ACTIVE VOICE

**Max** a réparé la voiture. | *Max repaired the car.*

PASSIVE VOICE

La voiture a été réparée **par Max.** | *The car was repaired by Max.*

---

ACTIVE VOICE

**Mes parents** ont acheté cet appartement. | *My parents bought this apartment.*

PASSIVE VOICE

Cet appartement a été acheté **par mes parents.** | *This apartment was bought by my parents.*

---

Note that the performer of the action in an agent phrase can be focused on, especially in contrasts.

La voiture a été réparée **par Max, pas par moi.** | *The car was repaired by Max, not by me.*

2. In the French passive voice, the past participle agrees in gender and number with the grammatical subject.

Les ordinateurs ont été vend**us.** | *The computers were sold.*
Les bicyclettes ont été vend**ues.** | *The bicycles were sold.*

3. The passive voice exists in all tenses.

| | |
|---|---|
| Les claviers ont été réparés par Danielle. | *The keyboards were repaired by Danielle.* |
| Les claviers sont réparés par Danielle. | *The keyboards are repaired by Danielle.* |
| Les claviers vont être réparés par Danielle. | *The keyboards are going to be repaired by Danielle.* |

4. After verbs of mental activity the agent phrase in a passive sentence may be introduced by **de** instead of **par.**

| | |
|---|---|
| Ce savant est respecté **de** tous ses collègues. | *This scholar is respected by all his colleagues.* |
| Ma grand-mère était aimée **de** tous ses petits-enfants. | *My grandmother was loved by all her grandchildren.* |

5. While in English the passive voice is relatively frequent, in French the passive voice belongs more to the written language than to everyday speech. To de-emphasize the performer of the action, spoken French usually uses the pronoun **on** or **ils** instead of the passive voice. Note that in sentences in which **on** or **ils** is the subject, an agent phrase beginning with **par** cannot be added.

| | |
|---|---|
| Ici on parle français. | *French is spoken here.* |
| Ils ont réparé la voiture. | *They've repaired the car.* |

**Activité 1** **Au bureau.** Refaites les phrases suivantes à la voix passive pour raconter ce qui se passe au bureau. Gardez le même temps verbal dans la phrase que vous formulez. Faites attention à l'accord du participe passé. Suivez le modèle.

> MODÈLE La secrétaire ouvre le bureau à huit heures.
> Le bureau est ouvert à huit heures par la secrétaire.

**Vocabulaire**

## Les affaires

**le chèque** *check*
**la demande d'emploi** *job application*
**l'échantillon** (*m.*) *sample*
**expédier** *to ship*
**la facture** *bill*
**faire un versement sur le compte de** *to make a deposit (in an account)*
**lancer un produit** *to launch a product*

**livrer des marchandises** *to deliver goods, merchandise*
**la marchandise** *merchandise, goods*
**le marché** *market*
**passer une commande** *to place an order*
**présenter une demande d'emploi** *to submit a job application*
**signer** *to sign*

1. La réceptionniste reçoit les clients.

   _____

2. Les employés passent des commandes.

   _____

(continued)

3. La secrétaire a fait un versement sur le compte de l'entreprise.

_____

4. Un camion a livré des marchandises.

_____

5. Le bureau a expédié des échantillons.

_____

6. Le patron a signé des chèques.

_____

7. La secrétaire envoie des factures.

_____

8. Une jeune femme a présenté une demande d'emploi.

_____

9. L'entreprise va lancer un nouveau produit.

_____

10. Des experts vont étudier le marché.

_____

**Activité 2**   **Le déménagement.**  Décrivez ce qui est arrivé pendant le déménagement des Martel. Formulez des phrases à la voix passive avec les éléments proposés en ajoutant **par** pour indiquer l'agent. Suivez le modèle.

> MODÈLE   les meubles / mettre dans le fourgon / les déménageurs
> Les meubles ont été mis dans le fourgon par les déménageurs.

**Vocabulaire**

### Le déménagement

**accrocher**  *to hang, hang up*
**brancher**  *to plug in*
**la caisse**  *crate, box*
**le/la déménageur(-euse)**
   *mover*
**le fauteuil**  *armchair*
**le fourgon (de déménagement)**
   *moving truck*

**la machine à laver**  *washing machine*
**les meubles**  *the furniture*
**la penderie**  *closet, walk-in closet*
**le placard**  *cupboard*
**le plombier**  *plumber*
**ranger**  *to put away*
**le sous-sol**  *basement*

1. les lits / monter / trois déménageurs

_____

2. les tableaux / accrocher au mur / Pierre et Solange

_____

3. la machine à laver / installer / un plombier

_____

4. le fauteuil / placer en face de la télé / M. Martel

_____

5. les vêtements / accrocher dans la penderie / Mme Martel

_____

6. deux grosses caisses en bois / laisser au sous-sol / les déménageurs

_____

7. la vaisselle / ranger dans les placards / Mme Martel

_____

8. les lampes / brancher / M. Martel

_____

**Activité 3** **La société idéale.** Édouard a une formule pour améliorer (*improve*) la société. Exprimez ses idées en formulant des phrases à la voix passive avec le verbe **devoir.** Suivez le modèle.

> MODÈLE    améliorer l'éducation
> L'éducation doit être améliorée.

1. protéger les enfants

_____

2. respecter les personnes âgées

_____

3. bien payer la police

_____

4. honorer le drapeau

_____

5. bien former (*to educate, train*) les professionnels

_____

6. subventionner (*to subsidize*) les musées

_____

7. moderniser les transports en commun (*public transportation*)

_____

8. encourager les petites entreprises (*small business*)

_____

# Substitutes for the passive voice

1. The passive voice is used less frequently in French than in English, and in French it has a slightly more formal or literary tone. French speakers often prefer the active voice.

   Le conte **a été écrit par Louis.** → **Louis a écrit** le conte.

2. When a speaker wants to focus on the person who performed an action, the passive can be replaced by a sentence beginning with **c'est... qui** or **ce sont... qui.**

   Le conte a été écrit **par Louis.** → **C'est Louis qui** a écrit le conte.

3. When the performer of the action is not expressed, or is not important, then the passive voice can be avoided by using the subject pronoun **on.**

   La chambre **sera nettoyée.** → **On nettoiera** la chambre.
   Ici le français **est parlé.** → Ici **on parle** français.

4. In French, unlike English, the *indirect* object of a sentence in the active voice may *not* be transposed into the subject of the sentence in the passive voice. In such cases, **on** must be used instead of the passive voice.

   *They were **told** the truth.*　　　*On leur a dit la vérité.*

5. In many cases, a pronominal construction (**se** + *verb*) can be used instead of the passive when the performer of the action is not expressed.

   Cette revue **est** beaucoup **lue.** → Cette revue **se lit** beaucoup.
   Ce mot **est** facilement **compris.** → Ce mot **se comprend** facilement.

   Additional examples of this common construction follow.

| | |
|---|---|
| **Ça ne se fait pas.** | *That's not done.* |
| **Ça ne se dit plus.** | *That's not said anymore.* |
| **Ce produit ne se vend qu'en** **pharmacie.** | *This product is only sold in pharmacies.* |
| **Les œufs ne se mangent pas le** **matin en France.** | *Eggs aren't eaten in the morning in France.* |
| **Les portes se ferment à six heures.** | *The doors are closed at six o'clock.* |

**Activité 4** **Comment se tenir à table en France.** Les bonnes manières à table ne sont pas les mêmes en France qu'aux États-Unis et au Canada. Refaites ces indications avec **on** pour faire une liste de conseils utiles au visiteur américain ou canadien. Suivez le modèle.

> MODÈLE　offrir des fleurs (mais pas des chrysanthèmes) à Madame
> On offre des fleurs (mais pas des chrysanthèmes) à Madame.

1. tenir toujours le couteau dans la main droite

   _____

2. tenir toujours la fourchette dans la main gauche

   _____

3. essuyer souvent la sauce avec un morceau de pain

_____

4. ne pas poser les coudes sur la table

_____

5. poser les poignets sur le bord de la table (plutôt que de tenir les mains sous la table)

_____

6. ne pas couper le pain avec le couteau

_____

7. casser son morceau de pain

_____

8. répondre «Avec plaisir» pour accepter de reprendre un des plats (*have a second helping of*)

_____

9. répondre «Merci» pour ne pas accepter de reprendre un des plats (plutôt que de dire «Non, merci»)

_____

**Activité 5**   **Conseils de cuisine.** Formulez ces conseils de cuisine de deux façons: avec **on** et avec la construction pronominale (**se** + verbe). Suivez le modèle.

> MODÈLE   prendre des amuse-gueules (*appetizer*) avant le repas
> **a.** On prend des amuse-gueules avant le repas.
> **b.** Des amuse-gueules se prennent avant le repas.

1. couper un fromage en cubes pour servir

   **a.** _____

   **b.** _____

2. préparer une bonne soupe la veille (*the day before*)

   **a.** _____

   **b.** _____

3. préparer ce plat une heure avant le repas

   **a.** _____

   **b.** _____

4. déguster un bon vin

   **a.** _____

   **b.** _____

(*continued*)

*Passive voice*   133

5. boire un café après le repas

   a. _____

   b. _____

6. servir des fruits comme dessert

   a. _____

   b. _____

**Activité 6** **Des renseignements utiles pour un ami étranger.** Roger reçoit John, un ami américain, à Paris. Il le renseigne sur la France en employant la construction pronominale équivalente à la voix passive. Écrivez ce que Roger dit à son ami. Suivez le modèle.

> MODÈLE    en France / les distances / calculer / en kilomètres
> En France les distances se calculent en kilomètres.

1. le base-ball / ne pas jouer / en France

   _____

2. les journaux américains / vendre / partout

   _____

3. les bouquinistes (*outdoor book sellers*)/ trouver / le long de la Seine

   _____

4. les films américains / projeter / dans beaucoup de cinémas

   _____

5. les chansons américaines / entendre / à la radio

   _____

6. des festivals de théâtre / donner / en été

   _____

7. un marché en plein air / installer / deux fois par semaine dans ce quartier

   _____

8. les billets de métro / vendre / en carnets de dix

   _____

**Activité 7** **C'est à vous d'être le professeur de français!** Exprimez les aspects suivants de la langue française à une classe d'anglophones. Employez la construction pronominale (**se** + verbe) dans chaque cas pour formuler les règles, en suivant le modèle.

> MODÈLE    **exagérer** / écrire / avec un seul **g**
> **Exagérer** s'écrit avec un seul **g.**

1. le verbe **devenir** / conjuguer / avec **être** au passé composé

   _____

2. dans le mot **clef** / le **f** final / ne pas prononcer

   _____

3. le subjonctif / utiliser / après l'expression **jusqu'à ce que**

   _____

4. le mot **rebuts** (*trash*) / employer / au Québec

   _____

5. *a silent film* / traduire en français / par **un film muet**

   _____

6. les mots **amoral** et **immoral** / confondre / souvent

   _____

7. la négation / placer / autour du verbe quand il est conjugué au présent

   _____

8. le vocabulaire technique / apprendre / sans difficulté

   _____

# DEUXIÈME PARTIE    Nouns, Adjectives, Adverbs, and Pronouns

## CHAPITRES

# 12 Nouns and articles

## Definite and indefinite articles

A noun (**un substantif**) is a word that names a person, a place, a thing, an idea, or a quality. Articles, which are used before nouns, are either definite or indefinite. A definite article identifies something or someone specific (*the* apple, *the* teacher). An indefinite article is more general (*an* apple, *a* teacher).

1. All nouns in French are either masculine or feminine. The article agrees in gender and number with the noun. There are four forms of the French definite article. Both masculine and feminine singular nouns beginning with a vowel or a mute **h** take the definite article **l'**.

|  | MASCULINE | FEMININE |
|---|---|---|
| **SINGULAR** | **le** crayon | **la** table |
|  | **l'**homme | **l'**école |
| **PLURAL** | **les** crayons | **les** tables |
|  | **les** hommes | **les** écoles |

2. There are three forms of the French indefinite article.

|  | MASCULINE | FEMININE |
|---|---|---|
| **SINGULAR** | **un** crayon | **une** table |
|  | **un** homme | **une** école |
| **PLURAL** | **des** crayons | **des** tables |
|  | **des** hommes | **des** écoles |

English has no plural indefinite article. The French **des** is often equivalent to *some* or *any*, but it is often not translated.

Il a **des** idées bizarres.      *He has odd ideas.*

**Activité 1**    **À l'école.** Ajoutez à chaque substantif l'article défini et écrivez le syntagme (*phrase*) au pluriel. Consultez un dictionnaire pour connaître le genre. Suivez le modèle.

| MODÈLE | le | garçon | les garçons |
|---|---|---|---|

1. _____ cahier _____

2. _____ calculette _____

3. _____ étudiant _____

4. _____ serviette _____

5. _____ papier _____

6. _____ stylo _____

7. _____ leçon _____

8. _____ calendrier _____

9. _____ bibliothèque _____

10. _____ dictionnaire _____

11. _____ histoire _____

12. _____ cloche _____

13. _____ exposé _____

14. _____ cantine _____

**Activité 2**  **Au magasin de vêtements.**  Ajoutez à chaque substantif l'article indéfini et écrivez le syntagme au pluriel, selon le modèle.

| MODÈLE | _____ un _____ garçon | _____ des garçons _____ |
|---|---|---|

1. _____ pull _____

2. _____ chemise _____

3. _____ pantalon _____

4. _____ cravate _____

5. _____ rayon _____

6. _____ vendeur _____

7. _____ vendeuse _____

8. _____ robe _____

9. _____ maillot de bain _____

10. _____ veste _____

11. _____ costume _____

12. _____ chemisier _____

13. _____ gant _____

14. _____ blouson _____

15. _____ anorak _____

# Gender of nouns

1. Most nouns referring to males are masculine. Most nouns referring to females are feminine.

| | |
|---|---|
| un homme | une femme |
| un garçon | une fille |
| un père | une mère |
| un oncle | une tante |

2. Many feminine nouns are formed by adding **-e** to the masculine form.

| | |
|---|---|
| un saint → une saint**e** | un employé → une employé**e** |
| un rival → une rival**e** | un ami → une ami**e** |
| un cousin → une cousin**e** | un commerçant → une commerçant**e** |
| un marchand → une marchand**e** | un Américain → une Américain**e** |

In many cases, the addition of **-e** involves more extensive changes in pronunciation and spelling.

| | |
|---|---|
| -i**en** → -i**enne** | un Ital**ien** → une Ital**ienne** |
| -**on** → -**onne** | un patr**on** → une patr**onne** |
| -**eur** → -**euse** | un vend**eur** → une vend**euse** |
| -**teur** → -**trice** | un ac**teur** → une ac**trice** |
| -**er** → -**ère** | un bouch**er** → une bouch**ère** |
| -**ier** → -**ière** | un épic**ier** → une épic**ière** |

The suffix **-esse** forms the feminine of some masculine nouns.

un prince → une princ**esse**
un dieu → une dé**esse**

3. Many nouns have the same form for both masculine and feminine; only the article changes to indicate the gender of the person referred to.

| | |
|---|---|
| un/une enfant | un/une élève |
| un/une camarade | un/une propriétaire |

4. Some nouns are masculine even when they refer to women.

| | | |
|---|---|---|
| un auteur | un juge | un poète |
| un docteur | un médecin | un professeur[††] |
| un écrivain[*] | un ministre[†] | un sculpteur |
| un ingénieur | un peintre | un témoin (*witness*) |

[*]**Une écrivaine** exists, but is used mainly in Québec.
[†]Traditionally, a government secretary in France has always been addressed as **Monsieur le Ministre,** and his wife as **Madame le Ministre.** However, due to the increasing number of women holding this position, the new official job title of **Madame *la* Ministre** has been created, along with **Monsieur *la* Ministre** to refer to her husband.
[††]**La prof** and **la professeur** exist in spoken French.

DEUXIÈME PARTIE

Ma femme est **un auteur** très connu.

*My wife is a very famous author.*

Ta sœur est **un** très bon **peintre.**

*Your sister is a very good painter.*

5. Other nouns are feminine even when they refer to men.

une brute
une personne

une vedette ( *film star*)
une victime

Marc est **une personne** sympathique, n'est-ce pas?

*Mark is a nice **person,** isn't he?*

Tu trouves? Tout le monde dit que c'est **une brute.**

*You think so? Everyone says that he's a **bully.***

---

**Activité 3**  **À compléter.**  Choisissez le mot qui complète ces phrases.

1. Dans mon quartier l'_____ et son mari sont très aimables. (épicier / épicière)

2. Élisabeth est devenue _____ (pharmacien / pharmacienne)

3. Cette étudiante est _____ artiste formidable. (un / une)

4. Notre ami Frédéric est _____ des victimes de l'accident. (un / une)

5. Tu connais _____ docteur? Il est italien, je crois. (le / la)

6. On dit que Joseph Mercier est _____ vedette de l'année. (le / la)

7. Leur fille est _____ enfant de sept ans. (un / une)

8. Ma mère est _____ seul ingénieur de l'équipe. (le / la)

---

**Activité 4**  **Elle aussi.**  Écrivez que les femmes mentionnées ont les mêmes caractéristiques que les hommes, selon le modèle.

> MODÈLE  Jacquot est clarinettiste. (sa sœur)
> Sa sœur est clarinettiste aussi.

1. Albert est musicien. (Marguerite)

_____

2. Louis? Il est épicier. (Émilie)

_____

3. Mon cousin est un élève de cette école primaire. (ma nièce)

_____

4. Loïc? C'est un Breton ( *from Brittany*). (Éloïse)

_____

*(continued)*

5. Jean-Paul Sartre est un écrivain célèbre. (Simone de Beauvoir)

   _____

6. Pierre a été victime de son imprudence. (Hélène)

   _____

7. Maurice est un instituteur formidable. (Lise)

   _____

8. M. Chauvin est le propriétaire de l'établissement. (Mme Chauvin)

   _____

9. Son mari est juge. (sa tante)

   _____

10. Olivier est un médecin respecté. (Chantal)

    _____

11. Cet homme est aviateur. (cette femme)

    _____

12. Roger est un nageur formidable. (Mireille)

    _____

13. Paul est notre champion. (Caroline)

    _____

14. Je connais M. Duval, le commerçant. (Mme Mercier)

    _____

## Gender of nouns (*continued*)

1. Although many French nouns give no clue as to their gender (**le peuple, la foule**), some have endings that do indicate gender. As a general rule, nouns ending in **e** tend to be feminine and nouns ending in other vowels or consonants tend to be masculine (**le contenu, le concept, le plan**). Many noun-ending combinations demonstrate this rule—and many contradict it, as illustrated by those endings marked with an asterisk (*) in the following tables.

### Masculine endings

| | | | |
|---|---|---|---|
| **-age\*** | un avantage, un orage, un voyage (*but* **la page, la plage**) | **-isme\*** | le socialisme, le communisme, le tourisme |
| **-amme\*** | le gramme, le programme | **-ment** | un bâtiment, le commencement, un monument |
| **-eau** | un bateau, un cadeau, un château (*but* **l'eau** [*f.*], **la peau**) | **-oir** | un espoir, le mouchoir, le trottoir |
| **-ème\*** | le problème, le système | **-ou** | le bijou, le clou, le genou |
| **-et** | le jouet, le secret, le sujet | **-re\*** | l'arbre, le cadavre, le cadre, le Havre |
| **-ing** | le camping, le dancing, le shopping | | |

## Feminine endings

| | | | |
|---|---|---|---|
| **-ace** | la glace, la menace, la surface | **-ise** | une chemise, une surprise, une valise |
| **-ade** | une ambassade, une promenade, une salade (*but* **le stade**) | **-sion*** | la décision, l'inversion, la télévision |
| **-ance** | la brillance, la chance, l'importance | **-té** | la liberté, la société, la spécialité (*but* **le comité, le pâté**) |
| **-esse** | la jeunesse, la politesse, la promesse | **-tion*** | la nation, la production, la programmation |
| **-ette** | une bicyclette, la calculette, la cassette | | |
| **-ière** | la frontière, la lumière, la manière | **-tude** | une attitude, la gratitude, la solitude |
| **-ine** | une aspirine, la cuisine, la piscine (*but* **le magazine**) | **-ure** | une aventure, la lecture, la voiture |

2. Some nouns can be either masculine or feminine, depending on their meaning.

| | | | |
|---|---|---|---|
| **le critique** *critic* | **le poste** *job, radio or TV (set)* | **le voile** *veil* |
| **la critique** *criticism, review* | **la poste** *mail, postal service* | **la voile** *sail* |
| **le livre** *book* | **le tour** *tour, trip* | |
| **la livre** *pound* | **la tour** *tower* | |

**Activité 5** **Masculin ou féminin?** Choisissez l'article correct dans chaque cas.

1. François s'est acheté _____ vélomoteur. (un / une)

2. Ce que tu as dit est vraiment _____ compliment. (un / une)

3. La natation est _____ activité agréable. (un / une)

4. _____ côtelette d'agneau, s'il vous plaît. (Un / Une)

5. _____ cyclisme est un sport important en France. (Le / La)

6. _____ émission comptez-vous regarder ce soir? (Quel / Quelle)

7. Je n'ai pas compris _____ message. (le / la)

8. Le pharmacien m'a donné _____ ordonnance. (un / une)

9. Elle aime _____ peinture. (le / la)

10. Est-ce que tu as vu _____ stade? (le / la)

11. Le petit Georges a mangé _____ tartine. (un / une)

12. J'ai perdu _____ rasoir. (mon / ma)

13–14. Il a _____ peau (le / la) très rouge après sa journée _____ (à la / au) plage.

15. Vous avez lu cet article? C'est _____ critique du film. (un / une)

16. Je veux voir les informations. Est-ce que je peux allumer _____ poste? (le / la)

17. Elle a acheté _____ livre de pommes. (un / une)

*(continued)*

18. _____ voile couvrait le visage de la mariée (*bride*). (Un / Une)

19. Ce bateau a fait _____ tour du monde. (le / la)

## Number (plural of nouns)

1. Most French nouns form their plural by adding **-s**.

> **NOTE**
>
> Although the **-f** ending of certain nouns (**un œuf, un bœuf**) is pronounced in the singular form, the **-f** becomes silent when followed by an **s** in the plural.
>
> | | |
> |---|---|
> | un œuf [œf] → des œufs [ø] | un bœuf [bœf] → des bœufs [bø] |

There are some exceptions. Singular nouns ending in **-s, -x,** or **-z** do not change their form in the plural.

| | | | |
|---|---|---|---|
| le cours | les cours | un prix | des prix |
| une fois | des fois | la voix | les voix |
| le mois | les mois | le nez | les nez |

2. Most nouns ending in **-al** have a plural form ending in **-aux.**

| | | | |
|---|---|---|---|
| l'animal | les animaux | l'hôpital | les hôpitaux |
| le cheval | les chevaux | l'idéal | les idéaux |
| le général | les généraux | le journal | les journaux |

There are some exceptions.

| | |
|---|---|
| le bal → les bals | le festival → les festivals |
| le carnaval → les carnavals | le récital → les récitals |

3. Nouns ending in **-au, -eau,** or **-eu** add **-x** to form the plural.

| | | | |
|---|---|---|---|
| le bateau | les bateaux | le cheveu | les cheveux |
| le bureau | les bureaux | le jeu | les jeux |
| | | *Exception:* | le pneu → les pneus |

4. Most nouns ending in **-ou** add **-s** to form the plural, but some add **-x.**

| | | | |
|---|---|---|---|
| le clou → les clous | *But:* | le chou → les choux | |
| le trou → les trous | | le genou → les genoux | |
| | | le bijou → les bijoux | |

5. Some nouns have irregular plurals.

| | | | |
|---|---|---|---|
| le ciel | les **cieux** | monsieur | **messieurs** |
| l'œil | les **yeux** | madame | **mesdames** |
| le travail | les **travaux** | mademoiselle | **mesdemoiselles** |
| le vitrail | les **vitraux** | | |

Family names in French do not change their form in the plural.

Vous connaissez **les Durand**?  
Non, mais je sais qu'ils sont les voisins **des Chevalier.**

*Do you know **the Durands**?*  
*No, but I know that they are neighbors **of the Chevaliers.***

6. Some nouns are used only in the plural.

| | |
|---|---|
| **les ciseaux** *scissors* | **les mœurs** *morals; customs* |
| **les frais** *expenses, cost* | **les vacances** *vacation* |
| **les mathématiques, les maths** *math* | |

Some nouns, especially abstract nouns, have no plural.

| | |
|---|---|
| **la foi** *faith* | **la patience** *patience* |
| **la paix** *peace* | |

Numbers and letters used as nouns also have no plural.

«Femme» s'écrit avec deux **m.**  
Il y a deux **cinq** dans mon numéro.

*"Femme" is written with two **m's.***  
*There are two **fives** in my number.*

**Activité 6**  **Pas un, mais deux.** Répondez dans chaque cas que vous cherchez (voulez, avez, etc.) **deux,** pas **un** des substantifs mentionnés, selon le modèle.

> MODÈLE  Vous cherchez un stylo?  
> Je cherche deux stylos.

1. Vous voulez un chapeau?

   _____

2. Vous assistez au festival?

   _____

3. Vous avez un neveu?

   _____

4. Votre nom s'écrit avec un l?

   _____

*(continued)*

5. Vous cherchez un monsieur?

   _____

6. Vous étudiez un vitrail?

   _____

7. Vous prononcez un discours?

   _____

8. Vous travaillez un métal?

   _____

9. Vous prenez un morceau?

   _____

10. Vous visitez un pays?

    _____

11. Vous avez un choix?

    _____

12. Vous préparez un repas?

    _____

13. Vous lisez un journal?

    _____

14. Vous changez un pneu?

    _____

15. Vous avez un rival?

    _____

# Identifying people: Il/Elle est vs. C'est

French has two constructions for identifying people.

1. **Il/elle est** and **ils/elles sont** are used before an unmodified noun of profession, religion, or nationality. Note that no indefinite article is used in this construction.

   | | |
   |---|---|
   | **Il est** médecin? | *Is he a doctor?* |
   | Non, sa femme est médecin. Lui, **il est** scientifique. | *No, his wife is a doctor. **He's a** scientist.* |
   | **Ils sont** protestants, les Duvalier? Lui, **il est** protestant. Elle, **elle est** catholique. | ***Are** the Duvaliers Protestants? **He's** a Protestant. **She's** a Catholic.* |

2. If the noun is modified (even by just an article), then **c'est** or **ce sont** must be used. **C'est un/une** is the most common construction to identify things.

| | |
|---|---|
| **C'est** un avocat? | *Is he a lawyer?* |
| Non, **ce n'est pas** un avocat. **C'est** un juge. | *No, he's not a lawyer. He's a judge.* |
| **Ce sont** des soldats? | *Are they soldiers?* |
| Non, **ce sont** des pilotes. | *No, they're pilots.* |
| **Il est** écrivain? | *Is he a writer?* |
| Oui, **c'est** un écrivain **célèbre.** | *Yes, he's a famous writer.* |

**Activité 7**  **Identifications.** Complétez ces phrases en indiquant le choix correct.

1. _____ un journal français. (C'est / Il est)

2. _____ vendeuse. (C'est / Elle est)

3. _____ français. (Ce sont / Ils sont)

4. _____ des commerçants. (Ce sont / Ils sont)

5. _____ le propriétaire de la boutique. (C'est / Il est)

6. _____ une salade délicieuse. (C'est / Elle est)

7. _____ notre patronne. (C'est / Elle est)

8. _____ vedette de cinéma. (C'est / Elle est)

9. _____ architecte. (C'est / Il est)

10. _____ professeurs. (Ce sont / Ils sont)

## The partitive

1. The partitive article is an indefinite article used to express an indefinite quantity or part of something (English: *some, any*). The partitive article consists of **de** + **le, la,** or **l'. De** + **le** contracts to **du.** The plural of the partitive article is **des** (which is also the plural indefinite article, as you will recall).

| DU | DE LA | DE L' | DES |
|---|---|---|---|
| **du** lait | **de la** crème | **de l'**eau | **des** haricots |
| **du** pain | **de la** patience | **de l'**huile | **des** sandwichs |
| | | | **des** verres |

2. After a negative, the partitive article is **de (d')** unless the verb is **être.** If the verb is **être,** the partitive article retains its full form. **De (D')** also replaces the indefinite article after a negative.

| | |
|---|---|
| Tu **n'as pas** encore acheté **de** pain! | *You **haven't** bought **any** bread yet!* |
| Tu **n'as** vraiment **pas de** patience. | *You really **don't** have **any** patience.* |

C'est du lait, ça?    *Is that milk?*
Non, **ce n'est pas du** lait. C'est de    *No, **it's not** milk. It's cream.*
    la crème.

Tu as **une** voiture?    *Do you have **a** car?*
Non, je **n'ai pas de** voiture.    *No, I **don't** have a car.*

**Activité 8**   **Il ne reste rien à la charcuterie.** Jean-Claude va chez le charcutier du quartier pour acheter quelque chose à manger, mais il ne reste rien à la charcuterie. Écrivez des échanges entre le charcutier et Jean-Claude en suivant le modèle.

> MODÈLE   œufs durs
> Vous avez des œufs durs?
> Non, monsieur. Il n'y a pas d'œufs durs.

1. jambon

   _____

   _____

2. salade niçoise

   _____

   _____

3. fromage

   _____

   _____

4. pâté

   _____

   _____

5. saucisson

   _____

   _____

6. saumon fumé

   _____

   _____

7. quiches

   _____

   _____

8. sandwichs

   _____

   _____

**Activité 9** **On a fait les courses à moitié.** Tout le monde va à l'épicerie, mais personne n'a acheté tout ce qu'il fallait. Employez le partitif pour le dire, en suivant le modèle.

> MODÈLE   Marc / acheter / lait / eau minérale
> Marc a acheté du lait, mais il n'a pas acheté d'eau minérale.

1. Suzanne / chercher / farine / œufs

   _____

2. moi / rapporter / pain / beurre

   _____

3. Laurent / trouver / champignons / salade

   _____

4. Élisabeth / prendre / pommes / oranges

   _____

5. toi et moi / acheter / petits pois / haricots verts

   _____

6. vous / rapporter / fromage / yaourt

   _____

7. toi / chercher / viande / poulet

   _____

8. les garçons / prendre / lait / coca

   _____

**Activité 10** **C'est quoi, ça?** Antoinette ne reconnaît pas tous les plats qu'on a préparés. Elle demande à son amie de lui expliquer ce qu'ils sont. Suivez le modèle.

> MODÈLE   crème / yaourt
> C'est de la crème, ça?
> Non, ce n'est pas de la crème. C'est du yaourt.

1. bœuf / porc

   _____

   _____

2. poulet / dindon (*turkey*)

   _____

   _____

3. haricots verts / endives

   _____

   _____

(continued)

4. riz / couscous

_____

_____

5. jus / limonade

_____

_____

6. thon / saumon

_____

_____

# Expressions of quantity: **de** vs. the partitive

1. After expressions of quantity, **de** is used instead of the partitive. The third-person plural of the verb is used after expressions of quantity when it is followed by a plural noun. Note that after expressions such as **une foule de,** the verb may be either singular or plural. After **la foule de,** the singular is commonly used.

| | | |
|---|---|---|
| **assez de** *enough* | **une foule de** *a crowd of* | **plus de** *more* |
| **autant de** *as much, as many* | **moins de** *less* | **tant de** *so much, so many* |
| **beaucoup de** *much, many* | **une multitude de** *a vast number of* | **trop de** *too much, too many* |
| **Combien de?** *How much?, How many?* | **peu de** *few, little, not much* | **un peu de** *a little (bit of)* |

Beaucoup de touristes visitent la ville. — *Many tourists visit the city.*

Une foule d'étudiants sont allés voir le directeur. — *A crowd of students went to see the director.*

La foule d'étudiants a été reçue par lui. — *The crowd of students was received by him.*

**NOTE** After approximate numbers ending in **-aine** and fractions, either the singular or the plural form of the verb is used.

Une vingtaine d'ingénieurs travaille/travaillent ici. — *About twenty engineers work here.*

2. **De** is also used in expressions of weights and measures.

| | |
|---|---|
| **une boîte de** *a box of* | **un kilo de** *a kilo of* |
| **une bouteille de** *a bottle of* | **une livre de** *a pound of* |

J'ai **deux bouteilles de** vin. — *I have **two bottles of** wine.*
Alors, j'ai **autant de** vin que toi. — *Then I have **as much** wine as you do.*

| | |
|---|---|
| **Combien de** viande as-tu achetée? | *How **much** meat did you buy?* |
| J'ai pris **un kilo de** bœuf et **une livre de** jambon. | *I got **a kilo of** beef and **a pound of** ham.* |

3. However, if the noun following the preposition **de** is specific in any of the preceding cases, the definite article is used and will contract with the preposition.

| | |
|---|---|
| Peu **des** étudiants ont compris. | *Few **of the** students understood.* |
| Les enfants ont mangé beaucoup **du** chocolat que je leur ai donné. | *The children ate much **of the** chocolate that I gave them.* |

**La plupart** (*most*) and **bien** (*a lot*) are followed by **de** + *article*.

| | |
|---|---|
| Il étudie **la plupart du** temps? | *Does he study **most of the** time?* |
| Oui, il a **bien des** livres à lire. | *Yes, he has **a lot of** books to read.* |

4. The phrase **ne** + *verb* + **que** (*only*) is not really a negative and is followed by the partitive.

| | |
|---|---|
| Tu **ne** dis **que des** sottises. | *You're saying **only** silly things.* |

5. Note the use of the partitive with school subjects after the verb **faire.**

| | |
|---|---|
| **faire des maths, de la physique** | *to study (major in) math, physics* |

6. In formal style, **de** replaces the partitive before an adjective that *precedes* the plural noun.

| | |
|---|---|
| Nous avons fait **de grands** efforts. | *We made **great** efforts.* |

However, this rule is increasingly disregarded in all styles.

| | |
|---|---|
| Elle a acheté **des belles** fleurs. | *She bought **some beautiful** flowers.* |

**NOTE**

**D'autres** is used in all styles.

| | |
|---|---|
| Avez-vous **d'autres** projets? | *Do you have **other** plans?* |
| Oui, on en a **d'autres.** | *Yes, we have **others.*** |

7. Do not confuse the preposition **de,** which is part of a verbal expression (for example, **avoir besoin de** [*to need*] and **se souvenir de** [*to remember*]), with the partitive article. In order to determine which of these two roles **de** occupies in a sentence, you must first know whether or not the conjugated verb takes **de** as a preposition before a complement.

| | |
|---|---|
| J'**ai besoin de** vin. | *I **need wine.*** (**avoir besoin de** = *verbal expression, so* **de** *is not a partitive here*) |
| Il me faut **du vin.** | *I **need wine.*** (**falloir** *does not take* **de** *before a complement, therefore* **du** = *partitive*) |

| Je **me souviens des** chevaux blancs dans mon rêve. | I *remember* the white horses in my dream. (**se souvenir de** = *verbal expression, so* **des** *is not a partitive here*) |
|---|---|
| Je **voyais des** chevaux blancs dans mon rêve. | I *saw* white horses in my dream. (**voir** *does not take* **de** *before a complement, therefore* **des** = *partitive*) |

**Note:** This distinction is important in determining what type of pronoun should replace a noun following **de, des, du,** and **de la.** When **de, des** (etc.) is a partitive or indefinite article, the object pronoun **en** replaces the noun and its article. However, when **de, des** (etc.) consists of the preposition **de** and the definite article, a disjunctive pronoun may be necessary instead, and it follows **de.** For this rule, see Chapter 16, p. 204.

**Activité 11**   **À compléter.**  Indiquez lequel des articles proposés est le choix correct.

1. Il prend _____ thé. (du / de)

2. Tu as besoin _____ courage. (du / de)

3. Ils m'ont servi _____ côtelettes de veau. (des / de)

4. Moi, je ne mange pas _____ veau. (un / du / de)

5. Elle ne fait que _____ bêtises (*mistakes, naughty things*). (des / de)

6. Nous cherchons _____ crayons. (des / de)

7. Ce soir on prépare _____ poulet. (du / de)

8. Combien _____ cours suivez-vous? (des / de)

9. Nous avons autant _____ problèmes que vous. (des / de)

10. L'association cherche _____ nouveaux membres. (des / de)

11. La plupart _____ étudiants sont sympathiques. (des / de)

12. Les professeurs donnent trop _____ travail. (du / de)

13. Il ne lit plus les mêmes livres. Il en lit _____ autres. (des / d')

14. Bien _____ journalistes ont écrit à ce sujet. (des / de)

**Activité 12**   **Comment est-ce que ça se dit?**  Traduisez les échanges suivants en français.

1. *We need coffee.*
   *I bought coffee.*
   *How much coffee did you buy?*
   *I bought enough coffee for us. I also bought three hundred grams of tea.*

   _____

   _____

   _____

   _____

2. *Most of the books that I read were interesting.*
   *Too many of the books that I read were boring.*

---

## More uses of the articles

1. The definite article designates a noun that refers to a specific person or thing.

   | | |
   |---|---|
   | Je vais te montrer **le dessert.** | *I'm going to show you **the dessert.*** |
   | **Le dessert** que tu as préparé? | ***The dessert** you prepared?* |

2. The French definite article also labels nouns used in a general sense. By contrast, in English no article is used when a noun refers to a general category.

   | | |
   |---|---|
   | **La technologie** est en train de transformer **la vie,** telle que nous la connaissons. | ***Technology** is in the process of transforming **life** as we know it.* |
   | Elle aime **les chiens.** | *She likes **dogs.*** |

   This is also true for names of countries and academic subjects.

   | | |
   |---|---|
   | **La Nouvelle-Zélande** se situe dans l'hémisphère sud. | ***New Zealand** is located in the southern hemisphere.* |
   | Il étudie **la littérature comparée** à la fac. | *He is studying **comparative literature** in college.* |

   The four verbs of preference (**adorer, aimer, détester, préférer**) all take a definite article (**le, la, les**) because, by definition, they generalize about an entire category. Contrast the general and specific use of the definite article in the following example.

   | | |
   |---|---|
   | J'adore **la viande,** mais je n'aime pas **la viande** qu'on sert dans ce bistrot. | *I love **meat** (in general), but I don't like **the meat** they serve in that bistro (specific).* |

3. By contrast, most other verbs (**avoir, boire, prendre, vouloir**) take a partitive article (**du, de la, des**) when the direct object is general since, by definition, these verbs refer to an indefinite quantity of an entire category.

   | | |
   |---|---|
   | Je **bois** souvent **de l'Orangina,** mais je **déteste le jus d'orange.** | *I often **drink Orangina,** but I **hate orange juice.*** |
   | Est-ce que vous **voyez des plats** végétariens sur la carte? Je **prends** rarement **de la viande** et je **déteste le bœuf.** | *Do you **see any** vegetarian **dishes** on the menu? I rarely **order meat,** and I hate beef.* |

4. The definite article is often used when ordering in a restaurant.

   | | |
   |---|---|
   | Pour moi, **le rosbif** et pour ma femme, **le canard à l'orange.** | *I'll have **roast beef,** and my wife will have **duck in orange sauce.*** |

   The indefinite article is often used to designate a serving of something.

   | | |
   |---|---|
   | **Un café** et **un chocolat chaud,** s'il vous plaît. | *A **cup of coffee** and **a cup of hot chocolate,** please.* |

5. The partitive article before names of foods and beverages designates an indefinite quantity. English may or may not use the words *some* or *any* in these cases.

Tu veux boire **du chocolat chaud?**　*Would you like to drink **hot chocolate?***
Non, merci. Tu as **du café?**　*No, thanks. Do you have **any coffee?***

Compare the use of the articles with the word **thé** in the following sentences.

**Le thé** est une boisson d'origine orientale.　*Tea is a drink that comes from Asia. (general)*
J'aime **le thé** que vous avez acheté.　*I like **the tea** that you bought. (specific)*
**Un thé,** s'il vous plaît.　***A cup of tea,** please. (a standard serving, said to a waiter)*
Après mon dîner, je bois **du thé.**　*After my dinner, I drink **tea.** (indefinite quantity)*

6. After the prepositions **avec** and **sans** no article is used unless the noun is modified.

Il a écouté **avec** attention.　*He listened with attention (attentively).*
Et il a rédigé une composition **sans** faute.　*And he wrote a composition without a mistake.*
Il a agi **avec** courage.　*He acted courageously.*
Il a agi **avec un** courage admirable.　*He acted with admirable courage.*

**Activité 13**　**Qu'est-ce qui manque?** Complétez les phrases suivantes avec l'article qui manque. Si aucun article ne manque, marquez le blanc avec un **X.**

1–2. Pour moi, _____ coq au vin et _____ pommes de terre à la lyonnaise.

3. Tu ne veux pas _____ bœuf?

4–5. Non, je mange très peu _____ viande. Je préfère _____ poulet.

6–7. Garçon! _____ vin rouge et _____ bière, s'il vous plaît.

8. Je regrette, mais nous n'avons plus _____ bière.

9. Alors, _____ jus d'orange.

10. Pour un étudiant en médecine, _____ diligence est très importante.

11. Il lui faut un peu _____ repos aussi.

12–13. Mais, en général, _____ étudiants en médecine ont très peu _____ temps pour se reposer.

14. Tu aimes _____ cinéma français?

15–16. Oui, il y a _____ films qui m'ont beaucoup plu. Mais je crois que je préfère _____ films italiens.

17. On passe _____ nouveaux films italiens au Pathé (*a French movie theater chain*) cette semaine. Tu veux aller les voir?

18–19. Oui, bien sûr. Mais j'ai tant _____ travail. On va voir. Si j'ai _____ temps libre, on ira au Pathé.

20–21. _____ ordinateur est essentiel dans _____ bureaux modernes.

22–23. C'est pour ça que beaucoup _____ étudiants font _____ informatique.

24. _____ informatique est une des matières les plus étudiées aujourd'hui.

# 13 Adjectives, comparatives, and superlatives

## Gender of adjectives

1. Adjectives give information about nouns and pronouns (a *small* box, a *different* book). Adjectives in French agree in gender and number with the noun or pronoun they modify. Most masculine adjectives add **-e** to form the feminine.

bleu → bleu**e** *blue*

compliqué → compliqué**e**
   *complicated*

espagnol → espagnol**e** *Spanish*

génial → génial**e** *brilliant, great*

grand → grand**e** *big*

gris → gris**e** *gray*

noir → noir**e** *black*

petit → petit**e** *little, small*

poli → poli**e** *polite*

prochain → prochain**e** *next*

2. Several groups of masculine adjectives do not follow this rule.

a. Adjectives with a masculine form ending in **-e** do not change in the feminine.

bizarr**e** → bizarr**e** *strange, peculiar*

difficil**e** → difficil**e** *difficult*

drôl**e** → drôl**e** *funny*

jaun**e** → jaun**e** *yellow*

logiqu**e** → logiqu**e** *logical*

roug**e** → roug**e** *red*

b. Most masculine adjectives ending in **-x** have feminine forms ending in **-se.**

dangereu**x** → dangereu**se**
   *dangerous*

généreu**x** → généreu**se** *generous*

jalou**x** → jalou**se** *jealous*

merveilleu**x** → merveilleu**se**
   *marvelous*

nerveu**x** → nerveu**se** *nervous*

sérieu**x** → sérieu**se** *serious*

c. Masculine adjectives ending in **-f** have feminine forms ending in **-ve.**

acti**f** → acti**ve** *active*

naï**f** → naï**ve** *naive*

neu**f** → neu**ve** *new*

sporti**f** → sporti**ve** *athletic*

d. Adjectives ending in **-el, -en,** or **-on** double the final consonant before adding **-e.**

actu**el** → actu**elle** *current,*
   *present-day*

b**on** → b**onne** *good*

canad**ien** → canad**ienne** *Canadian*

cru**el** → cru**elle** *cruel*

europé**en** → europé**enne** *European*

mign**on** → mign**onne** *cute*

**Gentil, pareil,** and **nul** also double the final **-l** before adding **-e: gentille, pareille, nulle.** The double l is pronounced /y/ in **gentille** and **pareille,** but /l/ in **nulle.**

e.  Some masculine adjectives ending in **-s** have a feminine form ending in **-sse.**

| | |
|---|---|
| bas → ba**sse** *low* | gras → gra**sse** *fat, fatty* |
| épais → épai**sse** *thick* | gros → gro**sse** *big, fat* |

f.  Some masculine adjectives ending in **-et** have feminine forms ending in **-ète.**

| | |
|---|---|
| compl**et** → compl**ète** *complete* | inqui**et** → inqui**ète** *restless,* |
| discr**et** → discr**ète** *discreet* | *upset* |
| | secr**et** → secr**ète** *secret* |

g.  Some masculine adjectives ending in **-et** or **-ot** double the final **-t** before adding **-e.**

| | |
|---|---|
| coqu**et** → coqu**ette** *flirtatious* | s**ot** → s**otte** *foolish* |
| mu**et** → mu**ette** *mute* | |

h.  Masculine adjectives ending in **-er** have feminine forms ending in **-ère.**

| | |
|---|---|
| am**er** → am**ère** *bitter* | étrang**er** → étrang**ère** *foreign* |
| derni**er** → derni**ère** *last* | lég**er** → lég**ère** *light* |

i.  Masculine adjectives derived from verbs and ending in **-eur** have feminine forms ending in **-euse.**

| | |
|---|---|
| flatter → flatt**eur** → flatt**euse** | tromper → tromp**eur** → tromp**euse** |
| *flattering* | *deceptive* |

3.  Some adjectives have irregular feminine forms.

| | | |
|---|---|---|
| **beau** → **belle** *beautiful, handsome* | **faux** → **fausse** *false* | **long** → **longue** *long* |
| **blanc** → **blanche** *white* | **favori** → **favorite** *favorite* | **nouveau** → **nouvelle** *new* |
| **bref** → **brève** *brief* | **fou** → **folle** *mad, crazy* | **public** → **publique** *public* |
| **doux** → **douce** *sweet, gentle, soft* | **frais** → **fraîche** *fresh* | **roux** → **rousse** *redheaded* |
| | **franc** → **franche** *frank* | **sec** → **sèche** *dry* |
| | **grec** → **grecque** *Greek* | **vieux** → **vieille** *old* |

4.  Some adjectives are invariable. They do not change form to reflect gender or number.

| | |
|---|---|
| un pantalon **chic** | *stylish pants* |
| une robe **chic** | *a stylish dress* |

Adjectives of color derived from nouns such as **marron, orange, rose,** are invariable.

| | |
|---|---|
| des chaussures **marron** | *brown shoes* |
| des chaussettes **rose** | *pink socks* |

Phrases referring to color containing **clair** (*light*) and **foncé** (*dark*) are also invariable.

une robe **vert clair**          *a light green dress*
une jupe **bleu foncé**          *a dark blue skirt*

**Activité 1**   **Tous les deux.**  Répondez aux questions en disant que la deuxième chose ou personne mentionnée a la même caractéristique que la première. Suivez le modèle.

> MODÈLE   Ce lycée est grand. Et cette école?
> Elle est grande aussi.

1. Ce Coca (*Coca-Cola*) est très frais. Et cette eau?

   _____

2. Ce café est amer. Et votre limonade?

   _____

3. Mon voisin est très sot. Et votre voisine?

   _____

4. Ce compte rendu est complet. Et cette page?

   _____

5. Ce tableau est ancien. Et cette sculpture?

   _____

6. Le frère de Rosette est brun. Et sa sœur?

   _____

7. Le concert est merveilleux. Et la pièce de théâtre?

   _____

8. Le président est très discret. Et sa secrétaire?

   _____

9. Son père est roux. Et sa tante?

   _____

10. Le film est sensationnel. Et la musique?

    _____

11. Leur cousin est sportif. Et leur cousine?

    _____

12. Leur fils est mignon. Et leur fille?

    _____

**Substitution.** Refaites les locutions suivantes en faisant les substitutions indiquées, selon le modèle.

> MODÈLE   un garçon intelligent (fille)
> une fille intelligente

1. le gouvernement actuel (administration)

_____

2. une histoire drôle (récit)

_____

3. un chapeau chic (écharpe)

_____

4. une conclusion logique (résultat)

_____

5. le théâtre grec (langue)

_____

6. l'ordre public (opinion)

_____

7. un enfant nerveux (mère)

_____

8. une valise légère (paquet)

_____

9. une chanson favorite (film)

_____

10. un fromage exquis (viande)

_____

11. un calme trompeur (tranquillité)

_____

12. un goût délicat (sensibilité)

_____

## Plural of adjectives

1. Most French adjectives are made plural by adding **-s** to the masculine or feminine singular form.

| | |
|---|---|
| blanche → blanche**s** | heureuse → heureuse**s** |
| bon → bon**s** | noir → noir**s** |
| drôle → drôle**s** | poli → poli**s** |

2. Masculine singular adjectives ending in **-s** or **-x** do not change form in the plural.

des gâteaux délicieu**x**          *delicious cakes*
des bâtiments ba**s**              *low buildings*

Adjectives ending in **-eau,** such as **beau, nouveau,** add **-x** to form the masculine plural.

de beau**x** jardins              *beautiful gardens*
des mots nouveau**x**            *new words*

3. Most masculine singular adjectives ending in **-al** have plural forms ending in **-aux.**

des plans géni**aux**             *brilliant plans*
des problèmes soci**aux**        *social problems*

But the adjectives **banal, fatal, final, natal,** and **naval** form the masculine plural by adding **-s.**

les examens final**s**            *final exams*
leurs pays natal**s**            *their native countries*

**Activité 3**   **Au pluriel.** Écrivez les expressions suivantes au pluriel. Suivez le modèle.

> MODÈLE   une enfant heureuse
>          des enfants heureuses

1. un examen oral

   _____

2. un film affreux

   _____

3. un film génial

   _____

4. un examen final

   _____

5. un garçon roux

   _____

6. un livre banal

   _____

7. un cas spécial

   _____

8. un voyage dangereux

_____

9. un mot nouveau

_____

10. un œuf frais

_____

11. un problème national

_____

12. un produit local

_____

**Activité 4**  **On court les magasins.** Vous demandez des choses dans différents magasins. Qu'est-ce que le vendeur ou la vendeuse vous répond? Suivez le modèle.

> MODÈLE  Je cherche une robe longue.
> Voici les robes longues.

1. Je cherche un parfum français.

_____

2. Je voudrais un légume frais.

_____

3. J'ai besoin d'un journal espagnol.

_____

4. Je veux acheter un fromage crémeux.

_____

5. Montrez-moi, s'il vous plaît, un fromage gras.

_____

6. J'ai besoin d'un pantalon gris.

_____

7. Vous avez un foulard bleu?

_____

8. Je voudrais lire un roman québécois.

_____

**La vie intellectuelle.** Formulez des phrases qui seraient utiles dans des discussions intellectuelles en ajoutant aux substantifs donnés la forme correcte des adjectifs.

1. **actuel**

   **a.** les élections

   _____

   **b.** l'économie

   _____

   **c.** les conflits

   _____

2. **international**

   **a.** des efforts

   _____

   **b.** des organisations

   _____

   **c.** une entreprise

   _____

3. **grec**

   **a.** la poésie

   _____

   **b.** les régions

   _____

   **c.** les dialectes (*m.*)

   _____

4. **classique**

   **a.** la musique

   _____

   **b.** les philosophes

   _____

   **c.** les chansons

   _____

5. **religieux**

   **a.** une croyance

   _____

   **b.** des sentiments

   _____

   **c.** des conceptions

   _____

6. **européen**

   **a.** l'Union

   _____

   **b.** les pays

   _____

   **c.** les langues

   _____

7. **concret**

   **a.** des exemples

   _____

   **b.** une application

   _____

   **c.** des actions

   _____

8. **étranger**

   **a.** des influences

   _____

   **b.** la littérature

   _____

   **c.** les ambassadeurs

   _____

9. **fictif** (*fictional*)

   **a.** des personnages

   _____

   **b.** une situation

   _____

   **c.** des histoires

   _____

10. **naval**

   **a.** l'école

   _____

   **b.** des combats

   _____

   **c.** les bases

   _____

# Position of adjectives

1. Most French adjectives follow the noun they modify.

    C'est un garçon **intelligent.**       *He's an **intelligent** boy.*
    C'est une femme **cultivée.**          *She's a **cultured** woman.*

2. Some common adjectives referring to beauty, age, goodness, and size usually precede the noun.

| | | |
|---|---|---|
| **beau** *beautiful, handsome* | **gros** *big, fat* | **mauvais** *bad* |
| **bon** *good* | **jeune** *young* | **nouveau** *new* |
| **gentil** *nice, friendly* | **joli** *pretty* | **petit** *small* |
| **grand** *big* | **long** *long* | **vieux** *old* |

    Nous sommes arrivés à ce **petit**        *We arrived at this **small** hotel after a*
        hôtel après un **long** voyage.            ***long** trip.*

    Special forms of **beau, nouveau,** and **vieux** are used before masculine singular nouns beginning with a vowel. These special forms are pronounced like the feminine forms of these adjectives, but spelled differently.

    un **beau** bâtiment                    un **bel** immeuble
    un **nouveau** bâtiment                 un **nouvel** immeuble
    un **vieux** bâtiment                   un **vieil** immeuble

3. Ordinal numbers and some other common adjectives usually precede the noun they modify.

| | | |
|---|---|---|
| **autre** *other* | **plusieurs** *several* | **quelques** (*pl.*) *a few* |
| **chaque** *each* | **premier** *first* | **tel** *such* |

    Prenez la **troisième** rue à gauche.     *Turn left at the **third** street.*
    **Chaque** étudiant a **plusieurs** livres.   *Each student has **several** books.*

4. When more than one adjective is used to describe a noun, each adjective is placed in its usual position. If two adjectives occupy the same position before or after the noun, they are joined by **et.**

    un **bon** compte rendu **intéressant**     *a **good, interesting** report*
    un compte rendu **intéressant et**          *an **interesting, comprehensive** report*
        **compréhensif**
    un **long et mauvais** compte rendu         *a **long, bad** report*

5. Some adjectives can either follow or precede a noun, but their meaning changes depending on their position. Usually, they have a literal meaning when they follow the noun and a figurative meaning when they precede it.

| | | |
|---|---|---|
| un **ancien** combattant *a **former** soldier (veteran)* | la **dernière** fois *the **last** (**final**) time* | un **sale** quartier *a **nasty** (**awful**) neighborhood* |
| une ville **ancienne** *an **old, ancient** city* | l'année **dernière** *last (**preceding**) year* | un quartier **sale** *a **dirty** neighborhood* |
| un **brave** homme *a **decent** man* | la **même** idée *the **same** idea* | la **seule** femme *the **only** woman* |
| un soldat **brave** *a **brave** soldier* | le jour **même** *the **very** day* | une femme **seule** *a woman **alone*** |
| **certains** pays *certain (**some**) countries* | un **pauvre** homme *a **poor** (**unfortunate**) man* | un **simple** citoyen *an **ordinary** citizen* |
| un échec **certain** *a **sure** failure* | un homme **pauvre** *a **poor** (**penniless**) man* | un texte **simple** *a **simple** text* |
| mon **cher** ami *my **dear** friend* | la **prochaine** fois *the **next** (**following**) time* | un **vrai** ami *a **real** friend* |
| une voiture **chère** *an **expensive** car* | la semaine **prochaine** *next week* | une histoire **vraie** *a **true** story* |
| | ma **propre** chambre *my **own** room* | |
| | une chambre **propre** *a **clean** room* | |

6. Note that the plural indefinite article **des** usually changes to **de** before an adjective.

**de** vrais amis *real friends*          **de** jeunes hommes *young men*

**Activité 6**    **Identifiez.** Complétez les réponses de Micheline aux questions de son amie Solange en écrivant un des adjectifs de la liste ci-dessus dans le blanc convenable. Faites attention au placement de l'adjectif pour exprimer l'idée communiquée par chaque échange entre les deux amies. Suivez le modèle.

> MODÈLE    SOLANGE:    Ta nouvelle jupe a coûté beaucoup d'argent?
>               MICHELINE:    Oui, c'est une _____ jupe ___chère___.

1.    SOLANGE:    Tu as déjà étudié avec M. Deschênes?

      MICHELINE:    Oui, c'est mon _____ professeur
      _____.

2.    SOLANGE:    Tu es allée en Bretagne il y a un mois?

      MICHELINE:    Oui, j'y suis allée le _____ mois
      _____.

3.    SOLANGE:    Tes voisins les Durand n'ont pas beaucoup d'argent, n'est-ce pas?

      MICHELINE:    C'est vrai. C'est une _____ famille
      _____.

4.    SOLANGE:    Tu n'as pas fait de fautes à l'examen de maths?

     MICHELINE:    J'étais la _____ étudiante / l'étudiante

                      _____ à résoudre tous les problèmes.

5.    SOLANGE:    Hélène est toujours disposée à nous aider.

     MICHELINE:    Oui, c'est une _____ amie

                      _____.

6.    SOLANGE:    Olivier ne nettoie jamais son appartement.

     MICHELINE:    Tu as raison. C'est un _____

                      appartement _____.

7.    SOLANGE:    Tous les détails de l'histoire sont exacts.

     MICHELINE:    Oui, c'est une _____ histoire

                      _____.

8.    SOLANGE:    Tes parents t'ont offert une bicyclette pour ton anniversaire, n'est-ce pas?

     MICHELINE:    Oui, j'ai ma _____ bicyclette

                      _____ maintenant.

**Activité 7**    **Décrivons!** Formez des descriptions en partant des éléments donnés, selon le modèle. Faites attention au genre, au nombre et aux formes spéciales des adjectifs.

> MODÈLE    jeune / professeurs
> de jeunes professeurs

1. beau / terrasse

     _____

2. vieux / églises

     _____

3. vieux / objet

     _____

4. nouveau / ordinateur

     _____

5. nouveau / industrie

     _____

6. vieux / instruments

     _____

*(continued)*

7. beau / accent

_____

8. beau / animaux

_____

9. vieux / assiette

_____

10. nouveau / avions

_____

## Expressions of comparison with adjectives, adverbs, verbs, and nouns

An object or a person may be seen as having more, less, or the same amount of a characteristic as another object or person. To express this, both French and English use comparative constructions with adjectives.

1. To make comparisons of superiority, French uses the construction **plus** + _adjective_ + **que.**

    | | |
    |---|---|
    | Le boulevard est **plus large que** notre rue. | _The boulevard is **wider than** our street._ |

    To make comparisons of inferiority, French uses the construction **moins** + _adjective_ + **que.**

    | | |
    |---|---|
    | Mais le boulevard est **moins large que** l'autoroute. | _But the boulevard is **less wide than** (**not as wide as**) the superhighway._ |

    To make comparisons of equality, French uses the construction **aussi** + _adjective_ + **que.**

    | | |
    |---|---|
    | Le boulevard est **aussi large que** l'avenue de la République. | _The boulevard is **as wide as** the Avenue of the Republic._ |

**NOTE**

The adjectives **bon** and **mauvais** have irregular comparative forms.

| | |
|---|---|
| bon(ne)(s) → **meilleur(e)(s)** | mauvais(e)(s) → **pire(s)** (**plus mauvais**) |
| Ce restaurant est **meilleur que** l'autre. | _This restaurant is **better than** the other one._ |
| Le bruit est **pire** (**plus mauvais**) ici **que** dans mon quartier. | _The noise is **worse** here **than** in my neighborhood._ |

2. Adverbs are compared in the same way as adjectives.

    | | |
    |---|---|
    | Elle répond **plus poliment que** lui. | _She answers **more politely than** he does._ |
    | Elle répond **moins poliment que** lui. | _She answers **less politely than** he does._ |
    | Elle répond **aussi poliment que** lui. | _She answers **as politely as** he does._ |

**NOTE**

The adverbs **bien** and **mal** have irregular comparative forms: **mieux** (*better*) and **pire** (*worse*). **Pire** may be replaced by **plus mal.** The comparative of **beaucoup** is **plus,** and the comparative of **peu** is **moins.**

| | |
|---|---|
| On dit que M. Morot enseigne **mieux que** Mme Richard. | *They say that Mr. Morot teaches **better than** Mrs. Richard.* |
| J'en doute. Ses étudiants écrivent **pire (plus mal) que** les étudiants de Mme Richard. | *I doubt it. His students write **worse than** Mrs. Richard's students do.* |

3. When verbs are compared, **autant** replaces **aussi** in comparisons of equality.

| | |
|---|---|
| Je travaille **plus/moins que** toi. | *I work **more/less than** you do.* |
| Je travaille **autant que** toi. | *I work **as much as** you do.* |

4. The comparison of nouns resembles the comparison of verbs. **De** is used before the noun.

| | |
|---|---|
| Il a **plus/moins de soucis que** nous. | *He has **more/fewer worries than** we do.* |
| Il a **autant de soucis que** nous. | *He has **as many worries as** we do.* |

In comparisons, **que** may be followed by a noun, a disjunctive pronoun, a demonstrative or possessive pronoun, a prepositional phrase, or an adjective. In the last case, when **que** is followed by an adjective, the adjective functions as a noun.

| | |
|---|---|
| Le chemisier jaune est plus chic que **le vert.** | *The yellow blouse is more stylish than **the green one.*** |
| Les petits enfants étudient autant que **les grands.** | *The little children study as much as **the big ones.*** |
| Ce roman est moins intéressant que **ceux de l'autre auteur.** | *This novel is not as interesting as **the ones by the other author.*** |

**Activité 8** **Notre ville.** Faites les comparaisons adjectivales indiquées par le signe arithmétique, +, – ou =.

> MODÈLE le lycée / – vieux / l'université
> Le lycée est moins vieux que l'université.

1. le stade / + grand / salle de concert

_____

2. les cinémas / + nombreux / les théâtres

_____

3. la faculté de médecine / = réputée / la faculté de droit

_____

4. le jardin zoologique est / = fréquenté / la bibliothèque municipale

_____

(*continued*)

5. le musée scientifique / – grand / le musée d'art

   _____

6. les restaurants ici / = chers / les restaurants parisiens

   _____

7. les rues de la vieille ville / + étroites / rues des quartiers modernes

   _____

8. le quartier des affaires / – animé / le quartier des étudiants

   _____

9. la piscine municipale / + bonne / la plage au bord du fleuve

   _____

**Activité 9** **Les professeurs parlent de leurs étudiants.** Exprimez ces idées avec le comparatif adverbial en refaisant les phrases, selon les modèles.

> MODÈLES  Jacques travaille sérieusement. Laurent, pas tellement.
> Jacques travaille plus sérieusement que Laurent.
>
> Jacques travaille sérieusement. Laurent, encore plus.
> Jacques travaille moins sérieusement que Laurent.
>
> Jacques travaille sérieusement. Laurent aussi.
> Jacques travaille aussi sérieusement que Laurent.

1. Monique répond intelligemment. Christine, encore plus.

   _____

2. Édouard rédige soigneusement. Louis, pas tellement.

   _____

3. Nicole travaille rapidement. Lucien aussi.

   _____

4. Anne-Marie écoute attentivement. Guillaume aussi.

   _____

5. Gérard oublie souvent. Paulette, encore plus.

   _____

6. François se comporte bien. Georges, pas tellement.

   _____

**Activité 10** **Et vous?** Faites des comparaisons entre cette année à l'université et l'année dernière quant aux choses indiquées. Utilisez des pronoms démonstratifs après **que** et faites attention à la forme des adjectifs. Suivez le modèle.

> MODÈLE  mes classes / difficile
> Mes classes sont plus/moins/aussi difficiles que celles de l'année dernière.

1. nos manuels / intéressant

   _____

2. mes camarades de classe / sympathique

   _____

3. les professeurs / exigeant

   _____

4. les devoirs / facile

   _____

5. la nourriture qu'on sert à la cantine (*lunchroom*) / bon

   _____

6. mon horaire / pratique

   _____

7. la classe de français / passionnant

   _____

8. les bals qu'on organise / amusant

   _____

**Activité 11**  **Un moment difficile à l'université.** Ces étudiants sont très occupés. Exprimez ce qu'ils font en employant la comparaison des substantifs (**plus de, moins de, autant de**). Suivez le modèle.

> MODÈLES  Richard lit trois romans. Odile en lit deux.
> Richard lit plus de romans qu'Odile.
>
> Richard lit trois romans. Odile en lit quatre.
> Richard lit moins de romans qu'Odile.
>
> Richard lit trois romans. Odile en lit trois aussi.
> Richard lit autant de romans qu'Odile.

1. Frédéric suit cinq cours. Marc en suit quatre.

   _____

2. Sylvie écrit deux thèmes. Robert en écrit un.

   _____

3. Monique subit trois examens. Marcelle en subit quatre.

   _____

4. Maurice résoud (*solves*) trois problèmes de maths. Philippe en résoud trois aussi.

   _____

5. Marie-Laure étudie deux langues étrangères. Alfred en étudie deux aussi.

   _____

(*continued*)

CHAPITRE 13

6. Claudine apprend trois poèmes. Chantal en apprend quatre.

   _____

7. Hervé analyse cinq œuvres. Charles en analyse quatre.

   _____

8. Julie fait six expériences de chimie. Serge en fait six aussi.

   _____

## Superlative of adjectives, adverbs, and nouns

1. The superlative of an adjective is formed by placing the definite article before **plus** or **moins** + _adjective._ When the adjective follows the noun, the definite article appears both before the noun and before **plus** or **moins.**

   | | |
   |---|---|
   | Où se trouve **le restaurant le plus connu** ici? | _Where is **the most well-known restaurant** here?_ |
   | **Les restaurants les plus célèbres** et **les plus chers** se trouvent dans ce quartier. | _**The most famous** and **the most expensive restaurants** are found in this neighborhood._ |

2. If an adjective usually precedes the noun, its superlative form also precedes the noun. Only one definite article is required.

   | | |
   |---|---|
   | Chantal est **la meilleure élève** de la classe. | _Chantal is **the best student** in the class._ |
   | Paris est **la plus grande ville** de France. | _Paris is **the biggest city** in France._ |
   | Philippe et Diane sont **les plus mauvais** (ou **les pires**) élèves de la classe. | _Philippe and Diane are **the worst students** in the class._ |

3. After a superlative, the English preposition _in_ is translated by **de.**

   | | |
   |---|---|
   | Quel est le magasin le plus élégant **de** cette ville? | _What is the most elegant store **in** this city?_ |
   | On dit que «Chez Cartier» est un des magasins les plus élégants **du** pays. | _They say that «Chez Cartier» is one of the most elegant stores **in the** country._ |

4. The superlative of an adverb is formed with **le plus** or **le moins.**

   | | |
   |---|---|
   | Lise s'exprime **le plus clairement de** tous les élèves. | _Lise expresses herself **the most clearly of** all the pupils._ |
   | Et elle parle **le moins lentement** aussi. | _And she speaks **the least slowly,** too._ |

5. The phrases **le plus de** (_the most_) and **le moins de** (_the least, the fewest_) are used before nouns.

   | | |
   |---|---|
   | Toi, tu manges **le plus de** viande. | _You eat **the most** meat._ |
   | Et **le moins de** légumes. | _And **the fewest** vegetables._ |

DEUXIÈME PARTIE

**NOTE**

The superlatives of the adverbs **bien** and **mal** are irregular: **le mieux** (*the best*), **le pis** (*the worst*). In modern usage, **le plus mal** is used instead of **le pis**.

| | |
|---|---|
| On dit que ce professeur enseigne **le mieux.** | *They say that this teacher teaches* **best.** |
| J'en doute. Ses étudiants écrivent **le plus mal de** tous. | *I doubt it. His students write* **the worst of** *all.* |

6. The phrases **le plus** (*the most*) and **le moins** (*the least*) can be used after verbs. These are the superlatives of **beaucoup** and **peu,** respectively.

| | |
|---|---|
| C'est Alain qui travaille **le plus** et qui gagne **le moins.** | *Alain is the one who works* **the most** *and who earns* **the least.** |

**Activité 12**   **Notre classe.** Formez des superlatifs pour décrire les étudiants de la classe. Faites attention aux signes arithmétiques, + ou −.

> MODÈLE   Charles / − attentif
> Charles est le moins attentif.

1. Marylène / + diligent

   _____

2. Jacques et Pierre / − obéissant

   _____

3. Solange / + sympathique

   _____

4. Irène et Marie / − travailleur

   _____

5. Olivier / + intelligent

   _____

6. Anne-Marie / + bavard

   _____

7. Jean-Paul / + charmant

   _____

8. Colette et Brigitte / − préparé

   _____

**Visite de la ville.** Rachelle fait visiter sa ville à ses amis. Elle leur explique tout en employant des superlatifs. Écrivez ce qu'elle leur dit, en suivant le modèle.

> MODÈLE    c'est / bibliothèque / complet / ville
> C'est la bibliothèque la plus complète de la ville.

1. voilà / place / imposant / ville

   _____

2. ici vous voyez / cathédrale / ancien / région

   _____

3. en face il y a / université / connu / pays

   _____

4. c'est / rue / long / ville

   _____

5. dans cette rue il y a / magasins / beau / région

   _____

6. voilà / charcuterie / apprécié / quartier

   _____

7. devant nous il y a / hôtel / élégant / pays

   _____

8. dans cette rue se trouvent / cafés / fréquenté / ville

   _____

9. ici vous voyez / maisons / vieux / ville

   _____

10. voilà / stade / grand / région

    _____

**Les meilleurs et les pires.** Dans ce groupe d'étudiants il y a des jeunes extraordinaires. Exprimez leurs distinctions (pas toutes sont positives) avec un superlatif adverbial. Faites attention aux signes arithmétiques, + ou −, et suivez le modèle.

> MODÈLE    Jean / courir / vite (+)
> C'est Jean qui court le plus vite.

1. Lucie / parler / poliment (+)

   _____

DEUXIÈME PARTIE

2. Olivier / travailler / efficacement (–)

_____

3. Albert / étudier / serieusement (–)

_____

4. Suzanne / chanter / bien (+)

_____

5. Hélène / arriver en retard / souvent (+)

_____

6. Roger / répondre / calmement (+)

_____

# 14 Adverbs

## Adverbs of manner

1. Adverbs give information about verbs, adjectives, other adverbs, or entire sentences. Adverbs of manner tell how something is done. Most adverbs of manner are formed by adding **-ment** to the feminine form of the adjective.

| MASCULINE | FEMININE | ADVERB |
|---|---|---|
| actif | active | **activement** *actively* |
| amer | amère | **amèrement** *bitterly* |
| certain | certaine | **certainement** *certainly* |
| cruel | cruelle | **cruellement** *cruelly* |
| doux | douce | **doucement** *gently, softly* |
| franc | franche | **franchement** *frankly* |
| lent | lente | **lentement** *slowly* |
| public | publique | **publiquement** *publicly* |
| sérieux | sérieuse | **sérieusement** *seriously* |

2. If the masculine singular form of an adjective ends in a vowel, you add **-ment** to that form to make it into an adverb.

| MASCULINE | ADVERB |
|---|---|
| absolu | **absolument** *absolutely* |
| électronique | **électroniquement** *electronically* |
| facile | **facilement** *easily* |
| gai | **gaiment** *happily* |
| poli | **poliment** *politely* |
| sincère | **sincèrement** *sincerely* |
| vrai | **vraiment** *really, truly* |

3. If the masculine singular form of an adjective ends in **-ant** or **-ent**, replacing these endings with **-amment** and **-emment**, respectively, will make such adjectives into adverbs.

| ADJECTIVE | ADVERB |
|---|---|
| constant | **constamment** *constantly* |
| courant | **couramment** *fluently* |
| intelligent | **intelligemment*** *intelligently* |
| prudent | **prudemment*** *carefully* |

*Note that **-emment** is always pronounced like **-amment**, with an initial /a/ sound.

4. Some adjectives become adverbs when **-ément** is added to the masculine form. Adjectives ending in **-e** drop the **-e** before the **-ément** ending is added.

| ADJECTIVE | ADVERB |
|---|---|
| aveugle | **aveuglément** *blindly* |
| commun | **communément** *commonly* |
| confus | **confusément** *unintelligibly* |
| énorme | **énormément** *enormously* |
| intense | **intensément** *intensely* |
| obscur | **obscurément** *obscurely* |
| précis | **précisément** *precisely* |
| profond | **profondément** *profoundly, deeply* |
| uniforme | **uniformément** *uniformly* |

5. A number of adjectives can be used as adverbs without having to alter their form in any way. This usage occurs mostly in set phrases. The masculine singular form of the adjective is used in these cases.

| | |
|---|---|
| **acheter/vendre cher** *to buy/ sell at a high price* | **parler (tout) bas** *to speak (very) softly* |
| **aller tout droit** *to go straight ahead* | **parler/crier fort** *to speak/ yell, cry out loudly* |
| **s'arrêter court** *to stop short* | **payer cher** *to pay a high price* |
| **chanter faux** *to sing off key* | **sentir bon/mauvais** *to smell good/bad* |
| **couper fin** *to slice thin* | |
| **coûter cher** *to cost a lot* | **tenir ferme** *to stand firm* |
| **lire tout haut** *to read aloud* | **travailler dur** *to work hard* |
| **mettre la radio plus haut** *to turn the radio up louder* | **viser juste** *to aim correctly* |
| | **voir clair** *to see clearly* |

6. Some adverbs are irregular.

| ADJECTIVE | ADVERB |
|---|---|
| bon | **bien** *well* |
| bref | **brièvement** *briefly* |
| gentil | **gentiment** *gently* |
| mauvais | **mal** *badly* |
| meilleur | **mieux** *better* |
| pire | **pis** *worse* |

7. Some other common adverbs of manner do not end in **-ment.**

| | | |
|---|---|---|
| **ainsi** *thus* | **exprès** *on purpose* | **volontiers** *gladly* |
| **debout** *up, awake, standing up* | **vite** *quickly* | |

**Activité 1** **Pour décrire des actions.** Formez les adverbes qui correspondent aux adjectifs suivants. Après cette activité, vous serez prêt(e) à décrire beaucoup d'autres actions. Suivez le modèle.

> MODÈLE  personnel
> personnellement

1. affreux _____
2. intelligent _____
3. correct _____
4. probable _____
5. gentil _____
6. triste _____
7. massif _____
8. gai _____
9. confus _____
10. fréquent _____

11. moral _____
12. pratique _____
13. généreux _____
14. cruel _____
15. évident _____
16. léger _____
17. long _____
18. précis _____
19. exact _____
20. complet _____

**Activité 2** **Comment est-ce qu'ils ont parlé?** Formez des adverbes pour décrire comment ces personnes s'adressent au professeur. Suivez le modèle.

> MODÈLE  Sarah est sincère quand elle parle avec le professeur?
> Oui, elle lui parle sincèrement.

1. Frédéric est nerveux quand il parle avec le professeur?

   _____

2. Lise est intense quand elle parle avec le professeur?

   _____

3. Paul est honnête quand il parle avec le professeur?

   _____

4. Anne et Barbara sont tristes quand elles parlent avec le professeur?

   _____

5. Luc et Jean-Claude sont discrets quand ils parlent avec le professeur?

   _____

6. Thérèse est patiente quand elle parle avec le professeur?

   _____

7. Odile et Marc sont polis quand ils parlent avec le professeur?

   _____

8. Serge est gentil quand il parle avec le professeur?

   _____

**Activité 3** | **Décrivez les actions.** Refaites les phrases suivantes en employant le verbe qui correspond au substantif et l'adverbe qui correspond à l'adjectif. Suivez le modèle.

> MODÈLE   Est-ce que les réponses de Victor sont intelligentes?
> Oui, il répond intelligemment.

1. Est-ce que le travail de Paulette est diligent?

   _____

2. Est-ce que les réactions de son frère sont violentes?

   _____

3. Est-ce que les dessins de cette artiste sont bons?

   _____

4. Est-ce que les sorties de votre sœur sont fréquentes?

   _____

5. Est-ce que la prononciation de ces élèves est mauvaise en français?

   _____

6. Est-ce que son amour pour elle est aveugle?

   _____

## The position and use of adverbs of manner

1. Adverbs of manner ending in **-ment** and the adverbs **bien, mal, mieux, pis,** and **vite** usually come directly after the verb they modify. In compound tenses, short adverbs usually come after the auxiliary verb, and longer adverbs usually come after the past participle.

| | |
|---|---|
| Julie et Bruno se disputent **constammant.** | *Julie and Bruno argue **constantly.*** |
| Après le dîner, ils se sont disputés **amèrement** et Julie a **vite** quitté le salon. | *After dinner, they argued **bitterly** and Julie **quickly** left the living room.* |

When an adverb modifies an adjective or another adverb, it precedes the word it modifies.

| | |
|---|---|
| Cette lettre est **très importante.** | *This letter is **very important.*** |
| Les spectateurs étaient **profondément émus.** | *The audience was **deeply moved.*** |

2. Adverbs of manner ending in **-ment** can be replaced by **avec** plus the corresponding noun.

joyeusement → **avec joie**          discrètement → **avec discrétion**
violemment → **avec violence**          amèrement → **avec amertume**

**Sans** + *noun* is often the equivalent of English adverbs ending in *-lessly* or English adverbs formed from negative adjectives.

**sans espoir** *hopelessly*          **sans hésitation** *unhesitatingly*
**sans honte** *shamelessly*          **sans succès** *unsuccessfully*

**D'une façon, d'une manière, d'un ton,** or **d'un air,** followed by an adjective, may be used in place of an adverb, when no adverb exists.

**d'une façon compétente**          **d'un ton moqueur** *mockingly*
  *competently*
**d'une manière compatible**          **d'un air indécis** *indecisively*
  *compatibly*

**Activité 4**   **Formulez vos phrases!** Organisez les éléments donnés pour former des phrases correctes. Faites attention au placement de l'adverbe, en suivant le modèle.

> MODÈLE   expliqué / bien / problème / le / a / le professeur
> Le professeur a bien expliqué le problème.

1. mal / le vocabulaire / connais / tu

   _____

2. nettoie / la cuisine / elle / soigneusement

   _____

3. ridicule / trouvons / ce projet / complètement / nous

   _____

4. étroitement / sont / les membres de cette famille / liés (*connected*)

   _____

5. sans / marche / il / empressement

   _____

6. d'une façon / les enfants / se sont conduits / déplaisante

   _____

7. dur / Marcelle / à / travaille / la bibliothèque

   _____

8. une / reçue / c'est / largement / idée

   _____

9. le / ont / ils / texte / compris / vite

_____

10. m' / elle / répondu / a / brusquement

_____

**Activité 5**   **L'expression adverbiale.** Consultez cette liste et associez les substantifs aux prépositions **avec** et **sans** pour traduire les adverbes anglais.

| | | |
|---|---|---|
| **la cérémonie** _ceremony_ | **le goût** _taste_ | **le tact** _tact_ |
| **la colère** _anger_ | **l'imagination** _imagination_ | **la tolérance** _tolerance_ |
| **l'effort** _effort_ | **l'indifférence** _indifference_ | |

1. _effortlessly_ _____

2. _tastefully_ _____

3. _unimaginatively_ _____

4. _indifferently_ _____

5. _angrily_ _____

6. _tolerantly_ _____

7. _unceremoniously_ _____

8. _tactlessly_ _____

## Adverbs of time and place

1. Adverbs of time tell when, or in what order, something happens.

| | | |
|---|---|---|
| **actuellement** _at present_ | **bientôt** _soon_ | **n'importe quand** _anytime_ |
| **alors** _then_ | **déjà** _already, ever_ | **parfois** _sometimes_ |
| **après** _after, afterward_ | **demain** _tomorrow_ | **précédemment** _previously_ |
| **après-demain** _the day after_ | **dernièrement** _lately_ | **quelquefois** _sometimes_ |
|   _tomorrow_ | **désormais** _from now on_ | **rarement** _rarely, seldom_ |
| **aujourd'hui** _today_ | **encore** _still, yet, again_ | **récemment** _recently_ |
| **auparavant** _previously,_ | **encore une fois** _again_ | **souvent** _often_ |
|   _beforehand_ | **enfin** _at last, finally_ | **tard** _late_ |
| **aussitôt** _immediately_ | **ensuite** _next, following that_ | **tôt** _early_ |
| **autrefois** _formerly, in the past_ | **hier** _yesterday_ | **toujours** _always_ |
| **avant** _before_ | **jamais** _never_ | **tout à l'heure** _a short while_ |
| **avant-hier** _the day before_ | **longtemps** _for a long time_ |   _ago, very soon_ |
|   _yesterday_ | **maintenant** _now_ | **tout de suite** _immediately_ |

Adverbs of time usually follow the verb, but they also often appear at the beginning of a sentence.

Je vais **quelquefois** au théâtre.      Il travaillait **auparavant** à Lille.

**Quelquefois** je vais au théâtre.      **Auparavant** il travaillait à Lille.

Many phrases that specify points in time function as adverbial phrases.

| | | |
|---|---|---|
| **une fois, deux fois,** *etc.* | **mardi prochain** | **tous les jours** |
| **une/deux fois par** | **le matin / l'après-midi** | **tous les mois** |
| **semaine/mois** | **la semaine dernière/** | **toute la journée** |
| **le lendemain** *the day after* | **prochaine** | **toutes les semaines** |
| **mardi** *Tuesday* | **en semaine** *during the week* | **la veille** *the evening before* |
| **le mardi** *(on) Tuesdays* | **le soir / la nuit** | **le week-end** |
| **mardi dernier** | **tous les ans** | |

2. Adverbs of place tell where something is located.

| | | |
|---|---|---|
| **ailleurs** *elsewhere,* | **dessus** *above* | **nulle part** *nowhere* |
| *somewhere else* | **devant** *in front* | **nulle part ailleurs** |
| **autour** *around* | **en bas** *down, downstairs* | *nowhere else* |
| **d'ailleurs** *besides* | **en haut** *up, upstairs* | **partout** *everywhere* |
| **dedans** *inside* | **ici** *here* | **partout ailleurs** |
| **dehors** *outside* | **là** *there* | *everywhere else* |
| **derrière** *behind* | **loin** *far away* | **près** *near* |
| **dessous** *below, under* | **n'importe où** *anywhere* | **quelque part** *somewhere* |

**NOTE**

**Nulle part** is a negative expression similar to **ne... pas** and **ne... jamais**. The **ne** must be included before the conjugated verb.

Je **ne** le trouve **nulle part.**          *I can't find it anywhere.*

In everyday language, both spoken and written, **ici** is often replaced by **là.**

Je regrette, mais Mme Poirier n'est          *I'm sorry, but Mrs. Poirier is not here.*
pas **là.**

The prefix **là-** can be added to some adverbs of place.

| | |
|---|---|
| **là-bas** *over there* | **là-dessus*** *on top of it, on it* |
| **là-dedans** *in there* | **là-haut** *up there* |
| **là-dessous*** *underneath there* | |

**Activité 6**   **Une belle maison.** Rendez plus précise cette description d'une belle maison en ajoutant les adverbes de lieu donnés entre parenthèses. On peut placer ces adverbes à la fin de la phrase, et parfois au début aussi. Suivez le modèle.

MODÈLE   Je remarque une maison. (là-bas)
Je remarque une maison là-bas.

1. Il y a des arbres. (autour)

_____

*****Ci-dessous** (*below* [here]) and **ci-dessus** (*above* [here]) also exist.

DEUXIÈME PARTIE

2. Il y a un jardin. (derrière)

   _____

3. Je regarde le salon. (en bas)

   _____

4. Je voudrais voir les chambres. (en haut)

   _____

5. Je cherche les propriétaires. (partout)

   _____

6. Je ne les vois pas. (nulle part)

   _____

7. Travaillent-ils? (dehors)

   _____

8. Je les entends. (quelque part)

   _____

9. Il y a deux personnes. (tout près)

   _____

10. Les voilà. (devant)

   _____

## Adverbial phrases

1. Prepositional phrases often function as adverbs of manner, time, and place. The preposition **dès** and the compound preposition **à partir de** combine with expressions of time to tell when something happened.

### Adverbial phrases of time with **dès** and **à partir de**

| | |
|---|---|
| **dès mon retour** *as soon as I get back* | **à partir d'aujourd'hui** *from today on* |
| **dès le matin** *from the morning on* | **à partir de demain** *from tomorrow on* |
| **dès le début** *from the beginning* | **à partir d'hier** *starting yesterday* |

### Adverbial phrases with **dans** and **en**

| | | |
|---|---|---|
| **dans l'avenir / le passé** *in the future/past* | **dans cinq minutes** *in five minutes ( five minutes from now)* | **d'aujourd'hui en huit** *a week from today* |
| **dans un mois** *in a month (a month from now)* | **en cinq minutes** *in five minutes (time it takes to do something)* | **en avance** *early (relative to a point in time)* |
| **dans un moment** *in a moment* | **d'ici une semaine** *a week from now* | **en retard** *late (relative to a point in time)* |
| **en ce moment** *at this time* | | |

## Adverbial phrases with **à**

à l'heure *on time*
à l'heure actuelle *at the present time (in this day and age)*
à temps *in time*
à l'époque *at the time, at that time*
à l'époque où nous sommes *in this day and age*

à leur arrivée *when they arrive(d) (upon their arrival)*
à leur retour *when they return(ed) (upon their return)*
à 3 kilomètres de la ville *3 kilometers from the city*
à 3 heures de Paris *3 hours from Paris*

à droite/gauche *to, on the right/left*
à cheval *on horseback*
à la hâte *hastily, in a rush*
à merveille *wonderfully*
à peine *hardly*
à pied *on foot*

## Adverbial phrases with **de**

d'abord *at first*
d'habitude, d'ordinaire *usually*
de bonne heure *early*

de jour en jour *from day to day*
de temps en temps *from time to time*

du matin au soir *from morning to night*
marcher d'un bon pas *to walk at a good pace*

## Adverbial phrases with **en**

en avant *in front, ahead*
en arrière *in back*
en face *opposite, across (the street)*

en désordre, en pagaille *in a mess*
en groupe *in a group*
en plus *moreover*

en tout cas *in any case*
en train/autobus/avion/ voiture *by train/bus/ plane/car*

## Adverbial phrases with **par**

par conséquent *consequently*
par écrit *in writing*
par la force *by force*
par hasard *by chance*
par ici/là *this way / that way*

par intervalles *intermittently*
par la poste *through the mail, by mail*
par un temps pareil *in such weather*

par terre *on the ground*
payer par chèque *to pay by check*

## Phrases of time with **sur**

sur une année *over (over the period of) a year*
sur le moment *at first*

sur les trois heures *at about three o'clock*

un jour sur deux *every other day*

The following miscellaneous phrases with **sans** are often translated by English adverbs.

sans but *aimlessly*
sans chaussures *barefoot*
sans doute *doubtless, probably*

sans faute *without fail*
sans mal *without any trouble, without difficulty*

**Mon rendez-vous.** M. Perrin explique les difficultés qu'il a eues pour ne pas manquer son rendez-vous. Ajoutez les prépositions qui manquent pour savoir ce qui lui est arrivé.

J'avais rendez-vous à trois heures. Je ne voulais pas arriver _____ 1

retard. Je suis donc parti _____ les deux heures pour
2

arriver un peu _____ avance. Il pleuvait. Je ne
3

pouvais pas aller _____ pied _____
4 5

un temps pareil. J'ai décidé d'aller _____ bus. Mais
6

le bus n'est pas venu. _____ conséquent, j'ai pris
7

un taxi. Je m'étais _____ peine installé quand le
8

taxi a eu un pneu crevé. Je suis descendu du taxi et j'ai commencé

à marcher _____ un bon pas. Je me trouvais
9

_____ vingt minutes du bureau où on m'attendait.
10

Tout à fait _____ hasard mon ami Michel est passé
11

dans sa voiture. Il a klaxonné pour attirer mon attention. Il m'a emmené

_____ voiture et on y est arrivés _____
12 13

cinq minutes. Je suis arrivé _____ temps!
14

**Activité 8** **Les soucis d'un jeune professeur.** Alfred Saint-Martin est un jeune professeur d'histoire dans un lycée à Tours. Il a une classe difficile. Pour savoir ce qu'il en pense et ce qu'il compte faire, refaites les phrases suivantes en y ajoutant la traduction française des phrases adverbiales données entre parenthèses.

1. J'ai fait un effort pour organiser la classe. (*right from the start*)

   _____

2. J'ai dit aux étudiants qu'il est défendu de venir en classe. (*barefoot*)

   _____

3. Je leur ai dit que je ne veux pas qu'ils laissent la salle de classe. (*in a mess*)

   _____

4. Ils ne doivent laisser ni leurs livres ni leurs papiers. (*on the ground*)

   _____

5. Jean-Claude Mercier vient au cours. (*every other day*)

   _____

6. Il prépare ses devoirs. (*in a rush*)

   _____

(*continued*)

7. Lise Monnet est la meilleure étudiante de la classe. (*doubtless*)

   _____

8. Les autres étudiants l'admirent. (*sincerely*)

   _____

9. Nous avons une semaine de congé. (*starting tomorrow*)

   _____

10. Je vais faire un effort pour améliorer cette classe. (*as soon as we get back*)

    _____

11. Nous allons faire des excursions. (*from time to time*)

    _____

12. Les vieilles méthodes ne sont pas toujours bonnes. (*in this day and age*)

    _____

## Disjunctive pronouns: forms and usage

Disjunctive pronouns (**les pronoms disjoints** or **les pronoms toniques**) are used to emphasize a noun or a pronoun that is used as a subject or as an object, or to replace a noun that is used as a subject or as an object. Disjunctive pronouns can stand by themselves; subject and object pronouns cannot.

|  | SINGULAR | PLURAL |
|---|---|---|
| **FIRST PERSON** | moi | nous |
| **SECOND PERSON** | toi | vous |
| **THIRD PERSON** | lui / elle | eux / elles |

| | |
|---|---|
| **Moi, je** fais du latin, mais **lui, il** fait du grec. | *I'm taking Latin, but **he**'s taking Greek.* |
| **Nous, on** travaille aujourd'hui. Et **toi?** | *We're working today. What about **you?*** |
| Je vais à la plage, **moi.** | *I'm going to the beach.* |

1. A disjunctive pronoun may stand alone in answer to a question.

   | | |
   |---|---|
   | Qui fait le ménage aujourd'hui? **Toi?** | *Who's doing the housework today? **You?*** |
   | Pas moi. **Eux.** | *Not me. **They are.*** |

2. The disjunctive pronouns are used after **c'est** and **ce sont** to identify people.

   | | |
   |---|---|
   | C'est moi. | C'est nous. |
   | C'est toi. | C'est vous. |
   | C'est lui. | **Ce sont** eux. |
   | C'est elle. | **Ce sont** elles. |

**NOTE** Colloquially one says **c'est eux / c'est elles;** in the negative, **ce n'est pas eux / ce n'est pas elles.** Note also the questions **qui est-ce?** (*formal*) and **c'est qui?** (*informal*).

3. The disjunctive pronouns are used after prepositions.

| | |
|---|---|
| Tu pars **sans elle**? | *Are you leaving **without her**?* |
| Pas du tout. Elle vient **chez moi** et nous partons ensemble. | *Not at all. She's coming **to my house** and we're leaving together.* |

4. The disjunctive pronouns are also used after **ne... que** (*only*).

| | |
|---|---|
| Je **ne** connais **que toi** à Paris. | *You're the **only** one I know in Paris.* |
| Il **n'**aime **qu'eux.** | *He likes **only them**.* |

5. The disjunctive pronoun **soi** (*himself, herself, themselves*) is used with indefinite pronouns or to avoid ambiguity.

| | |
|---|---|
| Chacun pour **soi.** | *Every man for **himself**.* |
| Il ne faut pas parler toujours de **lui.** | *One shouldn't talk about **him** all the time.* |
| Il ne faut pas parler toujours de **soi.** | *One shouldn't talk about **oneself** all the time.* |

**Activité 1**   **Vacances.** Formez des phrases exprimant un contraste avec les éléments proposés. Employez la forme tonique du pronom. Suivez le modèle.

> MODÈLE   je / aller au bord de la mer / ils / aller à la montagne
> Moi, je vais au bord de la mer. Eux, ils vont à la montagne.

1. nous / partir en Italie / elles / partir en Grèce

    _____

    _____

2. je / prendre le train / ils / partir en voiture

    _____

    _____

3. tu / faire de l'alpinisme / il / faire de la natation

    _____

    _____

4. ils / aller à la campagne / on /aller leur rendre visite

    _____

    _____

5. je / avoir trois semaines de vacances / vous / avoir un mois

    _____

    _____

6. je / préférer voyager seul / tu / préférer voyager en groupe

    _____

    _____

7. on / compter faire du cyclisme / il / vouloir faire du tourisme

_____

_____

8. elle / faire un stage linguistique en Allemagne / tu / te détendre

_____

_____

**Activité 2** **Tu as tort!** Un copain vous dit des choses erronées (*false*) sur vos habitudes. Corrigez ses impressions en formant une phrase négative. Mettez le pronom **moi** à la fin de chaque phrase. Suivez le modèle.

> MODÈLE   Je sais que tu aimes les films d'horreur.
> C'est faux! Je n'aime pas les films d'horreur, moi.

1. Je sais que tu sors avec Émilie.

_____

2. Je sais que tu te lèves à huit heures.

_____

3. Je sais que tu dors en classe.

_____

4. Je sais que tu joues de la clarinette.

_____

5. Je sais que tu cherches du travail.

_____

6. Je sais que tu vas chez Olivier après les cours.

_____

**Activité 3** **Mon ami Philippe? Jamais!** Un copain a des impressions fausses sur votre ami Philippe. Corrigez ses idées avec une phrase négative au passé composé en employant le mot **jamais.** Mettez le pronom **lui** à la fin de vos phrases, selon le modèle.

> MODÈLE   Ton ami Philippe sort avec Odile.
> Qu'est-ce que tu dis? Il n'est jamais sorti avec Odile, lui.

1. Ton ami Philippe dort en classe.

_____

2. Ton ami Philippe est toujours en retard.

_____

3. Ton ami Philippe interrompt le professeur.

_____

(*continued*)

4. Ton ami Philippe se dispute avec Serge.

_____

5. Ton ami Philippe se moque des cours.

_____

6. Ton ami Philippe dérange les autres étudiants.

_____

**Activité 4**    **Qui est-ce?** Écrivez des échanges pour vérifier l'identité des gens que vous voyez. Employez **c'est / ce sont** et une forme tonique du pronom, selon le modèle.

> MODÈLE    les Durand là-bas / les Devaux
> Ce sont les Durand là-bas?
> Non, ce n'est pas eux. Ce sont les Devaux.

1. toi sur la photo / ma sœur Barbara

_____

_____

2. moi le suivant (*next*) / lui

_____

_____

3. M. Charpentier assis sur le banc / notre voisin M. Beauchamp

_____

_____

4. Adèle Malmaison dans la boutique / Mlle Lachaux

_____

_____

5. nos amis là, à l'entrée du lycée / d'autres étudiants

_____

_____

6. Gisèle et Marie-Claire à l'arrêt du bus / Christine et Yvette

_____

_____

DEUXIÈME PARTIE

**Activité 5** | **Réponses mystérieuses.** Un copain curieux vous pose beaucoup de questions. Répondez-lui au négatif, en remplaçant la personne en italique par le pronom disjoint convenable. Suivez le modèle.

> MODÈLE   Tu es arrivé avec *Richard*?
> Non, je ne suis pas arrivé avec lui.

1. Ce cadeau est pour *moi*?

   _____

2. Tu comptes dîner avec *Janine et François*?

   _____

3. Tu as l'intention de passer chez *Paulette*?

   _____

4. Je peux compter sur *toi*?

   _____

5. Est-ce que Suzanne a été invitée par *Jacques*?

   _____

6. Est-ce que le professeur est fâché contre *Alice et toi*?

   _____

**Activité 6** | **Il n'y a pas d'autres.** Répondez aux questions suivantes à l'affirmatif. Utilisez l'expression **ne... que** suivi d'une forme tonique du pronom pour indiquer que la personne (les personnes) mentionnée(s) est (sont) le seul objet du sentiment exprimé. Suivez le modèle.

> MODÈLE   Elle invite M. Breuil?
> Oui. Elle n'invite que lui.

1. Tu m'aimes?

   _____

2. On respecte cet agent de police?

   _____

3. Les étudiants admirent le professeur Triquet?

   _____

4. Les juges estiment cette avocate?

   _____

5. Vous nous aidez?

   _____

(continued)

*Disjunctive pronouns*   189

6. Il apprécie les musiciens de cet orchestre?

   _____

7. Ils encouragent leurs filles?

   _____

**Activité 7** **Joyeux anniversaire!** Complétez ce paragraphe avec les pronoms qui manquent (toniques et autres) pour savoir ce qu'on a fait pour fêter l'anniversaire de Florence.

Demain, c'est l'anniversaire de Florence et moi, _____

voulais organiser une fête pour _____. J'ai téléphoné à

mon amie Hélène. _____, elle adore les fêtes, et je savais

qu'elle voudrait m'aider. «Qui est-ce que tu veux inviter?» m'a-t-elle demandé.

«Aide-_____ à faire la liste», lui ai-je répondu. «On invite

Serge?»

—Oui, _____, il est très sympathique et il aime danser.

—On invite Philippe et Charles?

—Oui, _____, ce sont de grands blagueurs et ils font rire

tout le monde.

—Et le cadeau de Florence? Qu'est-ce qu'on doit acheter pour

_____? Je n'ai vraiment pas d'idées,

_____. Tu peux proposer quelque chose,

_____?

—On va demander à Janine et à Claire. Elles, _____ ont

toujours de bonnes idées quand il s'agit de cadeaux.

Nous nous sommes réunies avec Janine et Claire et nous sommes allées avec

_____ aux grands magasins. Tout était très cher, et

_____, on n'avait pas beaucoup d'argent. Tout d'un coup,

Janine a dit: «Regarde! Des foulards de soie en solde. Allons les regarder.» Nous

en avons choisi un pour Florence et la vendeuse a fait un joli paquet.

La fête de Florence a été un grand succès. Nous avions invité une vingtaine

d'amis et ils sont tous venus. Florence a été vraiment très émue (*moved, touched*),

et le foulard lui a beaucoup plu.

—Vous êtes vraiment de très bonnes amies, _____. Vous

m'avez rendue très heureuse.

—Non, c'est _____ la bonne amie, Florence. C'est un
                          14

plaisir de faire tout ça pour _____.
                                           15

## Subject-verb agreement with disjunctive pronouns

After the phrase **c'est** + *disjunctive pronoun* + **qui,** the verb following **qui** agrees
with the disjunctive pronoun.

| | |
|---|---|
| **C'est toi qui t'en vas?** | *Are you the one who's leaving?* |
| Non. **C'est moi qui suis** de garde. | *No. **I'm the one who's** on duty.* |
| **Ce sont eux qui partent.** | *They're the ones who are leaving.* |
| **C'est vous qui faites** du japonais? | *Are you the ones who are studying Japanese?* |
| Non. **C'est nous qui étudions** le russe. | *No. **We're the ones who are studying** Russian.* |

---

**Activité 8**    **En français!** Traduisez ces phrases en français.

1. *He's buying bread. We're buying bottled water.*

    _____

2. *We saw Julien and Colette. We went over to (**s'approcher de**) them.*

    _____

3. *Gérard thinks only about himself.*

    _____

4. *We came in after him, but before you (singular).*

    _____

5. *And I thought you were inviting only me!*

    _____

6. *You're (informal) the one who is working.*

    _____

7. *They're the ones who are leaving (**s'en aller**).*

    _____

8. *He's the one who knows the answer.*

    _____

---

**Activité 9**    **Activité orale.** Apportez des photos de famille pour montrer à un(e)
camarade de classe. Il/Elle vous posera des questions au sujet des
personnes photographiées: «C'est toi? C'est ta cousine Agnès?» Utilisez
autant de pronoms disjoints que possible dans les questions et les
réponses.

# 16 Object pronouns

## Direct object pronouns

1. The direct object is the person or thing that serves as the complement of the verb. It is connected *directly* to the verb, without a preposition.

| | |
|---|---|
| Je vois **Jean.** | *I see **John.*** |
| Nous ne voyons pas **le magasin.** | *We don't see **the store.*** |
| J'ouvre **mon livre.** | *I open **my book.*** |
| Elle porte **ses lunettes.** | *She's wearing **her glasses.*** |

As a means of avoiding repetition, direct object nouns may be replaced by direct object pronouns.

| | SINGULAR | PLURAL |
|---|---|---|
| **FIRST PERSON** | **me** *me* | **nous** *us* |
| **SECOND PERSON** | **te** *you* | **vous** *you* |
| **THIRD PERSON** | **le** *him, it* | **les** *them* |
| | **la** *her, it* | |

2. Direct object pronouns precede the conjugated verb. Note that before a verb beginning with a vowel or mute **h**, the direct object pronouns **me, te, le, la** are elided and become **m', t', l'.**

| | |
|---|---|
| Est-ce que tu achètes **ce livre**? | *Are you buying **that book**?* |
| Non. Je **le** regarde tout simplement. | *No. I'm just looking at **it**.* |

| | |
|---|---|
| **Me** retrouvez-vous en ville? | *Will you meet **me** in town?* |
| Oui. Nous **t'**attendons au Café de la Gare. | *Yes. We'll wait for **you** at the Café de la Gare.* |

| | |
|---|---|
| Tu aimes **ces nouvelles chansons**? | *Do you like **these new songs**?* |
| Pas du tout. Je **les** déteste. | *Not at all. I hate **them**.* |

3. When a verb is followed by an infinitive, the direct object pronoun comes before the verb of which it is the direct object, which is usually the infinitive.

| | |
|---|---|
| Vous pouvez **nous** déposer en ville? | *Can you drop **us** off downtown?* |
| Je regrette, mais je ne peux pas **vous** prendre. | *I'm sorry, but I can't take **you** (give **you** a lift).* |

| | |
|---|---|
| Je peux **t'**aider? | *Can I help **you**?* |
| Non, merci. On **m'**a déjà aidé à monter mes valises à ma chambre. | *No, thank you. Someone has already helped **me** to carry my luggage up to my room.* |

4. Direct object pronouns precede the auxiliary verb in compound tenses. Remember that a past participle agrees in gender and number with a direct object noun or pronoun that precedes it.

| | |
|---|---|
| As-tu vu **Daniel**? | *Have you seen **Daniel**?* |
| Je **l'**ai cherché, mais je ne **l'**ai pas trouvé. | *I looked for **him**, but I didn't find **him**.* |
| Je **t'**ai appelé, mais tu ne **m'**as pas entendu. | *I called out to **you**, but you didn't hear **me**.* |
| Si, je **t'**ai salué, mais tu ne **m'**as pas vu. | *Yes, I waved hello to **you**, but you didn't see **me**.* |
| Et **les lettres**? Où est-ce que vous **les** avez mis**es**? | *What about **the letters**? Where did you put **them**?* |
| Je **les** ai jet**ées** à la poubelle. Je croyais que vous **les** aviez déjà lu**es**. | *I threw **them** into the garbage. I thought that you had already read **them**.* |

**NOTE**

Several verbs that take indirect objects in English take direct objects in French.

| | |
|---|---|
| **attendre quelqu'un / quelque chose** *to wait for someone/something* | **escalader quelque chose** *to climb over something* |
| **chercher quelqu'un / quelque chose** *to look for someone/something* | **payer quelque chose** *to pay for something* |
| **demander quelque chose** *to ask for something* | **regarder quelqu'un / quelque chose** *to look at someone/something* |
| **écouter quelqu'un / quelque chose** *to listen to someone/something* | |

**Activité 1** **Au magasin de vêtements.** Ombeline est dans une boutique. Continuez le récit qui raconte ce qu'elle fait pour acheter les vêtements qu'il lui faut. Utilisez les verbes entre parenthèses et les pronoms de complément direct. Suivez le modèle.

> MODÈLE   Voilà la porte du magasin. (ouvrir)
> Elle l'ouvre.

1. Voilà les robes. (regarder)

_____

2. Voilà une robe dans sa taille. (essayer)

_____

3. La robe ne lui plaît pas. (ne pas prendre)

_____

*(continued)*

4. Elle aime ce chemisier. (acheter)

   _____

5. Elle veut voir les foulards en soie. (chercher)

   _____

6. Elle trouve un foulard qui va bien avec son nouveau chemisier. (prendre)

   _____

7. Elle passe au rayon des chapeaux. (regarder)

   _____

8. Il y a deux chapeaux qui l'intéressent. (essayer)

   _____

9. Ils sont très chers. (ne pas acheter)

   _____

10. Mais elle va acheter le foulard. (payer)

   _____

**Activité 2**   **Emménagement.** La famille Jonquières est en train d'emménager dans leur nouvelle maison. Mme Jonquières répond aux questions des déménageurs sur l'emplacement des meubles. Employez les mots entre parenthèses pour écrire ses réponses et remplacez les compléments directs par des pronoms. Suivez le modèle.

> MODÈLE   Et le lave-vaisselle, Madame? (installer / cuisine)
> Vous pouvez l'installer dans la cuisine.

1. Et ce sofa, Madame? (mettre / salon)

   _____

2. Et ce lit, Madame? (monter / à la chambre de mon fils)

   _____

3. Et la machine à laver? (descendre / au sous-sol)

   _____

4. Et cette télévision? (laisser / salon)

   _____

5. Et cette table? (installer / salle à manger)

   _____

6. Et ces vêtements? (suspendre / penderie)

   _____

7. Et cet ordinateur? (monter / à la chambre de ma fille)

_____

8. Et ces fauteuils? (laisser / salon)

_____

**Activité 3**  **Pas possible!** Michel répond au négatif aux questions de son ami. Écrivez ce qu'il dit avec le pronom convenable, selon le modèle.

> MODÈLE  Tu m'aides?
>         Non, je ne peux pas t'aider.

1. Tu me déposes en ville?

_____

2. Tu m'emmènes à la poste?

_____

3. Tu me raccompagnes?

_____

4. Tu m'attends?

_____

5. Tu nous rejoins, Sara et moi?

_____

6. Tu nous appelles?

_____

**Activité 4**  **On s'organise.** Les étudiants s'organisent pour nettoyer le foyer d'étudiants avant de partir pour l'été. Employez le(s) nom(s) entre parenthèses pour répondre aux questions. Remplacez les compléments directs dans les questions par des pronoms en employant la construction **aller** + *infinitive*. Suivez le modèle.

> MODÈLE  Qui fait le linge? (Jean-Claude)
>         Jean-Claude va le faire.

**Vocabulaire**

## Le nettoyage

**balayer** *to sweep*
**la casserole** *pot*
**dépoussiérer** *to dust*
**faire le linge** *to do the laundry*
**faire le lit** *to make the bed*
**faire les carreaux** *to wash the windows*
**laver** *to wash*
**les meubles** (*m.*) *furniture*

**nettoyer** *to clean*
**les ordures** (*f.*) *garbage*
**le parquet** *wooden floor*
**passer l'aspirateur** *to vacuum*
**la poêle** *frying pan*
**récurer** *to scour*
**sortir** *to take out*
**les toilettes** (*f.*) *bathroom*

1. Qui balaie la cuisine? (Sabine)

   _____

2. Qui lave les verres? (Marc et David)

   _____

3. Qui nettoie les toilettes? (Élisabeth et Stéphanie)

   _____

4. Qui fait les lits? (moi)

   _____

5. Qui sort les ordures? (Édouard)

   _____

6. Qui passe l'aspirateur? (Barbara)

   _____

7. Qui dépoussière les meubles? (Charles et Michèle)

   _____

8. Qui fait les carreaux? (Odile et François)

   _____

9. Qui récure les casseroles et les poêles? (Louis et Denis)

   _____

10. Et qui lave tous les parquets? (toi!)

   _____

**Activité 5**  **Tout est déjà fait.** Répondez aux questions de votre ami(e) sur les devoirs en employant le passé composé. Remplacez les compléments directs par des pronoms. Faites attention à l'accord du participe passé. Suivez le modèle.

> MODÈLE   Tu ne lis pas le chapitre douze?
> Je l'ai déjà lu.

1. Tu n'écris pas la composition?

   _____

2. Marc et Paul ne rédigent pas le contrat?

   _____

3. Catherine et toi, vous ne faites pas les problèmes de maths?

   _____

4. Lise n'apprend pas les poèmes par cœur?

   _____

5. Tu n'étudies pas la pièce de théâtre?

   _____

6. Christine ne fait pas l'expérience au laboratoire?

   _____

7. Olivier ne révise pas les leçons d'histoire?

   _____

8. Baudouin et Philippe ne regardent pas les œuvres d'art?

   _____

9. Tu n'écoutes pas les CD pour le cours d'espagnol?

   _____

10. Tu ne relis pas tes notes de philosophie?

    _____

## Indirect object pronouns

1. An indirect object is the person to whom or for whom an action is done. It is connected to its verb by the preposition **à**.

   | | |
   |---|---|
   | J'écris **à Jean**. | *I write (**to**) **John**.* |
   | Les élèves parlent **au professeur**. | *The students talk **to the teacher**.* |
   | Nous donnons des cadeaux **à nos amis**. | *We give gifts **to our friends**.* |

   The French indirect object pronouns refer only to people. **Lui** means either *to/for him* or *to/for her*, depending on its context.

   | | SINGULAR | PLURAL |
   |---|---|---|
   | **FIRST PERSON** | me | nous |
   | **SECOND PERSON** | te | vous |
   | **THIRD PERSON** | lui | leur |

2. The indirect object pronouns follow the same rules for position as the direct object pronouns.

   | | |
   |---|---|
   | Les parents de cet enfant ont de la chance. Il **leur** obéit toujours. | *That child's parents are lucky. He always obeys **them**.* |
   | C'est vrai. Il ne **leur** désobéit jamais. | *That's true. He never disobeys **them**.* |
   | Ce chapeau **vous** va très bien. Il **vous** plaît? | *That hat looks very good **on you**. Do **you** like it?* |
   | Et Louis? Il avait faim? Oui. Je **lui** ai préparé un sandwich. | *What about Louis? Was he hungry? Yes. I made a sandwich **for him**.* |
   | Tu vas téléphoner aux parents? Oui. Je vais **leur** téléphoner ce soir. S'ils ne sont pas là, tu peux **leur** laisser un message au répondeur. | *Are you going to call Mom and Dad? I'm going to call **them** this evening. If they're not there, you can leave **them** a message on the answering machine.* |

3. Several verbs that take a direct object, or that have other constructions in English, take indirect objects in French.

| | |
|---|---|
| **aller bien à quelqu'un** *to look nice on someone* | **obéir à quelqu'un** *to obey someone* |
| **convenir à quelqu'un** *to suit someone, be convenient for someone* | **plaire à quelqu'un** *to please someone* |
| | **répondre à quelqu'un** *to answer someone* |
| **désobéir à quelqu'un** *to disobey someone* | **ressembler à quelqu'un** *to look like someone* |
| **nuire à quelqu'un** *to harm, hurt someone* | **téléphoner à quelqu'un** *to call, phone someone* |

4. Many verbs take two objects: a direct object (a thing) and an indirect object (a person).

| | |
|---|---|
| **apporter quelque chose à quelqu'un** *to bring something to someone* | **offrir quelque chose à quelqu'un** *to give something to someone (as a gift)* |
| **demander quelque chose à quelqu'un** *to ask something of/from someone* | **passer quelque chose à quelqu'un** *to pass something to someone* |
| **dire quelque chose à quelqu'un** *to tell/say something to someone* | **permettre quelque chose à quelqu'un** *to allow someone to do something* |
| **donner quelque chose à quelqu'un** *to give something to someone* | **prêter quelque chose à quelqu'un** *to lend something to someone* |
| **envoyer quelque chose à quelqu'un** *to send something to someone* | **promettre quelque chose à quelqu'un** *to promise someone to do something* |
| **expliquer quelque chose à quelqu'un** *to explain something to someone* | **rendre quelque chose à quelqu'un** *to give something back to someone* |
| **laisser quelque chose à quelqu'un** *to leave something for someone* | **vendre quelque chose à quelqu'un** *to sell something to someone* |
| **montrer quelque chose à quelqu'un** *to show something to someone* | |

> **NOTE**
>
> In **présenter quelqu'un à quelqu'un** (*to introduce someone to someone*), both the direct and the indirect objects refer to people.
>
> Je **lui** ai présenté **Nicole**.      *I introduced **Nicole** to **him/her**.*
> Je **l'**ai présenté(e) à **Nicole**.      *I introduced **him/her** to **Nicole**.*

5. With several French verbs, **à** is the equivalent of the English *from*. Thus, sentences such as **Je lui ai acheté la voiture** mean either *I bought the car from him/her* or *I bought the car for him/her*, depending on the context.

| | |
|---|---|
| **acheter quelque chose à quelqu'un** *to buy something for/from someone* | **enlever quelque chose à quelqu'un** *to take something away from someone* |
| **arracher quelque chose à quelqu'un** *to snatch something from someone* | **louer quelque chose à quelqu'un** *to rent something from someone* |
| **cacher quelque chose à quelqu'un** *to hide something from someone* | **prendre quelque chose à quelqu'un** *to take something from someone* |
| **emprunter quelque chose à quelqu'un** *to borrow something from someone* | **voler quelque chose à quelqu'un** *to steal something from someone* |

**Activité 6** **Oui et non.** Employez les mots entre parenthèses et un pronom complément d'objet indirect pour dire dans chaque cas ce qu'on ne fait pas. Suivez le modèle.

> MODÈLE  Je prête mon crayon à Luc. (mon stylo)
> Je ne lui prête pas mon stylo.

1. Nous donnons des conseils à nos voisins. (argent)

   _____

2. Annette me montre ses photos. (logiciels)

   _____

3. J'ai écrit une carte postale à mes cousins. (courriel)

   _____

4. Les Dufau vendent leur maison aux Masson. (voiture)

   _____

5. Je vais offrir une montre à ma petite amie. (collier)

   _____

6. Vous envoyez des dessins à votre frère. (affiches)

   _____

7. Mon chien m'apporte le journal. (mes pantoufles)

   _____

8. Il a donné son adresse au médecin. (son numéro de téléphone)

   _____

9. Le professeur a expliqué les problèmes à ses étudiants. (la méthode)

   _____

10. Je vais demander la voiture à mon père. (argent pour l'essence)

    _____

**Activité 7** **Ce qu'il faut faire.** Les employés d'un grand bureau demandent à leur chef ce qu'ils doivent faire aujourd'hui. Il leur répond avec l'expression **il faut** et un pronom complément d'objet indirect. Suivez le modèle pour savoir exactement ce qu'il leur dit.

> MODÈLE  Et pour nos clients en Tunisie? (envoyer le rapport)
> Il faut leur envoyer le rapport.

## Les affaires

**Vocabulaire**

l'**agence** (*f.*) *agency*
l'**annonce** (*f.*) *ad*
le/la **banquier(-ère)** *banker*
la **cargaison** *freight shipment*
la **facture** *invoice*
le/la **fournisseur(-se)** *supplier*
la **gamme** *range, line*
la **note** *bill*

le **produit** *product*
le **rapport** *report*
**régler la note** *to pay the bill, settle the account*
le/la **représentant(e)** *representative*
le/la **vendeur(-se)** *salesperson*

1. Et pour M. Delavigne? (écrire une lettre)

   _____

2. Et pour nos fournisseurs en Allemagne? (régler la dernière cargaison de marchandises)

   _____

3. Les Régnier n'ont pas encore réglé la facture. (envoyer la facture encore une fois)

   _____

4. M. Sarda a déjà appelé deux fois ce matin. (prêter trois cent mille euros)

   _____

5. L'agence Autos-Jour a téléphoné. (louer trois voitures et un camion)

   _____

6. Votre banquier a téléphoné. (emprunter un million d'euros)

   _____

7. La représentante du journal est arrivée. (montrer les nouvelles annonces)

   _____

8. Nos vendeurs vont arriver à onze heures. (présenter la nouvelle gamme de produits)

   _____

**Activité 8** **Conseils et recommandations.** Un groupe de copains parlent des camarades qui avaient besoin d'aide. Écrivez les solutions qu'ils ont trouvées en formant des phrases au passé composé avec des pronoms compléments d'objet indirect. Suivez le modèle.

> MODÈLE  Émile aimait bien mon ordinateur.
> tu accorder / une heure au clavier (*keyboard*)
> Tu lui as accordé une heure au clavier.

DEUXIÈME PARTIE

1. Marguerite ne pouvait pas aller à pied au lycée.
son père / prêter la voiture

_____

2. Albert a perdu sa montre.
nous / offrir une montre pour son anniversaire

_____

3. Monique ne comprenait pas ce texte.
moi, je / expliquer les idées du livre

_____

4. Richard et Serge voulaient jouer au football.
nous / demander de jouer avec nous

_____

5. Nathalie est malade et ne peut pas sortir.
vous / apporter des revues et des journaux

_____

6. Sylvie et Maude voulaient étudier pour l'examen d'histoire.
nous / rendre les livres que nous leur avions empruntés

_____

7. Mathieu a été absent hier. Il a manqué tous ses cours.
nous / montrer nos notes

_____

8. Hélène et Robert sont maintenant en Corse.
moi, je / envoyer une lettre

_____

9. Solange nous a écrit il y a deux semaines.
nous / répondre

_____

10. Alfred et Gilles ne savaient pas qu'il y a une fête vendredi.
nous / téléphoner

_____

## Pronoun y

1. A preposition of location (**à, en, dans, sur, sous, devant, derrière,** etc.), followed by a noun referring to a place or thing, can be replaced by the pronoun **y. Je** becomes **j'** before **y.**

| | |
|---|---|
| Vous allez tous **à Paris**? | _Are you all going **to Paris**?_ |
| Oui, nous **y** passons nos vacances. | _Yes, we're spending our vacation **there**._ |
| As-tu répondu **à sa lettre**? | _Have you answered **his letter**?_ |
| Oui. J'**y** ai déjà répondu. | _Yes. I have already answered **it**._ |

| | |
|---|---|
| Tu travailles **dans ce bureau**? | *Do you work **in this office**?* |
| Non, je n'**y** travaille plus. | *No, I don't work **there** anymore.* |
| | |
| Où est la monnaie? **Sur la table**? | *Where's the change? **On the table**?* |
| Oui. J'**y** ai laissé l'argent. | *Yes. I left the money **there**.* |

2. The pronoun **y** may refer to an entire phrase, clause, or idea, and sometimes **y** has no precise English equivalent. The pronoun **y** follows the rules for position that also govern direct and indirect object pronouns.

| | |
|---|---|
| Il est difficile de traverser la rue parce qu'il y a tant de voitures. | *It's hard to cross the street because there are so many cars.* |
| Tu as raison. Il faut **y** prendre garde. **(y = aux voitures)** | *You're right. We have to be careful (of them).* **(prendre garde à quelque chose)** |
| | |
| Alice n'aime pas son travail. | *Alice doesn't like her work.* |
| Elle doit **y** renoncer. **(y = à son travail)** | *She ought to quit.* **(renoncer à quelque chose)** |
| | |
| Les idées de cet auteur sont difficiles. | *This author's ideas are difficult.* |
| J'**y** réfléchis beaucoup. **(y = aux idées)** | *I think **about them** a lot.* **(réfléchir à quelque chose)** |

3. The reflexive pronouns **me, te,** and **se** elide to **m', t',** and **s'** before **y**.

| | |
|---|---|
| Tu **t'**es déjà mise **à travailler**, Christine? | *Have you already started working, Christine?* |
| Non, je ne **m'y** suis pas encore mise. | *No, I haven't started yet.* |

**Activité 9**   **Jamais de la vie!** Les gens ne font jamais ces activités. Dites-le en employant le pronom **y.**

> MODÈLE   Tu vas souvent à Lille?
> Non, je n'y vais jamais.

1. Lucie travaille au sous-sol?

_____

2. Maurice et François étudient à la terrasse du café du coin?

_____

3. Ton petit ami attend devant le cinéma?

_____

4. Vos parents passent leurs vacances au bord de la mer?

_____

5. Vous achetez à manger dans cette charcuterie?

_____

6. Les enfants jouent derrière l'immeuble?

_____

7. Les voisins se réunissent sur le toit?

_____

8. Tu laisses tes livres sur l'escalier?

_____

**Activité 10**  **Conseillez et rassurez.** Votre amie exprime ses doutes. Employez l'expression **il faut,** le pronom **y** et le verbe ou l'expression entre parenthèses pour lui donner un conseil ou pour la rassurer. Suivez le modèle.

> MODÈLE   J'ai du mal à me concentrer sur le livre de philosophie.
> (faire attention)
> Il faut y faire attention.

1. Je n'ai pas encore fait de projets de vacances. (penser)

_____

2. Je suis inquiète au sujet de mon avenir. (réfléchir)

_____

3. On dit que les rues de cette ville sont dangereuses la nuit. (prendre garde)

_____

4. Notre plan ne pourra pas réussir. (renoncer)

_____

5. Cette matière m'ennuie. C'est pour ça que mes notes sont mauvaises. (s'intéresser)

_____

6. Je ne sais pas si je pourrai devenir médecin. (rêver)

_____

7. J'ai des doutes sur ses explications. (croire)

_____

8. On m'attend au bureau du professeur. (aller)

_____

## Pronoun en

1. An indefinite or a partitive article plus a noun can be replaced by the pronoun **en. En** often means *some* or *any* in this context.

| | |
|---|---|
| Tu veux **du jus**? | *Do you want **any juice**?* |
| Non, je n'**en** veux pas. | *No, I don't want **any**.* |
| Connaissez-vous **des professeurs** ici? | *Do you know **any teachers** here?* |
| Oui, j'**en** connais. | *Yes, I know **some**.* |

2. The pronoun **en** may replace nouns used with expressions of quantity or numbers. In such cases, **en** may have no direct English equivalent.

| | |
|---|---|
| Tu as beaucoup **de travail**? | *Do you have a lot of **work**?* |
| J'**en** ai trop. (**en = de travail**) | *I have too much.* |

| | |
|---|---|
| Robert a des frères? | *Does Robert have any brothers?* |
| Oui, il **en** a trois. | *Yes, he has three (**brothers**).* |

| | |
|---|---|
| Tu n'as que trois cents euros? | *You have only three hundred euros?* |
| J'**en** ai dépensé deux cents. | *I spent two hundred (**euros**).* |

3. **En** may replace the construction **de** (*preposition*) + *noun or infinitive*, but only when the noun is inanimate (otherwise, a disjunctive pronoun would be necessary; for more on this, see p. 209).

| | |
|---|---|
| Pauline est-elle revenue **de France**? | *Has Pauline come back **from France**?* |
| Elle **en** revient jeudi. | *She's coming back (**from there**) Thursday.* (**revenir de quelque part**) |

| | |
|---|---|
| Les étés passés en Bretagne étaient merveilleux, n'est-ce pas? | *The summers spent in Brittany were wonderful, weren't they?* |
| Oui. Je m'**en** souviens. (**en = des étés**) | *Yes. I remember **them**.* (**se souvenir de quelque chose**) |

| | |
|---|---|
| Ton fils a-t-il peur **de nager dans l'océan**? | *Is your son afraid **to swim in the ocean**?* |
| Oui. Il **en** a peur. | *Yes. He's afraid (**to do that**).* (**avoir peur de [*faire*] quelque chose**) |

4. The pronoun **en** follows the same rules for position as direct and indirect object pronouns. In compound tenses, the past participle does not agree with **en**.

**Activité 11**   **Rectification.** Votre ami(e) se trompe sur les quantités. Corrigez ce qu'il/elle vous dit avec les chiffres donnés et le pronom **en.** Suivez le modèle.

> MODÈLE   Paulette a deux frères, n'est-ce pas? (quatre)
> Non, elle en a quatre.

1. Il y a vingt élèves dans cette classe, n'est-ce pas? (trente-deux)

   _____

2. Stéphane gagne trois cents euros par semaine, n'est-ce pas? (quatre cents)

   _____

3. Vous avez cent vingt pages à lire, n'est-ce pas? (deux cent cinquante)

   _____

4. Nous avons parcouru (*covered, traveled*) quatre cents kilomètres, n'est-ce pas? (trois cents)

   _____

5. Tu as eu soixante-dix dollars d'amende (*fine*), n'est-ce pas? (quatre-vingt-dix)

_____

6. Leur nouvelle maison a trois salles de bains, n'est-ce pas? (cinq)

_____

7. Nous allons acheter dix biftecks, n'est-ce pas? (quinze)

_____

8. Tu veux une douzaine d'œufs, n'est-ce pas? (deux douzaines)

_____

**Activité 12** **C'est déjà fait.** Répondez aux questions de votre ami(e) sur ce qui se passe à l'université en lui disant que tout s'est déjà accompli. Utilisez le pronom **en** dans chaque cas. Suivez le modèle.

> MODÈLE    Pierre va-t-il acheter des livres?
> Il en a déjà acheté.

1. Chantal et Odile comptent-elles suivre des cours de chimie?

_____

2. L'étudiant va-t-il se plaindre de ses classes?

_____

3. Est-ce que Bernard va être accablé de travail?

_____

4. M. Dumarier va-t-il se charger des inscriptions?

_____

5. Est-ce que Mme Martel va jouer du piano?

_____

6. François va-t-il se mêler des affaires des autres étudiants?

_____

7. Est-ce que Michel compte faire du japonais?

_____

8. Anne-Marie va-t-elle demander des conseils sur son programme d'études?

_____

9. Est-ce que Sylvie va revenir de la faculté?

_____

10. Le professeur Froissard va-t-il donner des devoirs?

_____

# Double object pronouns

When a sentence contains more than one object pronoun, the pronouns appear in the following order.

| me | | | | | | | |
|---|---|---|---|---|---|---|---|
| te | | le | | lui | | | |
| se | *before* | la | *before* | leur | *before* | y | *before* | **en** |
| nous | | les | | | | | |
| vous | | | | | | | |

The direct object pronouns **le** and **la** elide before **y** and **en.** However, the indirect object pronoun **lui** never elides. Double object pronouns follow the rules for position that govern single object pronouns.

| Est-ce que ton père te prête la voiture? | *Does your father lend you the car?* |
|---|---|
| Non, il ne **me la** prête jamais. | *No, he never lends **it to me.*** |
| | |
| Tu vas donner les cadeaux aux enfants? | *Are you going to give the gifts to the children?* |
| Oui, je vais **les leur** donner. | *Yes, I'm going to give **them to them.*** |
| | |
| Marcelle a sa calculatrice? | *Does Marcelle have her calculator?* |
| Oui, je **la lui** ai rendue hier. | *Yes, I returned **it to her** yesterday.* |
| | |
| Nos cousins ont besoin d'argent. | *Our cousins need money.* |
| Nous pouvons **leur en** envoyer. | *We can send **them some.*** |
| | |
| C'est une très belle avenue. | *This is a very beautiful avenue.* |
| Oui, nous **nous y** promenons souvent. | *Yes, we often take a walk **here.*** |

**Activité 13** **Ce qu'il faut faire.** Employez les verbes entre parenthèses et deux pronoms compléments d'objet pour dire ce qu'il faut faire (ou ce qu'on va faire) dans chaque cas. Suivez le modèle.

> MODÈLE   Odile ne sait pas l'adresse de Philippe. (je / aller / dire)
> Je vais la lui dire.

1. Marie-France ne reçoit pas de lettres. (nous / devoir / écrire)

   _____

2. Serge veut voir tes notes de physique. (je / aller / prêter)

   _____

3. Ousmane a besoin de son manuel de chimie. (nous / devoir / rendre)

   _____

4. Rachelle prend le déjeuner au bistrot d'en face. (tu / pouvoir / retrouver)

   _____

5. Suzanne et Ghislaine veulent voir tes photos. (je / avoir l'intention de / montrer)

   _____

6. Yves et Marc cherchent des affiches. (il faut / donner)

_____

7. Je ne comprends pas ces mots. (je / aller / expliquer)

_____

8. Nous voudrions du parfum de France. (Marguerite / pouvoir / rapporter)

_____

9. Les enfants adorent le jardin. (vous / pouvoir / amener)

_____

10. La vie ici n'est pas facile. (nous / devoir / s'habituer)

_____

11. Je voudrais du sel. (je / aller / passer)

_____

12. Ils ont besoin de ce logiciel. (il faut / apporter)

_____

**Activité 14**　**Mais si!** Votre ami se trompe. Les choses qui, selon lui, n'arrivent pas sont déjà arrivées. Dites-le-lui en employant le passé composé et deux pronoms compléments d'objet. Suivez le modèle.

> MODÈLE　Sabine n'offre jamais de cadeaux à ses frères.
> Mais si! Elle leur en a déjà offert.

1. Albert ne sert jamais de boissons à ses invités.

_____

2. Tu ne donnes jamais de conseils à Philippe.

_____

3. Serge et Robert ne s'opposent pas au programme politique de notre parti.

_____

4. Marc et Justine ne se servent jamais de cet ordinateur.

_____

5. Louise et toi, vous ne vous rendez pas compte du problème.

_____

6. Olivier ne nous rend jamais les choses qu'il nous emprunte.

_____

7. Cette femme ne lit jamais de livres à ses enfants.

_____

(continued)

8. Ces parents n'enseignent pas le français à leurs enfants.

   _____

9. Ce professeur ne propose jamais de thèmes intéressants à ses étudiants.

   _____

10. Toi, tu ne m'envoies jamais de cartes postales.

   _____

11. Tu ne me permets jamais de bonbons en semaine.

   _____

12. Ils ne nous promettent jamais leur soutien.

   _____

**Activité 15** **Proposons des solutions.** Employez **si** suivi de l'imparfait, les mots entre parenthèses, et deux pronoms compléments d'objet pour proposer des solutions aux problèmes posés par votre ami(e). Suivez le modèle.

> MODÈLE   Nathalie n'a pas de romans en français. (envoyer deux ou trois)
> Si on lui en envoyait deux ou trois?

1. Maurice et Frédéric admirent nos CD. (prêter)

   _____

2. Monique est à la bibliothèque de Beaubourg. (retrouver)

   _____

3. Madeleine et Lise n'ont pas la voiture pour aller au travail aujourd'hui. (amener)

   _____

4. Jean-Paul aime les croissants que nous faisons. (apporter une demi-douzaine)

   _____

5. Agnès sort du bureau à cinq heures. (aller attendre)

   _____

6. Cette rue a l'air dangereux. (s'éloigner)

   _____

7. Nous avons une lettre à écrire et cet ordinateur est disponible. (se servir pour la rédiger)

   _____

8. Philippe et son frère nous ont demandé le journal d'hier. (donner)

   _____

9. Eugénie a tous nos livres d'histoire. (demander)

   _____

10. Charles et sa femme s'intéressent à notre télé. (vendre)

   _____

# Restrictions on the use of object pronouns

The object pronouns **me, te, nous, vous, lui, leur** (which all refer solely to animate nouns) cannot follow a reflexive pronoun. The preposition **à** followed by a disjunctive pronoun must be used instead. If the noun is inanimate, **y** is used. In addition, **en** cannot replace **de** + *animate noun* when **de** is a preposition that is part of the verbal expression, as it is in **avoir peur de** and **s'approcher de.** Instead, disjunctive pronouns must be used after **de.** Compare the following examples.

---

Je me fie **à ce médecin.** → Je me fie **à lui.**
Je me fie **à ce dictionnaire.** → Je m'**y** fie.

J'ai peur **de nos professeurs.** → J'ai peur **d'eux.***
J'ai peur **des avions.** → J'**en** ai peur.

Nous nous approchons **de notre père.** → Nous nous approchons **de lui.**
Nous nous approchons **de la ville.** → Nous nous **en** approchons.

---

**Activité 16** **Oui, bien sûr.** Répondez aux questions de votre ami(e) à l'affirmatif. Remplacez les mots en italique par le pronom convenable.

> MODÈLE  Est-ce que vous vous fiez *à votre mémoire*?
> Oui, nous nous y fions.

1. Est-ce que tu te fies *à tes amis*?

   _____

2. Est-ce que Paulette s'intéresse *à la géologie*?

   _____

3. Est-ce que Jean-Luc s'intéresse *à Paulette*?

   _____

4. Est-ce que le petit Victor a honte *de ce qu'il a fait*?

   _____

5. Est-ce que son père a honte *du petit Victor*?

   _____

6. Est-ce que tu te souviens *de ton séjour en Espagne*?

   _____

7. Est-ce que tu te souviens *des gens que tu y as connus*?

   _____

*(continued)*

---

*In formal French, **en** can only replace **des** + *animate noun* when **des** is a partitive or indefinite article, as in: Je connais **des Québecois.** → J'**en** connais. However, in informal spoken French, **en** is often used to replace animate nouns following the preposition **de** + **les** (**des**): J'ai peur **des criminels.** → J'**en** ai peur. Nous nous souvenons bien **des amis de Pierre.** → Nous nous **en** souvenons bien.

8. Est-ce que le détective doute *de l'explication de M. Arnaud*?

   _____

9. Est-ce que le détective se doute *de M. Arnaud*?

   _____

10. Est-ce que vous avez peur *des voyages en bateau*?

    _____

## Object pronouns in affirmative commands

1. In affirmative commands, object pronouns follow the verb and are joined to it with a hyphen. **Me** and **te** become **moi** and **toi** after an imperative form.

   | | |
   |---|---|
   | Dites-**nous** ce qui est arrivé. | *Tell **us** what happened.* |
   | Les journaux? Mettez-**les** sur la table. | *The newspapers? Put **them** on the table.* |
   | Aide-**moi**! | *Help **me**!* |

   Although the final **-s** of the **tu** form of **-er** verbs is dropped in the imperative, it is restored (and pronounced) before **y** and **en** in affirmative commands.

   | | |
   |---|---|
   | J'ai envie de manger des pommes. Achète**s-en**. | *I feel like eating apples. Buy **some**.* |
   | J'aime mes vacances en Bretagne. Reste**s-y** plus longtemps. | *I love my vacation in Brittany. Stay **there** longer.* |

2. When an affirmative command contains two object pronouns, the pronouns take the order shown in the following chart. **Moi + en** becomes **m'en** and **toi + en** becomes **t'en**.

   | | | | | | | | | |
   |---|---|---|---|---|---|---|---|---|
   | | | | | **moi** | | | | |
   | Verb | | | | **toi** | | | | |
   | in | | **le** | | **lui** | | | | |
   | imperative | *before* | **la** | *before* | **nous** | *before* | **y** | *before* | **en** |
   | form | | **les** | | **vous** | | | | |
   | | | | | **leur** | | | | |

   | | |
   |---|---|
   | Je viens de recevoir mes photos. Montre-**les-moi**. | *I've just received my photos. Show **them to me**.* |
   | Regarde, j'ai du jus de fruits. Donne-**m'en**. J'ai très soif. | *Look, I have some fruit juice. Give **me some**. I'm very thirsty.* |
   | Je peux me servir de ton stylo? Volontiers. Sers-**t'en**. | *May I use your pen? Gladly. Use **it**.* |

   In affirmative commands, **y** is replaced by **là** or **là-bas** only after **me/moi, te/toi, le, la** *and* provided that **y** refers to a place.

   | | |
   |---|---|
   | Tu vas être à la bibliothèque? Oui, attends-**moi là-bas**. | *Are you going to be at the library? Yes, wait for **me there**.* |

**Activité 17** **On donne des ordres.** Répondez aux questions avec l'impératif des verbes entre parenthèses. Remplacez les substantifs des questions par des pronoms compléments d'objet.

> MODÈLE    Ces bonbons ont l'air délicieux. (tu / prendre / plusieurs)
> Prends-en plusieurs.

1. Je ne veux plus rester ici. (tu / s'en aller)

   _____

2. Veux-tu que je te dépose devant la faculté? (tu / déposer)

   _____

3. J'ai de la salade. En veux-tu? (tu / donner)

   _____

4. Nous n'aimons pas le programme du nouveau directeur. (vous / s'opposer)

   _____

5. Ces gens me rendent nerveux. (tu / s'éloigner)

   _____

6. Je vais m'habiller dans la salle de bains. Ça va? (tu / s'habiller)

   _____

7. Devons-nous nous arrêter à côté du parc? (vous / s'arrêter)

   _____

8. Qui va s'occuper du dîner? (tu / se charger)

   _____

9. Je crois que j'ai votre disquette. (vous / rendre)

   _____

10. Ils veulent des olives? (vous / passer)

    _____

**Activité 18** **En français.** Exprimez les idées suivantes en français.

1. *I asked him for his literature book, but he didn't give it to me.*

   _____

2. *He doesn't have his car anymore because someone stole it from him.*

   _____

3. *These people are interested in your house. Sell it to them. (formal)*

   _____

*(continued)*

4. *We asked (**poser**) the teacher questions about the lesson, but he didn't answer them.*

_____

5. *I looked for French newspapers and found two. I'll show them to you (familiar).*

_____

6. *She's on the third floor (**deuxième étage**). Go up (there) and you'll see her. (familiar)*

_____

7. *The children were playing on the roof, but they have come down (from there).*

_____

8. *You've made soup. Bring (**apporter**) me some and I'll taste (**essayer**) it.*

_____

**Activité 19**  **Activité orale.** Parlez avec un(e) camarade de classe au sujet des choses que vous avez et des plats que vous aimez manger. Formez des questions pour évoquer des réponses qui contiennent un ou deux pronoms compléments d'objet.

# 17 Possessive and demonstrative adjectives and pronouns

## Possessive adjectives

1. Possession in French is expressed by the preposition **de. De** is repeated before each noun that represents a possessor.

   | | |
   |---|---|
   | la maison **de** mon oncle | *my uncle's house* |
   | les cahiers **de** Janine et **d'**Alice | *Janine's and Alice's notebooks* |

   Possessive adjectives in French agree in gender and number with the nouns they modify.

   | BEFORE MASCULINE SINGULAR NOUNS | |
   |---|---|
   | **mon** vélo | **notre** vélo |
   | **ton** vélo | **votre** vélo |
   | **son** vélo | **leur** vélo |

   | BEFORE FEMININE SINGULAR NOUNS | |
   |---|---|
   | **ma** cassette | **notre** cassette |
   | **ta** cassette | **votre** cassette |
   | **sa** cassette | **leur** cassette |

   | BEFORE ALL PLURAL NOUNS | | | |
   |---|---|---|---|
   | **mes** vélos, | **mes** cassettes | **nos** vélos, | **nos** cassettes |
   | **tes** vélos, | **tes** cassettes | **vos** vélos, | **vos** cassettes |
   | **ses** vélos, | **ses** cassettes | **leurs** vélos, | **leurs** cassettes |

2. The possessive adjectives **son, sa, ses** may mean *his, her,* or *its,* depending on the possessor. The form of the adjective agrees with the noun possessed, not with the gender of the possessor.

   | | |
   |---|---|
   | Marie a **son** vélo et Pierre a **sa** moto. | *Marie has **her** bike and Pierre has **his** motorcycle.* |

3. Before a feminine noun beginning with a vowel or a mute **h,** the adjectives **mon, ton, son** replace **ma, ta, sa.**

   **mon** adresse  **ton** école  **son** histoire

4. To emphasize or clarify a possessor, French uses the preposition **à,** followed by a disjunctive pronoun.

   | | |
   |---|---|
   | Monique et Philippe ont pris sa voiture. | *Monique and Philippe took his/her car.* |
   | Sa voiture **à lui** ou sa voiture **à elle**? | *His car or **her** car?* |

| Mon ordinateur **à moi** est plus rapide que leur ordinateur **à eux**. | *My computer is faster than **their** computer.* |

5. The word **propre** (*own*) may also be used to add emphasis.

| Je l'ai vu de mes **propres** yeux. | *I saw it with my **own** eyes.* |

**Activité 1**

**Voilà.** Utilisez **voilà** suivi d'un adjectif possessif pour signaler à votre ami(e) que les objets dont il/elle parle sont tout près. Suivez le modèle.

> MODÈLE  Tu as un livre?
> Oui. Voilà mon livre.

1. Édouard a une voiture?

   _____

2. Nous avons une calculatrice?

   _____

3. Nos copains ont des disques?

   _____

4. Tu as des cartes?

   _____

5. J'ai des documents?

   _____

6. Odile a un chien?

   _____

7. Marc et Chantal ont des billets?

   _____

8. Les étudiants ont une salle de réunion?

   _____

9. Jean-Marc a une adresse?

   _____

10. Nathalie a un ordinateur?

   _____

**Activité 2**

**C'est sûrement à quelqu'un d'autre.** Dites dans chaque cas que le véhicule n'est pas à la personne présupposée. Utilisez les adjectifs possessifs dans vos réponses, selon le modèle.

> MODÈLE  Le quatre-quatre est à vous?
> Non. Ce n'est pas mon quatre-quatre.

## Les véhicules

| | |
|---|---|
| **un bateau** *boat* | **une moto** *motorcycle* |
| **une bicyclette** *bicycle* | **un quatre-quatre (4x4)** |
| **un bus** *bus* | *sport-utility vehicle (SUV)* |
| **un camion** *truck* | **un vélomoteur** *moped* |
| **une caravane** *trailer camper* | **une voiture de sport** *sports car* |

1. La moto est à tes cousins?

_____

2. Les voitures de sport sont à ton frère?

_____

3. La caravane est à toi et à ta famille?

_____

4. Le vélomoteur est à Paul?

_____

5. Le bus est à la compagnie?

_____

6. Le camion est à vous deux?

_____

7. Le bateau est à toi?

_____

8. La bicyclette est à Yves?

_____

**Activité 3**  **À qui?** Vous entendez une phrase dans laquelle l'identité du possesseur est ambiguë. Demandez des précisions au moyen de la préposition **à** et d'un pronom disjoint. Suivez le modèle.

> MODÈLE   Christine et Maurice sont venus avec ses parents.
> Ses parents à elle ou ses parents à lui?

1. Voilà Jacques et Madeleine avec sa mère.

_____

2. Monsieur Lachaux et sa nouvelle épouse vivent avec ses enfants.

_____

3. Les garçons et les filles sont arrivés dans leur voiture.

_____

*Possessive and demonstrative adjectives and pronouns*  215

4. J'ai vu Olivier et Suzanne avec son cousin.

   _____

5. Quand je vous ai vus, Anne-Marie et toi, vous promeniez un chien.

   _____

6. Il veut revoir Paulette avant son départ.

   _____

**Activité 4** **Le bureau du club des étudiants en biologie.** Les étudiants en biologie ont organisé un club et l'université leur a donné une petite salle pour installer leur bureau. Annette raconte ce que chaque étudiant a apporté au bureau. Employez des adjectifs possessifs pour savoir ce qu'elle dit, en suivant le modèle.

> MODÈLE   Georges / enveloppes
> Georges a apporté ses enveloppes.

**Vocabulaire**

## Au bureau

**une affiche** _poster_
**un annuaire** _telephone book_
**un calendrier** _calendar_
**un dictionnaire scientifique**
   _science dictionary_

**un feutre** _felt-tipped pen_
**une imprimante** _printer_
**du papier à lettres** _stationery_
**un répondeur** _answering machine_

1. Roger / affiche

   _____

2. Louise et Simone / répondeur

   _____

3. Charles / feutres

   _____

4. Hélène / imprimante

   _____

5. le professeur de biologie / papier à lettres

   _____

6. Albert et vous / calendrier

   _____

7. moi / annuaire

   _____

8. toi / dictionnaire scientifique

   _____

# Possessive pronouns

1. The English possessive pronouns are *mine, yours, his, hers, ours, theirs.* Those forms are used to replace a phrase consisting of a possessive adjective and a noun. The French possessive pronouns consist of the definite article and a special possessive form. A possessive pronoun agrees in gender and number with the noun it replaces.

| MASCULINE SINGULAR | FEMININE SINGULAR | MASCULINE PLURAL | FEMININE PLURAL |
|---|---|---|---|
| le mien | la mienne | les miens | les miennes |
| le tien | la tienne | les tiens | les tiennes |
| le sien | la sienne | les siens | les siennes |
| le nôtre | la nôtre | les nôtres | |
| le vôtre | la vôtre | les vôtres | |
| le leur | la leur | les leurs | |

2. **Le sien, la sienne, les siens, les siennes** may mean *his, hers,* or *its,* depending on the possessor. The form of the pronoun agrees with the noun it replaces.

| | |
|---|---|
| Moi, j'ai **ma calculatrice,** mais Pierre n'a pas **la sienne.** | *I have **my calculator,** but Pierre doesn't have **his.*** |
| Nous aimons **notre quartier,** mais elle préfère **le sien.** | *We like **our neighborhood,** but she prefers **hers.*** |

3. The articles **le** and **les** of the possessive pronouns contract with **à** and **de.**

| | |
|---|---|
| Tu penses à mon problème? | *Are you thinking about my problem?* |
| Non. Je pense **au mien.** | *No. I'm thinking **about mine.*** |
| | |
| Elle se souvient de nos idées? | *Does she remember our ideas?* |
| Non. Elle se souvient **des siennes.** | *No. She remembers **hers.*** |

**Activité 5** **On a tout laissé à l'amphi (*lecture hall*).** Employez un pronom possessif dans chaque cas pour dire que tout le monde a laissé ses affaires à l'université. Suivez le modèle.

> MODÈLE  toi / calculatrice / moi
> Toi, tu as ta calculatrice, mais moi, j'ai laissé la mienne à l'amphi.

1. moi / cahier / Françoise

_____

2. nous / stylos / nos copains

_____

3. toi / carte d'entrée / le professeur

_____

4. David / sac à dos / Christine

_____

5. Odile / bouquins / moi

_____

(continued)

6. vous / dictionnaire / nous

_____

7. mes amis / agendas / vous

_____

8. les étudiants / crayons / toi

_____

**Activité 6** **Ici et en bas.** La moitié des choses cherchées est ici, l'autre moitié est en bas (*downstairs*). Employez des pronoms possessifs pour le dire, comme dans le modèle.

> MODÈLE Je cherche tes livres et les livres de Jean-Pierre.
> Les miens sont ici, les siens sont en bas.

1. Je cherche mes copies et les copies des élèves.

_____

2. Je cherche votre carte de crédit et la carte de crédit de Renée.

_____

3. Je cherche notre carnet de chèques et le carnet de chèques de Rémi.

_____

4. Je cherche tes photographies et les photographies du professeur.

_____

5. Je cherche mes clés et les clés de nos amis.

_____

6. Je cherche mon manteau et le manteau de Jacqueline.

_____

**Activité 7** **C'est le mien.** Répondez aux questions suivantes avec la préposition qui est dans la question et le pronom possessif qui y correspond. Suivez le modèle.

> MODÈLE Avec quel professeur parles-tu?
> Avec le mien.

1. À quels amis téléphones-tu?

_____

2. Dans quel laboratoire travaillent-ils?

_____

3. De quelles clarinettes jouez-vous, vous deux?

_____

4. À quelle tragédie pense-t-il?

_____

5. De quelles affaires s'occupe-t-elle?

_____

6. De quel stylo vous servez-vous?

_____

## Demonstrative adjectives

In English, a demonstrative adjective points out a specific person or thing (*this* book, *that* story, *these* cassettes, *those* stores). In French, however, the demonstrative adjective by itself does not distinguish between *this* and *that*.

The French demonstrative adjective has four forms. Each form agrees with the noun it modifies.

|  | **MASCULINE** | | **FEMININE** | |
| --- | --- | --- | --- | --- |
| **SINGULAR** | **ce** crayon | *this/that pencil* | **cette** table | *this/that table* |
|  | **cet** homme | *this/that man* | | |
| **PLURAL** | **ces** crayons | *these/those pencils* | **ces** tables | *these/those tables* |

**NOTE**  Before a masculine singular noun beginning with a vowel or a mute **h,** the form **cet** is used.

To distinguish between *this* and *that,* French adds **-ci** to a noun to mean *this* or *these* and **-là** to a noun to mean *that* or *those*. These suffixes are used mainly for emphasis or contrast.

Votre classe lit **ce** livre-**ci** ou **ce** livre-**là**?
*Is your class reading **this** book or **that** book?*

Nous lisons **ce** livre-**ci. Ces** romans-**là** sont pour l'année prochaine.
*We're reading **this** book. **Those** novels are for next year.*

**Activité 8**  **Au rayon d'informatique.** Julie cherche un nouvel ordinateur et des accessoires. Elle demande au vendeur le prix de tout ce qu'elle voit. Écrivez ce qu'elle dit avec des adjectifs démonstratifs comme dans le modèle.

> MODÈLE   moniteur
> Vous pouvez me dire le prix de ce moniteur, s'il vous plaît?

**Vocabulaire**

### L'ordinateur

**le clavier** *keyboard*
**le disque dur** *hard drive*
**la disquette** *disquette*
**le lecteur de CD-ROM** *CD-ROM drive*

**le logiciel** *software package*
**la souris** *mouse*
**l'unité de disque** (*f.*) *disk drive*

1. ordinateur

   _____

2. unité de disque

   _____

3. disquettes

   _____

4. logiciel

   _____

5. lecteur de CD-ROM

   _____

6. disque dur

   _____

7. clavier

   _____

8. souris

   _____

**Activité 9**  **Préférences.**  Utilisez l'adjectif démonstratif convenable avec le suffixe **-là** pour indiquer quel objet on préfère dans chaque cas.

> MODÈLE   Tu aimes la cravate de Jacques?
> Oui, mais je préfère cette cravate-là.

1. Les étudiants aiment les livres d'histoire?

   _____

2. Tu aimes l'anorak de Fabien?

   _____

3. Germaine aime le chapeau de Colette?

   _____

4. Ta copine et toi, vous aimez les bijoux de Mme Deschamps?

   _____

5. Les voisins aiment leur appartement?

   _____

6. Tu aimes les quartiers du centre?

   _____

7. Tu aimes l'immeuble où habite Jean-Claude?

   _____

**Choisissez!** Vous travaillez au rayon de vêtements d'un grand magasin. Utilisez les adjectifs démonstratifs suivis des suffixes **-ci** et **-là** pour demander des précisions aux clients quand ils veulent voir quelque chose. Suivez le modèle.

> MODÈLE   Je voudrais voir le foulard, s'il vous plaît.
> Ce foulard-ci ou ce foulard-là?

1. Montrez-moi le pantalon, s'il vous plaît.

   _____

2. Je pourrais voir l'imperméable, s'il vous plaît?

   _____

3. Les chaussettes que vous avez derrière vous m'intéressent.

   _____

4. Voudriez-vous me montrer cette robe, s'il vous plaît?

   _____

5. Je voudrais essayer l'anorak, s'il vous plaît.

   _____

6. Un tee-shirt ferait mon affaire, s'il vous plaît.

   _____

7. Je voudrais voir les sandales, s'il vous plaît.

   _____

8. Vous me permettez d'essayer cette veste, s'il vous plaît?

   _____

## Demonstrative pronouns

1. Demonstrative pronouns in French (*this one, that one, the one; these, those, the ones*) agree with the nouns they refer to.

| | MASCULINE | FEMININE |
|---|---|---|
| **SINGULAR** | celui | celle |
| **PLURAL** | ceux | celles |

2. As with demonstrative adjectives, **-ci** and **-là** can be added to the noun to distinguish between *this/that* and *these/those*.

| | |
|---|---|
| Quel logiciel recommandez-vous? | *Which software package do you recommend?* |
| **Celui-ci** est plus utile que **celui-là**. | *This one is more useful than that one.* |
| Quelle est la différence entre ces imprimantes? | *What is the difference between these printers?* |
| **Celles-ci** sont plus chères que **celles-là**. | *These are more expensive than those.* |

*Demonstrative pronoun* + **-ci** and *demonstrative pronoun* + **-là** are also used to mean *the latter* and *the former*, respectively. The pronouns agree with the nouns they refer to. In French, *the latter* (**-ci**) precedes *the former* (**-là**).

| | |
|---|---|
| L'industrie et l'agriculture sont importantes en France. **Celle-ci** emploie moins d'ouvriers que **celle-là.** | *Industry and agriculture are important in France. **The latter** employs fewer workers than **the former.*** |

3. A demonstrative pronoun may be followed by the relative pronoun **qui** or **que** to mean *the one(s)*. The demonstrative pronoun may also be followed by **de** to signal possession.

| | |
|---|---|
| Quel livre a-t-il pris? **Celui qui** était sur la chaise? | *Which book did he take? **The one that** was on the chair?* |
| Oui, c'était **celui qu'**il cherchait. | *Yes. That was **the one that** he was looking for.* |
| Mais c'était **celui de mon frère.** | *But it was **my brother's.*** |
| J'ai lu les revues françaises—**celles qui** étaient sur votre bureau. | *I read the French magazines—**the ones that** were on your desk.* |
| **Celles de** la nouvelle étudiante française? | *The new **French student's**?* |
| Oui. **Celles qu'**elle a apportées de France. | *Yes. **The ones that** she brought from France.* |

4. The pronouns **ceci** (*this*) and **cela** (*that*) refer to situations rather than to specific nouns. In modern French, **cela** (or **ça** in spoken language) tends to be used instead of **ceci.**

| | |
|---|---|
| Et avec **ceci**? | *Anything else?* |
| **Cela** suffit, merci. | ***That's** enough, thank you.* |
| Il a perdu son travail. C'est dur, **ça.** | *He lost his job. **That's** a very difficult situation.* |
| Oui, mais c'est **ça,** la vie! | *Yes, but **that's** life!* |

**Activité 11**  **Les affaires qui traînent.** Formulez des échanges qui identifient les personnes à qui appartiennent les objets que les étudiants ont laissé traîner dans l'amphi (*lecture hall*). Suivez le modèle.

> MODÈLE  bonnet gris / Philippe / Stéphane
> Qui a oublié ce bonnet gris? Philippe?
> Non, je crois que c'est celui de Stéphane.

1. livre / Gisèle / Josette

   _____

   _____

2. stylo / Colin / Luc

   _____

   _____

3. chaussures / Fabien / Martin

_____

_____

4. gants / Julie / Hélène

_____

_____

5. cahiers / Eugénie et Colette / Élisabeth et Monique

_____

_____

6. calculatrice / Gérard / Paul

_____

_____

7. lunettes / Loïc / Thomas

_____

_____

**Activité 12**  **Quel bon goût!** Gabrielle aime tout ce que son amie Thérèse achète, possède, emploie, et ainsi de suite. Utilisez les pronoms démonstratifs et les verbes entre parenthèses pour voir ce qu'elle dit. Suivez le modèle.

> MODÈLE    Tu aimes les pulls en coton? (porter)
> Pas tellement. Mais j'aime celui que tu portes.

1. Tu aimes les petits pois? (préparer)

_____

2. Tu aimes la musique des années soixante? (jouer)

_____

3. Tu aimes les voitures allemandes? (conduire)

_____

4. Tu aimes la soupe à l'oignon? (servir)

_____

5. Tu aimes les lunettes de soleil? (porter)

_____

6. Tu aimes les spaghettis? (faire)

_____

7. Tu aimes les sandales? (acheter)

_____

# Relative pronouns and relative clauses

A relative clause describes a noun or pronoun mentioned in the main clause. A relative clause begins with a relative pronoun such as *who, whom, which,* or *that.* The noun that the relative pronoun refers to is called the *antecedent.* In the following examples, the relative clauses are in boldface.

| | |
|---|---|
| *the woman* **who** *studies a lot* | *Who* is the relative pronoun, *woman* is the antecedent. |
| *the students* **whom** *we helped* | *Whom* is the relative pronoun, *students* is the antecedent. |
| *the computer* **that** *I use* | *That* is the relative pronoun, *computer* is the antecedent. |

## The relative pronouns qui and que

1. In French, the relative pronouns **qui** and **que** are used for both people and things. **Qui** is used when the relative pronoun is the subject of the relative clause. **Que** is used when the relative pronoun is the direct object of the verb in the relative clause. In the following examples, the relative clauses are in boldface.

| | |
|---|---|
| la femme **qui** *étudie beaucoup* | **Qui** is the relative pronoun, subject of the verb **étudier.** |
| un ordinateur **qui** *est facile à utiliser* | **Qui** is the relative pronoun, subject of the verb **être.** |
| les étudiants **que** *nous avons aidés* | **Que** is the relative pronoun, direct object of the verb **aider.** |
| l'ordinateur **que** *j'ai utilisé* | **Que** is the relative pronoun, direct object of the verb **utiliser.** |

**NOTE** In relative clauses introduced by **qui,** the verb agrees with **qui,** which has the same person and number as the antecedent.

| | |
|---|---|
| les **amis qui vont** avec nous | *the friends* **who** *are going with us* |
| C'est **moi qui** vous le **dis.** | *I'm telling you.* |
| C'est **nous qui** le **savons.** | *We're the ones* **who** *know it.* |

2. Relative pronouns can never be omitted in French the way they often are in English.

| | |
|---|---|
| l'homme **que** je connais | *the man* (**whom**) *I know* |
| les articles **que** je lis | *the articles* (**that**) *I read* |

3. When the verb of the relative clause is in a compound tense conjugated with **avoir,** the past participle agrees with the relative pronoun **que,** which is a preceding direct object. The gender and number of **que** is determined by its antecedent.

   **les jeunes filles qu'**il a invité**es**     *the girls whom he invited*
   **la robe que** tu as mise                       *the dress you put on*

**NOTE**     The relative pronoun **que** becomes **qu'** before a vowel or a mute **h.**

4. When the verb of the relative clause is in a compound tense conjugated with **être,** the past participle agrees with the relative pronoun **qui** because **qui** is the subject of the verb in the relative clause. The antecedent determines the gender and number of **qui.**

   **les étudiantes qui** sont arrivé**es**     *the students who arrived*
   **l'assiette qui** est tombé**e**              *the plate that fell*

**Activité 1**     **Est-ce** *qui* **ou** *que*? Complétez les phrases suivantes avec **qui** ou **que.** Toutes les phrases ont quelque chose à voir avec le monde de l'université.

**Le cours de philo**

1. Voilà le professeur _____ enseigne le cours de philosophie.

2. C'est un cours _____ tout le monde aime bien.

3. Nous avons des lectures _____ sont très difficiles, mais passionnantes.

4. Les questions _____ le prof nous pose font réfléchir.

5. Voilà Jean-Claude. C'est lui _____ reçoit les meilleures notes en philo.

6. Il dit que c'est une matière _____ le passionne.

7. Notre professeur est un homme _____ Jean-Claude admire beaucoup.

**Le cours de chimie**

8. Ma meilleure amie est une fille _____ s'appelle Géraldine.

9. C'est quelqu'un _____ je connais depuis longtemps.

10. C'est le cours de chimie _____ nous intéresse le plus.

11. Géraldine et moi, nous faisons tous les problèmes _____ le prof nous donne à résoudre.

12. Notre professeur est une femme _____ a écrit plusieurs livres de chimie.

13. Géraldine et moi, nous avons acheté un des bouquins _____ elle a écrit.

(continued)

14. C'est un livre _____ est très utile pour l'étudiant.

15. C'est un livre _____ nous avons recommandé à tous nos amis.

16. Le prof de chimie est une femme _____ l'on respecte beaucoup.

**Activité 2** | **Des précisions.** Les propositions relatives, comme les adjectifs, servent à préciser, à identifier. Formez des propositions relatives pour mieux expliquer à votre ami(e) de qui ou de quoi il s'agit. Suivez les modèles.

> MODÈLES    Quel livre veux-tu? (Un livre est sur la table.)
> Le livre qui est sur la table.
>
> Quels gants est-ce Paulette va mettre? (Son petit ami lui a acheté des gants.)
> Les gants que son petit ami lui a achetés.

**Vocabulaire** 

## La santé

**agir** to work (*in reference to medicines*)
**le cabinet** *doctor's office*
**le centre diététique** *health food store*
**le comprimé** *tablet*
**conseiller** *to advise, recommend*
**la crème** *cream*
**donner le vertige à** *to make dizzy*

**l'infirmier(-ère)** *nurse*
**ordonner** *to prescribe*
**la pilule** *pill*
**la piqûre** *injection*
**le régime** *diet*
**le sirop pour la toux** *cough syrup*
**suivre un régime** *to follow a diet*
**le vertige** *dizziness*
**la vitamine** *vitamin*

1. Quel médecin est-ce que je dois aller voir? (Il a son cabinet dans ce bâtiment.)

   _____

2. Quels comprimés prends-tu? (Mon médecin m'a ordonné ces comprimés.)

   _____

3. Quel régime est-ce qu'il faut suivre? (Il a trouvé un régime au centre diététique.)

   _____

4. Quel sirop pour la toux agit vite? (J'ai laissé un sirop sur la table.)

   _____

5. Quelle piqûre t'a fait mal? (L'infirmière m'a fait une piqûre hier.)

   _____

6. Quelles pilules t'ont donné le vertige? (J'ai pris les pilules hier.)

   _____

7. Quelle crème utilises-tu pour la peau? (Le pharmacien m'a conseillé une crème.)

_____

8. Quelles vitamines prends-tu? (Les vitamines sont bonnes pour le cœur.)

_____

**Activité 3**    **Encore des précisions.** La personne qui parle emploie des propositions relatives pour identifier la personne ou la chose à laquelle elle fait allusion. Suivez les modèles.

> MODÈLES   Quel ordinateur?
> **a.** Olivier l'utilise.
> L'ordinateur qu'Olivier utilise.
> **b.** Il a beaucoup de mémoire.
> L'ordinateur qui a beaucoup de mémoire.

1. Quel professeur?

   **a.** Tous les étudiants l'adorent.

   _____

   **b.** Il enseigne le français et l'espagnol.

   _____

   **c.** Il vient de se marier.

   _____

   **d.** Mes parents le connaissent.

   _____

2. Quelle maison?

   **a.** Jeanne et Richard l'ont achetée.

   _____

   **b.** Elle a un jardin et une piscine.

   _____

   **c.** On l'a construite en 1975.

   _____

   **d.** Elle est en briques.

   _____

3. Quels cadeaux?

   **a.** Mon frère et moi, nous les avons reçus il y a une semaine.

   _____

   **b.** Mon oncle et ma tante nous les ont envoyés.

   _____

(continued)

**c.** Je te les ai montrés hier.

   _____

   **d.** Ils t'ont beaucoup plu.

   _____

4. Quel restaurant?

   **a.** Nos amis l'ont ouvert l'année dernière.

   _____

   **b.** Il a une ambiance alsacienne.

   _____

   **c.** Il a des nappes rouges.

   _____

   **d.** Beaucoup d'artistes le fréquentent.

   _____

5. Quel sénateur?

   **a.** Le peuple l'a élu l'année dernière.

   _____

   **b.** Il a promis de combattre l'inflation.

   _____

   **c.** Il est marié avec une journaliste.

   _____

   **d.** Les ouvriers le soutiennent.

   _____

## Relative pronouns preceded by à

1.  The relative pronoun **qui,** when it is preceded by the preposition **à,** refers only to people. There is no agreement of the past participle in compound tenses in such cases, since **à qui** represents the *indirect* object of the relative clause.

    | | |
    |---|---|
    | l'homme **à qui** je donne le livre | *the man I'm giving the book **to*** |
    | la femme **à qui** nous pensons | *the woman **that** we're thinking **of*** |
    | les étudiants **à qui** j'ai parlé | *the students **whom** I spoke **to*** |

2.  **Lequel** is the relative pronoun that refers primarily to things that are mentioned after a preposition. It agrees in gender and number with its antecedent.

    | | MASCULINE | FEMININE |
    |---|---|---|
    | **SINGULAR** | lequel | laquelle |
    | **PLURAL** | lesquels | lesquelles |

The preposition **à** combines with the forms of **lequel** as follows. The forms of **à** + **lequel** are used when the verb or expression of the relative clause requires the preposition **à** before an object.

|  | MASCULINE | FEMININE |
|---|---|---|
| **SINGULAR** | auquel | à laquelle |
| **PLURAL** | auxquels | auxquelles |

l'examen **auquel** j'ai réussi — *the test I passed* (**réussir à**)
la matière **à laquelle** je m'intéresse — *the subject I'm interested **in*** (**s'intéresser à**)

les bureaux **auxquels** vous téléphonez — *the offices you telephone* (**téléphoner à**)
les études **auxquelles** il s'applique — *the studies he applies himself **to*** (**s'appliquer à**)

**Activité 4**  **Continuons à préciser.** Formez des phrases qui ont des propositions relatives commençant par **à**. N'oubliez pas la différence de construction qu'il faut respecter entre les antécédents animés et inanimés.

> MODÈLE  Quel cours est bon? (J'ai assisté à un cours.)
> Le cours auquel j'ai assisté.

1. Avec quelle fille Roland va-t-il sortir? (Il pense à une fille tout le temps.)

   _____

2. Quelle lettre vas-tu me montrer? (J'ai répondu à cette lettre.)

   _____

3. Quel débat as-tu écouté? (Nos copains ont pris part à ce débat.)

   _____

4. De quelles habitudes le médecin parle-t-il? (Il faut renoncer à ces habitudes.)

   _____

5. Avec quel homme est-ce qu'elle s'est mariée? (Elle se fiait à cet homme.)

   _____

6. Quels clients sont venus? (Nous avons téléphoné à ces clients.)

   _____

7. Quels détails aimez-vous? (Vous avez veillé à ces détails.)

   _____

8. Quelles méthodes as-tu recommandées? (Je crois à ces méthodes.)

   _____

**Activité 5** **Quel drame!** Complétez les phrases suivantes avec le pronom relatif convenable. Toutes les phrases font allusion aux éléments d'une histoire d'amour entre Élisabeth et Antoine.

1. la lettre _____ Élisabeth a répondu

2. les parents _____ les deux jeunes gens n'ont pas obéi

3. le concert de rock _____ ils ont assisté

4. Georges, l'ami _____ Antoine se confiait

5. Odile, la fille _____ Antoine a connue dans la classe d'éducation civique

6. les rapports entre les deux _____ la jalousie d'Élisabeth a découragés

7. les conversations avec Odile _____ Antoine a dû renoncer

8. la querelle d'amour _____ Georges s'est mêlé

9. la mauvaise situation _____ l'intervention de Georges a remédié

10. le rapprochement _____ a eu lieu entre Élisabeth et Antoine

## Dont and relative pronouns preceded by de

The relative pronoun **dont** replaces the preposition **de** followed by a relative pronoun. **Dont** must immediately follow its antecedent and can refer to either people or things.

1. **Dont** is used when the verb or expression in the relative clause requires the preposition **de** before an object.

| | |
|---|---|
| un professeur **dont** je me souviens | a teacher (**whom**) I remember (**se souvenir de**) |
| les affaires **dont** il s'occupe | the matters **that** he's taking care of (**s'occuper de**) |
| les employés **dont** j'ai besoin | the employees **that** I need (**avoir besoin de**) |

2. **Dont** is used when **de** introduces a phrase that modifies another noun in the relative clause. (The English equivalent is usually *whose* or *of which*.)

| | |
|---|---|
| un étudiant **dont** je connais les parents | a student **whose** parents I know (**les parents de l'étudiant**) |
| une idée **dont** on comprend l'importance | an idea **whose** importance (the importance **of which**) we understand (**l'importance de l'idée**) |
| un auteur **dont** j'ai lu tous les livres | an author, all of **whose** books I have read (**tous les livres de l'auteur**) |

**NOTE**

Notice the word order in the clause introduced by **dont**: like the relative pronoun **que, dont** is immediately followed by a noun (or a subject pronoun) that functions as the subject of the relative clause.

3. When **dont** is used to express possession, the definite article is used in place of a possessive adjective.

| | |
|---|---|
| L'auteur a remporté plusieurs prix littéraires. | *The author has won several literary prizes.* |
| **Ses livres** sont passionnants. | ***His books** are fascinating.* |
| L'auteur dont **les livres** sont passionnants a remporté plusieurs prix littéraires. | *The author **whose books** are fascinating has won several literary prizes.* |

4. **Dont** is used with numbers and expressions of quantity.

| | |
|---|---|
| des articles **dont** j'ai lu **quelques-uns** | *articles, **some of which** I've read* (**quelques-uns des articles**) |
| des étudiants **dont une dizaine** sont français | *some students, **about ten of whom** are French* (**une dizaine des étudiants**) |
| trois hommes **dont deux** médecins | *three men, **of whom two** (are) doctors* (**deux des trois hommes**) |

5. **De qui** may also be used to refer to people, but **dont** is usually preferred.

| | |
|---|---|
| les étudiants **de qui** je parle ⎫ les étudiants **dont** je parle ⎭ | *the students **about whom** I'm speaking* |

6. **De + lequel** may also be used to refer to things, but **dont** is usually preferred.

| | MASCULINE | FEMININE |
|---|---|---|
| **SINGULAR** | duquel | de laquelle |
| **PLURAL** | desquels | desquelles |

| | |
|---|---|
| L'histoire **de laquelle** je me souviens est bonne. ⎫ L'histoire **dont** je me souviens est bonne. ⎭ | *The story **that** I remember is good.* |

7. After a compound preposition ending in **de** (such as **à cause de**) or a noun phrase ending in **de** (such as **dans la classe de**), **dont** must be replaced by **qui** (for people) or a form of **de + lequel** (for both things and people).

| | |
|---|---|
| **la gare près de laquelle** je travaille | *the station I work **near*** |
| **l'étudiante au sujet de qui** je vous ai parlé | *the student **about whom** I spoke to you* |
| **les voisins à cause de qui** nous avons dû déménager | *the neighbors **because of whom** we had to move* |

**Activité 6**  **De qui s'agit-il exactement?** Précisez la personne dont il s'agit en employant une proposition relative qui commence par **dont.** Dans chaque cas, l'équivalent en anglais commence par le mot *whose.*

> MODÈLE   Quel journaliste? (Tout le monde lit ses articles.)
> Le journaliste dont tout le monde lit les articles.

1. Quelle fille? (Sa mère est médecin.)

   _____

2. Quel ami? (Son oncle travaille au ministère.)

   _____

3. Quel sénateur? (Le pays entier a écouté son discours.)

   _____

4. Quels ouvriers? (Leur syndicat compte entreprendre une grève.)

   _____

5. Quels étudiants? (On a publié leur rapport.)

   _____

6. Quel professeur? (Son cours est toujours plein.)

   _____

7. Quelle infirmière? (Tout le monde admire son travail.)

   _____

8. Quel programmeur? (Ses logiciels se vendent très bien.)

   _____

9. Quels voisins? (Leurs enfants assistent à cette école.)

   _____

10. Quel groupe de rock? (Tous les jeunes écoutent ses chansons.)

    _____

**Activité 7**  **En une seule phrase, s'il vous plaît!**  Faites de chaque paire de phrases une seule phrase en vous servant du pronom relatif convenable. Choisissez parmi **qui, que, à qui, auquel** et **dont.** Suivez le modèle.

> MODÈLE   La cordonnerie est un métier. Ils vivent de ce métier.
> La cordonnerie est le métier dont ils vivent.

**Un séjour dans une ville de province**

1. Notre guide nous a montré un paysage. Nous nous sommes émerveillés de ce paysage.

   _____

2. Nous avons visité les murailles. La vieille ville est entourée de ces murailles.

   _____

3. Une amie nous a invités au festival de danse. Elle prenait part à ce festival.

   _____

4. Nous sommes allés voir une rue. On a transformé cette rue en rue piétonne.

   _____

5. On est allés voir une comédie. On a beaucoup ri de cette comédie.

   _____

6. Nous avons essayé la cuisine régionale. La ville se vante de (*boasts about*) sa cuisine.

   _____

7. On nous a signalé l'absence d'une université. Nous nous sommes aperçus de cette absence.

   _____

8. C'est la vie universitaire. La ville manquait de vie universitaire.

   _____

9. Nous avions des amis dans la région. Nous avons téléphoné à ces amis.

   _____

10. Nous avons passé une belle journée avec eux. Nous nous souvenons encore de cette journée.

    _____

**Une crise dans l'administration nationale**

11. La crise est arrivée. Tout le monde avait peur de cette crise.

    _____

12. Un ministre faisait mal les fonctions. Il était responsable de ces fonctions.

    _____

13. C'était un homme respecté. Personne ne se doutait de lui.

    _____

14. Ce ministre est un homme bien en vue (*prominent*). La nation entière se fiait à lui.

    _____

15. On dit qu'il a donné des emplois à des gens non qualifiés. Plusieurs de ces gens étaient ses parents et amis.

    _____

16. Ils faisaient un travail. On commençait à se plaindre de ce travail.

    _____

17. Il y avait cent employés au ministère. On a licencié (*fired*) une trentaine de ces employés.

    _____

18. C'est la confiance de la nation. Le ministre a abusé de la confiance de la nation.

    _____

# Relative pronouns preceded by other prepositions

1. Relative pronouns may follow other prepositions, such as **avec, chez, dans, devant, en, pour, sur,** and so on. After the prepositions **entre** and **parmi,** a form of **lequel** must be used to refer to both people and things.

**REFERRING TO PEOPLE**

| | |
|---|---|
| les amis **sur qui** je compte | *the friends I rely on* |
| mon ami **pour qui** je fais le marché | *my friend for whom I do the shopping* |
| le cousin **chez qui** j'habite | *the cousin at whose house I live* |
| les deux jeunes filles **entre lesquelles** il s'est assis | *the two girls he sat between* |
| les quatre garçons **parmi lesquels** Janine a choisi | *the four boys among whom Janine chose* |

**REFERRING TO THINGS**

| | |
|---|---|
| la table **sur laquelle** j'ai posé mes affaires | *the table I put my things on* |
| l'immeuble **dans lequel** elle habite | *the apartment house that she lives in* |
| la tente **sous laquelle** j'ai dormi | *the tent that I slept in* |
| la raison **pour laquelle** nous disputons | *the reason why we argue* |

2. Prepositions of location and direction followed by a relative pronoun can be replaced by **où.**

La table **sur laquelle** j'ai posé mes affaires. → La table **où** j'ai posé mes affaires.

L'immeuble **dans lequel** elle habite. → L'immeuble **où** elle habite.

**Où** can also be used as a relative pronoun after expressions of time. It is possible to substitute **que** in similar situations.

le jour **où** elle est partie  
le jour **qu'**elle est partie  } *the day she left*

**Activité 8**  **Gestion critiquée.** Ajoutez le pronom relatif convenable à ces phrases pour savoir pourquoi Philippe Duhamel et Micheline Arnaud ne sont pas d'accord avec les plans de leur entreprise. Dans plusieurs cas, il faut ajouter aussi la préposition qui manque.

**Vocabulaire**

## Avec et sur

**être d'accord avec** *to be in agreement with*
**se familiariser avec** *to familiarize oneself with*

**insister sur** *to insist on*
**se renseigner sur** *to get information about*

DEUXIÈME PARTIE

1. Nous n'avons pas assisté à la réunion pendant _____ on a pris la décision.

2. Ils commencent un programme d'action _____ nous ne sommes pas d'accord.

3. Ils ne peuvent pas assurer la qualité _____ nous insistons.

4. Ils ne connaissent pas le marché _____ nous nous sommes familiarisés.

5. Il y a trop de choses _____ ils ne se sont pas renseignés.

6. C'est un projet _____ nous allons protester.

7. On va exposer toutes les mauvaises conséquences _____ nous nous méfions.

**Activité 9**   **Au pays de mes ancêtres.** Christine montre à son amie Julie le village où elle est née et où sa famille a toujours vécu. Ajoutez le pronom relatif convenable à la conversation entre les deux filles. Dans plusieurs cas, il faut ajouter aussi la préposition qui manque.

**Vocabulaire**

## À la campagne

**au cours de**  *in the course of, during*
**chemin faisant**  *on the way*
**le chêne**  *oak tree*
**la clôture**  *fence*
**l'étang** (*m.*)  *pond*

**grimper aux arbres**  *to climb trees*
**le jardin potager**  *vegetable garden*
**le long de**  *along* (*the river*)
**le peuplier**  *poplar tree*

CHRISTINE:   Viens, je vais te montrer la maison dans _____
                 1
on habitait. La voilà.

JULIE:   La maison à côté de _____ il y a deux chênes?
                 2

CHRISTINE:   Justement. Ce sont les arbres _____ on
                 3
grimpait, mes frères et moi, quand on était petits et entre

_____ il y avait un petit banc en bois.
                 4

JULIE:   Est-ce que je peux voir ta chambre?

CHRISTINE:   Oui, montons. La voilà, la chambre dans _____
                 5
je couchais. Et voilà la fenêtre par _____ je
                 6
regardais la neige en hiver.

*(continued)*

JULIE:     Et cette clôture?

CHRISTINE: C'est la clôture derrière _____ il y a un
           champ.
           　　　　　　　　　　　　　　7

JULIE:     Je vois un chemin à gauche.

CHRISTINE: Oui, c'est un chemin le long _____ il y a des
           peupliers.
           　　　　　　　　　　　　　　8

JULIE:     Tu ne m'as pas dit qu'il y avait aussi un étang?

CHRISTINE: Ah, oui, l'étang sur _____ on patinait en
           　　　　　　　　　　　　9
           hiver. On peut y aller, ce n'est pas loin. Et chemin faisant, je
           te présenterais aux voisins chez _____ je
           　　　　　　　　　　　　　　　　　　　　10
           passais beaucoup de temps. Ils avaient un fils _____
           　　　　　　　　　　　　　　　　　　　　　　　　　　　　11
           j'étais amoureuse.

JULIE:     Et qu'est-ce qu'il est devenu, ce fils?

CHRISTINE: Il était beaucoup plus âgé que moi. Il a passé plusieurs années
           à Lyon au cours _____ il s'est marié.
           　　　　　　　　　　　　12

## Relative pronouns without antecedents

1. When there is no antecedent in the main clause, French uses **ce qui**
   if the relative pronoun is the subject of the relative clause or **ce que**
   if it is the direct object. The English equivalent is *what* or *that
   which.*

   Je ne vois pas **ce qui** t'inquiète.　　*I don't see **what's** upsetting you.*
   **Ce qui** reste à faire me tracasse.　　*What remains to be done is
   　　　　　　　　　　　　　　　　　　　　worrying me*

   Dis-moi **ce que** tu veux.　　　　　　*Tell me **what** you want.*
   **Ce que** tu dis, c'est intéressant.　　*What you say is interesting.*

   When there is no antecedent in the main clause and a verbal expression
   that takes **de** or **à** appears in the relative clause, **ce dont** and **ce à quoi** are
   used, respectively.

   Je n'ai pas trouvé **ce dont** j'avais　　*I haven't found **what** I needed.*
   　　besoin.　　　　　　　　　　　　　　**(avoir besoin de)**
   Tu veux que je te prête **ce dont** je　*You want me to lend you **what** I use?*
   　　me sers?　　　　　　　　　　　　　**(se servir de)**
   Explique-moi **ce à quoi** tu　　　　　*Explain to me **what** you're thinking*
   　　réfléchis.　　　　　　　　　　　　*about.* **(réfléchir à)**
   Je vais t'expliquer **ce à quoi** il　　*I'm going to explain to you **what** he*
   　　tient.　　　　　　　　　　　　　*insists **on**.* **(tenir à)**

2. **Ce qui, ce que,** and **ce dont** can also refer to a preceding clause.

| | |
|---|---|
| Il arrive toujours à l'heure, **ce qui** me plaît. | *He always arrives on time, **which** I like.* |
| Il parle trois langues, **ce que** j'admire. | *He speaks three languages, **which** I admire.* |
| Il est très travailleur, **ce dont** on s'est aperçu. | *He's very hard-working, **which** people have noticed.* |

**Ce qui** and **ce que** are used after **tout** to express *all that, everything that.*

| | |
|---|---|
| Il m'a montré **tout ce qu'**il a écrit. | *He showed me **everything that** he wrote.* |
| **Tout ce qui** est sur la table est pour toi. | ***Everything that** is on the table is for you.* |

3. The demonstrative pronouns **celui, celle, ceux, celles** are common before the relative pronouns **qui** and **que,** and mean *he/she who, they who, the one(s) who, those who.*

| | |
|---|---|
| **Ceux qui** le connaissent l'estiment. | ***Those who** know him think highly of him.* |
| **Celui qui** désobéit sera puni. | ***He who** disobeys will be punished.* |
| Il y a plusieurs étudiantes françaises, mais il faut parler avec **celles qui** connaissent Marseille. | *There are several (female) French students here, but you have to speak with **the ones who** are familiar with Marseilles.* |

**NOTE**

In proverbs, **qui** is often used by itself to mean *he who.*

| | |
|---|---|
| Rira bien **qui** rira le dernier. | *He who laughs last laughs best.* |
| **Qui** aime bien châtie bien. | *Spare the rod, spoil the child. (**He who** loves, punishes.)* |

**Activité 10** **À compléter.** Complétez les phrases suivantes avec les pronoms relatifs qui manquent. Parfois l'équivalent anglais sera donné pour vous aider.

1. —Avec qui comptes-tu parler? Avec Daniel ou Baudouin?
   —Peu importe. Avec _____ (*the one who*) je trouverai à la fac.

2. Tu veux un peu de _____ je mange?

3. _____ est arrivé est merveilleux.

4. Je trouve bête _____ (*everything that*) il dit.

5. Il s'est marié avec _____ (*the one who*) il a connue l'été dernier.

6. Il faut cacher tout _____ les enfants ont peur.

7. Nous n'avons pas accepté _____ ils nous ont offert.

(*continued*)

8. Il dit qu'il aura de bonnes notes, _____ je doute.

9. Elle est très cultivée, _____ nous plaît.

10. Je ne comprends pas _____ vous allez étudier en Belgique.

11. On se demande _____ (*what*) a pu l'offenser.

12. Je te remercie de tout _____ tu as fait pour moi.

**Activité 11** **Jacqueline est amoureuse.** Jacqueline a un petit ami, Luc, dont elle est amoureuse. Voici la lettre qu'elle écrit à son sujet à son amie Éliane. Complétez-la avec **ce qui, ce que** ou **ce dont**.

Ma chère Éliane:

Je te remercie de ta lettre. Luc et moi, on continue à sortir ensemble. Tu m'as demandé _____ il fait. Il est étudiant en sciences.

_____ l'intéresse, c'est la chimie. Je comprends

_____ Luc étudie parce que je m'intéresse à la chimie aussi.

Je vais t'expliquer _____ nous faisons quand nous sortons.

Nous allons beaucoup au cinéma et au théâtre. _____ nous attire,

ce sont les films étrangers. Nous en voyons beaucoup. _____ nous

avons besoin est un bon DVD pour pouvoir en regarder à la maison aussi. Tu

comprends que Luc et moi, nous avons les mêmes goûts, _____

est une bonne chose.

Je ne sais pas _____ nous allons faire pendant l'été. Luc veut

faire un stage dans une entreprise à Singapour, mais moi, je dois travailler ici.

C'est-à-dire que nous ne nous verrons pas pendant deux mois, _____

j'ai peur. Luc me rassure en disant que deux mois, ce n'est pas l'éternité,

_____ est vrai.

Bon, Éliane, écris-moi et dis-moi tout _____ tu fais maintenant.

Tu m'as écrit que tu penses changer de faculté, _____ je me

doutais. Je sais que tu trouves la médecine moins intéressante maintenant.

Qu'est-ce que tu comptes faire, alors? Écris-moi dès que tu auras une petite

minute de libre.

Je t'embrasse,
Jacqueline

**Activité d'ensemble.** Joignez les deux phrases en français en une seule au moyen d'un pronom relatif. Suivez le modèle.

> MODÈLE    J'ai écouté un CD. Je vais te le prêter.
> J'ai écouté un CD que je vais te le prêter.

### À la recherche d'un nouvel emploi

1. Élisabeth a un poste. Elle veut en démissionner.

   _____

2. Il y a d'autres emplois (*job openings*). Elle essaie de se renseigner sur ceux-là.

   _____

3. Elle manque de qualifications. Nous ne pouvons pas nous en passer dans mon bureau.

   _____

4. Elle a téléphoné à d'autres entreprises. Je lui en ai donné le nom.

   _____

5. Il y a des cours d'orientation (*career counseling*). Elle y assiste.

   _____

6. Il y a de nouveaux logiciels (*software*) pour le bureau. Élisabeth se familiarise avec eux.

   _____

7. Elle a déjà trouvé une entreprise. Elle voudrait travailler pour cette entreprise.

   _____

### Mon petit déjeuner

8. Je vais te montrer les choses. J'ai besoin de ces choses pour préparer mon petit déjeuner.

   _____

9. Voilà le réchaud (*hot plate*). Je fais mon café sur ce réchaud.

   _____

10. Voici le bol. Je bois mon café du matin dans un bol.

    _____

11. Voilà la boulangerie. J'achète mes croissants et mon pain dans cette boulangerie.

    _____

12. Voilà la porte de la boutique. Il y a une enseigne (*sign*) au-dessus de la porte.

    _____

# TROISIÈME PARTIE

# INTERROGATIVES AND NEGATIVES

# 19 INTERROGATIVE SENTENCES

## Question formation

There are three ways to change a statement into a question.

1. In spoken French, statements are turned into questions by raising the pitch of the voice at the end of the sentence. The word order is the same as that of a statement.

| | |
|---|---|
| Tu descends avec moi? | *Are you coming downstairs with me?* |
| Non, je reste ici. Tu retournes avant le dîner? | *No, I'm staying here. Are you coming back before dinner?* |
| Non. Je dîne en ville. | *No, I'm having dinner in town.* |

**NOTE**    Negative questions formed with rising intonation expect the answer to be *no*.

| | |
|---|---|
| Tu ne regardes pas la télé? | *You're not watching TV?* |
| Non, je téléphone. | *No, I'm making a phone call.* |

2. In both spoken and formal French, **est-ce que** may be placed at the beginning of a statement to turn it into a question.

| | |
|---|---|
| **Est-ce que** vous écoutez souvent les concerts à la radio? | *Do you often listen to the concerts on the radio?* |
| Oui, toujours. **Est-ce que** vous aimez la musique classique aussi? | *Yes, all the time. Do you like classical music, too?* |

3. In formal French, especially in writing, statements are turned into questions by placing the subject pronoun after the verb and joining the two with a hyphen. This is called *inversion*.

| | |
|---|---|
| **Travaillez-vous** ici, Madame? | ***Do you work*** *here, ma'am?* |
| Oui, Monsieur. **Cherchez-vous** un emploi? | *Yes, sir.* ***Are you looking for*** *a job?* |

**NOTES**
- The pronoun **je** is not used in inverted questions, except after certain monosyllabic verb forms in very formal style: **ai-je, suis-je, vais-je, sais-je** and with the formal variant of **je peux: puis-je.**

- If the third-person singular form of a verb ends in a vowel, **-t-** is added between the verb form and the inverted subject pronoun **il, elle,** or **on.**

| | |
|---|---|
| Parle-**t**-il français? | *Does he speak French?* |
| A-**t**-elle envie de sortir? | *Does she feel like going out?* |
| Salue-**t**-on le professeur en anglais? | *Does one greet the teacher in English?* |

- In an inverted question, a noun subject remains before the verb, and the corresponding pronoun is added after the verb.

| | |
|---|---|
| **Les étudiants** tutoient-**ils** leur professeur? | *Do the students use the **tu** form to their teacher?* |
| Jamais. Ils vouvoient le professeur. | *Never. They say **vous** to the teacher.* |
| **Le professeur** tutoie-**t-il** les étudiants? | *Does the teacher use the **tu** form to the students?* |
| Quelquefois. | *Sometimes.* |

- Negative questions with inversion are used mainly in formal style. The **ne** and **pas** surround the inverted pronoun and verb. These questions imply that the speaker expects the answer to be *yes.*

| | |
|---|---|
| **N'**appuie-**t-il pas** notre candidat? | *Doesn't he support our candidate?* |
| Si, bien sûr. **Ne** partage-**t-il pas** nos idées? | *Yes, of course. Doesn't he share our ideas?* |

- If the subject of a negative question is a noun, it remains in its position before **ne** and the corresponding pronoun is added after the verb.

| | |
|---|---|
| **Les musiciens** de cet orchestre **ne** jouent-**ils pas** merveilleusement? | *Don't the musicians in this orchestra play wonderfully?* |
| Si. Et regardez. **Le public n'**écoute-**t-il pas** avec beaucoup de plaisir? | *Yes. And look. Isn't the audience listening with great delight?* |

- Note that **si,** not **oui,** is used to answer *yes* to a negative question.

- **N'est-ce pas** can be added to the end of any statement to ask a question to which the speaker expects the answer to be *yes.* The meaning is similar to that of negative questions.

| | |
|---|---|
| Les musiciens jouent bien, **n'est-ce pas?** | *The musicians play well, **don't they?*** |

**Activité 1**    **Pour faire connaissance.** Vous faites la connaissance d'un vieux monsieur. Vous lui posez des questions en employant l'inversion. Après, vous posez les mêmes questions à une nouvelle étudiante. Formulez celles-ci avec **est-ce que.** Suivez le modèle.

> MODÈLE    parler français
> **a.** Parlez-vous français?
> **b.** Est-ce que vous parlez français?

1. inviter souvent vos amis à dîner

   **a.** _____

   **b.** _____

2. apprécier la musique classique

   **a.** _____

   **b.** _____

*(continued)*

CHAPITRE 19

3. habiter un beau quartier

   **a.** _____

   **b.** _____

4. chercher une maison à la campagne

   **a.** _____

   **b.** _____

5. travailler près de chez vous

   **a.** _____

   **b.** _____

6. dîner généralement au restaurant

   **a.** _____

   **b.** _____

**Activité 2** **L'amoureux.** Robert s'est entiché de (*has fallen for*) Chantal. Il se pose toutes sortes de questions à son sujet. Formulez ses questions en employant l'inversion, selon le modèle.

> MODÈLE   jouer au tennis
> Joue-t-elle au tennis?

1. aimer les maths comme moi

   _____

2. étudier les mêmes matières que moi

   _____

3. habiter près de l'université

   _____

4. penser à moi de temps en temps

   _____

5. travailler à la bibliothèque

   _____

6. déjeuner au restaurant universitaire

   _____

**Activité 3** **L'ami de l'amoureux.** Robert confie son amour à son ami Philippe. Philippe lui pose des questions sur Chantal. Formulez ses questions avec **est-ce que** en suivant le modèle.

> MODÈLE   tu / penser constamment à Chantal
> Est-ce que tu penses constamment à Chantal?

1. Chantal / habiter près de chez toi

_____

2. tu / arriver à la même heure que Chantal

_____

3. tu / saluer Chantal

_____

4. Chantal / aimer les mêmes activités que toi

_____

5. tu / déjeuner avec elle

_____

6. Chantal / bavarder avec toi de temps en temps

_____

**Activité 4**    **La section française.** Marie-Claire pose des questions à son conseiller d'orientation sur le département de langues étrangères de l'université. Elle emploie l'inversion. Que dit-elle?

> MODÈLE    M. Leclerc / apprécier la littérature française
> M. Leclerc apprécie-t-il la littérature française?

1. Mme Savignac / prononcer parfaitement l'anglais

_____

2. M. Paul / enseigner l'espagnol aussi

_____

3. Mlle Moreau / répondre toujours aux questions des étudiants

_____

4. M. Michelet / arriver à sept heures du matin

_____

5. M. et Mme Lamoureux / enseigner dans le même département

_____

6. Mme Leboucher / choisir des textes intéressants pour sa classe

_____

7. les professeurs / organiser des activités pour les étudiants

_____

8. les étudiants / aimer les cours de français

_____

**Activité 5** **Un succès sûr.** Dans une réunion d'affaires, M. Bertin explique à ses collègues les raisons pour lesquelles il croit que leur nouvelle affaire va réussir. Écrivez ce qu'il leur dit en employant des questions négatives formulées avec inversion du sujet. Le sujet est **nous** dans chaque cas. Suivez le modèle.

> MODÈLE  placer notre argent dans une excellente affaire
> Ne plaçons-nous pas notre argent dans une excellente affaire?

1. lancer une bonne affaire

   _____

2. diriger l'entreprise d'une façon intelligente

   _____

3. engager de bons travailleurs

   _____

4. aménager les bureaux

   _____

5. changer nos stratégies selon chaque situation

   _____

6. commencer à gagner de l'argent

   _____

**Activité 6** **Après la réunion.** Nous retrouvons M. Bertin avec un ami. Il lui explique les raisons pour lesquelles il croit que sa nouvelle affaire va réussir. Il utilise des questions négatives avec **on** au lieu de **nous.** Son ami lui répond avec **si.** Suivez le modèle.

> MODÈLE  placer notre argent dans une excellente affaire
> **a.** On ne place pas notre argent dans une excellente affaire?
> **b.** Si, on place notre argent dans une excellente affaire.

1. lancer une bonne affaire

   **a.** _____

   **b.** _____

2. diriger l'entreprise d'une façon intelligente

   **a.** _____

   **b.** _____

3. engager de bons travailleurs

   **a.** _____

   **b.** _____

4. aménager les bureaux

   a. _____

   b. _____

5. changer nos stratégies selon chaque situation

   a. _____

   b. _____

6. commencer à gagner de l'argent

   a. _____

   b. _____

**Activité 7**  **Au contraire.**  Quelle confusion! Alain pose des questions, mais dans chaque cas, c'est le contraire qui est vrai. Écrivez des échanges composés d'une question négative avec l'inversion et de la réponse qui indique l'inverse. Suivez le modèle.

> MODÈLE  les étudiants / être en retard / être en avance
> —Les étudiants ne sont-ils pas en retard?
> —Non, ils sont en avance.

1. Claire / arriver ce matin / arriver ce soir

   —_____

   —_____

2. Marc et Geneviève / être en classe / être malades

   —_____

   —_____

3. Richard / avoir sommeil / avoir envie de sortir

   —_____

   —_____

4. ma famille / avoir raison / avoir tort

   —_____

   —_____

5. ton frère et toi / prendre le petit déjeuner à la maison / prendre un café à l'université

   —_____

   —_____

6. Lise / suivre un régime / prendre du poids

   —_____

   —_____

*(continued)*

7. vos parents / être en colère / être de bonne humeur

—_____

—_____

8. Christophe / sortir / rester à la maison

—_____

—_____

**Activité 8** **Et en plus.** Écrivez de petits échanges composés d'une question négative et d'une réponse affirmative. Ajoutez à la réponse l'élément proposé entre parenthèses. Suivez le modèle.

> MODÈLE  toi / avoir faim (avoir soif)
> —Tu n'as pas faim?
> —Si, et j'ai soif aussi.

1. il / avoir mal au dos (avoir mal aux jambes)

—_____

—_____

2. faire du vent (faire froid)

—_____

—_____

3. toi / télécharger des chansons (télécharger des jeux vidéos)

—_____

—_____

4. Marianne / jouer du violon (chanter)

—_____

—_____

5. ta sœur et toi / apprendre à parler chinois (apprendre à l'écrire)

—_____

—_____

6. moi / pouvoir assister à la conférence (pouvoir aller au concert)

—_____

—_____

**Activité 9** **Activité orale.** Quelles questions poseriez-vous à un(e) nouvel(le) étudiant(e) pour parvenir à le (la) connaître? Avec un(e) camarade de classe jouez cette conversation entre deux jeunes qui font connaissance.

# Interrogative adjectives and pronouns

## Interrogative adjectives

1. The interrogative adjective **quel** (*which, what*) agrees in gender and number with the noun it modifies.

|  | MASCULINE | FEMININE |
|---|---|---|
| **SINGULAR** | **Quel** train? *Which train?* | **Quelle** classe? *Which class?* |
| **PLURAL** | **Quels** trains? *Which trains?* | **Quelles** classes? *Which classes?* |

2. **Quel(le)(s)** may be preceded by a preposition.

| | |
|---|---|
| **De quel** livre est-ce que vous parlez? | *What book are you talking **about**?* |
| **Pour quelle** compagnie travaille-t-il? | *What company does he work **for**?* |

   In French, prepositions must always stand before their noun object; they cannot appear at the end of the sentence, the way prepositions in English often do. Similarly, the prepositional phrase in French cannot be broken up the way prepositional phrases in English frequently are.

3. **Quel(le)(s)** is used before forms of **être** in sentences where English uses *what*.

| | |
|---|---|
| **Quelle** est la différence? | ***What's** the difference?* |
| **Quelles** sont vos idées? | ***What** are your ideas?* |

4. When a phrase consisting of **quel(le)(s)** + *noun* precedes a form of the passé composé or other compound tense and the verb is conjugated with **avoir,** the past participle will agree with the noun if the noun is the direct object of the verb.

| | |
|---|---|
| **Quels films** est-ce que tu as loué**s**? | *Which films did you rent?* |
| **Quelle chanson** est-ce qu'il a joué**e**? | *Which song did he play?* |

   But:

| | |
|---|---|
| **Quelle chanson** a joué tout à l'heure? | *What song just played?* |

   In the last sentence, no agreement is made between **quelle chanson** and the past participle, because **chanson** is the subject of the verb, not the direct object.

5. **Quel(le)(s)** may also be used in exclamations. The implication may be either positive or negative.

**Quelle** catastrophe!        *What a catastrophe!*
**Quels** restaurants!        *What restaurants!*

**Activité 1**    **Pour préciser.** Utilisez l'adjectif interrogatif **quel** pour demander des précisions sur les objets qu'on mentionne. Suivez le modèle.

> MODÈLE    Jacqueline s'est renseignée sur les possibilités.
>              Sur quelles possibilités?

1. Philippe m'a prêté le vélo.

   _____

2. Jocelyne et Vivienne ont écouté les CD.

   _____

3. Lucette a joué avec la raquette.

   _____

4. J'ai conduit la voiture.

   _____

5. Tu me donnes la carte, s'il te plaît.

   _____

6. Marc est sur la moto.

   _____

7. Montrez-moi la chambre.

   _____

8. J'ai perdu les jumelles (*binoculars*).

   _____

9. Serge se sert de la caméra.

   _____

10. Moi, je me sers de l'appareil-photo.

   _____

**Activité 2**    **Des précisions.** Dans chaque cas, demandez qu'on précise de quel article il s'agit. Utilisez l'adjectif interrogatif **quel** et faites attention aux prépositions et à l'accord du participe passé. Suivez le modèle.

> MODÈLE    Simone a acheté des livres.
>              Quels livres a-t-elle achetés?

TROISIÈME PARTIE

1. Monique a pris des billets.

   _____

2. Alain et Crispin sont entrés dans un magasin d'informatique.

   _____

3. Gabrielle a besoin d'une disquette.

   _____

4. Les étudiants ont parlé avec un de leurs professeurs.

   _____

5. Marc a réussi à un examen difficile.

   _____

6. Yves a reçu une mauvaise note dans une de ses classes.

   _____

7. Mes parents ont acheté des médicaments.

   _____

8. Les enfants ont regardé des émissions à la télé.

   _____

**Activité 3** **Exclamations!** Choisissez l'exclamation convenable dans chaque cas en écrivant la forme correcte de **quel** devant un seul des deux substantifs proposés.

1. Le cousin de Marie-Christine est blessé dans un accident de la route.

   a. _____ tragédie!

   b. _____ courage!

2. Eugène a gagné 40 000 euros à la loterie!

   a. _____ horreur!

   b. _____ chance!

3. Le toit de leur maison s'est effondré (*caved in*).

   a. _____ malheur!

   b. _____ merveille!

4. Germaine a séché (*cut*) tous ses cours cette semaine.

   a. _____ bêtise!

   b. _____ diligence!

5. Il y a eu un tremblement de terre en Italie.

   a. _____ plaisir!

   b. _____ catastrophe!

(continued)

6. Les grands-parents de François lui ont donné de l'argent pour acheter ses livres.

    a. _____ générosité!

    b. _____ politesse!

7. Julien refuse de travailler.

    a. _____ paresse!

    b. _____ talent!

## Interrogative pronoun lequel

1. French interrogative pronouns agree in gender and number with the noun they refer to.

|  | MASCULINE | FEMININE |
|---|---|---|
| SINGULAR | lequel *which (one)* | laquelle *which (one)* |
| PLURAL | lesquels *which (ones)* | lesquelles *which (ones)* |

| | |
|---|---|
| Un de nos élèves est tombé malade. **Lequel?** | *One of our students got sick.* ***Which one?*** |
| Mon frère travaille dans une banque. **Dans laquelle?** | *My brother works in a bank.* ***In which one?*** |
| Il y a deux robes qui sont pour toi. **Lesquelles?** | *There are two dresses that are for you.* ***Which ones?*** |

2. When the interrogative pronoun **lequel(le)(s)** precedes a form of the passé composé or other compound tense and when the verb is conjugated with **avoir,** the past participle agrees with the interrogative pronoun if that pronoun is the direct object of the verb.

| | |
|---|---|
| Elle a beaucoup de robes. Laquelle a-t-elle mis**e**? | *She has many dresses.* *Which one did she put on?* |
| Ils m'ont offert beaucoup de livres intéressants. Lesquels est-ce que tu as choisi**s**? | *They offered me a lot of interesting books.* *Which ones did you choose?* |

3. The prepositions **à** and **de** contract with the interrogative pronoun.

| | |
|---|---|
| Nous allons à un pays étranger. **Auquel?** | *We are going to a foreign country.* ***To which one?*** |
| J'ai besoin de ces journaux. **Desquels?** Il y en a tant. | *I need those newspapers.* ***Which ones?*** *There are so many.* |

**Activité 4**    **Ça m'intéresse.** Demandez à votre ami(e) quel objet l'intéresse. Employez le pronom interrogatif et le pronom démonstratif dans vos réponses, comme dans le modèle.

1. Ce film m'intéresse.

   _____

2. Ces revues m'intéressent.

   _____

3. Ce club d'informatique m'intéresse.

   _____

4. Ces émissions m'intéressent.

   _____

5. Cette photo m'intéresse.

   _____

6. Ces disques m'intéressent.

   _____

7. Cet itinéraire m'intéresse.

   _____

**Activité 5**  **Exactement.**  Posez des questions avec le pronom interrogatif **lequel** pour savoir exactement de quel objet il s'agit. Suivez le modèle et faites attention aux contractions obligatoires.

MODÈLE    Il cherche les chaussures de sport.
          Lesquelles cherche-t-il exactement?

1. Je veux l'anorak.

   _____

2. Elle met les bottes.

   _____

3. Nous lavons les pulls.

   _____

4. J'ai besoin des chaussettes de laine.

   _____

5. Elle cherche les collants.

   _____

6. Ils pensent aux vêtements.

   _____

7. Je prends le blue-jean.

   _____

CHAPITRE 20

**En colonie de vacances.** Les affaires des jeunes gens qui font un séjour dans cette colonie de vacances sont en pagaille. Les animateurs essaient de les restituer, ce qui n'est pas facile. Utilisez les pronoms interrogatifs, démonstratifs et possessifs pour écrire les réponses des jeunes gens aux questions des animateurs. Suivez le modèle.

> MODÈLE    Ce sont tes valises, Claudette?
> Lesquelles? Ah, non. Celles-là ne sont pas les miennes.

**Vocabulaire**

## On part en colonie

**la colonie de vacances** *summer camp*
**le couteau de poche** *pocketknife*
**la couverture** *blanket*
**les jumelles** *binoculars*

**la lampe de poche** *flashlight*
**la raquette de tennis** *tennis racket*
**le sac à dos** *backpack*
**le sac de couchage** *sleeping bag*
**la tente** *tent*

1. C'est ta raquette de tennis, Baudouin?

   _____

2. Ce sont tes pulls, Richard?

   _____

3. C'est le sac à dos d'Yvette?

   _____

4. Ce sont vos sacs de couchage, Marc et Paul?

   _____

5. Ce sont les lettres de Christine et Mireille?

   _____

6. C'est ta lampe de poche, Colin?

   _____

7. Ce sont vos couvertures, Ombeline et Josette?

   _____

8. Ce sont tes jumelles, Alice?

   _____

9. C'est ton couteau de poche, Serge?

   _____

10. C'est la tente de Michèle?

    _____

# Interrogative pronouns *who, whom, what,* and other question words

1. When *who* is the subject of the verb, it is usually rendered by **qui** in questions. No inversion of subject and verb takes place in this case.

   | | |
   |---|---|
   | **Qui** habite dans cet immeuble? | *Who lives in that apartment house?* |
   | **Qui** veut de l'eau minérale? | *Who wants some mineral water?* |

   **Qui** as a subject of the sentence may be replaced by **qui est-ce qui.**

   | | |
   |---|---|
   | **Qui est-ce qui** me demande au téléphone? | *Who wants to speak to me on the phone?* |

2. When *whom* is the direct object of the verb, **qui** may be used as the interrogative pronoun, followed by inversion. This construction, like all constructions using inversion, is characteristic of formal style.

   | | |
   |---|---|
   | **Qui voulez-vous** voir? | *Whom do you wish to see?* |
   | **Qui cherche-t-il?** | *Whom is he looking for?* |

   In all styles, when *whom* is the direct object of the verb, it may be expressed using **qui est-ce que.** The subject and verb are not inverted after **qui est-ce que.**

   | | |
   |---|---|
   | **Qui est-ce que** vous connaissez ici? | *Whom do you know here?* |
   | **Qui est-ce qu'**ils ont appelé? | *Whom did they call?* |

3. **What** as the subject of the sentence is expressed by **qu'est-ce qui.**

   | | |
   |---|---|
   | **Qu'est-ce qui** t'a fait mal? | *What hurt you?* |
   | **Qu'est-ce qui** t'embête? | *What is annoying you?* |

   **What** as the direct object of the verb is expressed by **qu'est-ce que.** The subject and verb are not inverted after **qu'est-ce que.**

   | | |
   |---|---|
   | **Qu'est-ce que** vous avez acheté? | *What did you buy?* |
   | **Qu'est-ce que** j'ai fait? | *What did I do?* |
   | **Qu'est-ce que** tu as pris comme dessert? | *What did you have for dessert?* |

   In formal style, **qu'est-ce que** may be replaced by **que** if the subject of the sentence is a pronoun. The subject and verb must be inverted after **que.**

   | | |
   |---|---|
   | **Que désirez-vous?** | *What would you like?* |
   | **Qu'ont-ils décidé?** | *What have they decided?* |

   If the subject of the sentence is a noun, **qu'est-ce que,** and not **que,** must be used.

   | | |
   |---|---|
   | **Qu'est-ce que** les touristes ont vu? | *What did the tourists see?* |
   | **Qu'est-ce que** le professeur a dit? | *What did the teacher say?* |

4. The interrogative pronoun **qui** is used after prepositions. However, the interrogative pronoun **que** is replaced by **quoi** when it follows a preposition.

**À qui** avez-vous demandé le
   chemin?
**À qui** est-ce que vous avez demandé
   le chemin? } *Who(m) did you ask directions of?*

**Sur qui** peut-elle compter?
**Sur qui** est-ce qu'elle peut compter? } *Who(m) can she rely on?*

**À quoi** pensez-vous?
**À quoi** est-ce que vous pensez? } *What are you thinking about?*

**De quoi** ont-ils besoin?
**De quoi** est-ce qu'ils ont besoin? } *What do they need?*

5. Here is a summary of the French equivalents of *who(m)* and *what.*

|  | SUBJECT | OBJECT | AFTER PREPOSITION |
|---|---|---|---|
| **WHO(M)** | Qui? / Qui est-ce qui? | Qui? / Qui est-ce que? | qui |
| **WHAT** | Qu'est-ce qui? | Que? / Qu'est-ce que? | quoi |

## Other question words in French

**Combien?** *How many?, How much?*
**Comment?** *How?*
**Depuis combien de temps?** *How long?*

**Depuis quand?** *Since when?*
**Lequel?/Laquelle?/ Lesquel(le)s?** *Which one(s)?*
**Où?** *Where?*

**D'où?** *From where?*
**Pourquoi?** *Why?*
**Quand?** *When?*
**Quel + noun?** *Which?*

6. Other interrogatives (*question words*) can be used with inversion or **est-ce que.** The forms with inversion are characteristic of formal style.

**Quand est-ce que** vous viendrez?
**Quand** viendrez-vous? } *When will you come?*

**Comment est-ce qu'**il le fera?
**Comment** le fera-t-il? } *How will he do it?*

**Combien est-ce que** vous me devez?
**Combien** me devez-vous? } *How much do you owe me?*

**Pourquoi est-ce que** tu ne l'as pas
   vendu?
**Pourquoi** ne l'as-tu pas vendu? } *Why didn't you sell it?*

7. In very formal style, a noun subject followed by an inverted pronoun and verb may follow an interrogative.

**Qui le juge a-t-il** accusé?      *Whom has the judge accused?*
**Pourquoi ce candidat n'a-t-il pas** été élu?      *Why wasn't this candidate elected?*
**Dans quelle revue cet article sera-t-il** publié?      *In which magazine will this article be published?*

After all interrogatives except for **qui** and **pourquoi**, French allows inversion of the subject and verb without adding a pronoun, as long as the verb is in a simple tense (the simple future, present, or **passé simple**) and there is no direct or indirect object after the verb and subject.

| | |
|---|---|
| Quand **viendra Lise**? | *When **will Lise arrive**?* |
| Depuis quand **étudie votre frère**? | *How long **has your brother been studying**?* |
| Combien de parfums **produit la France**? | *How many perfumes **does France produce**?* |
| Quelle langue **parlent vos amis**? | *What language **do your friends speak**?* |

But:

| | |
|---|---|
| **Pourquoi est-ce que Jean est sorti?** | ***Why did Jean go out?*** |
| **Quelle langue est-ce que vos amis parlent à leurs parents?** | ***What language do your friends speak with their parents?*** |

Or:

| | |
|---|---|
| **Pourquoi Jean est-il sorti?** | ***Why did Jean go out?*** |
| **Quelle langue vos amis parlent-ils à leurs parents?** | ***What language do your friends speak with their parents?*** |

8. In informal French there are different rules for question formation. These patterns are not acceptable in formal situations or in writing, but they are extremely common in speech.

   a. **Est-ce que** is dropped, but no inversion takes place.

   | | |
   |---|---|
   | Quand tu viens? | *When are you coming?* |
   | Pourquoi tu dis ça? | *Why do you say that?* |
   | Comment ils vont faire ça? | *How are they going to do that?* |
   | Où tu les as retrouvés? | *Where did you meet up with them?* |

   **Que** cannot be used in the preceding construction.

   b. The question word is not placed at the front of the sentence, but left where the element it asks about normally appears. **Que** is replaced by **quoi** in this structure.

   | | |
   |---|---|
   | Il vient **à trois heures.** | *He's coming at three o'clock.* |
   | Il vient **à quelle heure**? | ***What time** is he coming?* |
   | Il part **demain.** | *He's leaving tomorrow.* |
   | Il part **quand**? | ***When** is he leaving?* |
   | Ça coûte **cent** euros. | *It costs one hundred euros.* |
   | Ça coûte **combien**? | ***How much** does it cost?* |
   | Ils font **leurs devoirs.** | *They're doing their homework.* |
   | Ils font **quoi**? | ***What** are they doing?* |
   | Il veut **une tarte.** | *He wants a pastry.* |
   | Il veut **quoi**? | ***What** does he want?* |

**Activité 7**  **Des questions.** Complétez les questions suivantes avec le pronom qui manque.

1. _____ travaille ici? (*Who*)

2. _____ tu as fait hier? (*What*)

3. _____ vous avez acheté pour le déjeuner? (*What*)

4. _____ vous intéresse? (*What*)

5. Avec _____ tu es sorti? (*whom*)

6. Sur _____ avez-vous écrit? (*what*)


**Activité 8**  **Posez vos questions.** Indiquez le mot qui manque pour formuler une question correcte.

1. _____ voyez-vous?

   **a.** Qui est-ce que   **b.** Qui est-ce qui   **c.** Qui   **d.** Qu'est-ce que

2. _____ tu cherches dans ce tiroir?

   **a.** Qu'est-ce que   **b.** Que   **c.** Quoi   **d.** Qu'est-ce qui

3. Sur _____ insiste-t-elle?

   **a.** que   **b.** qu'est-ce que   **c.** qu'est-ce qui   **d.** quoi

4. À quelle heure _____ le train?

   **a.** part-il   **b.** part   **c.** il part   **d.** est-ce que part

5. Tu as acheté _____?

   **a.** que   **b.** qu'est-ce que   **c.** est-ce que   **d.** quoi

6. _____ allé _____?

   **a.** Est-il / où   **b.** Où / est-il   **c.** Il est / où   **d.** Où est / il

7. De _____ parlez-vous?

   **a.** quoi   **b.** quoi est-ce que   **c.** que   **d.** qu'est-ce que

8. _____ commandent ces clients?

   **a.** Qu'est-ce que   **b.** Que   **c.** Quoi   **d.** Qui


**Activité 9**  **Le style soutenu.** Refaites chaque question dans un style plus formel en enlevant **est-ce que.** Faites toutes les modifications nécessaires.

| MODÈLE | Où est-ce qu'elle habite? |
| --- | --- |
| | Où habite-t-elle? |

1. Qu'est-ce qu'ils ont préparé?

_____

2. Qui est-ce que Marie a vu?

_____

3. Quand est-ce que vos amis ont loué cet appartement?

_____

4. Quel logiciel est-ce que tu recommandes?

_____

5. Dans quel hôtel est-ce que Céline va rester?

_____

6. Pourquoi est-ce que cet enfant pleure?

_____

7. Combien est-ce qu'elles ont payé?

_____

**Activité 10** **Oh, Jacqueline!** Jean-Claude s'intéresse à Jacqueline, la cousine de son ami Gérard. Il veut se renseigner sur elle, sur ses goûts, et ainsi de suite. Lisez les informations que Gérard lui a données. Écrivez les questions que Jean-Claude a posées pour obtenir les réponses ci-dessous. Utilisez un style familier, selon le modèle.

> MODÈLE    Ma cousine s'appelle Jacqueline.
> Ta cousine s'appelle comment?

1. Elle habite Paris.

_____

2. Elle arrive dans une semaine.

_____

3. Jacqueline voyage avec son frère.

_____

4. Elle va rester un mois avec nous.

_____

5. Jacqueline s'intéresse à la chimie.

_____

6. Elle aime la cuisine japonaise.

_____

_(continued)_

7. Elle aime faire de la voile.

_____

8. Jacqueline a besoin d'une voiture.

_____

**Activité 11**    **Activité orale.** Jouez l'Activité 6 avec un(e) camarade en employant les objets qu'on trouve dans la salle de classe et vos affaires personnelles. Vous pouvez varier la structure des questions et des réponses, pourvu que vous utilisiez tous les pronoms que vous avez appris.

## Basic negative structures

1. Verbs are made negative in French by placing **ne** before the verb and **pas** after it.

| | |
|---|---|
| Je **ne** dîne **pas** au restaurant ce soir. Et toi? | *I'm **not** having dinner at the restaurant this evening. And you?* |
| Moi, je **ne** travaille **pas.** Donc, je sors. | *I'm **not** working. So, I'm going out.* |

**NOTE**

**Ne** becomes **n'** before a vowel.

| | |
|---|---|
| Je **n'**aime pas écouter cette musique. | *I **don't** like listening to this music.* |

2. Note the similar negative constructions **ne** + *verb* + **jamais** meaning *never* and **ne** + *verb* + **plus** meaning *not anymore, no more.*

| | |
|---|---|
| Tu **n'**invites **plus** Jeanine. | *You **don't** ask Jeanine out **anymore.*** |
| Ce n'est pas la peine. Elle **n'**accepte **jamais.** | *It doesn't pay to. She **never** accepts.* |

**NOTE**

Do not confuse the negative construction **ne... plus** (*no more*), in which the final **s** is not pronounced [ply], and the word **plus** (*more*), in which the final **s** is pronounced [plys].

| | |
|---|---|
| Oui, je voudrais **plus** [plys] de café, s'il te plaît. | *Yes, I'd like **more** coffee, please.* |
| Merci. Je **ne** voudrais **plus** [ply] de café. | *No, thanks. I **don't** care for **any more** coffee.* |

Note that in spoken French the negative particle **ne** often drops, thereby making the pronunciation of the final **s** of **plus** the only distinction between *more* and *no more.*

3. **Ne** + *verb* + **personne** means *no one, nobody;* **ne** + *verb* + **rien** means *nothing.*

| | |
|---|---|
| Vous cherchez quelqu'un, Monsieur? | *Are you looking for someone, sir?* |
| Non, Madame. Je **ne** cherche **personne.** | *No, ma'am. I'm **not** looking for **anyone.*** |

| | |
|---|---|
| J'entends un bruit. | *I hear a noise.* |
| Moi, je **n'**entends **rien.** | *I **don't** hear **anything.*** |

**Personne** and **rien** may be used as subjects. In this case, they precede the verb and are followed by **ne.**

| | |
|---|---|
| **Rien ne** change ici. | *Nothing changes here.* |
| C'est vrai. **Personne ne** déménage. Tout reste comme avant. | *It's true. **No one** moves out. Everything remains just as it was before.* |

## Positive and corresponding negative words

| | | | |
|---|---|---|---|
| **encore, toujours** *still* | | **plus** *no more, no longer* | |
| **encore, davantage** *more* | | **plus** *no more, not anymore* | |
| **quelquefois** *sometimes* | | **jamais** *never* | |
| **toujours** *always* | | **jamais** *never* | |
| **souvent** *often* | | **jamais** *never* | |
| **quelqu'un** *someone, somebody* | | **personne** *no one, nobody* | |
| **quelque chose** *something* | | **rien** *nothing* | |
| **quelque part** *somewhere* | | **nulle part** *nowhere* | |

**Activité 1**

**Comme c'est triste.** Pierrot n'est pas tout à fait content pendant ses premiers jours à l'université. Écrivez ses réponses négatives aux questions, en employant le mot négatif correspondant.

> MODÈLE   Est-ce que tu connais beaucoup de monde?
> Non, je ne connais personne.

1. Est-ce que ta petite amie te téléphone tous les jours?

   _____

2. Est-ce que tu manges avec quelqu'un?

   _____

3. Est-ce que tu regardes souvent la télé?

   _____

4. Est-ce que tu travailles encore?

   _____

5. Est-ce que quelqu'un organise des activités pour les nouveaux étudiants?

   _____

6. Est-ce que tu aimes quelque chose ici?

   _____

**Activité 2**

**Ça va mieux.** Pierrot est content à l'université maintenant. Écrivez ses réponses négatives aux questions, en employant le mot négatif correspondant.

1. Est-ce que tu es encore seul?

   _____

2. Est-ce que tu es triste quelquefois?

_____

3. Est-ce que tu désires encore rentrer chez toi?

_____

4. Est-ce que quelqu'un dérange les étudiants quand ils travaillent?

_____

5. Est-ce que tu trouves quelque chose à critiquer?

_____

6. Est-ce que quelque chose te fait peur maintenant?

_____

**Activité 3** **Jamais!** Les étudiants racontent ce qu'ils ne font jamais à l'école. Écrivez ce qu'ils disent en employant **ne... jamais.**

| MODÈLE | fumer en classe |
| | Nous ne fumons jamais en classe. |

1. arriver en retard

_____

2. interrompre le professeur

_____

3. oublier nos devoirs

_____

4. perdre nos livres

_____

5. applaudir après la classe

_____

6. jeter nos stylos en l'air

_____

7. confondre les rois de France dans la classe d'histoire

_____

8. jouer aux cartes en classe

_____

**Tout change.** Josette retourne à son quartier après plusieurs années d'absence. Son amie Valérie lui raconte comment les choses ont changé. Écrivez ce qu'elle dit à Josette en employant **ne... plus.**

> MODÈLE    mon frère / travailler à la bibliothèque
> Mon frère ne travaille plus à la bibliothèque.

1. les Dulac / habiter l'immeuble en face

   _____

2. M. Beauchamp / vendre sa poterie aux voisins

   _____

3. nous / acheter le journal au kiosque du coin

   _____

4. ma mère / descendre faire les courses tous les jours

   _____

5. moi / jouer du piano

   _____

6. Mme Duverger / enseigner au lycée du quartier

   _____

7. nos amis / passer beaucoup de temps dans le quartier

   _____

## Other negative structures

1. **Aucun(e)** means *no, not any* and precedes a noun. **Ne** precedes the verb.

   Tu crois qu'il va rentrer?          *Do you think he's coming back?*
   Je **n'**ai **aucune idée.**          *I have **no idea.***

   Ce cours est très difficile.          *This course is very difficult.*
   C'est que le professeur **ne** nous          *That's because the teacher **doesn't***
   donne **aucun exemple.**          *give us **any examples.***

**NOTE**    Aucun(e) always takes a verb conjugated in the singular.

2. **Aucun(e)** + *noun* or **aucun(e) des** + *plural noun* means *no, none* and may function as the subject of a sentence. **Ne** precedes the verb.

   **Aucun ami n'**accepte son          *No friend accepts his invitation.*
   invitation.

   **Aucun de ses amis n'**accepte son          *None of his friends accepts his*
   invitation.          *invitation.*

3. **Ni... ni...** means *neither . . . nor . . .* Like **aucun(e)**, **personne**, and **rien**, it may either follow or precede the verb. **Ne** precedes the verb in both cases. When **ni... ni...** refers to the subject of the sentence, a plural verb is used.

Je **ne** vois **ni Charles ni Hélène.**　　　*I don't see **either Charles or Hélène.***
**Ni Charles ni Hélène ne** sont là.　　　***Neither Charles nor Hélène** is here.*

Je **n'**aime **ni** le café **ni** le thé.　　　*I like **neither** coffee **nor** tea.*

4. **(Ni)... non plus** means *neither* or *not either* in a sentence in which the French equivalent of *nor* does not appear.

Charles n'est pas là.　　　*Charles isn't here.*
**(Ni) Hélène non plus.**　　　***Neither is Hélène. (Hélène isn't
　　　　　　　　　　　　　　　　　　　　either.)***

Je n'aime pas le professeur　　　*I don't like the computer science
　d'informatique.　　　　　　　　　teacher.*
**Moi non plus.**　　　　　　　　　***Neither do I.***

5. **Ne** + *verb* + **guère** means *hardly.*

Il **n'**est **guère** content.　　　*He's **hardly** happy.*

**Activité 5**　**Un professeur paresseux.** Utilisez **ne... aucun** pour savoir pourquoi les étudiants ne sont pas contents dans la classe du professeur Malherbe.

> MODÈLE　donner / devoir
> 　　　　Il ne donne aucun devoir.

1. expliquer / texte

　_____

2. corriger / composition

　_____

3. recommander / livre

　_____

4. proposer / thème de discussion

　_____

5. présenter / idée

　_____

6. analyser / problème

　_____

**Activité 6**　**Un étudiant en difficulté.** Jean-Marc a beaucoup de problèmes à l'université. Décrivez-les en employant **ni... ni...** dans chaque cas, selon le modèle.

> MODÈLE　arriver / en avance / à l'heure
> 　　　　Il n'arrive ni en avance ni à l'heure.

1. aimer / la physique / la littérature

_____

2. finir / ses devoirs / ses compositions

_____

3. étudier / à la bibliothèque / à la maison

_____

4. réfléchir / à son travail / à son avenir

_____

5. demander des conseils / à ses amis / à ses professeurs

_____

6. écouter / les conférences / les discussions

_____

## Ne... que and ne... pas que

**Ne... que** is a false negation that means *only*. **Ne** precedes the verb and **que** precedes the word or words to be emphasized. Because **ne... que** is a restrictive rather than a negative construction, indefinite and partitive articles immediately following it do not become **de** as they do with other negative words.*

| | |
|---|---|
| Paulette aime la musique classique? | *Does Paulette like classical music?* |
| Non, elle **n'**écoute **que des** chansons populaires. | *No, she listens **only** to popular songs.* |
| | |
| Tu veux aller à Avignon par le train? | *Do you want to go to Avignon by train?* |
| Je **ne** voyage **qu'**en voiture. | *I travel **only** by car.* |

**NOTE**

**Ne faire que...** + *verb* means *to do nothing but . . .*

| | |
|---|---|
| Quand elle était malade, elle **n'a fait que dormir.** | *When she was sick, she **did nothing but sleep.*** |

**Ne... pas que** means *not all / not the only*.

| | |
|---|---|
| Il **n'**y a **pas que** le travail. Il faut s'amuser aussi. | *Work **isn't all there is.** You have to have fun too.* |
| Il **n'**aime **pas que** la physique. Il adore la géographie aussi. | *Physics is not the only subject he likes. He loves geography, too.* |

*See p. 147 of Chapter 12 for this rule.

**Il n'y en a pas d'autre.** Refaites les phrases suivantes avec **ne... que,** selon les modèles.

> MODÈLE  La chimie est la seule classe que j'aime.
> Je n'aime que la chimie.
>
> Je parle seulement en français avec Pierre.
> Je ne parle qu'en français avec Pierre.
>
> Il ne s'arrête pas de se plaindre.
> Il ne fait que se plaindre.

1. Philippe est la seule personne que je respecte ici.

_____

2. Ma chambre est la seule que je nettoie.

_____

3. Alice est la seule personne que j'invite.

_____

4. Elle apprécie seulement la littérature française.

_____

5. L'avenir est la seule chose à laquelle ils réfléchissent.

_____

6. Odile ne s'arrête pas de parler au téléphone.

_____

7. Je joue seulement au football.

_____

8. Elle mange seulement des fruits et des légumes.

_____

**Activité orale.** Avec un(e) camarade de classe, discutez des choses que vous ne faites pas chez vous. Comparez les règles. Présentez à la classe les choses à ne pas faire que votre camarade et vous partagez.

CHAPITRE 21

# 22 Negatives and indefinites

## Negative words: forms and uses

1. In Chapter 21 we reviewed the following affirmative and corresponding negative words.

| | |
|---|---|
| **encore, toujours** *still* | **plus** *no more* |
| **encore, davantage** *more* | **plus** *no more, not anymore* |
| **quelquefois** *sometimes* | **jamais** *never* |
| **toujours** *always* | **jamais** *never* |
| **souvent** *often* | **jamais** *never* |
| **quelqu'un** *someone, somebody* | **personne** *no one, nobody* |
| **quelque chose** *something* | **rien** *nothing* |
| **quelque part** *somewhere* | **nulle part** *nowhere* |

Here are some additional pairs of corresponding affirmative and negative expressions.

| | |
|---|---|
| **déjà** *ever* | **jamais** *never* |
| **déjà** *already* | **pas encore** *not yet* |
| **ou** *or* | **ni** *neither, nor* |
| **soit... soit / soit... ou** *either . . . or* | **ni... ni** *neither . . . nor* |

2. In both simple and compound tenses, **ne** precedes the conjugated verb, and the negative word usually follows the conjugated verb.

Est-ce que tu as déjà été en Belgique? *Have you ever been to Belgium?*
Non, je **n'**y suis **jamais** allé. *No, I've **never** gone there.*

Nous passerons l'été soit à Nice, *We'll spend the summer **either** in*
  soit en Espagne. Et vous? *Nice **or** in Spain. How about you?*
Nous **ne** partons **ni** dans le Midi, **ni** *We won't be going **either** to the south*
  à l'étranger. Nous travaillons *of France **or** abroad. We're working*
  cet été. *this summer.*

3. Both **ne** and the negative words **pas, rien, jamais,** and **plus** precede an infinitive. **Personne,** however, follows an infinitive.

Je vous conseille de **ne pas** y **aller.** *I advise you **not to go** there.*
Il m'a dit de **ne jamais revenir.** *He told me **never to come back.***
On passe la journée à **ne rien faire.** *We spend the day **doing nothing.***
Je préfère **ne voir personne.** *I prefer **not to see anyone.***

4. More than one negative word can be used in a sentence: **ne... plus jamais** or **ne... jamais plus** (*never again*), **ne... plus rien** (*nothing else, nothing more*), **ne... plus personne** (*nobody else, no one anymore*), and so on.

| | |
|---|---|
| Il **n'**y a **jamais personne** ici. | *There's **never anyone** here.* |
| C'est qu'il **n'**y a **plus rien** à faire. | *That's because there's **nothing more** to do.* |

5. Negative words can stand by themselves.

| | |
|---|---|
| Connais-tu beaucoup de monde ici? | *Do you know a lot of people here?* |
| **Personne.** | *No one.* |
| Qu'est-ce que vous cherchez? | *What are you looking for?* |
| **Rien.** | *Nothing.* |

6. After the word **que** in comparisons, French may use a negative word.

| | |
|---|---|
| J'ai l'impression que Vincent est **plus paresseux que jamais.** | *I have the impression that Vincent is **lazier than ever.*** |
| Vous vous trompez. Il travaille **mieux que personne.** | *You're mistaken. He works **better than anyone.*** |

7. Before adjectives, nouns, pronouns, or adverbs, **non** or **pas** is usually used. **Non** is more formal; **pas** is more colloquial.

| | |
|---|---|
| Tu es épuisé? | *Are you exhausted?* |
| **Pas épuisé (Non épuisé),** mais un peu fatigué. | ***Not exhausted,** but a little tired.* |
| Il travaille mardi, **pas jeudi (non jeudi).** | *He's working Tuesday, **not Thursday.*** |

**Activité 1**   **Hubert le rêveur.**  Hubert passe son temps à rêver. Essayez de le ramener à la réalité en employant les mots négatifs nécessaires.

> MODÈLE     Je gagne toujours à la loterie.
> Ne dis pas d'idioties! Tu ne gagnes jamais à la loterie.

1. Quelqu'un me donnera un million d'euros.

   _____

2. Quelques filles me croient le plus beau garçon de la classe.

   _____

3. J'ai souvent cent à l'examen de philo.

   _____

4. La femme du président de la République m'a envoyé quelque chose.

   _____

5. Mon père va m'offrir soit une voiture soit une moto.

   _____

6. Il me reste toujours l'argent que j'ai reçu pour mon anniversaire.

   _____

(continued)

7. Je connais quelqu'un à Casablanca.

_____

8. Je connais quelqu'un à Rabat aussi.

_____

9. J'irai au Maroc avec Solange.

_____

10. Si je n'aime pas mes cadeaux, on m'offrira quelque chose d'autre.

_____

**Activité 2**  **Marceline la trouble-fête (*party-pooper*).**  Marceline est tellement pessimiste au sujet de la fête qu'on a organisée qu'elle donne le cafard (*depresses*) à tout le monde. Écrivez les réactions de Marceline aux idées de ses copains en employant les mots négatifs convenables.

> MODÈLE  Tout le monde viendra à notre fête.
> Personne ne viendra à notre fête.

1. Chacun apportera quelque chose à manger.

_____

2. Nous boirons quelque chose.

_____

3. Nous écouterons soit des cassettes soit des CD.

_____

4. Jeanine a déjà acheté du vin.

_____

5. Olivier a un nouveau DVD.

_____

6. Odile amène toujours quelqu'un d'intéressant.

_____

7. Ces fêtes sont toujours amusantes.

_____

8. Après la fête, nous irons nous promener quelque part.

_____

## Indefinite words and expressions

1. Many indefinite expressions in English begin with the word *some*. They are often the affirmative counterparts of negative words.

| quelque chose *something* | quelquefois *sometimes* |
| quelque part *somewhere* | quelqu'un *someone, somebody* |

2. In French, the word *some* before a noun is expressed either by the partitive article or by the adjective **quelques,** which is more emphatic.

Je n'ai que **quelques** mots à vous dire.

*I have only **a few** words to say to you.*

Vous trouverez **quelques** idées intéressantes dans cet article.

*You'll find **some** interesting ideas in this article.*

3. The pronoun *some,* when used emphatically, is expressed in French using **quelques-uns, quelques-unes.** The pronoun **en** usually appears in the sentence.

As-tu acheté des journaux français?
J'**en** ai acheté **quelques-uns.**

*Did you buy any French newspapers?*
*I bought **some** (a few).*

As-tu acheté des revues françaises?
J'**en** ai acheté **quelques-unes.**

*Did you buy any French magazines?*
*I bought **some** (a few).*

4. When *some* is the subject of the sentence and means *some people,* its French equivalent is **certains,** which often occurs in conjunction with **d'autres** (*others*).

**Certains** appuient cette nouvelle loi; **d'autres** sont contre.

***Some** support this new law; **others** are against (it).*

In everyday French, **certains** and **d'autres** as subjects are often replaced by **il y en a qui** and **il y en a d'autres qui,** respectively.

**Il y en a qui** appuient cette nouvelle loi; **il y en a d'autres qui** sont contre.

5. To express *someone or other, somewhere or other, something or other,* and so on, French uses **je ne sais,** followed by the appropriate interrogative word.

| **je ne sais combien** *I'm not sure how much/many* | **je ne sais quand** *sometime or other* |
| **je ne sais comment** *somehow* | **je ne sais quel + noun** *some + (noun) or other* |
| **je ne sais où** *somewhere or other* | **je ne sais qui** *someone or other* |
| **je ne sais pourquoi** *for some reason or other* | **je ne sais quoi** *something or other* |

Jacqueline est allée **je ne sais où** aujourd'hui.

*Jacqueline went **somewhere or other** today.*

Oui. Le dimanche elle va rendre visite à **je ne sais qui** à Fontainebleau.

*Yes. On Sundays she goes to visit **someone** in Fontainebleau.*

Il s'est sauvé de l'accident **je ne sais comment.**

***Somehow or other** he saved himself from the crash.*

Quelle chance! Cette tragédie a fait **je ne sais combien** de victimes.

*What luck! That tragedy caused **I don't know how many** deaths.*

6. *Any* in the sense of *it doesn't matter which one* is expressed in French by **n'importe** followed by the appropriate interrogative word.

| | |
|---|---|
| **n'importe qui**  *anyone* | **n'importe lequel, laquelle,** |
| **n'importe quoi**  *anything* | **lesquels, lesquelles**  *whichever* |
| **n'importe où**  *anywhere* | *one(s), any one(s)* |
| **n'importe comment**  *anyhow* | **n'importe quand**  *at any time* |
| **n'importe quel + *noun*** | **n'importe combien**  *any amount, no* |
| *any + (noun)* | *matter how much/many* |

Qu'est-ce que tu veux manger?     *What do you want to eat?*
**N'importe quoi.**     *Anything.*
Et où est-ce que tu veux aller après?     *And where do you want to go afterward?*
**N'importe où.**     *Anywhere.*

7. Remember that the English word *any* and the words it appears in (*anyone, anything, anywhere*) are translated by negative words in French if the sentence is negative, and by indefinite words and expressions if the sentence is affirmative. Contrast the following pairs of sentences.

Est-ce qu'il en sait **quelque chose**?     *Does he know **anything** about it?*
Non. Il **n'**en sait **rien**.     *No. He **doesn't** know **anything** about it.*

Allez-vous **quelque part** cette semaine?     *Are you going **anywhere** this week?*
Non, nous **n'**allons **nulle part**.     *No, we're **not** going **anywhere**.*

However, expressions with **n'importe** may be used in sentences that include a negation, in order to express the French equivalent of *just any*.

Je ne vais pas offrir **n'importe quoi**.     *I'm not going to give **just anything** as a gift.*

Nous ne voulons pas passer le temps avec **n'importe qui**.     *We don't want to spend time with **just anyone**.*

**Activité 3**    **On n'est pas au courant.** Refaites les phrases suivantes en employant une des expressions avec **je ne sais.** Les deux phrases doivent signifier plus ou moins la même chose. Suivez le modèle.

> MODÈLE    Je n'ai pas la moindre idée de ce qu'elle va nous offrir.
> Elle va nous offrir je ne sais quoi.

1. Marc ne se souvient pas de la personne à qui il a donné le message.

    _____

2. On ignore avec quel professeur elle va parler.

    _____

3. Personne ne comprend pourquoi elles se sont mises en colère.

    _____

4. Personne ne savait combien de gâteaux le malade avait mangés.

_____

5. Je ne vois pas comment il a réussi aux examens.

_____

6. On ne nous a pas dit quand nos cousins arrivent.

_____

**Activité 4**    **Exprimez votre indifférence.** Répondez aux questions suivantes en employant une des expressions avec **n'importe.** Par vos réponses, vous montrez que le choix entre les possibilités vous est égal. Suivez le modèle.

> MODÈLE    Avec qui est-ce que je dois parler?
> Avec n'importe qui.

1. Qu'est-ce que tu veux boire?

_____

2. Où est-ce que tu veux manger?

_____

3. Quel journal est-ce que je dois acheter?

_____

4. Quand est-ce que tu veux partir?

_____

5. À quel cinéma veux-tu aller?

_____

6. Combien d'argent vas-tu payer?

_____

7. Comment est-ce que tu comptes le convaincre?

_____

8. À qui est-ce que nous pouvons demander le chemin?

_____

## More expressions with indefinite words

1. When an indefinite or negative word is followed by an adjective, the preposition **de** is added before the adjective, which is always masculine singular.

| | |
|---|---|
| **quelqu'un/personne d'intelligent** | _someone / no one intelligent_ |
| **quelque chose/rien de délicieux** | _something/nothing delicious_ |
| **un je ne sais quoi de fascinant** | _something fascinating_ |

2.  **Quelqu'un, quelque chose, personne,** and **rien** can also be modified by **d'autre.**

---

**personne d'autre** *nobody / no one else*
**quelque chose d'autre** *something else*

**quelqu'un d'autre** *somebody else*
**rien d'autre** *nothing else*

---

**NOTE**

Different parts of speech, such as interrogatives, can also be modified by **de** + *adjective.*

| | |
|---|---|
| **Qu'est-ce qu'il y a de plus amusant** pour les enfants que le guignol? | *What **is more fun** for children than a puppet show?* |
| C'est **ce qu'il y a de** plus **intéressant.** | *That's **what's** most **interesting.*** |
| **Quoi de neuf?** | *What's new?* |
| **Quoi d'autre?** | *What else?* |

3.  The indefinite adjective **chaque** means *each.*

| | |
|---|---|
| Avez-vous apporté quelque chose pour **chaque** enfant? | *Have you brought something for **each** child?* |

4.  The word **tout** has several uses in French. As an indefinite adjective it has four forms: **tout, toute, tous, toutes.**

    • When it directly precedes a singular noun, it means *every.*

| | |
|---|---|
| **Tout enfant** doit aller à l'école. | ***Every child** must go to school.* |

    • **Tout/toute** + *definite article* + *noun* means *the whole, all (of) (the).*

| | |
|---|---|
| **toute la ville** | *the whole city* |
| **Tous les enfants** doivent aller à l'école. | *All ([of] the) children must go to school.* |

    • Note also the meanings of **tous/toutes les** + *number.*

| | |
|---|---|
| Il vient **tous les trois mois.** | *He comes **every three months** (**every third month**).* |
| Prenez. C'est pour **tous les deux.** | *Take it. It's for **both of you.*** |
| **Nous** sommes sortis **tous les quatre.** | *All four of us went out.* |

**NOTE**

**Tout** and its forms can also be nouns, pronouns, adjectives, and adverbs.

    • **Tout** as a pronoun means *everything.*

| | |
|---|---|
| J'espère que **tout** va bien. | *I hope **everything** is all right.* |
| **Tout** est en règle. | ***Everything** is in order.* |

    • **Tous** as a pronoun means *all* or *everyone.* It takes a plural verb when it is the subject of the sentence.

| | |
|---|---|
| Ils sont **tous** revenus. | *They **all** came back.* |
| **Tous** ont demandé de vous voir. | ***Everyone** has asked to see you.* |

    • **Tout le monde** is the most common way to express *everyone.* Note that when **tout le monde** is the subject, the verb must be in the singular. To express *the whole world,* French uses **le monde entier.**

**NOTE**

> **Tout le monde** a demandé de te voir.    *Everyone has asked to see you.*
>
> Cet auteur est connu **dans le**    *This author is known **the world***
> **monde entier.**    *over.*

● **Tout** as an adverb before an adjective means *quite, completely, fully.* It is invariable (**tout,** pronounced /tu/, /tut/ before a vowel) before a singular or plural masculine adjective, but shows gender and number agreement with a following feminine adjective. These agreements reflect the fact that before a feminine adjective, the adverb **tout** is always pronounced /tut/.

> Il est **tout** content.    *He's **quite** happy.*
> Ces logiciels sont **tout** neufs.    *These software packages are brand-new.*
> Elle est **toute** contente.    *She's **quite** happy.*
> Ces maisons sont **toutes** neuves.    *These houses are brand-new.*

Before a feminine adjective beginning with a vowel or a mute **h,** the agreement of **tout** is optional since the final **t** is pronounced before the following vowel (liaison).

> Elle a été **tout(e)** étonnée.    *She was **thoroughly** amazed.*
> Elles sont **tout(es)** heureuses.    *They are **completely** happy.*

---

**Activité 5**    **À compléter.** Choisissez parmi les possibilités proposées celle qui complète correctement la phrase.

1. Le médecin m'a dit de ne rien manger _____ sucré. (quelque chose / de / *no word required*)

2. Si Jean-Marc ne peut pas le faire, on va demander à quelqu'un

   _____. (d'autre / autre / ailleurs)

3. _____ étudiant doit rédiger une composition. (Quelqu'un / Toutes les / Chaque)

4. Ils sont _____ contents de nous voir. (tous / toutes / tout)

5. Il y a trois belles églises dans la ville et nous les avons visitées

   _____. (tous / toutes / tout)

## Idioms and expressions with negative and indefinite words

| Expressions with **jamais** | |
| --- | --- |
| **Il n'en manque jamais une!** *He's always blundering. / He always puts his foot in it.* <br> **à jamais** *forever* | **à tout jamais** *forever and ever* <br> **Jamais de la vie!** *Not on your life!* <br> **Jamais deux sans trois.** *Misfortunes always come in threes.* |

## Expressions with **quelque(s)**

**Ils sont quelque peu déçus.*** *They're a little disappointed.*

**Il est trois heures et quelques.** *It's a little past three.*

## Expressions with **ni... ni**

**Cela ne me fait ni chaud ni froid.** *It's all the same to me. / I don't feel strongly about it.*

**Cette histoire n'a ni queue ni tête.** *This story doesn't make any sense at all.*

## Expressions with **rien**

**Ça ne fait rien.** *It doesn't matter. That's OK. (In response to* **Pardon.***)*

**Ce n'est pas pour rien qu'il t'a dit ça.** *It's not without good reason that he told you that.*

**C'est un/une rien du tout.** *He/She is a nobody. / He/She is a worthless person.*

**Cet article n'a rien à voir avec nos recherches.** *This article has nothing to do with our research.*

**Comme si de rien n'était.** *As if nothing had happened.*

**De rien.** *You're welcome.*

**Il a peur d'un rien.** *He's afraid of every little thing.*

**Je veux te parler, rien que cinq minutes.** *I want to talk to you, just five minutes.*

**Moi, j'y mettrais un rien de poivre.** *I'd add a dash of pepper.*

**Rien ne sert de pleurer.** *It's no use crying.*

**Rien qu'à le voir, on sait qu'il est gentil.** *Just by looking at him you know he's nice.*

**Si cela ne vous fait rien.** *If you don't mind.*

**Tu dis ça rien que pour m'embêter.** *You're saying that just to annoy me.*

**Un rien la fait rire.** *She laughs at every little thing.*

## Expressions with **chacun**

**Chacun à son tour.** *Each one in his/her turn.*

**Chacun pour soi!** *Everyone for himself/herself!*

**À chacun son goût. / À chacun ses goûts.** *To each his/her own.*

## Expressions with **certain**

**d'un certain âge** *older (middle-aged).*

**Elle a un certain charme.** *She has a certain charm.*

*Note that **quelque** becomes an adverb when it modifies an adjective and therefore remains invariable.

## Expressions with **ailleurs**

**d'ailleurs** *moreover, besides*
**Il est ailleurs. / Il a l'esprit
    ailleurs.** *He's miles away (not
    paying attention).*

**partout ailleurs** *everywhere else*

## Expressions with **nul**

**C'est une vraie nullité.** *He/She is a
    real washout.*
**faire match nul** *to tie (sports)*
**Il est nul / Elle est nulle en
    philosophie.** *He/She is a very
    poor philosophy student.*

**un travail nul; une composition
    nulle** *a worthless piece of work; a
    worthless composition*

**Activité 6**  **Comment l'exprimer?** Choisissez la possibilité qui exprime l'idée
indiquée.

1. *You want to tell a friend that he's not paying attention.*

    **a.** Tu es une vraie nullité.
    **b.** Tu as l'esprit ailleurs.

2. *You want to say that a certain place is not very selective in its admission policies.*

    **a.** On admet tout un chacun.
    **b.** C'est un rien du tout.

3. *You want to say that a friend is always putting his foot in his mouth.*

    **a.** Rien qu'à le voir, on s'en rend compte.
    **b.** Il n'en manque jamais une.

4. *You react to a story that makes no sense to you.*

    **a.** Cette histoire n'a ni queue ni tête.
    **b.** Cette histoire ne me fait ni chaud ni froid.

5. *You reassure someone who said "excuse me" because he thought he stepped on
    your toe.*

    **a.** Si cela ne vous fait rien.
    **b.** Cela ne fait rien.

6. *You tell someone that you won't take much of her time.*

    **a.** Rien que cinq minutes.
    **b.** Une heure et quelques.

7. *You tell someone it's no use crying.*

    **a.** Rien ne sert de pleurer.
    **b.** Tu pleures pour un rien.

*(continued)*

8. *You want to say that Mr. Jarre is a nobody.*

   **a.** C'est un rien du tout.
   **b.** C'est un travail nul.

9. *You want to express a categorical refusal.*

   **a.** Comme si de rien n'était.
   **b.** Jamais de la vie!

10. *You want to deny any connection between something and yourself.*

   **a.** Cela ne me fait rien du tout.
   **b.** Ça n'a rien à voir avec moi.

**Activité 7** **Qu'est-ce que cela veut dire?** Choisissez la possibilité qui exprime la même idée que la première phrase.

1. Un rien l'effraie.

   **a.** Rien ne l'effraie.
   **b.** Tout l'effraie.

2. Mets un rien de sel dans la soupe.

   **a.** La soupe a besoin d'un peu de sel.
   **b.** Ne mets plus de sel dans la soupe.

3. C'est un homme d'un certain âge.

   **a.** Il a environ cinquante ans.
   **b.** Je sais exactement quel âge il a.

4. Il fait ça rien que pour nous faire peur.

   **a.** Il évite de faire des choses qui nous feraient peur.
   **b.** La seule raison pour laquelle il fait ça est pour nous faire peur.

5. Ils ont fait match nul.

   **a.** Les deux équipes n'ont pas joué.
   **b.** Les deux équipes ont eu le même nombre de points.

6. Rien qu'à l'entendre, on sait qu'elle a du talent.

   **a.** Si tu l'entendais seulement, tu te rendrais compte de son talent.
   **b.** En l'entendant, tu te rends compte qu'elle n'a pas de talent.

7. Il est trois heures et quelques.

   **a.** Il est presque quatre heures.
   **b.** Il est entre trois heures et trois heures dix.

8. Ce n'est pas pour rien que je t'ai dit ça.

   **a.** Je n'ai dit ça pour aucune raison.
   **b.** J'avais une très bonne raison pour te le dire.

# QUATRIÈME PARTIE    PREPOSITIONS

## CHAPITRE

# 23 PREPOSITIONS

A preposition is a word that links two elements of a sentence: **le livre** *de* **Janine, entrer** *dans* **la cuisine, parler** *à* **lui, finir** *de* **travailler.**

## The preposition à

The preposition **à** has many uses in French. Remember its contractions are **à + le → au; à + les → aux. À** is also used before infinitives, as presented in Chapter 10 and Appendix III.

1. a. **À** is used in expressions of measurement.

| | |
|---|---|
| faire du 70 **à l'heure** | *to do 70 kilometers **an hour*** |
| vendre **au kilo, au mètre** | *to sell **by the kilogram, by the meter*** |
| être payé **au mois** | *to be paid **by the month*** |
| **un à un, peu à peu** | *one by one, little by little* |
| **tour à tour** | *alternately, in turn* |

   b. **À** expresses direction and location in space.

| | |
|---|---|
| aller **à la banque** | *to go **to the bank*** |
| être **à la banque** | *to be **at the bank*** |

   c. **À** labels distance in time and space.

| | |
|---|---|
| habiter **à quinze kilomètres** de Paris | *to live **fifteen kilometers** from Paris* |
| être **à trois heures** de Marseille | *to be **three hours** from Marseilles* |

   d. **À** expresses the point in time at which something happens (clock time, age).

| | |
|---|---|
| **À quelle heure** le train part-il? | ***What time** does the train leave?* |
| arriver **à sept heures du soir** | *to arrive **at seven in the evening*** |
| **à dix-huit ans** | *at (**the age of**) eighteen* |

2. a. **À** expresses the manner or style in which something is done.

| | |
|---|---|
| manger **à la française** | *to eat **French style*** |
| coucher **à quatre dans une chambre** | *to sleep **four to a room*** |

   b. **À** expresses the means by which something is done.

| | |
|---|---|
| fait, écrit **à la main** | *made, written **by hand*** |
| aller **à bicyclette, à pied** | *to go **by bike, on foot*** |
| écrire **au crayon** | *to write **in pencil*** |

3. **À** expresses possession or belonging to someone after the verb **être.**

| | |
|---|---|
| Ce stylo est **au prof.** | *This pen is **the teacher's.*** |
| C'est bien gentil **à toi.** | *That's really nice **of you.*** |

4. a. **À** indicates the purpose for which an object is intended.

| | |
|---|---|
| une tasse **à** thé | *a teacup* |
| sandwichs **à** emporter | *sandwiches to take out* |

  b. **À** labels the principal ingredient in a dish or a characteristic feature.

| | |
|---|---|
| un sandwich **au fromage** | *a **cheese** sandwich* |
| une glace **aux fraises** | ***strawberry** ice cream* |
| la femme **au chapeau** | *the woman **in** (**wearing**) **a hat*** |
| une chemise **à manches longues** | *a **long-sleeved** shirt* |

5. a. **À** is used with nouns derived from verbs or with infinitives as a replacement for a subordinate clause.

| | |
|---|---|
| à mon arrivée | *when I got there (upon my arrival)* |
| à notre retour | *when we got back (upon our return)* |
| à l'entendre chanter | *when I heard him/her sing (upon hearing him/her sing)* |
| à la réflexion | *if you think about it (on second thought)* |

  b. **À** translates as *at* and *to* with certain nouns.

| | |
|---|---|
| à ma grande surprise, joie | *to my great surprise, joy* |
| à sa consternation | *to his dismay* |
| à la demande de tous | *at everyone's request* |

  c. **À** expresses a standard for judging or knowing (and means *by, according to, from*).

| | |
|---|---|
| reconnaître quelqu'un **à sa voix** | *to recognize someone **by his/her** voice* |
| **À ce que j'ai compris,** il ne viendra pas. | ***From what I understood,** he won't come.* |
| juger quelque chose **aux résultats** | *to judge something **by the results*** |

## Idioms and expressions with à

### Location (spatial and figurative)

| | |
|---|---|
| **à côté** *next door, nearby* | **être à la page** *to be up-to-date* |
| **à côté de** *next to* | **Je ne me sens pas à la hauteur.** *I don't feel up to the task.* |
| **à deux pas de chez moi** *right near my house* | **Qui est à l'appareil?** *Who's calling?* |
| **à la une** *on the front page (of a newspaper)* | |

## Time

| | |
|---|---|
| **à la fois** *at the same time* | **à plusieurs reprises** *several times* |
| **à l'instant** *a moment ago* | **à ses heures (libres)** *in one's free time* |

## Manner

| | |
|---|---|
| **à juste titre** *rightfully* | **aimer quelqu'un à la folie** *to be mad/wild about someone* |
| **à la perfection** *perfectly, just right* | |
| **à souhait** *to perfection* | **être à l'étroit** *to be cramped for space* |
| **à titre confidentiel** *off the record* | |
| **à titre de père/mère** *as a father/mother; in my role as a father/mother* | **étudier quelque chose à fond** *to study something thoroughly* |
| **à tort** *wrongfully* | **lire à haute voix** *to read aloud* |
| **à tour de rôle** *in turn* | **un vol à main armée** *armed robbery* |

## Price, purpose, and degree

| | |
|---|---|
| **à la longue** *in the long run* | **faire les choses à moitié** *to do things halfway* |
| **à peine** *hardly* | |
| **à tout prix** *at all costs* | **tout au plus** *at the very most* |
| **acheter quelque chose à prix d'or** *to pay through the nose for something* | |

## Sentences, interjections, and exclamations

| | |
|---|---|
| **À la ligne.** *New paragraph (in dictation).* | **au fait** *by the way* |
| **À la poubelle!** *Get rid of it!; Throw it out!* | **Au feu!** *Fire!* |
| **à propos** *by the way* | **Au secours!** *Help!* |
| **À quoi bon?** *What's the use?* | **Au suivant!** *Next!; Who's next?* |
| **À suivre.** *To be continued.* | **Au voleur!** *Thief!* |
| **À votre santé!** *To your health!* | |

**Activité 1** **Expliquez les différences.** Comprenez-vous la différence de sens qui existe entre les deux expressions de chaque paire? Expliquez-la en anglais.

1. à la une / à la page

   _____

2. à plusieurs reprises / à la fois

   _____

3. à l'étroit / à la hauteur

   _____

4. une bouteille à lait / une tasse à thé

_____

5. au suivant / à suivre

_____

**Synonymes ou antonymes?** Indiquez si les expressions suivantes sont synonymes ou antonymes.

|  | SYNONYMES | ANTONYMES |
|---|---|---|
| 1. à juste titre / à tort | _____ | _____ |
| 2. à souhait / à la perfection | _____ | _____ |
| 3. à l'appareil / au téléphone | _____ | _____ |
| 4. à propos / au fait | _____ | _____ |
| 5. à tour de rôle / tour à tour | _____ | _____ |

**On cause.** Complétez ces échanges avec les expressions qui manquent.

1. **a.** —Tu as le journal. Qu'est-ce qu'il y a _____?
   on the front page

   **b.** —Un vol _____ dans le métro.
   armed

2. **a.** —Tu sais, papa, j'aime Philippe _____.
   madly

   **b.** —Babette, ma fille, _____, je te dirai que tu es
   as a father
   trop jeune.

3. **a.** —Marie-Claude a appris son rôle _____.
   perfectly

   **b.** —Oui, elle ne fait pas les choses _____.
   halfway

# The preposition **de**

Like **à**, the preposition **de** has many uses in French. Remember its two contractions: **de + le → du; de + les → des. De** is also used as the partitive article (see Chapter 12) and before infinitives in many constructions (see Chapter 10 and Appendix III).

1. a. **De** is used in many expressions of measurement.

   | | |
   |---|---|
   | un bifteck **de 500 grammes** | _a **500-gram** steak_ |
   | augmenter son salaire **de 100 euros** | _to raise someone's salary **by 100 euros**_ |
   | plus grand(e) **d'une tête** | _a **head** taller_ |
   | Ce fleuve a **850 mètres de large** et **100 mètres de profondeur.** | _This river is **850 meters wide** and **100 meters deep.**_ |

b. **De** is used in some expressions of place and time.

| | |
|---|---|
| **de ce côté** | *on this side* |
| **de l'autre côté** | *on the other side* |
| **du côté de** la bibliothèque | *in the direction of the library* |
| **de côté et d'autre** | *here and there; on both sides* |
| **du temps de** Napoléon | *in Napoleon's time* |
| **de** nos jours | *in our day* |
| travailler **de jour, de nuit** | *to work days, nights* |
| Ils n'ont rien fait **de toute l'année.** | *They've done nothing all year.* |
| Je n'ai rien fait de pareil **de toute ma vie.** | *I've done nothing like that in my entire life.* |

c. **De** introduces phrases that express the manner in which something is done.

| | |
|---|---|
| connaître quelqu'un **de vue** | *to know someone by sight* |
| répéter **de mémoire** | *to repeat from memory* |

2. a. **De** introduces nouns in apposition.

| | |
|---|---|
| la région **de Bourgogne** | *the Burgundy region* |
| le nom **de Maubrey** | *the name Maubrey* |
| Quel temps **de chien**! | *What lousy weather!* |

b. **De** expresses starting point or origin.

| | |
|---|---|
| partir **de Paris** | *to leave from Paris* |
| sortir **de la boutique** | *to go out of the shop* |
| Il est **du Sénégal.** | *He's from Senegal.* |

3. a. **De** expresses possession.

| | |
|---|---|
| le livre **de l'étudiant** | *the student's book* |
| les rues **de Paris** | *the streets of Paris* |
| le contenu **du livre** | *the contents of the book* |

b. **De** expresses the contents of something.

| | |
|---|---|
| une tasse **de thé** | *a cup of tea* |
| une collection **de poupées** | *a doll collection* |

4. a. **De** labels the characteristic feature. The English equivalent is often a compound noun (*noun + noun*).

| | |
|---|---|
| la société **de consommation** | *the consumer society* |
| une classe **d'anglais** | *an English class* |

b. **De** labels the means by which something is done.

| | |
|---|---|
| écrire **de la main gauche** | *to write with one's left hand* |
| faire quelque chose **de ses propres mains** | *to do something with one's own hands* |

5. **De** is used in **changer de** + *singular noun* to express *to change + singular or plural noun.*

| | |
|---|---|
| changer **de train, d'avion** | *to change **trains, planes*** |
| changer **de direction** | *to change **direction*** |
| changer **d'avis, d'idée** | *to change **one's mind*** |

6. **De** labels the cause.

| | |
|---|---|
| mourir **de faim** | *to die **of hunger*** |
| fatigué **du voyage** | *tired **from the trip*** |

## Idioms and expressions with de

### Time

| | |
|---|---|
| **d'abord** *first* | **de bonne heure** *early* |
| **de bon matin** *early in the morning* | **trois jours de suite** *three days in a row* |

### Appositions

| | |
|---|---|
| **C'est un drôle de numéro.** *He/She is a strange character.* | **C'est une drôle d'idée.** *It's a strange idea.* |

### Origin, manner, and other categories

| | |
|---|---|
| **C'est de la part de qui, s'il vous plaît?** *Who's calling, please?* | **du reste** *moreover* |
| **Cette pièce sert d'étude.** *This room is used as a study.* | **ne pas être d'attaque** *not to feel up to it* |
| **d'autre part** *on the other hand* | **poser une question de but en blanc** *to ask a question just like that / point-blank / suddenly* |
| **du coup** *as a result* | **se heurter de face, de front** *to collide head-on* |
| | **un billet de faveur** *complimentary ticket* |

**Activité 4** **Est-ce *à* ou *de*?** Complétez ces phrases avec **à** ou **de**. Si aucune préposition n'est nécessaire, marquez l'espace d'un X. N'oubliez pas que dans certains cas, il faudra employer les contractions **au, aux, du, des**.

1. Elle est contente _____ notre travail.

2. J'ai soif. Je vais acheter une bouteille _____ jus de pomme.

3. Tu prends ta soupe dans une tasse _____ thé? Comme c'est bizarre.

4. Si tu veux écrire à tes parents, je te donnerai du papier _____ lettres.

*(continued)*

5. Je lui ai demandé s'il voulait m'accompagner. Il a fait «non»

_____ la tête.

6. _____ secours! Je suis tombé et je ne peux pas me lever!

7. Nous n'avons rien fait _____ toute la semaine.

8. Nous allons _____ côté de la place. Tu viens avec nous?

9. Ma chambre a trois mètres _____ large.

**Activité 5** **Expliquez les différences.** Comprenez-vous la différence de sens qui existe entre les deux expressions de chaque paire? Expliquez-la en anglais.

1. de suite / à suivre

_____

2. de hauteur / à la hauteur

_____

3. à côté / de côté

_____

4. Il est au Japon. / Il est du Japon.

_____

5. une corbeille à papier / une corbeille de papier

_____

6. travailler de jour / travailler à la journée

_____

**Activité 6** **La vie en famille.** Mme Gilbert écrit à son amie Vivienne Mauriac pour lui donner des nouvelles de sa famille. Pour savoir ce qu'elle dit, complétez son courriel avec des prépositions ou des phrases qui contiennent **à** ou **de.**

Ma chère Vivienne:

Tu me pardonneras de ne pas avoir écrit avant. Tout va très bien ici. Les

enfants grandissent. Mon fils Paul est déjà plus grand que moi

_____. Il dit qu'il veut être pilote. C'est une
        (1) *by a head*

_____, n'est-ce pas? J'espère qu'il va
        (2) *strange idea*

_____.
        (3) *change his mind*

Brigitte étudie à la _____. Elle se lève tous les jours
                            (4) *medical school*

_____ pour lire. Ses cours sont difficiles et il faut qu'elle
        (5) *early in the morning*

étudie tout _____. Paul va au lycée qui est
(6) *thoroughly*

_____ de chez nous.
(7) *right near*

Mon mari voyage beaucoup pour affaires. Demain il revient

_____ New York et la semaine prochaine il prend le
(8) *from*

train pour Genève où il va passer une semaine. Il n'a jamais autant

voyagé _____.
(9) *in his whole life*

Et toi, qu'est-ce que tu deviens? J'attends tes nouvelles avec impatience.

Toutes mes amitiés,
Sylvie

**Activité 7**  **Comprenez-vous?** Laquelle des deux possibilités signifie plus ou moins la même chose que l'expression donnée?

1. C'est un drôle de numéro.
   **a.** C'est une personne bizarre.
   **b.** Elle n'a pas de numéro de téléphone.

2. Je la connais de vue.
   **a.** Je la vois.
   **b.** Je sais qui c'est quand je la vois.

3. Jacquot est plus petit de trois centimètres.
   **a.** Jacquot mesure trois centimètres de moins que quelqu'un.
   **b.** Jacquot mesure moins de trois centimètres.

4. Il fait un temps de chien.
   **a.** Il ne fait pas du tout beau.
   **b.** Il fait les choses en peu de temps.

5. On a donné un billet de faveur à Marc.
   **a.** Le billet était un cadeau.
   **b.** Marc n'a pas voulu le billet.

6. Il m'a posé la question de but en blanc.
   **a.** Il a hésité à me poser la question.
   **b.** Il m'a posé la question brusquement.

7. Mon oncle m'a servi de professeur de maths.
   **a.** Mon oncle a trouvé quelqu'un pour m'enseigner les maths.
   **b.** Mon oncle m'a enseigné les maths lui-même.

8. C'est une classe d'arabe.
   **a.** Les étudiants sont arabes.
   **b.** On y enseigne l'arabe.

9. C'est de la part de qui?
   **a.** Qui est à l'appareil?
   **b.** Qui est celui qui part?

CHAPITRE 23

# The prepositions avec and sans

1.  a.  **Avec** expresses accompaniment, much like English *with*.

    | | |
    |---|---|
    | Attends, j'irai **avec toi**. | *Wait, I'll go **with you**.* |
    | Je suis d'accord **avec vous**. | *I agree **with you**.* |

    b.  **Avec** labels the cause.

    | | |
    |---|---|
    | **Avec** l'inflation, tout le monde parle des prix. | *With inflation as high as it is, everyone is talking about prices.* |
    | J'ai peur de conduire **avec toute cette neige**. | *I'm afraid to drive **with all of this snow**.* |

    c.  **Avec** expresses *in addition to*.

    | | |
    |---|---|
    | Et **avec cela** (ça), madame? | *Anything else, madam? (in a store)* |
    | Il n'a pas étudié et **avec ça** il a séché le cours. | *He didn't study, and **on top of that** he cut class.* |

    d.  **Avec** + *noun* is often the equivalent of an English adverb, as reviewed in Chapter 14.

    | | |
    |---|---|
    | **avec** plaisir, **avec** colère | *gladly, angrily* |

2.  a.  **Sans** is the equivalent of the English *without*.

    | | |
    |---|---|
    | Notre équipe a dû jouer **sans** notre meilleur joueur. | *Our team had to play **without** our best player.* |
    | **Sans** argent on ne peut rien faire. | ***Without** money you can't do anything.* |
    | Je me suis couché **sans** avoir fini mon travail. | *I went to bed **without** having finished my work.* |

    b.  **Sans** can mean *if it weren't for ...*, *but for ....*

    | | |
    |---|---|
    | **Sans ce plan,** on se serait perdus. | ***If it weren't for this street map**, we would have gotten lost.* |

    c.  The preposition **sans** + *noun* is often the equivalent of an English adjective ending in *-less* or an adjective with a negative prefix such as *un-* or *in-*.

    | | |
    |---|---|
    | **sans doute, sans effort** | *doubtless, effortless* |
    | **un sans-abri, sans domicile fixe (S.D.F.)** | *a **homeless** person* |
    | une situation **sans remède** | *a **hopeless** situation* |
    | un film **sans intérêt** | *an **uninteresting** film* |
    | une femme **sans préjugés** | *an **unprejudiced, unbiased** woman* |

    d.  The use of **sans** with negative words eliminates the need for **ne.** The partitive article often becomes **de** after **sans** because of the implied negative meaning of the preposition.

    | | |
    |---|---|
    | **sans** parler à personne | ***without** speaking to anyone* |
    | **sans** rien faire | ***without** doing anything* |
    | **sans** jamais l'avoir vu | ***without** ever having seen him* |
    | sortir **sans** faire **de** bruit | *to go out **without** making **any** noise* |

## Idioms and expressions with **avec** and **sans**

**se fâcher avec quelqu'un** *to get angry with someone*
**se lever avec le jour** *to get up at the crack of dawn*
**se mettre en rapport/relation avec** *to get in touch with*
**prendre des gants avec quelqu'un** *to handle someone with kid gloves*
**être sans le sou** *to be broke*
**être sans travail, sans emploi** *to be out of work, unemployed*
**être un sans-gêne** *to be inconsiderate*

**sans aucun doute** *without a doubt*
**Sans façons!** *Let's not stand on ceremony!; I really mean it!*
**sans broncher** *without flinching*
**sans ça** *otherwise*
**sans faute** *without fail*
**sans oublier** *last but not least*
**sans plus** *that's all, nothing more*
**les sans-emploi** *the unemployed*

**Activité 8**    *Sans* ou *avec*? Complétez les phrases en français avec la préposition **sans** ou **avec** pour qu'elles aient à peu près le même sens que leur traduction anglaise.

1. *He's an unimaginative man.*    C'est un homme _____ imagination.

2. *She answered bitterly.*    Elle a répondu _____ amertume.

3. *They write effortlessly.*    Ils écrivent _____ effort.

4. *Come eat with us! I really mean it!*    Viens manger avec nous! _____ façons!

5. *If it weren't for her, we wouldn't have finished the job.* _____ elle, nous n'aurions pas fini le travail.

6. *With the ice on the road, driving is difficult.*    _____ le verglas, il est difficile de conduire.

7. *You have to handle him carefully.*    Il faut prendre des gants _____ lui.

8. *You have to speak sweetly to her.*    Il faut lui parler _____ douceur.

9. *He threw himself into the fray unflinchingly.*    Il s'est lancé au combat _____ broncher.

# The prepositions en and dans

En and dans both mean *in*. En is used directly before a noun; dans must be followed by an article (definite, indefinite, or partitive) or by some other determiner, such as a possessive or demonstrative adjective.

| | |
|---|---|
| aller **en ville** | *to go **downtown*** |
| **dans la** ville | *in the city* |
| | |
| être **en prison** | *to be **in jail*** |
| **dans cette** prison | *in this jail* |

1.  a.  **En** is used to mean *as* or *like*.

   | | |
   |---|---|
   | Je te parle **en ami.** | *I'm speaking to you **as a friend.*** |
   | Il agit **en prince.** | *He's acting **like a prince.*** |

   b.  **En** is used to express location within a period of time or duration.

   | | |
   |---|---|
   | **en** automne, **en** juillet, en 2006 | *in the fall, **in** July, **in** 2006* |
   | **de** jour **en** jour | ***from** day **to** day, daily* |
   | faire quelque chose **en** deux semaines | *to do ( finish) something **in** two weeks* |

   c.  **En** labels the means of transportation.

   | | |
   |---|---|
   | voyager **en** train, **en** avion | *to travel **by** train, **by** plane* |
   | rentrer **en** taxi, **en** car | *to go back **by** cab, **by** intercity bus* |

   d.  **En** marks the condition or appearance of something.

   | | |
   |---|---|
   | être **en** nage | *to be sweaty* |
   | être **en** bonne santé | *to be **in** good health* |
   | être **en** pyjama | *to be **in** one's pajamas* |
   | être **en** guerre | *to be **at** war* |
   | **en** hâte, **en** désordre, **en** pagaille | *in a hurry, **in** disorder, **in** a mess* |

   e.  **En** marks transformation into something else.

   | | |
   |---|---|
   | transformer la ferme **en** atelier | *to transform the farm **into** a workshop* |
   | se déguiser **en** avocat | *to disguise oneself **as** a lawyer* |
   | traduire **en** italien | *to translate **into** Italian* |

   f.  **En** marks the material of which something is made (as does **de**).

   | | |
   |---|---|
   | un collier **en or** | *a **gold** necklace* |
   | un couteau **en acier inoxidable** | *a **stainless steel** knife* |
   | une jupe **en laine** | *a **woolen** skirt* |
   | C'est **en quoi?** | *What's it **made of?*** |

   g.  **En** is used before **plein** to mean *in the middle of*.

   | | |
   |---|---|
   | **en pleine** ville | ***right in the middle of** the city* |
   | **en plein** hiver | ***in the middle of** winter* |
   | être **en plein** travail | *to be **in the middle of** one's work* |

h. **En** is used to form some common adverbial expressions.

| | |
|---|---|
| **en** haut, **en** bas | *upstairs, downstairs* |
| **en** avant, **en** arrière | *forward, backward* |
| **en** face | *opposite* |
| **en** tout cas | *in any case* |
| **en** plus | *besides, in addition* |

i. **En** is followed by an article or determiner in a few expressions.

| | |
|---|---|
| **en l'honneur de** | *in honor of* |
| **en l'absence de** | *in the absence of* |
| **en mon nom** | *in my name* |
| **en sa faveur** | *in his/her favor* |

2. a. **Dans** is used to express location (English *in*).

| | |
|---|---|
| **dans** la boîte, **dans** la rue, **dans** le train | *in the box, **in** the street, **in** the train* |

b. **Dans** is used to express location in time (English *in, in the course of, during*).

| | |
|---|---|
| **dans** la journée, la soirée | ***in the course of** the day, the evening* |
| **dans** la matinée, l'après-midi | ***during** the morning, afternoon* |
| Il partira **dans** cinq jours. | *He will leave **in** five days, ( five days from today).*\* |

c. **Dans** is used to express figurative location.

| | |
|---|---|
| **dans** la situation actuelle | ***in** the present situation* |
| **dans** ces conditions | ***given** these conditions* |
| être **dans** les affaires | *to be **in** business* |

d. **Dans** is used in contexts in which English uses *from, on,* or *into*.

| | |
|---|---|
| boire **dans** une tasse | *to drink **from** a cup* |
| prendre quelque chose **dans** une boîte | *to take something **from** a box* |
| copier quelque chose **dans** un livre | *to copy something **from** a book* |
| **dans** l'avion | *on the plane* |
| mettre quelque chose **dans** le tiroir | *to put something **into** the drawer* |
| monter **dans** le train | *to get **on** the train* |
| On s'est croisés **dans** l'escalier. | *We ran into each other **on** the stairs.* |

e. **Dans** is used for approximations or estimates.

| | |
|---|---|
| Il a payé **dans** les dix mille euros. | *He paid something **in the area of** ten thousand euros.* |

---

### Idioms and expressions with **en** and **dans**

**Avez-vous cette serviette en cuir noir?** *Do you have this briefcase in black leather?*
**avoir confiance en quelqu'un** *to have confidence in someone*

**C'est sa mère en plus jeune.** *She's a younger version of her mother.*
**en danger** *in danger*

*(continued)*

---

\***Dans cinq jours** means *five days from today,* whereas **en cinq jours** means *in (within the duration of ) five days:* **Son voyage commencera dans un mois. Il traversera l'océan en un mois.**

**Activité 9**    Est-ce *en* ou *dans*? Complétez les paragraphes suivants avec **en** ou **dans**.

### Le nouvel appartement des Truffaut

Les Truffaut ont acheté un nouvel appartement. Je crois qu'il leur a coûté

_____ les cent mille euros. L'appartement n'est pas
<br>         1

_____ la ville de Paris parce qu'ils préfèrent habiter
<br>         2

_____ banlieue. Mais leur bureau est
<br>         3

_____ ville. Ils y vont _____ train.
<br>         4                                   5

### Christine Urbain parle de ses vacances.

J'ai envie de partir _____ vacances. J'aime passer mes
<br>                            6

vacances _____ les Alpes. J'adore partir
<br>                7

_____ été. Il fait beau et je mets un short
<br>         8

_____ coton tous les jours. Je commence à faire mes
<br>         9

préparatifs. Tout sera prêt _____ cinq jours et je
<br>                             10

pourrai partir!

### Un collègue en difficulté

Je ne sais pas ce qui se passe avec Édouard. Son bureau est

_____ pagaille. Lui qui était toujours
<br>         11

_____ pleine forme ne fait plus d'exercice. Je me demande
<br>         12

ce qui se passe _____ sa tête. Le chef n'a plus confiance

           13

_____ lui. J'ai l'impression que son poste est

           14

_____ jeu et Édouard ne semble pas s'en rendre compte.

           15

## Sous, sur, and related prepositions

There are cases in which the French prepositions **sous** (*under*) and **sur** (*on*) have unexpected English equivalents.

1. a. **Sous** may correspond to the English *at* or *in*.

| | |
|---|---|
| **sous** l'équateur | *at the equator* |
| **sous** la tente | *in the tent* |
| **sous** la pluie, **sous** le soleil | *in the rain, in the sun* |
| avoir quelque chose **sous** les yeux | *to have something **before** one's eyes* |
| avoir quelque chose **sous** la main | *to have something **at** hand* |

   b. **Sous** may express location in time, usually within a period or historical event.

| | |
|---|---|
| **sous** la Révolution | ***at the time of** the Revolution* |
| **sous** le règne de Napoléon | ***during/in** Napoleon's reign* |
| **sous peu** | *shortly* |

2. a. **Sur** may correspond to the English *at* or *in* in an expression of position.

| | |
|---|---|
| **sur** le stade | *at the stadium* |
| **sur** la place (du marché) | *at the marketplace* |
| **sur** la chaussée | *in the roadway* |
| **sur** la photo | *in the photo* |
| acheter quelque chose **sur** le marché | *to buy something **at** the market* |
| Il pleut **sur** toute la France. | *It's raining all **over** France.* |

   b. **Sur** expresses approximate time.

| | |
|---|---|
| arriver **sur** les trois heures | *to arrive at **around** three o'clock* |
| Elle va **sur** ses dix-huit ans. | *She's going **on** eighteen.* |

   c. **Sur** expresses the English *out of* in statements of proportion and measure.

| | |
|---|---|
| deux fois **sur** trois | *two times **out** of three* |
| une femme **sur** dix | *one woman **in** ten* |
| un jour **sur** trois | *every third day* |
| un lundi **sur** deux | *every other Monday* |

   d. **Sur** labels the subject of a piece of writing or conversation (English *about*).

| | |
|---|---|
| un article **sur** la santé | *an article **about** health* |
| interroger le soldat **sur** son régiment | *to question the soldier **about** his regiment* |

**étudier la question sous tous les angles** *to study the question from every angle*

**présenter sous un jour favorable** *to present in a favorable light*

**sous l'influence de** *under the influence of*

**sous peine d'amende** *on penalty of a fine*

**sous une identité d'emprunt** *under an assumed identity*

**Cet enfant a eu grippe sur grippe.** *This child has had one flu after another.*

**Elle est revenue sur son idée.** *She thought better of it.*

**être sur la bonne/mauvaise piste** *to be on the right/wrong track*

**Il revient toujours sur la même question.** *He keeps going back to the same matter.*

**Je n'ai pas les documents sur moi.** *I don't have the documents on me.*

**La clé est restée sur la porte.** *The key was left in the door.*

**revenir sur ses pas** *to retrace one's steps*

**vivre les uns sur les autres** *to live one on top of the other*

## Dessus and dessous

1. **Sur** and **sous** have corresponding adverbs—**dessus** (*over it, on top of it*) and **dessous** (*beneath it, underneath it*).

| | |
|---|---|
| La chaise boite. Ne mets pas ta valise **dessus.** | *The chair is uneven. Don't put your suitcase **on top of it.*** |
| Tu vois tous ces papiers? La lettre est **dessous.** | *Do you see all those papers? The letter is **underneath them.*** |

2. The adverbs have compound forms **au-dessus** and **au-dessous.**

habiter **au-dessus/au-dessous**    *to live **upstairs/downstairs***

**Au-dessus de** and **au-dessous de** are compound prepositions.

| | |
|---|---|
| les enfants **au-dessus de** dix ans | *children **over** ten years of age* |
| Il fait dix degrés **au-dessus de** zéro. | *It's ten degrees **above** zero.* |
| rien **au-dessus de** cent euros | *nothing **over** one hundred euros* |
| C'est **au-dessus de** mes forces. | *It's **too much** for me.* |

| | |
|---|---|
| les jeunes **au-dessous de** dix-huit ans | *young people **under** eighteen years old* |
| être **au-dessous de** sa tâche | *not to be **up** to one's task* |
| Il croit que c'est **au-dessous de** lui de faire le ménage. | *He thinks that it's **beneath** him to do the housework.* |

3. **Par-dessus de** and **en dessous de** also appear in some expressions.

| | |
|---|---|
| J'en ai **par-dessus** la tête. | *I'm fed up with it.* |
| **par-dessus le marché** | *on top of everything, in addition to everything* |

| | |
|---|---|
| faire quelque chose **en dessous** | *to do something underhanded* |
| être **en dessous de la moyenne** | *to be below average* |

4. Some common expressions with **dessus** and **dessous:**

| aller bras dessus, bras dessous | to walk arm in arm |
| sens dessus-dessous | topsy-turvy; in complete disorder |

**Activité 10** **Exprimez en français!** Écrivez les phrases suivantes en français.

1. *I'm fed up with it.*

   _____

2. *Jacques and Marie walk arm in arm.*

   _____

3. *These students are below average.*

   _____

4. *The detective is on the right track.*

   _____

5. *We bought apples at the marketplace.*

   _____

6. *I like to take walks in the rain.*

   _____

7. *I'm free every other Saturday.*

   _____

8. *He works under an assumed identity.*

   _____

9. *She thinks work is beneath her.*

   _____

10. *Children below ten years of age don't pay.*

    _____

11. *It's too much for me.*

    _____

12. *He wrote an article about Tunisia.*

    _____

# The prepositions **entre, pour,** and **par**

1. a. The preposition **entre** means *between.*

   Il y a un jardin **entre** les deux      There is a garden **between** the two
   maisons.                                houses.

b. **Entre** has many figurative uses.

| | |
|---|---|
| **entre** parenthèses/guillemets | *in parentheses/quotation marks* |
| enfermé **entre** quatre murs | *shut in* |
| **entre** nous | *just between us* |
| Il n'y a rien de commun **entre** eux. | *They have nothing in common.* |
| J'ai cette revue **entre** les mains. | *I have that magazine in my hands.* |

c. **Entre** appears in some important idioms.

| | |
|---|---|
| **entre** chien et loup | *at twilight* |
| **entre** la poire et le fromage | *at the end of a meal* |
| parler **entre** ses dents | *to mumble* |

d. Note the use of **d'entre** to translate *of* before a disjunctive pronoun after expressions of quantity, numbers, negative words, and interrogatives.

| | |
|---|---|
| beaucoup **d'entre** nous | *many of us* |
| deux **d'entre** eux | *two of them* |
| Qui **d'entre** vous? | *Who among you?* |

2. a. The preposition **pour** usually translates into English as *for*.

| | |
|---|---|
| J'ai apporté quelque chose **pour** toi. | *I've brought something for you.* |

b. **Pour** means *for* with expressions of time. It usually indicates future time.

| | |
|---|---|
| Je pars **pour** trois jours. | *I'm leaving for three days.* |
| J'en ai **pour** cinq minutes. | *I'll be done in five minutes.* |

c. **Pour** means *to* or *in order to* before an infinitive.

| | |
|---|---|
| Tu ne dis ça que **pour** me fâcher. | *You're only saying that to make me angry.* |

d. **Pour** occurs in idiomatic expressions.

| | |
|---|---|
| Tant d'histoires **pour** si peu de chose! | *So much fuss over such a small thing!* |
| garder le meilleur **pour** la fin | *to save the best for last* |
| être **pour** la peine de mort | *to be for (in favor of) the death penalty* |
| Et **pour** cause! | *And for good reason!* |
| **Pour** être fâché, je le suis! | *Talk about being angry, I am angry!* |

3. a. **Par** usually translates into English as *through* or *by*, especially with the passive voice.

| | |
|---|---|
| Il est sortie **par** la porte de devant. | *He went out through the front door.* |
| jeter quelque chose **par** la fenêtre | *to throw something out the window* |
| obtenir quelque chose **par** la force | *to get something by force* |
| un tableau peint **par** Louis David | *a picture painted by Louis David* |

b. **Par** is used to denote position in certain expressions of place and time.

| | |
|---|---|
| Tu ne vas pas sortir **par** un temps pareil! | *You're not going to go out **in** weather like this!* |
| être/tomber **par** terre | *to be/fall **on** the ground* |
| deux fois **par** mois | *twice a month* |
| **par** les temps qui courent | *these days* |

c. **Par** occurs in idiomatic expressions.

| | |
|---|---|
| **par ici, par là** | *this way, that way* |
| **par conséquent** | *consequently* |
| **par mégarde** | ***by** accident* |
| **par intervalles** | *intermittently* |
| **par cœur** | ***by** heart* |
| faire quelque chose **par** amitié, **par** amour | *to do something **out of** friendship, **out of** love* |
| Il a fini **par** ennuyer tout le monde. | *He wound up annoying everyone.* |

**Activité 11**  **La vie est parfois compliquée.**  Complétez les narrations suivantes avec les prépositions **entre, d'entre, pour** ou **par.**

### La mère de Maurice est furieuse!

Ma mère est furieuse. _____ être furieuse, elle l'est! Elle dit que
<br>1

c'est _____ cause. Je vais vous dire ce qui s'est passé. J'étais avec mes
<br>2

amis. Il faisait très mauvais. Plusieurs _____ nous sommes sortis
<br>3

_____ la tempête. Moi, je me suis enrhumé. Maintenant je prends du
<br>4

sirop contre la toux et de l'aspirine plusieurs fois _____ jour. Et je garde
<br>5

le meilleur _____ la fin. Ma mère a attrapé mon rhume.
<br>6

_____ conséquent, elle prend le sirop et l'aspirine avec moi.
<br>7

### Les problèmes de Philippe

_____ nous, je crois que Philippe est déprimé. Il dit des
<br>8

bêtises _____ mégarde et parle souvent _____ ses dents. Il
<br>9       10

laisse ses papiers _____ terre et il se fâche _____ un rien. Il va
<br>11       12

finir _____ ennuyer tout le monde.
<br>13

## Other prepositions

1. **Devant** (*in front of*) and **derrière** (*behind*) are used to express position and location.

| | |
|---|---|
| **devant** le lycée | ***in front of** the high school* |
| **derrière** l'arbre | ***behind** the tree* |

2. **Avant** (*before*), like **après** (*after*), is used to talk about time.

| | |
|---|---|
| **avant** huit heures | *before eight o'clock* |
| **après** l'examen | *after the test* |

**Avant** becomes **avant de** before an infinitive.

| | |
|---|---|
| **avant de** partir | *before leaving* |

**Après** is usually used with the perfect infinitive (**avoir** or **être** + *past participle*).

| | |
|---|---|
| **après avoir fini** le travail | *after finishing the work* |
| **après être sorti(e)(s)** | *after going out* |

3. **À travers** means *through, across.*

| | |
|---|---|
| partir **à travers** champs/bois | *to set off across country, through the woods* |
| voir le paysage **à travers** la vitre | *to see the scenery through the window* |

4. **Chez** means *at the house of, at the store of,* or, figuratively, *with, among.*

| | |
|---|---|
| passer le dimanche **chez mon oncle** | *to spend Sunday at my uncle's house* |
| acheter du poulet **chez le boucher** | *to buy chicken at the butcher's* |
| aller **chez le dentiste** | *to go to the dentist* |
| C'est une coutume **chez les Allemands.** | *It's a custom among the Germans.* |

5. **Contre** means *against.*

| | |
|---|---|
| s'appuyer **contre** le mur | *to lean against the wall* |

**Contre** has other English equivalents in certain contexts.

| | |
|---|---|
| se fâcher / être en colère **contre** quelqu'un | *to get/be angry with someone* |
| Nous sommes tout à fait **contre.** | *We're totally against (it).* |
| dix voix **contre** cinq | *ten votes to five* |
| un sirop **contre** la toux | *a cough syrup* |
| échanger/troquer un livre **contre** un logiciel | *to exchange/swap a book for a software program* |

6. **Vers** means *toward* in space and time; **envers** means *toward* figuratively, in the sense of an attitude or gesture toward someone.

| | |
|---|---|
| aller **vers** Lille | *to go toward Lille* |
| **vers** cinq heures | *around five o'clock* |
| votre gentillesse **envers** moi | *your kindness toward me* |

7. **Hors de** and **en dehors de** mean *outside of* when referring to spatial position.

| | |
|---|---|
| **hors de / en dehors** de l'appartement | *out of / outside of the apartment* |

**Hors de** and **hors** (in certain fixed expressions only) can be used figuratively.

| | |
|---|---|
| **hors d'**haleine, **hors de** danger | *out of breath, out of danger* |
| **hors jeu** | *offside (sports), out of play* |

## More prepositions

| | | | |
|---|---|---|---|
| **à cause de** | *because of* | **parmi** | *among* |
| **au sujet de** | *about* (*on the subject of*) | **pendant** | *during* |
| **d'après** | *according to* | **près de** | *near* |
| **durant** | *during* | **quant à** | *as for* |
| **environ** | *about* (*approximately*) | **selon** | *according to* |
| **loin de** | *far from* | **suivant** | *according to* |
| **malgré** | *in spite of* | | |

**Activité 12**    **Comprenez-vous?** Écrivez l'équivalent anglais de ces phrases.

1. On se verra vers six heures.

   _____

2. D'après le médecin, il n'est pas hors de danger.

   _____

3. On vit mieux en dehors de la ville.

   _____

4. Il a été très généreux envers ses enfants.

   _____

5. Elle regarde à travers la fenêtre.

   _____

6. Le professeur a parlé au sujet de l'examen.

   _____

7. Il me faut passer chez mon avocat.

   _____

8. Je te donne ces timbres contre cette pièce.

   _____

**Activité 13**    **Et en français?** Écrivez ces phrases en français.

1. *according to the newspapers* _____
2. *during the class* _____
3. *in spite of the difficulty* _____
4. *near the station* _____
5. *as for me* _____
6. *three votes to two* _____

*(continued)*

7. *about ten students* _____

8. *offside (out of play)* _____

9. *across country* _____

10. *with, among French people* _____

11. *before going downstairs* _____

12. *after going downstairs* _____

## Prepositions with geographical names

1. French uses the definite article before names of countries, provinces, regions, and continents.

**la France** *France*　　　　　　　　**le Midi** *the south of France*
**la Bretagne** *Brittany*　　　　　　　**l'Europe** *Europe*

2. French uses the preposition **en** to express motion toward or location in a country (or province or region) if the place name is feminine singular. The definite article is not used.

aller **en** Italie　　　　　　　　　　*to go **to** Italy*
partir **en** Pologne　　　　　　　　*to leave **for** Poland*
faire un voyage **en** Chine　　　　*to take a trip **to** China*

3. **En** is also used before masculine singular countries beginning with a vowel. The definite article is not used.

aller **en** Irak　　　　　　　　　　*go to Iraq*
émigrer **en** Israël　　　　　　　　*to emigrate **to** Israel*

**NOTE**　　**Israël** is not usually accompanied by the definite article: **Israël est un pays du Moyen-Orient.**

4. To express *from* with the previously listed place names, **de** or **d'** is substituted for **en.**

revenir **d'**Italie　　　　　　　　　*to return **from** Italy*
être **de** Pologne　　　　　　　　　*to be **from** Poland*
partir **d'**Israël　　　　　　　　　*to leave **from** Israel*

5. For masculine singular place names that do not begin with a vowel, and masculine and feminine plural place names, *to* or *in* is expressed by **à** + *definite article* (**au** or **aux**).

aller/être **au** Portugal　　　　　　*to go to / be **in** Portugal*
aller/être **au** Japon　　　　　　　*to go to / be **in** Japan*
aller/être **aux** États-Unis　　　　*to go to / be **in** the United States*
aller/être **aux** Antilles　　　　　*to go to / be **in** the West Indies**

*Martinique and Guadeloupe are the most well-known islands in **les Antilles,** which comprise the French-speaking islands of the Caribbean.

6. To express *from* with the previously listed place names, **de** + *definite article* (**du** or **des**) is used.

revenir **du** Danemark, **du** Canada
*to come back **from** Denmark, **from** Canada*

revenir **du** Viêt-Nam, **des** Pays-Bas
*to come back **from** Vietnam, **from** the Netherlands*

7. With the names of most islands, French uses **à** (sometimes **à la** for feminine names) to express *to* and **de** (sometimes **de la**) to express *from*.

à (l'île) Maurice / **de** (l'île) Maurice    ***to* / *from** Mauritius*
à **la** Réunion / **de la** Réunion    ***to* / *from** Reunion Island*
à Porto Rico / **de** Porto Rico    ***to* / *from** Puerto Rico*
à **la** Guadeloupe / **de la** Guadeloupe    ***to* / *from** Guadeloupe*
à **la** Martinique / **de la** Martinique    ***to* / *from** Martinique*

**NOTE**   Some islands, however, take **en: en Sicile, en Corse, en Sardaigne.**

8. Before names of cities, French uses **à** to express *to* or *in* and **de** to express *from*.

à Montréal, **de** Montréal    ***to*/*in** Montreal, **from** Montreal*
à Genève, **de** Genève    ***to*/*in** Geneva, **from** Geneva*
à New York, **de** New York    ***to*/*in** New York, **from** New York*
à Dakar, **de** Dakar    ***to*/*in** Dakar, **from** Dakar*

9. Some cities have a definite article as part of their name: **Le Havre, La Rochelle, Le Caire** (*Cairo*), **La Havane** (*Havana*), **La Nouvelle-Orléans** (*New Orleans*). The article is kept when **à** or **de** is used with these names, and the appropriate contractions are made.

**Le** Havre: **au** Havre, **du** Havre    *Le Havre: **to*/*in** Le Havre, **from** Le Havre*

**La** Rochelle: **à La** Rochelle, **de La** Rochelle    *La Rochelle: **to*/*in** La Rochelle, **from** La Rochelle*

10. All place names take the definite article when modified. **En** becomes **dans** when the article is used. The preposition **à** also changes to **dans** when the place name is modified.

**dans** l'Europe du vingtième siècle    *in twentieth-century Europe*

11. French uses **en** to express *in* or *to* and **de** to express *from* before the following U.S. states that are grammatically feminine: **Californie, Caroline du Nord/Sud, Floride, Géorgie, Louisiane, Pennsylvanie, Virginie, Virginie-Occidentale.** The rest of the U.S. states are grammatically masculine, and either **dans le** or **au** may be used in almost all cases. Before states beginning with a vowel, **dans l'** or **en** may be used.

**dans le** Colorado, **au** Colorado, **du** Colorado
**dans l'**Alabama, **en** Alabama, **de l'**Alabama, **d'**Alabama

<table>
</table>

**NOTE**  Notice the differences in the prepositions used with place names that refer to both a province/state and a city.

| | |
|---|---|
| le Québec, Québec | Quebec **Province**, Quebec **City** |
| au Québec, à Québec | to/in Quebec **Province**, to/in Quebec **City** |
| du Québec, de Québec | from Quebec **Province**, from Quebec **City** |
| l'état de New York, New York | New York **State**, New York **City** |
| dans l'état de New York, à New York | to/in New York **State**, to/in New York **City** |
| de l'état de New York, de New York | from New York **State**, from New York **City** |

Other examples: **l'état de Washington** (*Washington state*) and **Washington** (*Washington D.C.*); **le Mexique** (*Mexico*) and **Mexico** (*Mexico City*).

## Feminine countries

### l'Europe

| | | |
|---|---|---|
| **l'Allemagne** *Germany* | **l'Espagne** *Spain* | **la République tchèque** *Czech Republic* |
| **l'Angleterre** *England* | **la France** *France* | **la Russie** *Russia* |
| **l'Autriche** *Austria* | **la Grèce** *Greece* | **la Serbie** *Serbia* |
| **la Belgique** *Belgium* | **l'Irlande** *Ireland* | **la Slovaquie** *Slovakia* |
| **la Bosnie** *Bosnia* | **l'Italie** *Italy* | **la Suède** *Sweden* |
| **la Croatie** *Croatia* | **la Norvège** *Norway* | **la Suisse** *Switzerland* |
| **l'Écosse** *Scotland* | **la Pologne** *Poland* | |

### l'Afrique

| | | |
|---|---|---|
| **l'Afrique du Sud** *South Africa* | **l'Égypte** *Egypt* | **la République démocratique du Congo** *Democratic Republic of Congo* |
| **l'Algérie** *Algeria* | **la Guinée** *Guinea* | |
| **la Côte d'Ivoire** *Ivory Coast* | **la Libye** *Libya* | **la Tunisie** *Tunisia* |
| | **la Mauritanie** *Mauretania* | |

### l'Asie et l'Océanie

| | | |
|---|---|---|
| **l'Arabie saoudite** *Saudi Arabia* | **l'Inde** *India* | **la Syrie** *Syria* |
| **l'Australie** *Australia* | **la Jordanie** *Jordan* | **la Thaïlande** *Thailand* |
| **la Chine** *China* | **la Nouvelle-Zélande** *New Zealand* | **la Turquie** *Turkey* |
| **la Corée (du Nord, du Sud)** *Korea (North, South)* | **les Philippines** *the Philippines* | |

### l'Amérique

| | | |
|---|---|---|
| **les Antilles** *West Indies* | **la Colombie** *Colombia* | **la République dominicaine** *Dominican Republic* |
| **l'Argentine** *Argentina* | | |

## Masculine countries

### l'Europe

**le Danemark** *Denmark*
**le Luxembourg** *Luxemburg*

**les Pays-Bas** *Netherlands*

**le Portugal** *Portugal*

### l'Afrique

**le Congo** *the Congo*
**le Mali** *Mali*

**le Maroc** *Morocco*
**le Mozambique** *Mozambique*

**le Sénégal** *Senegal*
**le Soudan** *Sudan*

### l'Asie et l'Océanie

**l'Afghanistan** *Afghanistan*
**le Cambodge** *Cambodia*
**l'Irak** *Iraq*
**l'Iran** *Iran*

**Israël** *Israel*
**le Japon** *Japan*
**le Koweït** *Kuwait*
**le Liban** *Lebanon*

**le Pakistan** *Pakistan*
**le Viêt-Nam** *Vietnam*

### l'Amérique

**le Brésil** *Brazil*
**le Canada** *Canada*
**le Chili** *Chile*

**les États-Unis** *United States*
**le Guatemala** *Guatemala*
**Haïti** *Haiti*

**le Mexique** *Mexico*
**le Pérou** *Peru*
**Le Salvador** *El Salvador*

---

**Activité 14** **Des étudiants à l'étranger.** Un groupe de jeunes Belges font un stage d'un an dans différents pays. Dites en chaque cas le pays et la ville où ils se trouvent, selon le modèle.

> MODÈLE   Willie / France / Paris
> Willie travaille en France, à Paris.

1. Monique / Canada / Québec

   _____

2. Olivier / États-Unis / La Nouvelle-Orléans

   _____

3. Mariek / Japon / Tokyo

   _____

4. Fernand / Brésil / São Paulo

   _____

5. Gérard / Mexique / Mexico

   _____

(continued)

CHAPITRE 23

6. Stella / Haïti / Port-au-Prince

_____

7. Luc / Sénégal / Dakar

_____

8. Brigitte / Pays-Bas / Amsterdam

_____

9. Sylvie / Égypte / Le Caire

_____

10. Béatrice / Portugal / Lisbonne

_____

11. Jan / Viêt-Nam / Hô Chi Minh-Ville

_____

12. Raymond / Israël / Jérusalem

_____

**Activité 15** **D'où sont-ils?** Faites des phrases pour exprimer l'origine de ces étudiants étrangers. Suivez le modèle.

> MODÈLE    Jacques / France
> Jacques est de France.

1. Fatima / Irak

_____

2. Lise / Bruxelles

_____

3. Martin et Santos / Chili

_____

4. Sven / Danemark

_____

5. Rosa et Laura / Naples

_____

6. Mei-Li / Chine

_____

7. Amalia / Mexico

_____

8. Fred et Jane / Californie

_____

9. Kimberly / Vermont

_____

10. Odile / Luxembourg

_____

11. Corazon / Philippines

_____

12. Mies / Pays-Bas

_____

13. Hanako et Hiro / Japon

_____

14. Bill / États-Unis

_____

15. Olivier / Le Havre

_____

# 24 PRESENT AND PAST SUBJUNCTIVE

## Moods of verbs

The mood of a verb indicates how the speaker views a statement. The indicative mood is used to state facts and describe reality. The imperative mood is used to make commands. The subjunctive mood is used to express wishes, desires, necessities, emotions, opinions, doubts, suppositions, and other more subjective conditions.

**Indicative mood**

> **Nous faisons** nos devoirs.

> *We do our homework.*

**Imperative mood**

> **Faisons** nos devoirs tout de suite!

> *Let's do our homework right away!*

**Subjunctive mood**

> Le professeur exige **que nous fassions** nos devoirs tous les soirs.

> *The teacher demands that we do our homework every night.*

The subjunctive mood is used much more frequently in French than in English. It typically appears in dependent and relative clauses.

## Forms of the present subjunctive

1. To form the present subjunctive of most verbs, drop the **-ent** ending from the present tense **ils/elles** form and add the endings **-e, -es, -e, -ions, -iez, -ent.**

| RENTRER | | | |
|---|---|---|---|
| que je | rentr**e** | que nous | rentr**ions** |
| que tu | rentr**es** | que vous | rentr**iez** |
| qu'il/qu'elle | rentr**e** | qu'ils/qu'elles | rentr**ent** |

| FINIR | | | |
|---|---|---|---|
| que je | finiss**e** | que nous | finiss**ions** |
| que tu | finiss**es** | que vous | finiss**iez** |
| qu'il/qu'elle | finiss**e** | qu'ils/qu'elles | finiss**ent** |

| VENDRE | | | |
|---|---|---|---|
| que je | vend**e** | que nous | vend**ions** |
| que tu | vend**es** | que vous | vend**iez** |
| qu'il/qu'elle | vend**e** | qu'ils/qu'elles | vend**ent** |

Regular **-er** verbs that have changes in the vowel in the present-tense stem, such as **acheter** and **compléter,** have those changes in the subjunctive as well.

que j'ach**è**te / que nous ach**e**tions

que je compl**è**te / que nous compl**é**tions

2. The subjunctive forms of most irregular verbs follow the same pattern as the regular verbs. For example, study the subjunctive of **lire, écrire,** and **joindre.**

| LIRE | | | |
|---|---|---|---|
| que je | lis**e** | que nous | lis**ions** |
| que tu | lis**es** | que vous | lis**iez** |
| qu'il/qu'elle | lis**e** | qu'ils/qu'elles | lis**ent** |

| ÉCRIRE | | | |
|---|---|---|---|
| que j' | écriv**e** | que nous | écriv**ions** |
| que tu | écriv**es** | que vous | écriv**iez** |
| qu'il/qu'elle | écriv**e** | qu'ils/qu'elles | écriv**ent** |

| JOINDRE | | | |
|---|---|---|---|
| que je | joign**e** | que nous | joign**ions** |
| que tu | joign**es** | que vous | joign**iez** |
| qu'il/qu'elle | joign**e** | qu'ils/qu'elles | joign**ent** |

3. Irregular verbs such as **boire, prendre,** and **venir,** which have variations in the stem in the present indicative, show similar changes in the present subjunctive.

| BOIRE | | | |
|---|---|---|---|
| que je | **boiv**e | que nous | **buv**ions |
| que tu | **boiv**es | que vous | **buv**iez |
| qu'il/qu'elle | **boiv**e | qu'ils/qu'elles | **boiv**ent |

| PRENDRE | | | |
|---|---|---|---|
| que je | **prenn**e | que nous | **pren**ions |
| que tu | **prenn**es | que vous | **pren**iez |
| qu'il/qu'elle | **prenn**e | qu'ils/qu'elles | **prenn**ent |

| VENIR | | | |
|---|---|---|---|
| que je | **vienn**e | que nous | **ven**ions |
| que tu | **vienn**es | que vous | **ven**iez |
| qu'il/qu'elle | **vienn**e | qu'ils/qu'elles | **vienn**ent |

4. The verbs **aller, avoir, être, faire, pouvoir, savoir,** and **vouloir** are irregular in the subjunctive.

| ALLER | | | |
|---|---|---|---|
| que j' | **aille** | que nous | **allions** |
| que tu | **ailles** | que vous | **alliez** |
| qu'il/qu'elle | **aille** | qu'ils/qu'elles | **aillent** |

| AVOIR | | | |
|---|---|---|---|
| que j' | **aie** | que nous | **ayons** |
| que tu | **aies** | que vous | **ayez** |
| qu'il/qu'elle | **ait** | qu'ils/qu'elles | **aient** |

| ÊTRE | | | |
|---|---|---|---|
| que je | **sois** | que nous | **soyons** |
| que tu | **sois** | que vous | **soyez** |
| qu'il/qu'elle | **soit** | qu'ils/qu'elles | **soient** |

| FAIRE | | | |
|---|---|---|---|
| que je | **fasse** | que nous | **fassions** |
| que tu | **fasses** | que vous | **fassiez** |
| qu'il/qu'elle | **fasse** | qu'ils/qu'elles | **fassent** |

| POUVOIR | | | |
|---|---|---|---|
| que je | **puisse** | que nous | **puissions** |
| que tu | **puisses** | que vous | **puissiez** |
| qu'il/qu'elle | **puisse** | qu'ils/qu'elles | **puissent** |

| SAVOIR | | | |
|---|---|---|---|
| que je | **sache** | que nous | **sachions** |
| que tu | **saches** | que vous | **sachiez** |
| qu'il/qu'elle | **sache** | qu'ils/qu'elles | **sachent** |

| VOULOIR | | | |
|---|---|---|---|
| que je | **veuille** | que nous | **voulions** |
| que tu | **veuilles** | que vous | **vouliez** |
| qu'il/qu'elle | **veuille** | qu'ils/qu'elles | **veuillent** |

The verb **valoir** is conjugated somewhat like **aller** in the present subjunctive: **que je vaille, que nous valions** (versus **que nous allions**). **Falloir,**

which is conjugated only in the third person singular, resembles **valoir** in the subjunctive: **qu'il faille.** The subjunctive of **pleuvoir** is **qu'il pleuve.**

## Uses of the subjunctive: getting or wanting someone to do something

1. The subjunctive is used after verbs that express wanting, preferring, needing, making, or forcing someone to do something.

| | |
|---|---|
| **Je** ne **veux** pas **qu'il parte.** | *I don't want him to leave.* |
| Alors **je vais empêcher qu'il s'en aille.** | *Then I'll keep him from going away.* |

| | |
|---|---|
| **J'exige que Philippe soit** là. | *I demand that Philippe be here.* |
| **Il faut que nous l'invitions,** alors. | *We must invite him then.* |

| | |
|---|---|
| **Je suggère que vous traduisiez** l'article. | *I suggest that you translate the article.* |
| **Il est nécessaire que vous** m'**aidiez.** | *It's necessary for you to help me.* |

2. The following verbs and expressions are followed by the subjunctive because they express an imposition of will.

| | | |
|---|---|---|
| **aimer mieux que** *to prefer* | **empêcher que** *to prevent, keep* | **recommander que** |
| **attendre que** *to wait until,* | **exiger que** *to demand* | *to recommend* |
| *wait for* | **ordonner que** *to order* | **souhaiter que** *to wish* |
| **avoir besoin que** *to need* | **permettre que** *to allow* | **suggérer que** *to suggest* |
| **demander que** *to request, ask* | **préférer que** *to prefer* | **vouloir que** *to want* |
| **désirer que** *to desire, want, wish* | | |

3. The following impersonal expressions signifying imposition of will are followed by the subjunctive.

| | | |
|---|---|---|
| **il est essentiel/important que** | **il est nécessaire/urgent que** | **il faut que** *it is necessary* |
| *it is essential/important that* | *it is necessary/urgent that* | *that; one has to* |
| **il est indispensable/utile que** | | |
| *it is indispensable/useful that* | | |

4. For the subjunctive to be used, the subjects of the main clause and the subordinate clause have to be different. If the subjects of the two clauses are the same, the infinitive is used in the subordinate clause.

| | |
|---|---|
| **Je** veux que **tu** reviennes. | *I want you to come back.* |
| **Je** veux revenir. | *I want to come back.* |

| | |
|---|---|
| **Ils** préfèrent que **nous** restions. | *They prefer that we stay.* |
| **Ils** préfèrent rester. | *They prefer to stay.* |

5. The present subjunctive can be used after any tense.

| | |
|---|---|
| Je voulais qu'il **vienne.** | *I wanted him to come.* |
| Il voudra que nous le **fassions.** | *He'll want us to do it.* |

| Nous aurions voulu que vous **puissiez venir**. | *We would have wanted you to be able to come.* |

**Activité 1** **Moi, je ne veux pas.** Un ami vous dit ce que font les autres. Répondez-lui dans chaque cas que vous, vous ne voulez pas que les autres fassent ces choses-là. Employez le subjonctif dans la proposition subordonnée, suivant le modèle.

> MODÈLE   Marie étudie huit heures par jour.
> Moi, je ne veux pas qu'elle étudie huit heures par jour.

1. Serge fait du japonais.

   _____

2. Élisabeth laisse les fenêtres ouvertes.

   _____

3. Richard sort avec Hélène.

   _____

4. Louis boit du coca.

   _____

5. Je vois un vieux film.

   _____

6. Michel sait où tu habites.

   _____

7. Chantal est triste.

   _____

8. Robert et Thérèse ont peur.

   _____

9. Daniel maigrit.

   _____

10. Moi, je grossis.

    _____

**Activité 2** **La fête de samedi soir.** C'est à vous d'organiser la fête de samedi. Dites ce que chacun doit faire, selon le modèle.

> MODÈLE   je veux / Marie / inviter ses cousins
> Je veux que Marie invite ses cousins.

1. je préfère / Marc / choisir le gâteau

_____

2. il est nécessaire / Lise et Rachelle / aller chercher les boissons

_____

3. il est important / Roland et Jacqueline / pouvoir venir

_____

4. je veux / Janine / faire les amuse-gueules

_____

5. il faut / tu / faire quelques coups de fil (_phone calls_)

_____

6. il est essentiel / Olivier / être / là

_____

7. je préfère / nous / acheter des plats préparés chez le charcutier

_____

8. je veux / tu / venir m'aider samedi après-midi

_____

---

**Activité 3**  **Des étudiants à Paris.** Un groupe d'étudiants de province vont passer une semaine à Paris. Où est-ce qu'ils veulent aller? Ils ne sont pas d'accord. Construisez des phrases avec les éléments donnés pour savoir ce que chacun souhaite faire. Employez le subjonctif dans les propositions subordonnées. Suivez le modèle.

> MODÈLE  Paul / vouloir / on / aller / d'abord / aux Champs-Élysées
> Paul veut qu'on aille d'abord aux Champs-Élysées.

1. le professeur / exiger / nous / visiter tous les monuments de Paris

_____

2. Barbara / souhaiter / nous / commencer / par la visite du Louvre

_____

3. Martin / désirer / le groupe / faire / le tour de Paris en bus

_____

4. Monique / demander / on / voir / les Tuileries

_____

(continued)

5. Georges / recommander / tous les étudiants / aller / à l'Arc de Triomphe

_____

6. Gustave / suggérer / nous / monter / à Montmartre

_____

7. Diane / ordonner / tout le monde / suivre l'itinéraire

_____

8. Édouard / aimer mieux / on / faire une promenade dans le Marais

_____

9. Renée / vouloir / nous / prendre le déjeuner

_____

10. Véronique / ne pas vouloir / nous / passer / toute la journée à discuter

_____

**Activité 4** **Nos souhaits et désirs.** Joignez les éléments donnés en une seule phrase qui exprime le désir que les actions se réalisent. Employez le subjonctif dans la proposition subordonnée. Suivez le modèle.

> MODÈLE Tu fais le linge. (j'ai besoin)
> J'ai besoin que tu fasses le linge.

1. Tout est en règle. (j'exige)

_____

2. Les enfants ont peur. (je ne veux pas)

_____

3. Cette famille vit mal. (nous ne voulons pas)

_____

4. Il boit trop de coca. (ses parents empêcheront)

_____

5. Il apprend les réponses. (je recommande)

_____

6. Ils conduisent prudemment. (je demande)

_____

7. Elle rejoint son fiancé. (ses parents aiment mieux)

_____

8. Elle sort avec Jean-Philippe. (ses parents ne permettent pas)

_____

## Uses of the subjunctive: emotion and opinion

The subjunctive is used following verbs and impersonal expressions that express emotion.

### Fear

**avoir peur que** *to be afraid that*   **craindre que** *to fear that*

### Surprise or curiosity

**cela m'étonne que** *I'm surprised that*
**Comment cela se fait que...?** *How is it that . . . ?*
**s'étonner que** *to be surprised that*

**il est bizarre/curieux/ extraordinaire que** *it's strange/extraordinary that*

**il est étonnant que** *it's surprising that*

### Happiness and sadness

**être content(e)/heureux(-se)/ triste que** *to be happy/sad that*

**être ravi(e)/satisfait(e)/ désolé(e)/navré(e) que** *to be delighted/satisfied/sorry/ so sorry that*

**regretter que** *to be sorry that*
**se réjouir que** *to rejoice, be glad that*

### Annoyance and anger

**avoir honte que** *to be ashamed that*
**cela m'ennuie/m'agace/ m'énerve que** *it annoys me that*

**être fâché(e)/furieux(-se) que** *to be angry/furious that*
**se fâcher que** *to get angry that, because*

**il est ennuyeux/agaçant/ énervant que** *it's annoying/ irritating that*
**se plaindre que** *to complain that*

| | |
|---|---|
| **Le chef est ravi que vous puissiez** l'aider. | *The boss is delighted that you can help him.* |
| **Je suis heureux qu'il ait** confiance en moi. | *I'm happy that he has confidence in me.* |
| **Je m'étonne que le travail ne soit pas fini.** | *I'm surprised that the work is not finished.* |
| **Cela m'ennuie qu'il** nous **fasse** attendre. | *I'm annoyed that he's keeping us waiting.* |

The subjunctive is used after verbs and impersonal expressions that show that the action of the subordinate clause is an opinion, an evaluation, or a possibility.

## Opinion and evaluation

**accepter que** *to accept that*
**approuver que** *to approve of someone's doing something*
**ce n'est pas la peine que** *it's not worth it that*
**c'est une chance que** *it's lucky that*
**désapprouver que** *to disapprove of someone's doing something*

**il convient que** *it is suitable, advisable that*
**il est logique/normal/ naturel/juste que** *it's logical/normal/natural/right that*
**il est rare que** *it is not often that*

**il importe que** *it matters that, is important that*
**il suffit que** *it is enough that*
**il vaut mieux que** *it is better that*
**peu importe que** *it matters little that*

## Possibility

**il est possible/impossible que** *it's possible/impossible that*
**il n'y a aucune chance que** *there's no chance that*

**il n'y a pas de danger que** *there's no danger that*
**il se peut que** *it's possible that*

**il semble que\*** *it appears that (but it's not definite)*

---

**Activité 5**  **C'est bien.**  On raconte à Marcelle tout ce qu'il y a de neuf. Dans chaque cas, elle exprime sa satisfaction en disant qu'elle est contente de ce qui arrive. Écrivez ce que dit Marcelle en employant le subjonctif dans la proposition subordonnée, selon le modèle.

> MODÈLE   Pierre ne travaille pas aujourd'hui.
> Je suis contente qu'il ne travaille pas aujourd'hui.

1. Marianne et Justine sont là.

   _____

2. Gérard vend son vélo.

   _____

3. Mes parents partent en vacances.

   _____

4. Jean-Claude nous attend.

   _____

\*Note that **il semble que** takes the subjunctive, but **il *me* semble que** takes the indicative (in the affirmative), since it is the equivalent of **je pense que.**

5. Le petit Charles ne désobéit jamais.

   _____

6. Christine et moi, nous dînons ensemble.

   _____

7. Toi et moi, nous terminons le programme cette année.

   _____

8. Frédéric connaît Odile.

   _____

**Activité 6** **En une seule phrase, s'il vous plaît.** Changez l'ordre des deux phrases données pour en faire une seule. Faites les modifications nécessaires en suivant les modèles.

> MODÈLES    Il n'est pas encore là. C'est étonnant.
> Il est étonnant qu'il ne soit pas encore là.
>
> Je maigris. Le médecin se réjouit.
> Le médecin se réjouit que je maigrisse.

1. Tu comprends tout. Je suis ravi.

   _____

2. Ils ne veulent pas nous aider. Nous sommes furieux.

   _____

3. Le prof ne nous reconnaît pas. Cela m'étonne.

   _____

4. Il y a un accident. J'ai peur.

   _____

5. Tu ne peux pas venir. Elle est navrée.

   _____

6. Elle met le foulard que je lui ai offert. Je suis content.

   _____

7. Philippe n'apprend pas beaucoup. Son professeur se plaint.

   _____

8. Ces enfants se battent tout le temps. Je suis fâchée.

   _____

*(continued)*

9. Un professeur perd son travail. C'est rare.

_____

10. Vous me le dites. Cela suffit.

_____

**Activité 7**  **Quel fouillis! Et voilà les parents qui débarquent!**  Vous habitez un appartement avec trois colocataires. Cette fin de semaine les parents viennent voir leurs enfants à l'université. Vous êtes contents de voir vos parents, mais l'état de l'appartement vous inquiète un peu. Pour décrire la situation, joignez les verbes et les expressions entre parenthèses aux phrases. Suivez le modèle.

> MODÈLE  Nos parents viennent nous rendre visite.
> (nous sommes contents)
> Nous sommes contents que nos parents viennent nous
> rendre visite.

**Vocabulaire**

## Pour une demeure propre

**balayer le parquet** *to sweep the floor*
**la bibliothèque** *bookcase*
**cirer le parquet** *to wax the floor*
**dépoussiérer les meubles**
   **(je dépoussière)** *to dust the furniture*

**faire le ménage** *to do the housework*
**le fouillis** *mess*
**ranger** *to put away*
**récurer les casseroles** *to scour the pots*
**la toile d'araignée** *spiderweb, cobweb*

1. Je vis dans le désordre. (ma mère n'acceptera pas)

_____

2. Nous faisons le ménage. (il est essentiel)

_____

3. Nous dépoussiérons les meubles. (il faut que)

_____

4. Bernard et toi, vous récurez les casseroles. (je suis content)

_____

5. Toi et moi, nous balayons le parquet. (il convient que)

_____

6. Nous cirons le parquet aussi. (il est possible)

_____

7. Paul et Marc, vous rangez les livres dans les bibliothèques. (il vaut mieux)

_____

8. Bernard enlève les toiles d'araignée. (je me réjouis)

_____


**Activité 8**  **La flemme (_laziness_) de fin de cours.** C'est le mois de juin et tout le monde a la flemme, sauf vous. Vous essayez de remonter leur morale (_motivate them; get them going again_) en leur conseillant de travailler avec un peu de diligence. Employez le subjonctif dans l'expression de vos conseils. Suivez le modèle.

> MODÈLE  Charles: Je ne veux pas assister au cours de chimie aujourd'hui. (il est important)
> Vous: Écoute, Charles. Il est important que tu assistes au cours de chimie.

1. Annette: Je n'étudie pas pour les examens. (il est bizarre)

_____

2. Michel: Je n'ai aucune envie de travailler à la bibliothèque. (ça m'étonne)

_____

3. Françoise: Je n'écris pas la dissertation de philosophie. (il vaut mieux que)

_____

4. André: Je n'écoute pas les CD sur l'ordinateur. (il est utile)

_____

5. Sylvie: Je ne prends plus de notes dans la classe d'histoire. (il est indispensable)

_____

6. Albert: Je ne fais pas mes devoirs. (les profs seront fâchés)

_____

7. Catherine: Je ne lis plus le livre de biologie. (je regrette)

_____

8. Corine: Je m'endors dans la classe d'anglais. (je n'approuve pas)

_____

9. Sébastien: Je fais des dessins dans mon cahier dans la classe de maths. (il n'est pas normal)

_____

10. Bruno: Je perds mes disquettes. (il est agaçant)

_____

# Uses of the subjunctive: negation of fact and opinion

1. The subjunctive is used after verbs and expressions that negate the action or idea of the subordinate clause.

| | | |
|---|---|---|
| **douter** *to doubt*<br>**il est douteux que** *it is doubtful that* | **il est exclu que** *it's out of the question that* | **nier** *to deny* |

**Je doute qu'il sache** le faire.
**Mais il n'est pas exclu qu'il puisse** nous aider.

*I doubt that he knows how to do it.*
*But it isn't out of the question that he can help us.*

**NOTE** The indicative is usually used after the *negative* of **douter** and **nier,** because when those verbs are used in the negative, they no longer negate facts.

**Je ne doute pas qu'il sait le faire.**     *I don't doubt he knows how to do it.*

2. When the following verbs and expressions are negative, they are followed by the subjunctive. When they are affirmative, they are followed by the indicative.

| | | |
|---|---|---|
| **ça ne veut pas dire que** *it doesn't mean that*<br>**ce n'est pas que** *it's not that*<br>**il est peu probable que** *it's not probable that*<br>**il ne me semble pas que** *it doesn't seem to me that*<br>**il n'est pas certain que** *it's not certain that* | **il n'est pas clair que** *it's not clear that*<br>**il n'est pas évident que** *it's not evident/obvious that*<br>**il n'est pas exact que** *it's not correct, accurate that*<br>**il n'est pas sûr que** *it's not certain that* | **il n'est pas vrai que** *it's not true that*<br>**il ne paraît pas que** *it doesn't seem that*<br>**je ne dis pas que** *I'm not saying that*<br>**je ne suis pas sûr(e) que** *I'm not sure that* |

**Il n'est pas certain qu'il vienne.**
**Ça ne veut pas dire qu'il ne veuille pas** nous voir.

*It's not certain that he's coming.*
*That doesn't mean that he doesn't want to see us.*

**Il n'est pas évident qu'elle sache** la réponse.
Moi, **je suis sûr qu'elle** la **sait.**

*It is not evident that she knows the answer.*
*I'm sure that she knows it.*

3. The verbs **croire, espérer,** and **penser** are followed by the indicative when affirmative, but by the subjunctive when negative or interrogative.

**Je ne crois pas que cet étranger** te **comprenne.**
**Penses-tu que je doive** tout répéter?

*I don't think that that foreigner understands you.*
*Do you think that I ought to repeat everything?*

**Oui, je crois que c'est** nécessaire.

*Yes, I think it's necessary.*

4. The indicative may be used after the negative and interrogative of **croire** and **penser** instead of the subjunctive to convey that the speaker is certain about the action.

| | |
|---|---|
| **Je ne crois/pense pas que tu as raison.** | *I don't think you're right.* (*I think you're wrong.*) |
| **Je ne crois/pense pas que tu aies raison.** | *I don't think you're right.* (*But I'm not sure.*) |

**Activité 9**  **Conversation.** Perrine et Joceline causent ensemble. Perrine demande à son amie si elle sait ce que leurs amis vont faire. Joceline répond dans chaque cas qu'elle ne croit pas que leurs amis comptent faire tout ça. Reconstruisez leur conversation en employant le subjonctif dans la proposition subordonnée de la réponse de Joceline. Suivez le modèle.

> MODÈLE    Stéphane / arriver aujourd'hui
> Perrine: Tu sais si Stéphane arrivera aujourd'hui?
> Joceline: Je ne crois pas qu'il arrive aujourd'hui.

1. notre professeur / finir la leçon

   PERRINE: _____

   JOCELINE: _____

2. Ghislaine / rompre avec son petit ami

   PERRINE: _____

   JOCELINE: _____

3. ton cousin / revenir cette semaine

   PERRINE: _____

   JOCELINE: _____

4. Nadine / servir une pizza à la fête

   PERRINE: _____

   JOCELINE: _____

5. Philippe / sortir avec Mireille

   PERRINE: _____

   JOCELINE: _____

6. Paul / pouvoir nous rejoindre

   PERRINE: _____

   JOCELINE: _____

7. Alice / être là ce soir

   PERRINE: _____

   JOCELINE: _____

*(continued)*

8. toi et moi / étudier assez

PERRINE: _____

JOCELINE: _____

9. Chloë / aller au concert

PERRINE: _____

JOCELINE: _____

10. Daniel / prendre un taxi

PERRINE: _____

JOCELINE: _____

**Activité 10**  **Exprimez vos doutes.**  Utilisez les expressions données entre parenthèses pour exprimer vos doutes sur les faits suivants, selon le modèle.

> MODÈLE   Nous avons un examen aujourd'hui. (je doute)
> Je doute que nous ayons un examen aujourd'hui.

1. Laurence réussit à tous ses examens. (il n'est pas sûr)

   _____

2. Nous offrons des CD à Renée. (il est douteux)

   _____

3. Tu suis un cours d'histoire. (il n'est pas exclu)

   _____

4. Il fait des progrès en anglais. (ça ne veut pas dire)

   _____

5. Lucie t'écrit. (il est peu probable)

   _____

6. Il nous reconnaît. (je ne suis pas sûr)

   _____

7. L'élève apprend tout ça. (je doute)

   _____

8. Ce pays produit des voitures. (il n'est pas clair)

   _____

**Activité 11**  **Au sujet des amis.**  Deux étudiants parlent de leurs amis de l'université. Ils confirment et nient ce qu'on dit à leur sujet. Écrivez ce qu'ils disent en joignant les deux phrases données en une seule. Choisissez entre l'indicatif et le subjonctif dans les propositions subordonnées. Suivez le modèle.

MODÈLE    Marcelle suit un cours de maths. (je crois)
          Je crois que Marcelle suit un cours de maths.

1. La voiture de Jean-François est toujours en panne. (je ne pense pas)

   _____

2. Gisèle compte abandonner ses études. (il est évident)

   _____

3. Luc peut s'acheter un ordinateur. (je doute)

   _____

4. Michèle sort avec Hervé Duclos. (tout le monde sait)

   _____

5. Paul ne fait pas attention en classe. (Marc nie)

   _____

6. Chantal se plaint de tout. (il n'est pas exact)

   _____

7. Martin étudie beaucoup. (je suis sûr que)

   _____

8. Éliane va en France cette année. (il est peu probable)

   _____

## Uses of the subjunctive: special cases

1. After expressions of fear, after **empêcher que,** and after the interrogative of **douter,** the word **ne** may be placed before the verb in the subjunctive. This **ne** does not make the verb negative, but rather makes the style more formal. This **ne explétif** is omitted in informal speech and writing.

   **J'ai peur qu'**il **ne** comprenne.          *I'm afraid he understands.*
   **J'ai empêché qu'**il **ne** sorte.            *I kept him from going out.*
   **Doutez-vous que** ce livre **ne**             *Do you doubt that this book is*
       soit utile?                                    *useful?*

2. The subjunctive can be used to express an indirect command for third-person subjects. The English equivalent is *have* or *let him/her/them do something.*

   Suzanne a besoin de nous parler.               *Suzanne needs to speak to us.*
   **Qu'elle vienne** nous voir, alors.           **Let her come** *see us then.*

   Monsieur, l'avocat est arrivé.                 *Sir, the lawyer is here.*
   Je descends tout suite. **Qu'il attende**      *I'm coming right down.* **Have him**
       dans mon bureau.                               **wait** *in my office.*

   Les étudiants ne comprennent pas               *The students don't understand your*
       vos conférences, monsieur.                     *lectures, sir.*
   **Qu'ils fassent** attention.                  **Let them pay** *attention.*

*Present and past subjunctive*    323

**Activité 12** **Le style soutenu.** Refaites les phrases suivantes dans le style soutenu en ajoutant le **ne** explétif.

1. J'ai peur que vous preniez froid.

   _____

2. Elle craint que nous soyons en colère.

   _____

3. Doutez-vous qu'il soit d'accord?

   _____

4. Elle empêche que nous finissions notre travail.

   _____

   _____

**Activité 13** **C'est aux autres de le faire!** Employez **que** suivi du subjonctif pour donner des ordres à une troisième personne. Remplacez les compléments directs et indirects par les pronoms convenables. Suivez le modèle.

> MODÈLE   Marc veut suivre le cours de philosophie.
> Qu'il le suive alors.

1. Marianne et Lisette veulent apprendre le japonais.

   _____

2. Serge veut rejoindre ses amis.

   _____

3. Simone doit faire un virement (_transfer of funds_).

   _____

4. Alexandre doit prendre le train.

   _____

5. Les Durand veulent vendre leur voiture.

   _____

6. Monique peut nous rendre l'argent.

   _____

7. Christian veut traduire le document.

   _____

8. Stéphane doit finir le travail.

   _____

# Forms and uses of the past subjunctive

1. The past subjunctive in French is composed of the subjunctive of the auxiliary verb (**avoir** or **être**), followed by the past participle. The same rules of agreement apply as in the passé composé.

VERBS CONJUGATED WITH **avoir**

que j'**aie parlé, fini, perdu**
que tu **aies parlé, fini, perdu**
qu'il/qu'elle **ait parlé, fini, perdu**
que nous **ayons parlé, fini, perdu**
que vous **ayez parlé, fini, perdu**
qu'ils/qu'elles **aient parlé, fini, perdu**

VERBS CONJUGATED WITH **être**

que je **sois parti(e)**
que tu **sois parti(e)**
qu'il/qu'elle **soit parti(e)**
que nous **soyons parti(e)s**
que vous **soyez parti(e)(s)**
qu'ils/qu'elles **soient parti(e)s**

2. The past subjunctive is used to indicate that the action of the subordinate clause happened before the action of the main clause. Compare the following pairs of sentences.

Je suis désolé **que tu perdes.**     *I'm sorry **that you're losing.***
Je suis désolé **que tu aies perdu.**     *I'm sorry **that you lost.***

Tu crains **qu'elle ne** te **comprenne pas.**     *You fear **that she won't understand** you.*
Tu crains **qu'elle ne** t'**ait pas compris.**     *You fear **that she didn't understand** you.*

Il est content **que nous venions.**     *He's happy **that we're coming.***
Il est content **que nous soyons venus.**     *He's happy **that we've come.***

3. In everyday French, the present subjunctive is used to describe events that happened in the past, when the action of the subordinate clause happened *at the same time* or *after* the action of the main clause. Only when the action of the subordinate clause happened *before* the action of the main clause can one use the past subjunctive.* Compare the following pairs of sentences.

Elle **était** étonnée **qu'il pleuve.**     *She **was** surprised **that it was raining.***
Elle **était** étonnée **qu'il ait plu.**     *She **was** surprised **that it had rained.***

Il **était** content **que nous venions.**     *He **was** happy **that we were coming.***
Il **était** content **que nous soyons venus.**     *He **was** happy **that we had come.***

**Activité 14**   **Les sentiments.** Claudine est en train de vivre un moment difficile. Elle exprime ses sentiments dans cette situation. Écrivez ce qu'elle dit en formant une seule phrase avec les éléments donnés. Employez le passé du subjonctif dans les propositions subordonnées, en suivant le modèle.

*In formal, written French, the imperfect and the pluperfect tenses of the subjunctive may be used instead of the present and past subjunctive in these contexts. See Appendix IV for more on these two literary tenses.

> MODÈLE    Mon petit ami Jacques est tombé malade. (je suis désolée)
> Je suis désolée que mon petit ami Jacques soit tombé
> malade.

1. **a.** Il a pris une bronchite. (je crains)

   _____

   **b.** Il est allé voir le médecin. (je doute)

   _____

2. **a.** Ma sœur a reçu une mauvaise note en français. (j'ai peur)

   _____

   **b.** Elle a étudié pour l'examen. (je ne crois pas)

   _____

   **c.** Elle a eu des ennuis avec son petit ami. (je soupçonne)

   _____

   **d.** Elle ne nous a pas montré son examen. (je n'approuve pas)

   _____

   **e.** Sylvie ne nous en a pas parlé. (ma mère se plaint)

   _____

3. **a.** Le prof d'histoire nous a demandé une dissertation de quinze pages.
      (je suis furieuse)

   _____

   **b.** Il ne nous en a pas demandé deux! (c'est une chance que)

   _____

**Activité 15**    **Au passé!** Refaites les échanges suivants en changeant le verbe de la
proposition subordonnée au passé du subjonctif. Suivez le modèle.

> MODÈLE    —Je suis content que tu reviennes.
> —Et moi, je suis contente que tu m'attendes.
> —Je suis content que tu sois revenue.
> —Et moi, je suis contente que tu m'aies attendue.

1. —Le prof est content que Jean-Yves réponde.
   —Ça ne veut pas dire qu'il comprenne.

   _____

   _____

2. —Je suis ravi qu'elle puisse venir.
   —Mais il est agaçant que son mari ne vienne pas avec elle.

   —_____

   —_____

3. —Colette se réjouit que son chef ait confiance en elle.
   —Il faut qu'elle fasse un excellent travail.

   —_____

   —_____

4. —Ma mère regrette que ma sœur ne mette pas son nouveau pull.
   —Il est curieux que ce pull ne plaise pas à ta sœur.

   —_____

   —_____

5. —Je suis surpris qu'Irène ne m'attende pas.
   —Ça ne veut pas dire qu'elle sorte.

   —_____

   —_____

**Activité 16** **Contrastes.** Traduisez ces paires de phrases en français en faisant attention à l'emploi du présent et du passé du subjonctif.

1. **a.** _I'm happy that they're leaving._

   _____

   **b.** _I'm happy that they left._

   _____

2. **a.** _I'm not sure that she's taking a course._

   _____

   **b.** _I'm not sure that she took a course._

   _____

3. **a.** _I don't think the boy is reading the book._

   _____

   **b.** _I don't think the boy read the book._

   _____

4. **a.** _It's improbable that they're on vacation._

   _____

   **b.** _It was improbable that they were on vacation._

   _____

(continued)

5. **a.** *We're surprised that the children don't fight.* (**se battre**)

_____

**b.** *We're surprised that the children didn't fight.*

_____

6. **a.** *He doubted that she was seriously (**gravement**) ill.*

_____

**b.** *He doubted that she had been seriously ill.*

_____

**Activité 17**  **Activité orale: Impressions et réactions.**  Avec un(e) camarade, parlez de ce qui vous surprend à l'université, de ce qui vous rend heureux(heureuse) ou triste, de ce qui vous paraît bizarre, des changements que vous voudriez voir. Parlez aussi de vos craintes et doutes. Employez le subjonctif autant que possible.

# CHAPITRE 25 — OTHER USES OF THE SUBJUNCTIVE

## The subjunctive after certain conjunctions

1. The subjunctive is used after the following conjunctions.

| | | |
|---|---|---|
| **à condition que** *on the condition that, provided that* <br> **à moins que** *unless* <br> **afin que** *so that, in order that* (*formal*) <br> **avant que** *before* <br> **bien que** *although* | **de crainte que** *for fear that* <br> **de façon que** *so that, in order that* <br> **de peur que** *for fear that* <br> **en attendant que** *until* <br> **encore que** *although* (*literary*) <br> **jusqu'à ce que** *until* | **pour que** *so that, in order that* <br> **pourvu que** *provided that, as long as; let's hope* <br> **quoique** *although* <br> **sans que** *without* |

Partons **sans que personne ne s'en rende compte.**
*Let's leave **without anyone's noticing.***

Alors, parlons tout bas **pour qu'on ne nous entende pas.**
*Then let's speak very softly **so that people don't hear us.***

Il faut continuer à travailler **bien qu'il fasse chaud.**
*It's necessary to continue working **although it's hot.***

Je vais t'aider **pour que tu puisses** finir.
*I'll help you **so that you can** finish.*

Allons-nous-en **avant que Paul revienne.**
*Let's go away **before Paul comes back.***

Je préfère rester **jusqu'à ce qu'il vienne.**
*I prefer to stay **until he comes.***

J'irai **pourvu que vous puissiez** m'accompagner.
*I'll go **as long as you can** accompany me.*

D'accord. Je vais chercher mon parapluie **de peur qu'il pleuve.**
*OK. I'll go get my umbrella **for fear that it may rain.***

**Pourvu qu'il ne pleuve pas!**
*Let's hope (**that**) it **doesn't** rain!*

2. In formal style, the **ne explétif** (see p. 323) may precede the subjunctive after **à moins que, avant que, de crainte que,** and **de peur que.**

Il viendra **à moins qu'**il **ne** soit malade.
*He'll come **unless** he's sick.*

Allons-nous-en **avant que** Paul **ne** revienne.
*Let's go **before** Paul comes back.*

Je vais chercher mon parapluie **de peur qu'**il **ne** pleuve.
*I'm going to look for my umbrella **for fear that** it will rain.*

An infinitive construction replaces the subjunctive if the subject of both clauses is the same.

| | |
|---|---|
| J'écris l'adresse **pour que tu ne l'oublies pas.** | *I'll write down the address **so that you won't forget it.*** |
| J'écris l'adresse **pour ne pas l'oublier.** | *I'll write down the address **so that I won't forget it.*** |
| Il mangera **avant que nous partions.** | *He'll eat **before we leave.*** |
| Il mangera **avant de partir.** | *He'll eat **before he leaves.*** |

**Activité 1**

**Jusqu'à quand?** Un groupe de garçons attendent leurs petites amies, mais elles sont en retard. Ils parlent entre eux pour décider combien de temps ils vont attendre. Écrivez ce qu'ils disent en utilisant la conjonction **jusqu'à ce que.** Suivez le modèle.

> MODÈLE Marc: j'attendrai / Cybèle / arriver
> Marc: J'attendrai jusqu'à ce que Cybèle arrive.

1. Paul: j'attendrai / Marie-Claire / m'appeler

_____

2. Philippe: j'attendrai / Yvette / venir

_____

3. Serge: j'attendrai / le bus / arriver pour me ramener

_____

4. Luc: j'attendrai / Robert / revenir de la cabine téléphonique

_____

5. Baudouin: j'attendrai / vous / s'en aller

_____

6. Maurice: j'attendrai / nous / pouvoir vérifier où elles sont

_____

7. Daniel: j'attendrai / nous / savoir par quel moyen elles viennent

_____

8. Richard: j'attendrai / ma petite amie / apparaître sous mes yeux

_____

**Activité 2**

**À ceci près (*with this exception*).** Un groupe d'amis parlent de ce qu'ils feront, mais posent dans chaque cas une condition qui pourrait les en empêcher. Écrivez ce qu'ils disent en employant **à moins que,** selon le modèle.

> MODÈLE Marc: J'irai au cinéma.
> Lise: Mais si nous avons une dissertation à rédiger...
> Marc: Oui. J'irai au cinéma à moins que nous ayons une dissertation à rédiger.

1. RENÉE: Hélène sortira avec Nicolas.

   MARIE: Mais si elle est occupée...

   RENÉE: _____

2. DAVID: Jocelyne partira en Italie.

   ALICE: Mais si son père lui défend d'y aller...

   DAVID: _____

3. PAUL: Christophe t'expliquera la leçon.

   LUC: Mais s'il ne fait pas attention en classe...

   PAUL: _____

4. JULIE: Michel veut inviter tous ses amis chez lui.

   SARA: Mais si ses parents reviennent...

   JULIE: _____

5. PAPA: On peut aller chez les Laurentin.

   MAMAN: Mais s'ils ont des choses à faire...

   PAPA: _____

6. ODILE: Il faudra partir sans Jacqueline.

   DIANE: Mais si elle peut se manifester d'ici cinq minutes...

   ODILE: _____

7. JOSEPH: Nous pouvons faire un pique-nique demain.

   ANDRÉ: Mais s'il fait mauvais...

   JOSEPH: _____

**Activité 3** **Pas si vite!** Luc veut sortir, voir ses amis, et ainsi de suite, mais sa mère pose des conditions. Écrivez ce que sa mère lui dit en formant des phrases avec **pourvu que,** selon le modèle.

> MODÈLE  Maman, je vais au cinéma avec Albert ce soir.
>   (tu / finir tes devoirs avant)
>   Oui, pourvu que tu finisses tes devoirs avant.

1. Maman, je sors prendre un café avec Éloïse ce soir. (tu / prendre le dessert avec nous)

   _____

2. Maman, je vais à la fête chez Victor. (tu / être de retour avant minuit)

   _____

3. Maman, je veux aller voir le match de football dimanche. (ton frère / pouvoir t'accompagner)

   _____

*(continued)*

4. Maman, je dois aller à la bibliothèque. (tu / mettre de l'ordre dans ta chambre)

_____

5. Maman, Guy m'invite à passer l'après-midi chez lui. (tu / faire les courses avant)

_____

6. Maman, je veux inviter Lise à manger avec nous. (elle / ne pas venir avant huit heures)

_____

7. Maman, je peux prendre la voiture ce soir? (ton père / te le permettre)

_____

8. Maman, je peux dîner dans un restaurant de luxe? (nous / pouvoir aller avec toi)

_____

**Activité 4**  **C'est pour ça.** Formez des phrases avec **pour que** pour expliquer ce qui motive, en suivant le modèle.

> MODÈLE   L'agent de police parle lentement. (l'étranger / le comprendre)
> L'agent de police parle lentement pour que l'étranger
> le comprenne.

**François est souffrant.**

1. Le médecin lui ordonne des antibiotiques. (il / se remettre [_recover_])

_____

2. Sa mère a baissé les stores (_blinds_). (François / dormir)

_____

3. Elle prépare une bonne soupe. (il / prendre quelque chose de chaud)

_____

4. On lui donne trois couvertures (_blankets_). (il / ne pas avoir froid)

_____

**M. et Mme Durand essaient d'orienter un étudiant étranger qui habite chez eux.**

5. Nous allons t'acheter un poste de télé. (tu / regarder des émissions en français)

_____

6. On va te dessiner un petit plan du quartier. (tu / ne pas te perdre)

_____

7. On te donne une carte avec notre numéro de téléphone. (tu / pouvoir nous appeler)

_____

8. Nous allons inviter nos neveux et nos nièces. (tu / faire leur connaissance)

_____

**Activité 5** **Courage!** Vous encouragez votre ami à faire ce qu'il doit faire malgré les ennuis qui se présentent. Employez une proposition avec **bien que** pour lui dire qu'il faut surmonter les obstacles. Suivez le modèle.

> MODÈLE —Tu ne sors pas?
> —Il pleut.
> —Tu dois sortir bien qu'il pleuve.

1. —Tu ne fais pas tes devoirs?

   —Je suis fatigué.

   —_____

2. —Tu ne descends pas faire les courses?

   —Il fait mauvais.

   —_____

3. —Tu ne lis pas le livre de chimie?

   —Je n'en ai pas envie.

   —_____

4. —Tu ne téléphones pas à Renée?

   —Nous sommes brouillés (*mad at each other*).

   —_____

5. —Tu ne vas pas au cours?

   —Je ne me sens pas bien.

   —_____

6. —Tu ne mets pas de cravate?

   —J'ai chaud.

   —_____

7. —Tu n'écris rien?

   —Je ne sais pas la réponse.

   —_____

8. —Tu ne finis pas ta rédaction?

   —Il est tard.

   —_____

**Activité 6**  **Sans ça.** Joignez chaque paire de phrases en une seule avec la conjonction **sans que** de façon à ce que la nouvelle phrase exprime la même idée. Suivez les modèles.

> MODÈLES  Elle part. Je ne la vois pas.
> Elle part sans que je la voie.
>
> Elle est partie. Je ne l'ai pas vue.
> Elle est partie sans que je l'aie vue.

1. Il entre doucement. On ne s'en aperçoit pas.

   _____

2. Cet étudiant copie. Le professeur ne s'en rend pas compte.

   _____

3. Marc a eu des ennuis avec la police. Ses parents ne sont pas au courant.

   _____

4. Il parle au téléphone. Je ne peux pas entendre ce qu'il dit.

   _____

5. Je te passerai un petit mot (*note*). Le prof ne me verra pas.

   _____

6. Il est parti. Nous ne le savions pas.

   _____

7. Il est rentré. Nous ne l'avons pas vu.

   _____

8. Elle s'est fâchée. Je ne lui ai rien dit.

   _____

**Activité 7**  **On fait les courses.**  Un groupe d'amis sont en train de faire leurs courses. Décrivez leur activité en formant des phrases avec une proposition adverbiale. Employez les conjonctions indiquées, selon le modèle.

> MODÈLE  j'irai à la boucherie / avant / vous / revenir / de la charcuterie
> J'irai à la boucherie avant que vous (ne) reveniez de
>    la charcuterie.

**Vocabulaire**

## Les boutiques / les commerçants

### Les boutiques

| | |
|---|---|
| **la blanchisserie** *laundry* | **la pâtisserie** *pastry shop* |
| **la boutique du coiffeur** *barbershop* | **la pharmacie** *the drugstore* |
| **le kiosque (à journaux)** *newsstand* | **le pressing** *dry cleaners* |
| **la librairie** *bookstore* | **la station-service** *gas station* |

1. je ne passerai pas à la blanchisserie / jusqu'à / Louise / descendre au marché

   _____

2. Marc ira à la pâtisserie / pour / nous / prendre un bon dessert ce soir

   _____

3. Claire ira au kiosque du coin / pourvu / nous / l'accompagner

   _____

4. je vais vite au pressing / de peur / ils / fermer pour le déjeuner

   _____

5. nous attendrons Chantal à la station-service / jusqu'à / elle / faire le plein

   _____

6. Philippe attendra à la station-service / jusqu'à / le mécanicien / changer l'huile

   _____

7. nous regarderons l'étalage (*display*) de la librairie / en attendant / Jean / sortir de la boutique du coiffeur

   _____

8. Odile veut passer à la pharmacie / à moins / vous / être pressés pour rentrer

   _____

   _____

## The subjunctive in relative clauses

1. The subjunctive is used in a relative clause if the antecedent in the main clause is hypothetical or indefinite.

   | | |
   |---|---|
   | Il n'y a **personne qui** me **comprenne.** | *There's **no one who understands** me.* |
   | Je ne vois **pas d'endroit où nous puissions** nous asseoir. | *I don't see **any place where we can** sit down.* |
   | L'entreprise a besoin de **secrétaires qui sachent** trois langues. | *The firm needs **secretaries who know** three languages.* |
   | Je cherche **une voiture qui fasse** du cent cinquante à l'heure. | *I'm looking for **a car that does** one hundred fifty kilometers per hour.* |
   | Connaissez-vous **quelqu'un qui puisse** nous aider? | *Do you know **someone who can** help us?* |

2. If the antecedent in the main clause is not hypothetical and actually exists, the indicative is used in the relative clause.

   | | |
   |---|---|
   | J'ai besoin **des secrétaires qui savent** trois langues. | *I need **the secretaries who know** three languages.* |
   | J'ai acheté **la voiture qui fait** du cent cinquante à l'heure. | *I bought **the car that does** one hundred fifty kilometers per hour.* |
   | Voilà **quelqu'un qui peut** nous aider. | *There's **someone who can** help us.* |

**Activité 8** **On cherche un logement.** David cherche un appartement avec trois autres étudiants. Il décrit ce que chacun désire dans un logement. À partir des éléments donnés, formez des phrases qui expriment ce qu'il dit. Suivez le modèle.

> MODÈLE  nous / chercher un appartement / avoir quatre chambres à coucher
>
> Nous cherchons un appartement qui ait quatre chambres à coucher.

1. toi, tu / vouloir un appartement / avoir deux salles de bains

   _____

2. Mathieu / avoir besoin d'un appartement / être climatisé

   _____

3. Philippe et moi, nous / préférer un appartement / être près de la faculté

   _____

4. nous / vouloir un appartement / ne pas avoir besoin de beaucoup de rénovation

   _____

5. moi, je / chercher un appartement / avoir le confort moderne

   _____

6. Charles / désirer un appartement / se trouver dans un immeuble neuf

   _____

7. Mathieu et Philippe / chercher un appartement / être en face de l'arrêt de bus

   _____

8. nous / chercher un voisin / ne pas se plaindre des fêtes

   _____

**Activité 9** **L'ami idéal.** Pour savoir ce que Stéphane dit sur l'ami idéal qu'il cherche, complétez les propositions relatives avec le subjonctif du verbe entre parenthèses.

1. Je veux trouver un ami avec qui je _____ parler facilement. (pouvoir)

2. J'ai besoin d'un ami qui me _____. (comprendre)

3. Je préférerais un ami qui _____ très intelligent. (être)

4. Je veux un ami qui _____ de l'humour. (avoir)

5. J'ai besoin d'un ami qui me _____ toujours la vérité. (dire)

6. Je cherche un ami qui _____ des études dans notre faculté. (faire)

**Au bureau.** La compagnie où travaille Chantal cherche des employés. Complétez les phrases suivantes avec le subjonctif ou l'indicatif, selon le cas, pour savoir quels candidats doivent faire une demande d'emploi auprès de son bureau.

**Vocabulaire**

## Le bureau moderne

**l'infographie** (*f.*) *computer graphics*
**l'interconnexion de réseau** (*f.*)
  *networking*
**le représentant / la représentante
de commerce** *traveling
  salesperson*

**le traitement de données** *data
  processing*
**le traitement de texte** *word
  processing*

1. Nous avons une représentante de commerce qui _____
   parler l'espagnol. (savoir)

2. Nous cherchons quelqu'un qui _____ parler l'italien.
   (savoir)

3. Nous avons besoin d'un secrétaire qui _____ bien les
   programmes pour le traitement de texte. (connaître)

4. Il faut trouver quelqu'un qui _____ des connaissances
   d'infographie. (avoir)

5. Nous n'avons personne qui _____ mettre à jour nos
   systèmes de traitement de données. (pouvoir)

6. Nous n'avons pas encore de collègue qui _____
   spécialisé dans l'interconnexion de réseau. (être)

7. Nous avons des employés qui _____ une expérience
   internationale. (avoir)

8. Mais il n'y a personne qui _____ capable d'ouvrir des
   bureaux en Asie. (être)

## The subjunctive after superlatives

1. The subjunctive is used in clauses after superlatives. These sentences
   usually express a subjective or personal opinion or evaluation.

| | |
|---|---|
| C'est l'entreprise **la plus dynamique que je connaisse.** | *It's **the most dynamic** company that I know.* |
| Et ses produits sont **les plus solides qu'on puisse** trouver. | *And its products are **the most dependable** ones that you can find.* |
| C'est **le meilleur** livre **que j'aie lu.** | *It's **the best** book **that I have** read.* |
| C'est la dissertation **la plus difficile que nous ayons écrite.** | *It's **the hardest** term paper **that we have written.*** |

2. The subjunctive is also used after **dernier, premier, seul,** and **unique.**

Vous êtes la **seule** personne **qui**      *You're the **only** person **who can***
   **puisse** comprendre.                   *understand.*
C'est le **premier** livre **qui soit** utile.     *It's the **first** book **that is** useful.*

**Activité 11**    **Un peu d'enthousiasme!** Joignez les deux phrases en une seule. Employez un superlatif (ou un de ces adjectifs: **dernier, premier, seul, unique**). Utilisez le subjonctif dans la proposition subordonnée. Suivez les modèles.

> MODÈLES    Ce roman est facile. Nous le lisons.
> C'est le roman le plus facile que nous lisions.
>
> Vous êtes la seule personne. Vous m'avez téléphoné.
> Vous êtes la seule personne qui m'ait téléphoné.

1. Cette fille est belle. Je la connais.

   _____

2. Ce cours est ennuyeux. Je le suis.

   _____

3. Ce compte-rendu est intéressant. Marc l'écrit.

   _____

4. Ce village est joli. Vous le visitez.

   _____

5. Ce patient est le premier. Il vient au cabinet du dentiste.

   _____

6. Vous êtes la seule étudiante. Vous faites du chinois.

   _____

7. Cette employée est la dernière. Elle s'en va du bureau.

   _____

8. Ce repas est mauvais. On l'a servi à la cantine.

   _____

9. Ce restaurant est bon. Nous le fréquentons.

   _____

10. Ce tableau est beau. Tu l'as peint.

    _____

11. Ce loyer est élevé. Je l'ai payé.

    _____

12. Tu es le seul ami. Tu me comprends.

    _____

# The subjunctive in certain types of indefinite clauses (for recognition only)

French uses the following construction to express *however + adjective* or *no matter how + adjective.*

aussi  
pour  
quelque  } + *adjective* + **que** + *subjunctive of* **être, paraître,** etc.  
si  
tout(e)  

| | |
|---|---|
| **aussi fort que ce pays soit** | *however strong this country is* |
| **pour petit qu'il paraisse** | *as small as he may seem* |
| **quelque timides qu'ils paraissent\*** | *however shy they may appear* |
| **si peu que ce soit** | *however little it may be* |
| **toute confiante que vous soyez** | *however confident you may be* |

**Quel(le)(s)** + **que** + *subjunctive of* **être** + *noun* expresses the idea of *whatever.*

| | |
|---|---|
| **quel que soit l'obstacle** | *whatever the obstacle may be* |
| **quels que soient les problèmes** | *whatever the problems may be* |
| **quelles que soient vos craintes** | *whatever your fears may be* |

**Qui que** and **quoi que** + *subjunctive* mean *whoever* and *whatever,* respectively. **Où que** + *subjunctive* means *wherever.*

| | |
|---|---|
| **qui que vous soyez** | *whoever you may be* |
| **qui que ce soit** | *whoever, anyone* |
| **quoi que vous fassiez** | *whatever you're doing* |
| **quoi que ce soit** | *anything* |
| **où que tu ailles** | *wherever you go* |

---

**Activité 12**   **À traduire.**  Traduisez les phrases suivantes en anglais.

1. Qui qu'elle soit, elle n'a pas le droit d'entrer.

   _____

2. Si riches qu'ils soient devenus, ils ne peuvent oublier la pauvreté de leur jeunesse.

   _____

3. Tout doué que tu sois, il faut que tu étudies.

   _____

4. Il comptait nous offrir quoi que ce soit.

   _____

*(continued)*

\*When **quelque** precedes an adjective, it plays the role of adverb and is therefore invariable.

5. Je ne lui pardonnerai jamais, quoi qu'il dise.

   _____

6. Ce candidat accepte l'argent de qui que ce soit.

   _____

7. Quelle que soit la somme offerte, elle ne sera pas suffisante.

   _____

8. Où que tu ailles, tu trouveras les mêmes difficultés.

   _____

# APPENDICES

# APPENDICE I: WRITTEN CONVENTIONS

The French language is written in the same alphabet as English, but conventions of writing are different. French makes use of a series of diacritical marks called *accent marks* that appear over vowels and are part of French spelling.

There are four accent marks in French. All may occur over the letter **e.**

- é  **e accent aigu** (*acute accent*)
- è  **e accent grave** (*grave accent*)
- ê  **e accent circonflexe** (*circumflex accent*)
- ë  **e tréma** (*diaeresis*)

## L'accent aigu

The acute accent appears only on the letter **e** in French. The original function of **accent aigu** was to indicate that the **e** was pronounced as a closed vowel. The closest English sound to **é** is the first part of the diphthong *ai* in *wait*. The acute accent is written on the past participle of all **-er** verbs: **allé, parlé, remboursé, gagné**, etc. The letter **é** corresponds to the English *y* in the suffix **-té: liberté, hostilité, qualité, quantité,** etc. It appears in the prefixes **é-** corresponding to the English *ex-*, and **dé-** corresponding to the English *dis-, de-, un-*: **échange, découvrir, déduire, défaire.** The initial **é** often corresponds to *s-* in English: **étrange, école, écriture, épice.**

## L'accent grave

The grave accent in French may appear over the vowels **a, e, u. Accent grave** appears over the vowel **a** in the preposition **à** and in the adverb **là.** The accent mark distinguishes those words from other very common words.

| | |
|---|---|
| **à** *to, at* | **a** *has* |
| **là** *there* | **la** *the* (*f.*) |

Aside from this use, **accent grave** appears over the vowel **u** in the adverb **où** (*where*). The accent mark distinguishes it from **ou** (*or*).

Thus, **accent grave** is used almost exclusively over the letter **e.** Its original function was to indicate that the **e** was pronounced as an open vowel. The closest English sound to **è** is the *e* in *bet*.

The vowels **é** and **è** often contrast in verbs: **nous préférons** vs. **je préfère.** The vowel **è** is used in several common words before **s: après, dès, près, très.**

## L'accent circonflexe

The circumflex accent may appear over any vowel. The original purpose of **accent circonflexe** was to indicate a long vowel resulting from the dropping of a consonant, usually **s.** It can be useful to think of cognate English words with **s** to remember which French words have the circumflex accent. Compare the following examples: **la bête** (*beast*), **la fête** (*holiday, party, festival*), **Pâques** (*Easter, paschal*), **la pâte** (*dough, paste*), **râper** (*to grate, rasp*).

The circumflex accent is used to distinguish pairs of words in writing.

| | |
|---|---|
| **je crois** *I believe* | **je croîs** *I grow* |
| **cru** (past participle of **croire**) | **crû** (past participle of **croître**) |
| **du** *of the; some* | **dû** (past participle of **devoir**) |

## Le tréma

The **tréma** occurs over **e** or **i.** It indicates that the vowel has its full sound and is not part of a diphthong. It can also indicate that a preceding **u** should be pronounced (that the **u** is not merely showing the pronunciation of the preceding **g**).

| | |
|---|---|
| **Noël** | *Christmas* |
| **aiguë** | *feminine form of* **aigu** |

## Cédille

French also uses a diacritical mark called a *cedilla* (**cédille**) under the letter **c** to indicate that the **c** is pronounced /s/ before the vowels **a, o, u.** Compare the following pairs of words: **ça** and **cas; commençons** and **flocon; reçu** and **recul.**

# APPENDICE II: NUMBERS, TELLING TIME, AND DATES

## A. Cardinal numbers to 99

The cardinal numbers from 0 to 59 are:

| | | | |
|---|---|---|---|
| 0 | zéro | 18 | dix-huit |
| 1 | un, une | 19 | dix-neuf |
| 2 | deux | 20 | vingt |
| 3 | trois | 21 | vingt et un(e) |
| 4 | quatre | 22 | vingt-deux |
| 5 | cinq | 23 | vingt-trois |
| 6 | six | 24 | vingt-quatre |
| 7 | sept | 25 | vingt-cinq |
| 8 | huit | 26 | vingt-six |
| 9 | neuf | 27 | vingt-sept |
| 10 | dix | 28 | vingt-huit |
| 11 | onze | 29 | vingt-neuf |
| 12 | douze | 30 | trente |
| 13 | treize | 31 | trente et un(e) |
| 14 | quatorze | 40 | quarante |
| 15 | quinze | 50 | cinquante |
| 16 | seize | 59 | cinquante-neuf |
| 17 | dix-sept | | |

**Un** and **une** are the only numbers that agree in gender with the following noun. The forms for *one* are the same as the indefinite article.

From 60 to 99, French counts by twenties. The units 1 through 19 are added to the multiple of twenty. **Un(e)** is joined by a hyphen, not by **et,** to **quatre-vingts.** Note also that **quatre-vingts** loses its final **-s** before another number.

| | |
|---|---|
| 60 | soixante |
| 61 | soixante et un(e) |
| 62 | soixante-deux |
| 63 | soixante-trois |
| 70 | soixante-dix |
| 71 | soixante et onze |
| 72 | soixante-douze |
| 73 | soixante-treize |
| 74 | soixante-quatorze |
| 75 | soixante-quinze |
| 76 | soixante-seize |
| 77 | soixante-dix-sept |
| 78 | soixante-dix-huit |
| 79 | soixante-dix-neuf |
| 80 | quatre-vingts |
| 81 | quatre-vingt-un(e) |
| 82 | quatre-vingt-deux |
| 83 | quatre-vingt-trois |
| 84 | quatre-vingt-quatre |
| 85 | quatre-vingt-cinq |
| 86 | quatre-vingt-six |
| 87 | quatre-vingt-sept |
| 88 | quatre-vingt-huit |
| 89 | quatre-vingt-neuf |
| 90 | quatre-vingt-dix |
| 91 | quatre-vingt-onze |
| 99 | quatre-vingt-dix-neuf |

# B. Cardinal numbers 100 and above

Multiples of 100 are written with a final **-s.**

| | |
|---|---|
| 100 | cent |
| 200 | deux cents |
| 300 | trois cents |
| 400 | quatre cents |
| 500 | cinq cents |
| 600 | six cents |
| 700 | sept cents |
| 800 | huit cents |
| 900 | neuf cents |

The final **-s** of **cents** drops before another number.

| | |
|---|---|
| 201 | deux cent un |
| 326 | trois cent vingt-six |

French counts by hundreds through 1900.

| | |
|---|---|
| 1200 | douze cents |
| 1610 | seize cent dix |
| 1900 | dix-neuf cents |

2.100 is, however, **deux mille cent.**

The word for *thousand*, **mille,** is invariable. Note that neither **cent** (*100*) nor **mille** (*1000*) are preceded by **un.** (Compare English *one hundred, one thousand.*)

| | |
|---|---|
| 1.000 | mille |
| 2.000 | deux mille |
| 3.500 | trois mille cinq cents |
| 10.000 | dix mille |
| 100 000 | cent mille |
| 200 000 | deux cent mille |

Note that French uses a period or a space to separate thousands where English uses a comma. The comma is used in French numbers as a decimal point: **2,5 = deux virgule cinq** (*2.5*).

The word for *million* is a noun and is followed by **de** before another noun. However, if other numbers come between *million* and the noun, **de** is not used. Note that **cent** is pluralized directly before the word **million.**

| | | |
|---|---|---|
| **un million de livres** | *1,000,000* | *books* |
| **deux millions d'habitants** | *2,000,000* | *inhabitants* |
| **trois millions trois cent mille étudiants** | *3,300,000* | *students* |
| **deux cents millions d'euros** | *200,000,000* | *euros* |

A *billion* in French is **un milliard.** The French term **un billion** means *a trillion.* Like **million,** the noun **milliard** is followed by **de** before another noun: **Milliard cinq milliards d'êtres humains** *5,000,000,000 human beings.*

# C. Ordinal numbers

To form ordinal numbers in French, the suffix **-ième** is added to the cardinal number, except for **un/une** which have the ordinal number **premier/première.** Numbers ending in **-e** drop the **-e** before adding the suffix **-ième.** The ordinal **second(e)** is synonymous with **deuxième.** Note the spellings of the words for *fifth* and *ninth*:

| | |
|---|---|
| **deuxième** *second* | **quatorzième** *fourteenth* |
| **quatrième** *fourth* | **dix-septième** *seventeenth* |
| **cinquième** *fifth* | **vingtième** *twentieth* |
| **huitième** *eighth* | **centième** *hundredth* |
| **neuvième** *ninth* | **millième** *thousandth* |
| **dixième** *tenth* | **trois mille cinq centième** *thirty-five hundredth* |

The word **premier/première** is only used to mean *first*. Ordinals such as *twenty-first, one hundred and first*, etc., are formed regularly.

| | |
|---|---|
| **vingt et unième** *twenty-first* | **quatre-vingt-unième** *eighty-first* |
| **soixante et onzième** *seventy-first* | **cent unième** *one hundred and first* |

Ordinal numbers in French are often abbreviated by a raised **-ème** or **-e**: $20^{\text{ème}}$, $4^{\text{e}}$.

# D. Telling time

To ask the time in French, the question **Quelle heure est-il?** (or more colloquially, **Il est quelle heure?**) is used. Time is told in French by the phrase **il est,** followed by the hour.

| | |
|---|---|
| Il est **une heure.** | *It's one o'clock.* |
| Il est **onze heures.** | *It's eleven o'clock.* |

Minutes past the hour until the half hour are added directly to the hour. The words **quart** and **demi(e)** are joined by **et.**

| | |
|---|---|
| Il est **quatre heures cinq.** | *It's five past four.* |
| Il est **quatre heures et quart.** | *It's a quarter past four.* |
| Il est **quatre heures vingt.** | *It's twenty past four.* |
| Il est **quatre heures et demie.** | *It's four-thirty.* |

Minutes before the hour are expressed by the word **moins. Moins** *le* **quart** mean *a quarter to the hour*.

| | |
|---|---|
| Il est cinq heures **moins vingt.** | *It's twenty to five.* |
| Il est cinq heures **moins le quart.** | *It's a quarter to five.* |

For *twelve noon* French uses **il est midi**, and for *twelve midnight* **il est minuit**. Minutes past these hours are expressed as above.

| | |
|---|---|
| Il est **midi moins le quart.** | *It's **a quarter to twelve** (A.M.).* |
| Il est **midi et demi.*** | *It is **half past noon**.* |
| Il est **minuit dix.** | *It's **ten past twelve** (A.M.).* |

The preposition **à** is used to label the time at which something happens.

| | |
|---|---|
| —**À** quelle heure est-elle arrivée? | *What time did she arrive?* |
| —**À** huit heures moins le quart. | *At a quarter to eight.* |

French also uses a 24-hour clock for official purposes, such as transportation and entertainment schedules. In this system of telling time, **douze heures** and **vingt-quatre heures** replace **midi** and **minuit**, respectively. Minutes after the hour are counted from one to fifty-nine. **Et, moins, quart,** and **demi(e)** are not used. Phrases such as **du matin, de l'après-midi, du soir,** and **de la nuit,** which are French equivalents of A.M. and P.M., are also not used in the 24-hour system, as they would be redundant.

| | |
|---|---|
| La première séance du film est à **18 h 14.** | *The first showing of the film is at **6:14** P.M.* |
| Le train pour Berlin part à **13 h 48.** | *The train for Berlin leaves at **1:48** P.M.* |
| Boutique fermée entre **12 h** et **14 h.** | *Shop closed between **noon** and 2 P.M.* |

## E. Days of the Week

| | | |
|---|---|---|
| **lundi** *Monday* | **jeudi** *Thursday* | **dimanche** *Sunday* |
| **mardi** *Tuesday* | **vendredi** *Friday* | |
| **mercredi** *Wednesday* | **samedi** *Saturday* | |

### Months of the Year

| | | |
|---|---|---|
| **janvier** *January* | **mai** *May* | **septembre** *September* |
| **février** *February* | **juin** *June* | **octobre** *October* |
| **mars** *March* | **juillet** *July* | **novembre** *November* |
| **avril** *April* | **août** *August* | **décembre** *December* |

Note that in French (unlike English) both days and months are written with the first letter in lowercase.

1. No preposition is used before days of the week.

| | |
|---|---|
| Il arrivera **lundi.** | *He'll arrive **on Monday**.* |
| Je l'ai vue **dimanche.** | *I saw her **on Sunday**.* |

2. **Le** is used before the days of the week to indicate repeated or regular action.

| | |
|---|---|
| —Je n'ai pas de cours **le mardi.** | *I don't have classes **on Tuesdays**.* |
| —Et moi, je travaille **le vendredi.** | *And I work **on Fridays**.* |

*Note that **demi** does not end in an **e** after **midi** and **minuit,** because they are both masculine nouns. Elsewhere, **demie** is in agreement with **heure,** which is feminine.

## F. Dates and years

1. To express dates, French uses cardinal numbers with the exception of **le premier.** The definite article **le** precedes the date. Note that, as with days of the week, no preposition is used for *on*.

—Je croyais que tes cousins arrivaient le trente novembre.
*I thought your cousins were arriving on November thirtieth.*

—Non, ils arrivent le premier décembre.
*No, they're arriving on the first of December.*

2. When dates are written in figures, the day precedes the month.

**4.3.06**         *March 4, 2006*

3. Years are usually expressed in hundreds, although **mil** may also be used. **En** is used to express the year in which something happened.

**en dix-sept cent quatre-vingt-neuf**
**en mil sept cent quatre-vingt-neuf** } *in 1789*

Je suis né **en dix-neuf cent quatre-vingt-cinq.**
*I was born in 1985.*

4. In French, as in English, the last two numbers are often used in speech to express the years of the twentieth century. To date, this pattern has not been universally adopted for expressing dates in the twenty-first century. However, for some speakers **'04, '05, '06,** and so on, are acceptable in speaking but never in writing.

Elle est partie en **quatre-vingt-onze.**
*She left in '91.*

## Expressions relating to the days and dates

| | |
|---|---|
| **Quelle est la date (aujourd'hui)?** | *What's today's date?* |
| **Le combien sommes-nous?** | *What's today's date?* |
| **C'est le premier juin.** | *It's June first.* |
| **Nous sommes le premier juin.** | *It's June first.* |
| **Quel jour sommes-nous?** | *What day is it?* |
| **C'est mercredi.** | *It's Wednesday.* |
| **Nous sommes mercredi aujourd'hui.** | *It's Wednesday today.* |
| **au début de juin** | *at the beginning of June* |
| **à la mi-juin** | *in the middle of June* |
| **vers la fin de juin** | *toward the end of June* |
| **Il te rendra ton argent la semaine des quatre jeudis.** | *You'll never get your money back from him. (English: in a month of Sundays)* |
| **des gens endimanchés** | *people dressed in their Sunday best* |
| **un peintre du dimanche** | *an amateur painter* |
| **Poisson d'avril!** | *April fool!* |

# APPENDICE III: THE INFINITIVE AS COMPLEMENT OF ANOTHER VERB

## A. Verb + infinitive

The following verbs are followed directly by an infinitive (no preposition). In the lists **qqn** stands for **quelqu'un** and indicates an animate subject or object, and **qqch** stands for **quelque chose** and designates an inanimate subject or object. **Faire** stands for any infinitive.

**adorer faire qqch** *to love to do something*

**aimer faire qqch** *to like to do something*

**aimer mieux faire qqch** *to prefer to do something*

**aller faire qqch** *to be going to do something (future meaning)*

**avoir beau faire qqch** *to do something in vain*

**compter faire qqch** *to intend to do something*

**daigner faire qqch** *to deign to do something*

**désirer faire qqch** *to want to do something*

**détester faire qqch** *to hate to do something*

**devoir faire qqch** *should, must/ought to, have to do something*

**espérer faire qqch** *to hope to do something*

**oser faire qqch** *to dare to do something*

**penser faire qqch** *to intend to do something, be thinking of doing something*

**pouvoir faire qqch** *to be able to do something*

**préférer faire qqch** *to prefer to do something*

**reconnaître faire qqch** *to admit to doing something*

**savoir faire qqch** *to know how to do something*

**sembler faire qqch** *to seem to be doing something*

**souhaiter faire qqch** *to wish to do something*

**vouloir faire qqch** *to want to do something*

The impersonal expressions **il faut** (*one must, you have to*) and **il vaut mieux** (*it's better to*) are also followed directly by an infinitive.

Many verbs of motion are also followed directly by the infinitive in French.

**aller faire qqch** *to be going to do something*

**s'en aller faire qqch** *to go off to do something*

**amener qqn faire qqch** *to bring someone to do something*

**descendre faire qqch** *to go down to do something*

**emmener qqn faire qqch** *to take someone to do something*

**entrer faire qqch** *to go inside to do something*

**monter faire qqch** *to go up to do something*

**rentrer faire qqch** *to go home to do something*

**revenir faire qqch** *to come back to do something*

**sortir faire qqch** *to go out to do something*

**venir faire qqch** *to come to do something*

## B. Verb + à + infinitive

Verbs expressing beginnings or the starting points of actions often require **à** before a following infinitive.

| | |
|---|---|
| **apprendre à**  *to learn how to* | **hésiter à**  *to hesitate to* |
| **s'apprêter à**  *to get ready to* | **s'intéresser à**  *to be interested in* |
| **s'attendre à**  *to expect to* | **se mettre à**  *to begin to* |
| **avoir à**  *to have to* | **penser à**  *to be thinking of (doing something)* |
| **commencer à**  *to begin to* | **se préparer à**  *to get ready to* |
| **consentir à**  *to consent to* | **se résoudre à**  *to resolve to* |
| **se décider à**  *to make up one's mind to* | **songer à**  *to be thinking of (doing something)* |
| **s'habituer à**  *to get used to* | **tenir à**  *to insist on* |

Many verbs expressing effort or involvement require **à** before a following infinitive.

| | |
|---|---|
| **s'acharner à**  *to try desperately to* | **s'éreinter à**  *to tire oneself by* |
| **s'adonner à**  *to devote oneself to* | **s'essouffler à**  *to get out of breath* |
| **s'amuser à**  *to enjoy oneself* | **s'exercer à**  *to practice* |
| **s'appliquer à**  *to apply oneself to* | **se fatiguer à**  *to tire oneself by* |
| **s'apprêter à**  *to prepare oneself to* | **s'irriter à**  *to get annoyed* |
| **se borner à**  *to limit oneself to* | **s'obstiner à**  *to persist stubbornly in* |
| **chercher à**  *to try to* | **passer son temps à**  *to spend one's time* |
| **se complaire à**  *to take pleasure in* | **perdre son temps à**  *to waste one's time* |
| **se consacrer à**  *to devote oneself to* | **persister à**  *to persist in* |
| **s'énerver à**  *to get annoyed* | **se plaire à**  *to take pleasure in* |
| **s'ennuyer à**  *to get/be bored* | **prendre plaisir à**  *to take pleasure in* |
| **s'entraîner à**  *to train to, practice* | **se résigner à**  *to resign oneself to* |

Several verbs expressing the achievement or failure of an action require **à** before an infinitive.

| | |
|---|---|
| **arriver à**  *to manage to* | **renoncer à**  *to give up* |
| **continuer à**  *to continue to* | **réussir à**  *to succeed in* |
| **parvenir à**  *to manage to, succeed in* | |

## Verb + direct object + à + infinitive

Many verbs taking an animate direct object are connected by the preposition **à** to a following infinitive. These verbs express the idea of getting someone to do something.

**accoutumer qqn à faire qqch** *to get someone used to doing something*

**aider qqn à faire qqch** *to help someone do something*

**autoriser qqn à faire qqch** *to authorize someone to do something*

**condamner qqn à faire qqch** *to condemn someone to do something*

**contraindre qqn à faire qqch** *to compel someone to do something*

**décider qqn à faire qqch** *to help someone decide to do something*

**encourager qqn à faire qqch** *to encourage someone to do something*

**engager qqn à faire qqch** *to urge someone to do something*

**forcer qqn à faire qqch** *to force someone to do something*

**inciter qqn à faire qqch** *to incite someone to do something*

**inviter qqn à faire qqch** *to invite someone to do something*

**obliger qqn à faire qqch** *to oblige someone to do something*

**pousser qqn à faire qqch** *to talk someone into doing something*

**préparer qqn à faire qqch** *to prepare someone to do / for doing something*

Note that **apprendre** when it means *to teach* resembles **enseigner:** they both take an indirect object for the person being taught.

**apprendre/enseigner à qqn à faire qqch**   *to teach someone to do something*

## C. Verb + **de** + infinitive

Many verbs and verbal expressions require **de** before an infinitive complement. Among them are verbs signifying an interruption of the action expressed by the infinitive and verbs conveying an attitude toward the action expressed by the infinitive.

**s'abstenir de** *to refrain from*
**accepter de** *to agree to*
**achever de** *to finish*
**affecter de** *to pretend to*
**s'arrêter de** *to stop*
**avoir peur de** *to be afraid of*
**avoir raison de** *to be right to*
**avoir tort de** *to be wrong to*
**brûler de** *to be burning to, dying to*
**cesser de** *to stop*
**craindre de** *to fear*
**se dépêcher de** *to hurry to*
**s'empêcher de** *to refrain from, keep oneself from*
**s'empresser de** *to hurry, rush to*
**entreprendre de** *to undertake to*
**s'étonner de** *to marvel at*
**éviter de** *to avoid*
**s'excuser de** *to apologize for*
**faire semblant de** *to pretend to*

**finir de** *to finish*
**se garder de** *to be wary of, to be careful not to*
**se hâter de** *to hasten to*
**s'inquiéter de** *to worry about*
**manquer de** *to fail to*
**mériter de** *to deserve to*
**négliger de** *to neglect to*
**omettre de** *to omit, neglect to*
**oublier de** *to forget to*
**se presser de** *to hurry, rush to*
**parler de** *to talk about*
**refuser de** *to refuse to*
**redouter de** *to dread*
**regretter de** *to regret*
**se réjouir de** *to be delighted to*
**se repentir de** *to regret*
**rougir de** *to be ashamed of*
**se soucier de** *to care about*
**se vanter de** *to boast of*

Verbs expressing an effort or plan to perform the action expressed by the infinitive use the preposition **de** before the infinitive complement.

| | |
|---|---|
| **avoir l'intention de** *to intend to* | **menacer de** *to threaten to* |
| **se charger de** *to make sure to, to see to it that something is done* | **promettre de** *to promise to* |
| **choisir de** *to choose to* | **se proposer de** *to set out, mean, intend to* |
| **décider de** *to decide to* | **résoudre de** *to resolve to* |
| **essayer de** *to try to* | **risquer de** *to risk, run the risk of* |
| **être forcé/obligé de*** *to be forced/obliged to* | **tâcher de** *to try to* |
| **jurer de** *to swear to* | **tenter de** *to try to* |

*Some special cases:*

1. **S'indigner de** is usually translated as *it makes someone indignant that*.

2. **Se souvenir de** is most often followed by the infinitive of the auxiliary + past participle (the perfect infinitive).

   In French, **n'oubliez pas de** is used to tell someone to remember to do something.

   **N'oubliez pas de** prendre les billets.    *Remember to buy the tickets.*

3. **Bien faire de** means *to be right in doing something, to do the wise thing by doing something*.

   Tu **as bien fait d'**arriver en avance.    *You were wise to get here early.*

4. **Venir de** means *to have just done something*.

   Il **vient de renoncer** à son poste.    *He has just quit his job.*

## Verb + direct object + **de** + infinitive

Many verbs taking an animate direct object take **de** before a following infinitive in French.

| | |
|---|---|
| **accuser qqn de faire qqch** *to accuse someone of doing something* | **dissuader qqn de faire qqch** *to dissuade someone from doing something* |
| **avertir qqn de (ne pas) faire qqch** *to warn someone (not) to do something* | **empêcher qqn de faire qqch** *to prevent someone from doing something* |
| **contraindre qqn de faire qqch** *to compel someone to do something* | **excuser qqn de faire qqch** *to excuse, forgive someone for doing something* |
| **convaincre qqn de faire qqch** *to convince someone to do something* | **féliciter qqn d'avoir fait qqch** *to congratulate someone for having done something* |
| **décourager qqn de faire qqch** *to discourage someone from doing something* | **louer qqn d'avoir fait qqch** *to praise someone for having done something* |
| **défier qqn de faire qqch** *to challenge someone to do something* | **menacer qqn de faire qqch** *to threaten someone with doing something* |

*Note that when **obliger** is used in the passive voice it takes **de**, but when used in the active voice it takes **à**, before a following infinitive.

**persuader qqn de faire qqch** *to persuade someone to do something*

**presser qqn de faire qqch** *to pressure someone to do something*

**prier qqn de faire qqch** *to beg someone to do something*

**remercier qqn de faire qqch** *to thank someone for doing something*

**soupçonner qqn de faire qqch** *to suspect someone of doing something*

**supplier qqn de faire qqch** *to beg someone to do something*

Another group of verbs that take **de** before the following infinitive take an indirect object. Examine the following expressions in which **quelqu'un** is both the indirect object of the first verb and the subject of the infinitive.

# Verb + indirect object + de + infinitive

**commander à qqn de faire qqch** *to order someone to do something*

**conseiller à qqn de faire qqch** *to advise someone to do something*

**déconseiller à qqn de faire qqch** *to advise someone not to do something*

**défendre à qqn de faire qqch** *to forbid someone to do something*

**demander à qqn de faire qqch** *to ask someone to do something*

**dire à qqn de faire qqch** *to tell someone to do something*

**faire signe à qqn de faire qqch** *to signal someone to do something*

**interdire à qqn de faire qqch** *to forbid someone to do something*

**ordonner à qqn de faire qqch** *to order someone to do something*

**pardonner à qqn de faire qqch** *to forgive someone for doing something*

**permettre à qqn de faire qqch** *to allow someone to do something*

**proposer à qqn de faire qqch** *to suggest to someone that he/she do something*

**reprocher à qqn de faire qqch** *to reproach someone for doing something*

**suggérer à qqn de faire qqch** *to suggest to someone that he/she to do something*

## D. Verbs of perception + infinitive

Verbs of perception such as **voir, regarder, entendre, écouter,** and the verb **laisser** (*to leave, let*) are followed directly by the infinitive. The direct object of these verbs is the subject of the infinitive and can be placed either before or after the infinitive if it is a noun.

Nous voyons **les acteurs** jouer.
Nous voyons jouer **les acteurs.**　　*We see **the actors** act.*

On va entendre **l'horloge** sonner.
On va entendre sonner **l'horloge.**　　*We'll hear **the clock** strike the hour.*

Elle a laissé **les étudiants** sortir.
Elle a laissé sortir **les étudiants.**　　*She let **the students** go out.*

When the direct object noun is replaced by a direct object pronoun with verbs of perception or **laisser,** it must stand before the verb of perception or **laisser.**

Nous **les** voyons jouer.　　*We see **them** act.*
On va **l'**entendre sonner.　　*We'll hear **it** strike the hour.*
Elle **les** a laissés sortir.　　*She let **them** go out.*

Verbs of perception and **laisser** may appear in sentences with two direct objects, a direct object of the verb of perception and a direct object of the infinitive.

Nous écoutons **les oiseaux** chanter **une mélodie** familière.

*We listen to **the birds** sing a familiar **song**.*

J'ai laissé **ma fille** acheter **ce jouet.**

*I let **my daughter** buy **that toy**.*

## Verb + **par/pour** + infinitive

**commencer par faire qqch** *to begin by doing something*

**finir par faire qqch** *to wind up doing something*

**suffire pour faire qqch** *to be enough to, adequate for doing something*

# APPENDICE IV: ADDITIONAL LITERARY TENSES

## A. Forms and uses of the imperfect subjunctive

1. The imperfect subjunctive is a literary form, reserved for formal writing. It is formed by adding the following endings to the stem of **-er** verbs: **-asse, -asses, -ât, -assions, -assiez, -assent.**

2. For **-ir** and **-re** verbs and for irregular verbs, the endings of the imperfect subjunctive are added to the **tu** form of the **passé simple** minus the final **-s.** The imperfect subjunctive endings for this group of verbs are **-sse, -sses, -^t, -ssions, -ssiez, -ssent.**

| PARLER | | | |
|---|---|---|---|
| que je | **parlasse** | que nous | **parlassions** |
| que tu | **parlasses** | que vous | **parlassiez** |
| qu'il/qu'elle | **parlât** | qu'ils/qu'elles | **parlassent** |

| FINIR | | | |
|---|---|---|---|
| que je | **finisse** | que nous | **finissions** |
| que tu | **finisses** | que vous | **finissiez** |
| qu'il/qu'elle | **finît** | qu'ils/qu'elles | **finissent** |

| VENDRE | | | |
|---|---|---|---|
| que je | **vendisse** | que nous | **vendissions** |
| que tu | **vendisses** | que vous | **vendissiez** |
| qu'il/qu'elle | **vendît** | qu'ils/qu'elles | **vendissent** |

**NOTE** The spelling changes for verbs such as **commencer** and **manger** occur in all persons of the imperfect subjunctive: **que je commençasse, que tu mangeasses,** etc.

3. Here are the imperfect subjunctive forms of **avoir, être, faire,** and **venir.**

| AVOIR | | | |
|---|---|---|---|
| que j' | **eusse** | que nous | **eussions** |
| que tu | **eusses** | que vous | **eussiez** |
| qu'il/qu'elle | **eût** | qu'ils/qu'elles | **eussent** |

| ÊTRE | | | |
|---|---|---|---|
| que je | **fusse** | que nous | **fussions** |
| que tu | **fusses** | que vous | **fussiez** |
| qu'il/qu'elle | **fût** | qu'ils/qu'elles | **fussent** |

| FAIRE | | | |
|---|---|---|---|
| que je | **fisse** | que nous | **fissions** |
| que tu | **fisses** | que vous | **fissiez** |
| qu'il/qu'elle | **fît** | qu'ils/qu'elles | **fissent** |

| VENIR | | | |
|---|---|---|---|
| que je | **vinsse** | que nous | **vinssions** |
| que tu | **vinsses** | que vous | **vinssiez** |
| qu'il/qu'elle | **vînt** | qu'ils/qu'elles | **vinssent** |

4. In formal written French, the imperfect subjunctive is used in a subordinate clause when 1) the subjunctive is required, 2) the verb in the main clause is in a past tense, and 3) the action of the subordinate clause occurs at the same time or after the action of the main clause.

| EVERYDAY FRENCH | FORMAL FRENCH |
|---|---|
| Je veux **qu'il vienne.** | Je veux **qu'il vienne.** |
| Je voulais **qu'il vienne.** | Je voulais **qu'il vînt.** |
| Je ne crois pas **qu'il puisse** le faire. | Je ne crois pas **qu'il puisse** le faire. |
| Je ne croyais pas **qu'il puisse** le faire. | Je ne croyais pas **qu'il pût** le faire. |
| Il faut **qu'il réponde.** | Il faut **qu'il réponde.** |
| Il a fallu **qu'il réponde.** | Il a fallu **qu'il répondît.** |

5. An inverted third-person singular imperfect subjunctive (especially of **être**) often means *even if*. This construction is commonly used for stylistic effect in newspaper writing.

| | |
|---|---|
| Il ne pourrait pas agir seul, **fût-il** le président. | *He couldn't act alone, **even if he were** the president.* |
| Elle rêvait d'être à Paris, ne **fût-ce** que pour deux ou trois jours. | *She dreamed of being in Paris, **even if it were** only for two or three days.* |

In everyday French the preceding sentences would be phrased as follows:

Il ne pourrait pas agir seul, **même s'il était** le président.
Elle rêvait d'être à Paris, **même si ce n'était que** pour deux ou trois jours.

# B. Forms and uses of the pluperfect subjunctive

1. The pluperfect subjunctive consists of the imperfect subjunctive of the auxiliary verb (**avoir** or **être**) plus the past participle.

| VERBS CONJUGATED WITH **avoir** | VERBS CONJUGATED WITH **être** |
|---|---|
| que j'**eusse parlé, fini, perdu** | que je **fusse parti(e)** |
| que tu **eusses parlé, fini, perdu** | que tu **fusses parti(e)** |
| qu'il/qu'elle **eût parlé, fini, perdu** | qu'il/qu'elle **fût parti(e)** |
| que nous **eussions parlé, fini, perdu** | que nous **fussions parti(e)s** |
| que vous **eussiez parlé, fini, perdu** | que vous **fussiez parti(e)(s)** |
| qu'ils/qu'elles **eussent parlé, fini, perdu** | qu'ils/qu'elles **fussent parti(e)s** |

2. The pluperfect subjunctive is used to indicate that the action of the subordinate clause happened before the action of the main clause, when the verb of the main clause is in the past. Compare the following pairs of sentences in formal language.

| | |
|---|---|
| J'étais heureux **qu'il fût** là. | *I was happy **that he was there.*** |
| J'étais heureux **qu'il eût été** là. | *I was happy **that he had been** there.* |
| On ne croyait pas **qu'il partît.** | *We didn't think **he was leaving.*** |
| On ne croyait pas **qu'il fût parti.** | *We didn't think **he had left.*** |

Here are those same sentences in less formal French.

J'étais heureux **qu'il soit** là.
J'étais heureux **qu'il ait été** là.

On ne croyait pas **qu'il parte.**
On ne croyait pas **qu'il soit parti.**

3. The pluperfect subjunctive can also replace the pluperfect and the conditional perfect in both parts of a conditional sentence.

| | |
|---|---|
| S'**il** me l'**eût dit, j'eusse compris.** | *If **he had told** me, **I would have understood.*** |
| S'**il fût venu, nous eussions parlé.** | *If **he had come, we would have talked.*** |

Here are those same sentences in everyday French.

S'il me l'**avait dit, j'aurais compris.**
S'il **était venu, nous aurions parlé.**

As in the case of the imperfect subjunctive, you only need to recognize the forms of the pluperfect subjunctive.

# C. Forms and uses of the *passé antérieur*

In addition to the pluperfect tense consisting of the imperfect subjunctive of the auxiliary and the past participle, French has a literary tense called the **passé antérieur** which is made up of the **passé simple** of the auxiliary, followed by the past participle.

| FINIR | | | |
|---|---|---|---|
| j' | **eus fini** | nous | **eûmes fini** |
| tu | **eus fini** | vous | **eûtes fini** |
| il/elle/on | **eut fini** | ills/elles | **eurent fini** |

| ALLER | | | |
|---|---|---|---|
| je | **fus allé(e)** | nous | **fûmes allé(e)s** |
| tu | **fus allé(e)** | vous | **fûtes allé(e)(s)** |
| il | **fut allé** | ils | **furent allés** |
| elle | **fut allée** | elles | **furent allées** |

The **passé antérieur** is used in formal literary French after conjunctions such as **quand, lorsque, aussitôt que, dès que, après que.** Note that the **passé antérieur** is used in texts where the **passé simple** is used.

**Après qu'il eut mis la table,** il servit le dîner.

*After he had set the table, he served dinner.*

Je la vis **dès qu'elle fut entrée.**

*I saw her as soon as she came in.*

# APPENDICE V: VERB CHARTS

## Regular verbs

### -er verbs

**PARLER** *to speak*

### Indicative mood

| | |
|---|---|
| PRESENT | parle, parles, parle, parlons, parlez, parlent |
| IMPERFECT | parlais, parlais, parlait, parlions, parliez, parlaient |
| FUTURE | parlerai, parleras, parlera, parlerons, parlerez, parleront |
| CONDITIONAL | parlerais, parlerais, parlerait, parlerions, parleriez, parleraient |
| PASSÉ COMPOSÉ | ai parlé, as parlé, a parlé, avons parlé, avez parlé, ont parlé |
| PASSÉ SIMPLE | parlai, parlas, parla, parlâmes, parlâtes, parlèrent |
| PLUPERFECT | avais parlé, avais parlé, avait parlé, avions parlé, aviez parlé, avaient parlé |
| FUTURE PERFECT | aurai parlé, auras parlé, aura parlé, aurons parlé, aurez parlé, auront parlé |
| CONDITIONAL PERFECT | aurais parlé, aurais parlé, aurait parlé, aurions parlé, auriez parlé, auraient parlé |

### Subjunctive mood

| | |
|---|---|
| PRESENT | parle, parles, parle, parlions, parliez, parlent |
| PAST | aie parlé, aies parlé, ait parlé, ayons parlé, ayez parlé, aient parlé |
| IMPERFECT | parlasse, parlasses, parlât, parlassions, parlassiez, parlassent |

### Imperative mood

parle (*but:* parles-en), parlons, parlez

### Present participle

parlant

# -ir verbs

## FINIR *to finish*

### Indicative mood

| | |
|---|---|
| PRESENT | finis, finis, finit, finissons, finissez, finissent |
| IMPERFECT | finissais, finissais, finissait, finissions, finissiez, finissaient |
| FUTURE | finirai, finiras, finira, finirons, finirez, finiront |
| CONDITIONAL | finirais, finirais, finirait, finirions, finiriez, finiraient |
| PASSÉ COMPOSÉ | ai fini, as fini, a fini, avons fini, avez fini, ont fini |
| PASSÉ SIMPLE | finis, finis, finit, finîmes, finîtes, finirent |
| PLUPERFECT | avais fini, avais fini, avait fini, avions fini, aviez fini, avaient fini |
| FUTURE PERFECT | aurai fini, auras fini, aura fini, aurons fini, aurez fini, auront fini |
| CONDITIONAL PERFECT | aurais fini, aurais fini, aurait fini, aurions fini, auriez fini, auraient fini |

### Subjunctive mood

| | |
|---|---|
| PRESENT | finisse, finisses, finisse, finissions, finissiez, finissent |
| PAST | aie fini, aies fini, ait fini, ayons fini, ayez fini, aient fini |
| IMPERFECT | finisse, finisses, finît, finissions, finissiez, finissent |

### Imperative mood

finis, finissons, finissez

### Present participle

finissant

## -re verbs

**VENDRE** *to sell*

### Indicative mood

| | |
|---|---|
| PRESENT | vends, vends, vend, vendons, vendez, vendent |
| IMPERFECT | vendais, vendais, vendait, vendions, vendiez, vendaient |
| FUTURE | vendrai, vendras, vendra, vendrons, vendrez, vendront |
| CONDITIONAL | vendrais, vendrais, vendrait, vendrions, vendriez, vendraient |
| PASSÉ COMPOSÉ | ai vendu, as vendu, a vendu, avons vendu, avez vendu, ont vendu |
| PASSÉ SIMPLE | vendis, vendis, vendit, vendîmes, vendîtes, vendirent |
| PLUPERFECT | avais vendu, avais vendu, avait vendu, avions vendu, aviez vendu, avaient vendu |
| FUTURE PERFECT | aurai vendu, auras vendu, aura vendu, aurons vendu, aurez vendu, auront vendu |
| CONDITIONAL PERFECT | aurais vendu, aurais vendu, aurait vendu, aurions vendu, auriez vendu, auraient vendu |

### Subjunctive mood

| | |
|---|---|
| PRESENT | vende, vendes, vende, vendions, vendiez, vendent |
| PAST | aie vendu, aies vendu, ait vendu, ayons vendu, ayez vendu, aient vendu |
| IMPERFECT | vendisse, vendisses, vendît, vendissions, vendissiez, vendissent |

### Imperative mood

vends, vendons, vendez

### Present participle

vendant

## Verbs conjugated with **être** in compound tenses

The following verbs are conjugated with **être** as the auxiliary in compound tenses.

| | | | |
|---|---|---|---|
| **aller** | **monter** | **rentrer** | **tomber** |
| **arriver** | **mourir** | **rester** | **venir** |
| **descendre** | **naître** | **retourner** | |
| **devenir** | **partir** | **revenir** | |
| **entrer** | **passer** | **sortir** | |

## ARRIVER *to arrive*

### Indicative mood

| | |
|---|---|
| PASSÉ COMPOSÉ | suis arrivé(e), es arrivé(e), est arrivé(e), sommes arrivé(e)s, êtes arrivé(e)(s), sont arrivé(e)s |
| PLUPERFECT | étais arrivé(e), étais arrivé(e), était arrivé(e), étions arrivé(e)s, étiez arrivé(e)(s), étaient arrivé(e)s |
| FUTURE PERFECT | serai arrivé(e), seras arrivé(e), sera arrivé(e), serons arrivé(e)s, serez arrivé(e)(s), seront arrivé(e)s |
| CONDITIONAL PERFECT | serais arrivé(e), serais arrivé(e), serait arrivé(e), serions arrivé(e)s, seriez arrivé(e)(s), seraient arrivé(e)s |

### Subjunctive mood

| | |
|---|---|
| PAST | sois arrivé(e), sois arrivé(e), soit arrivé(e), soyons arrivé(e)s, soyez arrivé(e)(s), soient arrivé(e)s |

## Verbs with spelling changes

Verbs whose stems end in **c,** such as **commencer,** add a cedilla under the **c (ç)** before the letters **a** and **o.**

## COMMENCER *to begin*

| | |
|---|---|
| PRESENT | commence, commences, commence, commençons, commencez, commencent |
| IMPERFECT | commençais, commençais, commençait, commencions, commenciez, commençaient |
| PASSÉ SIMPLE | commençai, commenças, commença, commençâmes, commençâtes, commencèrent |
| PRESENT PARTICIPLE | commençant |

Verbs whose stems end in **g,** such as **manger,** add an **e** after the **g** before the letters **a** and **o.**

## MANGER *to eat*

| | |
|---|---|
| PRESENT | mange, manges, mange, mangeons, mangez, mangent |
| IMPERFECT | mangeais, mangeais, mangeait, mangions, mangiez, mangeaient |
| PASSÉ SIMPLE | mangeai, mangeas, mangea, mangeâmes, mangeâtes, mangèrent |
| PRESENT PARTICIPLE | mangeant |

Verbs whose stems end in **y,** such as **nettoyer,** change the **y** to **i** before a mute **e.**

## NETTOYER *to clean*

| | |
|---|---|
| PRESENT | nettoie, nettoies, nettoie, nettoyons, nettoyez, nettoient |
| PRESENT SUBJUNCTIVE | nettoie, nettoies, nettoie, nettoyions, nettoyiez, nettoient |
| FUTURE | nettoierai, nettoieras, nettoiera, nettoierons, nettoierez, nettoieront |
| CONDITIONAL | nettoierais, nettoierais, nettoierait, nettoierions, nettoieriez, nettoieraient |
| IMPERATIVE | nettoie, nettoyons, nettoyez |

**NOTE**

Verbs ending in **-ayer** may either change **y** to **i** before a mute **e** or keep the **y** in all forms: **je paie** or **je paye.** Verbs in **-oyer** and **-uyer** must change **y** to **i** before a mute **e.**

In **-er** verbs that have mute **e** as their stem vowel (**acheter, appeler, jeter, mener,** etc.), the mute **e** is pronounced **è** in those forms where the ending has a mute **e.** In the present tense, this occurs in all singular forms and the third-person plural. This change in sound may be spelled in one of two ways.

• Verbs such as **lever** change the **e** to **è** to show the change in pronunciation.

## LEVER *to raise*

| | |
|---|---|
| PRESENT | lève, lèves, lève, levons, levez, lèvent |
| PRESENT SUBJUNCTIVE | lève, lèves, lève, levions, leviez, lèvent |
| FUTURE | lèverai, lèveras, lèvera, lèverons, lèverez, lèveront |
| CONDITIONAL | lèverais, lèverais, lèverait, lèverions, lèveriez, lèveraient |
| IMPERATIVE | lève, levons, levez |

• The verbs **appeler** and **jeter** double the consonant before the mute **e** to show the sound change of mute **e** to **è.**

## APPELER *to call*

| | |
|---|---|
| PRESENT | appelle, appelles, appelle, appelons, appelez, appellent |
| PRESENT SUBJUNCTIVE | appelle, appelles, appelle, appelions, appeliez, appellent |
| FUTURE | appellerai, appelleras, appellera, appellerons, appellerez, appelleront |
| CONDITIONAL | appellerais, appellerais, appellerait, appellerions, appelleriez, appelleraient |
| IMPERATIVE | appelle, appelons, appelez |

## JETER  *to throw*

| | |
|---|---|
| PRESENT | jette, jettes, jette, jetons, jetez, jettent |
| PRESENT SUBJUNCTIVE | jette, jettes, jette, jetions, jetiez, jettent |
| FUTURE | jetterai, jetteras, jettera, jetterons, jetterez, jetteront |
| CONDITIONAL | jetterais, jetterais, jetterait, jetterions, jetteriez, jetteraient |
| IMPERATIVE | jette, jetons, jetez |

- First-conjugation verbs such as **espérer** that have **é** as the stem vowel change **é** to **è** when the ending has a mute **e.** However, unlike verbs like **lever,** verbs like **espérer** keep the acute accent in the future and conditional.

## ESPÉRER  *to hope*

| | |
|---|---|
| PRESENT | espère, espères, espère, espérons, espérez, espèrent |
| PRESENT SUBJUNCTIVE | espère, espères, espère, espérions, espériez, espèrent |
| FUTURE | espérerai, espéreras, espérera, espérerons, espérerez, espéreront |
| CONDITIONAL | espérerais, espérerais, espérerait, espérerions, espéreriez, espéreraient |
| IMPERATIVE | espère, espérons, espérez |

# Irregular verbs

## ALLER  *to go, be going (to)*

| | |
|---|---|
| PRESENT | vais, vas, va, allons, allez, vont |
| IMPERFECT | allais, allais, allait, allions, alliez, allaient |
| PASSÉ COMPOSÉ | suis allé(e), *etc.* |
| FUTURE | irai, iras, ira, irons, irez, iront |
| CONDITIONAL | irais, irais, irait, irions, iriez, iraient |
| PASSÉ SIMPLE | allai, allas, alla, allâmes, allâtes, allèrent |
| PRESENT SUBJUNCTIVE | aille, ailles, aille, allions, alliez, aillent |
| IMPERATIVE | va, allons, allez |
| PRESENT PARTICIPLE | allant |

## S'ASSEOIR  *to sit down*

| | |
|---|---|
| PRESENT | m'assieds, t'assieds, s'assied, nous asseyons, vous asseyez, s'asseyent |
| IMPERFECT | m'asseyais, t'asseyais, s'asseyait, nous asseyions, vous asseyiez, s'asseyaient |
| PASSÉ COMPOSÉ | me suis assis(e), *etc.* |
| FUTURE | m'assiérai, t'assiéras, s'assiéra, nous assiérons, vous assiérez, s'assiéront |
| CONDITIONAL | m'assiérais, t'assiérais, s'assiérait, nous assiérions, vous assiériez, s'assiéraient |
| PASSÉ SIMPLE | m'assis, t'assis, s'assit, nous assîmes, vous assîtes, s'assirent |
| PRESENT SUBJUNCTIVE | m'asseye, t'asseyes, s'asseye, nous asseyions, vous asseyiez, s'asseyent |
| IMPERATIVE | assieds-toi, asseyons-nous, asseyez-vous |
| PRESENT PARTICIPLE | s'asseyant |

## AVOIR  *to have*

| | |
|---|---|
| PRESENT | ai, as, a, avons, avez, ont |
| IMPERFECT | avais, avais, avait, avions, aviez, avaient |
| PASSÉ COMPOSÉ | ai eu, *etc.* |
| FUTURE | aurai, auras, aura, aurons, aurez, auront |
| CONDITIONAL | aurais, aurais, aurait, aurions, auriez, auraient |
| PASSÉ SIMPLE | eus, eus, eut, eûmes, eûtes, eurent |
| PRESENT SUBJUNCTIVE | aie, aies, ait, ayons, ayez, aient |
| IMPERATIVE | aie (*but:* aies-en), ayons, ayez |
| PRESENT PARTICIPLE | ayant |

## BATTRE  *to beat, strike, hit*

| | |
|---|---|
| PRESENT | bats, bats, bat, battons, battez, battent |
| IMPERFECT | battais, battais, battait, battions, battiez, battaient |
| PASSÉ COMPOSÉ | ai battu, *etc.* |
| FUTURE | battrai, battras, battra, battrons, battrez, battront |
| CONDITIONAL | battrais, battrais, battrait, battrions, battriez, battraient |
| PASSÉ SIMPLE | battis, battis, battit, battîmes, battîtes, battirent |
| PRESENT SUBJUNCTIVE | batte, battes, batte, battions, battiez, battent |
| IMPERATIVE | bats, battons, battez |
| PRESENT PARTICIPLE | battant |
| Conjugated like **battre:** | **combattre** *to fight, combat* |

## BOIRE *to drink*

| | |
|---|---|
| PRESENT | bois, bois, boit, buvons, buvez, boivent |
| IMPERFECT | buvais, buvais, buvait, buvions, buviez, buvaient |
| PASSÉ COMPOSÉ | ai bu, *etc.* |
| FUTURE | boirai, boiras, boira, boirons, boirez, boiront |
| PASSÉ SIMPLE | bus, bus, but, bûmes, bûtes, burent |
| PRESENT SUBJUNCTIVE | boive, boives, boive, buvions, buviez, boivent |
| IMPERATIVE | bois, buvons, buvez |
| PRESENT PARTICIPLE | buvant |

## CONDUIRE *to drive*

| | |
|---|---|
| PRESENT | conduis, conduis, conduit, conduisons, conduisez, conduisent |
| IMPERFECT | conduisais, conduisais, conduisait, conduisions, conduisiez, conduisaient |
| PASSÉ COMPOSÉ | ai conduit, *etc.* |
| FUTURE | conduirai, conduiras, conduira, conduirons, conduirez, conduiront |
| CONDITIONAL | conduirais, conduirais, conduirait, conduirions, conduiriez, conduiraient |
| PASSÉ SIMPLE | conduisis, conduisis, conduisit, conduisîmes, conduisîtes, conduisirent |
| PRESENT SUBJUNCTIVE | conduise, conduises, conduise, conduisions, conduisiez, conduisent |
| IMPERATIVE | conduis, conduisons, conduisez |
| PRESENT PARTICIPLE | conduisant |
| Conjugated like **conduire:** | **construire** *to build,* **détruire** *to destroy,* **produire** *to produce,* **réduire** *to reduce,* **traduire** *to translate* |

## CONNAÎTRE _to know (a person, place, etc.)_

| | |
|---|---|
| PRESENT | connais, connais, connaît, connaissons, connaissez, connaissent |
| IMPERFECT | connaissais, connaissais, connaissait, connaissions, connaissiez, connaissaient |
| PASSÉ COMPOSÉ | ai connu, _etc._ |
| FUTURE | connaîtrai, connaîtras, connaîtra, connaîtrons, connaîtrez, connaîtront |
| CONDITIONAL | connaîtrais, connaîtrais, connaîtrait, connaîtrions, connaîtriez, connaîtraient |
| PASSÉ SIMPLE | connus, connus, connut, connûmes, connûtes, connurent |
| PRESENT SUBJUNCTIVE | connaisse, connaisses, connaisse, connaissions, connaissiez, connaissent |
| IMPERATIVE | connais, connaissons, connaissez |
| PRESENT PARTICIPLE | connaissant |
| Conjugated like **connaître:** | **apparaître** _to appear,_ **disparaître** _to disappear,_ **paraître** _to seem, appear,_ **reconnaître** _to recognize_ |

## COURIR _to run_

| | |
|---|---|
| PRESENT | cours, cours, court, courons, courez, courent |
| IMPERFECT | courais, courais, courait, courions, couriez, couraient |
| PASSÉ COMPOSÉ | ai couru, _etc._ |
| FUTURE | courrai, courras, courra, courrons, courrez, courront |
| CONDITIONAL | courrais, courrais, courrait, courrions, courriez, courraient |
| PASSÉ SIMPLE | courus, courus, courut, courûmes, courûtes, coururent |
| PRESENT SUBJUNCTIVE | coure, coures, coure, courions, couriez, courent |
| IMPERATIVE | cours, courons, courez |
| PRESENT PARTICIPLE | courant |

## CRAINDRE _to fear_

| | |
|---|---|
| PRESENT | crains, crains, craint, craignons, craignez, craignent |
| IMPERFECT | craignais, craignais, craignait, craignions, craigniez, craignaient |
| PASSÉ COMPOSÉ | ai craint, _etc._ |
| FUTURE | craindrai, craindras, craindra, craindrons, craindrez, craindront |
| CONDITIONAL | craindrais, craindrais, craindrait, craindrions, craindriez, craindraient |
| PASSÉ SIMPLE | craignis, craignis, craignit, craignîmes, craignîtes, craignirent |
| PRESENT SUBJUNCTIVE | craigne, craignes, craigne, craignions, craigniez, craignent |
| IMPERATIVE | crains, craignons, craignez |
| PRESENT PARTICIPLE | craignant |
| Conjugated like **craindre:** | **plaindre** _to pity_ |

## CROIRE *to believe, think*

| | |
|---|---|
| PRESENT | crois, crois, croit, croyons, croyez, croient |
| IMPERFECT | croyais, croyais, croyait, croyions, croyiez, croyaient |
| PASSÉ COMPOSÉ | ai cru, *etc.* |
| FUTURE | croirai, croiras, croira, croirons, croirez, croiront |
| CONDITIONAL | croirais, croirais, croirait, croirions, croiriez, croiraient |
| PASSÉ SIMPLE | crus, crus, crut, crûmes, crûtes, crurent |
| PRESENT SUBJUNCTIVE | croie, croies, croie, croyions, croyiez, croient |
| IMPERATIVE | crois, croyons, croyez |
| PRESENT PARTICIPLE | croyant |

## CUEILLIR *to gather, pick (flowers)*

| | |
|---|---|
| PRESENT | cueille, cueilles, cueille, cueillons, cueillez, cueillent |
| IMPERFECT | cueillais, cueillais, cueillait, cueillions, cueilliez, cueillaient |
| PASSÉ COMPOSÉ | ai cueilli, *etc.* |
| FUTURE | cueillerai, cueilleras, cueillera, cueillerons, cueillerez, cueilleront |
| CONDITIONAL | cueillerais, cueillerais, cueillerait, cueillerions, cueilleriez, cueilleraient |
| PASSÉ SIMPLE | cueillis, cueillis, cueillit, cueillîmes, cueillîtes, cueillirent |
| PRESENT SUBJUNCTIVE | cueille, cueilles, cueille, cueillions, cueilliez, cueillent |
| IMPERATIVE | cueille, cueillons, cueillez |
| PRESENT PARTICIPLE | cueillant |
| Conjugated like **cueillir:** | **accueillir** *to welcome* |

## DEVOIR *to owe; must, should, ought to*

| | |
|---|---|
| PRESENT | dois, dois, doit, devons, devez, doivent |
| IMPERFECT | devais, devais, devait, devions, deviez, devaient |
| PASSÉ COMPOSÉ | ai dû, *etc.* |
| FUTURE | devrai, devras, devra, devrons, devrez, devront |
| CONDITIONAL | devrais, devrais, devrait, devrions, devriez, devraient |
| PASSÉ SIMPLE | dus, dus, dut, dûmes, dûtes, durent |
| PRESENT SUBJUNCTIVE | doive, doives, doive, devions, deviez, doivent |
| IMPERATIVE | dois, devons, devez |
| PRESENT PARTICIPLE | devant |

## DIRE *to say, tell*

| | |
|---|---|
| PRESENT | dis, dis, dit, disons, dites, disent |
| IMPERFECT | disais, disais, disait, disions, disiez, disaient |
| PASSÉ COMPOSÉ | ai dit, *etc.* |
| FUTURE | dirai, diras, dira, dirons, direz, diront |
| CONDITIONAL | dirais, dirais, dirait, dirions, diriez, diraient |
| PASSÉ SIMPLE | dis, dis, dit, dîmes, dîtes, dirent |
| PRESENT SUBJUNCTIVE | dise, dises, dise, disions, disiez, disent |
| IMPERATIVE | dis, disons, dites |
| PRESENT PARTICIPLE | disant |
| Conjugated like **dire:** | **contredire** *to contradict* (*but:* **vous contredisez** [*present*])<br>**interdire** *to forbid* (*but:* **vous interdisez** [*present*]) |

## ÉCRIRE *to write*

| | |
|---|---|
| PRESENT | écris, écris, écrit, écrivons, écrivez, écrivent |
| IMPERFECT | écrivais, écrivais, écrivait, écrivions, écriviez, écrivaient |
| PASSÉ COMPOSÉ | ai écrit, *etc.* |
| FUTURE | écrirai, écriras, écrira, écrirons, écrirez, écriront |
| CONDITIONAL | écrirais, écrirais, écrirait, écririons, écririez, écriraient |
| PASSÉ SIMPLE | écrivis, écrivis, écrivit, écrivîmes, écrivîtes, écrivirent |
| PRESENT SUBJUNCTIVE | écrive, écrives, écrive, écrivions, écriviez, écrivent |
| IMPERATIVE | écris, écrivons, écrivez |
| PRESENT PARTICIPLE | écrivant |
| Conjugated like **écrire:** | **décrire** *to describe* |

## ENVOYER *to send*

| | |
|---|---|
| PRESENT | envoie, envoies, envoie, envoyons, envoyez, envoient |
| IMPERFECT | envoyais, envoyais, envoyait, envoyions, envoyiez, envoyaient |
| PASSÉ COMPOSÉ | ai envoyé, *etc.* |
| FUTURE | enverrai, enverras, enverra, enverrons, enverrez, enverront |
| CONDITIONAL | enverrais, enverrais, enverrait, enverrions, enverriez, enverraient |
| PASSÉ SIMPLE | envoyai, envoyas, envoya, envoyâmes, envoyâtes, envoyèrent |
| PRESENT SUBJUNCTIVE | envoie, envoies, envoie, envoyions, envoyiez, envoient |
| IMPERATIVE | envoie, envoyons, envoyez |
| PRESENT PARTICIPLE | envoyant |

## ÊTRE *to be*

| | |
|---|---|
| PRESENT | suis, es, est, sommes, êtes, sont |
| IMPERFECT | étais, étais, était, étions, étiez, étaient |
| PASSÉ COMPOSÉ | ai été, *etc.* |
| FUTURE | serai, seras, sera, serons, serez, seront |
| CONDITIONAL | serais, serais, serait, serions, seriez, seraient |
| PASSÉ SIMPLE | fus, fus, fut, fûmes, fûtes, furent |
| PRESENT SUBJUNCTIVE | sois, sois, soit, soyons, soyez, soient |
| IMPERATIVE | sois, soyons, soyez |
| PRESENT PARTICIPLE | étant |

## FAIRE *to do, make*

| | |
|---|---|
| PRESENT | fais, fais, fait, faisons, faites, font |
| IMPERFECT | faisais, faisais, faisait, faisions, faisiez, faisaient |
| PASSÉ COMPOSÉ | ai fait, *etc.* |
| FUTURE | ferai, feras, fera, ferons, ferez, feront |
| CONDITIONAL | ferais, ferais, ferait, ferions, feriez, feraient |
| PASSÉ SIMPLE | fis, fis, fit, fîmes, fîtes, firent |
| PRESENT SUBJUNCTIVE | fasse, fasses, fasse, fassions, fassiez, fassent |
| IMPERATIVE | fais, faisons, faites |
| PRESENT PARTICIPLE | faisant |
| Conjugated like **faire:** | **défaire** *to undo,* **refaire** *to redo* |

## FALLOIR *to be necessary*

| | |
|---|---|
| PRESENT | il faut |
| IMPERFECT | il fallait |
| PASSÉ COMPOSÉ | il a fallu |
| FUTURE | il faudra |
| CONDITIONAL | il faudrait |
| PASSÉ SIMPLE | il fallut |
| PRESENT SUBJUNCTIVE | il faille |

## JOINDRE *to join*

| | |
|---|---|
| PRESENT | joins, joins, joint, joignons, joignez, joignent |
| IMPERFECT | joignais, joignais, joignait, joignions, joigniez, joignaient |
| PASSÉ COMPOSÉ | ai joint, *etc.* |
| FUTURE | joindrai, joindras, joindra, joindrons, joindrez, joindront |
| CONDITIONAL | joindrais, joindrais, joindrait, joindrions, joindriez, joindraient |
| PASSÉ SIMPLE | joignis, joignis, joignit, joignîmes, joignîtes, joignirent |
| PRESENT SUBJUNCTIVE | joigne, joignes, joigne, joignions, joigniez, joignent |
| IMPERATIVE | joins, joignons, joignez |
| PRESENT PARTICIPLE | joignant |

## LIRE *to read*

| | |
|---|---|
| PRESENT | lis, lis, lit, lisons, lisez, lisent |
| IMPERFECT | lisais, lisais, lisait, lisions, lisiez, lisaient |
| PASSÉ COMPOSÉ | ai lu, *etc.* |
| FUTURE | lirai, liras, lira, lirons, lirez, liront |
| CONDITIONAL | lirais, lirais, lirait, lirions, liriez, liraient |
| PASSÉ SIMPLE | lus, lus, lut, lûmes, lûtes, lurent |
| PRESENT SUBJUNCTIVE | lise, lises, lise, lisions, lisiez, lisent |
| IMPERATIVE | lis, lisons, lisez |
| PRESENT PARTICIPLE | lisant |

## METTRE *to put*

| | |
|---|---|
| PRESENT | mets, mets, met, mettons, mettez, mettent |
| IMPERFECT | mettais, mettais, mettait, mettions, mettiez, mettaient |
| PASSÉ COMPOSÉ | ai mis, *etc.* |
| FUTURE | mettrai, mettras, mettra, mettrons, mettrez, mettront |
| CONDITIONAL | mettrais, mettrais, mettrait, mettrions, mettriez, mettraient |
| PASSÉ SIMPLE | mis, mis, mit, mîmes, mîtes, mirent |
| PRESENT SUBJUNCTIVE | mette, mettes, mette, mettions, mettiez, mettent |
| IMPERATIVE | mets, mettons, mettez |
| PRESENT PARTICIPLE | mettant |
| Conjugated like **mettre:** | **admettre** *to admit*, **permettre** *to permit*, **promettre** *to promise*, **remettre** *to delay, postpone, put on again* |

## MOURIR  *to die*

| | |
|---|---|
| PRESENT | meurs, meurs, meurt, mourons, mourez, meurent |
| IMPERFECT | mourais, mourais, mourait, mourions, mouriez, mouraient |
| PASSÉ COMPOSÉ | suis mort(e), *etc.* |
| FUTURE | mourrai, mourras, mourra, mourrons, mourrez, mourront |
| CONDITIONAL | mourrais, mourrais, mourrait, mourrions, mourriez, mourraient |
| PASSÉ SIMPLE | mourus, mourus, mourut, mourûmes, mourûtes, moururent |
| PRESENT SUBJUNCTIVE | meure, meures, meure, mourions, mouriez, meurent |
| IMPERATIVE | meurs, mourons, mourez |
| PRESENT PARTICIPLE | mourant |

## NAÎTRE  *to be born*

| | |
|---|---|
| PRESENT | nais, nais, naît, naissons, naissez, naissent |
| IMPERFECT | naissais, naissais, naissait, naissions, naissiez, naissaient |
| PASSÉ COMPOSÉ | suis né(e), *etc.* |
| FUTURE | naîtrai, naîtras, naîtra, naîtrons, naîtrez, naîtront |
| CONDITIONAL | naîtrais, naîtrais, naîtrait, naîtrions, naîtriez, naîtraient |
| PASSÉ SIMPLE | naquis, naquis, naquit, naquîmes, naquîtes, naquirent |
| PRESENT SUBJUNCTIVE | naisse, naisses, naisse, naissions, naissiez, naissent |
| IMPERATIVE | nais, naissons, naissez |
| PRESENT PARTICIPLE | naissant |

## OUVRIR  *to open*

| | |
|---|---|
| PRESENT | ouvre, ouvres, ouvre, ouvrons, ouvrez, ouvrent |
| IMPERFECT | ouvrais, ouvrais, ouvrait, ouvrions, ouvriez, ouvraient |
| PASSÉ COMPOSÉ | ai ouvert, *etc.* |
| FUTURE | ouvrirai, ouvriras, ouvrira, ouvrirons, ouvrirez, ouvriront |
| CONDITIONAL | ouvrirais, ouvrirais, ouvrirait, ouvririons, ouvririez, ouvriraient |
| PASSÉ SIMPLE | ouvris, ouvris, ouvrit, ouvrîmes, ouvrîtes, ouvrirent |
| PRESENT SUBJUNCTIVE | ouvre, ouvres, ouvre, ouvrions, ouvriez, ouvrent |
| IMPERATIVE | ouvre, ouvrons, ouvrez |
| PRESENT PARTICIPLE | ouvrant |
| Conjugated like **ouvrir:** | **couvrir** *to cover,* **découvrir** *to discover,* **offrir** *to offer,* **souffrir** *to suffer* |

## PARTIR  *to leave*

| | |
|---|---|
| PRESENT | pars, pars, part, partons, partez, partent |
| IMPERFECT | partais, partais, partait, partions, partiez, partaient |
| PASSÉ COMPOSÉ | suis parti(e), *etc.* |
| FUTURE | partirai, partiras, partira, partirons, partirez, partiront |
| CONDITIONAL | partirais, partirais, partirait, partirions, partiriez, partiraient |
| PASSÉ SIMPLE | partis, partis, partit, partîmes, partîtes, partirent |
| PRESENT SUBJUNCTIVE | parte, partes, parte, partions, partiez, partent |
| IMPERATIVE | pars, partons, partez |
| PRESENT PARTICIPLE | partant |
| Conjugated like **partir:** | **dormir**  *to sleep,* **mentir**  *to lie,* **sentir**  *to feel,* **servir**  *to serve,* **sortir**  *to go out* |

## PEINDRE  *to paint*

| | |
|---|---|
| PRESENT | peins, peins, peint, peignons, peignez, peignent |
| IMPERFECT | peignais, peignais, peignait, peignions, peigniez, peignaient |
| PASSÉ COMPOSÉ | ai peint, *etc.* |
| FUTURE | peindrai, peindras, peindra, peindrons, peindrez, peindront |
| CONDITIONAL | peindrais, peindrais, peindrait, peindrions, peindriez, peindraient |
| PASSÉ SIMPLE | peignis, peignis, peignit, peignîmes, peignîtes, peignirent |
| PRESENT SUBJUNCTIVE | peigne, peignes, peigne, peignions, peigniez, peignent |
| IMPERATIVE | peins, peignons, peignez |
| PRESENT PARTICIPLE | peignant |
| Conjugated like **peindre:** | **atteindre**  *to reach, attain,* **éteindre**  *to put out, extinguish* |

## PLAIRE  *to please*

| | |
|---|---|
| PRESENT | plais, plais, plaît, plaisons, plaisez, plaisent |
| IMPERFECT | plaisais, plaisais, plaisait, plaisions, plaisiez, plaisaient |
| PASSÉ COMPOSÉ | ai plu, *etc.* |
| FUTURE | plairai, plairas, plaira, plairons, plairez, plairont |
| CONDITIONAL | plairais, plairais, plairait, plairions, plairiez, plairaient |
| PASSÉ SIMPLE | plus, plus, plut, plûmes, plûtes, plurent |
| PRESENT SUBJUNCTIVE | plaise, plaises, plaise, plaisions, plaisiez, plaisent |
| IMPERATIVE | plais, plaisons, plaisez |
| PRESENT PARTICIPLE | plaisant |
| Conjugated like **plaire:** | **se taire**  *to keep quiet* |

## PLEUVOIR *to rain*

| | |
|---|---|
| PRESENT | il pleut |
| IMPERFECT | il pleuvait |
| PASSÉ COMPOSÉ | il a plu |
| FUTURE | il pleuvra |
| CONDITIONAL | il pleuvrait |
| PASSÉ SIMPLE | il plut |
| PRESENT SUBJUNCTIVE | il pleuve |
| PRESENT PARTICIPLE | pleuvant |

## POUVOIR *can, to be able to*

| | |
|---|---|
| PRESENT | peux, peux, peut, pouvons, pouvez, peuvent |
| IMPERFECT | pouvais, pouvais, pouvait, pouvions, pouviez, pouvaient |
| PASSÉ COMPOSÉ | ai pu, *etc.* |
| FUTURE | pourrai, pourras, pourra, pourrons, pourrez, pourront |
| CONDITIONAL | pourrais, pourrais, pourrait, pourrions, pourriez, pourraient |
| PASSÉ SIMPLE | pus, pus, put, pûmes, pûtes, purent |
| PRESENT SUBJUNCTIVE | puisse, puisses, puisse, puissions, puissiez, puissent |
| IMPERATIVE | (*not used*) |
| PRESENT PARTICIPLE | pouvant |

## PRENDRE *to take*

| | |
|---|---|
| PRESENT | prends, prends, prend, prenons, prenez, prennent |
| IMPERFECT | prenais, prenais, prenait, prenions, preniez, prenaient |
| PASSÉ COMPOSÉ | ai pris, *etc.* |
| FUTURE | prendrai, prendras, prendra, prendrons, prendrez, prendront |
| CONDITIONAL | prendrais, prendrais, prendrait, prendrions, prendriez, prendraient |
| PASSÉ SIMPLE | pris, pris, prit, prîmes, prîtes, prirent |
| PRESENT SUBJUNCTIVE | prenne, prennes, prenne, prenions, preniez, prennent |
| IMPERATIVE | prends, prenons, prenez |
| PRESENT PARTICIPLE | prenant |
| Conjugated like **prendre:** | **apprendre** *to learn,* **comprendre** *to understand,* **reprendre** *to take again, resume,* **surprendre** *to surprise* |

## RECEVOIR  *to receive*

| | |
|---|---|
| PRESENT | reçois, reçois, reçoit, recevons, recevez, reçoivent |
| IMPERFECT | recevais, recevais, recevait, recevions, receviez, recevaient |
| PASSÉ COMPOSÉ | ai reçu, *etc.* |
| FUTURE | recevrai, recevras, recevra, recevrons, recevrez, recevront |
| CONDITIONAL | recevrais, recevrais, recevrait, recevrions, recevriez, recevraient |
| PASSÉ SIMPLE | reçus, reçus, reçut, reçûmes, reçûtes, reçurent |
| PRESENT SUBJUNCTIVE | reçoive, reçoives, reçoive, recevions, receviez, reçoivent |
| IMPERATIVE | reçois, recevons, recevez |
| PRESENT PARTICIPLE | recevant |
| Conjugated like **recevoir:** | **apercevoir**  *to perceive,* **décevoir**  *to disappoint* |

## RIRE  *to laugh*

| | |
|---|---|
| PRESENT | ris, ris, rit, rions, riez, rient |
| IMPERFECT | riais, riais, riait, riions, riiez, riaient |
| PASSÉ COMPOSÉ | ai ri, *etc.* |
| FUTURE | rirai, riras, rira, rirons, rirez, riront |
| CONDITIONAL | rirais, rirais, rirait, ririons, ririez, riraient |
| PASSÉ SIMPLE | ris, ris, rit, rîmes, rîtes, rirent |
| PRESENT SUBJUNCTIVE | rie, ries, rie, riions, riiez, rient |
| IMPERATIVE | ris, rions, riez |
| PRESENT PARTICIPLE | riant |
| Conjugated like **rire:** | **sourire**  *to smile* |

## SAVOIR  *to know*

| | |
|---|---|
| PRESENT | sais, sais, sait, savons, savez, savent |
| IMPERFECT | savais, savais, savait, savions, saviez, savaient |
| PASSÉ COMPOSÉ | ai su, *etc.* |
| FUTURE | saurai, sauras, saura, saurons, saurez, sauront |
| CONDITIONAL | saurais, saurais, saurait, saurions, sauriez, sauraient |
| PASSÉ SIMPLE | sus, sus, sut, sûmes, sûtes, surent |
| PRESENT SUBJUNCTIVE | sache, saches, sache, sachions, sachiez, sachent |
| IMPERATIVE | sache, sachons, sachez |
| PRESENT PARTICIPLE | sachant |

## SUIVRE *to follow*

| | |
|---|---|
| PRESENT | suis, suis, suit, suivons, suivez, suivent |
| IMPERFECT | suivais, suivais, suivait, suivions, suiviez, suivaient |
| PASSÉ COMPOSÉ | ai suivi, *etc.* |
| FUTURE | suivrai, suivras, suivra, suivrons, suivrez, suivront |
| CONDITIONAL | suivrais, suivrais, suivrait, suivrions, suivriez, suivraient |
| PASSÉ SIMPLE | suivis, suivis, suivit, suivîmes, suivîtes, suivirent |
| PRESENT SUBJUNCTIVE | suive, suives, suive, suivions, suiviez, suivent |
| IMPERATIVE | suis, suivons, suivez |
| PRESENT PARTICIPLE | suivant |
| Conjugated like **suivre:** | **poursuivre** *to pursue, continue* |

## TENIR *to hold*

| | |
|---|---|
| PRESENT | tiens, tiens, tient, tenons, tenez, tiennent |
| IMPERFECT | tenais, tenais, tenait, tenions, teniez, tenaient |
| PASSÉ COMPOSÉ | ai tenu, *etc.* |
| FUTURE | tiendrai, tiendras, tiendra, tiendrons, tiendrez, tiendront |
| CONDITIONAL | tiendrais, tiendrais, tiendrait, tiendrions, tiendriez, tiendraient |
| PASSÉ SIMPLE | tins, tins, tint, tînmes, tîntes, tinrent |
| PRESENT SUBJUNCTIVE | tienne, tiennes, tienne, tenions, teniez, tiennent |
| IMPERATIVE | tiens, tenons, tenez |
| PRESENT PARTICIPLE | tenant |
| Conjugated like **tenir:** | **appartenir** *to belong,* **contenir** *to contain,* **maintenir** *to maintain,* **obtenir** *to get, obtain,* **retenir** *to retain,* **soutenir** *to sustain, support* |

## VALOIR *to be worth*

| | |
|---|---|
| PRESENT | vaux, vaux, vaut, valons, valez, valent |
| IMPERFECT | valais, valais, valait, valions, valiez, valaient |
| PASSÉ COMPOSÉ | ai valu, *etc.* |
| FUTURE | vaudrai, vaudras, vaudra, vaudrons, vaudrez, vaudront |
| CONDITIONAL | vaudrais, vaudrais, vaudrait, vaudrions, vaudriez, vaudraient |
| PASSÉ SIMPLE | valus, valus, valut, valûmes, valûtes, valurent |
| PRESENT SUBJUNCTIVE | vaille, vailles, vaille, valions, valiez, vaillent |
| IMPERATIVE | vaux, valons, valez |
| PRESENT PARTICIPLE | valant |

## VENIR *to come*

| | |
|---|---|
| PRESENT | viens, viens, vient, venons, venez, viennent |
| IMPERFECT | venais, venais, venait, venions, veniez, venaient |
| PASSÉ COMPOSÉ | suis venu(e), *etc.* |
| FUTURE | viendrai, viendras, viendra, viendrons, viendrez, viendront |
| CONDITIONAL | viendrais, viendrais, viendrait, viendrions, viendriez, viendraient |
| PASSÉ SIMPLE | vins, vins, vint, vînmes, vîntes, vinrent |
| PRESENT SUBJUNCTIVE | vienne, viennes, vienne, venions, veniez, viennent |
| IMPERATIVE | viens, venons, venez |
| PRESENT PARTICIPLE | venant |
| Conjugated like **venir:** | **devenir** *to become,* **prévenir** *to forewarn,* **revenir** *to come back,* **se souvenir** *to remember* |

## VIVRE *to live*

| | |
|---|---|
| PRESENT | vis, vis, vit, vivons, vivez, vivent |
| IMPERFECT | vivais, vivais, vivait, vivions, viviez, vivaient |
| PASSÉ COMPOSÉ | ai vécu, *etc.* |
| FUTURE | vivrai, vivras, vivra, vivrons, vivrez, vivront |
| CONDITIONAL | vivrais, vivrais, vivrait, vivrions, vivriez, vivraient |
| PASSÉ SIMPLE | vécus, vécus, vécut, vécûmes, vécûtes, vécurent |
| PRESENT SUBJUNCTIVE | vive, vives, vive, vivions, viviez, vivent |
| IMPERATIVE | vis, vivons, vivez |
| PRESENT PARTICIPLE | vivant |

## VOIR *to see*

| | |
|---|---|
| PRESENT | vois, vois, voit, voyons, voyez, voient |
| IMPERFECT | voyais, voyais, voyait, voyions, voyiez, voyaient |
| PASSÉ COMPOSÉ | ai vu, *etc.* |
| FUTURE | verrai, verras, verra, verrons, verrez, verront |
| CONDITIONAL | verrais, verrais, verrait, verrions, verriez, verraient |
| PASSÉ SIMPLE | vis, vis, vit, vîmes, vîtes, virent |
| PRESENT SUBJUNCTIVE | voie, voies, voie, voyions, voyiez, voient |
| IMPERATIVE | vois, voyons, voyez |
| PRESENT PARTICIPLE | voyant |
| Conjugated like **voir:** | **prévoir** *to foresee, provide,* **revoir** *to see again* |

## VOULOIR  *to want*

| | |
|---|---|
| PRESENT | veux, veux, veut, voulons, voulez, veulent |
| IMPERFECT | voulais, voulais, voulait, voulions, vouliez, voulaient |
| PASSÉ COMPOSÉ | ai voulu, *etc.* |
| FUTURE | voudrai, voudras, voudra, voudrons, voudrez, voudront |
| CONDITIONAL | voudrais, voudrais, voudrait, voudrions, voudriez, voudraient |
| PASSÉ SIMPLE | voulus, voulus, voulut, voulûmes, voulûtes, voulurent |
| PRESENT SUBJUNCTIVE | veuille, veuilles, veuille, voulions, vouliez, veuillent |
| IMPERATIVE | veuille, veuillez |
| PRESENT PARTICIPLE | voulant |

# ANSWER KEY

## PREMIÈRE PARTIE

### Chapitre 1

*Activité 1*
1. Moi, je prépare un bon dîner.
2. Papa finit son livre.
3. Ma fille Lise attend un coup de téléphone.
4. Mon fils écoute un nouveau CD.
5. On invite nos cousins à prendre le dessert avec nous.
6. Mon cousin Philippe joue de la guitare.
7. Nous chantons ensemble.
8. Nous applaudissons.

*Activité 2*

| | |
|---|---|
| 1. attendons | 5. apporte |
| 2. dînent | 6. remercie |
| 3. arrivent | 7. passe |
| 4. salue | 8. remplit |

*Activité 3*

| | |
|---|---|
| 1. entre | 6. arrives |
| 2. choisissons | 7. répond |
| 3. regardent | 8. finit |
| 4. cherche | 9. fermons |
| 5. écoute | 10. attendons |

*Activité 4*

| | |
|---|---|
| 1. rangeons | 4. commençons |
| 2. balaie / balaye | 5. essuient |
| 3. nettoie | 6. essaie / essaye |

*Activité 5*
1. Oui, nous commençons / Non, nous ne commençons pas à lire des livres en français.
2. Oui, nous corrigeons / Non, nous ne corrigeons pas nos copies en classe.
3. Oui, nous effaçons / Non, nous n'effaçons pas les mots mal écrits.
4. Oui, nous employons / Non, nous n'employons pas le français dans nos conversations.
5. Oui, nous dérangeons / Non, nous ne dérangeons pas les autres étudiants.
6. Oui, nous tutoyons / Non, nous ne tutoyons pas le professeur.
7. Oui, nous prononçons / Non, nous ne prononçons pas correctement.
8. Oui, nous rédigeons des / Non, nous ne rédigeons pas de courriels en français.

*Activité 6*
1. Est-que tu préfères travailler en été ou en hiver?
2. Qu'est-ce que tu espères faire après l'université?
3. Combien est-ce que tu pèses?
4. Comment est-ce que tu épelles ton nom?
5. Est-ce que tu rejettes les idées extrémistes?
6. Où est-ce que tu achètes les livres pour les cours?

*Activité 7*
1. Jean-Claude espère devenir interprète.
2. Il préfère les langues.
3. Il projette un voyage aux États-Unis.
4. Il feuillette des brochures de l'agence de voyages.

5. Il renouvelle son passeport.
6. Ses idées reflètent l'influence de sa mère.
7. Elle lui répète toujours l'importance d'une orientation internationale.

*Activité 8*

| | |
|---|---|
| 1. change | 5. répète |
| 2. travaille | 6. cherchent |
| 3. gagne | 7. désirent |
| 4. demande | 8. annoncent |

*Activité 9*
1. Il y a / Voilà dix ans que Mme Ferron enseigne dans notre université. / Mme Ferron enseigne dans notre lycée depuis dix ans.
2. Il y a / Voilà huit ans qu'elle encourage les étudiants à étudier à l'étranger. / Elle encourage les étudiants à étudier à l'étranger depuis huit ans.
3. Il y a / Volià huit ans qu'elle organise des voyages pour les étudiants. / Elle organise des voyages pour les étudiants depuis huit ans.
4. Il y a / Voilà quatre ans que les étudiants passent un semestre au Québec chaque année. / Les étudiants passent un semestre au Québec chaque année depuis quatre ans.
5. Il y a / Voilà trois ans que mon ami Charles étudie l'allemand. / Mon ami Charles étudie l'allemand depuis trois ans.
6. Il y a / Voilà deux mois qu'il projette un voyage d'études en Allemagne. / Il projette un voyage d'études en Allemagne depuis deux mois.
7. Il y a / Voilà six semaines que Charles feuillette des brochures. / Charles feuillette des brochures depuis six semaines.
8. Il y a / Voilà un mois que Mme Ferron cherche le programme idéal pour Charles. / Mme Ferron cherche le programme idéal pour Charles depuis un mois.

*Activité 10 Answers will vary.*

### Chapitre 2

*Activité 1*
1. Je dois passer la journée à la bibliothèque, mais je ne veux pas.
2. Elle doit rester à la maison, mais elle ne veut pas.
3. Ils doivent aller chez le médecin, mais ils ne veulent pas.
4. Nous devons rentrer tôt, mais nous ne voulons pas.
5. Tu dois préparer le dîner, mais tu ne veux pas. / Vous devez préparer le dîner, mais vous ne voulez pas.
6. Vous devez prendre un taxi, mais vous ne voulez pas.

*Activité 2*
1. Papa et moi, nous faisons la vaisselle.
2. Les parents font le jardin.
3. David et moi, nous faisons les courses.
4. Grand-mère fait la lessive.
5. Moi, je fais les carreaux.
6. Maman et toi, vous faites les lits.

*Activité 3*
1. Je veux aller au concert ce soir, mais je ne peux pas.
2. Ils veulent vous (nous) accompagner au café, mais ils ne peuvent pas.

3. Elle veut passer ses vacances à Tahiti, mais elle ne peut pas.
4. Tu veux chercher Laurent à la gare, mais tu ne peux pas.
5. Nous voulons regarder un film à la télé, mais nous ne pouvons pas.
6. Elles veulent faire du shopping, mais elles ne peuvent pas.

## Activité 4
1. Pierre et Michèle ont mal aux jambes.
2. Frédéric a mal aux bras.
3. Rachelle a mal au dos.
4. Toi, tu as mal à l'épaule droite.
5. Moi, j'ai mal aux genoux.
6. Alfred et moi, nous avons mal aux pieds.

## Activité 5
1. Il a sommeil.
2. J'ai faim.
3. Nous avons soif.
4. Elles ont chaud.
5. Tu as froid.
6. Il a peur.
7. Vous avez raison.
8. On a honte.
9. Tu as tort.
10. Elle a de la chance.

## Activité 6
1. sont
2. ont
3. fait
4. fait
5. ont
6. prennent
7. font
8. faites
9. prennent

## Activité 7
1. Eux aussi, ils prennent un café.
2. Nous aussi, nous avons faim / on a faim.
3. Eux aussi, ils font les courses maintenant.
4. Eux aussi, ils ont vingt ans.
5. Vous aussi, vous êtes en vacances la semaine prochaine.
6. Lui aussi, il est en retard.
7. Moi aussi, je prends du poids en hiver.
8. Toi aussi, tu as raison.

## Activité 8
1. Le journal est sous le banc.
2. Moi, je suis à côté du banc.
3. Mes amis sont assis sur le banc.
4. Les arbres sont derrière le banc.
5. Toi et moi, nous sommes près du lac.
6. Nous sommes en face du café.
7. Le lac est entre la forêt et le pré.
8. Vous êtes au café.

## Activité 9
1. fait
2. fait
3. suis
4. ai
5. fais
6. prends
7. fais
8. faisons
9. faisons
10. prenons

## Activité 10
1. Non, je ne crains rien.
2. Non, je ne reçois rien.
3. Non, je ne dois rien.
4. Non, je ne construis rien.
5. Non, je ne reconnais rien.
6. Non, je ne peins rien.
7. Non, je ne traduis rien.
8. Non, je ne découvre rien.

## Activité 11
1. Nicole peint tous les jours.
2. La nature apparaît dans ses tableaux.
3. Nous apercevons son talent.
4. Nous découvrons de nouveaux thèmes.
5. Maintenant, Nicole introduit la vie de la ville dans son art.
6. Ses nouveaux tableaux ne déçoivent pas.
7. Le public accueille son art avec enthousiasme.

## Activité 12
1. Moi aussi, j'ouvre toutes les fenêtres en été.
2. Moi aussi, j'accueille souvent des étudiants étrangers à la maison.
3. Moi aussi, je mets toutes les plantes à l'extérieur au mois de mars.
4. Moi aussi, je découvre de nouveaux paysages.
5. Moi aussi, je souffre du dos quand il fait froid et humide.
6. Moi aussi, je pars en vacances au mois de juillet.
7. Moi aussi, je dors dans le jardin quand il fait beau.
8. Moi aussi, je permets aux enfants de jouer sur la pelouse.

## Activité 13
1. Josette part en vacances.
2. Elle rejoint des amis.
3. Elle conduit une vieille voiture.
4. Elle dort dans des hôtels très modestes.
5. Elle arrive dans le désert.
6. Elle sent la chaleur.
7. Elle souffre d'allergies.
8. Elle repart à la maison.

## Activité 14
1. Elle croit que ça va être amusant.
2. Elle écrit des courriels aux copains pour les inviter.
3. Elle sait arriver à la plage.
4. Elle boit de l'eau parce qu'il fait chaud.
5. Elle meurt de soif.
6. Elle court sur la plage pour faire de l'exercice.
7. Elle voit le coucher du soleil sur la mer.
8. Elle dit que c'est très joli.
9. Le soir, elle lit des blagues en ligne.
10. Elle suit l'actualité à la télé.
11. Elle vit des jours heureux au bord de la mer.

## Activité 15
1. J'apprends à danser le tango. Tu sais danser le tango, toi?
   Non, pas encore, mais je veux danser le tango.
2. J'apprends à jouer au golf. Tu sais jouer au golf, toi?
   Non, pas encore, mais je veux jouer au golf.
3. J'apprends à chanter du jazz. Tu sais chanter du jazz, toi?
   Non, pas encore, mais je veux chanter du jazz.
4. J'apprends à conduire une Ferrari. Tu sais conduire une Ferrari, toi?
   Non, pas encore, mais je veux conduire une Ferrari.
5. J'apprends à faire la cuisine. Tu sais faire la cuisine, toi?
   Non, pas encore, mais je veux faire la cuisine.
6. J'apprends à programmer l'ordinateur. Tu sais programmer l'ordinateur, toi?
   Non, pas encore, mais je veux programmer l'ordinateur.

## Activité 16
1. Est-ce que tu vas faire du jogging?
   Mais, je viens de faire du jogging!
2. Est-ce que les gestionnaires vont placer cet argent?
   Mais, ils viennent de placer cet argent!
3. Est-ce que vous allez télécharger un document?
   Mais, nous venons / on vient de télécharger un document!
4. Est-ce que Christine va téléphoner à ses parents?
   Mais, elle vient de téléphoner à ses parents!
5. Est-ce que nous allons visiter les monuments?
   Mais, vous venez de visiter les monuments!
6. Est-ce que je vais voir un film?
   Mais, vous venez / tu viens de voir un film!

### Activité 17

1. Ils savent qu'ils doivent marcher tous les jours, mais ils disent qu'ils ne peuvent pas et qu'ils ne veulent pas.
2. Nous savons que nous devons faire de l'exercice, mais nous disons que nous ne pouvons pas et que nous ne voulons pas.
3. Tu sais / Vous savez que tu dois / vous devez nager une heure tous les jours, mais tu dis / vous dites que tu ne peux pas / vous ne pouvez pas et que tu ne veux pas / vous ne voulez pas.
4. Je sais que je dois faire du sport, mais je dis que je ne peux pas et que je ne veux pas.
5. Elle sait qu'elle doit suivre un régime pour maigrir, mais elle dit qu'elle ne peut pas et qu'elle ne veut pas.
6. Vous savez que vous devez faire du vélo, mais vous dites que vous ne pouvez pas et que vous ne voulez pas.

### Activité 18 *Answers will vary.*

## Chapitre 3

### Activité 1

1. Non. Mais il a nagé hier.
2. Non. Mais nous avons déjeuné en ville hier.
3. Non. Mais il a pris de l'essence hier.
4. Non. Mais nous avons nettoyé notre chambre hier.
5. Non. Mais ils ont rédigé un thème hier.
6. Non. Mais j'ai appris le vocabulaire hier.
7. Non. Mais il a fait le linge hier.
8. Non. Mais nous avons fini le travail hier.
9. Non. Mais j'ai attendu mes amis hier.
10. Non. Mais elle a répondu en classe hier.
11. Non. Mais ils ont obtenu les résultats de l'examen hier.
12. Non. Mais le film a repris hier.
13. Non. Mais j'ai eu mal à l'estomac hier.
14. Non. Mais tu as été / vous avez été en avance hier.
15. Non. Mais il a fait un gâteau hier.

### Activité 2

1. J'ai invité mon copain Serge à faire une promenade en voiture avec moi.
2. Serge a voulu faire le plein avant de partir.
3. Tout d'un coup, nous avons entendu un bruit.
4. Nous avons eu un pneu crevé.
5. Nous avons poussé la voiture au bord de la rue.
6. Nous avons acheté un nouveau pneu à la station-service.
7. Nous avons dû dépenser tout notre argent.
8. Nous n'avons pas pu aller à la campagne.
9. Nous avons remonté la rue.
10. Tu nous as vus de la fenêtre.
11. J'ai garé la voiture devant mon immeuble.
12. Sylvie et toi, vous avez ri de notre histoire.

### Activité 3

1. J'ai convaincu mon père d'acheter un nouvel ordinateur.
2. Mon père et moi, nous avons lu une brochure ensemble.
3. Nous avons demandé d'autres brochures.
4. Mon père a trouvé un revendeur bien informé.
5. Nous avons posé beaucoup de questions au revendeur.
6. Il a répondu patiemment à nos questions.
7. Nous avons choisi une imprimante aussi.
8. J'ai acheté des logiciels.
9. Mon père a trouvé des CD-ROM intéressants.
10. J'ai mis le nouvel ordinateur dans ma chambre.

### Activité 4

1. Marie a reçu un courriel.
2. Elle a ouvert le message.
3. Elle a lu le texte.
4. Son cousin François a écrit le courriel.
5. Il a joint une photo au courriel.
6. Il a été malade pendant un mois.
7. Il a passé deux semaines à l'hôpital.
8. Marie a imprimé le courriel pour ses parents.
9. Ils ont dit à Marie de téléphoner à François.
10. Elle a invité François à passer les vacances chez elle.
11. Il a été très content d'accepter son invitation.
12. Il a promis d'arriver au début du mois de juillet.

### Activité 5

1. Je suis arrivée chez moi vers cinq heures et demie.
2. Je suis repartie à six heures.
3. Je suis allée au supermarché pour acheter quelque chose à manger.
4. Je suis rentrée tout de suite.
5. Lise et Solange sont venues chez moi vers sept heures.
6. Elles sont restées une heure.
7. Elles sont parties à huit heures.
8. Je suis montée dans ma chambre faire mes devoirs.
9. Je suis redescendue regarder les informations à la télé.
10. Je suis remontée dans ma chambre pour me coucher.
11. Je suis tombée dans mon lit, épuisée.

### Activité 6

1. Cette fois ils sont arrivés en avance.
2. Cette fois ils ont pris le métro.
3. Cette fois ils ont parlé de leurs cours.
4. Cette fois ils ont lu *Le Monde.*
5. Cette fois ils ont commandé un steak-frites.
6. Cette fois ils ont bu beaucoup d'eau minérale.
7. Cette fois ils ont mangé lentement.
8. Cette fois ils sont restés une demi-heure après le repas.
9. Cette fois ils ont laissé un pourboire de deux euros.
10. Cette fois ils sont allés en ville après le déjeuner.

### Activité 7

1. avons voulu
2. sommes allés
3. avons installé
4. avons fait
5. ont dressé
6. avons mangé
7. sommes entrés
8. est entré
9. j'ai entendu
10. a remarqué
11. sont sortis
12. avons été
13. est parti
14. a eu
15. avons arrêté
16. est rentré
17. n'a fermé
18. avons plié
19. sommes retournés
20. a été

### Activité 8

1. a sorti
2. est parti
3. a monté
4. a vu
5. a dû
6. est arrivé
7. a demandé
8. est sortie
9. a fait
10. a étendu
11. sont descendues
12. ont descendu
13. sont rentrées
14. ont monté
15. sont entrées
16. a commencé
17. a dit
18. ont rentré

### Activité 9

1. quitté
2. offert
3. accepté
4. fait
5. pris
6. arrivée
7. commencé
8. lues
9. vus
10. donné
11. trouvée
12. entrée
13. demandé
14. montrés
15. choisi
16. trouvée
17. commencé
18. présentée
19. accueillie

### Activité 10

1. Les devoirs que j'ai faits hier?
2. La lettre que j'ai reçue hier?
3. La composition que j'ai rédigée hier?
4. Le nouveau sac à dos que j'ai acheté hier?
5. L'appareil-photo que j'ai utilisé hier?
6. Le nouveau DVD que j'ai regardé hier?
7. Les nouveaux CD que j'ai écoutés hier?
8. Les chaussures que j'ai mises hier?
9. Les lunettes de soleil que j'ai portées hier?
10. Les revues que j'ai lues hier?

**Activité 11** *Answers will vary.*

## Chapitre 4

### Activité 1

1. Vous ne croyez plus à cette histoire. Avant, vous croyiez à cette histoire.
2. Il ne lit plus en allemand. Avant, il lisait en allemand.
3. Elles ne font plus les carreaux. Avant, elles faisaient les carreaux.
4. Tu n'habites plus en ville. Avant, tu habitais en ville.
5. Ils ne vivent plus bien. Avant, ils vivaient bien.
6. Mon chien n'obéit plus. Avant, il obéissait.
7. Elle ne rougit plus. Avant, elle rougissait.
8. Je ne réponds plus en classe. Avant, je répondais en classe.
9. Tu ne voyages plus. Avant, tu voyageais.
10. Elle ne prononce plus correctement. Avant, elle prononçait correctement.
11. Vous n'appréciez plus la musique classique. Avant, vous appréciiez la musique classique.
12. Ils ne rangent plus leurs affaires. Avant, ils rangeaient leurs affaires.

### Activité 2

1. Nous avions une maison dans un quartier tranquille.
2. Elle était grande.
3. La maison avait dix pièces.
4. Mes parents travaillaient en ville.
5. Ils allaient au bureau en bus.
6. L'arrêt était au coin de la rue.
7. Beaucoup d'autres jeunes filles habitaient dans notre rue.
8. Je jouais avec elles.
9. Nous allions à l'école ensemble.
10. Je gardais souvent ma petite sœur Marguerite.
11. Maman nous conduisait au parc.
12. Nous étions tous très contents.

### Activité 3

1. Nous vivions à la campagne.
2. Je partageais une chambre avec ma sœur.
3. Nous n'avions pas beaucoup d'argent.
4. Mais on était heureux.
5. Je nageais dans le lac.
6. Mes parents élevaient des vaches.
7. Les enfants buvaient du lait frais.
8. Nous vendions le lait.
9. Ton grand-père commençait à passer me voir.
10. J'avais dix-huit ans.

### Activité 4

1. Je passais souvent les vacances chez ma tante.
2. Je voulais toujours aller au bord de la mer.
3. Ma famille et moi, nous visitions chaque été une région de France.
4. Mes cousins m'invitaient tous les ans chez eux.
5. On prenait le plus souvent les vacances en hiver.
6. Ma cousine Élisabeth venait en général chez nous à Paris.

7. Nous partions d'habitude en Suisse.
8. Mon père louait tous les étés un appartement à Nice.
9. Ma famille allait chaque année pour Noël chez nos grands-parents.
10. Nous passions le week-end toutes les semaines à la ferme.

### Activité 5

1. Il faisait du vent quand je suis arrivée à l'arrêt.
2. Il pleuvinait quand le bus est arrivé.
3. Il pleuvait quand je suis montée dans le bus.
4. Il gelait quand je suis arrivée à la faculté.
5. Il grêlait quand j'ai retrouvé mon amie Hélène.
6. Il neigeait quand nous sommes entrées dans l'amphithéâtre.
7. Il tonnait quand le professeur a commencé sa conférence.
8. Il grêlait quand nous sommes sorties de l'amphithéâtre.

### Activité 6

1. Il était huit heures et demie quand mon train est venu.
2. Il était neuf heures pile quand je suis arrivé en ville.
3. Il était un peu tard quand je suis arrivé au bureau.
4. Il était midi quand mon collègue m'a invité à déjeuner.
5. Il était une heure et demie quand nous avons fini de manger.
6. Il était tard dans l'après-midi quand j'ai quitté le bureau.
7. Il était déjà sept heures quand j'ai retrouvé ma fiancée pour dîner.
8. Il était presque minuit quand je suis rentré chez moi.

### Activité 7

1. Il a nettoyé la cuisine pendant que les enfants jouaient dans le jardin.
2. Il a fait le linge pendant que sa mère promenait le chien.
3. Il a préparé le dîner pendant que sa sœur faisait les courses.
4. Il a mis la table pendant que son fils aîné réparait la voiture.
5. Il a étudié ses dossiers pendant que sa fille bricolait au sous-sol.
6. Il a ciré les meubles pendant que son frère lisait le journal.

### Activité 8

1. Je ne suis pas allé(e) au restaurant parce que je n'avais pas envie de sortir.
2. Nous n'avons pas fait une promenade parce que nous n'avions pas le temps.
3. Je n'ai pas lu le chapitre parce que j'avais mal à la tête.
4. Albert n'a pas pris le petit déjeuner parce qu'il était trop pressé.
5. Chantal n'est pas venue à la réunion parce qu'elle travaillait.
6. Nos copains ne sont pas allés au concert parce qu'ils n'avaient pas d'argent.
7. Les voisins ne sont pas sortis parce que leur voiture était en panne.
8. Tu n'as pas répondu au professeur parce que tu ne faisais pas attention à sa question.

### Activité 9

1. Le ciel était couvert pendant qu'ils cherchaient un endroit pour camper.
2. Il pleuvinait pendant que les deux garçons dressaient leur tente.
3. Il pleuvait pendant que Guy faisait un feu de camp.
4. Il faisait du vent pendant qu'Alain cuisinait.
5. La température baissait pendant qu'ils mangeaient.
6. Des éclairs illuminaient le ciel pendant qu'ils ouvraient les sacs de couchage.

7. Il tonnait pendant que les deux garçons essayaient de dormir.
8. Mais le matin, il faisait beau pendant qu'ils pliaient leur tente.

### Activité 10
1. Vous attendiez le bus depuis vingt minutes quand Jean-Claude est venu vous prendre avec sa voiture. / Il y avait (Ça faisait) vingt minutes que vous attendiez le bus quand Jean-Claude est venu vous prendre avec sa voiture. / *You had been waiting for the bus for twenty minutes when Jean-Claude came by to get you in his car.*
2. Nous étudiions à la bibliothèque depuis six heures quand Christine nous a invités à dîner chez elle. / Il y avait (Ça faisait) six heures que nous étudiions à la bibliothèque quand Christine nous a invités à dîner chez elle./ *We had been studying in the library for six hours when Christine invited us to have dinner at her house.*
3. Odile dormait depuis dix minutes quand le téléphone a sonné. / Il y avait (Ça faisait) dix minutes qu'Odile dormait quand le téléphone a sonné. / *Odile had been sleeping for ten minutes when the telephone rang.*
4. Sylvain entrait des données depuis deux heures quand il y a eu une panne d'électricité. / Il y avait (Ça faisait) deux heures que Sylvain entrait des données quand il y a eu une panne d'électricité. / *Sylvain had been entering data for two hours when there was a power failure.*
5. Brigitte faisait du jogging depuis une heure quand il a commencé à pleuvoir. / Il y avait (Ça faisait) une heure que Brigitte faisait du jogging quand il a commencé à pleuvoir. / *Brigitte had been jogging for an hour when it began to rain.*
6. Alain rangeait ses affaires depuis dix minutes quand ses amis l'ont appelé pour jouer au football. / Il y avait (Ça faisait) dix minutes qu'Alain rangeait ses affaires quand ses amis l'ont appelé pour jouer au football. / *Alain had been straightening up his things for ten minutes when his friends called him to play soccer.*

### Activité 11
1. Si nous naviguions sur Internet? / Si on naviguait sur Internet?
2. Si nous achetions le journal? / Si on achetait le journal?
3. Si nous passions chez Françoise? / Si on passait chez Françoise?
4. Si nous regardions une vidéo? / Si on regardait une vidéo à la télé?
5. Si nous mangions au restaurant? / Si on mangeait au restaurant?
6. Si nous commencions nos devoirs? / Si on commençait nos devoirs?

### Activité 12
1. voulais
2. suis entré(e)
3. étaient
4. avait
5. ai vu
6. suis passé(e)
7. suis monté(e)
8. ai trouvé
9. suis descendu(e)
10. voulais
11. ai remarqué
12. intéressaient
13. n'avais
14. n'ai acheté
15. ai décidé

### Activité 13
1. a quitté
2. a pris
3. est arrivé
4. avait
5. connaissait
6. a trouvé
7. fallait
8. recevait
9. vivait
10. a renoncé
11. a invité
12. a mis
13. ont ouvert
14. étaient
15. sont devenus

**Activité 14** *Answers will vary.*

## Chapitre 5

### Activité 1
1. Non, je ferai le ménage demain.
2. Non, ils reviendront demain.
3. Non, il ira à la fac demain.
4. Non, vous travaillerez demain.
5. Non, tu répondras demain.
6. Non, je saurai la réponse demain.
7. Non, tu enverras le colis demain.
8. Non, vous emmènerez les enfants au zoo demain.
9. Non, nous projetterons le film demain.
10. Non, ils compléteront leur travail demain.

### Activité 2
1. Je crois que tu réussiras.
2. Je crois qu'ils descendront.
3. Je crois qu'il ira en cours.
4. Je crois qu'il neigera.
5. Je crois que je sortirai.
6. Je crois que vous arriverez à l'heure.
7. Je crois qu'ils nous prêteront la voiture.
8. Je crois que je compléterai mes devoirs.

### Activité 3
1. Je ne sais pas s'ils partiront.
2. Je ne sais pas si je travaillerai / nous travaillerons.
3. Je ne sais pas si tu passeras / vous passerez l'examen.
4. Je ne sais pas s'il reviendra.
5. Je ne sais pas s'ils iront à la réunion.
6. Je ne sais pas si je conduirai.
7. Je ne sais pas s'ils liront.
8. Je ne sais pas si on projettera un film.
9. Je ne sais pas si je voudrai venir.
10. Je ne sais pas s'il pourra rentrer.

### Activité 4
1. Le fils aîné fera les valises.
2. Papa s'occupera des petits.
3. Maman se chargera de la voiture.
4. Tout le monde se réveillera à sept heures du matin.
5. Tous les membres de la famille se dépêcheront.
6. Personne ne regardera la télé.
7. Les enfants s'aideront mutuellement.
8. Les grands-parents prépareront le petit déjeuner.
9. Personne ne verra le temps passer.
10. Les Ramonet se mettront en route vers dix heures du matin.

### Activité 5
1. Je ferai ma valise dès que le linge sera sec.
2. Les enfants s'habilleront quand ils rentreront de l'école.
3. Nous mangerons quand maman reviendra du marché.
4. Mon frère mettra les valises dans la voiture aussitôt que papa reviendra de la station-service.
5. Nous choisirons la route quand je trouverai la carte.
6. Nous partirons quand il fera beau.
7. Nous chercherons un hôtel lorsque nous arriverons à Strasbourg.
8. Je me coucherai aussitôt que nous serons à l'hôtel.

### Activité 6
1. Sortez dès que la cloche sonnera.
2. Téléphone aussitôt qu'Albert arrivera.
3. Mettez-vous à prendre des notes quand le professeur commencera sa conférence.
4. Descends à la cuisine quand je t'appellerai.
5. Venez me voir quand vous pourrez.
6. Ferme la porte à clé quand tu t'en iras.
7. Dites bonjour de ma part à votre fils quand vous le verrez.

8. Lisez ma lettre dès que vous la recevrez.
9. Ne fais pas de bruit après que le bébé s'endormira.

*Activité 7*
1. Oui, tu rentrerais si tu pouvais. / Vous rentreriez si vous pouviez.
2. Oui, elles feraient du ski si elles pouvaient.
3. Oui, je deviendrais programmeur si je pouvais.
4. Oui, vous vous verriez tous les jours si vous pouviez.
5. Oui, tu te mettrais en route si tu pouvais. / Vous vous mettriez en route si vous pouviez.
6. Oui, il se promènerait s'il pouvait.
7. Oui, nous achèterions du pain si nous pouvions.
8. Oui, vous seriez chez vous si vous pouviez.

*Activité 8*
1. Moi non plus, je ne prendrais pas la voiture.
2. Moi non plus, je ne ferais pas la vaisselle.
3. Moi non plus, je ne m'assoirais / m'assiérais pas dans le jardin.
4. Moi non plus, je ne regarderais pas la télé aujourd'hui.
5. Moi non plus, je n'enlèverais pas mon pull.
6. Moi non plus, je ne projetterais pas ce film.
7. Moi non plus, je ne répéterais pas ces slogans.
8. Moi non plus, je ne courrais pas.

*Activité 9*
1. Impossible! Je ne renoncerais pas à mon travail.
2. Impossible! Elle ne rejetterait pas notre offre.
3. Impossible! Il ne se lèverait pas pendant la classe.
4. Impossible! Ils ne feraient pas grève.
5. Impossible! Je n'exagérerais pas.
6. Impossible! Tu ne perdrais pas les billets.
7. Impossible! Il ne tomberait pas en faisant du ski.
8. Impossible! Il ne jetterait pas son dîner à la poubelle.

*Activité 10*
1. Si Jean-Pierre s'habillait bien, les autres étudiants ne se moqueraient pas de lui.
2. Si Jean-Pierre faisait du sport, il connaîtrait beaucoup de monde.
3. Si Jean-Pierre s'intéressait à ses études, il serait préparé en classe.
4. Si Jean-Pierre ne s'absentait pas souvent, les professeurs ne se fâcheraient pas contre lui.
5. Si Jean-Pierre ne lisait pas de bandes dessinées en classe, les profs ne seraient pas furieux.
6. Si Jean-Pierre ne mangeait pas toujours seul, il parlerait avec les autres étudiants.

*Activité 11*
1. Si vous installez la machine à laver au sous-sol, nous aurons plus de place dans la cuisine.
2. Si je mets la lampe à côté du fauteuil, je pourrai lire.
3. Si nous nettoyons le tapis, nous le mettrons dans le salon.
4. Si tu trouves la table en plastique, tu pourras la mettre sur la terrasse.
5. Si on laisse l'ordinateur dans ma chambre, je ferai mes devoirs sans déranger les autres.
6. Si les déménageurs montent une étagère dans ma chambre, je rangerai tous mes livres.

*Activité 12*
1. Si on avait deux télés, on pourrait regarder la télé dans le séjour.
2. Si cette maison avait un grenier, il y aurait de la place pour les boîtes.
3. Si la cheminée fonctionnait, nous pourrions faire un feu.
4. Si on avait des tableaux dans le salon, il serait douillet.

5. Si j'avais un lecteur CD dans ma chambre, je n'écouterais pas mes CD dans le séjour.
6. Si le frigo n'était pas tellement petit, Papa ne ferait pas les courses plusieurs fois par semaine.
7. Si tu décrochais les rideaux, je pourrais les laver.
8. Si cette fenêtre se fermait bien, il ne ferait pas froid dans ma chambre.

*Activité 13*
1. Si je me sentais mal, j'irais chez le médecin.
2. Si je ne mangeais que des fruits et des légumes, je maigrirais.
3. S'il sortait sous la pluie, il attraperait un rhume.
4. Si elle tombait malade, elle se reposerait.
5. Si nous allions pieds nus, nous nous ferions mal aux pieds.
6. Si tu avais mal à la tête, tu prendrais des comprimés d'aspirine.
7. Si le médecin m'ordonnait des antibiotiques, je les prendrais.
8. Si j'étais en forme, je ne me fatiguerais pas tellement.

*Activité 14* *Answers will vary.*

**Chapitre 6**

*Activité 1*
1. Non, ne partons pas la semaine prochaine. Attendons la fin du mois.
2. Non, ne prenons pas l'avion. Prenons le train.
3. Non, ne descendons pas dans un hôtel de luxe. Choisissons une auberge.
4. Non, ne visitons pas les monuments en taxi. Louons une voiture.
5. Non, n'assistons pas à un concert. Allons voir une pièce de théâtre.
6. Non, ne mangeons pas dans le restaurant de l'hôtel. Dînons dans un restaurant en ville.

*Activité 2*
1. D'abord, descends dans la rue.
2. Ensuite, cherche une librairie.
3. Là-bas, demande un livre sur les Antilles.
4. Rentre tout de suite à ton appartement.
5. Après, lis le livre.
6. Choisis ton itinéraire.
7. Après, réserve une place dans l'avion et une chambre d'hôtel sur Internet.
8. Finalement, fais les valises.

*Activité 3*
1. Lis les annonces.
2. Sache ce que tu veux.
3. Regarde les soldes.
4. Va aux grands magasins.
5. Essaie / Essaye les vêtements qui te plaisent.
6. Sois patiente.
7. Choisis une robe.
8. Paie / Paye avec la carte de crédit.
9. Reviens à la maison.
10. Mets ta nouvelle robe.

*Activité 4*
1. Allons en ville.
2. Prenons le train de neuf heures.
3. Descendons à la gare centrale.
4. Faisons une promenade.
5. Déjeunons dans un bon restaurant.
6. Cherchons un bon film.
7. Achetons des livres dans une librairie.
8. Rentrons par le train de cinq heures.

*Activité 5*

1. Non, ne mens pas. Dis la vérité.
2. Non, ne descends pas. Reste en haut.
3. Non, ne lis pas le texte. Écris la composition.
4. Non, ne suis pas ce régime. Fais du sport.
5. Non, ne mincis pas. Prends du poids.
6. Non, ne prépare pas le déjeuner. Fais la vaisselle.
7. Non, ne nettoie pas la cuisine. Balaie / Balaye l'escalier.
8. Non, ne jette pas cette cravate. Offre les vieux vêtements aux voisins.

*Activité 6*

1. Descendez à six heures et demie.
2. Allez à la boulangerie.
3. Faites les courses.
4. Choisissez des légumes frais chez le marchand.
5. Prenez un kilo d'asperges et de la salade.
6. Soyez de retour à la maison avant sept heures et demie.
7. Sortez les verres et mettez le couvert.
8. Commencez à préparer le dîner.
9. Sachez que les invités arriveront sûrement en retard.

*Activité 7*

1. Arrive / Arrivez à l'heure.
2. Écoute / Écoutez le professeur.
3. Ne dors / dormez pas en classe.
4. N'oublie / N'oubliez jamais le livre.
5. Réponds / Répondez aux questions.
6. Répète / Répétez après le professeur.
7. Essaie (Essaye) / Essayez de comprendre le professeur.
8. Ne dérange / Ne dérangez pas les autres étudiants.

*Activité 8* Answers will vary.

## Chapitre 7

*Activité 1*

1. Je me lève tout de suite. Jérôme se lève tout de suite aussi.
2. Je me brosse les dents. Jérôme se brosse les dents aussi.
3. Je me peigne. Jérôme se peigne aussi.
4. Je me rase. Jérôme se rase aussi.
5. Je m'habille. Jérôme s'habille aussi.
6. Je me lave les mains. Jérôme se lave les mains aussi.
7. Je me lave la figure. Jérôme se lave la figure aussi.
8. Je me repose. Jérôme se repose aussi.
9. Je me couche à onze heures. Jérôme se couche à onze heures aussi.
10. Je m'endors tout de suite. Jérôme s'endort tout de suite aussi.

*Activité 2*

1. Ils se lèvent tout de suite.
2. Ils se brossent les dents.
3. Ils se peignent.
4. Ils se rasent.
5. Ils s'habillent.
6. Ils se lavent les mains.
7. Ils se lavent la figure.
8. Ils se reposent.
9. Ils se couchent à onze heures.
10. Ils s'endorment tout de suite.

*Activité 3*

1. Nous nous levons immédiatement.
2. Nous nous lavons les mains et la figure.
3. Nous nous brossons les dents.
4. Nous nous lavons les cheveux.
5. Nous nous séchons les cheveux.
6. Nous nous maquillons.
7. Nous nous peignons.
8. Nous nous brossons les cheveux.
9. Nous nous limons les ongles.
10. Nous nous habillons avec soin.

*Activité 4*

1. Je me joins à mes copains.
2. Ils se trouvent dans un café du centre.
3. Je m'approche du café.
4. Mes copains se lèvent.
5. Nous nous éloignons du café.
6. Nous nous dirigeons vers le cinéma.
7. Nous nous dépêchons.
8. Nous nous arrêtons au guichet pour prendre les billets.
9. Nous entrons dans le cinéma et nous nous asseyons.

*Activité 5*

1. Je ne veux pas m'inquiéter.
2. Vous devez vous calmer.
3. Il ne peut pas se sentir triste.
4. Elles ne veulent pas s'ennuyer.
5. Tu ne dois pas te mettre en colère.
6. Nous n'allons pas nous offenser.
7. Le professeur va s'impatienter.
8. Tu dois t'animer.

*Activité 6*

1. En général, je ne me fâche pas, mais cette fois-ci je vais me fâcher.
2. En général, elles ne s'énervent pas, mais cette fois-ci elles vont s'énerver.
3. En général, tu ne t'impatientes pas, mais cette fois-ci tu vas t'impatienter.
4. En général, il ne s'offense pas, mais cette fois-ci il va s'offenser.
5. En général, nous ne nous inquiétons pas, mais cette fois-ci nous allons nous inquiéter.
6. En général, vous ne vous embêtez pas, mais cette fois-ci vous allez vous embêter.
7. En général, je ne me sens pas de trop, mais cette fois-ci je vais me sentir de trop.
8. En général, tu ne te passionnes pas, mais cette fois-ci tu vas te passionner.

*Activité 7*

1. Vous devez vous calmer.
2. Elle doit s'amuser un peu.
3. Je dois me sentir heureux(-se).
4. Nous ne devons pas nous mettre en colère.
5. Ils doivent s'enthousiasmer.
6. Tu ne dois pas t'impatienter.
7. Je dois m'animer un peu.
8. Vous ne devez pas vous offenser.

*Activité 8*

1. Quand est-ce que tu vas te mettre à préparer le dîner? Je me suis déjà mise à préparer le dîner.
2. Quand est-ce que les enfants vont se coucher? Ils se sont déjà couchés.
3. Quand est-ce que vous allez vous occuper du linge, Josette et toi? Nous nous sommes déjà occupées du linge.
4. Quand est-ce que tu vas te reposer? Je me suis déjà reposé(e).
5. Quand est-ce qu'Elvire va se laver les cheveux? Elle s'est déjà lavé les cheveux.

6. Quand est-ce que tu vas te limer les ongles?
   Je me suis déjà limé les ongles.
7. Quand est-ce que Carole et Paulette vont se calmer?
   Elles se sont déjà calmées.
8. Quand est-ce que je vais me brosser les cheveux?
   Tu t'es déjà brossé les cheveux.

### Activité 9
1. Non, je ne me suis pas encore levée.
2. Non, je ne me suis pas encore rasé.
3. Non, nous ne nous sommes pas encore brossé les dents.
4. Non, je ne me suis pas encore lavé les cheveux.
5. Non, je ne me suis pas encore habillé.
6. Non, nous ne nous sommes pas encore peignés.

### Activité 10
1. Olivier et Jean se sont réveillés de bonne heure.
2. Christine s'est lavé les cheveux.
3. Monique et Véronique se sont préparées pour le départ.
4. Mireille s'est dépêchée comme une folle.
5. Christian et Pierre se sont chargés de la nourriture.
6. Tous les étudiants se sont réunis devant la Faculté des Lettres.
7. Ils se sont assis dans les autocars.
8. Les autocars se sont éloignés de l'université.

### Activité 11
1. Le petit Claude s'est mouillé la chemise en buvant un coca.
2. Marlise s'est salie dans le garage.
3. Les jumeaux se sont moqués du voisin.
4. Les parents de Philippe se sont mis en panique.
5. Leur fils s'est échappé de la maison.
6. Caroline s'est plainte de tout.
7. Le petit Baudouin s'est caché au sous-sol.
8. Odile s'est coupé le doigt avec un couteau.
9. Moi, je me suis fatiguée.
10. Je me suis couchée de bonne heure.

### Activité 12
1. Oui, mais hier nous ne nous sommes pas vus.
2. Oui, mais hier nous ne nous sommes pas écrit.
3. Oui, mais hier nous ne nous sommes pas parlé.
4. Oui, mais hier nous ne nous sommes pas téléphoné.
5. Oui, mais hier nous ne nous sommes pas donné rendez-vous.
6. Oui, mais hier nous ne nous sommes pas aidés.
7. Oui, mais hier nous ne nous sommes pas envoyé de courriels.
8. Oui, mais hier nous ne nous sommes pas posé de questions.

### Activité 13
1. Ils se sont vus.
2. Ils se sont connus.
3. Ils se sont parlé.
4. Ils se sont compris.
5. Ils se sont plu.
6. Ils sont tombés amoureux.
7. Ils se sont acheté de petits cadeaux.
8. Ils se sont fiancés.
9. Après un temps, ils se sont disputés.
10. Ils se sont menti.
11. Ils ont rompu.
12. Ils ne se sont pas mariés.

### Activité 14
1. Lève-toi. Levez-vous.
2. Habille-toi. Habillez-vous.
3. Dépêche-toi. Dépêchez-vous.
4. Lave-toi les mains. Lavez-vous les mains.

5. Ne t'énerve pas. Ne vous énervez pas.
6. Ne te repose plus. Ne vous reposez plus.
7. Ne te dispute pas. Ne vous disputez pas.
8. Ne te recouche pas. Ne vous recouchez pas.
9. Dirige-toi vers la porte. Dirigez-vous vers la porte.
10. Prépare-toi pour partir. Préparez-vous pour partir.

### Activité 15
1. Habillons-nous.
2. Dépêchons-nous.
3. Lavons-nous les mains.
4. Ne nous énervons pas.
5. Ne nous reposons plus.
6. Ne nous disputons pas.
7. Aidons-nous.
8. Dirigeons-nous vers la porte.
9. Préparons-nous pour partir.

### Activité 16
1. Ce produit se vend-il bien?
2. Les étudiants s'amusent-ils au bal?
3. Ne vous dirigez-vous pas vers la sortie?
4. Se sont-ils approchés du guichet?
5. Ne nous éloignons-nous pas du centre de la ville?
6. Pourquoi vos amis ne se voient-ils plus?
7. Pourquoi ne t'intéresses-tu plus au cinéma?
8. À quelle heure se sont-elles mises en route?
9. Ne se sont-ils pas offensés?
10. S'est-elle souvenue de moi?
11. Pourquoi ne s'est-elle pas habituée à la vie française?
12. Vous attendez-vous à le voir?

### Activité 17 *Answers will vary.*

## Chapitre 8

### Activité 1
1. Le professeur a demandé pourquoi Jacques n'était pas venu.
2. Les étudiants ont répondu que Jacques était resté chez lui.
3. Le professeur a voulu savoir si Jacques était tombé malade.
4. On nous a dit que Jacques était arrivé à la cantine.
5. Jacques nous a demandé si nous avions assisté à la classe du professeur Jourdain.
6. Hélène lui a répondu que nous avions tous été présents.
7. Je lui ai prêté les notes que j'avais prises.

### Activité 2
1. C'est qu'elle m'avait déjà téléphoné avant-hier.
2. C'est qu'elle était déjà venue me voir avant-hier.
3. C'est qu'ils avaient déjà demandé le nom du médecin avant-hier.
4. C'est que j'avais déjà passé mon permis de conduire avant-hier.
5. C'est qu'elles avaient déjà fait leur travail avant-hier.
6. C'est que j'avais déjà posté la lettre avant-hier.
7. C'est qu'il avait déjà fait le plein avant-hier.
8. C'est que nous avions déjà balayé la chambre avant-hier.

### Activité 3
1. À huit heures et demie, ma sœur avait déjà pris une douche.
2. À huit heures et demie, ma mère avait déjà préparé le petit déjeuner.
3. À huit heures et demie, je m'étais déjà levé(e).
4. À huit heures et demie, mon amie Ghislaine avait déjà téléphoné deux fois.
5. À huit heures et demie, mon père n'était pas encore parti pour le bureau.
6. À huit heures et demie, j'avais déjà relu mes notes de biologie.

7. À huit heures et demie, mes frères avaient déjà mis leurs papiers dans leurs serviettes.
8. À huit heures et demie, je ne m'étais pas encore habillé(e).

## Activité 4
1. Claude et Alain auront cherché les boissons.
2. Sylvie aura mis le couvert.
3. Jean-Paul aura choisi les DVD.
4. Sophie et Odile auront invité tout le monde.
5. Hervé et Nathalie auront décoré la salle.
6. Marguerite aura acheté les gobelets.
7. Robert aura organisé les attractions.

## Activité 5
1. Il m'offrira un coup de main après que j'aurai fini.
2. Elle sonnera à la porte après que nous nous serons couché(e)s.
3. Tu viendras après que tout le monde sera parti.
4. Ils trouveront la carte routière après que nous nous serons perdu(e)s.
5. Nous arriverons après qu'ils auront fermé le restaurant.
6. Il nous renseignera après que nous aurons trouvé la solution.
7. Elle apportera le pain après que nous aurons fini de manger.
8. Vous viendrez nous prendre en voiture après que nous serons partis en autocar.

## Activité 6
1. Tu recevras une bonne note parce que tu auras étudié sérieusement.
2. On donnera un prix à Marc parce qu'il aura rédigé la meilleure composition.
3. On récompensera les étudiants parce qu'ils se seront conduits comme il faut.
4. Les journaux loueront cet agent de police parce qu'il aura agi héroïquement.
5. Le petit Pierrot sera grondé parce qu'il n'aura pas rangé ses affaires.
6. Michèle se fera gronder par ses parents parce qu'elle aura séché ses cours.
7. Je répondrai à toutes les questions à l'examen parce que j'aurai compris la matière.
8. Tout le monde sera déçu parce que nos cousins ne seront pas arrivés avant le match.

## Activité 7
1. Nous mangerons un dîner magnifique que nous aurons cuisiné.
2. J'écouterai le CD que j'aurai acheté.
3. Papa servira un dessert formidable avec la pâtisserie qu'il aura achetée.
4. Ma sœur nous racontera l'histoire du roman qu'elle aura lu.
5. Ma mère lira des articles dans la revue qu'elle aura achetée.
6. Nous regarderons le film que nous aurons loué.
7. Ma mère et moi, nous parlerons des articles qu'elle aura lus.
8. Mon frère chantera les nouvelles chansons qu'il aura apprises à l'école.

## Activité 8
1. Moi, je ne me serais pas couché(e) à cinq heures du matin.
2. Moi, je n'aurais pas pris rendez-vous avec le professeur Bouvard.
3. Moi, je ne me serais pas mis(e) en route sous la pluie.
4. Moi, je n'aurais pas fait dix kilomètres à pied.
5. Moi, je n'aurais pas cueilli des fleurs dans le jardin public.
6. Moi, je n'aurais pas cru à l'histoire que Marc a racontée.
7. Moi, je n'aurais pas dépensé tout mon argent.
8. Moi, je n'aurais pas oublié la date de la réception.

## Activité 9
1. Vraiment? Guillaume aurait conduit la voiture d'André.
2. Vraiment? Jacqueline et Martin seraient descendus.
3. Vraiment? Vincent et moi, nous aurions interrompu.
4. Vraiment? Moi, je me serais exprimé(e).
5. Vraiment? Albert aurait employé ce mot.
6. Vraiment? Simone et moi, nous aurions plongé.
7. Vraiment? Ségolène aurait répondu à Georges.
8. Vraiment? Solange et Marie se seraient disputées avec lui.

## Activité 10
1. Mais si elle était allée en ville hier, moi aussi je serais allé(e) en ville.
2. Mais si elle avait acheté le logiciel hier, moi aussi j'aurais acheté le logiciel.
3. Mais si elle s'était promenée hier, moi aussi je me serais promené(e).
4. Mais si elle avait envoyé ses paquets hier, moi aussi j'aurais envoyé mes paquets.
5. Mais si elle avait pris son billet hier, moi aussi j'aurais pris mon billet.
6. Mais si elle s'était préparée pour partir hier, moi aussi je me serais préparé(e) pour partir.
7. Mais si elle avait écouté le CD hier, moi aussi j'aurais écouté le CD.
8. Mais si elle avait travaillé hier, moi aussi j'aurais travaillé.

## Activité 11
1. Si Rachelle avait rédigé sa composition, elle se serait réunie avec ses amis.
2. Si Philippe avait relu ses leçons de chimie, il aurait joué au football.
3. Si Louise et Danielle avaient préparé le compte rendu, elles seraient allées aux grands magasins.
4. Si Olivier et Jean-Luc étaient allés au laboratoire de langues, ils auraient assisté au concert.
5. Si Françoise et Guy avaient étudié l'histoire du dix-septième siècle, ils seraient allés danser.
6. Si Mireille avait fait les problèmes de maths, elle serait sortie avec Charles.
7. Si Monique et Édouard avaient révisé leurs notes de littérature française, ils auraient dîné en ville.
8. Si Jean-François avait appris le poème par cœur, il aurait joué aux jeux vidéo.

## Activité 12
1. Michèle aurait salué Yves à la cantine si elle l'avait vu.
2. Sylvie aurait téléphoné à Roger si elle n'avait pas passé toute la journée à la bibliothèque.
3. Damien aurait dit à Judith qu'il y avait un examen aujourd'hui s'il s'en était souvenu.
4. Ariane aurait suivi son régime si elle n'avait pas eu envie de manger du chocolat.
5. Nicolas aurait fait le ménage s'il avait eu le temps.
6. Patrick aurait pris sa bicyclette s'il ne s'était pas foulé la cheville.
7. Paul et Virginie seraient sortis s'ils n'avaient pas dû étudier.
8. Louis serait venu à la faculté s'il n'était pas allé chez le médecin.

*Activité 13* Answers will vary.

*Activité 14* Answers will vary.

## Chapitre 9

### Activité 1
1. je gagnai
2. tu commenças
3. elle choisit
4. elles attendirent
5. vous espérâtes
6. tu nageas

7. il encouragea
8. nous déménageâmes
9. je descendis
10. tu annonças
11. ils rangèrent
12. elles défendirent
13. vous obéîtes
14. nous entendîmes
15. je remplaçai
16. on rédigea
17. nous réfléchîmes
18. vous essayâtes
19. tu allas
20. nous partageâmes

## Activité 2
1. La nuit tomba sur Versailles et son château.
2. La ville devint silencieuse.
3. Les habitants rentrèrent chez eux.
4. On ferma les magasins.
5. J'entrai dans un bistrot.
6. Je m'assis à une petite table.
7. J'attendis Michèle.
8. Elle voulut me voir.
9. Elle me rejoignit à sept heures.
10. Nous prîmes un café ensemble.
11. Nous sortîmes.
12. Nous nous promenâmes près du château.
13. Nous rentrâmes chez nous.

## Activité 3
1. Le soleil s'est levé.
2–3. Le ciel bleu est devenu écarlate et les nuages pâles se sont couchés derrière la montagne.
4–5. Sylvaine a été sublime dans cette lumière pourpre et Baptiste n'a pas pu s'empêcher de lui en toucher un mot.
6–7. «Vous êtes née sous un soleil céleste, Sylvaine», lui a-t-il dit.
8–9. Elle a souri en entendant ces mots, mais elle n'y a point répondu.
10. Il a fallu des remarques plus étincelantes pour retenir l'attention de la jeune rêveuse.
11–12. Elle a descendu la route qui l'a menée vers la ville.
13. Sa tête s'est remplie d'images d'une vie sophistiquée et suave.
14. Baptiste a voulu la suivre, mais il n'a pas eu le courage.

# Chapitre 10

## Activité 1
1. Tu auras une bonne note en faisant tes devoirs de maths tous les jours.
2. Tu arriveras à l'heure en quittant la maison à sept heures et demie.
3. En apprenant toutes les dates par cœur, on évite beaucoup de problèmes dans le cours d'histoire.
4. En écoutant des programmes en anglais sur Internet, tu te prépareras pour l'examen oral.
5. On évite la fatigue en organisant son travail.
6. En regardant très peu la télé, on peut toujours finir son travail.

## Activité 2
1. Les voyageurs partant pour le Nord sont priés de passer au quai numéro 3.
2. Nous annonçons un retard pour tous les avions provenant d'Afrique.
3. Le docteur Gobert verra les malades souffrant d'un problème gastrique.
4. Les étudiants passant leurs examens demain doivent arriver à l'université à huit heures.
5. C'est un manuel d'anglais contenant tout le vocabulaire essentiel.
6. Voici une carte montrant le site des centrales nucléaires.

## Activité 3
1. Les Maurois aiment faire un grand réveillon pour la Saint-Sylvestre.
2. Ils vont s'offrir des étrennes le jour de l'An.
3. Le 6 janvier ils espèrent inviter des amis pour la fête des Rois.
4. La grand-mère veut passer le dimanche de Pâques avec eux.
5. Le 8 mai, ils comptent aller en Normandie pour commémorer la victoire des Alliés en 1945.
6. Pour Noël, ils désirent être dans leur maison à la campagne.
7. Ils doivent aller fleurir les tombes de leurs parents décédés le 2 novembre.
8. Ils vont aller à la messe de minuit le 24 décembre.

## Activité 4
1. Alice et Géraldine ont pu faire du tourisme.
2. Georges ne savait pas nager très bien.
3. Il n'osait pas s'éloigner de la plage.
4. Claudette et Brigitte préféraient jouer au tennis.
5. Louis aimait visiter les petits villages en dehors de la ville.
6. Solange n'a pas pu acheter de souvenirs.
7. Richard a dû envoyer beaucoup de courriels.

## Activité 5
1. X
2. à
3. X
4. X
5. à
6. à
7. à
8. X

## Activité 6
1. Le professeur nous encourage à lire un livre par semaine.
2. J'aime mieux faire mes recherches sur Internet.
3. Jacques réussira à finir son compte rendu demain.
4. Son patron engage Philomène à faire de l'allemand.
5. L'administration de l'école vous autorise à chercher du travail.
6. Henri et Jules se résignent à recevoir une mauvaise note en maths.
7. Chantal continue à réviser ses notes d'informatique.
8. Odile passe son temps à recopier ses notes.

## Activité 7
1. d'
2. à
3. X
4. X
5. d'
6. à
7. de
8. de
9. à
10. à
11. X
12. de

## Activité 8
1. Loïc et Charles tiennent à voir un match de football.
2. Marie-Noëlle s'empresse de s'acheter des livres.
3. Albert se flatte de connaître parfaitement toutes les lignes de métro.
4. Berthe et Christine entreprennent d'organiser une sortie aux cabarets.
5. Philippe compte visiter la Cité des Sciences et de l'Industrie.
6. Chantal passe son temps à regarder les robes aux grands magasins.
7. Tous les étudiants brûlent de visiter le Louvre.
8. Paulette et Mireille espèrent avoir le temps de voir Montmartre.

## Activité 9
1. Il faut l'encourager à apprendre les mots.
2. Il faut le convaincre de faire attention.
3. Il faut lui déconseiller de sortir tous les jours.
4. Il faut le persuader de participer en classe.
5. Il faut leur dire de se taire.
6. Il faut leur conseiller de se concentrer sur leurs études.

7. Il faut l'aider à résoudre les problèmes.
8. Il faut les dissuader de le faire.

*Activité 10*
1. Le grand-père a convaincu son gendre Guillaume de ne pas quitter son travail.
2. Les enfants de Guillaume et Sylvie se sont empressés d'apporter des fleurs à la tante Émilie.
3. Le petit Bertrand a demandé à sa mère de lui acheter une bicyclette.
4. La grand-mère a pardonné à sa petite-fille Giselle d'avoir oublié son anniversaire.
5. Guillaume et Sylvie ont félicité leur fille Christine d'avoir eu la meilleure note de la classe en biologie.
6. L'oncle François a enseigné à sa nièce à se servir de l'ordinateur.
7. Anne-Marie a interdit à sa fille Mireille de sortir avec Frédéric.
8. Nadine a prié ses parents de l'emmener au bord de la mer.
9. Sylvie a invité ses beaux-parents à dîner.
10. Guillaume a proposé à ses parents de passer leurs vacances avec sa famille.

*Activité 11*
1. à
2. de
3. à
4. de
5. à
6. pour
7. de
8. de
9. à
10. pour

*Activité 12*
1. Il faut le faire retapisser.
2. Il faut la faire réparer.
3. Il faut le faire nettoyer.
4. Il faut la faire remplacer.
5. Il faut le faire paver.
6. Il faut les faire plâtrer.
7. Il faut le faire débarrasser.

*Activité 13*
1. Mlle Arnaud lui fait réciter des poèmes.
2. Mlle Arnaud lui fait présenter son travail devant un petit groupe.
3. Mlle Arnaud leur fait écrire une composition.
4. Mlle Arnaud lui fait relire l'explication dans son livre.
5. Mlle Arnaud leur fait regarder un film.
6. Mlle Arnaud leur fait aider leurs camarades.
7. Mlle Arnaud lui fait observer une leçon de français.
8. Mlle Arnaud nous fait écouter la chanson que les élèves ont apprise.

*Activité 14*
1. Son petit ami l'a fait pleurer.
2. Le vent les a fait trembler.
3. Mon voisin les a fait pousser.
4. Leur institutrice les a fait lire.
5. Le clown les a fait rire.
6. Le mécanicien l'a fait démarrer.
7. Ses enfants l'ont fait sourire.
8. La chaleur l'a fait soupirer.
9. Le froid l'a fait grelotter.
10. La vendeuse l'a fait rager.

*Activité 15* *Answers will vary.*

## Chapitre 11

*Activité 1*
1. Les clients sont reçus par la réceptionniste.
2. Des commandes sont passées par les employés.
3. Un versement sur le compte de l'entreprise a été fait par la secrétaire.
4. Des marchandises ont été livrées par un camion.
5. Des échantillons ont été expédiés par le bureau.
6. Des chèques ont été signés par le patron.
7. Des factures sont envoyées par la secrétaire.
8. Une demande d'emploi a été présentée par une jeune femme.
9. Un nouveau produit va être lancé par l'entreprise.
10. Le marché va être étudié par des experts.

*Activité 2*
1. Les lits ont été montés par trois déménageurs.
2. Les tableaux ont été accrochés au mur par Pierre et Solange.
3. La machine à laver a été installée par un plombier.
4. Le fauteuil a été placé en face de la télé par M. Martel.
5. Les vêtements ont été accrochés dans la penderie par Mme Martel.
6. Deux grosses caisses en bois ont été laissées au sous-sol par les déménageurs.
7. La vaisselle a été rangée dans les placards par Mme Martel.
8. Les lampes ont été branchées par M. Martel.

*Activité 3*
1. Les enfants doivent être protégés.
2. Les personnes âgées doivent être respectées.
3. La police doit être bien payée.
4. Le drapeau doit être honoré.
5. Les professionnels doivent être bien formés.
6. Les musées doivent être subventionnés.
7. Les transports en commun doivent être modernisés.
8. Les petites entreprises doivent être encouragées.

*Activité 4*
1. On tient toujours le couteau dans la main droite.
2. On tient toujours la fourchette dans la main gauche.
3. On essuie souvent la sauce avec un morceau de pain.
4. On ne pose pas les coudes sur la table.
5. On pose les poignets sur le bord de la table (plutôt que de tenir les mains sous la table).
6. On ne coupe pas le pain avec le couteau.
7. On casse son morceau de pain.
8. On répond «Avec plaisir» pour accepter de reprendre un des plats.
9. On répond «Merci» pour ne pas accepter de reprendre un des plats (plutôt que de dire «Non, merci»).

*Activité 5*
1. On coupe un fromage en cubes pour servir. / Un fromage se coupe en cubes pour servir.
2. On prépare une bonne soupe la veille. / Une bonne soupe se prépare la veille.
3. On prépare ce plat une heure avant le repas. / Ce plat se prépare une heure avant le repas.
4. On déguste un bon vin. / Un bon vin se déguste.
5. On boit un café après le repas. / Un café se boit après le repas.
6. On sert des fruits comme dessert. / Des fruits se servent comme dessert.

*Activité 6*
1. Le base-ball ne se joue pas en France.
2. Les journaux américains se vendent partout.
3. Les bouquinistes se trouvent le long de la Seine.
4. Les films américains se projettent dans beaucoup de cinémas.
5. Les chansons américaines s'entendent à la radio.
6. Des festivals de théâtre se donnent en été.
7. Un marché en plein air s'installe deux fois par semaine dans ce quartier.
8. Les billets de métro se vendent en carnets de dix.

## Activité 7
1. Le verbe **devenir** se conjugue avec **être** au passé composé.
2. Dans le mot **clef,** le **f** final ne se prononce pas.
3. Le subjonctif s'utilise après l'expression **jusqu'à ce que.**
4. Le mot **rebuts** s'emploie au Québec.
5. *A silent film* se traduit en français par **un film muet.**
6. Les mots **amoral** et **immoral** se confondent souvent.
7. La négation se place autour du verbe quand il est conjugué au présent.
8. Le vocabulaire technique s'apprend sans difficulté.

## DEUXIÈME PARTIE

### Chapitre 12

#### Activité 1
1. le / les cahiers
2. la / les calculettes
3. l' / les étudiants
4. la / les serviettes
5. le / les papiers
6. le / les stylos
7. la / les leçons
8. le / les calendriers
9. la / les bibliothèques
10. le / les dictionnaires
11. l' / les histoires
12. la / les cloches
13. l' / les exposés
14. la / les cantines

#### Activité 2
1. un / des pulls
2. une / des chemises
3. un / des pantalons
4. une / des cravates
5. un / des rayons
6. un / des vendeurs
7. une / des vendeuses
8. une / des robes
9. un / des maillots de bain
10. une / des vestes
11. un / des costumes
12. un / des chemisiers
13. un / des gants
14. un / des blousons
15. un / des anoraks

#### Activité 3
1. épicière
2. pharmacienne
3. une
4. une
5. le
6. la
7. une
8. le

#### Activité 4
1. Marguerite est musicienne aussi.
2. Émilie? Elle est épicière aussi.
3. Ma nièce est une élève de cette école primaire aussi.
4. Éloïse? C'est une Bretonne aussi.
5. Simone de Beauvoir est un écrivain célèbre aussi.
6. Hélène a été victime de son imprudence aussi.
7. Lise est une institutrice formidable aussi.
8. Mme Chauvin est la propriétaire de l'établissement aussi.
9. Sa tante est juge aussi.
10. Chantal est un médecin respecté aussi.
11. Cette femme est aviatrice aussi.
12. Mireille est une nageuse formidable aussi.
13. Caroline est notre championne aussi.
14. Je connais Mme Mercier, la commerçante, aussi.

#### Activité 5
1. un
2. un
3. une
4. Une
5. Le
6. Quelle
7. le
8. une
9. la
10. le
11. une
12. mon
13–14. la/à la
15. une
16. le
17. une
18. Un
19. le

#### Activité 6
1. Je veux deux chapeaux.
2. J'assiste à deux festivals.
3. J'ai deux neveux.
4. Mon nom s'écrit avec deux **l.**
5. Je cherche deux messieurs.
6. J'étudie deux vitraux.
7. Je prononce deux discours.
8. Je travaille deux métaux.
9. Je prends deux morceaux.
10. Je visite deux pays.
11. J'ai deux choix.
12. Je prépare deux repas.
13. Je lis deux journaux.
14. Je change deux pneus.
15. J'ai deux rivaux.

#### Activité 7
1. C'est
2. Elle est
3. Ils sont
4. Ce sont
5. C'est
6. C'est
7. C'est
8. Elle est
9. Il est
10. Ils sont

#### Activité 8
1. Vous avez du jambon? Non, monsieur. Il n'y a pas de jambon.
2. Vous avez de la salade niçoise? Non, monsieur. Il n'y a pas de salade niçoise.
3. Vous avez du fromage? Non, monsieur. Il n'y a pas de fromage.
4. Vous avez du pâté? Non, monsieur. Il n'y a pas de pâté.
5. Vous avez du saucisson? Non, monsieur. Il n'y a pas de saucisson.
6. Vous avez du saumon fumé? Non, monsieur. Il n'y a pas de saumon fumé.
7. Vous avez des quiches? Non, monsieur. Il n'y a pas de quiches.
8. Vous avez des sandwichs? Non, monsieur. Il n'y a pas de sandwichs.

#### Activité 9
1. Suzanne a cherché de la farine, mais elle n'a pas cherché d'œufs.
2. Moi, j'ai rapporté du pain, mais je n'ai pas rapporté de beurre.
3. Laurent a trouvé des champignons, mais il n'a pas trouvé de salade.
4. Élisabeth a pris des pommes, mais elle n'a pas pris d'oranges.
5. Toi et moi, nous avons acheté des petits pois, mais nous n'avons pas acheté de (d')haricots verts.
6. Vous avez rapporté du fromage, mais vous n'avez pas rapporté de yaourt.
7. Toi, tu as cherché de la viande, mais tu n'as pas cherché de poulet.
8. Les garçons ont pris du lait, mais ils n'ont pas pris de coca.

#### Activité 10
1. C'est du bœuf, ça? Non, ce n'est pas du bœuf. C'est du porc.
2. C'est du poulet, ça? Non, ce n'est pas du poulet. C'est du dindon.
3. Ce sont des haricots verts, ça? Non, ce ne sont pas des haricots verts. Ce sont des endives.
4. C'est du riz, ça? Non, ce n'est pas du riz. C'est du couscous.
5. C'est du jus, ça? Non, ce n'est pas du jus. C'est de la limonade.
6. C'est du thon, ça? Non, ce n'est pas du thon. C'est du saumon.

#### Activité 11
1. du
2. de
3. des
4. de
5. des
6. des

7. du
8. de
9. de
10. de
11. des
12. de
13. d'
14. des

### Activité 12
1. Nous avons besoin de café. J'ai acheté du café. Combien de café as-tu acheté? J'ai acheté assez de café pour nous. J'ai acheté trois cents grammes de thé aussi.
2. La plupart des livres que j'ai lus étaient intéressants. Trop des livres que j'ai lus étaient ennuyeux.

### Activité 13
| | |
|---|---|
| 1–2. le / les | 12–13. les / de |
| 3. de | 14. le |
| 4–5. de / le | 15–16. des / les |
| 6–7. Un / une | 17. de (des) |
| 8. de | 18–19. de / du |
| 9. un | 20–21. L' / les |
| 10. la | 22–23. d' / de l' |
| 11. de | 24. L' |

## Chapitre 13

### Activité 1
1. Elle est très fraîche aussi.
2. Elle est amère aussi.
3. Elle est très sotte aussi.
4. Elle est complète aussi.
5. Elle est ancienne aussi.
6. Elle est brune aussi.
7. Elle est merveilleuse aussi.
8. Elle est très discrète aussi.
9. Elle est rousse aussi.
10. Elle est sensationnelle aussi.
11. Elle est sportive aussi.
12. Elle est mignonne aussi.

### Activité 2
1. l'administration actuelle
2. un récit drôle
3. une écharpe chic
4. un résultat logique
5. la langue grecque
6. l'opinion publique
7. une mère nerveuse
8. un paquet léger
9. un film favori
10. une viande exquise
11. une tranquillité trompeuse
12. une sensibilité délicate

### Activité 3
1. des examens oraux
2. des films affreux
3. des films géniaux
4. des examens finals
5. des garçons roux
6. des livres banals
7. des cas spéciaux
8. des voyages dangereux
9. des mots nouveaux
10. des œufs frais
11. des problèmes nationaux
12. des produits locaux

### Activité 4
1. Voici les parfums français.
2. Voici les légumes frais.
3. Voici les journaux espagnols.
4. Voici les fromages crémeux.
5. Voici les fromages gras.
6. Voici les pantalons gris.
7. Voici les foulards bleus.
8. Voici les romans québécois.

### Activité 5
1. les élections actuelles / l'économie actuelle / les conflits actuels
2. des efforts internationaux / des organisations internationales / une entreprise internationale
3. la poésie grecque / les régions grecques / les dialectes grecs
4. la musique classique / les philosophes classiques / les chansons classiques
5. une croyance religieuse / des sentiments religieux / des conceptions religieuses
6. l'Union européenne / les pays européens / les langues européennes
7. des exemples concrets / une application concrète / des actions concrètes
8. des influences étrangères / la littérature étrangère / les ambassadeurs étrangers
9. des personnages fictifs / une situation fictive / des histoires fictives
10. l'école navale / des combats navals / les bases navales

### Activité 6
1. mon ancien professeur
2. le mois dernier
3. une famille pauvre
4. la seule étudiante
5. une vraie amie
6. un appartement sale
7. une histoire vraie
8. ma propre bicyclette

### Activité 7
1. une belle terrasse
2. de vieilles églises
3. un vieil objet
4. un nouvel ordinateur
5. une nouvelle industrie
6. de vieux instruments
7. un bel accent
8. de beaux animaux
9. une vieille assiette
10. de nouveaux avions

### Activité 8
1. Le stade est plus grand que la salle de concert.
2. Les cinémas sont plus nombreux que les théâtres.
3. La faculté de médecine est aussi réputée que la faculté de droit.
4. Le jardin zoologique est aussi fréquenté que la bibliothèque municipale.
5. Le musée scientifique est moins grand que le musée d'art.
6. Les restaurants ici sont aussi chers que les restaurants parisiens.
7. Les rues de la vieille ville sont plus étroites que les rues des quartiers modernes.
8. Le quartier des affaires est moins animé que le quartier des étudiants.
9. La piscine municipale est meilleure que la plage au bord du fleuve.

### Activité 9
1. Monique répond moins intelligemment que Christine.
2. Édouard rédige plus soigneusement que Louis.
3. Nicole travaille aussi rapidement que Lucien.
4. Anne-Marie écoute aussi attentivement que Guillaume.
5. Gérard oublie moins souvent que Paulette.
6. François se comporte mieux que Georges.

### Activité 10 *Answers may vary but may include:*
1. Nos manuels sont plus / moins / aussi intéressants que ceux de l'année dernière.
2. Mes camarades de classe sont plus / moins / aussi sympathiques que ceux de l'année dernière.
3. Les professeurs sont plus / moins / aussi exigeants que ceux de l'année dernière.
4. Les devoirs sont plus / moins / aussi faciles que ceux de l'année dernière.
5. La nourriture qu'on sert à la cantine est meilleure / pire / aussi bonne que celle de l'année dernière.
6. Mon horaire est plus / moins / aussi pratique que celui de l'année dernière.
7. La classe de français est plus / moins / aussi passionnante que celle de l'année dernière.
8. Les bals qu'on organise sont plus / moins / aussi amusants que ceux de l'année dernière.

### Activité 11

1. Frédéric suit plus de cours que Marc.
2. Sylvie écrit plus de thèmes que Robert.
3. Monique subit moins d'examens que Marcelle.
4. Maurice résoud autant de problèmes de maths que Philippe.
5. Marie-Laure étudie autant de langues étrangères qu'Alfred.
6. Claudine apprend moins de poèmes que Chantal.
7. Hervé analyse plus d'œuvres que Charles.
8. Julie fait autant d'expériences de chimie que Serge.

### Activité 12

1. Marylène est la plus diligente.
2. Jacques et Pierre sont les moins obéissants.
3. Solange est la plus sympathique.
4. Irène et Marie sont les moins travailleuses.
5. Olivier est le plus intelligent.
6. Anne-Marie est la plus bavarde.
7. Jean-Paul est le plus charmant.
8. Colette et Brigitte sont les moins préparées.

### Activité 13

1. Voilà la place la plus imposante de la ville.
2. Ici vous voyez la cathédrale la plus ancienne de la région.
3. En face il y a l'université la plus connue du pays.
4. C'est la rue la plus longue de la ville.
5. Dans cette rue il y a les plus beaux magasins de la région.
6. Voilà la charcuterie la plus appréciée du quartier.
7. Devant nous il y a l'hôtel le plus élégant du pays.
8. Dans cette rue se trouvent les cafés les plus fréquentés de la ville.
9. Ici vous voyez les plus vieilles maisons de la ville.
10. Voilà le plus grand stade de la région.

### Activité 14

1. C'est Lucie qui parle le plus poliment.
2. C'est Olivier qui travaille le moins efficacement.
3. C'est Albert qui étudie le moins sérieusement.
4. C'est Suzanne qui chante le mieux.
5. C'est Hélène qui arrive en retard le plus souvent.
6. C'est Roger qui répond le plus calmement.

## Chapitre 14

### Activité 1

| | |
|---|---|
| 1. affreusement | 11. moralement |
| 2. intelligemment | 12. pratiquement |
| 3. correctement | 13. généreusement |
| 4. probablement | 14. cruellement |
| 5. gentiment | 15. évidemment |
| 6. tristement | 16. légèrement |
| 7. massivement | 17. longuement |
| 8. gaiment | 18. précisément |
| 9. confusément | 19. exactement |
| 10. fréquemment | 20. complètement |

### Activité 2

1. Oui, il lui parle nerveusement.
2. Oui, elle lui parle intensément.
3. Oui, il lui parle honnêtement.
4. Oui, elles lui parlent tristement.
5. Oui, ils lui parlent discrètement.
6. Oui, elle lui parle patiemment.
7. Oui, ils lui parlent poliment.
8. Oui, il lui parle gentiment.

### Activité 3

1. Oui, elle travaille diligemment.
2. Oui, il réagit violemment.
3. Oui, elle dessine bien.
4. Oui, elle sort fréquemment.
5. Oui, ils prononcent mal en français.
6. Oui, il l'aime aveuglément.

### Activité 4

1. Tu connais mal le vocabulaire.
2. Elle nettoie soigneusement la cuisine.
3. Nous trouvons ce projet complètement ridicule.
4. Les membres de cette famille sont étroitement liés.
5. Il marche sans empressement.
6. Les enfants se sont conduits d'une façon déplaisante.
7. Marcelle travaille dur à la bibliothèque.
8. C'est une idée largement reçue.
9. Ils ont vite compris le texte.
10. Elle m'a répondu brusquement.

### Activité 5

| | |
|---|---|
| 1. sans effort | 5. avec colère |
| 2. avec goût | 6. avec tolérance |
| 3. sans imagination | 7. sans cérémonie |
| 4. avec indifférence | 8. sans tact |

### Activité 6

1. Il y a des arbres autour.
2. Il y a un jardin derrière.
3. Je regarde le salon en bas.
4. Je voudrais voir les chambres en haut.
5. Je cherche les propriétaires partout.
6. Je ne les vois nulle part.
7. Travaillent-ils dehors?
8. Je les entends quelque part.
9. Il y a deux personnes tout près.
10. Les voilà devant.

### Activité 7

| | |
|---|---|
| 1. en | 8. à |
| 2. sur | 9. d' |
| 3. en | 10. à |
| 4. à | 11. par |
| 5. par | 12. en |
| 6. en | 13. en |
| 7. Par | 14. à |

### Activité 8

1. J'ai fait un effort pour organiser la classe dès le début.
2. J'ai dit aux étudiants qu'il est défendu de venir en classe sans chaussures.
3. Je leur ai dit que je ne veux pas qu'ils laissent la salle de classe en désordre / pagaille.
4. Ils ne doivent laisser ni leurs livres ni leurs papiers par terre.
5. Jean-Claude Mercier vient au cours un jour sur deux.
6. Il prépare ses devoirs à la hâte.
7. Lise Monnet est sans doute la meilleure étudiante de la classe.
8. Les autres étudiants l'admirent sincèrement.
9. À partir de demain, nous avons une semaine de congé.
10. Je vais faire un effort pour améliorer cette classe dès notre retour.
11. Nous allons faire des excursions de temps en temps.
12. Les vieilles méthodes ne sont pas toujours bonnes à l'époque où nous sommes.

## Chapitre 15

### Activité 1

1. Nous, nous partons en Italie. Elles, elles partent en Grèce.
2. Moi, je prends le train. Eux, ils partent en voiture.

3. Toi, tu fais de l'alpinisme. Lui, il fait de la natation.
4. Eux, ils vont à la campagne. Nous, on va leur rendre visite.
5. Moi, j'ai trois semaines de vacances. Vous, vous avez un mois.
6. Moi, je préfère voyager seul. Toi, tu préfères voyager en groupe.
7. Nous, on compte faire du cyclisme. Lui, il veut faire du tourisme.
8. Elle, elle fait un stage linguistique en Allemagne. Toi, tu te détends.

### Activité 2

1. C'est faux! Je ne sors pas avec Émilie, moi.
2. C'est faux! Je ne me lève pas à huit heures, moi.
3. C'est faux! Je ne dors pas en classe, moi.
4. C'est faux! Je ne joue pas de la clarinette, moi.
5. C'est faux! Je ne cherche pas de travail, moi.
6. C'est faux! Je ne vais pas chez Olivier après les cours, moi.

### Activité 3

1. Qu'est-ce que tu dis? Il n'a jamais dormi en classe, lui.
2. Qu'est-ce que tu dis? Il n'a jamais été en retard, lui.
3. Qu'est-ce que tu dis? Il n'a jamais interrompu le professeur, lui.
4. Qu'est-ce que tu dis? Il ne s'est jamais disputé avec Serge, lui.
5. Qu'est-ce que tu dis? Il ne s'est jamais moqué des cours, lui.
6. Qu'est-ce que tu dis? Il n'a jamais dérangé les autres étudiants, lui.

### Activité 4

1. C'est toi sur la photo? Non, ce n'est pas moi. C'est ma sœur Barbara.
2. C'est moi le suivant? Non, ce n'est pas toi/vous. C'est lui.
3. C'est M. Charpentier assis sur le banc? Non, ce n'est pas lui. C'est notre voisin M. Beauchamp.
4. C'est Adèle Malmaison dans la boutique? Non, ce n'est pas elle. C'est Mlle Lachaux.
5. Ce sont nos amis, là, à l'entrée du lycée? Non, ce n'est pas / ce ne sont pas eux. Ce sont d'autres étudiants.
6. Ce sont Gisèle et Marie-Claire à l'arrêt du bus? Non, ce n'est pas / ce ne sont pas elles. Ce sont Christine et Yvette.

### Activité 5

1. Non, il / ce cadeau n'est pas pour toi.
2. Non, je ne compte pas dîner avec eux.
3. Non, je n'ai pas l'intention de passer chez elle.
4. Non, tu ne peux pas compter sur moi.
5. Non, elle n'a pas été invitée par lui.
6. Non, il n'est pas fâché contre nous.

### Activité 6

1. Oui. Je n'aime que toi.
2. Oui. On ne respecte que lui.
3. Oui. Ils n'admirent que lui.
4. Oui. Ils n'estiment qu'elle.
5. Oui. Nous n'aidons que vous.
6. Oui. Il n'apprécie qu'eux.
7. Oui. Ils n'encouragent qu'elles.

### Activité 7

| | |
|---|---|
| 1. je | 9. toi |
| 2. elle | 10. elles |
| 3. Elle | 11. elles |
| 4. moi | 12. nous |
| 5. lui | 13. vous |
| 6. eux | 14. toi |
| 7. elle | 15. toi |
| 8. moi | |

### Activité 8

1. Lui, il achète du pain. Nous, on achète de l'eau minérale.
2. Nous avons vu Julien et Colette. Nous nous sommes approchés d'eux.
3. Gérard ne pense qu'à lui-même.
4. Nous sommes entrés après lui mais avant toi.
5. Et je croyais que vous n'invitiez que moi!
6. C'est toi qui travailles.
7. Ce sont eux qui s'en vont.
8. C'est lui qui sait la réponse.

### Activité 9 *Answers will vary.*

## Chapitre 16

### Activité 1

| | |
|---|---|
| 1. Elle les regarde. | 6. Elle le prend. |
| 2. Elle l'essaie. | 7. Elle les regarde. |
| 3. Elle ne la prend pas. | 8. Elle les essaie. |
| 4. Elle l'achète. | 9. Elle ne les achète pas. |
| 5. Elle les cherche. | 10. Elle le paie. |

### Activité 2

1. Vous pouvez le mettre dans le salon.
2. Vous pouvez le monter à la chambre de mon fils.
3. Vous pouvez la descendre au sous-sol.
4. Vous pouvez la laisser dans le salon.
5. Vous pouvez l'installer dans la salle à manger.
6. Vous pouvez les suspendre dans la penderie.
7. Vous pouvez le monter à la chambre de ma fille.
8. Vous pouvez les laisser dans le salon.

### Activité 3

1. Non, je ne peux pas te déposer (en ville).
2. Non, je ne peux pas t'emmener (à la poste).
3. Non, je ne peux pas te raccompagner.
4. Non, je ne peux pas t'attendre.
5. Non, je ne peux pas vous rejoindre.
6. Non, je ne peux pas vous appeler.

### Activité 4

1. Sabine va la balayer.
2. Marc et David vont les laver.
3. Élisabeth et Stéphanie vont les nettoyer.
4. Moi, je vais les faire.
5. Édouard va les sortir.
6. Barbara va le passer.
7. Charles et Michèle vont les dépoussiérer.
8. Odile et François vont les faire.
9. Louis et Denis vont les récurer.
10. Toi, tu vas les laver!

### Activité 5

| | |
|---|---|
| 1. Je l'ai déjà écrite. | 6. Elle l'a déjà faite. |
| 2. Ils l'ont déjà rédigé. | 7. Il les a déjà révisées. |
| 3. Nous les avons déjà faits. | 8. Ils les ont déjà regardées. |
| 4. Elle les a déjà appris. | 9. Je les ai déjà écoutés. |
| 5. Je l'ai déjà étudiée. | 10. Je les ai déjà relues. |

### Activité 6

1. Nous ne leur donnons pas d'argent.
2. Elle ne me montre pas ses logiciels.
3. Je ne leur ai pas écrit un courriel.
4. Ils ne leur vendent pas leur voiture.
5. Je ne vais pas lui offrir un collier.
6. Vous ne lui envoyez pas d'affiches.
7. Il ne m'apporte pas mes pantoufles.
8. Il ne lui a pas donné son numéro de téléphone.
9. Il ne leur a pas expliqué la méthode.
10. Je ne vais pas lui demander d'argent pour l'essence.

*Activité 7*
1. Il faut lui écrire une lettre.
2. Il faut leur régler la dernière cargaison de marchandises.
3. Il faut leur envoyer la facture encore une fois.
4. Il faut lui prêter trois cent mille euros.
5. Il faut lui/leur louer trois voitures et un camion.
6. Il faut lui emprunter un million d'euros.
7. Il faut lui montrer les nouvelles annonces.
8. Il faut leur présenter la nouvelle gamme de produits.

*Activité 8*
1. Son père lui a prêté la voiture.
2. Nous lui avons offert une montre pour son anniversaire.
3. Moi, je lui ai expliqué les idées du livre.
4. Nous leur avons demandé de jouer avec nous.
5. Vous lui avez apporté des revues et des journaux.
6. Nous leur avons rendu les livres que nous leur avions empruntés.
7. Nous lui avons montré nos notes.
8. Moi, je leur ai envoyé une lettre.
9. Nous lui avons répondu.
10. Nous leur avons téléphoné.

*Activité 9*
1. Non, elle n'y travaille jamais.
2. Non, ils n'y étudient jamais.
3. Non, il n'y attend jamais.
4. Non, ils n'y passent jamais leurs vacances.
5. Non, je n'y achète / nous n'y achetons jamais à manger.
6. Non, ils n'y jouent jamais.
7. Non, ils ne s'y réunissent jamais.
8. Non, je n'y laisse jamais mes livres.

*Activité 10*
1. Il faut y penser.
2. Il faut y réfléchir.
3. Il faut y prendre garde.
4. Il faut y renoncer.
5. Il faut s'y intéresser.
6. Il faut y rêver.
7. Il faut y croire.
8. Il faut y aller.

*Activité 11*
1. Non, il y en a trente-deux.
2. Non, il en gagne quatre cents.
3. Non, j'en ai deux cent cinquante.
4. Non, nous en avons parcouru trois cents.
5. Non, j'en ai eu quatre-vingt-dix.
6. Non, elle en a cinq.
7. Non, nous allons en acheter quinze.
8. Non, j'en veux deux douzaines.

*Activité 12*
1. Elles en ont déjà suivi.
2. Il s'en est déjà plaint.
3. Il en a déjà été accablé.
4. Il s'en est déjà chargé.
5. Elle en a déjà joué.
6. Il s'en est déjà mêlé.
7. Il en a déjà fait.
8. Elle en a déjà demandé.
9. Elle en est déjà revenue.
10. Il en a déjà donné.

*Activité 13*
1. Nous devons lui en écrire.
2. Je vais les lui prêter.
3. Nous devons le lui rendre.
4. Tu peux l'y retrouver.
5. J'ai l'intention de les leur montrer.
6. Il faut leur en donner.
7. Je vais te les/vous les expliquer.
8. Marguerite peut vous en rapporter.
9. Vous pouvez les y amener.
10. Nous devons nous y habituer.
11. Je vais vous en / t'en passer.
12. Il faut le leur apporter.

*Activité 14*
1. Mais si! Il leur en a déjà servi.
2. Mais si! Je lui en ai déjà donné.
3. Mais si! Ils s'y sont déjà opposés.
4. Mais si! Ils s'en sont déjà servis.
5. Mais si! Nous nous en sommes déjà rendu compte.
6. Mais si! Il nous les a déjà rendues.
7. Mais si! Elle leur en a déjà lu.
8. Mais si! Ils le leur ont déjà enseigné.
9. Mais si! Il leur en a déjà proposé.
10. Mais si! Je t'en ai déjà envoyé.
11. Mais si! Je t'en ai déjà permis.
12. Mais si! Il nous/vous l'a déjà promis.

*Activité 15*
1. Si on les leur prêtait?
2. Si on l'y retrouvait?
3. Si on les y amenait?
4. Si on lui en apportait une demi-douzaine?
5. Si on allait l'y attendre?
6. Si on s'en éloignait?
7. Si on s'en servait pour la rédiger?
8. Si on le leur donnait?
9. Si on les lui demandait?
10. Si on la leur vendait?

*Activité 16*
1. Oui, je me fie à eux.
2. Oui, elle s'y intéresse.
3. Oui, il s'intéresse à elle.
4. Oui, il en a honte.
5. Oui, il a honte de lui.
6. Oui, je m'en souviens.
7. Oui, je me souviens d'eux.
8. Oui, il en doute.
9. Oui, il se doute de lui.
10. Oui, j'en ai peur. / Oui, nous en avons peur.

*Activité 17*
1. Va t'en.
2. Dépose-moi là(-bas).
3. Donne-m'en.
4. Opposez-vous-y.
5. Éloigne-toi d'eux.
6. Habille-toi là(-bas).
7. Arrêtez-vous-y.
8. Charge-t'en.
9. Rendez-la-moi.
10. Passez-leur-en.

*Activité 18*
1. Je lui ai demandé son livre de littérature, mais il ne me l'a pas donné.
2. Il n'a plus sa voiture parce que quelqu'un la lui a volée.
3. Ces gens s'intéressent à votre maison. Vendez-la-leur.
4. Nous avons posé des questions sur la leçon au professeur, mais il n'y a pas répondu.
5. J'ai cherché des journaux français et j'en ai trouvé deux. Je te les montrerai.
6. Elle est au deuxième étage. Montes-y et tu la verras.
7. Les enfants jouaient sur le toit, mais ils en sont descendus.
8. Tu as fait de la soupe. Apporte-m'en et je l'essaierai.

*Activité 19* Answers will vary.

## Chapitre 17

*Activité 1*
1. Oui. Voilà sa voiture.
2. Oui. Voilà notre calculatrice.
3. Oui. Voilà leurs disques.
4. Oui. Voilà mes cartes.
5. Oui. Voilà tes documents.
6. Oui. Voilà son chien.

7. Oui. Voilà leurs billets.
8. Oui. Voilà leur salle de réunion.
9. Oui. Voilà son adresse.
10. Oui. Voilà son ordinateur.

*Activité 2*
1. Non. Ce n'est pas leur moto.
2. Non. Ce ne sont pas ses voitures de sport.
3. Non. Ce n'est pas notre caravane.
4. Non. Ce n'est pas son vélomoteur.
5. Non. Ce n'est pas son bus.
6. Non. Ce n'est pas notre camion.
7. Non. Ce n'est pas mon bateau.
8. Non. Ce n'est pas sa bicyclette.

*Activité 3*
1. Sa mère à lui ou sa mère à elle?
2. Ses enfants à lui ou ses enfants à elle?
3. Leur voiture à eux ou leur voiture à elles?
4. Son cousin à lui ou son cousin à elle?
5. Son chien à elle ou mon chien à moi?
6. Son départ à lui ou son départ à elle?

*Activité 4*
1. Roger a apporté son affiche.
2. Louise et Simone ont apporté leur répondeur.
3. Charles a apporté ses feutres.
4. Hélène a apporté son imprimante.
5. Le professeur de biologie a apporté son papier à lettres.
6. Albert et vous, vous avez apporté votre calendrier.
7. Moi, j'ai apporté mon annuaire.
8. Toi, tu as apporté ton dictionnaire scientifique.

*Activité 5*
1. Moi, j'ai mon cahier, mais Françoise a laissé le sien à l'amphi.
2. Nous, nous avons nos stylos, mais nos copains ont laissé les leurs à l'amphi.
3. Toi, tu as ta carte d'entrée, mais le professeur a laissé la sienne à l'amphi.
4. David a son sac à dos, mais Christine a laissé le sien à l'amphi.
5. Odile a ses bouquins, mais moi, j'ai laissé les miens à l'amphi.
6. Vous, vous avez votre dictionnaire, mais nous avons laissé le nôtre à l'amphi.
7. Mes amis ont leurs agendas, mais vous, vous avez laissé les vôtres à l'amphi.
8. Les enfants ont leurs crayons, mais toi, tu as laissé les tiens à l'amphi.

*Activité 6*
1. Les tiennes sont ici, les leurs sont en bas.
2. La nôtre/ La mienne est ici, la sienne est en bas.
3. Le vôtre est ici, le sien est en bas.
4. Les miennes sont ici, les siennes sont en bas.
5. Les tiennes sont ici, les leurs sont en bas.
6. Le tien est ici, le sien est en bas.

*Activité 7*
1. Aux miens.
2. Dans le leur.
3. De la nôtre. / Des nôtres.
4. À la sienne.
5. Des siennes.
6. Du mien. / Du nôtre.

*Activité 8*
1. Vous pouvez me dire le prix de cet ordinateur, s'il vous plaît?
2. Vous pouvez me dire le prix de cette unité de disque, s'il vous plaît?
3. Vous pouvez me dire le prix de ces disquettes, s'il vous plaît?
4. Vous pouvez me dire le prix de ce logiciel, s'il vous plaît?
5. Vous pouvez me dire le prix de ce lecteur de CD-ROM, s'il vous plaît?

6. Vous pouvez me dire le prix de ce disque dur, s'il vous plaît?
7. Vous pouvez me dire le prix de ce clavier, s'il vous plaît?
8. Vous pouvez me dire le prix de cette souris, s'il vous plaît?

*Activité 9*
1. Oui, mais ils préfèrent ces livres-là.
2. Oui, mais je préfère cet anorak-là.
3. Oui, mais elle préfère ce chapeau-là.
4. Oui, mais nous préférons ces bijoux-là.
5. Oui, mais ils préfèrent cet appartement-là.
6. Oui, mais je préfère ces quartiers-là.
7. Oui, mais je préfère cet immeuble-là.

*Activité 10*
1. Ce pantalon-ci ou ce pantalon-là?
2. Cet imperméable-ci ou cet imperméable-là?
3. Ces chaussettes-ci ou ces chaussettes-là?
4. Cette robe-ci ou cette robe-là?
5. Cet anorak-ci ou cet anorak-là?
6. Ce tee-shirt-ci ou ce tee-shirt-là?
7. Ces sandales-ci ou ces sandales-là?
8. Cette veste-ci ou cette veste-là?

*Activité 11*
1. Qui a oublié ce livre? Gisèle? Non, je crois que c'est celui de Josette.
2. Qui a oublié ce stylo? Colin? Non, je crois que c'est celui de Luc.
3. Qui a oublié ces chaussures? Fabien? Non, je crois que ce sont celles de Martin.
4. Qui a oublié ces gants? Julie? Non, je crois que ce sont ceux d'Hélène.
5. Qui a oublié ces cahiers? Eugénie et Colette? Non, je crois que ce sont ceux d'Élisabeth et Monique.
6. Qui a oublié cette calculatrice? Gérard? Non, je crois que c'est celle de Paul.
7. Qui a oublié ces lunettes? Loïc? Non, je crois que ce sont celles de Thomas.

*Activité 12*
1. Pas tellement. Mais j'aime ceux que tu prépares.
2. Pas tellement. Mais j'aime celle que tu joues.
3. Pas tellement. Mais j'aime celle que tu conduis.
4. Pas tellement. Mais j'aime celle que tu sers.
5. Pas tellement: Mais j'aime celles que tu portes.
6. Pas tellement. Mais j'aime ceux que tu fais.
7. Pas tellement. Mais j'aime celles que tu achètes.

## Chapitre 18

*Activité 1*

| | | | |
|---|---|---|---|
| 1. | qui | 9. | que |
| 2. | que | 10. | qui |
| 3. | qui | 11. | que |
| 4. | que | 12. | qui |
| 5. | qui | 13. | qu' |
| 6. | qui | 14. | qui |
| 7. | que | 15. | que |
| 8. | qui | 16. | que |

*Activité 2*
1. Le médecin qui a son cabinet dans ce bâtiment.
2. Les comprimés que mon médecin m'a ordonnés.
3. Le régime qu'il a trouvé au centre diététique.
4. Le sirop que j'ai laissé sur la table.
5. La piqûre que l'infirmière m'a faite hier.
6. Les pilules que j'ai prises hier.
7. La crème que le pharmacien m'a conseillée.
8. Les vitamines qui sont bonnes pour le cœur.

## Activité 3

1. a. Le professeur que tous les éudiants adorent.
   b. Le professeur qui enseigne le français et l'espagnol.
   c. Le professeur qui vient de se marier.
   d. Le professeur que mes parents connaissent / que connaissent mes parents.
2. a. La maison que Jeanne et Richard ont achetée.
   b. La maison qui a un jardin et une piscine.
   c. La maison qu'on a construite en 1975.
   d. La maison qui est en briques.
3. a. Les cadeaux que mon frère et moi, nous avons reçus il y a une semaine.
   b. Les cadeaux que mon oncle et ma tante nous ont envoyés.
   c. Les cadeaux que je t'ai montrés hier.
   d. Les cadeaux qui t'ont beaucoup plu.
4. a. Le restaurant que nos amis ont ouvert l'année dernière.
   b. Le restaurant qui a une ambiance alsacienne.
   c. Le restaurant qui a des nappes rouges.
   d. Le restaurant que beaucoup d'artistes fréquentent / que fréquentent beaucoup d'artistes.
5. a. Le sénateur que le peuple a élu l'année dernière.
   b. Le sénateur qui a promis de combattre l'inflation.
   c. Le sénateur qui est marié avec une journaliste.
   d. Le sénateur que les ouvriers soutiennent / que soutiennent les ouvriers.

## Activité 4

1. Il va sortir avec la fille à qui il pense tout le temps.
2. Je vais te montrer la lettre à laquelle j'ai répondu.
3. J'ai écouté le débat auquel nos copains ont pris part.
4. Il parle des habitudes auxquelles il faut renoncer.
5. Elle s'est mariée avec l'homme à qui elle se fiait.
6. Les clients à qui nous avons téléphoné sont venus.
7. J'aime / Nous aimons les détails auxquels vous avez veillé.
8. J'ai recommandé les méthodes auxquelles je crois.

## Activité 5

1. à laquelle
2. à qui
3. auquel
4. à qui
5. qu'
6. que
7. auxquelles
8. à laquelle
9. à laquelle
10. qui

## Activité 6

1. La fille dont la mère est médecin.
2. L'ami dont l'oncle travaille au ministère.
3. Le sénateur dont le pays entier a écouté le discours.
4. Les ouvriers dont le syndicat compte entreprendre une grève.
5. Les étudiants dont on a publié le rapport.
6. Le professeur dont le cours est toujours plein.
7. L'infirmière dont tout le monde admire le travail.
8. Le programmeur dont les logiciels se vendent très bien.
9. Les voisins dont les enfants assistent à cette école.
10. Le groupe de rock dont tous les jeunes écoutent les chansons.

## Activité 7

1. Notre guide nous a montré un paysage dont nous nous sommes émerveillés.
2. Nous avons visité les murailles dont la vieille ville est entourée.
3. Une amie nous a invités au festival de danse auquel elle prenait part.
4. Nous sommes allés voir une rue qu'on a transformée en rue piétonne.
5. On est allés voir une comédie dont on a beaucoup ri.
6. Nous avons essayé la cuisine régionale dont la ville se vante.
7. On nous a signalé l'absence d'une université dont nous nous sommes aperçus.
8. C'est la vie universitaire dont la ville manquait.
9. Nous avions des amis dans la région à qui nous avons téléphoné.
10. Nous avons passé une belle journée avec eux dont nous nous souvenons encore.
11. La crise dont tout le monde avait peur est arrivée.
12. Un ministre faisait mal les fonctions dont il était responsable.
13. C'était un homme respecté dont personne ne se doutait.
14. Ce ministre est un homme bien en vue à qui la nation entière se fiait.
15. On dit qu'il a donné des emplois à des gens non qualifiés, dont plusieurs étaient ses parents et ses amis.
16. Ils faisaient un travail dont on commençait à se plaindre.
17. Il y avait cent employés au ministère dont on a licencié une trentaine.
18. C'est la confiance de la nation dont le ministre a abusé.

## Activité 8

1. laquelle
2. avec lequel
3. sur laquelle
4. avec lequel
5. sur lesquelles
6. contre lequel
7. dont / desquelles

## Activité 9

1. laquelle
2. laquelle
3. auxquels
4. lesquels
5. laquelle
6. laquelle
7. laquelle
8. duquel
9. lequel
10. qui
11. dont
12. desquelles

## Activité 10

1. celui qui
2. ce que
3. Ce qui
4. tout ce qu'
5. celle qu'
6. ce dont
7. ce qu'
8. ce dont
9. ce qui
10. ce que
11. ce qui
12. ce que

## Activité 11

1. ce qu'
2. Ce qui
3. ce que
4. ce que
5. Ce qui
6. Ce dont
7. ce qui
8. ce que
9. ce dont
10. ce qui
11. ce que
12. ce dont

## Activité 12

1. Élisabeth a un poste dont elle veut démissionner.
2. Il y a d'autres emplois sur lesquels elle essaie de se renseigner.
3. Elle manque de qualifications dont nous ne pouvons pas nous passer dans mon bureau.
4. Elle a téléphoné à d'autres entreprises dont je lui ai donné le nom.
5. Il y a des cours d'orientation auxquels elle assiste.
6. Il y a de nouveaux logiciels pour le bureau avec lesquels Élisabeth se familiarise.
7. Elle a déjà trouvé une entreprise pour laquelle elle voudrait travailler.
8. Je vais te montrer les choses dont j'ai besoin pour préparer mon petit déjeuner.
9. Voici le réchaud sur lequel je fais mon café.
10. Voici le bol dans lequel je bois mon café du matin.
11. Voilà la boulangerie dans laquelle / où j'achète mes croissants et mon pain.
12. Voilà la porte de la boutique au-dessus de laquelle il y a une enseigne.

## TROISIÈME PARTIE

### Chapitre 19

*Activité 1*
1. a. Invitez-vous souvent vos amis à dîner?
   b. Est-ce que vous invitez souvent vos amis à dîner?
2. a. Appréciez-vous la musique classique?
   b. Est-ce que vous appréciez la musique classique?
3. a. Habitez-vous un beau quartier?
   b. Est-ce que vous habitez un beau quartier?
4. a. Cherchez-vous une maison à la campagne?
   b. Est-ce que vous cherchez une maison à la campagne?
5. a. Travaillez-vous près de chez vous?
   b. Est-ce que vous travaillez près de chez vous?
6. a. Dînez-vous généralement au restaurant?
   b. Est-ce que vous dînez généralement au restaurant?

*Activité 2*
1. Aime-t-elle les maths comme moi?
2. Étudie-t-elle les mêmes matières que moi?
3. Habite-t-elle près de l'université?
4. Pense-t-elle à moi de temps en temps?
5. Travaille-t-elle à la bibliothèque?
6. Déjeune-t-elle au restaurant universitaire?

*Activité 3*
1. Est-ce que Chantal habite près de chez toi?
2. Est-ce que tu arrives à la même heure que Chantal?
3. Est-ce que tu salues Chantal?
4. Est-ce que Chantal aime les mêmes activités que toi?
5. Est-ce que tu déjeunes avec elle?
6. Est-ce que Chantal bavarde avec toi de temps en temps?

*Activité 4*
1. Mme Savignac prononce-t-elle parfaitement l'anglais?
2. M. Paul enseigne-t-il l'espagnol aussi?
3. Mlle Moreau répond-elle toujours aux questions des étudiants?
4. M. Michelet arrive-t-il à sept heures du matin?
5. M. et Mme Lamoureux enseignent-ils dans le même département?
6. Mme Leboucher choisit-elle des textes intéressants pour sa classe?
7. Les professeurs organisent-ils des activités pour les étudiants?
8. Les étudiants aiment-ils les cours de français?

*Activité 5*
1. Ne lançons-nous pas une bonne affaire?
2. Ne dirigeons-nous pas l'entreprise d'une façon intelligente?
3. N'engageons-nous pas de bons travailleurs?
4. N'aménageons-nous pas les bureaux?
5. Ne changeons-nous pas nos stratégies selon chaque situation?
6. Ne commençons-nous pas à gagner de l'argent?

*Activité 6*
1. a. On ne lance pas une bonne affaire?
   b. Si, on lance une bonne affaire.
2. a. On ne dirige pas l'entreprise d'une façon intelligente?
   b. Si, on dirige l'entreprise d'une façon intelligente.
3. a. On n'engage pas de bons travailleurs?
   b. Si, on engage de bons travailleurs.
4. a. On n'aménage pas les bureaux?
   b. Si, on aménage les bureaux.
5. a. On ne change pas nos stratégies selon chaque situation?
   b. Si, on change nos stratégies selon chaque situation.
6. a. On ne commence pas à gagner de l'argent?
   b. Si, on commence à gagner de l'argent.

*Activité 7*
1. —Claire n'arrive-t-elle pas ce matin? —Non, elle arrive ce soir.
2. —Marc et Geneviève ne sont-ils pas en classe? —Non, ils sont malades.
3. —Richard n'a-t-il pas sommeil? —Non, il a envie de sortir.
4. —Ma famille n'a-t-elle pas raison? —Non, ils ont / elle a tort.
5. —Ton frère et toi, ne prenez-vous pas le petit déjeuner à la maison? —Non, nous prenons un café à l'université.
6. —Lise ne suit-elle pas un régime? —Non, elle prend du poids.
7. —Vos parents ne sont-ils pas en colère? —Non, ils sont de bonne humeur.
8. —Christophe ne sort-il pas? —Non, il reste à la maison.

*Activité 8*
1. —Il n'a pas mal au dos? —Si, et il a mal aux jambes aussi.
2. —Il ne fait pas de vent? —Si, et il fait froid aussi.
3. —Toi, tu ne télécharges pas de chansons? —Si, et je télécharge des jeux vidéos aussi.
4. —Marianne ne joue pas du violon? —Si, et elle chante aussi.
5. —Ta sœur et toi, vous n'apprenez pas à parler chinois? —Si, et nous apprenons à l'écrire aussi.
6. —Moi, je ne peux pas assister à la conférence? —Si, et tu peux aller au concert aussi.

*Activité 9* Answers will vary.

### Chapitre 20

*Activité 1*
1. Quel vélo?
2. Quels CD?
3. Avec quelle raquette?
4. Quelle voiture?
5. Quelle carte?
6. Sur quelle moto?
7. Quelle chambre?
8. Quelles jumelles?
9. De quelle caméra?
10. De quel appareil-photo?

*Activité 2*
1. Quels billets a-t-elle pris?
2. Dans quel magasin sont-ils entrés?
3. De quelle disquette a-t-elle besoin?
4. Avec quel professeur ont-ils parlé?
5. À quel examen difficile a-t-il réussi?
6. Dans quelle classe a-t-il reçu une mauvaise note?
7. Quels médicaments ont-ils achetés?
8. Quelles émissions ont-ils regardées à la télé?

*Activité 3*
1. a. Quelle tragédie!
2. b. Quelle chance!
3. a. Quel malheur!
4. a. Quelle bêtise!
5. b. Quelle catastrophe!
6. a. Quelle générosité!
7. a. Quelle paresse!

*Activité 4*
1. Lequel? Celui-là?
2. Lesquelles? Celles-là?
3. Lequel? Celui-là?
4. Lesquelles? Celles-là?
5. Laquelle? Celle-là?
6. Lesquels? Ceux-là?
7. Lequel? Celui-là?

*Activité 5*
1. Lequel veux-tu/voulez-vous exactement?
2. Lesquelles met-elle exactement?
3. Lesquels lavez-vous exactement?
4. Desquelles as-tu/avez-vous besoin exactement?
5. Lesquels cherche-t-elle exactement?
6. Auxquels pensent-ils exactement?
7. Lequel prends-tu/prenez-vous exactement?

*Activité 6*
1. Laquelle? Ah, non. Celle-là n'est pas la mienne.
2. Lesquels? Ah, non. Ceux-là ne sont pas les miens.
3. Lequel? Ah, non. Celui-là n'est pas le sien.

4. Lesquels? Ah, non. Ceux-là ne sont pas les nôtres.
5. Lesquelles? Ah, non. Celles-là ne sont pas les leurs.
6. Laquelle? Ah, non. Celle-là n'est pas la mienne.
7. Lesquelles? Ah, non. Celles-là ne sont pas les nôtres.
8. Lesquelles? Ah, non. Celles-là ne sont pas les miennes.
9. Lequel? Ah, non. Celui-là n'est pas le mien.
10. Laquelle? Ah, non. Celle-là n'est pas la sienne.

*Activité 7*

1. Qui
2. Qu'est-ce que
3. Qu'est-ce que
4. Qu'est-ce qui
5. qui
6. quoi

*Activité 8*

1. c
2. a
3. d
4. b
5. d
6. c
7. a
8. b

*Activité 9*

1. Qu'ont-ils préparé?
2. Qui Marie a-t-elle vu?
3. Quand vos amis ont-ils loué cet appartement?
4. Quel logiciel recommandes-tu?
5. Dans quel hôtel Céline va-t-elle rester?
6. Pourquoi cet enfant pleure-t-il?
7. Combien ont-elles payé?

*Activité 10*

1. Elle habite où?
2. Elle arrive quand?
3. Jacqueline voyage avec qui?
4. Elle va rester combien de temps avec vous?
5. Jacqueline s'intéresse à quoi?
6. Elle aime quoi? / Elle aime quelle cuisine?
7. Elle aime faire quoi?
8. Jacqueline a besoin de quoi?

*Activité 11 Answers will vary.*

## Chapitre 21

*Activité 1*

1. Non, elle ne me téléphone jamais.
2. Non, je ne mange avec personne.
3. Non, je ne regarde jamais la télé.
4. Non, je ne travaille plus.
5. Non, personne n'organise d'activités pour les nouveaux étudiants.
6. Non, je n'aime rien ici.

*Activité 2*

1. Non, je ne suis plus seul.
2. Non, je ne suis jamais triste.
3. Non, je ne désire plus rentrer chez moi.
4. Non, personne ne dérange les étudiants quand ils travaillent.
5. Non, je ne trouve rien à critiquer.
6. Non, rien ne me fait peur maintenant.

*Activité 3*

1. Nous n'arrivons jamais en retard.
2. Nous n'interrompons jamais le professeur.
3. Nous n'oublions jamais nos devoirs.
4. Nous ne perdons jamais nos livres.
5. Nous n'applaudissons jamais après la classe.
6. Nous ne jetons jamais nos stylos en l'air.
7. Nous ne confondons jamais les rois de France dans la classe d'histoire.
8. Nous ne jouons jamais aux cartes en classe.

*Activité 4*

1. Les Dulac n'habitent plus l'immeuble en face.
2. M. Beauchamp ne vend plus sa poterie aux voisins.
3. Nous n'achetons plus le journal au kiosque du coin.
4. Ma mère ne descend plus faire les courses tous les jours.
5. Moi, je ne joue plus du piano.
6. Mme Duverger n'enseigne plus au lycée du quartier.
7. Nos amis ne passent plus beaucoup de temps dans le quartier.

*Activité 5*

1. Il n'explique aucun texte.
2. Il ne corrige aucune composition.
3. Il ne recommande aucun livre.
4. Il ne propose aucun thème de discussion.
5. Il ne présente aucune idée.
6. Il n'analyse aucun problème.

*Activité 6*

1. Il n'aime ni la physique ni la littérature.
2. Il ne finit ni ses devoirs ni ses compositions.
3. Il n'étudie ni à la bibliothèque ni à la maison.
4. Il ne réfléchit ni à son travail ni à son avenir.
5. Il ne demande des conseils ni à ses amis ni à ses professeurs.
6. Il n'écoute ni les conférences ni les discussions.

*Activité 7*

1. Je ne respecte que Philippe ici.
2. Je ne nettoie que ma chambre.
3. Je n'invite qu'Alice.
4. Elle n'apprécie que la littérature française.
5. Ils ne réfléchissent qu'à l'avenir.
6. Je ne téléphone qu'à Odile.
7. Je ne joue qu'au football.
8. Elle ne mange que des fruits et des légumes.

*Activité 8 Answers will vary.*

## Chapitre 22

*Activité 1*

1. Ne dis pas d'idioties! Personne ne te donnera un million d'euros.
2. Ne dis pas d'idioties! Aucune fille ne te croit le plus beau garçon de la classe.
3. Ne dis pas d'idioties! Tu n'as jamais cent à l'examen de philo.
4. Ne dis pas d'idioties! La femme du président de la République ne t'a rien envoyé.
5. Ne dis pas d'idioties! Ton père ne va t'offrir ni une voiture ni une moto.
6. Ne dis pas d'idioties! Il ne te reste plus l'argent que tu as reçu pour ton anniversaire.
7. Ne dis pas d'idioties! Tu ne connais personne à Casablanca.
8. Ne dis pas d'idioties! Tu ne connais personne à Rabat non plus.
9. Ne dis pas d'idioties! Tu n'iras nulle part avec Solange.
10. Ne dis pas d'idioties! On ne t'offrira rien d'autre si tu n'aimes pas tes cadeaux.

*Activité 2*

1. Personne n'apportera rien à manger.
2. Nous ne boirons rien.
3. Nous n'écouterons ni des cassettes ni des CD.
4. Jeanine n'a pas encore acheté de vin.
5. Olivier n'a aucun nouveau DVD.
6. Odile n'amène jamais personne d'intéressant.
7. Ces fêtes ne sont jamais amusantes.
8. Après la fête, nous n'irons nous promener nulle part.

*Activité 3*

1. Marc a donné le message à je ne sais qui.
2. Elle va parler avec je ne sais quel professeur.
3. Elles se sont mises en colère je ne sais pourquoi.
4. Le malade avait mangé je ne sais combien de gâteaux.
5. Il a réussi aux examens je ne sais comment.
6. Nos cousins arriveront je ne sais quand.

*Activité 4*

1. N'importe quoi.
2. N'importe où.
3. N'importe lequel.
4. N'importe quand.
5. À n'importe lequel.
6. N'importe combien.
7. N'importe comment.
8. À n'importe qui.

*Activité 5*

1. de
2. d'autre
3. Chaque
4. tout
5. toutes

*Activité 6*

1. b
2. a
3. b
4. a
5. b
6. a
7. a
8. a
9. b
10. b

*Activité 7*

1. b
2. a
3. a
4. b
5. b
6. a
7. b
8. b

# QUATRIÈME PARTIE

## Chapitre 23

*Activité 1*

1. à la une: *on the front page* / à la page: *up-to-date, in the know*
2. à plusieurs reprises: *several times* / à la fois: *at the same time*
3. à l'étroit: *crowded, short of space* / à la hauteur: *up to a task, capable of doing*
4. une bouteille à lait: *a milk bottle* / une tasse à thé: *a teacup*
5. au suivant: *Who's next?* / à suivre: *to be continued*

*Activité 2*

1. antonymes
2. synonymes
3. synonymes
4. synonymes
5. synonymes

*Activité 3*

1. a. à la une
   b. à main armée
2. a. à la folie
   b. à titre de père
3. a. à la perfection
   b. à moitié

*Activité 4*

1. de
2. de
3. à
4. à
5. de
6. Au
7. de
8. du
9. de

*Activité 5*

1. de suite: *in a row* / à suivre: *to be continued*
2. de hauteur: *in height* / à la hauteur: *up to the task*
3. à côté: *next door, close by* / de côté: *aside*
4. Il est au Japon.: *He's in Japan.* /Il est du Japon.: *He's from Japan.*
5. une corbeille à papier: *a wastepaper basket* / une corbeille de papier: *a wastepaper basket full of paper*
6. travailler de jour: *to work days* / travailler à la journée: *to work by the day, be paid by the day*

*Activité 6*

1. d'une tête
2. drôle d'idée
3. changer d'avis
4. faculté de médecine
5. de bonne heure
6. à fond
7. à deux pas
8. de
9. de toute sa vie

*Activité 7*

1. a
2. b
3. a
4. a
5. a
6. b
7. b
8. b
9. a

*Activité 8*

1. sans
2. avec
3. sans
4. Sans
5. Sans
6. Avec
7. avec
8. avec
9. sans

*Activité 9*

1. dans
2. dans
3. en
4. en
5. en
6. en
7. dans
8. en
9. en
10. dans
11. en
12. en
13. dans
14. en
15. en

*Activité 10*

1. J'en ai par-dessus la tête.
2. Jacques et Marie marchent bras dessus, bras dessous.
3. Ces étudiants sont en dessous de la moyenne.
4. Le détective est sur la bonne piste.
5. Nous avons acheté des pommes sur le marché.
6. J'aime me promener sous la pluie.
7. Je suis libre un samedi sur deux.
8. Il travaille sous une identité d'emprunt.
9. Elle pense que le travail est au-dessous d'elle.
10. Les enfants au-dessous de dix ans ne paient pas.
11. C'est au-dessus de mes forces.
12. Il a écrit un article sur la Tunisie.

*Activité 11*

1. Pour
2. pour
3. d'entre
4. par
5. par
6. pour
7. Par
8. Entre
9. par
10. entre
11. par
12. pour
13. par

*Activité 12*

1. *We'll see each other around six o'clock.*
2. *According to the doctor he is not out of danger.*
3. *You / We live better outside the city.*
4. *He was very generous to his children.*
5. *She looks out the window.*
6. *The teacher spoke about the test.*
7. *I have to go see my lawyer (at his office).*
8. *I'll give you these stamps for that coin.*

*Activité 13*

1. selon/d'après les journaux
2. pendant la classe
3. malgré la difficulté
4. près de la gare
5. quant à moi
6. trois voix contre deux

7. environ dix étudiants
8. hors jeu
9. à travers champs
10. chez les Français
11. avant de descendre
12. après être descendu(e)(s)

### Activité 14

1. Monique travaille au Canada, à Québec.
2. Olivier travaille aux États-Unis, à La Nouvelle-Orléans.
3. Mariek travaille au Japon, à Tokyo.
4. Fernand travaille au Brésil, à São Paulo.
5. Gérard travaille au Mexique, à Mexico.
6. Stella travaille à Haïti, à Port-au-Prince.
7. Luc travaille au Sénégal, à Dakar.
8. Brigitte travaille aux Pays-Bas, à Amsterdam.
9. Sylvie travaille en Égypte, au Caire.
10. Béatrice travaille au Portugal, à Lisbonne.
11. Jan travaille au Viêt Nam, à Hô Chi Minh-Ville.
12. Raymond travaille en Israël, à Jérusalem.

### Activité 15

1. Fatima est d'Irak.
2. Lise est de Bruxelles.
3. Martin et Santos sont du Chili.
4. Sven est du Danemark.
5. Rosa et Laura sont de Naples.
6. Mei-Li est de Chine.
7. Amalia est de Mexico.
8. Fred et Jane sont de Californie.
9. Kimberly est du Vermont.
10. Odile est du Luxembourg.
11. Corazon est des Philippines.
12. Mies est des Pays-Bas.
13. Hanako et Hiro sont du Japon.
14. Bill est des États-Unis.
15. Olivier est du Havre.

## CINQUIÈME PARTIE

### Chapitre 24

#### Activité 1

1. Moi, je ne veux pas qu'il fasse du japonais.
2. Moi, je ne veux pas qu'elle laisse les fenêtres ouvertes.
3. Moi, je ne veux pas qu'il sorte avec Hélène.
4. Moi, je ne veux pas qu'il boive du coca.
5. Moi, je ne veux pas que tu voies un vieux film.
6. Moi, je ne veux pas qu'il sache où j'habite.
7. Moi, je ne veux pas qu'elle soit triste.
8. Moi, je ne veux pas qu'ils aient peur.
9. Moi, je ne veux pas qu'il maigrisse.
10. Moi, je ne veux pas que tu grossisses.

#### Activité 2

1. Je prefère que Marc choisisse le gâteau.
2. Il est nécessaire que Lise et Rachelle aillent chercher les boissons.
3. Il est important que Roland et Jacqueline puissent venir.
4. Je veux que Janine fasse les amuse-gueules.
5. Il faut que tu fasses quelques coups de fil.
6. Il est essentiel qu'Olivier soit là.
7. Je préfère que nous achetions des plats préparés chez le charcutier.
8. Je veux que tu viennes m'aider samedi après-midi.

#### Activité 3

1. Le professeur exige que nous visitions tous les monuments de Paris.
2. Barbara souhaite que nous commencions par la visite du Louvre.
3. Martin désire que le groupe fasse le tour de Paris en bus.
4. Monique demande qu'on voie les Tuileries.
5. Georges recommande que tous les étudiants aillent à l'Arc de Triomphe.
6. Gustave suggère que nous montions à Montmartre.
7. Diane ordonne que tout le monde suive l'itinéraire.
8. Édouard aime mieux qu'on fasse une promenade dans le Marais.
9. Renée veut que nous prenions le déjeuner.
10. Véronique ne veut pas que nous passions toute la journée à discuter.

#### Activité 4

1. J'exige que tout soit en règle.
2. Je ne veux pas que les enfants aient peur.
3. Nous ne voulons pas que cette famille vive mal.
4. Ses parents empêcheront qu'il boive trop de coca.
5. Je recommande qu'il apprenne les réponses.
6. Je demande qu'ils conduisent prudemment.
7. Ses parents aiment mieux qu'elle rejoigne son fiancé.
8. Ses parents ne permettent pas qu'elle sorte avec Jean-Philippe.

#### Activité 5

1. Je suis contente qu'elles soient là.
2. Je suis contente qu'il vende son vélo.
3. Je suis contente qu'ils partent en vacances.
4. Je suis contente qu'il nous attende.
5. Je suis contente qu'il ne désobéisse jamais.
6. Je suis contente que vous dîniez ensemble.
7. Je suis contente que nous terminions le programme cette année.
8. Je suis contente qu'il connaisse Odile.

#### Activité 6

1. Je suis ravi que tu comprennes tout.
2. Nous sommes furieux qu'ils ne veuillent pas nous aider.
3. Il m'étonne que le prof ne nous reconnaisse pas.
4. J'ai peur qu'il y ait un accident.
5. Elle est navrée que tu ne puisses pas venir.
6. Je suis content qu'elle mette le foulard que je lui ai offert.
7. Son professeur se plaint que Philippe n'apprenne pas beaucoup.
8. Je suis fâchée que ces enfants se battent tout le temps.
9. C'est rare qu'un professeur perde son travail.
10. Il suffit que vous me le disiez.

#### Activité 7

1. Ma mère n'acceptera pas que je vive dans le désordre.
2. Il est essentiel que nous fassions le ménage.
3. Il faut que nous dépoussiérions les meubles.
4. Je suis content(e) que toi et Bernard, vous récuriez les casseroles.
5. Il convient que toi et moi, nous balayions le parquet.
6. Il est possible que nous cirions le parquet aussi.
7. Paul et Marc, il vaut mieux que vous rangiez les livres dans les bibliothèques.
8. Je me réjouis que Bernard enlève les toiles d'araignée.

#### Activité 8

1. Il est bizarre que tu n'étudies pas pour les examens.
2. Ça m'étonne que tu n'aies aucune envie de travailler à la bibliothèque.
3. Il vaut mieux que tu écrives la dissertation de philosophie.
4. Il est utile que tu écoutes les CD sur l'ordinateur.
5. Il est indispensable que tu prennes des notes dans la classe d'histoire.
6. Les profs seront fâchés que tu ne fasses pas tes devoirs.
7. Je regrette que tu ne lises plus le livre de biologie.
8. Je n'approuve pas que tu t'endormes dans la classe d'anglais.

9. Il n'est pas normal que tu fasses des dessins dans ton cahier dans la classe de maths.
10. Il est agaçant que tu perdes tes disquettes.

### Activité 9

1. Tu sais si notre professeur finira la leçon?
   Je ne crois pas qu'il finisse la leçon.
2. Tu sais si Ghislaine rompra avec son petit ami?
   Je ne crois pas qu'elle rompe avec son petit ami.
3. Tu sais si ton cousin reviendra cette semaine?
   Je ne crois pas qu'il revienne cette semaine.
4. Tu sais si Nadine servira une pizza à la fête?
   Je ne crois pas qu'elle serve une pizza à la fête.
5. Tu sais si Philippe sortira avec Mireille?
   Je ne crois pas qu'il sorte avec Mireille.
6. Tu sais si Paul pourra nous rejoindre?
   Je ne crois pas qu'il puisse nous rejoindre.
7. Tu sais si Alice sera là ce soir?
   Je ne crois pas qu'elle soit là ce soir.
8. Tu sais si toi et moi, nous étudierons assez?
   Je ne crois pas que nous étudiions assez.
9. Tu sais si Chloë ira au concert?
   Je ne crois pas qu'elle aille au concert.
10. Tu sais si Daniel prendra un taxi?
    Je ne crois pas qu'il prenne un taxi.

### Activité 10

1. Il n'est pas sûr que Laurence réussisse à tous ses examens.
2. Il est douteux que nous offrions des CD à Renée.
3. Il n'est pas exclu que tu suives un cours d'histoire.
4. Ça ne veut pas dire qu'il fasse des progrès en anglais.
5. Il est peu probable que Lucie t'écrive.
6. Je ne suis pas sûr qu'il nous reconnaisse.
7. Je doute que l'élève apprenne tout ça.
8. Il n'est pas clair que ce pays produise des voitures.

### Activité 11

1. Je ne pense pas que la voiture de Jean-François soit toujours en panne.
2. Il est évident que Gisèle compte (*indicatif*) abandonner ses études.
3. Je doute que Luc puisse s'acheter un ordinateur.
4. Tout le monde sait que Michèle sort avec Hervé Duclos.
5. Marc nie que Paul ne fasse pas attention en classe.
6. Il n'est pas exact que Chantal se plaigne de tout.
7. Je suis sûr que Martin étudie (*indicatif*) beaucoup.
8. Il est peu probable qu'Éliane aille en France cette année.

### Activité 12

1. J'ai peur que vous ne preniez froid.
2. Elle craint que nous ne soyons en colère.
3. Doutez-vous qu'il ne soit d'accord?
4. Elle empêche que nous ne finissions notre travail.

### Activité 13

1. Qu'elles l'apprennent alors.
2. Qu'il les rejoigne alors.
3. Qu'elle le fasse alors.
4. Qu'il le prenne alors.
5. Qu'ils la vendent alors.
6. Qu'elle nous le rende alors.
7. Qu'il le traduise alors.
8. Qu'il le finisse alors.

### Activité 14

1. a. Je crains qu'il ait pris une bronchite.
   b. Je doute qu'il soit allé voir le médecin.
2. a. J'ai peur que ma sœur (n')ait reçu une mauvaise note en français.
   b. Je ne crois pas qu'elle ait étudié pour l'examen.

c. Je soupçonne qu'elle ait eu des ennuis avec son petit ami.
d. Je n'approuve pas qu'elle ne nous ait pas montré son examen.
e. Ma mère se plaint que Sylvie ne nous en ait pas parlé.
3. a. Je suis furieuse que le prof d'histoire nous ait demandé une dissertation de quinze pages.
   b. C'est une chance qu'il ne nous en ait pas demandé deux!

### Activité 15

1. —Le prof est content que Jean-Yves ait répondu.
   —Ça ne veut pas dire qu'il ait compris.
2. —Je suis ravi qu'elle ait pu venir.
   —Mais il est agaçant que son mari ne soit pas venu avec elle.
3. —Colette se réjouit que son chef ait eu confiance en elle.
   —Il faut qu'elle ait fait un excellent travail.
4. —Ma mère regrette que ma sœur n'ait pas mis son nouveau pull.
   —Il est curieux que ce pull n'ait pas plu à ta sœur.
5. —Je suis surpris qu'Irène ne m'ait pas attendu.
   —Ça ne veut pas dire qu'elle soit sortie.

### Activité 16

1. a. Je suis content(e)/heureux(se) qu'ils partent.
   b. Je suis content(e)/heureux(se) qu'ils soient partis.
2. a. Je ne suis pas sûr(e) qu'elle suive un cours.
   b. Je ne suis pas sûr(e) qu'elle ait suivi un cours.
3. a. Je ne crois pas que le garçon lise le livre.
   b. Je ne crois pas que le garçon ait lu le livre.
4. a. Il est peu probable qu'ils soient en vacances.
   b. Il était peu probable qu'ils soient en vacances.
5. a. Nous sommes surpris / étonnés que les enfants ne se battent pas.
   b. Nous sommes surpris / étonnés que les enfants ne se soient pas battus.
6. a. Il doutait qu'elle soit gravement malade.
   b. Il doutait qu'elle ait été gravement malade.

*Activité 17 Answers will vary.*

## Chapitre 25

### Activité 1

1. J'attendrai jusqu'à ce que Marie-Claire m'appelle.
2. J'attendrai jusqu'à ce qu'Yvette vienne.
3. J'attendrai jusqu'à ce que le bus arrive pour me ramener.
4. J'attendrai jusqu'à ce que Robert revienne de la cabine téléphonique.
5. J'attendrai jusqu'à ce que vous vous en alliez.
6. J'attendrai jusqu'à ce que nous puissions vérifier où elles sont.
7. J'attendrai jusqu'à ce que nous sachions par quel moyen elles viennent.
8. J'attendrai jusqu'à ce que ma petite amie apparaisse sous mes yeux.

### Activité 2

1. Oui. Hélène sortira avec Nicolas à moins qu'elle soit occupée.
2. Oui. Jocelyne partira en Italie à moins que son père lui défende d'y aller.
3. Oui. Christophe t'expliquera la leçon à moins qu'il ne fasse pas attention en classe.
4. Oui. Michel veut inviter tous ses amis chez lui à moins que ses parents reviennent.
5. Oui. On peut aller chez les Laurentin à moins qu'ils aient des choses à faire.
6. Oui. Il faudra partir sans Jacqueline à moins qu'elle puisse se manifester d'ici cinq minutes.

7. Oui. Nous pouvons faire un pique-nique demain à moins qu'il fasse mauvais.

### Activité 3

1. Oui, pourvu que tu prennes le dessert avec nous.
2. Oui, pourvu que tu sois de retour avant minuit.
3. Oui, pourvu que ton frère puisse t'accompagner.
4. Oui, pourvu que tu mettes de l'ordre dans ta chambre.
5. Oui, pourvu que tu fasses les courses avant.
6. Oui, pourvu qu'elle ne vienne pas avant huit heures.
7. Oui, pourvu que ton père te le permette.
8. Oui, pourvu que nous puissions aller avec toi.

### Activité 4

1. Le médecin lui ordonne des antibiotiques pour qu'il se remette.
2. Sa mère a baissé les stores pour que François dorme.
3. Elle prépare une bonne soupe pour qu'il prenne quelque chose de chaud.
4. On lui donne trois couvertures pour qu'il n'ait pas froid.
5. Nous allons t'acheter un poste de télé pour que tu regardes des émissions en français.
6. On va te dessiner un petit plan du quartier pour que tu ne te perdes pas.
7. On te donne une carte avec notre numéro de téléphone pour que tu puisses nous appeler.
8. Nous allons inviter nos neveux et nos nièces pour que tu fasses leur connaissance.

### Activité 5

1. —Tu dois faire tes devoirs bien que tu sois fatigué.
2. —Tu dois descendre faire les courses bien qu'il fasse mauvais.
3. —Tu dois lire le livre de chimie bien que tu n'en aies pas envie.
4. —Tu dois téléphoner à Renée bien que vous soyez brouillés.
5. —Tu dois aller au cours bien que tu ne te sentes pas bien.
6. —Tu dois mettre une cravate bien que tu aies chaud.
7. —Tu dois écrire quelque chose bien que tu ne saches pas la réponse.
8. —Tu dois finir ta rédaction bien qu'il soit tard.

### Activité 6

1. Il entre doucement sans qu'on s'en aperçoive.
2. Cet étudiant copie sans que le professeur s'en rende compte.
3. Marc a eu des ennuis avec la police sans que ses parents soient au courant.
4. Il parle au téléphone sans que je puisse entendre ce qu'il dit.
5. Je te passerai un petit mot sans que le prof me voie.
6. Il est parti sans que nous le sachions.
7. Il est rentré sans que nous l'ayons vu.
8. Elle s'est fâchée sans que je lui aie rien dit.

### Activité 7

1. Je ne passerai pas à la blanchisserie jusqu'à ce que Louise descende au marché.
2. Marc ira à la pâtisserie pour que nous prenions un bon dessert ce soir.
3. Claire ira au kiosque du coin pourvu que nous l'accompagnions.

4. Je vais vite au pressing de peur qu'ils (ne) ferment pour le déjeuner.
5. Nous attendrons Chantal à la station-service jusqu'à ce qu'elle fasse le plein.
6. Philippe attendra à la station-service jusqu'à ce que le mécanicien change l'huile.
7. Nous regarderons l'étalage de la librairie en attendant que Jean sorte de la boutique du coiffeur.
8. Odile veut passer à la pharmacie à moins que vous (ne) soyez pressés pour rentrer.

### Activité 8

1. Toi, tu veux un appartement qui ait deux salles de bains.
2. Mathieu a besoin d'un appartement qui soit climatisé.
3. Philippe et moi, nous préférons un appartement qui soit près de la faculté.
4. Nous voulons un appartement qui n'ait pas besoin de beaucoup de rénovation.
5. Moi, je cherche un appartement qui ait le confort moderne.
6. Charles désire un appartement qui se trouve dans un immeuble neuf.
7. Mathieu et Philippe cherchent un appartement qui soit en face de l'arrêt de bus.
8. Nous cherchons un voisin qui ne se plaigne pas des fêtes.

### Activité 9

| | |
|---|---|
| 1. puisse | 4. ait |
| 2. comprenne | 5. dise |
| 3. soit | 6. fasse |

### Activité 10

| | |
|---|---|
| 1. sait | 5. puisse |
| 2. sache | 6. soit |
| 3. connaisse | 7. ont |
| 4. ait | 8. soit |

### Activité 11

1. C'est la plus belle fille que je connaisse.
2. C'est le cours le plus ennuyeux que je suive.
3. C'est le compte rendu le plus intéressant que Marc écrive.
4. C'est le village le plus joli que vous visitiez.
5. C'est le premier patient qui vienne au cabinet du dentiste.
6. Vous êtes la seule étudiante qui fasse du chinois.
7. C'est la dernière employée qui s'en aille du bureau.
8. C'est le pire repas qu'on ait servi à la cantine.
9. C'est le meilleur restaurant que nous fréquentions.
10. C'est le plus beau tableau que tu aies peint.
11. C'est le loyer le plus élevé que j'aie payé.
12. Tu es le seul ami qui me comprenne.

### Activité 12

1. *Whoever she may be, she doesn't have the right to go in.*
2. *However rich they may have become, they cannot forget the poverty of their youth.*
3. *However gifted you may be, you must study.*
4. *He was planning to offer us (just about) anything.*
5. *I will never forgive him, whatever he says (no matter what he says).*
6. *This candidate accepts money from (just about) anyone.*
7. *Whatever the sum offered may be, it will never be enough.*
8. *Wherever you go, you will find the same problems.*

# LEXIQUE

This end vocabulary provides contextual meanings of French words used in this text. It includes place names and all cognate nouns (to indicate gender), most abbreviations, and regular past participles used as adjectives. Adjectives are listed in the masculine forms, with the feminine forms in parentheses. Verbs are listed in their infinitive forms; irregular forms of the verbs and irregular past participles are listed in parentheses. An asterisk (*) indicates words beginning with an aspirate *h* (an *h* that is treated like a consonant). A dagger (†) indicates verbs that are conjugated with **être** in compound tenses; a double dagger (‡) indicates verbs that can be conjugated with both **être** or **avoir** in compound tenses, depending on the context.

## Abbreviations

| | | | |
|---|---|---|---|
| *adj.* | adjective | *m.* | masculine |
| *adv.* | adverb | *n.* | noun |
| *art.* | article | *o.s.* | oneself |
| *conj.* | conjunction | *pl.* | plural |
| *f.* | feminine | *p.p.* | past participle |
| *fam.* | familiar | *prep.* | preposition |
| *gram.* | grammatical term | *pron.* | pronoun |
| *impers.* | impersonal verb | *Q.* | Quebec usage |
| *indic.* | indicative mood | *qch.* | **quelque chose** |
| *inf.* | infinitive | *qn.* | **quelqu'un** |
| *interj.* | interjection | *s.* | singular |
| *interr.* | interrogative | *s.o.* | someone |
| *inv.* | invariable | *s.th.* | something |
| *irreg.* | irregular | *subj.* | subjunctive mood |

## A

**abandonner** to abandon; give up
**abord: d'abord** *adv.* first, first of all, at first
**abri** *m.* shelter; **sans-abri** homeless
**absence** *f.* absence, lack; **en l'absence de** in the absence of
**s'absenter (de)** to be absent (from), be away (from)
**absolu(e)** *adj.* absolute
**s'abstenir (de)** *irreg.* (**je m'abstiens**; *p.p.* **abstenu**) to refrain (from)
**abuser (de)** to abuse
**accablé(e) (de)** *adj.* overwhelmed (by/with)
**accent** *m.* accent; *gram.* **accent aigu (circonflexe, grave)** acute [é] (circumflex [ê], grave [è]) accent
**accepter** to accept; **accepter de** to agree to
**accessoire** *m.* accessory
**accident** *m.* accident
**accompagner** to accompany, go along, go with
**accompli(e)** *adj.* accomplished
**accord** *m.* agreement; **d'accord** *interj.* all right; **être d'accord** to agree; *gram.* agreement
**accorder** to grant, give; **s'accorder** *gram.* to agree
**accrocher** to hang, hang up
**accueillir** *irreg.* (**j'accueille**) to welcome

**accuser** to accuse
**acheter (j'achète)** to buy
**acier** *m.* steel; **acier inoxidable** stainless steel
**acquérir** *irreg.* (*p.p.* **acquis**) to acquire, purchase
**acteur/trice** *m., f.* actor, actress
**actif/ive** *adj.* active
**action** *f.* action
**activité** *f.* activity
**actualité** *f.* current events; **suivre l'actualité** to keep up with the news
**actuel(le)** *adj.* present, current
**actuellement** *adv.* at the moment
**adjectif** *m., gram.* adjective
**admettre** *irreg.* (*p.p.* **admis**) to admit
**administratif/ve** *adj.* administrative
**administration** *f.* administration
**admirer** to admire
**adorer** to love, adore
**adresse** *f.* address
**s'adresser à** to speak to (*s.o.*)
**adverbe** *m.* adverb
**affaire** *f.* affair, business, matter; **affaires** *pl.* things, personal possessions; **bonne affaire** good deal; **quartier des affaires** business district; **voyager pour affaires** to travel on business
**affiche** *f.* poster

affirmatif/ve *adj.* affirmative
affreusement *adv.* dreadfully
affreux/euse *adj.* horrible; dreadful
Afghanistan *m.* Afghanistan
afin que *conj.* + *subj.* so that, in order that
Afrique *f.* Africa
agaçant(e) *adj.* irritating
agacer (nous agaçons) to annoy
âge *m.* age; **d'un certain âge** older (*over fifty*); **quel âge avez-vous?** how old are you?
âgé(e) *adj.* old; elderly
agence *f.* agency; **agence de voyages** travel agency; **agence immobilière** real estate agency
agenda *m.* engagement book
agent *m.* agent; **agent de police** police officer; *gram.* agent
agir to act; to work (*medicines*); **il s'agit de** *impers.* it's about, it's a question of
agneau *m.* lamb; **côtelette d'agneau** lamb chop
agréable *adj.* pleasant, nice
agriculture *f.* agriculture
ah *interj.* oh
aide *f.* help, assistance; **avoir besoin d'aide** to need help
aider to help
aigu (aigüe) *adj.* acute; *gram.* **accent** (*m.*) **aigu** acute accent (é)
ail *m.* garlic
ailleurs *adv.* elsewhere, somewhere else
aimable *adj.* friendly, likable
aimer to like; to love; **aimer à la folie** to be crazy about (*s.o.*); **aimer bien** to like; **aimer mieux** to prefer; **Qui aime bien, châtie bien.** Spare the rod, spoil the child.
aîné(e) *adj.* older, elder
ainsi *conj.* thus
air *m.* air; look; **avoir l'air (d'un[e])** to look (like a); **d'un air indécis** indecisively; **en l'air** up in the air; **en plein air** outdoor(s)
ajouter to add
Allemagne *f.* Germany
allemand(e) *adj.* German; *m.* German (*language*); **Allemand(e)** *m., f.* German (*person*)
†aller *irreg.* (je vais) to go; **aller** + *inf.* to be going (*to do s.th.*); **aller à bicyclette** to ride a bicycle; **aller à pied** to walk; **aller bien** to feel well; **aller pieds nus** to walk barefoot; **s'en aller** to go away, leave
allergie *f.* allergy; **souffrir d'allergies** suffer from allergies
allié(e) *m., f.* ally; **la victoire des alliés** Allied victory
allumer to light; turn on (*appliance*)
allusion *f.* allusion; **faire allusion à** to allude, refer to
alors *adv.* so; then, in that case
Alpes (les) *f. pl.* the Alps
alpinisme *m.* mountaineering, climbing
alsacien(ne) *adj.* Alsatian; *m.* Alsatian (*language*); **Alsacien(ne)** *m., f.* Alsatian (*person*)
ambassade *f.* embassy
ambassadeur/drice *m., f.* ambassador
ambiance *f.* atmosphere, surroundings
ambigu(ë) *adj.* ambiguous
améliorer to improve
aménager (nous aménageons) to move in (*house*); to fix up, convert (*room, etc.*)

amende *f.* fine
amener (j'amène) to bring (*s.o.*)
amer (amère) *adj.* bitter
amèrement *adv.* bitterly
américain(e) *adj.* American; **Américain(e)** *m., f.* American (*person*)
Amérique *f.* America
amertume *f.* bitterness
ami(e) *m., f.* friend; **entre amis** among friends; **parents et amis** friends and family; **petit(e) ami(e)** *m., f.* boyfriend, girlfriend
amicalement *adv.* cordially
amitié *f.* friendship; **par amitié** out of friendship; **toutes mes amitiés** my best wishes
amour *m.* love; **par amour** out of love
amoureux/euse (de) *adj.* in love (with)
amphithéâtre *m.* (*fam.* **amphi**) lecture hall, amphitheater
amusant(e) *adj.* amusing, fun, funny
amuse-gueule *m. inv.* appetizer, snack
s'amuser to enjoy o.s., have fun
an *m.* year; **jour** (*m.*) **de l'an** New Year's Day
analyser to analyse
ancêtre *m., f.* ancestor
ancien(ne) *adj.* ancient; former, old
anglais(e) *adj.* English; *m.* English (*language*); **Anglais(e)** *m., f.* English (*person*)
angle *m.* angle; **sous tous les angles** from all angles, from all points of view
Angleterre *f.* England
anglophone *adj.* English-speaking; *m., f.* English speaker
animal *m.* animal
animateur/trice *m., f.* group leader
animé(e) *adj.* animated, lively
s'animer to liven up
année *f.* year
anniversaire *m.* anniversary; birthday
annonce *f.* ad
annoncer (nous annonçons) to announce, tell
annuaire *m.* phone book
anorak *m.* anorak, waterproof winter jacket
antécédent *m., gram.* antecedent
antérieur(e) *adj.*: **futur antérieur** future perfect
antibiotique *m.* antibiotic
Antilles (les) *f. pl.* the West Indies, French-speaking islands in the Caribbean
antonyme *m.* antonym
août *m.* August
apercevoir *irreg.* (j'aperçois, *p.p.* aperçu) to see; **s'apercevoir de** to notice
apparaître *irreg.* (j'apparais; *p.p.* apparu) to appear
appareil *m.*: **à l'appareil** on the phone, speaking; **appareil photo** camera
appartement *m.* apartment
appartenir à *irreg.* (j'appartiens, *p.p.* appartenu) to belong to
appeler (j'appelle) to call; **s'appeler** to be called, named
applaudir to applaud
application *f.* application
s'appliquer to apply o.s.
apporter to bring
apprécier to appreciate, value, rate highly
apprendre *irreg.* (nous apprenons; *p.p.* appris) to learn; **apprendre à** to learn how to; to teach

s'approcher (de) to approach
approprié(e) *adj.* appropriate, suitable
approuver to approve; to agree with
appuyer (j'appuie) to support; (s')appuyer contre to lean against
après *prep.* after; afterwards
après-demain *adv.* the day after tomorrow
après-midi *m.* afternoon
arabe *adj.* Arab; Arabe *m., f.* Arab (*person*); *m.* Arabic (*language*)
Arabie (*f.*) saoudite Saudi Arabia
araignée *f.* spider; toile (*f.*) d'araignée spiderweb
arbre *m.* tree
arc *m.* arch
architecte *m., f.* architect
architecture *f.* architecture
argent *m.* money; gagner de l'argent to earn money
Argentine *f.* Argentina
armé(e) *adj.* armed; vol (*m.*) à main armée armed robbery
arracher to pull up; arracher (qch à qn) to snatch
arranger (nous arrangeons) to arrange
arrêt *m.* stop; arrêt d'autobus bus stop
arrêter to stop; s'arrêter court to stop short
arrière *adv.* back; en arrière behind
arrivée *f.* arrival
†arriver to arrive; arriver en avance (en retard, à l'heure) to be early, late, on time; arriver à to manage to
arrondissement *m.* district
art *m.* art; œuvre d'art *f.* work of art
article *m.* article
artiste *m., f.* artist
Asie *f.* Asia
aspect *m.* aspect
asperge *f.* asparagus
aspirateur *m.* vacuum cleaner; passer l'aspirateur to vacuum
aspirine *f.* aspirin
asseoir *irreg.* (*p.p.* assis) to seat; s'asseoir to sit down
assez (de) *adv.* enough
assiette *f.* plate
assister à to attend, go to (*event*)
assurer to assure; to guarantee
atelier *m.* workshop
attaquer to attack
atteindre *irreg.* (j'atteins, nous atteignons; *p.p.* atteint) to reach; attain
attendre to wait (for); attendre que + *subj.* to wait until; s'attendre à (ce que + *subj.*) to expect to
attentif/ve *adj.* attentive
attention *f.* attention; faire attention (à) to watch out (for), pay attention
atterrir to land (*plane*)
attirer to attract
attitude *f.* attitude
attraction *f.* attraction
attraper to catch
auberge *f.* inn
aucun(e) (ne... aucun[e]) *adj.* no, not any; *pron.* not one, none; sans aucun doute without a doubt
augmentation *f.* raise, increase

augmenter to raise, increase
aujourd'hui *adv.* today
auparavant *adv.* previously, beforehand
auprès de *prep.* with, to
aussi *adv.* also, as well; aussi... que as . . . as; moi aussi me too
aussitôt *adv.* immediately, at once; aussitôt que *conj.* as soon as
Australie *f.* Australia
autant (que) *adv.* as much (as); autant de... que as much/many . . . as
auteur *m., f.* author
autobus *m.* (city) bus; arrêt d'autobus bus stop; en autobus by bus
autocar *m.* coach, (interurban) bus; en autocar by bus
automne *m.* autumn, fall; en automne in the fall
automobile *f.* automobile, car
autoriser (à) to authorise (to)
autoroute *f.* highway, freeway
autour (de) *prep.* around
autre *adj.* other, different; *pron.* another, other; d'autre part on the other hand; personne d'autre nobody else; quelque chose d'autre something else; quelqu'un d'autre somebody else; quoi d'autre? what else?; rien d'autre nothing else; vivre les uns sur les autres to live on top of one another
autrefois *adv.* formerly, in the past
Autriche *f.* Austria
Auvergne *f.* Auvergne
auxiliaire *m.* auxiliary
avaler to swallow
avance *f.* advance; être en avance to be early
avancer (nous avançons) to advance
avant *adv., prep.* before; avant de + *inf.*; avant que *conj.* + *subj.*; avant-hier the day before yesterday; en avant in front
avantage *m.* advantage
avenir *m.* future; à l'avenir from now on, in the future
aventure *f.* adventure
avenue *f.* avenue
avertir to warn
aveugle *adj., m., f.* blind
aveuglément *adv.* blindly
aviateur/trice *m., f.* aviator, pilot
avion *m.* airplane; en avion by plane
avis *m.* opinion; changer d'avis to change one's mind
avocat(e) *m., f.* lawyer
avoir *irreg.* (*p.p.* eu) to have; avoir à to have to; avoir l'air (d'un[e]) to look (like a); avoir beau to do something in vain; avoir besoin de to need; avoir de la chance to be lucky; avoir chaud to be hot; avoir confiance en to trust (*s.o.*); avoir faim to be hungry; avoir envie de to feel like; avoir fini to be finished; avoir froid to be cold; avoir honte (de) to be ashamed (of); avoir l'intention de to intend to; avoir mal à la tête to have a headache; avoir mal au cœur to feel nauseous; avoir peur (de) to be afraid (of); avoir raison (de) to be right (to); avoir soif to be thirsty; avoir tort (de) to be wrong (to); avoir 20 ans to be 20 years old; *impers.* il y a there is/are
avril *m.* April

# B

**bagages** *m. pl.* luggage
**se baigner** to bathe (*o.s.*); to swim
**bain** *m.* bath; **maillot de bain** swimsuit; **salle de bains** bathroom
**baisser** to lower; to go down
**bal** *m.* bal
**balayer (je balaie)** to sweep
**balcon** *m.* balcony
**banal(e)** *adj.* banal, ordinary
**banc** *m.* bench
**bande** *f.* strip; **bande dessinée** comic strip
**banlieue** *f.* suburbs
**banque** *f.* bank
**banquier/ère** *m., f.* banker
**bas(se)** *adj.* low; **en bas** downstairs, down below; **là-bas** over there; **parler tout bas** to speak in a low voice; **les Pays-Bas** the Netherlands
**base** *f.* base
**base-ball** *m.* baseball
**bateau** *m.* boat; **en bateau** by boat
**bâtiment** *m.* building
**bâtir** to build
**battre** *irreg.* (*p.p.* **battu**) to beat, strike, hit; **se battre** to fight
**bavard(e)** *adj.* talkative
**bavarder** to chat
**beau (bel, belle, beaux, belles)** *adj.* beautiful, nice; **avoir beau** + *inf.* to do (*s.th.*) in vain; **beaux-parents** parents in-law; **à la belle étoile** under the stars; **il fait beau** it's nice outside
**bébé** *m.* baby
**Belgique** *f.* Belgium
**besoin** *m.* need; **avoir besoin de** to need
**bête** *f.* beast; *adj.* silly, idiotic
**bêtise** *f.* foolishness
**beurre** *m.* butter
**bibliothèque** *f.* library; bookcase
**bicyclette** *f.* bicycle; **aller à bicyclette** to ride a bicycle
**bien** *adv.* well; **aimer bien** to like; **aller bien** to feel well; **aller bien à** to look good on (*s.o.*); **aller bien avec** to go well with; **bien de** a lot of, many; **bien en vue** prominent; **bien que** *conj.* + *subj.* even though; **être bien** to be nice looking; **Qui aime bien, châtie bien.** Spare the rod, spoil the child; **Rira bien qui rira le dernier.** He who laughs last laughs best.
**bientôt** *adv.* soon
**bière** *f.* beer
**bifteck** *m.* steak
**bijou** *m.* (*pl.* **bijoux**) jewel
**bilingue** *adj.* bilingual
**billet** *m.* ticket; **billet de faveur** complimentary ticket
**biologie** *f.* biology
**bistrot** *m.* pub, bar
**bizarre** *adj.* strange, peculiar; **il est bizarre que** + *subj.* it's strange that
**blagueur/euse** *m., f.* joker
**blanc(he)** *adj.* white
**blanc** *m.* blank; **de but en blanc** point-blank
**blanchisserie** *f.* laundromat

**blessé(e)** *adj.* hurt, wounded
**bleu(e)** *adj.* blue
**blouson** *m.* jacket
**bœuf** *m.* beef; ox
**boire** *irreg.* (**nous buvons**, *p.p.* **bu**) to drink
**bois** *m.* wood; **caisse** (*f.*) **en bois** wooden box
**boisson** *f.* drink
**boîte** *f.* box; nightclub
**boiter** to limp; to wobble (*furniture*)
**bol** *m.* bowl
**bon(ne)** *adj.* good; **à quoi bon?** what is the use? **bonne affaire** good deal; **de bon matin** early in the morning; **de bonne heure** early; **de bonne humeur** in a good mood; **en bonne santé** in good health; **d'un bon pas** at a good pace; **sur la bonne piste** on the right track
**bonbon** *m.* candy
**bonjour** *interj.* hello, good day
**bonnet** *m.* hat
**bord** *m.* side, edge; **le bord de la mer** the seashore; **le bord de la rue** the side of the street
**Bosnie** *f.* Bosnia
**botte** *f.* boot
**boucher/ère** *m., f.* butcher
**boucherie** *f.* butcher shop
**boulangerie** *f.* bakery
**boulevard** *m.* boulevard
**boum** *f.* party
**bouquin** *m.* book
**bouquiniste** *m., f.* secondhand bookseller
**Bourgogne** *f.* Burgundy
**bourse** (*f.*) **d'études** grant, scholarship
**bouteille** *f.* bottle
**boutique** *f.* shop, store
**branché(e)** *adj., fam.* with it
**brancher** to plug in
**bras** *m.* arm; **bras dessus, bras dessous** arm in arm
**brave** *adj.* brave, courageous
**bref (brève)** *adj.* brief
**Brésil** *m.* Brazil
**Bretagne** *f.* Brittany
**breton(ne)** *adj.* Breton; *m.* Breton (*language*); **Breton(ne)** *m., f.* Breton (*person*)
**bricoler** to fix things, tinker
**brièvement** *adv.* briefly
**brillance** *f.* brilliance
**brillant(e)** *adj.* shiny; brilliant
**brique** *f.* brick
**brochure** *f.* brochure
**broncher** to stumble; **sans broncher** without flinching
**bronchite** *f.* bronchitis
**se brosser (les cheveux, les dents)** to brush (one's hair, one's teeth)
**brouillé(e)** *adj.*: **être brouillé avec** to be on bad terms with (*s.o.*)
**se brouiller (avec qn)** to fall out (with s.o.)
**bruit** *m.* noise
**brûler (de)** to be dying, very eager (to)
**brun(e)** *adj.* brown; dark-haired
**brusquement** *adv.* abruptly, bluntly
**brute** *f.* brute, bully
**bureau** *m.* office
**bus** *m.* (city) bus
**but** *m.* objective; **de but en blanc** point-blank

**ça** *pron., fam.* this, that; it; **ça fait... que** it has been . . . that (*time*); **ça se dit** one can say that; **ça veut dire** it means; **ça va mieux** things are going better; **c'est pour ça** that's why; **c'est quoi ça?** what is that?

**cabaret** *m.* nightclub

**cabine** *f.*: **cabine téléphonique** phone booth

**cabinet** *m.*: **cabinet du médecin/dentiste** doctor's/dentist's office

**cacher** to hide; **se cacher** to hide o.s.

**cadavre** *m.* cadaver

**cadeau** *m.* gift

**cadet(te)** *adj.* younger, youngest; *m., f.* the youngest child

**cadre** *m.* frame

**cafard** *m.*: **donner le cafard à** to depress, get (*s.o.*) down

**café** *m.* coffee; coffeehouse, café

**cahier** *m.* workbook; notebook

**Caire (Le)** *m.* Cairo (*Egypt*)

**caisse** *f.* crate, box

**calculatrice** *f.* calculator

**calculer** to calculate

**calculette** *f.* (pocket) calculator

**calendrier** *m.* calendar

**Californie** *f.* California

**calme** *m.* calm, peacefulness

**calmement** *adv.* calmly

**se calmer** to calm down

**camarade** *m., f.* friend; **camarade de classe** classmate

**Cambodge** *m.* Cambodia

**caméra** *f.* video camera

**camion** *m.* truck

**camp** *m.* camp; **feu** (*m.*) **de camp** campfire

**campagne** *f.* country, countryside; campaign (*politics*)

**camper** to camp

**camping** *m.* camping; **faire du camping** to go camping

**Canada** *m.* Canada

**canadien(ne)** *adj.* Canadian; **Canadien(ne)** *m., f.* Canadian (*person*)

**canard** *m.* duck

**candidat(e)** *m., f.* candidate; applicant; **se porter candidat à** to apply for

**cantine** *f.* canteen

**capable** *adj.* able

**capitale** *f.* capital (*city*)

**car** *m.* bus; van

**caractère** *m.* character; **caractère gras** boldface

**caractéristique** *f.* characteristic, feature

**caravane** *f.* caravan, trailer

**cargaison** *f.* cargo, freight

**carnaval** *m.* carnival

**carnet** *m.* notebook; **se vendre en carnets de dix** can be bought in books of ten tickets

**carreau** *m.* pane; **faire les carreaux** to wash the windows

**carte** *f.* card; map; menu; **carte de crédit** credit card; **carte postale** postcard

**cas** *m.* case; **en tout cas** in any case; **selon le cas** as the case may be

**casser** to break

**casserole** *f.* saucepan

**cassette** *f.* cassette

**catastrophe** *f.* catastrophe, disaster

**cathédrale** *f.* cathedral

**catholique** *adj., m., f.* Catholic

**causatif/ve** *adj.* causal

**cause** *f.* cause; **à cause de** because of; **et pour cause** for good reason

**causer** to chat, talk

**CD** *m. inv.* compact disc

**CD-ROM** *m. inv.* CD-ROM

**ce (cet, cette, ces)** *adj.* this, that, these, those

**ceci** *pron.* this, that; **à ceci près** with this exception

**céder (je cède)** to yield

**cédille** *f.* cedilla (ç)

**cela (ça)** *pron.* this, that

**célébration** *f.* celebration

**célèbre** *adj.* famous

**célébrer (je célèbre)** to celebrate

**céleste** *adj.* celestial, heavenly

**celui (celle, ceux, celles)** *pron.* the one, the ones; this one, that one; these, those

**cent** *adj.* one hundred

**centaine** *f.* a hundred or so; **des centaines** hundreds (of)

**centimètre** *m.* centimeter

**central(e)** *adj.* central; **gare** (*f.*) **centrale** central station

**centre** *m.* center; **centre de la ville** city center; **centre diététique** health food store

**cérémonie** *f.* ceremony; **sans cérémonie** informally

**certain(e)** *adj.* certain, sure; some; **il est certain que** + *indic.* **une personne d'un certain âge** older (*over fifty*)

**certainement** *adv.* certainly

**cesser** to stop

**chacun(e)** *pron.* each one, everyone; **chacun pour soi** every man for himself

**chaise** *f.* chair

**chaleur** *f.* heat

**chambre** *f.* room; **chambre à coucher** bedroom

**champ** *m.* field; **à travers champs** across fields

**champignon** *m.* mushroom

**champion(ne)** *m., f.* champion

**chance** *f.* luck; **avoir de la chance** to be lucky

**changement** *m.* change

**changer (nous changeons)** to change

**chanson** *f.* song

**chanter** to sing; **chanter faux** to sing off-key

**chapeau** *m.* hat

**chaque** *adj.* each, every

**charcuterie** *f.* delicatessen

**charcutier/ère** *m., f.* pork butcher, delicatessen owner

**se charger (nous nous chargeons) de** to take care, charge of

**charmant(e)** *adj.* charming

**charme** *m.* charm

**chasser** to drive away

**chasseur** *m.* bellboy (*hotel*)

**château** *m.* castle, chateau

**châtier** to punish; **Qui aime bien, châtie bien.** Spare the rod, spoil the child.

**chaud(e)** *adj.* hot; **avoir chaud** to be hot; **faire chaud** to be hot (*weather*)

**chaussée** *f.* road, roadway

**chaussette** *f.* sock

**chaussure** *f.* shoe

**chef** *m.* boss; leader

**chef-lieu** *m.* county seat

**chemin** *m.* road, path; **chemin de fer** railroad; **chemin faisant** on the way

**cheminée** *f.* chimney

**chemise** *f.* shirt; **chemise à manches longues** long-sleeve shirt

**chemisier** *m.* blouse

**chêne** *m.* oak tree

**chèque** *m.* check

**cher (chère)** *adj.* expensive; dear; **acheter (vendre) cher** to buy (sell) at a high price; **coûter cher** to cost a lot; **payer cher** to pay a high price

**chercher** to look for; **chercher à** to try to

**chéri(e)** *m., f.* dear, honey

**cheval** *m.* horse

**cheveu** *m.* hair; **se brosser (se couper, se laver, se sécher) les cheveux** to brush (cut, wash, dry) one's hair

**cheville** *f.* ankle; **se fouler la cheville** to sprain one's ankle

**chez** *prep.*: **chez moi** at my home; **chez le médecin** at the doctor's office

**chic** *adj. inv.* chic, stylish

**chien(ne)** *m., f.* dog; **temps** (*m.*) **de chien** foul weather; **entre chien et loup** at dusk

**chiffre** *m.* numeral

**Chili** *m.* Chile

**chimie** *f.* chemistry

**Chine** *f.* China

**chinois(e)** *adj.* Chinese; *m.* Chinese (*language*); **Chinois(e)** *m., f.* Chinese (*person*)

**chocolat** *m.* chocolate

**choisir** to choose

**choix** *m.* choice

**chose** *f.* thing; **quelque chose** *pron. indef.* something

**chou** *m.* (*pl.* **choux**) cabbage

**chrysanthème** *m.* chrysanthemum

**ciel** *m.* (*pl.* **cieux**) sky; heavens

**cinéma** *m.* movie theater; **vedette** (*f.*) **de cinéma** movie star

**cinquante** *adj.* fifty

**circonflexe** *m.* circumflex; *gram.* **accent circonflexe** circumflex accent (ê)

**circonstances** *f. pl.* circumstances

**cirer** to wax; **cirer le parquet** to wax the floor

**ciseaux** *m. pl.* scissors

**cité** *f.*: **Cité des sciences et de l'industrie** Museum of Science and Industry

**citoyen(ne)** *m., f.* citizen

**citron** *m.* lemon

**civique** *adj.* civic

**clair(e)** *adj.* clear; light (*color*); **voir clair** to see clearly

**clarinette** *f.* clarinet

**clarinettiste** *m., f.* clarinettist

**classe** *f.* class; classroom; **de première classe** first-rate; **en première classe** in first class

**classique** *adj.* classical

**clavier** *m.* keyboard

**clé (clef)** *f.* key; **mot clef** keyword

**client(e)** *m., f.* client; customer

**climatisation** *f.* air conditioning

**climatisé(e)** *adj.* with air conditioning

**cliquer** to click

**cloche** *f.* bell

**clôture** *f.* fence

**clou** *m.* nail

**clown** *m.* clown

**club** *m.* club

**coca** *m.* Coca Cola

**cœur** *m.* heart; **par cœur** by heart

**coiffeur/euse** *m., f.* hairdresser

**coin** *m.* corner; **du coin** local

**colère** *f.* anger; **être en colère** to be angry; **se mettre en colère** to get angry

**collants** *m.* tights

**collection** *f.* collection

**collège** *m.* middle school

**collègue** *m., f.* colleague

**collier** *m.* necklace

**colocataire** *m., f.* roommate, housemate

**Colombie** *f.* Colombia

**colonie** *f.*: **colonie de vacances** summer camp

**combat** *m.* fight, fighting

**combattant(e)** *m., f.*: **anciens combattants** war veterans

**combattre** *irreg.* (*p.p.* **combattu**) to fight, combat

**combien (de)** *adv.* how much/many; **depuis combien de temps** + *pres.* ? how long + *pres. perf. progr.*?

**comédie** *f.* comedy

**comité** *m.* committee

**commande** *f.* order; **passer une commande** to place an order

**commander** to order, command

**comme** *adv.* as, like; how; **comme il faut** properly; **comme c'est bizarre!** how strange!; **comme dessert** for dessert

**commémorer** to commemorate

**commencement** *m.* beginning

**commencer (nous commençons)** to begin

**comment** *adv.* how; what; **n'importe comment** anyhow; **je ne sais comment** somehow

**commerçant(e)** *m., f.* shopkeeper; merchant

**commerce** *m.* trade, commerce, business; **représentant** (*m.*) **de commerce** traveling salesperson

**commercial(e)** *adj.* commercial, trading

**commun(e)** *adj.* common; **en commun** in common

**communément** *adv.* commonly

**communion** *f.* communion

**communiquer** to communicate, convey

**communisme** *m.* communism

**compact(e)** *adj.* compact; **disque compact** compact disc

**compagnie** *f.* company

**comparaison** *f.* comparison

**comparatif** *m., gram.* comparative

**comparé(e)** *adj.*: **littérature** (*f.*) **comparée** comparative literature

**comparer** to compare

**compétent(e)** *adj.*: **d'une façon compétente** competently

**complément** *m., gram.* object; **complément d'objet direct (indirect)** direct (indirect) object

**complet/ète** *adj.* complete

**complètement** *adv.* completely

**compléter (je complète)** to complete

**compliment** *m.* compliment

**compliqué(e)** *adj.* complicated

**se comporter** to behave

**composé(e)** *adj.* compound; **passé composé** past tense (*compound*)

**composition** *f.* essay, composition

**compréhensif/ve** *adj.* comprehensive

**comprendre** *irreg.* (**nous comprenons;** *p.p.* **compris**) to understand; **se comprendre** to understand each other

**comprimé** *m.* tablet

**compte** *m.* account; **compte rendu** account, report; **se rendre compte (de)** to realize

**compter** to intend; **compter sur** to count on; **compter à rebours** to count down

**se concentrer** to concentrate

**concept** *m.* concept

**conception** *f.* conception, conceiving

**concert** *m.* concert; **salle** (*f.*) **de concert** concert hall

**conclusion** *f.* conclusion

**concret/ète** *adj.* concrete

**condition** *f.* condition; **à condition que** + *subj.* on the condition that, provided that

**conditionnel** *m., gram.* conditional

**conduire** *irreg.* (*p.p.* **conduit**) to drive; **permis** (*m.*) **de conduire** driver's license; **se conduire** to behave

**conduite** *f.* behavior; **zéro de conduite** no marks for conduct

**conférence** *f.* lecture; conference

**confiance** *f.* confidence, trust; **avoir confiance (en)** to have confidence (faith) (in)

**confiant(e)** *adj.* confident

**confidentiel(le)** *adj.* confidential; **à titre confidentiel** confidentially

**confier** to confide; **se confier à** to confide in

**confirmer** to confirm

**conflit** *m.* conflict

**confondre** to mix up, confuse

**confort** *m.* comfort

**confus(e)** *adj.* embarrassed; ashamed

**confusément** *adv.* unintelligibly

**confusion** *f.* confusion

**congé** *m.* vacation, holiday; **une semaine de congé** one week off

**Congo** *m.* Congo

**conjonction** *f., gram.* conjunction

**conjuguer** to conjugate; **ce verbe se conjugue avec avoir** this verb is conjugated with **avoir**

**connaissance** *f.* acquaintance; **faire la connaissance** to get acquainted

**connaître** *irreg.* (*p.p.* **connu**) to know; to be familiar with; to meet

**se consacrer à** to devote o.s. to

**conseil** *m.* advice; council; **conseil d'administration** board of directors

**conseiller** to advise, recommend

**consentir (à)** *irreg.* (**je consens**) to consent (to)

**conséquence** *f.* consequence

**conséquent(e)** *adj.* logical; **par conséquent** *adv.* consequently, therefore

**conserve** *f.* canned food; **en conserve** canned

**consommation** *f.* consumption; **société** (*f.*) **de consommation** consumer society

**consommer** to eat, consume

**constamment** *adv.* constantly

**consternation** *f.* consternation, dismay

**construction** *f.* construction

**construire** *irreg.* (*p.p.* **construit**) to build

**consulter** to consult, refer to

**conte** *m.* tale

**contenir** *irreg.* (**je contiens;** *p.p.* **contenu**) to contain

**content(e)** *adj.* happy, pleased; **être content de/que** to be happy about (that)

**contenu** *m.* contents

**continuer** to continue

**contraction** *f., gram.* contraction

**contraire** *m.* opposite; **au contraire** on the contrary

**contraste** *m.* contrast

**contrat** *m.* contract

**contre** *prep.* against; **trois voix contre deux** three votes to two

**contredire** *irreg.* (**vous contredisez,** *p.p.* **contredit**) to contradict

**convaincre** *irreg.* (**je convaincs, nous convainquons;** *p.p.* **convaincu**) to convince

**convenable** *adj.* appropriate; proper

**convenir (à qn)** *irreg.* (**je conviens;** *p.p.* **convenu**) to suit; **il convient que** + *subj.* it is proper that

**conversation** *f.* conversation

**converser** to converse

**copain (copine)** *m., f.* friend, pal

**copie** *f.* exercise (*homework*)

**copier** to copy, reproduce

**coq** *m.* cock, rooster

**coquet(te)** *adj.* flirtatious

**corbeille** *f.* basket; **corbeille à papiers** wastepaper basket

**cordonnerie** *f.* shoe repair shop

**Corée** *f.* Korea

**correspondre** to correspond

**corriger (nous corrigeons)** to correct

**Corse** *f.* Corsica

**costume** *m.* costume; suit

**côté** *m.* side; **de côté et d'autre** here and there; **à côté de** *prep.* next to, beside

**Côte d'Ivoire** *f.* Ivory Coast

**côtelette** *f.* chop; **côtelette d'agneau (de veau)** lamb (veal chop)

**coton** *m.* cotton

**couchage** *m.*: **sac de couchage** sleeping bag

**coucher** *m.* bedtime; **coucher du soleil** sunset

**se coucher** to go to bed

**coude** *m.* elbow

**coulisse** *f.*: **dans les coulisses** in the wings

**coup** *m.*: **coup de main** helping hand; **coup de téléphone** phone call; **du coup** suddenly; **tout d'un coup** all of a sudden

**couper** to cut; **couper fin** to slice thin; **se couper** to cut o.s.; **se couper les cheveux (les ongles)** to cut one's hair (nails)

**courage** *m.* courage

**couramment** *adv.* fluently

**courant(e)** *adj.* current; **eau** (*f.*) **courante** running water; **courant** *m.*: **être au courant (de)** to know (about)

**courir** (*p.p.* **couru**) to run; **par les temps qui courent** nowadays

**courriel** *m.* e-mail; e-mail message

**cours** *m.* course; classe; **au cours de** in the course of, during; **sécher un cours** to cut class; **suivre un cours** to take a course

**course** *f.* errand; **faire les courses** to do errands

**court(e)** *adj.* short; **s'arrêter court** to stop short

**couscous** *m.* couscous (*North African wheat dish*)

**cousin(e)** *m., f.* cousin
**couteau** *m.* knife
**coûter** to cost; **coûter cher** to cost a lot
**coutume** *f.* custom
**couvert(e)** *adj.* overcast (sky); **couvert** *m.* place setting; **mettre le couvert** to set the table
**couverture** *f.* blanket
**couvrir** *irreg.* (**je couvre**; *p.p.* **couvert**) to cover
**craindre** *irreg.* (**je crains, nous craignons**; *p.p.* **craint**) to fear
**crainte** *f.* fear
**cravate** *f.* tie
**crayon** *m.* pencil
**crédit** *m.* credit; **carte** (*f.*) **de crédit** credit card
**crème** *f.* cream
**crémeux/se** *adj.* creamy
**crevassé(e)** *adj.* cracked (*ground*)
**crevé(e)** *adj.* burst, punctured (*tire*)
**cri** *m.* scream
**crier** to yell, scream
**crise** *f.* crisis
**critique** *m., f.* critic (*person*); *f.* review, criticism
**critiquer** to criticize
**Croatie** *f.* Croatia
**croire** *irreg.* (**nous croyons**; *p.p.* **cru**) to believe, think
**croissant** *m.* croissant (*butter roll*)
**croître** *irreg.* (**je croîs, nous croissons**; *p.p.* **crû**) to grow
**croyance** *f.* belief
**cru(e)** *adj.* raw
**cube** *m.* cube; **couper en cubes** to dice
**cueillir** *irreg.* (**je cueille**) to gather, pick (*flowers*)
**cuir** *m.* leather
**cuire** *irreg.* (**il cuit**; *p.p.* **cuit**) to cook
**cuisine** *f.* kitchen; **faire la cuisine** to cook
**cuit(e)** *adj.* cooked
**cultivé(e)** *adj.* cultured, cultivated
**culture** *f.* culture
**culturel(le)** *adj.* cultural
**curieux/euse** *adj.* curious
**cyclisme** *m.* cycling; **faire du cyclisme** to ride a bicycle

# D

**d'abord** *adv.* first, first of all, at first
**d'accord** *interj.* all right; **être d'accord** to agree
**dame** *f.* lady, woman
**dancing** *m.* dance hall
**Danemark** *m.* Denmark
**danger** *m.* danger; **en danger** in danger; **hors de danger** out of danger; **il n'y a pas de danger** it is not dangerous
**dangereux/euse** *adj.* dangerous
**dans** *prep.* in; within; **dans le Midi** in the South of France; **dans les coulisses** in the wings
**danse** *f.* dance
**danser** to dance
**date** *f.* date; **quelle est la date aujourd'hui?** what is the date today?
**davantage** *adv.* more
**débarquer** *fam.* to turn up
**débarrasser** to clear; **se débarrasser de** to get rid of
**débat** *m.* debate

**débattre** *irreg.* (*p.p.* **débattu**) to debate
**debout** *adv.* up, awake, standing up
**début** *m.* beginning; **au début** at the beginning
**décédé(e)** *adj.* deceased
**décembre** *m.* December
**décevoir** *irreg.* (**je déçois**; *p.p.* **déçu**) to disappoint
**décider** to decide; **se décider à** to make up one's mind to
**décision** *f.* decision
**se décoller** to peel off, come unstuck
**déconseiller** to advise against
**décorer** to decorate
**décourager** (**nous décourageons**) to discourage
**découverte** *f.* discovery; **partir à la découverte** to go off in a spirit of discovery
**découvrir** *irreg.* (*p.p.* **découvert**) to discover
**décrire** *irreg.* (**nous décrivons**; *p.p.* **décrit**) to describe
**décrocher** to take down (*from wall*)
**déçu(e)** *adj.* disappointed
**déduire** *irreg.* (*p.p.* **déduit**) to deduct
**déesse** *f.* goddess
**défaire** *irreg.* (**nous défaisons**) to undo
**défendre (à qn)** to forbid
**défini(e)** *adj.* definite
**degré** *m.* degree
**se déguiser (en)** to dress up (as)
**dehors** *adv.* outside; **en dehors de** outside of
**déjà** *adv.* already; ever
**déjeuner** to have lunch
**déjeuner** *m.* lunch; **petit déjeuner** breakfast; **prendre le petit déjeuner** to have breakfast
**délicat(e)** *adj.* delicate; refined
**délicieux/euse** *adj.* delicious
**demain** *adv.* tomorrow; **après-demain** the day after tomorrow
**demande** *f.* demand; request; **faire une demande d'emploi** to apply for a job; **à la demande de tous** by popular request
**demander (de)** to ask (for, to); **se demander** to wonder
**démarrer** to start (*car*)
**déménagement** *m.* move (*house*); **fourgon** (*m.*) **de déménagement** moving truck
**déménager** (**nous déménageons**) to move (out), change residence
**déménageur** *m.* mover
**demeure** *f.* residence
**demi** *adj.* (*inv. before noun with a hyphen*) half; **demi-douzaine** half a dozen; **demi-heure** half an hour; **et demie** half past the hour
**démissionner** to quit, resign (*job*)
**démocratie** *f.* democracy
**démonstratif/ve** *adj., gram.* demonstrative
**dent** *f.* tooth; **parler entre ses dents** to mumble; **se brosser les dents** to brush one's teeth
**dentiste** *m., f.* dentist
**départ** *m.* departure
**département** *m.* department
**se dépêcher (de)** to hurry (to)
**dépenser** to spend (money)
**déplaisant(e)** *adj.* unpleasant
**déposer** to give a lift; **déposer en ville** to drop (*s.o.*) off in town
**dépoussiérer** (**je dépoussière**) to dust

**déprimé(e)** *adj.* depressed

**depuis** *prep.* since, for; **depuis combien de temps** how long . . .; **depuis quand...** since when . . .

**déranger (nous dérangeons)** to bother, disturb

**dernier/ère** *adj.* last, most recent; **Rira bien qui rira le dernier.** He who laughs last laughs best.

**dernièrement** *adv.* lately

**derrière** *adv.* behind; in back of

**désapprouver** to disapprove

**‡descendre** to go down, downstairs; to stay (*hotel*); **descendre (de)** to get off (*bus, train*); to take down

**description** *f.* description

**désert** *m.* desert

**se déshabiller** to get undressed

**désir** *m.* desire, wish

**désirer** to desire, want

**désobéir (à)** to disobey

**désolé(e)** *adj.* sorry

**désordre** *m.* untidiness; **être en désordre** to be untidy

**désormais** *adv.* from now on

**dessert** *m.* dessert

**dessin** *m.* drawing

**dessiné(e)** *adj.*: **bande** (*f.*) **dessinée** comic strip, cartoon

**dessiner** to draw

**dessous** *adv.* under, beneath; beneath it, underneath it; **au-dessous (de)** below, underneath; **bras dessus, bras dessous** arm in arm; **ci-dessous** below; **en-dessous** underneath, below; **là-dessous** underneath there; **sens dessus-dessous** upside down

**dessus** *adv.* over it, on top of it; **au-dessus** above, on top of; **au-dessus de mes forces** beyond me, too much for me; **bras dessus, bras dessous** arm in arm; **ci-dessus** above; **en-dessus** on top of; **là-dessus** on top of it; **par-dessus** over; **sens dessus-dessous** upside down

**détail** *m.* detail

**détective** *m., f.* detective

**se détendre** to relax

**déterminé(e)** *adj.*: **être déterminé à** to be determined to

**détester** to hate

**détruire** *irreg.* (*p.p.* **détruit**) to destroy

**deux** *adj.* two; **à deux pas de** just a few minutes from

**deuxième** *adj.* second

**devant** *prep.* in front of, before

**†devenir** *irreg.* (**je deviens**; *p.p.* **devenu**) to become

**devoir** *irreg.* (**je dois**; *p.p.* **dû**) to owe; must, should, ought to; *m. pl.* homework

**dialecte** *m.* dialect

**dictionnaire** *m.* dictionary

**diététique** *adj.* dietary; **centre diététique** health food store

**dieu** *m.* god

**différé(e)** *adj.* pre-recorded (*TV*); **émission en différé** pre-recorded broadcast

**différemment** *adv.* differently

**différence** *f.* difference

**différent(e)** *adj.* different, various

**difficile** *adj.* difficult

**difficulté** *f.* difficulty; **être en difficulté** to be in trouble

**diligemment** *adv.* diligently

**diligence** *f.* diligence, conscientiousness

**diligent(e)** *adj.* diligent, conscientious

**dimanche** *m.* Sunday; **dimanche de Pâques** Easter Sunday

**dindon** *m.* turkey

**dîner** to have dinner; *m.* dinner

**dire** *irreg.* (**vous dites**; *p.p.* **dit**) to say, tell; **c'est-à-dire** that is to say; **vouloir dire** to mean

**direct(e)** *adj.* direct; *gram.* **complément** (*m.*) **d'objet direct** direct object; **en direct** live (*TV*)

**directeur/trice** *m., f.* manager, head; **directeur d'école** school principal

**direction** *f.* direction

**diriger (nous dirigeons)** to direct; **se diriger vers** to head toward

**discours** *m.* speech

**discret/ète** *adj.* discrete

**discrétion** *f.* discretion

**discussion** *f.* discussion

**discuter** to discuss

**disjoint(e)** *adj., gram.* disjunctive

**disparaître** *irreg.* (*p.p.* **disparu**) to disappear

**disponible** *adj.* available

**disposé(e)** *adj.* ready to, available (*person*)

**se disputer** to argue

**disque** *m.*: **disque compact** CD; **disque dur** hard drive; **unité** (*f.*) **de disque** disk drive

**disquette** *f.* floppy disk

**dissertation** *f.* essay

**dissuader** to dissuade

**distinction** *f.* distinction

**distrait(e)** *adj.* absentminded

**divers(e)** *adj.* various

**divorcer (nous divorçons)** to (get a) divorce

**dizaine** *f.* about ten

**docteur** *m.* doctor

**document** *m.* document

**doigt** *m.* finger

**dollar** *m.* dollar

**domicile** *m.* residence; *m., f. inv.* **sans domicile fixe (SDF)** homeless person

**donc** *conj.* therefore

**donnée** *f.* data; **système** (*m.*) **de traitement de données** data processing system

**donner (qch à qn)** to give (*s.th. to s.o.*); **donner des conseils** to give advice; **donner le vertige** to make dizzy

**dont** *pron.* whose, of whom, of which; **ce dont** what, that of which

**dormir** *irreg.* (**je dors**) to sleep; **dormir à la belle étoile** to sleep outdoors

**dos** *m.* back; **sac** (*m.*) **à dos** backpack; **avoir mal au dos** to have a backache

**dossier** *m.* file

**doucement** *adv.* gently, softly

**douceur** *f.* softness; **en douceur** gently

**douche** *f.* shower

**douillet(e)** *adj.* cozy

**doute** *m.* doubt; **être dans le doute** to be doubtful, uncertain; **sans doute** no doubt; **sans aucun doute** without a doubt

**douter que** + *subj.* to doubt; **douter de** to be suspicious of; **se douter de** to suspect (*s.th.*)

**douteux/euse** *adj.* doubtful, uncertain; **il est douteux que** + *subj.* it's doubtful that

**doux (douce)** *adj.* sweet, gentle, soft
**douzaine** *f.* dozen; **demi-douzaine** half a dozen
**douze** *adj.* twelve
**drame** *m.* tragedy; drama
**drapeau** *m.* flag
**dresser** to put up, erect
**droguerie** *f.* hardware store
**droit** *m.* law (*university*); **faculté de droit** law school
**droit(e)** *adj.* straight; right; **aller (tout) droit** to go straight ahead; **à droite** *adv.* to, on the right
**drôle** *adj.* funny; strange; **drôle de** (+ *noun*) strange, peculiar
**dur(e)** *adj., adv.* hard; difficult; **disque** (*m.*) **dur** hard drive; **œuf** (*m.*) **dur** hard-boiled egg; **travailler dur** to work hard
**DVD** *m. inv.* DVD
**dynamique** *adj.* dynamic

# E

**eau** *f.* water; **eau courante** running water; **eau minérale** mineral water
**écarlate** *adj.* scarlet
**échange** *m.* exchange
**échanger (nous échangeons)** to exchange
**échantillon** *m.* sample
**s'échapper (de)** to escape (from)
**écharpe** *f.* scarf
**échec** *m.* failure; **jouer aux échecs** to play chess
**éclair** *m.* lightning
**école** *f.* school; **école primaire** elementary school; **école navale** naval college; **suivre bien à l'école** to be a good student
**économie** *f.* economy; *pl.* savings
**Écosse** *f.* Scotland
**écouter** to listen (to)
**écrire** *irreg.* (**nous écrivons;** *p.p.* **écrit**) (**à**) to write (to); **écrire à la main** to write by hand; **écrire de la main gauche (droite)** to be left- (right-)handed; **s'écrire** to write to each other
**écriture** *f.* (hand)writing
**écrivain** *m., f.* writer; **écrivaine** *f., Q.* (woman) writer
**éditer** to edit
**éducation** *f.* education; **éducation secondaire** high school education
**effacer (nous effaçons)** to erase
**efficacement** *adv.* efficiently
**effort** *m.* effort; **sans effort** effortless(ly)
**effrayer (j'effraie)** to frighten
**égal(e)** *adj.:* **ça m'est égal** I don't mind
**église** *f.* church
**Égypte** *f.* Egypt
**élections** *f. pl.* elections
**électricité** *f.* electricity; **panne d'électricité** power outage
**élégant(e)** *adj.* elegant
**élément** *m.* element
**élève** *m., f.* pupil, student
**élevé(e)** *adj.* high
**élever** *irreg.* (**j'élève**) to rear, breed
**élire** *irreg.* (**nous élisons;** *p.p.* **élu**) to elect
**s'éloigner de** to move away from

**s'embêter** to be bored
**embrasser** to kiss
**émerveillé(e)** *adj.* to be filled with wonder
**émigrer** to emigrate
**émission** *f.* show (*TV*)
**emménagement** *m.* moving in
**emménager (nous emménageons)** to move in
**emmener (j'emmène)** to take (*s.o.*)
**émotion** *f.* emotion, feeling
**empêcher que** + *subj.* to prevent from; **elle n'a pas pu s'empêcher de...** she could not help . . .
**emplacement** *m.* location
**emploi** *m.* job; *gram.* usage; **demande d'emploi** job application; **sans-emploi** *m., f. inv.* unemployed
**employé(e)** *m., f.* employee
**employer (j'emploie)** to use; **ce mot s'emploie** this word is used
**emporter** to carry, take away, carry off
**empressement** *m.* eagerness; **sans empressement** slowly
**s'empresser (de)** to hurry, rush
**emprunt** *m.* borrowing; **identité** (*f.*) **d'emprunt** assumed identity
**emprunter (qch à qn)** to borrow (*s.th. from s.o.*)
**ému(e)** *adj.* touched, moved
**enchanté(e)** *adj.* delighted
**encore** *adv.* again; still; **encore plus** even more; **encore que** although; **encore une fois** once again; **pas encore** not yet
**encourager (nous encourageons) (à)** to encourage (to)
**endive** *f.* endive
**s'endormir** *irreg.* (*p.p.* **endormi**) to fall asleep
**endroit** *m.* place
**énervant(e)** *adj.* annoying
**s'énerver** to get upset; **ne pas s'énerver** to stay calm
**enfance** *f.* childhood
**enfant** *m., f.* child; **petit-enfant** grandchild
**enfin** *adv.* finally, at last
**engager (nous engageons)** to hire, to urge
**enlever (j'enlève)** to remove; to take off (*clothing*); **enlever (qch à qn)** to take away (*s.th. from s.o.*)
**ennui** *m.* boredom; trouble; **mourir d'ennui** to be bored to death
**ennuyer (j'ennuie)** to bore; to irritate (*s.o.*); **s'ennuyer** to get bored
**ennuyeux/euse** *adj.* boring; very annoying
**énorme** *adj.* enormous
**énormément** *adv.* enormously
**s'enrhumer** to catch a cold
**enseigne** *f.* sign
**enseignement** *m.* education; learning
**enseigner (qch à qn)** to teach (*s.o. s.th.*)
**ensemble** *adv.* together; **d'ensemble** overall, comprehensive
**ensuite** *adv.* then, next
**entendre** to hear
**enthousiasme** *m.* enthusiasm
**s'enthousiasmer** to get enthusiastic
**s'enticher (de)** to become infatuated (with)
**entier/ère** *adj.* entire, whole
**entouré(e) de** *adj.* surrounded by

**entre** *prep.* between; among; **entre chien et loup** at dusk; **entre les mains** in one's hands; **entre nous** between you and me; **(dire qch) entre la poire et le fromage** (*to say s.th.*) casually; **parler entre ses dents** to mumble

**entrée** *f.* entrance

**entreprendre** *irreg.* (**nous entreprenons;** *p.p.* **entrepris**) **de** to undertake

**entreprise** *f.* firm; **petite (grosse) entreprise** small (big) firm

‡**entrer** to come in, enter

**enveloppe** *f.* envelope

**envers** *prep.* toward, to

**envie** *f.* desire; **avoir envie de** to want

**environ** *adv.* about

**envoyer** (**j'envoie**) to send

**épais(se)** *adj.* thick

**épaule** *f.* shoulder

**épeler** (**j'épelle**) to spell

**épice** *f.* spice

**épicerie** *f.* grocery store

**épicier/ère** *m., f.* grocer

**époque** *f.* time; **à l'époque** at the time

**épuisé(e)** *adj.* exhausted

**équateur** *m.* equator

**équipe** *f.* team

**équivalent** *m.* equivalent

**errer** to wander

**erroné(e)** *adj.* erroneous

**escalader** to climb

**escalier** *m.* stairs

**espace** *m.* space; blank

**Espagne** *f.* Spain

**espagnol(e)** *adj.* Spanish; *m.* Spanish (*language*); **Espagnol(e)** *m., f.* Spaniard

**espérer** (**j'espère**) to hope

**espoir** *m.* hope; **sans espoir** hopelessly

**esprit** *m.* mind; **avoir l'esprit ailleurs** to have one's mind elsewhere

**essayer** (**j'essaie**) (**de**) to try (to); to try on (*clothes*)

**essence** *f.* gasoline; **prendre de l'essence** to buy, get gasoline

**essentiel(le)** *adj.* essential; **il est essentiel que** + *subj.* it is essential that

**essuyer** (**j'essuie**) to wipe

**estimer** to estimate

**estomac** *m.* stomach; **avoir mal à l'estomac** to have a stomachache

**établir** to establish

**établissement** *m.* establishment

**étage** *m.* floor, story

**étagère** *f.* bookshelf

**étalage** *m.* display

**étang** *m.* pond

**état** *m.* state; **les États-Unis** United States

**été** *m.* summer

**éteindre** *irreg.* (**nous éteignons**) to put out, extinguish (*fire*); turn off (*TV*)

**étendre** to hang out (*laundry*)

**éternité** *f.* eternity; **pour l'éternité** eternally, forever

**étincelant(e)** *adj.* sparkling; brilliant

**étoile** *f.* star; **dormir à la belle étoile** to sleep outdoors

**étonnant(e)** *adj.* amazing, surprising

**étonner** to surprise; **s'étonner de** + *inf.* (**que** + *subj.*) to marvel at (that)

**étrange** *adj.* strange

**étranger/ère** *adj.* foreign; *m., f.* foreigner; **à l'étranger** abroad, in a foreign country

**être** *irreg.* (*p.p.* **été**) to be; **être amoureux/euse (de)** to be in love (with); **être d'accord avec** to be in agreement with; **être de retour** to be back; **être en bonne santé** to be in good health; **être en forme** to be in good shape; **être en guerre** to be at war; **être pour** to be in favor of

**être** *m.* being

**étreindre** *irreg.* (**nous étreignons**) to embrace

**étrennes** *f. pl.* New Year's gift

**étroit(e)** *adj.* narrow; **à l'étroit** cramped

**étroitement** *adv.* closely

**étude** *f.* office; *f. pl.* studies

**étudiant(e)** *m., f.* student

**étudier** to study

**euro** *m.* euro (*currency*)

**Europe** *f.* Europe

**européen(ne)** *adj.* European; **Européen(ne)** *m., f.* European (*person*); **Union européenne** European Union (*EU*)

**eux** *pron., m. pl.* them; **chez eux** at their house

**évidemment** *adv.* obviously

**évident(e)** *adj.* obvious, clear; **il est évident que** + *indic.* it is clear that

**éviter de** to avoid

**évoluer** to evolve

**évoquer** to recall, evoke

**exagérer** (**j'exagère**) to exaggerate

**examen** *m.* test; **passer un examen** to take an exam; **réussir à un examen** to pass an exam; **subir un examen** to undergo an examination

**exception** *f.* exception

**exclu(e)** *adj.* excluded

**excursion** *f.* excursion

**s'excuser (de)** to apologize (for)

**exercice** *m.* exercise; **faire de l'exercice** to exercise

**exigeant(e)** *adj.* demanding

**exiger** (**nous exigeons**) to demand

**expédier** to ship

**expérience** *f.* experience; experiment (*lab.*)

**expert(e)** *m., f.* expert

**explication** *f.* explanation

**expliquer** to explain

**exposé** *m.* oral presentation

**exposer** to expose, show

**exprès** *adv.* on purpose

**expression** *f.* expression

**exprimer** to express

**exquis(e)** *adj.* exquisite

**extérieur** *m.* exterior; **à l'extérieur** outside

**extraordinaire** *adj.* extraordinary

**extrémiste** *adj., m., f.* extremist

# F

**fabuleux/euse** *adj.* fabulous, extraordinary

**face** *f.*: **de face** frontal; **en face (de)** across from

**fâché(e)** *adj.* angry

**se fâcher (avec/contre)** to get angry (*with s.o.*)

**facile** *adj.* easy

**facilement** *adv.* easily

**faciliter** to make easier

**façon** *f.* way; **de façon à ce que** + *subj.* so that, in order that; **d'une façon...** in a . . . way; **sans façon** without fuss

**facteur** *m.* mail carrier

**facture** *f.* bill

**faculté** *f.* (*fam.* **fac**) university department or school

**faim** *f.* hunger; **avoir faim** to be hungry; **mourir de faim** to starve, to be very hungry

**faire** *irreg.* (**vous faites;** *p.p.* **fait**) to do, make; **ça fait deux jours (que)** it has been two days (since); **chemin faisant** on the way; **faire** + *inf.* to have (*s.o. do s.th.*); **faire attention (à)** to pay attention (to); to watch out (for); **faire de** + *school subject* to study; **faire de l'exercice** to exercise; **faire des dessins** to draw; **faire du bruit** to make noise; **faire du sport (du jogging, du vélo)** to play sports (jog, bike ride); **faire dix kilomètres** to travel, cover 10 kilometers; **faire du tourisme** to do some sightseeing; **faire la connaissance de** to meet (*s.o.*); **faire la cuisine** to cook; **faire la lessive / le linge** to do the laundry; **faire la vaisselle** to wash the dishes; **faire le lit** to make the bed; **faire le ménage** to do the housework; **faire le plein (d'essence)** to fill it up (with gas); **faire les carreaux** to wash the windows; **faire les choses à moitié** to do things only halfway; **faire les courses** to do errands; **faire les valises** to pack one's bags; **faire sa toilette** to wash and get dressed; **faire un pique-nique** to go on a picnic; **faire un stage** to do an internship; **faire un versement sur le compte de** to make a deposit; **faire un voyage** to take a trip; **faire une demande d'emploi** to apply for a job; **faire une promenade** to go for a stroll; **il fait du vent (beau, mauvais)** *impers.* it's windy (the weather is nice, bad)

**fait** *m.* fact

**falloir** *irreg., impers.* (**il faut;** *p.p.* **fallu**) to be necessary; **il faut** + *inf.* one must, you have to; **il faut que** + *subj.* it is necessary that one, one has to; **il faut** + *noun* one needs

**familial(le)** *adj.* family

**se familiariser (avec)** to familiarize o.s. (with)

**familier/ère** *adj.* familiar; informal

**famille** *f.* family; **en famille** with one's family

**farine** *f.* flour

**fascinant(e)** *adj.* fascinating

**fatal(e)** *adj.* fatal

**fatigant(e)** *adj.* tiring

**fatigue** *f.* fatigue

**fatigué(e)** *adj.* tired

**fatiguer** to make tired, to tire

**faut (il)** (see **falloir**)

**faute** *f.* mistake, error; **sans faute** *adv.* without fail

**fauteuil** *m.* armchair

**faux (fausse)** *adj.* false; wrong; **chanter faux** to sing off-key

**faveur** *f.* favor; **billet** (*m.*) **de faveur** complimentary ticket; **en sa faveur** in his/her favor

**favorable** *adj.* favorable; **sous un jour favorable** in a favorable light

**favori(te)** *adj.* favorite

**féliciter** to congratulate

**féminin** *m., gram.* feminine

**femme** *f.* woman; wife

**fenêtre** *f.* window; **par la fenêtre** through, out of the window

**fer** *m.* iron; **Société Nationale des Chemins de Fer Français (SNCF)** French national railway company

**ferme** *f.* farm

**ferme** *adj.* firm; **tenir ferme** to stand firm

**fermer** to close

**festival** *m.* festival

**fête** *f.* holiday, party, festival; **trouble-fête** *m., f.* party-pooper

**feu** *m.* fire; **faire un feu** to make a fire; **Au feu!** Fire!

**feuilleter (je feuillette)** to leaf through

**feutre** *m.* felt-tip pen

**février** *m.* February

**fiancé(e)** *m., f.* fiancé, fiancée

**se fiancer (nous nous fiançons)** to get engaged

**fictif/ve** *adj.* fictional

**se fier (à)** to trust

**figure** *f.* face

**fil** *m.:* **coup de fil** phone call

**fille** *f.* girl; daughter; **petite-fille** granddaughter

**film** *m.* movie; **film étranger (d'horreur, muet)** foreign (horror, silent) movie

**fils** *m.* son

**fin** *f.* end; **fin de semaine** weekend; **garder le meilleur pour la fin** to keep the best for last

**finir (de)** to finish; **finir par** to end by (*doing s.th.*)

**fixe** *adj.* steady; **sans domicile fixe (SDF)** *m., f. inv.* homeless person

**se flatter de** to claim to (*be able to*)

**flatteur/euse** *adj.* flattering

**flemme** *f.* laziness

**fleur** *f.* flower

**fleurir** to blossom; **aller fleurir les tombes** to put flowers on graves

**fleuve** *m.* (large) river

**flocon** *m.* flake

**flûte** *f.* flute

**foi** *f.* faith

**fois** *f.* time; **à la fois** at the same time; **encore une fois** once again; **deux fois** twice; **une fois** once

**folie** *f.* madness; **aimer qn à la folie** to be madly in love

**foncé(e)** *adj.* dark (color)

**fonctionner** to work

**fonctions** *f. pl.* duties

**fond:** **à fond** thoroughly

**fonder** to found

**football** *m.* soccer

**force** *f.* strength; **obtenir par la force** to force s.o. to give you (*s.th.*)

**forcer (nous forçons)** to force

**forêt** *f.* forest

**formater** to format

**forme** *f.* form; shape; **être en pleine forme** to be in great shape; **sous forme de gélules** in capsule form

**formel(le)** *adj.* formal

**former** to form, create

**formidable** *adj.* wonderful, great

**formule** *f.* way, system

**formuler** to formulate, express

**fort** *adv.* hard; **crier fort** to yell

**fou (folle)** *adj.* mad, crazy

**fouillis** *m.* mess

**foulard** *m.* scarf

**foule** *f.* crowd; **une foule de** a crowd of

**se fouler (la cheville)** to sprain (one's ankle)
**fourchette** *f.* fork
**fourgon** *m.* truck; **fourgon de déménagement** moving truck
**fournisseur/euse** *m. f.* supplier
**foyer** *m.* residence; **foyer d'étudiants** student residence
**frais** *m.* expense, cost
**frais (fraîche)** *adj.* fresh
**fraise** *f.* strawberry
**franc(he)** *adj.* frank, honest
**franchement** *adv.* frankly
**francophone** *adj.* French-speaking; *m., f.* French speaker
**frapper** to strike, hit
**fréquemment** *adv.* frequently
**fréquent(e)** *adj.* frequent
**fréquenté(e)** *adj.* busy, much visited (*place*)
**fréquenter** to frequent, to go to often
**frère** *m.* brother
**frigo** *m. fam.* refrigerator
**frites** *f. pl.* French fries; **steak-frites** steak with French fries
**froid** *m.* cold
**froid(e)** *adj.;* **avoir froid** to be cold; **il fait froid** it's cold; **prendre froid** to catch cold
**fromage** *m.* cheese; **(dire qch) entre la poire et le fromage** (*to say s.th.*) casually
**front** *m.* forehead; **se heurter de front** to collide, clash head-on
**frontière** *f.* border
**fruit** *m.* fruit
**fumé(e)** *adj.* smoked
**fumer** to smoke
**furieux/euse** *adj.* furious
**futur** *m., gram.* future; **futur antérieur** future perfect; **futur proche** immediate future

# G

**gagnant(e)** *adj.* winning; *m. f.* winner
**gagner** to earn; win
**gai(e)** *adj.* happy
**gaiment** *adv.* happily
**gamme** *f.* range, line (*products*)
**gant** *m.* glove; **prendre des gants avec** to be as gentle as possible, use kid gloves with (*s.o.*)
**garage** *m.* garage
**garçon** *m.* boy; young man; waiter
**garde** *f.:* **être de garde** to be on duty; **prendre garde** to watch, be careful
**garder** to keep
**gare** *f.* station; **gare centrale** central station
**garer** to park (*car*)
**gastrique** *adj.* gastric
**gâteau** *m.* cake
**gauche** *adj., f.* left; **à gauche** on the left; **écrire de la main gauche** to be left-handed
**geler (je gèle)** to freeze
**gélule** *f.* capsule
**gémir** to moan
**gendre** *m.* son-in-law
**gêne** *f.* discomfort; **sans-gêne** *adj.* inconsiderate
**général(e)** *adj.* general; **en général** *adv.* usually

**général** *m.* general
**généreux/euse** *adj.* generous
**générosité** *f.* generosity
**génial(e)** *adj.* brilliant
**genou** *m.* (*pl.* **genoux**) *m.* knee
**genre** *m., gram.* gender
**gens** *m. pl.* people; **jeunes gens** young people
**gentil(le)** *adj.* nice, friendly
**gentillesse** *f.* kindness
**gentiment** *adv.* gently
**géographie** *f.* geography
**géologie** *f.* geology
**gérondif** *m., gram.* gerund
**gestion** *f.* management
**glace** *f.* ice cream; **glace aux fraises** strawberry ice cream
**gobelet** *m.* tumbler
**goût** *m.* taste; **avec goût** tastefully
**gouvernement** *m.* government
**grammaire** *f.* grammar
**gramme** *m.* gram
**grand(e)** *adj.* big; tall; large; great; **grand magasin** *m.* department store
**grand-mère** *f.* grandmother
**grand-père** *m.* grandfather
**grandir** to grow up
**grands-parents** *m. pl.* grandparents
**gras(se)** *adj.* fat; fatty; **faire la grasse matinée** to sleep late
**gratitude** *f.* gratitude
**grave** *adj.* grave; *gram.* **accent** (*m.*) **grave** grave accent (**è**)
**grec(que)** *adj.* Greek; *m.* Greek (*language*); **Grec(que)** Greek (*person*)
**Grèce** *f.* Greece
**grêler** *impers.* to hail
**grelotter** to shiver
**grenier** *m.* attic
**grève** *f.* strike; **faire grève** to be on strike
**grimper** to climb; **grimper aux arbres** to climb trees
**grippe** *f.* flu
**gris(e)** *adj.* gray
**gronder** to scold
**gros(se)** *adj.* big; fat
**grossir** to gain weight
**groupe** *m.* group; **en groupe** in, as a group; **groupe de rock** rock band
**Guadeloupe (la)** *f.* Guadeloupe
**Guatemala** *m.* Guatemala
**guère** *adv.:* **ne... guère** scarcely, hardly
**guérir** to cure, make better, heal
**guerre** *f.* war; **être en guerre** to be at war
**gueule** *f.* mouth; **amuse-gueule** *m. inv.* appetizer, snack
**guichet** *m.* box office, ticket window
**guide** *m. f.* guide
**guillemet** *m., gram.* quotation mark
**guitare** *f.* guitar; **jouer de la guitare** to play the guitar

# H

**s'habiller** to get dressed
**habitant(e)** *m., f.* inhabitant

**habiter** to live, reside
**habitude** *f.* habit; **d'habitude** *adv.* usually
**habitué(e)** **à** *adj.* accustomed to
**s'habituer à** to get used to
***Haïti** *m.* Haiti
**haleine** *f.* breath; **hors d'haleine** out of breath
***haricot** *m.* bean; **haricots verts** green beans
***hasard** *m.*: **par hasard** by chance
***hâte** *f.* haste; **à la hâte** hastily
***haut(e)** *adj.* high; **haut** *adv.* **en haut** at the top;
   upstairs; **là-haut** up there; **tout haut / à haute
   voix** aloud, out loud
***hauteur** *f.* height; **à la hauteur de** up to the task;
   **deux mètres** (*m.*) **de hauteur** two meters high
***havre** *m.* haven
**hémisphère** *m.* hemisphere
**héroïquement** *adv.* heroically
**hésitation** *f.* hesitation
**hésiter** to hesitate
**heure** *f.* hour; time; **à l'heure** on time; **à ses heures**
   when he/she feels like it; **de bonne heure** early;
   **demi-heure** half an hour; **être à l'heure** to be on
   time; **il est deux heures** it's two o'clock; **quelle
   heure est-il?** what time is it?; **tout à l'heure** a
   short while ago; very soon
**heureux/euse** *adj.* happy
**se *heurter (de front)** to collide, clash head-on
**hier** *adv.* yesterday; **avant-hier** the day before
   yesterday
**histoire** *f.* history; story
**hiver** *m.* winter; **en hiver** in the winter
**homme** *m.* man
**honnête** *adj.* honest
**honnêtement** *adv.* honestly
**honneur** *m.* honor; **en l'honneur de** in honor of
**honoré(e)** *adj.* honored
***honte** *f.* shame; **avoir honte de** to be ashamed of;
   **sans honte** shamelessly
**hôpital** *m.* hospital
**horaire** *m.* schedule
**horreur** *f.*: **film d'horreur** horror movie
***hors** *prep.* outside; **hors de** out of; **hors jeu** *adj., inv.*
   offside; out of play; **hors d'haleine** out of breath
***hors-d'œuvre** *m. inv.* appetizer
**hostilité** *f.* hostility
**hôtel** *m.* hotel
**huile** *f.* oil
***huit** *adj.* eight
***huitième** *adj.* eighth
**humain(e)** *adj.* human; **être** (*m.*) **humain** human
   being
**humeur** *f.* mood; **être de bonne (mauvaise) humeur**
   to be in a good (bad) mood
**humide** *adj.* damp
**humour** *m.* humor; **avoir de l'humour** to have a
   sense of humor
**hurler** to scream
**hypothétique** *adj.* hypothetical

# I

**ici** *adv.* here
**idéal(e)** *adj.* ideal; **idéal** *m.* ideal
**idée** *f.* idea

**identification** *f.* identification
**identifier** to identify
**identité** *f.* identity; **identité d'emprunt** assumed
   identity
**idiotie** *f.* idiocy, stupidity
**ignorer** not to know
**image** *f.* image
**imagination** *f.* imagination; **sans imagination**
   without imagination
**immédiatement** *adv.* immediately
**immeuble** *m.* building
**immobilier/ère** *adj.*: **agence immobilière** real
   estate agency
**immoral(e)** *adj.* immoral
**imparfait** *m., gram.* imperfect (*verb tense*)
**impatience** *f.* impatience; **avec impatience**
   impatiently
**s'impatienter** to get impatient, lose patience
**impératif** *m., gram.* imperative (*mood*)
**imperméable** *m.* raincoat
**importance** *f.* importance
**important(e)** *adj.* important; **il est important que**
   + *subj.* it's important that
**importer** to matter; **n'importe comment** anyhow;
   **n'importe combien** any number; **n'importe
   lequel** anyone; **n'importe où** anywhere;
   **n'importe quand** anytime; **n'importe qui**
   anybody; **n'importe quoi** anything; **peu importe**
   it does not matter
**imposant(e)** *adj.* imposing
**impression** *f.* impression; **avoir l'impression que**
   to have the feeling that
**imprévu(e)** *adj.* unexpected
**imprimante** *f.* printer
**imprimer** to print
**imprudence** *f.* carelessness
**inanimé(e)** *adj.* lifeless
**Inde** *f.* India
**indécis(e)** *adj.* indecisive
**indéfini(e)** *adj.* indefinite; *gram.* **article** (*m.*) **indéfini**
   indefinite article
**indicatif** *m., gram.* indicative (*mood*)
**indication** *f.* information
**indifférence** *f.* indifference
**indiqué(e)** *adj.* appropriate
**indiquer** to point out, show
**indirect(e)** *adj., gram.* indirect; **pronom** (*m.*) **d'objet
   indirect** indirect object pronoun
**indispensable** *adj.*: **il est indispensable que** +
   *subj.* it's indispensable that
**industrie** *f.* industry; **Cité** (*f.*) **des sciences et de
   l'industrie** Museum of Science and Industry
**infinitif** *m., gram.* infinitive (*mood*)
**infirmier/ère** *m., f.* nurse
**inflation** *f.* inflation
**influence** *f.* influence; **sous l'influence de** under
   the influence of
**infographie** *f.* computer graphics
**informations** *f. pl.* news (*broadcast*)
**informatique** *f.* computer science
**informé(e)** *adj.* informed
**ingénieur** *m.* engineer
**inoxidable** *adj.* stainless; **acier** (*m.*) **inoxidable**
   stainless steel
**inquiet/ète** *adj.* worried, restless
**s'inquiéter (je m'inquiète)** to worry

**inscription** *f.* enrollment, registration
**insister (sur)** to insist (on)
**installer** to install; **s'installer** to move in, settle in
**instant** *m.* instant; **à l'instant** at this very instant; **dans un instant** in a moment
**instituteur/trice** *m., f.* elementary school teacher
**instrument** *m.* instrument
**insuffisant(e)** *adj.* insufficient
**intellectuel(le)** *adj.* intellectual
**intelligemment** *adv.* intelligently
**intelligent(e)** *adj.* intelligent
**intensément** *adv.* intensively
**intention** *f.* intention; **avoir l'intention de** to intend to
**interconnexion** *f.*: **interconnexion de réseau** networking
**interdire (de)** *irreg.* (**nous interdisons**) to forbid
**intéressant(e)** *adj.* interesting
**intéresser** to interest; **s'intéresser (à)** to be interested (in)
**intérêt** *m.* interest; **film** (*m.*) **sans intérêt** movie devoid of interest
**Internet** *m.* Internet
**interprète** *m., f.* interpreter
**interrogatif/ve** *adj., gram.* interrogative
**interroger** (**nous interrogeons**) to interrogate
**interrompre** *irreg.* (**il interrompt**; *p.p.* **interrompu**) to interrupt
**intervalle** *m.* interval, space; **par intervalles** at intervals
**intervention** *f.* intervention, intercession
**introduire** *irreg.* (**nous introduisons**) to introduce, put into
**inverse** *f.* opposite; **à l'inverse** conversely
**inversion** *f.* inversion
**invitation** *f.* invitation
**invité(e)** *m., f.* guest
**inviter** to invite
**Irak** *m.* Iraq
**Iran** *m.* Iran
**Israël** *m.* Israel
**Italie** *f.* Italy
**italien(ne)** *adj.* Italian; *m.* Italian (*language*); **Italien(ne)** Italian (*person*)
**italique** *adj.*: **caractères italiques** italics
**itinéraire** *m.* itinerary, route

## J

**jalousie** *f.* jealousy
**jamais** *adv.* never (*with or without* **ne**); ever (*without* **ne**); **à tout jamais** forever; **jamais de la vie!** never! not on your life!; **ne... jamais plus** never again; **plus... que jamais** more . . . than ever
**jambe** *f.* leg
**jambon** *m.* ham
**janvier** *m.* January
**Japon** *m.* Japan
**japonais(e)** *adj.* Japanese; *m.* Japanese (*language*); **Japonais(e)** Japanese (*person*)
**jardin** *m.* garden; **faire le jardin** to do the gardening; **jardin potager** vegetable garden; **jardin zoologique** zoo
**jaune** *adj.* yellow

**jeter (je jette)** to throw
**jeu** *m.* game; **jeu vidéo** video game; **hors jeu** *adj. inv.* offside; out of play
**jeudi** *m.* Thursday
**jeune** *adj.* young; **jeunes gens** young people; **les jeunes** *m. pl.* young people
**jeunesse** *f.* youth; young people
**jogging** *m.* jogging; **faire du jogging** to run, jog
**joie** *f.* joy
**joindre** *irreg.* (**nous joignons**; *p.p.* **joint**) to join; to reach (*s.o.*) (*by phone*); **se joindre à** to join (*s.o.*)
**joli(e)** *adj.* pretty
**Jordanie** *f.* Jordan
**jouer** to play; **jouer à** to play (*a sport, a game*); **jouer de** to play (*a musical instrument*)
**jouet** *m.* toy
**joueur/euse** *m., f.* player
**jour** *m.* day; **il fait jour** it's daytime; **jour de Noël** Christmas Day; **travailler de jour** to work during the day; **8 heures par jour** 8 hours a day
**journal** *m.* newspaper
**journaliste** *m., f.* journalist
**journée** *f.* (whole) day
**joyeusement** *adv.* joyfully
**joyeux/euse** *adj.* joyful
**juge** *m., f.* judge
**juger** (**nous jugeons**) to judge
**juillet** *m.* July
**juin** *m.* June
**jumeau** *m.* (**jumelle**) *f.* twin
**jumelles** *f. pl.* binoculars
**jupe** *f.* skirt
**jus** *m.* juice
**jusqu'à** *prep.* until; **jusqu'à ce que** *conj. + subj.* until
**juste** *adj.* just, fair; **à juste titre** with good reason; **viser juste** to aim correctly
**justement** *adv.* precisely, exactly; in fact

## K

**kilogramme** *m.* (*fam.* **kilo**) kilogram
**kilomètre** *m.* (**km**) kilometer
**kiosque** *m.* kiosk, stall
**klaxonner** to honk the horn
**Koweit** *m.* Kuwait

## L

**laboratoire** *m.* laboratory
**lac** *m.* lake
**laine** *f.* wool
**laisser** to leave; to let; to allow
**lait** *m.* milk
**lampe** *f.* lamp; **lampe de poche** flashlight
**lancer** (**nous lançons**) to launch; **se lancer au combat** to launch into fighting
**langue** *f.* language; **langue étrangère** foreign language
**Languedoc** *m.* region of southern France
**large** *adj.* wide
**largement** *adv.* widely
**latin** *m.* Latin

**laver** to wash; **machine à laver** washing machine; **se laver les mains (la figure, les cheveux, la tête)** to wash one's hands (face, hair)

**lave-vaisselle** *m.* dishwasher

**leçon** *f.* lesson

**lecteur** *m.*: **lecteur CD** CD player; **lecteur de CD-ROM** CD-ROM drive

**lecture** *f.* reading

**léger/ère** *adj.* light

**légèrement** *adv.* lightly

**légume** *m.* vegetable

**lentement** *adv.* slowly

**lenteur** *f.* slowness

**lequel (laquelle, lesquels, lesquelles)** *pron.* which (one), who, whom

**lessive** *f.* laundry; **faire la lessive** to do the laundry

**lettre** *f.* letter; **papier** (*m.*) **à lettres** stationery; *pl.* arts (*subject*)

**leur(s)** *adj.* (*m., f.*) their; **leur** *pron.* (*m., f.*) to them; **le/la/les leur(s)** *pron.* theirs

**lever (je lève)** to lift, raise; **se lever** to get up; to stand up; to rise (*sun*); **se lever avec le jour / de bonne heure** to get up early

**se lézarder** to crack (*wall*)

**Liban** *m.* Lebanon

**liberté** *f.* liberty, freedom

**librairie** *f.* bookstore

**libre** *adj.* available; free; **une minute de libre** a free moment

**Libye** *f.* Libya

**licencier** to fire

**lié(e)** *adj.*: **étroitement lié** very closely related

**lieu** *m.* place; **avoir lieu** to take place; **au lieu de** *prep.* instead of

**ligne** *f.* line; **à la ligne** new paragraph; **ligne de métro** subway line

**se limer les ongles** to file one's nails

**limonade** *f.* lemon-lime soft drink

**linge** *m.* wash; **étendre le linge** to hang out one's washing; **faire le linge** to do the laundry

**linguistique** *adj.* linguistic; **stage** (*m.*) **linguistique** intensive language course

**lire** *irreg.* (**nous lisons**; *p.p.* **lu**) **lire tout haut / à haute voix** to read aloud

**lit** *m.* bed

**littéraire** *adj.* literary; **prix** (*m.*) **littéraire** literary award

**littérature** *f.* literature

**livre** *m.* book; *f.* pound

**livrer** to deliver; **livrer des marchandises** to deliver goods

**local(e)** *adj.* local

**locution** *f., gram.* phrase, locution

**logé(e)** *adj.*: **être logé** to be housed, have lodging

**logement** *m.* housing, lodging

**loger (nous logeons)** to house, put (*s.o.*) up

**logiciel** *m.* software

**logique** *adj.* logical

**loi** *f.* law

**loin** *prep.* far; **loin de** far from

**long(ue)** *adj.* long; **à la longue** eventually; **le long de** *adv.* along; **chemise** (*f.*) **à manches longues** long-sleeve shirt

**longtemps** *adv.* (for) a long time

**longuement** *adv.* for a long time; in detail

**longueur** *f.* length; **dans le sens de la longueur** lengthwise

**lorsque** *conj.* when

**loterie** *f.* lottery; **gagner à la loterie** to win the lottery

**louer** to rent

**Louisiane** *f.* Louisiana

**loup** *m.* wolf; **entre chien et loup** at dusk

**loyer** *m.* rent

**lumière** *f.* light

**lundi** *m.* Monday

**lunettes** *f. pl.* glasses; **lunettes de soleil** sunglasses; **porter des lunettes** to wear glasses

**luxe** *m.* luxury; **hôtel** (*m.*) **de luxe** luxury hotel

**Luxembourg** *m.* Luxembourg

**lycée** *m.* high school

**lycéen(ne)** *m., f.* high-school student

# M

**ma** *adj., f.* my

**machine** *f.*; **machine à laver** washing machine

**madame** *f.* (**M^me**) (*pl.* **mesdames**) Madam, Mrs. (Ma'am)

**mademoiselle** *f.* (**M^lle**) (*pl.* **mesdemoiselles**) Miss

**magasin** *m.* store; **grand magasin** department store

**magazine** *m.* magazine

**magnifique** *adj.* magnificent

**mai** *m.* May

**maigrir** to lose weight

**maillot** *m.*: **maillot de bain** swimsuit

**main** *f.* hand; **coup** (*m.*) **de main** helping hand; **écrire à la main** to write by hand; **écrire de la main gauche (droite)** to write with one's left (right) hand; **entre ses mains** in one's hands; **faire de ses propres mains** to make (*s.th.*) yourself; **sous la main** handy

**maintenant** *adv.* now

**maintenir** *irreg.* (**je maintiens**; *p.p.* **maintenu**) to maintain

**mais** *conj.* but; **mais si** of course there is (*affirmative answer to a negative question*)

**maison** *f.* house; home; **à la maison** at home; **maison de campagne** country house

**maîtriser** to control

**mal** *adv.* badly; **avoir mal à la tête (à l'estomac)** to have a headache (stomachache); **faire mal** to hurt; **avoir mal au cœur** to feel nauseous; **pas mal de** quite a lot of; **sans mal** without any trouble

**malade** *m., f.* sick person, patient; *adj.* sick; **tomber malade** to get sick

**maladroit(e)** *adj.* clumsy

**malgré** *prep.* in spite of

**Mali** *m.* Mali

**maman** *f., fam.* mom, mommy

**manche** *f.* sleeve; **chemise** (*f.*) **à manches longues** long-sleeve shirt

**manger (nous mangeons)** to eat

**manière** *f.* manner, way

**se manifester** to appear, turn up (*person*)

**manque (de)** *m.* lack (of)

**manquer** to miss; to be missing; **manquer de** to be short of, lack

**manteau** *m.* coat

**manuel** *m.* manual, handbook

**se maquiller** to put on make-up

**marais** *m.* marshland; **le Marais** the Marais (*district of Paris*)

**marchand(e)** *m., f.* merchant, vendor

**marchandise** *f.* merchandise; **cargaison** (*f.*) **de marchandises** cargo of merchandise; **livrer des marchandises** to deliver goods

**marché** *m.* market; **faire le marché** to go to the market; **par-dessus le marché** on top of that; **marché en plein air** open-air market

**marcher** to walk; to work (*appliance*)

**mardi** *m.* Tuesday

**mari** *m.* husband

**mariée** *f.* bride

**se marier** to get married

**Maroc** *m.* Morocco

**marquer** to mark off

**marron** *adj. inv.* brown

**mars** *m.* March

**Martinique (la)** *f.* Martinique

**masculin(e)** *adj.* masculine

**massif/ve** *adj.* built (*person*)

**massivement** *adv.* massively

**match** *m.* game (*sport*)

**mathématiques** *f. pl.* (*fam.* **maths**) mathematics

**matière** *f.* academic subject; matter

**matin** *m.* morning; **de bon matin** early in the morning

**matinée** *f.* morning (*duration*); **faire la grasse matinée** to sleep late

**Mauritanie** *f.* Mauretania

**mauvais(e)** *adj.* bad; **être sur la mauvaise piste** to be on the wrong track; **il fait mauvais** it's bad weather out

**mécanicien(ne)** *m., f.* mechanic

**médecin** *m.* doctor; **chez le médecin** at the doctor's office

**médecine** *f.* medicine (*science*); **faculté** (*f.*) **de médecine** Medical School

**médicament** *m.* medication; drug

**se méfier (de)** to mistrust

**mégarde** *f.*: **par mégarde** accidentally

**meilleur(e)** *adj.* better; **le/la/les meilleur(e)(s)** the best

**se mêler de** to meddle in; **se mêler des affaires des autres** to meddle in other people's business

**membre** *m.* member

**même** *adj.* same; self; *adv.* even; *pron.* **les mêmes** the same (ones); **lui-même** himself; **même pas** not even; **même si** even if

**mémoire** *f.* memory; **de mémoire** from memory

**menace** *f.* threat

**menacer (nous menaçons)** to threaten

**ménage** *m.* housekeeping; **faire le ménage** to do the housework

**mener (je mène)** to lead

**mentionner** to mention

**mentir** *irreg.* (**je mens**) to lie

**mer** *f.* sea, ocean; **bord** (*m.*) **de la mer** seashore

**merci** *interj.* thank you

**mercredi** *m.* Wednesday

**mère** *f.* mother; **grand-mère** grandmother

**mériter** to deserve

**merveille** *f.*: **à merveille** perfectly

**merveilleux/euse** *adj.* marvelous

**mes** *adj.*, (*m. f., pl.*) my

**mésaventure** *f.* misadventure

**mesdames** *f. pl.* ladies

**mesdemoiselles** *f. pl.* young ladies

**message** *m.* message

**messe** *f.* mass; **messe de minuit** midnight mass

**messieurs** *m. pl.* men; gentlemen

**mesurer** to measure

**métal** *m.* metal

**méthode** *f.* method

**métier** *m.* job, occupation; trade

**mètre** *m.* meter

**métro** *m.* subway; **ligne** (*f.*) **de métro** subway line

**mettre** *irreg.* (*p.p.* **mis**) to put; to wear; **mettre à jour** to update; **mettre la maison en ordre** to clean up the house; **mettre la radio plus haut** to turn the radio up; **mettre la table / le couvert** to set the table; **se mettre à** to start (*doing s.th.*); **se mettre en colère** to get angry; **se mettre en route** to start out, set off

**meuble** *m.* piece of furniture

**mexicain(e)** *adj.* Mexican; **Mexicain(e)** *m., f.* Mexican (*person*)

**Mexico** Mexico City

**Mexique** *m.* Mexico

**midi** *m.* noon; **après-midi** afternoon; **dans le Midi** in the South of France

**mien(ne)(s) (le/la/les)** *pron.* (*m., f.*) mine

**mieux** *adv.* better; **aimer mieux** to prefer, like best; **bien, mieux, le mieux** well, better, the best; **ça va mieux** things are going better; **il vaut mieux que** + *subj.* it's better that

**mignon(ne)** *adj.* sweet, cute

**mille** *adj.* (*also* **mil** *for years*) (one) thousand

**milliard** *adj.* billion

**million** *adj.* million

**mincir** to get thin

**minéral(e)** *adj.* mineral; **eau** (*f.*) **minérale** mineral water

**ministère** *m.* ministry

**ministre** *m., f.* minister

**minuit** midnight; **messe** (*f.*) **de minuit** midnight mass

**minute** *f.* minute; **avoir une minute de libre** to have a free moment

**mode** *f.* fashion

**modèle** *m.* example

**moderne** *adj.* modern

**modernisé(e)** *adj.* modernized

**modeste** *adj.* modest, simple

**modification** *f.* modification

**modifier** to modify

**mœurs** *f. pl.* morals

**moi** *pron.* I; me; **chez moi** at my house; **moi aussi** me too; **pas moi** not me

**moindre(s) (le/la/les)** *adj.*: **je n'en ai pas la moindre idée** I don't have the slightest idea

**moins** *adv.* less; **à moins que** *conj.* + *subj.* unless; **moins de... que** less . . . than; **moins le quart** quarter to (*the hour*); **le moins** the least; **en moins de** in less than

**mois** *m.* month; **par mois** per month

**moitié** *f.* half; **à moitié** half; **à moitié prix** half price

**moment** *m.* while, moment; **dans un moment** in a moment; **en ce moment** at the moment, at this time; **vivre un moment difficile** to be having a difficult time

**monde** *m.* world; **faire le tour du monde** to travel around the world; **tout le monde** everybody

**moniteur/trice** *m., f.* instructor, counselor

**monnaie** *f.* change

**monsieur** *m.* (**M.**) (*pl.* **Messieurs**) Mister, Mr.; gentleman; Sir

**montagne** *f.* mountain

‡**monter** to go up (*stairs*); to get on (*bicycle, bus, train*); to take up

**montre** *f.* watch

**montrer** to show

**monument** *m.* monument

**se moquer (de)** to make fun (of)

**moqueur/euse** *adj.* mocking

**moral** *m.*: **remonter le moral de** to raise the spirits (*of s.o.*)

**morceau** *m.* piece

**mordre** to bite

**mort** *f.* death; **peine** (*f.*) **de mort** death penalty

**mot** *m.* word; **en toucher un mot à** to let (*s.o.*) know; **un petit mot** a note

**motiver** to justify (*actions*)

**moto** *f.* motorcycle

**mouchoir** *m.* tissue, handkerchief

**se mouiller** to get wet

†**mourir** (**je meurs**; *p.p.* **mort**) to die; **mourir de faim** to starve, be very hungry; **mourir d'ennui** to be bored to death **mourir de soif** to be very thirsty

**moyen** *m.* mean; **au moyen de** by means of; **le Moyen-Orient** the Middle East

**moyenne** *f.* average; **en-dessous de la moyenne** below the average; **en moyenne** on average

**Mozambique** *m.* Mozambique

**muet(te)** *adj.* mute; **film** (*m.*) **muet** silent movie

**multitude** *f.*: **une multitude de** a vast number of

**municipal(e)** *adj.* municipal

**mur** *m.* wall

**muraille** *f.* high wall

**musée** *m.* museum

**musicien(ne)** *m., f.* musician

**musique** *f.* music

**mutuellement** *adv.* each other, mutually

**mystérieux/euse** *adj.* mysterious

# N

**nager** (**nous nageons**) to swim

**nageur/euse** *m., f.* swimmer

**naif** (**naïve**) *adj.* naive

†**naître** *irreg.* (**je nais**; *p.p.* **né**) to be born

**nappe** *f.* tablecloth

**narration** *f.* narration

**natal(e)** *adj.* native; **pays** (*m.*) **natal** native land

**natation** *f.* swimming

**nation** *f.* nation

**national(e)** *adj.* national; **Société** (*f.*) **Nationale de Chemins de Fer (SNCF)** French national railway company

**nature** *f.* nature

**naturel(le)** *adj.* natural

**naval(e)** *adj.* naval; **école** (*f.*) **navale** naval college

**navré(e)** *adj.* sorry

**nécessaire** *adj.* necessary; **il est nécessaire que** + *subj.* it is necessary that

**négatif/ve** *adj.* negative

**négation** *f.* negation

**neige** *f.* snow

**neiger** *impers.* to snow

**nerveux/euse** *adj.* nervous

**nerveusement** *adv.* nervously

**nettoyage** *m.* cleaning

**nettoyer** (**je nettoie**) to clean

**neuf** *adj. inv.* nine

**neuf/ve** *adj.* new

**neuvième** *adj.* ninth

**neveu** (**nièce**) *m., f.* nephew (niece)

**nez** *m.* nose

**ni** *conj.* neither; nor; **ne... ni... ni** neither . . . nor

**niçois(e)** *adj.* from Nice; **salade** (*f.*) **niçoise** salad made with anchovies, potatoes, hard-boiled eggs, and green beans

**nier** to deny

**Noël** *m.* Christmas; **jour** (*m.*) **de Noël** Christmas Day

**noir(e)** *adj.* black

**nom** *m.* name

**nombre** *m.* number

**nombreux/euse** *adj.* numerous, many

**nord** *m.* north

**normal(e)** *adj.* normal; **il est normal que** + *subj.*

**nos** *adj.* (*m., f. pl.*) our

**note** *f.* note; bill; score; **régler la note** to pay the bill, settle the account

**notre** *adj.* (*m., f. s.*) our

**nôtre(s): le/la/ les nôtre(s)** *pron.* (*m., f.*) ours; our own

**nourriture** *f.* food

**nous** *pron.* we; **chez nous** at our house

**nouveau** (**nouvelle**) *adj.* new; **la Nouvelle-Orléans** New Orleans; **Nouvelle-Zélande** (*f.*) New Zealand

**nouvelles** *f. pl.* news

**novembre** *m.* November

**noyer** (**je noie**) to drown

**nuage** *m.* cloud

**nuire** (**à**) *irreg.* (**nous nuisons**; *p.p.* **nui**) to harm, hurt

**nuit** *f.* night; **il fait nuit** it's nighttime; **travailler de nuit** to work the night shift

**nul(le)** *adj.* useless, hopeless; worthless; **faire match nul** to tie (*sport*)

**nulle part** *adv.* nowhere

**nullité** *f.* nonentity (*person*)

**numéro** *m.* number; **numéro de téléphone** phone number; **numéro gagnant** winning number

**nu(e)** *adj.*: **pieds nus** barefoot

# O

**obéir** to obey

**obéissant(e)** *adj.* obedient

**objet** *m.* object; **objet direct (indirect)** *gram.* direct (indirect) object

**obligatoire** *adj.* compulsory

**obliger** (**nous obligeons**) to oblige

**obscur(e)** *adj.* dark; obscure

**obscurément** *adv.* obscurely

observation *f.* observation

observer to observe

obstacle *m.* obstacle; **surmonter des obstacles** to overcome obstacles

s'obstiner (à) to persist stubbornly (in)

obtenir *irreg.* (**nous obtenons**; *p.p.* **obtenu**) to obtain, get

occasion *f.* occasion

occidental(e) *adj.* western; **Virginie-occidentale** West Virginia

occupation *f.* occupation

occupé(e) *adj.* busy

s'occuper (de) to deal (with), take care (of)

Océanie *f.* Oceania

octobre *m.* October

œil *m.* (*pl.* **yeux**) eye; **personne ne ferme l'œil de la nuit** nobody gets a wink of sleep

œuf *m.* egg; **œuf dur** hard-boiled egg

œuvre *f.* (**d'art**) work of art, works (*art*)

offenser to offend, hurt; **s'offenser** to get insulted, offended

offert(e) *adj.* offered

officiel(le) *adj.* official

offre *f.* offer

offrir *irreg.* (**j'offre**; *p.p.* **offert**) to offer

oignon *m.* onion

olive *f.* olive

omettre (*p.p.* **omis**) to omit

oncle *m.* uncle

ongle *m.* nail; **se limer les ongles** to file one's nails

onze *adj.* eleven

opinion *f.* opinion

s'opposer (à) to oppose, be against

optimiste *adj.* optimistic

or *m.* gold; **en or** gold, *made of gold*

orage *m.* thunderstorm

oral(e) *adj.* oral

orange *f.* orange

orchestre *m.* orchestra

ordinaire: **d'ordinaire** usually

ordinal(e) *adj.* ordinal

ordinateur *m.* computer

ordonnance *f.* prescription

ordonner to prescribe; to order; **ordonner que +** *subj.* to order that

ordre *m.* order; **donner des ordres** to give orders; **en ordre** tidy, orderly; **mettre de l'ordre** to tidy up; **ordre public** law and order; **par ordre chronologique** in chronological order

ordures *f. pl.* garbage

organisation *f.* organization

organiser to organize

orient *m.* east; **Moyen-Orient** Middle East

oriental(e) *adj.* eastern

orientation *f.* orientation; positioning

orienter to orient

origine *f.* origin

oser to dare

oublier to forget

ouest *m.* west

oui *adv.* yes

ouvert(e) *adj.* open

ouverture *f.* opening

ouvrier/ère *m., f.* worker

ouvrir *irreg.* (**j'ouvre**; *p.p.* **ouvert**) to open

pagaille *f.:* **en pagaille** in chaos

page *f.* page; **à la page** up-to-date

pain *m.* bread

paire *f.* pair

paix *f.* peace

Pakistan *m.* Pakistan

pâle *adj.* pale

panique *f.* panic; **être pris de panique** to be panic-stricken; **se mettre en panique** to fly into a panic

panne *f.* breakdown (*machine*); **être en panne** to break down; **panne d'électricité** power failure

pansement *m.* bandage; **mettre un pansement** to put on a bandage

pantalon *m. s.* pants

pantoufle *f.* slipper

papa *m.* dad, daddy

papier *m.* paper; **corbeille** (*f.*) **à papiers** wastepaper basket; **papier à lettres** stationery; **papier peint** wallpaper

Pâques *f. pl.* Easter

paquet *m.* parcel

par *prep.* by; per; **commencer par** to begin by (*doing s.th.*); **finir par** to end by (*doing s.th.*); **par amitié/amour** out of friendship, love; **par cœur** by heart; **par conséquent** consequently; **par écrit** in writing; **par hasard** by chance; **par ici** this way; **par là** that way; **par intervalles** intermittently; **par la force** by force; **par la porte** through the door; **par la poste** through the mail; **par le train** by train; **par les temps qui courent** these days; **par mégarde** accidentally; **par mois** per month; **par terre** on the floor/ground; **par un temps pareil** in such weather; **payer par chèque** to pay by check

paragraphe *m.* paragraph

paraître *irreg.* (**nous paraissons**; *p.p.* **paru**) to seem, appear

parc *m.* park

par-dessus *prep.* over; **par-dessus le marché** on top of all that; **en avoir par-dessus la tête** to be sick and tired (*of s.th.*)

pardon *m.* sorry!

pardonner (à) to forgive

pareil(le) *adj.* such; similar

parenthèse *f.* parenthesis; **entre parenthèses** in parentheses

parent *m.* parent; **beaux-parents** mother- and father-in-law; **grands-parents** grandparents

paresse *f.* laziness

paresseux/euse *adj.* lazy

parfait(e) *adj.* perfect

parfaitement *adv.* perfectly

parfois *adv.* sometimes

parfum *m.* perfume

parisien(ne) *adj.* Parisian; **Parisien(ne)** Parisian (*person*)

parler to speak; **parler de** to talk about; **parler tout bas** to speak softly; **se parler** to speak to each other

parmi *prep.* among

parquet *m.* wooden floor; **balayer (cirer) le parquet** to sweep (wax) the floor

**part** f. portion, share; **à part** except for; **de ma part** on my behalf; **nulle part** nowhere; **prendre part** to participate in; **quelque part** somewhere

**partager (nous partageons)** to share

**participe** m. gram. participle; **participe (présent, passé)** (present, past) participle

**participer (à)** to participate (in)

**partie** f. part

†**partir** irreg. (**je pars**) to leave; **à partir de** from; **partir en vacances** to leave on vacation

**partitif/ve** adj., gram. partitive

**partout** adv. everywhere

**parvenir (à)** irreg. (**je parviens**; p.p. **parvenu**) to manage (to)

**passé(e)** adj. past; last; **passé** m., gram. past; **participe passé** past participle; **passé composé** past tense (compound tense); **passé du subjonctif** past subjunctive; **passé simple** past tense (literary)

‡**passer** to pass; to spend; to happen; **passer qch à qn** to lend s.th. to s.o.; **passer l'aspirateur** to vacuum; **passer le temps** to pass the time; **passer son temps à** to spend one's time (doing s.th.); **passer un examen** to take an exam; **passer une commande** to place an order; **se passer de** to do without; **voir le temps passer** to see time go by

**passionnant(e)** adj. fascinating

**passionner** to fascinate; **se passionner pour** to get excited (about)

**passif/ve** adj. passive; **voix** (f.) **passive** gram. passive voice

**pastille** f. lozenge, drop

**pâte** f. dough; paste

**pâté** m. liver paste, pâté

**patiemment** adv. patiently

**patience** f. patience

**patient(e)** adj. patient; m., f. patient (hospital)

**patiner** to skate

**pâtisserie** f. pastry shop; pastry

**patron(ne)** m., f. boss, employer

**pauvre** adj. poor; unfortunate

**paver** to pave

**payé(e)** adj. paid

**payer (je paie)** to pay; **payer cher** to pay a high price; **payer par chèque** to pay by check; **payer qch** to pay for s.th.

**pays** m. country; **les Pays-bas** the Netherlands; **pays natal** native land

**paysage** m. landscape; scenery

**peau** f. skin

**peigner** to comb; **se peigner** to comb one's hair

**peindre** irreg. (**nous peignons**) to paint

**peine** f.; **à peine** hardly; **ce n'est pas la peine** it's not worth it; **peine de mort** death penalty; **se donner la peine de** to go to the trouble of; **sous peine de** in fear of

**peint(e)** adj. painted

**peintre** m., f. painter

**peinture** f. painting; paint

**pelouse** f. lawn

**pendant** prep. during; for; **pendant que** conj. while

**penderie** f. closet

**penser** to think; to intend; **penser à** to think of, think about; **penser** + inf. to plan on (doing s.th.)

**perdre** to lose; to waste; **perdre son temps** to waste time; **se perdre** to get lost

**père** m. father; **grand-père** grandfather

**perfection** f. perfection; **à la perfection** to perfection

**périr** to perish

**permanence** f.: **salle** (f.) **de permanence** study hall

**permettre** irreg. (p.p. **permis**) to allow, let, permit

**permis** m. permit; **permis de conduire** driving license

**Pérou** m. Peru

**personnel(le)** adj. personal

**personnage** m. (fictional) character; personality

**personne** f. person; **ne... personne** nobody, no one; **personne d'autre** nobody else

**persuader** to persuade

**peser (je pèse)** to weigh

**pessimiste** adj. pessimistic

**petit(e)** adj. small; little; **petit(e) ami(e)** boyfriend (girlfriend); **petit déjeuner** breakfast; **petit-enfant** grandchild; **petit mot** note; **petits pois** green peas; **petite sœur** younger sister; pl. **les petits** young children

**peu** adv. little; few; not very; hardly; **à peu près** about, near; **en peu de temps** quickly, soon; **il est peu probable que** + subj. it's doubtful that; **peu à peu** little by little; **peu importe** it does not matter; **un peu (de)** a little (of); **sous peu** soon

**peuple** m. people (of a country)

**peuplier** m. poplar tree

**peur** f. fear; **avoir peur de** to be afraid of; **de peur que** conj. + subj. for fear that; **faire peur à** to scare

**pharmacie** f. pharmacy

**pharmacien(ne)** m., f. pharmacist

**Philippines (les)** the Philippines

**philosophe** m., f. philosopher

**philosophie** f. (fam. **philo**) philosophy

**photocopier** to photocopy

**photographie** f. (fam. **photo**) picture; **appareil photo** m. (still) camera

**photographié(e)** adj. photographed

**phrase** f. sentence

**physique** f. physics

**piano** m. piano; **jouer du piano** to play the piano

**pièce** f. room; **pièce de monnaie** coin; **pièce de théâtre** play

**pied** m. foot; **à pied** on foot; **aller pieds nus** to walk barefoot; **se faire mal au pied** to hurt one's foot

**piéton(ne)** adj. pedestrian; **rue** (f.) **piétonne** pedestrian zone

**pile** adv. sharp (time)

**pilote** m., f. pilot

**pilule** f. pill

**pique-nique** m. picnic

**piqûre** f. injection

**pire (pis)** adj. worse; **le/la/les pire(s)** the worst

**piscine** f. pool

**piste** f. track, trail

**pizza** f. pizza

**placard** m. cupboard

**place** f. place; plaza; room, space

**placement** m. investment (financial)

**placer (nous plaçons)** to put; to invest

**plage** f. beach

**plaindre** irreg. (**je plains, nous plaignons**; p.p. **plaint**) to pity; **se plaindre (de)** to complain about

**plaire** irreg. (**nous plaisons**; p.p. **plu**) to please; **se plaire** to like each other; **s'il vous plaît** please

**plaisir** m. pleasure; **avec plaisir** gladly

**plan** *m.* plan; map
**plancher** *m.* floor
**plante** *f.* plant
**plastique** *m.* plastic
**plat** *m.* dish
**plâtrer** to plaster
**plein(e)** *adj.* full; **en pleine forme** in great shape; **en pleine ville** in the middle of the city; **être en plein travail** to be in the middle of one's work; **marché en plein air** outdoor market; *m.* **faire le plein** to fill up (*with gas*)
**pleurer** to cry
**pleuviner** *irreg., impers.* to drizzle
**pleuvoir** *impers.* (**il pleut**; *p.p.* **plu**) to rain
**plier** to fold
**plombier/ière** *m., f.* plumber
**plonger (nous plongeons)** to dive
**pluie** *f.* rain; **sous la pluie** in the rain
**plupart: la plupart (de)** most (of)
**pluriel** *m., gram.* plural
**plus** *adv.* more; **en plus** moreover; **plus rien à faire** nothing left to do; **le plus** + *adv.* most; **le/la/les plus** + *adj.* most; **moi non plus** me neither; **ne... plus** no longer, no more; **plus de** + *noun* **que** more + *noun* than; **plus** + *adj.* **que** more + *adj.* than; **tout au plus** at the very most
**plusieurs (de)** *adj., pron.* many, several; **à plusieurs reprises** on many occasions; **dans plusieurs cas** in many cases
**plus-que-parfait** *m., gram.* pluperfect
**plutôt** *adv.* **(que de)** instead (of), rather (than)
**pneu** *m.* tire; **pneu crevé** flat tire
**poche** *f.* pocket; **couteau** (*m.*) **de poche** pocket knife; **lampe** (*f.*) **de poche** flashlight
**poêle** *f.* frying pan
**poème** *m.* poem
**poésie** *f.* poetry
**poète** *m., f.* poet
**poids** *m.* weight; **prendre du poids** to gain weight
**poignet** *m.* wrist
**point** *m.* point; **être sur le point de** to be about to; **ne... point** *adv.* not at all (*literary*); **point de vue** point of view
**poire** *f.* pear; **(dire qch) entre la poire et le fromage** (*to say s.th.*) casually
**pois** *m.* pea; **petits pois** green peas
**poisson** *m.* fish
**poivre** *m.* pepper
**poli(e)** *adj.* polite
**police** *f.* police; **agent** (*m.*) **de police** police officer
**poliment** *adv.* politely
**politesse** *f.* politeness
**politique** *f.* politics
**Pologne** *f.* Poland
**pomme** *f.* apple; **pomme de terre** potato
**populaire** *adj.* popular
**porc** *m.* pork
**port** *m.* port, harbor
**porte** *f.* door; **frapper à la porte** to knock at the door; **sonner à la porte** to ring the doorbell
**porter** to carry; to wear; **se porter candidat** to run for office
**portrait** *m.* portrait, description
**Portugal** *m.* Portugal
**poser des questions** to ask questions; to put down; **se poser des questions** to ask each other questions

**positif/ve** *adj.* positive
**posséder (je possède)** to possess
**possessif/ve** *adj.* possessive
**possibilité** *f.* possibility
**possible** *adj.*; **il est possible que** + *subj.* it's possible that
**postal(e)** *adj.*: **carte** (*f.*) **postale** postcard
**poste** *m.* position, job; *f.* mail; post office **par la poste** by mail
**poster** to mail
**potager** *m.* vegetable garden
**poterie** *f.* pottery
**poubelle** *f.* garbage can; **à la poubelle** in the garbage
**poulet** *m.* chicken
**poupée** *f.* doll
**pour** *prep.* for; in order to; **c'est pour ça** that's why; **et pour cause** for good reason; **être pour qch** to be in favor of; **garder le meilleur pour la fin** to keep the best for last
**pourboire** *m.* tip
**pourpre** *adj.* crimson
**pourquoi** *adv., conj.* why; **je ne sais pourquoi** for some reason or other
**poursuivre** *irreg.* (**je poursuis**; *p.p.* **poursuivi**) to pursue, continue
**pourvoir** *irreg.* (**nous pourvoyons**; *p.p.* **pourvu**) to provide
**pourvu que** *conj.* + *subj.* as long as; provided that; let's hope that
**pousser** to push; to grow
**pouvoir** *irreg.* (**je peux**; *p.p.* **pu**) to be able to; can
**pratique** *adj.* practical
**pratiquement** *adv.* practically
**pratiquer** to practice
**pré** *m.* meadow
**précédemment** *adv.* previously
**précis(e)** *adj.* precise, clear, accurate
**précisément** *adv.* precisely
**préciser** to specify
**précision** *f.* point, piece of information
**préférence** *f.* preference
**préférer (je préfère)** to prefer; **préférer que** + *subj.* to prefer that
**préjugé** *m.* prejudice
**premier/ère** *adj.*, first; **de première classe** first-rate; **en première classe** in first class; **le premier / la première** *m., f.* the first (one)
**prendre** *irreg.* (**nous prenons**; *p.p.* **pris**) to take; **prendre de l'essence** to get gas; **prendre des gants avec qn** to be as gentle as possible; **prendre du poids** to gain weight; **prendre froid** to catch cold; **prendre garde** to be careful, take care; **prendre le (petit) déjeuner** to have lunch (breakfast); **prendre pour un autre** to mistake (*s.o.*) for s.o. else; **passer prendre qn** to go pick s.o. up; **prendre un rhume** to catch a cold; **prendre un verre** to have a drink
**préoccupation** *f.* worry
**se préoccuper** to worry
**préparatifs** *m. pl.* preparations
**préparer** to prepare; **se préparer à** to get ready to
**préposition** *f.* preposition
**près** *adv.* near; **à ceci près** with this exception; **à peu près** about, almost; **près de** close to; **tout près** very close
**présent(e)** *adj.* present; **participe** (*m.*) **présent** *gram.* present participle; *m.* present (time)

**présenter** to present; to introduce; **se présenter** to introduce o.s.; **se présenter sous un jour favorable** to show o.s. in a favorable light

**président(e)** *m., f.* president

**presque** *adv.* almost, nearly

**pressé(e)** *adj.* in a hurry; **citron** (*m.*) **pressé** lemonade

**pressing** *m.* dry cleaner's

**présupposé(e)** *adj.* presupposed

**prêt(e)** *adj.* **(à)** ready (to)

**prétendre** to pretend; to claim

**prêter (à)** to lend (to)

**prévenir** *irreg.* (**je préviens**; *p.p.* **prévenu**) to forewarn

**prévoir** *irreg.* (**nous prévoyons**; *p.p.* **prévu**) to foresee

**prévu(e)** *adj.* expected, anticipated

**prier** to pray; to invite; to ask; to request; to beg

**primaire** *adj.* **école** (*f.*) **primaire** elementary school

**prince(sse)** *m., f.* prince (princess)

**principal(e)** *adj.* principal, main; *gram.* **proposition** (*f.*) **principale** main clause

**printemps** *m.* spring

**prison** *f.* prison

**prisonnier/ère** *m., f.* prisoner

**se priver de** to deprive o.s. of s.th

**prix** *m.* price; **à moitié prix** half price; **à prix d'or** real bargain; **prix littéraire** literary award

**probable** *adj.* probable; **il est probable que** + *indic.*; **il est peu probable que** + *subj.* it's doubtful, improbable that

**probablement** *adv.* probably

**problème** *m.* problems

**procéder** *irreg.* (**je procède**) **(à)** to proceed

**prochain(e)** *adj.* next

**proche** *adj., adv.* near; **futur** (*m.*) **proche** *gram.* immediate future

**production** *f.* production

**produire** *irreg.* (**nous produisons**) to produce

**produit** *m.* product

**professeur** (*fam.* **le/la prof**) *m.* professor, instructor

**professionnel(le)** *m., f.* professional

**profiter de** to take advantage of; to enjoy

**profond(e)** *adj.* deep

**profondément** *adv.* profoundly, deeply

**profondeur** *f.* depth; **deux mètres** (*m.*) **de profondeur** two meters deep

**programmation** *f.* programming

**programme** *m.* program; agenda; show (*TV, radio*)

**programmer** to program

**programmeur/euse** *m., f.* programmer

**progrès** *m.* progress

**progresser** to progress

**projet** *m.* project; plan; **faire des projets** to make plans

**projeter (je projette)** to project; to plan; to throw

**promenade** *f.* ride; **faire une promenade** to take a ride; **faire une promenade à pied (en voiture)** to go for a walk (a car ride)

**promener (je promène)** to take for a walk or a drive (*person, dog*); **se promener** to take a walk

**promesse** *f.* promise

**promettre** *irreg.* (**nous promettons**, *p.p.* **promis**) **(de)** to promise

**pronom** *m., gram.* pronoun; **pronom complément d'objet direct (indirect), démonstratif, disjoint, interrogatif, possessif, relatif** direct (indirect) object, demonstrative, disjunctive, interrogative, possessive, relative pronoun

**pronominal(e)** *adj., gram.* pronominal; **verbe** (*m.*) **pronominal** reflexive verb

**prononcer (nous prononçons)** to pronounce

**prononciation** *f.* pronunciation

**propos** *m.*: **à propos** by the way, incidentally; **à propos de** about

**proposé(e)** *adj.* suggested

**proposer** to suggest; **se proposer de** to set out, mean, intend

**proposition** *f., gram.* clause; **proposition adverbiale (principale, relative, subordonnée)** adverbiale (main, relative, subordinate) clause

**propre** *adj.* clean; own; **voir de ses propres yeux** to see with one's own eyes

**propriétaire** *m., f.* owner

**protéger (nous protégeons)** to protect

**protestant(e)** *adj.* Protestant

**protester** to protest

**provenir** *irreg.* (**je proviens**; *p.p.* **provenu**) **de** to come from

**province** *f.* province (*France: outside Paris*)

**prudemment** *adv.* carefully

**prudent(e)** *adj.* careful

**psychologique** *adj.* psychological

**public (publique)** *adj.* public; *m.* public

**publicité** *f.* advertisement, commercial

**publier** to publish

**publiquement** *adv.* publicly

**puis** *adv.* then, next

**puisque** *conj.* since, as, seeing that

**pull** *m.* sweater

**pyjama** *m. s.* pyjamas

## Q

**quai** *m.* platform (*train station*)

**qualification** *f.* qualification

**qualifié(e)** *adj.* qualified

**quand** *adv., conj.* when; **depuis quand** since when; **je ne sais quand** sometime or other; **n'importe quand** at any time

**quant à** *adv.* as for, as to; **quant à moi** as for me

**quantité** *f.* quantity

**quart** *m.* quarter; **et quart** quarter past (the hour); **le quart de** a fourth of; **moins le quart** quarter to (the hour)

**quartier** *m.* neighborhood; **quartier des affaires** business district

**quatorze** *adj.* fourteen

**quatre** *adj.* four

**Québec** *m.* Quebec

**québécois(e)** *adj.* from / of Quebec; **québécois** *m.* Quebecois (*language*); **Québécois(e)** *m., f.* Quebecois (*person*)

**quel(le)(s)** *adj.* what; which; what (a); **n'importe quel** + *noun* any + *noun*; **quel âge a-t-il?** how old is he?; **quel que soit l'obstacle** whatever the obstacle may be; **quel temps fait-il?** what is the weather like?

**quelque(s)** *adj.* some, any; **quelque chose** *pron. indef.* something; **quelque chose de** + *adj.* something; **quelque part** *adv.* somewhere

**quelquefois** *adv.* sometimes

**quelques-uns/-unes** *pron., pl.* a few, some

**quelqu'un** *pron. neu.* someone, somebody; **quelqu'un d'autre** someone else

**quémander** to beg for

**querelle** *f.* quarrel

**question** *f.* question; **(se) poser des questions** to ask (each other) questions

**queue** *f.* tail; **histoire sans queue ni tête** cock-and-bull story

**quiche** *f.* quiche

**quinze** *adj.* fifteen

**quinzième** *m.* fifteenth

**quitter** to leave (*person or place*)

**quoi** *pron.* what; **à quoi bon?** what's the use?; **c'est en quoi?** what is it made of?; *fam.* **c'est quoi ça?** what is this?; **n'importe quoi** anything; **quoi d'autre?** what else?; **quoi que ce soit** anything

**quoique** *conj.* + *subj.* although

# R

**rabais** *m.* discount, reduction

**raccompagner** to take, accompany (*s.o.*) home

**raconter** to tell, tell about, relate

**radio** *f.* radio; **à la radio** on the radio

**rager (nous rageons)** to fume (with anger)

**raison** *f.* reason; **avoir raison** to be right

**ramener (je ramène)** to bring back, take back; **ramener en voiture** to drive (*s.o.*) back home

**ramper** to crawl; to creep (*plant*)

**randonnée** *f.* ride; drive; hike

**ranger (nous rangeons)** to put away; to tidy up

**râper** to scrap, rasp

**rapide** *adj.* fast, speedy

**rapidement** *adv.* quickly, rapidly

**rappeler (je rappelle)** to call back; **se rappeler qch** to recall, remember

**rapport** *m.* report; relationship; **par rapport à** in comparison with; **se mettre en rapport avec** to get in touch with (*s.o.*)

**rapporter** to bring back

**rapprochement** *m.* bringing closer, together

**raquette** *f.* racket

**se raser** to shave (*o.s.*)

**rasoir** *m.* razor

**rassurer** to reassure

**ravi(e)** *adj.* delighted

**rayer** *irreg.* **(je raie)** to cross out

**rayon** *m.* department (*store*)

**réaction** *f.* reaction

**réagir** to react

**réaliser** to bring about, make real; **se réaliser** to happen

**réalité** *f.* reality

**rebours** *m.*: **compter à rebours** to count backwards

**rebut** *m., Q.* garbage

**récemment** *adv.* recently

**réception** *f.* reception

**réceptionniste** *m., f.* receptionist

**recevoir** *irreg.* **(je reçois;** *p.p.* **reçu)** to receive

**réchaud** *m.* hot plate

**recherche** *f.* research; **à la recherche de** in search of; **faire des recherches** to do research

**récit** *m.* account, story

**récital** *m.* recital

**réciter** to recite

**recommandation** *f.* recommendation

**recommander** to recommend

**récompenser** to reward

**récompense** *f.* reward

**réconfortant(e)** *adj.* fortifying (*medicine*)

**reconnaître** *irreg.* **(nous reconnaissons;** *p.p.* **reconnu)** to recognize

**reconstruire** *irreg.* (*p.p.* **reconstruit**) to rebuild

**recopier** to copy out, write out

**se recoucher** to go back to bed

**rectification** *f.* rectification, correction

**recul** *m.* retreat

**récurer** to scour

**rédaction** *f.* written composition

**redécorer** to redecorate

‡**redescendre** to go back down again

**rédiger (nous rédigeons)** to write, draft

**réduction** *f.* discount

**réduire (nous reduisons)** to reduce

**réécrire** *irreg.* **(vous réécrivez)** to rewrite

**refaire** *irreg.* **(vous refaites)** to redo; to make again

**réfléchir (à)** to think (about); to reflect (upon)

**refléter (je reflète)** to reflect

**réflexion** *f.* reflection; **à la réflexion** on second thought

**reformuler** to re-write

**refus** *m.* refusal

**refuser (de)** to refuse

**regarder** to look at; to watch; **se regarder** to look at each other

**régime** *m.* diet; **suivre un régime** to be on a diet

**régiment** *m.* regiment

**région** *f.* region; area

**régional(e)** *adj.* local, of the district

**règle** *f.* rule; **tout est en règle** everything is in order

**régler** to settle up; **régler la note / la facture** to pay the bill

**règne** *m.* reign; **sous le règne de** in the reign of

**regretter (de)** to regret; **regretter que** + *subj.* to regret that

**rejeter (je rejette)** to reject

**rejoindre** *irreg.* **(nous rejoignons)** to rejoin, meet up

**se réjouir que** + *subj.* to be delighted that

**relatif/ve** *adj., gram.* relative

**relation** *f.* relation(ship); **en relation avec** in touch with (*s.o.*)

**religieux/euse** *adj.* religious

**relire** *irreg.* **(nous relisons;** *p.p.* **relu)** to re-read

**remarquer** to notice

**rembourser** to pay back

**remède** *m.* remedy; **la situation est sans remède** the situation is hopeless

**remédier** to remedy, put right

**remercier** to thank

**remettre** *irreg.* to delay, postpone; **se remettre de** to recover, get better

‡**remonter** to go back up; **remonter le moral de** to raise the spirits (*of s.o.*)

**remplacer (nous remplaçons)** to replace

**remplir** to fill

**rencontrer** to meet (by chance); **se rencontrer** to meet; to get together

**rendez-vous** *m.* meeting; **se donner rendez-vous** to make an appointment; to arrange to meet

**rendre** to give back; **rendre visite à** to visit (*s.o.*); **se rendre à** to go to; **se rendre compte de** to realize

**Renaissance (la)** *f.* the Renaissance

**renoncer (nous renonçons) à** to renounce, give up the idea

**renouveler (je renouvelle)** to renew

**rénovation** *f.* restoration

**renseignement** *m.* (piece of) information

**renseigner** to inform; **se renseigner (sur)** to get information (about)

‡ **rentrer** to return, go home; to take inside

**renvoyer (je renvoie)** to send back; to dismiss

**réparer** to fix, repair

†**repartir (je repars)** to leave again

**repas** *m.* meal

**repeindre** *irreg.* (**nous repeignons**) to repaint

**répéter (je répète)** to repeat

**répondeur** *m.* answering machine

**répondre (à)** to answer, respond

**réponse** *f.* answer, response

**repos** *m.* rest

**se reposer** to rest

**reprendre** *irreg.* (**nous reprenons**; *p.p.* **repris**) to take up again, resume

**représentant(e)** *m., f.* representative; **représentant de commerce** traveling salesperson

**reprise** *f.*: **à plusieurs reprises** on many occasions

**reprocher (qch à qn)** to reproach (*s.o. for s.th.*)

**reproduire (nous reproduisons)** to reproduce, duplicate

**république** *f.* republic; **République démocratique du Congo** Democratic Republic of Congo; **République dominicaine** Dominican Republic; **République tchèque** Czech Republic

**réputé(e)** *adj.* renowned

**réseau** *m.* network; **interconnexion de réseau** networking

**se résigner (à)** to resign o.s. (to)

**résoudre (de)** *irreg.* (**je résous**; *p.p.* **résolu**) to solve, resolve

**respecter** to respect

**responsable** *adj.* responsible

**ressembler à qn** to look like s.o.; **se ressembler** to look alike

**restaurant** *m.* restaurant

†**rester** to stay, remain; to be remaining

**restituer** to return, restore

**résultat** *m.* result

**résumer** to summarize

**retapisser** to re-paper

**retard** *m.* delay; **être en retard** to be late

**retarder: ma montre retarde de cinq minutes** my watch is five minutes slow

**retenir (je retiens**; *p.p.* **retenu)** to retain

**retour** *m.* homecoming, return home; **être de retour** to be back (home); **dès mon retour** as soon as I get (got) back

†**retourner** to return; to come, go back

**retrouver** to find (again); to meet up again

**réuni(e)** *adj.* reunited

**réunion** *f.* meeting; reunion; **assister à la réunion** to attend the meeting

**se réunir** to get together

**réussir (à)** to succeed (in); to pass (*a test*)

**rêve** *m.* dream

**se réveiller** to wake up

**réveillon** *m.* holiday dinner; **réveillon de la Saint-Sylvestre** New Year's Eve party

**révéler (je révèle)** to reveal

**revendeur/euse** *m., f.* secondhand dealer

†**revenir** *irreg.* (**je reviens**; *p.p.* **revenu**) to return; to come back

**rêver (de)** to dream (of/about)

**rêveur/euse** *m., f.* dreamer

**réviser** to review

**revoir** *irreg.* (**nous revoyons**; *p.p.* **revu**) to see again

**révolution** *f.* revolution

**revue** *f.* magazine; review; journal

**rhume** *m.* cold; **attraper un rhume** to catch a cold

**riche** *adj.* rich

**rideau** *m.* curtain

**ridicule** *adj.* ridiculous

**rien** *pron.* nothing; **c'est un rien du tout** he is a nobody; **ça n'a rien à voir avec** it has nothing to do with; **ne... rien** nothing, not anything; **pour un rien** at the drop of a hat; **rien d'autre** nothing else; **rien que pour** only to

**rire** *irreg.* (**nous rions**; *p.p.* **ri**) to laugh; **Rira bien qui rira le dernier.** He who laughs last laughs best.

**risquer (de)** to risk, run the risk of

**rival(e)** *m., f.* rival

**riz** *m.* rice

**robe** *f.* dress

**rock** *m.* rock and roll

**roi (reine)** *m., f.* king (queen); **la fête des rois,** Epiphany (*January 6, the Feast of the Kings*)

**rôle** *m.* part; character; **à tour de rôle** in turn, by turns

**roman** *m.* novel

**rompre** *irreg.* (**il rompt**) to break; to break up

**rosbif** *m.* roast beef

**rose** *adj.* pink; *f.* rose (*flower*)

**rouge** *adj.* red

**rougir** to blush

**rouler** to drive in a vehicle

**roulette** *f.*: **comme sur des roulettes** like clockwork

**route** *f.* road; **se mettre en route** to start out

**routier/ière** *adj.* road; **carte routière** road map

**rouvrir** to reopen

**roux (rousse)** *adj.* red (hair)

**rue** *f.* street; **rue piétonne** pedestrian street

**ruisseau** *m.* stream

**russe** *adj.* Russian; *m.* Russian (*language*); **Russe** Russian (*person*)

**Russie** *f.* Russia

**S**

**sac** *m.* bag; **sac à dos** backpack; **sac de couchage** sleeping bag

**saint(e)** *adj.* saint; **la Saint-Sylvestre** New Year's Eve

**saison** *f.* season

**salade** *f.* salad; lettuce

**salaire** *m.* salary

**sale** *adj.* dirty; **il fait un sale temps** the weather is lousy

salir to make dirty; **se salir** to get dirty

salle *f.* room; auditorium; **salle à manger** dining room; **salle de bains** bathroom; **salle de classe** classroom; **salle de concert** concert hall; **salle de permanence** study hall; **salle de réunion** meeting room; **salle de séjour** living room

salon *m.* living room

saluer to greet

Salvador (Le) *m.* El Salvador

samedi *m.* Saturday

sandale *f.* sandal

sandwich *m.* sandwich

sans *prep.* without; **sans broncher** without flinching; **(manger) sans cérémonie** (eat) informally; **sans doute** doubtless; **sans espoir** hopelessly; **sans façon** without fuss; **sans honte** shamelessly; **sans hésitation** unhesitatingly; **sans mal** without any trouble; **sans que** + *subj.* without; **sans plus** no more than that; **sans succès** unsuccessfully; **sans-abri** *m., f.* / **sans domicile fixe** homeless; **sans-emploi** *m., f., inv.* unemployed; **sans le sou** *m., f., inv.* penniless; **sans faute** *adv.* without fail; **sans-gêne** *adj., inv.* inconsiderate

santé *f.* health; **à votre santé!** *interj.* cheers!, to your health!; **être en bonne santé** to be in good health

satisfaction *f.* satisfaction

satisfait(e) *adj.* satisfied

sauce *f.* sauce; gravy

saucisson *m.* sausage

sauf *prep.* except

saumon *m.* salmon

se sauver (de) to save o.s. (from)

sauvegarder to save (*computer file*)

savoir *irreg.* (**je sais**; *p.p.* **su**) to know (how)

scène *f.* scene

science *f.* science; **Cité** (*f.*) **des sciences et de l'industrie** Museum of Science and Industry

scientifique *adj.* scientific; *m., f.* scientist

sculpteur (femme sculpteur) *m., f.* sculptor

sculpture *f.* sculpture

séance *f.* performance; representation; **la première séance du film** the first showing

sec (sèche) *adj.* dry

sécher (il sèche) to dry; **sécher un cours** to skip a class; **se sécher les cheveux** to dry one's hair

second(e) *adj.* second; *m., f.* the second (one)

secondaire *adj.* secondary

secours *m.*: **au secours!** help!

secret/ète *adj.* secretive

secrétaire *m., f.* secretary

section *f.* section

seize *adj.* sixteen

séjour *m.* stay, sojourn; **salle de séjour** living room

sel *m.* salt

selon *prep.* according to

semaine *f.* week; **une semaine de congé** a week off; **la semaine prochaine (dernière)** next (last) week

sembler to seem, appear; *impers.* **il semble que** + *subj.* it seems that

semestre *m.* semester

sénateur *m.* senator

Sénégal *m.* Senegal

sens *m.* meaning; direction; **dans le sens de la longueur** lengthwise

sensationnel(le) *adj.* terrific

sensibilité *f.* sensibility

sentiment *m.* feeling

sentir *irreg.* (**je sens**) to smell; to feel; **se sentir** to feel; **sentir bon (mauvais)** to smell good (bad); **se sentir de trop** to feel in the way

sept *adj.* seven

septembre *m.* September

septième *adj.* seventh

Serbie *f.* Serbia

sérieusement *adv.* seriously

sérieux/euse *adj.* serious

serpent *m.* snake

service *m.* service; **station-service** *f.* service station, garage

serviette *f.* briefcase

servir *irreg.* (**je sers**) to serve; **se servir de** to use; **rien ne sert de pleurer** it's no use crying

seul(e) *adj.* alone; only; single

seulement *adv.* only

shopping *m.*: **faire du shopping** to go shopping

short *m. s.* shorts

siècle *m.* century

sien(ne)(s): **le/la/les sien(ne)(s)** *pron. m., f.* his/hers

signaler to indicate, point out

signe *m.* sign

signer to sign

signifier to mean, signify

silencieux/euse *adj.* silent, quiet

similarité *f.* similarity

sirop *m.* syrup; **sirop contre la toux** cough syrup

situation *f.* situation

situé(e) *adj.* located

se situer to be located

six *adj.* six

sixième *adj.* sixth

ski *m.* ski; **faire du ski** to ski

slogan *m.* slogan

Slovaquie *f.* Slovakia

SNCF *f.* **Société** (*f.*) **Nationale de Chemins de Fer** French national railway company

socialisme *m.* socialism

société *f.* society

sœur *f.* sister

sofa *m.* sofa

soi *pron., neu.* oneself; **chacun pour soi** every man for himself

soie *f.* silk

soif *f.* thirst; **avoir soif** to be thirsty; **mourir de soif** to be very thirsty

se soigner to take care of o.s.

soigneusement *adv.* carefully

soin *m.* care

soir *m.* evening; **ce soir** tonight

soirée *f.* evening

soit... soit *conj.* either . . . or

soixante *adj.* sixty

sol *m.*: **sous-sol** basement

soldat *m.* soldier

solde *m.* sale; **en solde** on sale

soleil *m.* sun; **coucher** (*m.*) **du soleil** sunset; **faire du soleil** to be sunny; **lunettes** (*f.*) **de soleil** sunglasses

solitude *f.* loneliness

solution *f.* solution

sommeil *m.* sleep; **avoir sommeil** to be sleepy

**songer (à) (nous songeons)** to be thinking (of)
**sonner** to ring; **on sonne** someone is at the door
**sophistiqué(e)** *adj.* sophisticated
**sortie** *f.* exit; night out
‡**sortir** *irreg.* (**je sors**) to leave; to go out; to take out
**sot(te)** *adj.* silly
**sottise** *f.* stupidity, foolishness
**sou** *m.*: **sans-le-sou** penniless
**se soucier (de)** to worry (about)
**souci** *m.* worry
**soudain** *adv.* suddenly
**Soudan** *m.* Sudan
**souffrir** *irreg.* (**je souffre**; *p.p.* **souffert**) to suffer
**souhait** *m.* wish; **à souhait** as one could wish
**souhaiter** (**que** + *subj.*) to wish (that)
**soupçonner** to suspect
**soupe** *f.* soup; **soupe aux légumes (au poulet, en conserve)** vegetable (chicken, canned) soup
**soupirer** to sigh
**sourire** *irreg.* (**je souris**; *p.p.* **souri**) to smile
**souris** *f.* mouse
**sous** *prep.* under, beneath; in (*sun, rain*); **sous l'influence de** under the influence of; **sous la main** handy; **sous la pluie** in the rain; **sous la Révolution** at the time of the Revolution; **sous la tente** in a tent; **sous le règne de** under, during the reign of; **sous les yeux** right in front of you; **sous peu** soon; **sous tous les angles** from all angles, from all points of view; **sous une identité d'emprunt** under an assumed identity
**sous-sol** *m.* basement
**soutenir** *irreg.* (**je soutiens**; *p.p.* **soutenu**) to sustain, support
**soutien** *m.* support
**souvenir** *m.* memory, recollection; souvenir
**se souvenir (de)** *irreg.* (**je me souviens**; *p.p.* **souvenu**) to remember
**souvent** *adv.* often
**spaghettis** *m. pl.* spaghetti
**spécialisé(e)** *adj.* specialized
**spécialité** *f.* specialty
**spectateur/trice** *m., f.* viewer, spectator
**sport** *m.* sport; **faire du sport** to do, practice sports; **voiture** (*f.*) **de sport** sports car
**sportif/ve** *adj.* athletic; sports-minded
**stade** *m.* stadium
**stage** *m.* training course; **faire un stage linguistique** to participate in a language program
**station-service** *f.* service station, garage
**steak-frites** *m.* steak with French fries
**store** *m.* blind (*window*)
**stratégie** *f.* strategy
**structure** *f.* structure
**style** *m.* style ; **style familier (soutenu)** informal (formal) style
**stylo** *m.* pen
**suave** *adj.* suave, smooth
**subir** to undergo
**subjonctif** *m., gram.* subjunctive (mood)
**sublime** *adj.* sublime
**subordonné(e)** *adj., gram.* subordinate
**substantif** *m., gram.* noun
**substitution** *f.* substitution
**subventionner** to subsidize
**sucré(e)** *adj.* sweetened

**sud** *m.* south; **hémisphère** (*m.*) **sud** south hemisphere; **Afrique** (*f.*) **du Sud** South Africa
**Suède** *f.* Sweden
**suffire**: **il suffit que** + *subj.* it will be enough if you
**suffixe** *m.* suffix
**suggérer** (**il suggère**) to suggest
**Suisse** *f.* Switzerland
**suite** *f.*: **tout de suite** immediately; **trois jours de suite** three days in a row
**suivant(e)** *adj.* following; **suivant** *prep.* according to
**suivre** *irreg.* (**je suis**; *p.p.* **suivi**) to follow; **à suivre** to be continued; **suivre bien à l'école** to be a good student; **suivre l'actualité** to keep up with the news; **suivre un cours** to take a class; **suivre un régime** to be on a diet
**sujet** *m.* topic; *gram.* subject; **au sujet de** about
**superlatif** *m., gram.* superlative
**supermarché** *m.* supermarket
**supporter** to bear, stand
**supposition** *f.* supposition
**supprimer** to eliminate
**sur** *prep.* on; **deux sur trois** two out of three; **il a eu rhume sur rhume** he had one cold after the other; **sur le moment** at first; **sur toute la France** in all of France; **sur une année** over a period of a year; **un jour sur deux** every other day
**sûr(e)** *adj.* sure, certain; **bien sûr** of course; **il est sûr que** + *indic.* it is certain that; **il n'est pas sûr que** + *subj.* it is uncertain whether
**sûrement** *adv.* certainly
**surface** *f.* surface
**surfer** to surf (the Internet)
**surmonter** to overcome
**surprendre** *irreg.* (**nous surprenons**; *p.p.* **surpris**) to surprise
**suspendre** to hang up
**sympathique** *adj.* (*fam.* **sympa**) nice, friendly
**syndicat** *m.* union (*work*)
**synonyme** *m.* synonym; *adj.* synonymous
**syntagme** *m., gram.* word group, phrase
**Syrie** *f.* Syria
**système** *m.* system; **système de traitement de données** data processing system

## T

**ta** *adj.* (*f. s.*), *fam.* your
**table** *f.* table; **à table** at the table
**tableau** *m.* painting
**tâche** *f.* task, work
**tact** *m.* tact; **sans tact** tactless
**Tahiti** *f.* Tahiti
**taille** *f.* size
**se taire** *irreg.* (**nous nous taisons**; *p.p.* **tu**) to keep quiet
**talent** *m.* talent
**tant (de)** *adv.* so much, so many
**tante** *f.* aunt
**tapis** *m.* rug, carpet
**tard** *adv.* late
**tarte** *f.* pie, tart
**tartine** *f.* slice of bread with butter or jam

**tasse** *f.* cup; **une tasse de thé** a cup of tea; **une tasse à thé** a teacup

**taxi** *m.* taxi

**tchèque** *adj.* Czech; *m.* Czech (*language*); **Tchèque** *m., f.* Czech (*person*)

**te (t')** *pron.* (*s.*) *fam.* you; to you, for you

**technique** *adj.* technical

**tee-shirt** *m.* T-shirt

**télécharger (nous téléchargeons)** to download (*Internet*)

**téléphone** *m.* telephone; **coup de téléphone** phone call; **numéro de téléphone** phone number

**téléphoner (à)** to phone; **se téléphoner** to call one another

**téléphonique** *adj.*: **cabine téléphonique** phone booth

**télévision** *f.* (*fam.* **télé**) television

**tellement** *adv.* so; so much; **pas tellement** not that much

**témoin** *m.* witness

**température** *f.* temperature

**tempête** *f.* storm

**temps** *m., gram.* tense; time; weather; **après un temps** after a while; **avoir le temps** to have time; **depuis combien de temps... / il y a combien de temps...** since when . . ., how long . . .; **du temps de** in the time of; **la plupart du temps** most of the time; **par les temps qui courent** nowadays; **par un temps pareil** in such weather; **passer son temps** to spend one's time; **temps de chien** foul weather; **tout le temps** all the time

**tendre** to stretch out

**tenir** *irreg.* (**je tiens**; *p.p.* **tenu**) to hold; **tenir à** to insist on; **se tenir** to behave

**tennis** *m.* tennis

**tente** *f.* tent; **sous la tente** in a tent

**terminale** *f.* last year of French secondary school

**terminer** to end, finish

**terrasse** *f.* terrace, patio

**terre** *f.* ground; **par terre** on the floor / ground; **pomme de terre** potato; **tremblement de terre** earthquake

**tes** *adj.* (*m., f. pl.*), *fam.* your

**tête** *f.* head; **avoir mal à la tête** to have a headache; **en avoir par-dessus la tête** to be sick and tired (*of s.th.*); **être plus grand d'une tête** to be a head taller; **histoire sans queue ni tête** cock-and-bull story; **se laver la tête** to wash one's hair

**Texas** *m.* Texas

**texte** *m.* text; **traitement** (*m.*) **de texte** word processing

**TGV (Train à Grande Vitesse)** *m.* French high-speed train

**Thaïlande** *f.* Thailand

**théâtre** *m.* theater; **pièce** (*f.*) **de théâtre** play

**thème** *m.* theme; composition

**thon** *m.* tuna

**tien(ne)(s): le/la/les** *pron., (m., f.), fam.* yours

**timbre** *m.* stamp

**tiré(e) (de)** *adj.* taken (from)

**tiroir** *m.* drawer

**titre** *m.*: **à juste titre** with good reason; **à titre confidentiel** confidentially; **à titre de père** as a father

**toile** *f.* web; **toile d'araignée** spider web

**toilette** *f.*: **faire sa toilette** to wash and get dressed; *f. pl.* bathroom

**toit** *m.* roof

**tolérance** *f.* tolerance

**†tomber** to fall; **tomber amoureux** to fall in love; **tomber malade** to get sick; **tomber par terre** to fall on the ground

**ton** *adj.* (*m., s.*), *fam.* your

**ton** *m.* tone

**tonique** *adj.* accented

**tonner** to thunder

**tordre** to twist

**tort** *m.*: **à tort** wrongly; **avoir tort** to be wrong

**tôt** *adv.* early

**touchant(e)** *adj.* touching

**toucher** to touch; **en toucher un mot à** to let (*s.o.*) know

**toujours** *adv.* always; still

**tour** *m.* turn; **à tour de rôle / tour à tour** in turn; **faire le tour du monde** to go around the world; **tour de ville** city tour; *f.* tower

**tourisme** *m.* tourism; **faire du tourisme** to go sightseeing

**touriste** *m., f.* tourist

**tournée** *f.* tour; **être en tournée** to be on tour

**tourner** to turn

**tournure** *f.* turn of phrase

**tout(e)** (*pl.* **tous, toutes**) *adj., pron.* all, every; everything; each; any; **tout** *adv.* wholly, entirely, quite, very, all; **à tout jamais** forever; **à tout prix** at all cost; **à toute vitesse** very fast; **aller tout droit** to go straight ahead; **en tout cas** in any case; **parler tout bas** to speak very softly; **pas du tout** not at all; **tout à fait** entirely; **tout à l'heure** a short while ago; very soon; **tout au plus** at the most; **tout de suite** immediately; **tout droit** straight ahead; **tout d'un coup** suddenly; **tout est en règle** everything is in order; **tout le monde** everybody; **tout le temps** all the time; **tout près** very close; **tout un chacun** everybody; **tout va bien** everything is going fine; **tous les ans** every year

**toux** *f.* cough; **sirop contre la toux** cough syrup

**tracasser** to worry, bother

**traduction** *f.* translation

**traduire** *irreg.* (**nous traduisons**) to translate

**tragédie** *f.* tragedy

**train** *m.* train; **billet** (*m.*) **de train** train ticket; **en train** by train; **être en train de** to be in the process of; **prendre le train** to take the train

**traîner** to lie around; **laisser traîner ses affaires** to leave one's things lying around

**trait** *m.* feature, trait

**traitement** *m.* processing; **traitement de données** data processing; **traitement de texte** word processing

**tranquille** *adj.* quiet, calm

**tranquillité** *f.* quiet, peacefulness

**transformation** *f.* change, transformation

**transformer** to transform, change, convert

**transport** *m.*: **les transports en commun** public transportation

**travail** *m.* (*pl.* **travaux**) work; project; job; employment

**travailler** to work; **travailler dur** to work hard

**travailleur/euse** *m., f.* worker; *adj.* hardworking

**travers** *m.*: **à travers** through

**traverser** to cross

treize *adj.* thirteen

tréma *m.* dieresis (*accent*); **e tréma** (ë)

tremblement *m.*: **tremblement de terre** earthquake

trembler to shake, tremble

trentaine *f.* about thirty

trente *adj.* thirty

très *adv.* very; most; very much

triste *adj.* sad

tristement *adv.* sadly

troisième *adj.* third

tromper to deceive; **se tromper (de)** to make a mistake; to be wrong (about)

trompeur/euse *adj.* deceptive

trop (de) *adv.* too; too much/many (of); **se sentir de trop** to feel in the way

troquer to trade, swap (*s.th. for s.th. else*)

trottoir *m.* sidewalk

trou *m.* hole

trouble-fête *m., f.* party-pooper

trouver to find; **se trouver** to be located

Tunisie *f.* Tunisia

Turquie *f.* Turkey

tutoyer (**je tutoie**) to use **tu** when speaking with s.o.

typique *adj.* typical

# U

un(e) (*pl.* **des**) *art.* a, an; *adj., pron.* one; **vivre les uns sur les autres** to live on top of one another

uni(e) *adj.* united; **États-Unis** *m. pl.* United-States

uniforme *adj.* uniform

uniformément *adv.* uniformly

union *f.* union; **Union** (*f.*) **européenne** European Union

unique *adj.* only

unité *f.* unit: **unité de disque** disk drive

universitaire *adj.* (*of or belonging to the*) university

urgent(e) *adj.* urgent; **il est urgent que** + *subj.* it is urgent that

utile *adj.* useful; **il est utile que** + *subj.* it is useful that

utiliser to use

# V

vacances *f. pl.* vacation; **colonie** (*f.*) **de vacances** summer camp; **partir en vacances** to go away on vacation; **trois semaines de vacances** three weeks of vacation

vache *f.* cow

vaincre *irreg.* (**nous vainquons**; *p.p.* **vaincu**) to conquer, vanquish

vaisselle *f.* dishes; **faire la vaisselle** to wash the dishes; **lave-vaisselle** *m.* dishwasher

valise *f.* suitcase

valoir *irreg.* (**il vaut**; *p.p.* **valu**) to be worth; **il vaut mieux** + *inf.* it is better to; **il vaut mieux que** + *subj.* it is better that

se vanter (de) to pride o.s. (on)

variable *adj.* unsettled (*weather*)

varier to change, vary

vaut (il) (*see* **valoir**)

veau *m.* veal

vedette *f.* star, celebrity

véhicule *m.* vehicle

veille *f.* the day before; the evening before

veiller (à) to attend to, see to

vélo *m.* bicycle; **faire du vélo** to go cycling

vélomoteur *m.* moped, light motorcycle

vendeur/euse *m., f.* salesman/saleswoman

vendre to sell

vendredi *m.* Friday

†venir *irreg.* (**je viens**; *p.p.* **venu**) to come; **venir de** + *inf.* to have just (*done s.th.*)

vent *m.* wind; **il fait du vent** it's windy

venter *impers.* to be windy

verbal(e) *adj., gram.* verbal

verbe *m., gram.* verb

verglas *m.* ice (*on road*)

vérifier to verify, check

vérité *f.* truth

Vermont *m.* Vermont

verre *m.* glass; drink; **prendre un verre** to have a drink

vers *prep.* towards; around, about (*time*)

versement *m.* payment; **faire un versement (sur le compte de)** to make a deposit (in an account)

vert(e) *adj.* green; **haricots** (*m.*) **verts** green beans

vertige *m.* dizziness; vertigo; **donner le vertige** to make dizzy

veste *f.* sport jacket

vêtement *m.* clothing

viande *f.* meat

victime *f.* victim; **être victime de son imprudence** to be victim of one's own imprudence

victoire *f.* victory; **la victoire des alliés** Allied victory

vidéo *f.* video; **jeu** (*m.*) **vidéo** video game

vie *f.* life; **jamais de la vie!** never! not on your life!

Viêt-Nam *m.* Vietnam

vieux (**vieil, vieille**) *adj.* old; ancient

village *m.* village

ville *f.* town, city; **en ville** in town, in the city; **en pleine ville** in the middle of the city

vin *m.* wine

vingt *adj.* twenty

vingtaine *f.* around twenty

violemment *adv.* violently

violence *f.* violence

violent(e) *adj.* violent

violon *m.* violin

Virginie *f.* Virginia

visage *m.* face

visite *f.* visit; **rendre visite à** to visit (*s.o.*)

visiter to visit (*a place*)

visiteur/euse *m., f.* visitor

vitamine *f.* vitamin

vite *adv.* fast, quickly

vitesse *f.* speed; **à toute vitesse** very fast

vitrail *m.* (*pl.* **vitraux**) stained-glass window

vitre *f.* pane (of glass)

vivre *irreg.* (**je vis**; *p.p.* **vécu**) to live

vocabulaire *m.* vocabulary

voilà *prep.* there is, there are; **voilà un an que j'habite ce quartier** I have been living in this neighborhood for a year; **le/la voilà!** here he/she comes!

voile *m.* veil

voir *irreg.* (**nous voyons**; *p.p.* **vu**) to see; **se voir** to see each other

voisin(e) *m., f.* neighbor

voiture *f.* car; **voiture de sport** sports car

voix *f.* voice; **à haute voix** aloud, out loud; **trois voix contre deux** three votes to two; *gram.* **voix passive (active)** passive (active) voice

vol *m.* theft; **vol à main armée** armed robbery

voler to fly; to steal

voleur/euse *m., f.* thief

volontiers *adv.* gladly

vôtre(s): le/la/les vôtre(s) *pron., m., f.* yours

vouloir *irreg.* (**je veux**; *p.p.* **voulu**) to want, wish; **vouloir dire** to mean

vouvoyer (je vouvoie) to use **vous** when speaking with s.o

voyage *m.* trip; **agence** (*f.*) **de voyages** travel agency; **faire un voyage** to take a trip

voyager (nous voyageons) to travel

voyageur/euse *m., f.* traveler

vrai(e) *adj.* true; **il est vrai que** + *indic.* it is true that

vraiment *adv.* truly, really

vue *f.*: **bien en vue** prominent (*person*)

Web *m.*: **surfer le Web** to surf the Web

week-end *m.* weekend

yaourt *m.* yogurt

yeux *m. pl.* (*sing.* **œil**) eyes; **avoir mal aux yeux** to have sore eyes; **sous les yeux** right in front of you; **voir de ses propres yeux** to see with one's own eyes

zéro *m.* zero; **il fait 10 degrés au-dessus de zéro** it's 10 degrees above freezing (point)

zoo *m.* zoo

zoologique *adj.* zoological; **jardin** (*m.*) **zoologique** zoo

# INDEX